JOSEPH STALIN:
MAN AND LEGEND

RONALD HINGLEY

Joseph Stalin:
Man and Legend

McGRAW-HILL BOOK COMPANY
New York St. Louis San Francisco

Library of Congress Cataloging in Publication Data

Hingley, Ronald.
Joseph Stalin: man and legend.

1. Stalin, Iosif, 1879-1935.
2. Russia – History – 1925-1953. I. Title.

DK268.S8H56   947.084′2′0924   74-991

ISBN 0 07 028943 3

Printed in Great Britain

... dove l'argomento de la mente
s'aggiugne al mal volere ed alla possa,
nessun riparo vi può far la gente

DANTE, *Inferno*, Canto xxxi

Contents

List of Illustrations

Picture research by Angela Murphy

Frontispiece: Stalin on his fiftieth birthday, 1929 [*Staadtsbibliothek*]

Between pages 106 and 107

Legend-Stalin in boyhood, 1880s [*SCR: photo by John Freeman*]
Stalin at Gori Ecclesiastical School, c. 1888 [*Sueddeutscher Verlag*]
Stalin the seminarist, 1894 [*Staadtsbibliothek*]
Tiflis Orthodox Theological Seminary [*Photo by John Freeman*]
Stalin at Kutaisi Prison, 1903 [*Snark International*]
Stalin's first wife, Yekaterina Svanidze, c. 1905 [*Popperfoto*]
Legend-Stalin receives Lenin's 'letter', 1903
Legend-Stalin first meets Lenin, 1905 [*Mansell Collection*]
Legend-Stalin as Lenin's closest comrade-in-arms, 1917 [*SCR*]
A larger-than-life Stalin addresses railway workers, 1926 [*Planet News*]
Stalin 'at the front', 1941 [*Photo by John Freeman*]
Police record, St Petersburg Okhrana files, c. 1913 [*Hulton Picture Library*]
'Mug shot' from Okhrana files, c. 1910 [*Archiv Gerstenberg*]
Stalin at Kureyka, central Siberia, during his last period of exile (1913-17) [*Snark International*]
Stalin and Trotsky, October 1917 [*Popperfoto*]
Stalin as People's Commissar for Nationalities [*Topix*]
Voroshilov, Mikoyan, Molotov, Stalin and Dimitrov as Lenin's pall-bearers, 1924 [*Hulton Picture Library*]

Between pages 234 and 235

Voroshilov and Budyonny, 1920 [*Archiv Gerstenberg*]
Stalin with Rykov, Zinovyev and Bukharin, early 1920s [*Archiv Gerstenberg*]
Stalin with Mikoyan and Ordzhonikidze: Tiflis, 1926 [*Sueddeutscher Verlag*]
Stalin and Kirov: Leningrad, 1926 [*SCR: photo by John Freeman*]
Trotsky in exile with his wife and son: Alma Ata, 1928 [*Archiv Gerstenberg*]

List of Illustrations

Stalin and his second wife, Nadezhda Alliluyeva, picnicking with the Voroshilovs: Sochi, 1929 [*Snark International/Colonel Emmanuel D'Astier*]

Stalin and Gorky [*SCR: photo by John Freeman*]

Industrial Party trial: Moscow, 1931 [*Archiv Gerstenberg*]

Industrial Party trial: the accused hear the sentence [*Archiv Gerstenberg*]

Kalinin, Stalin, Voroshilov and Molotov follow Kirov's coffin, 1934 [*Archiv Gerstenberg*]

Kaganovich, Ordzhonikidze, Stalin, Voroshilov and Kirov, early 1930s [*Archiv Gerstenberg*]

The agricultural front: collectivized Uzbek farmworkers [*Archiv Gerstenberg*]

Heads of the secret police: Dzerzhinsky (1917-26) [*Hulton Picture Library*]; Yagoda (1934-6) [*Sueddeutscher Verlag*]; Yezhov (1936-8) [*Sueddeutscher Verlag*]; Beria (from 1938) [*Hulton Picture Library*]

Zinovyev and Kamenev (d. 1936) [*Archiv Gerstenberg*]

Pyatakov (d. 1937) and Radek (d. 1939) [*Archiv Gerstenberg*]

Bukarin and Rykov (d. 1938) [*Archiv Gerstenberg*]

Tomsky (d. 1936) and Ordzhonikidze (d. 1937) [*Archiv Gerstenberg; Hulton Picture Library*]

May Day Parade: Red Square, Moscow [*Camera Press*]

Trotsky on his death-bed: Mexico City, 1940 [*Archiv Gerstenberg*]

Between pages 362 and 363

Stalin, 1920 [*Camera Press*]

Stalin, 1927 [*Planet News*]

'Candid camera' shots which escaped the vigilance of Stalin's censors [*Imperial War Museum; Illustrationsfoto*]

Stalin's mother, Yekaterina Dzhugashvili (d. 1936) [*Sueddeutscher Verlag*]

Stalin with Svetlana: Kuntsevo, 1935

Stalin's elder son, Yakov Dzhugashvili, as a German prisoner [*Keystone*]

Stalin's younger son, Vasily Stalin, as an air force commander [*Popperfoto*]

Supreme Soviet, January 1938: Bulganin, Zhdanov, Stalin, Voroshilov, Khrushchev [*Staadtsbibliothek*]

Molotov signs the Treaty between the USSR and Germany, 4 October 1939, watched by Ribbentrop and Stalin [*Popperfoto*]

Churchill and Stalin at the Kremlin, 1942 [*SCR*]

Teheran (1943); Roosevelt, Churchill, Stalin and Major Birse celebrate Churchill's sixty-ninth birthday [*Camera Press*]

Yalta (1945): Churchill, Roosevelt and Stalin [*Camera Press*]

Potsdam (July-August 1945): Attlee, Truman and Stalin [*Archiv Gerstenberg*]

List of Illustrations

Mao Tse-tung, Ulbricht, Stalin and Khrushchev on Stalin's seventieth birthday, 1949 [*Sueddeutscher Verlag*]

Stalin lies in state, 10 March 1953

Soviet leaders (including Voroshilov, Malenkov, Molotov, Beria, Khrushchev) follow Stalin's glass coffin [*Popperfoto*]

The Red Square Mausoleum during the period when it bore Stalin's name as well as Lenin's; and the same monument destalinized [*Sueddeutscher Verlag*]

Preface

LIVES of Stalin are not so numerous that one need apologize for attempting a new one, especially as the present study falls outside the categories to which the best-known existing (pre-1973) biographies belong: the popular and the Marxist.

I have tried to use the sources more critically than have those popularizers who seem to measure the reliability of evidence by the degree to which its contents are sensational. As for professedly Marxist biographies, those published in the Soviet Union provide valuable evidence on the Cult of Stalin - but on little else. Some western-published Marxist biographies are, by contrast, comparatively serious in their approach, and I have found four - those of Souvarine, Trotsky, Deutscher and Roy Medvedev - particularly stimulating. But their picture of Stalin, while differing between author and author, differs far more from mine. They base their work on rigid presuppositions about the nature of history and about the part played in it by the various Russian revolutions. Their work is also marked - and, for many, marred - in varying degrees by Leninist piety. Far more damaging to their achievement, though, is the prejudice against Stalin from which they all suffer in some degree - despite sharing, as I do not, the dictator's political creed.

Accepting Stalin's ultimate premises, while yet rejecting his methods, anti-Stalinist Marxist chroniclers of Stalin underestimate his dexterity and acumen. They also manifest - as is only natural - a strong personal dislike of one who, by causing such widespread suffering in the name of their political faith, has done much to discredit it; and it is this dislike, seemingly, which has deceived them into underrating Stalin's intelligence. But a very evil man may yet be very clever, as I hope to demonstrate. Moreover, reluctant though one may be to accept the fact, he may also be found personally sympathetic in some degree, even by those who most deplore his actions. On this point I again disagree with the anti-Stalinist Marxist biographers, siding rather with Winston Churchill and Franklin D. Roosevelt – who both liked Stalin, but were thereby betrayed into political error. I also concur with General de Gaulle, who has attributed to the Soviet dictator 'a certain sinister charm'.[1] I do not, however, go as far as the anonymous junior American diplomat's wife who once described the great dictator as 'dreamy'.[2]

So much for biographies of Stalin published before 1973. Late in that year – too late, unfortunately, to be taken into consideration in the text of the present volume, which was already with the printers – two new and substantial studies of Stalin appeared almost simultaneously: those of Robert C. Tucker and Adam B. Ulam. Free from over-sensationalism and damaging political preconceptions, abundantly documented and respectful to their source material, these works have set entirely new standards in the elucidation of the great dictator; to neither of them do the above-mentioned strictures apply. It so happens, however, that both also pursue aims very different from my own ... and from each other's. Professor Tucker's book is the first volume of a projected trilogy which will eventually run to some fifteen hundred pages; it deals in great detail, and with considerable emphasis on matters ideological, with the period up to 1929. Professor Ulam has not only written the history of Stalin, but has combined it with that of Russia in the Stalin period.

My own approach has involved a more rigorous concentration on Stalin the man, on his impact and on his Legend. An attempt has been made to contribute a serious, comprehensive and accurate account, but one which also expresses a personal attitude, since I do not share the fashionable view that a historian must always abstain from 'value judgements' explicit or implied.

This, then, is what I (a private individual) think of a public individual. The approach is based on philosophical assumptions which I partly share with Stalin's *bêtes noires* Dostoyevsky and Milovan Djilas: that the claim to organize one's fellow-men politically for their own good is a sign of depravity rather than of virtue; that the purported promotion of a sectional interest – especially of a nation or a class – as an end in itself, is apt to provoke disaster, most particularly for the nation or class which is the object of such benevolence (Germans and the proletariat, for example, as benefited by Hitler and Stalin respectively); that the drive to substitute for an imperfect real society a notional perfect society tends to create hell on earth; that the claim to promote unlimited freedom for humanity is a factor favouring the development of unlimited collective slavery; that most individuals who seek or claim to build a Utopia by political means do more harm than good; that the harm which they do is proportionate to their intelligence ... but that they are often – by a merciful dispensation – rather stupid, their capacity for mischief being thereby fortunately much reduced.

Stalin was the exception: a politician who was yet truly intelligent. Let us hope that we shall never look upon his like again.

Frilford   RONALD HINGLEY

Names, Dates, Acknowledgements

RUSSIAN names are transliterated along lines laid down at length in the prefaces to volumes 1–8 of *The Oxford Chekhov*, edited and translated by myself and published by the Oxford University Press. In the Reference Notes and Bibliography only, the authors' (or their translators') own spellings of their names have been retained in cases where these diverge from the above. Georgian names which would – if strictly transliterated from their Russian form – end in -iya, are given the ending -ia: e.g., Beria, Zhordania. To avoid confusion, the traditional russified name for the Georgian capital – Tiflis – is everywhere used instead of Tbilisi, despite the fact that the latter is now the correct form. Russian first names are given in transliterated form, except that Stalin's Christian name appears as the familiar 'Joseph', not as the transliterated 'Iosif'. The conventional spelling of 'Khrushchev' and certain other well-known names is retained. Eastern European names are printed without diacritical signs. The words 'Caucasus' and 'Caucasian' refer (unless otherwise specified) not to the mountain range but to the area corresponding with the former Imperial Russian Viceroyalty of the Caucasus. Though this included substantial areas north of the main mountain range, its most important regions (including Stalin's native Georgia) were and are, from the Russian point of view, on the *other* (southern) side of the Caucasus: for this reason the forms 'Transcaucasian' and 'Transcaucasia' are also used in the text, and often interchangeably with 'Caucasian' and 'Caucasus'.

Dates relating to the period between 1 January 1700 and 1 February 1918 accord with the Julian Calendar used in Russia at that time. This means that they lag behind the dates used in western Europe: by thirteen days in the twentieth century and by twelve days in the nineteenth century.

For their kindness in helping me to prepare this book I am much indebted to the following: to Dr C. D. Kernig, Editor-in-Chief, *The Soviet System and Democratic Society: a Comparative Encyclopedia*, Freiburg,

Germany, for permission to make use (largely in Chapter Sixteen, below) of material from the article 'Stalin and Stalinism' written for his publication by myself; to Mrs Schiff and to Mr Byron S. Greenberg of the New York Post for sending me a copy of the article on Stalin's mother by H. R. Knickerbocker (see Bibliography); to Mr Bruce Parrott of the University of Columbia for obtaining for me a copy of *Stalin und die Tragoedie Georgiens* by J. Iremashvili (Iremaschwili); to Miss Jane Grayson of St Hilda's College, Oxford, for obtaining for me various rare materials from Russian émigré journals published in Paris. To Professor Ralph Carter Elwood of Carleton University I am most particularly grateful for his generosity in showing me material (then unpublished, but now available in his 'Lenin and *Pravda*' – see Bibliography) on Stalin's relations with Lenin in 1912–13, and also for the light which he shed in personal discussions on various aspects of Stalin's life over which Trotsky – and later biographers following Trotsky – have gone astray. For the account given below in Chapter Three, Sections 2 and 3 (*Lenin's Man in St Petersburg ?* and *The Austrian Episode*) I naturally take sole responsibility, but while gladly acknowledging that many of the ideas there expounded were first suggested to me by Professor Elwood. Mrs Ann Shukman of Lady Margaret Hall, Oxford, and Mr Jeremy Newton of The Queen's College, Oxford, have each, independently, twice vetted drafts of my manuscript in detail, making many sensitive and useful suggestions; for their skilled editorial services and for their encouragement I am grateful indeed. An early draft of the text was read by Professor M. H. Futrell of the University of British Columbia, to whose insights and suggestions I am also greatly indebted, as I am to my sons Peter and Martin, who have also advised me. For the loan or gift of material, and/or for much valued advice, I am most grateful to Dr Patrick Boyde, to Mr Richard Luckett, to Professor Richard Pipes, and also to the following fellow-members of St Antony's College, Oxford: Chimen Abramsky, Eddie Bolland, Constantine Brancovan, Raymond Carr, Norman Davies, Michael Glenny, Max Hayward, George Katkov, Dennis O'Flaherty, Tony Nicholls, Harry Shukman and Harry Willetts. To the College librarians, especially to Anne Abley and Valerie Jensen, I owe a special debt for their unfailing patience and for their kindness towards a colleague who has made so many claims on their time and skill. I am also most grateful to Joan Clifton for secretarial assistance.

Above all I wish to thank my wife for the valuable criticism which she has offered at all stages in the preparation of this book; for sustaining me with her sympathy on the many occasions when the exhilaration of the Marvellous Georgian's company threatened to sap my energies; and for typing more drafts of the manuscript than we can now remember.

Introduction

The Sources, the Legend and the Cult

THE biographer of Stalin labours under difficulties greater than those besetting the chronicler of any other outstanding modern figure.

Firstly there is the virtual absence of archive material. The Soviet Union maintains no Public Record Office in which scholars could obtain access to unpublished documents on Stalin. And though one does occasionally come across obscure references to a Stalin Archive in the USSR, it has never been opened and its location is unknown. Even if it exists, and should ever disgorge its secrets, disappointment might well result. Stalin was not the man to rest content with merely concealing material compromising himself (and, in the present context, this means practically any kind of material conceivable) – he would have destroyed it utterly. The dictator's secret files, if such indeed exist, might therefore turn out almost as unproductive in new biographical insights as those of the Okhrana's Foreign Department (at Stanford University), and as the Trotsky Archive (at Harvard University), have so far proved with regard to the limited areas of Stalin's activities which they embrace. Unless there should ever be a spectacular change of political climate in Moscow, no startling new material on Stalin is ever likely to come out of the Soviet Union; nor is any new material at all likely to surface except for what the authorities themselves may from time to time publish on a subject which still remains political dynamite.

Another relatively ordinary obstacle to the study of Stalin derives from his obscurity as a young man. Not until late in his fourth decade did he become sufficiently important to merit biographical treatment. Until then no one had any interest in preserving material on so insignificant a member of a minor and semi-outlawed political party: a late developer whose potentialities were evident to no one – except, possibly, to the leader of his faction, Lenin. Within Lenin's Bolshevik faction, moreover, Stalin was often occupied on sensitive 'cloak-and-dagger' operations about which many other Bolsheviks – themselves often living under aliases, often hunted by the police – were not informed for security reasons, and on which they have therefore been unable to bear witness.

Only in October 1917, when Stalin took office in the first Soviet Government, did he suddenly attain sufficient stature to attract attention. By that time, though, he was already in a position to suppress inconvenient facts – of which there were many – about his background and history. We shall observe him doing so in due course. We shall also observe that, while he could already (in the 1920s) censor his biography negatively, he could not – yet – do so positively and creatively: that is, he could not yet insert into it the spurious episodes with which it was later to be so lavishly enriched. If we remember that the dictator's pre-revolutionary role had been modest – and that even this modest role had been performed in secrecy for security reasons – we shall not be surprised that the young Stalin is often ignored, or assigned only an insignificant part, in the many historical studies and memoirs of pre-revolutionary Bolshevism published in Soviet Russia between 1917 and 1928. That period is, accordingly, by no means as rich in information about the dictator's early life as might have been expected in view of the fact that censorship conditions still remained relatively favourable for the preservation of evidence.

Another point must also be borne in mind. From October 1917 (and especially from 1923) onwards Stalin was a public figure whose actions were a matter of public record. Admittedly these actions were being distorted, even as they were performed, by Stalinist propaganda, and on an ever increasing scale. But there was a limit, even under conditions of rigorous Stalinist thought control from 1929 onwards, to the degree in which the dictator's post-1917 doings could be retrospectively reshaped in the form of a substantially spurious biography or Stalin Legend. There was less need, too, for such fabrications in respect of the post-revolutionary period, when Stalin's role – if not invariably glorious – was at least comparatively prominent. In its impact on the period from 1917 onwards, therefore, the official Stalinist version of Stalin's doings (in the canonical form which it eventually assumed) depends less on sheer invention than it does in its picture of the younger Stalin. By no means, however, did this consideration prevent Stalin's later propagandists from presenting his whole achievement in distortedly heroic form.

It is from 1929 onwards – with Stalin's attainment of unchallenged ascendancy – that the material of his biography begins to assume its unique and peculiarly perverse form. The dictator has become a prime target for biographical research at the very time when he has just gained full control of the Soviet sources, human and documentary, relevant to his biography.

Far from allowing scholars access to this material, he proceeds to destroy – in the full and strictly literal sense – many of the scholars and (probably) much of the material. It is now that he launches or sponsors the corpus of spurious and ennobling accounts of himself by others – and especially of his early life up to the death of Lenin – which we call the Stalin Legend. During the 1930s this Legend becomes increasingly fraudulent in its claims about Stalin's youthful activities. Authors of previous, less pretentious versions of the Leader's doings are exterminated; their places are taken by new, yet more mendacious evangelists. No longer content with the mere suppression of inconvenient information, the Legend's creators are now issuing successive relays of specially concocted myths, each more uplifting than the last. By about 1936 the Stalin Legend has assumed the essential form in which it is to be propagated, subject to continuing new embellishment, throughout the rest of the dictator's life. Hence the extreme unreliability of Soviet-published material on the early Stalin dating from 1929–53 – and most especially (within that same period) from 1936–53.

As for the Legend's contents, which will be described in greater detail below, their general burden is as follows. From his schooldays onwards Comrade Stalin is a phenomenally heroic underground revolutionary politician. He is the premier Caucasian Bolshevik and a major leader of the all-Russian Bolshevik movement; he is a close collaborator and disciple of Lenin from early manhood onwards; he is a leading ideologist, but also a man of action who marches in the forefront of all important pre-1917 revolutionary initiatives; he is, with Lenin, the chief architect of the Bolshevik October *coup* of 1917; he does more than anyone else to win the Civil War of 1918-21; he is Lenin's most faithful ally and comrade-in-arms during Lenin's last years.

As we shall see below, these claims are all false or grossly exaggerated, while many of the details which embellish them are wholly bogus.

How closely did Stalin, in person, direct the detailed fabrication of his Legend-biography? Unfortunately, little evidence survives on this point. We shall occasionally find him inserting self-boosting claims in the material; but we shall also discover him deprecating, from time to time, the very Stalin Cult and the Legend which formed part of it. In one memorable instance we shall see him combining both conflicting tendencies – by slotting into the *Short Biography* of himself, prepared by others, the deliciously ironical claim that: 'Stalin never allowed his work to be marred by the slightest hint of vanity, conceit or self-adulation.'[1] Clearly his attitude was ambivalent, the very policy of self-glorification cultivated for reasons of expediency by Stalin the Dictator being highly distasteful to Stalin the Man. In view of this, and of what is known about his methods and character in general, it seems unlikely that he habitually issued detailed directives to the manufacturers of his pseudo-biography. It was simpler, far, just to shoot those whose copy did not come up to scratch, while leaving the menaced survivors to draw the consequences.

In considering the Legend as a whole, we must remember that two distinct time scales are involved: (*a*) that of the period in Stalin's biography to which the Legend applies; (*b*) that of the much later Cult period in which the Legend was invented. These facts and their timetable may be summarized (in deliberately simplified form), as follows:

1879 to 1923 (especially 1899 to 1917): period to which the Stalin Legend applies.

1924 to 1928: period to which the Stalin Legend no longer applies, but in which the Stalin Cult has not yet been launched on a comprehensive scale.

1929 to 1953 (especially 1936 to 1953): period of the Cult, of which the fabrication of the Legend is a part.

After considering Soviet-published material of the Cult period 1929-53, one is relieved to turn to Soviet published disclosures dating from the destalinizing years – and even from the (later) restalinizing years – following the dictator's death. Though such publications have also been rigorously controlled from above (along the lines described in Chapter Sixteen, below) they are voluminous and – if carefully used – extremely valuable.

So much for material on Stalin published in Russia. It can be supplemented by material published in the West, where Soviet censorship does not operate. But these western-published sources too have their defects. Many have been contributed by authors driven into emigration by Stalin – authors who were, and had good reason to be, violently biased against him and all his works. Moreover, certain extremely important memoirs remained unrecorded for forty and more years after some of the events which they describe: for example, the reminiscences (1932) of Iremashvili (sole independent first-hand witness to the dictator's childhood) and the accounts given later still (in 1967-9) by Stalin's daughter of what her father confided in her about his early life. Other important western-published defector sources suffer from obvious symptoms of 'ghosting': in particular, they are apt to contain long passages of verbatim dialogue such as only persons endowed with an unprecedented capacity for total recall could have reconstituted in so detailed a form after so long an interval.

An additional problem has been posed by the publication in the West of numerous wholly spurious memoirs by persons purporting to have been Stalin's or Beria's nephews and the like. Many of these – such as those described in Paul Blackstock's admirably entitled ' "Books for Idiots":

False Soviet "Memoirs" ' – must be discounted entirely. But what of the intermediate category – such as Elizabeth Lermolo's suspect and highly fictionalized *Face of a Victim*? What of the mysterious, recently published *Khrushchev Remembers*, which we can neither link positively with the Khrushchev nor prove to have been concocted independently of him? These and similar works have often been treated as serious sources by authorities on the period. But neither possesses, to put it mildly, the credentials for which one looks in historical evidence. The Stalin material abounds in such documents, of which it can only be said (as has been noted in another context) that the marks of genuineness are too strong to permit one to view them as totally fraudulent, but the marks of fraudulence too strong to permit one to view them as totally genuine.[2] I have tried to quarry them for what ore may be separated from the dross, and have therefore found occasion to quote from them guardedly in my text.

On the unsatisfactory nature of the material the assassination of Kirov in 1934 provides an eloquent comment. This was, perhaps, the single most important event of Stalin's career, since it led to the notorious purge trials of 1936–8 which consolidated his power. The murder has to be reconstructed in part from confessions extracted during the Bukharin Trial of 1938 ... confessions long recognized as spurious, being part of a deliberate judicial frame-up. This tainted data must be combined with the 'revelations' sprung in 1956 and 1961 by Nikita Khrushchev. Unlike the suspect *Khrushchev Remembers*, this particular material is at least known to have originated with Khrushchev. But we must remember that this same Khrushchev was not, even in his real persona, the most reliable of witnesses, since he was so outstanding a practitioner of *vranyo*: the special Russian art form for which 'blarney' is the nearest translation. To such dubious evidence on the Kirov affair must be added the reminiscences – some seemingly ghosted – of certain Soviet defectors to the West. This material can, fortunately, be tested in part against a more trustworthy source: the account given by Boris Nikolayevsky of statements made to him in person by the doomed Bukharin during his last trip outside the USSR. But a mystery Kirov's murder still remains, and a similar degree of obscurity surrounds many other episodes in the dictator's life.

As these considerations suggest, the biographer of Stalin has much to learn from historians of the ancient world, for his task in many ways resembles theirs more closely than it compares with the work of scholars dealing with less problematical figures from our own age. The comparative assessment of late and disputed sources has almost as important a part to play in tracing Stalin's activities as it has in the investigation of an Alcibiades, an Alexander the Great, a Nero or a Caligula. The main difference is the extent to which, in Stalin's case, the biographical sources have been deliberately and systematically suppressed over a long period by the very subject of the biography.

In dealing with such problems it is often better to stop arguing about sources, and to let the sources argue for themselves. This policy has been adopted the more readily for two reasons. Firstly, investigation of the evidence on Stalin has an interest in its own right: it sheds on the dictator's epoch a light such as no other line of study can supply. Secondly, the story of Stalin's sources (which he controlled in so dictatorial and effective a manner) *is* – to a considerable extent – the story of Stalin himself.

They remained good friends throughout their schooldays. Iremashvili it was who survived and became the sole witness of Stalin's childhood to publish his recollections outside the purview of Kremlinite censorship.

Another account of these years has Dzhugashvili riding about on the back of another boy and shouting *Ya stal, ya stal* ('I am steel, I am steel');[21] this is the first foretaste of the name Stalin on which Soso was eventually to settle in 1912 after taking up and discarding a dozen other revolutionary aliases.

As such episodes show, the future dictator was assertive from an early age. He would walk about with his long, hooked nose in the air, and it could be unwise to come between him and anything on which he had set his mind, for he showed limitless passion in the pursuit of predetermined goals. Curt of speech, he was never seen to cry, and would sneer at his companions' misfortunes, requiring of others only that they should submit to his will. His greatest triumph was to feel victorious and feared.[22] Such, again, is the version of his closest schoolfriend, Iremashvili, who well may (as Trotsky suggests) have unintentionally coloured his reminiscences in retrospect;[23] these were not published until 1932, long after the earliest events which they describe and at a time when Stalin had already acquired dictatorial powers. Still, such as they are, they remain the best evidence on Stalin's schooldays which we are ever likely to have.

Wrestling was by no means Stalin's only pastime as a boy. His chief delights were rambling, rock-climbing and pot-holing in the local hills dominated by the snow-capped Caucasian mountain range. 'Soso loved Nature; it could fill him with genuine enthusiasm.' But his love was for inarticulate scenery, not for living beings; one of his favourite pastimes was to throw stones at birds.[24]

A great reader from early in life, Soso frequented a Gori bookshop, where (as later in Tiflis) he could obtain works banned by the school authorities. He steeped himself in the classics of Georgian literature, and one of these – a novel by Kazbegi – supplied him with a hero in the romantically vengeful character Koba; Soso even insisted that his classmates should call him Koba, and was still addressed by this nickname by his few surviving intimates in the years of his prime. There are also allusions to Joseph's natural singing talent and to his organizing a church choir, besides which he would lead his friends in renderings of Georgian folk songs. Nor can it still be maintained that Stalin was never heard to sing after 1917, since his daughter Svetlana remembers his pleasing light tenor voice.[25] Other reports credit the boy dictator with a talent for sketching. The general picture is of a gifted but modest all-rounder.

So far Stalin's story has been told as if it were the life of some more ordinary man, and with no reference to a factor which uniquely complicates his biography: the existence of an official Legend. By this is meant the elaborate pseudo-biography of the dictator's early life, as concocted in his political prime from 1929 onwards. Foisted on the Soviet and world public by countless propagandists and policemen, the Legend has masked the Leader's real career by suppressing inconvenient episodes and substituting others more ennobling. The Legend cannot be ignored on these pages – as noted in the Introduction, the very existence of so spurious a phenomenon is itself a crucial element in the dictator's real biography. Nor can it be assumed that every item in the Legend is false, for its compilers were more concerned to twist than to replace the truth. In what is – taken as a whole – designedly a bogus amalgam many a nugget of useful information will, accordingly, be found embedded.

Bearing these considerations in mind, we can now graft on to our narrative of Stalin's childhood – hitherto based on sources little contaminated by the Cult – mythopoeic material such as is found in various Legend-biographies, as also in such collected accounts of the child Stalin as that published to coincide with his sixtieth birthday in 1939.[26] Discussing the dictator's infancy, these authorities piously reproduce the alleged memoirs of ageing Georgians who claimed association with the boy Joseph half a century or so earlier. Though such material must naturally be treated with extreme caution, there is no need to suspend belief entirely – except for those items stressing the precocity of Soso's political activities and ascribing to him various heroic or semi-divine attributes. It must, of course, never be forgotten that all these contributions were recorded, compiled, edited, censored and read during the peak period of Stalin's great persecutions, and by individuals who were all living under the shadow of the executioner's pistol. When G. Elisabedashvili speaks of little Soso as a 'hero in all respects first and foremost among his comrades',[27] we must remember that this evidence surfaced only a year or two after many of Stalin's leading political colleagues had publicly confessed to such imaginary crimes as infecting Soviet pigs with erysipelas, putting ground glass into butter, attempting to assassinate Lenin and spying for Germany and Japan. Against so grotesque a background, friendly and admiring references to the boy wonder were, presumably, to be had on demand and in any required form.

This being the case, one should perhaps praise the restraint of the Legend-builders who covered the dictator's childhood, for mendacious though accounts of the boy Dzhugashvili certainly are in some respects, they do not have an excessively extravagant ring – not, at least, when compared with some of the wilder claims made for Comrade Stalin as a young adult by the same Legend-building industry. The trend is to present the infant and adolescent Leader as a sober, reliable, helpful schoolboy . . . and not so much of a rebel either; Stalin was, after all, in full control of the government at the time when these memoirs were published, and there was no call to sanctify subversion by invoking the image of a mischievous Soso. The various terrorized evangelists of the late 1930s accordingly depict Comrade Stalin as a model pupil. 'Like Lenin, he was a diligent scholar and always obtained the highest marks. He was first in study and play, a leader in all games, a good friend and a favourite among his schoolfellows.'[28] Possessed of a phenomenal memory, the Comrade gladly coaches his less gifted fellows, occasionally correcting a teacher who lapses into error. Once the Comrade intervenes successfully with the school authorities on behalf of a friend prevented from sitting his examinations by illness. Serene and effortlessly master of his environment, he displays the easy assurance of a child Christ discoursing with His elders in the Temple. As for athletic prowess, there are references to Comrade Stalin taking the lead in informal games, and to his being the best swimmer in town – at the age of six! During races in the near-by rivers, the Kura and the Lyakhva, the infant Comrade reputedly outdistances a local greengrocer called Mikha Bitsadze.[29]

Turning from such frivolities to the sensitive topic of politics, we find one gospeller of the developed Cult period – Yaroslavsky – antedating the boy's active interest in this key theme. He has the child Joseph haranguing the workers and peasants of Gori on the causes of their poverty. 'Comrade Stalin explained step by step why the peasants lived so poorly, who exploited them, who were their friends, and who their enemies. He spoke so simply and interestingly that the peasants begged him to come and talk to them again.'[30] Yet Stalin himself had already virtually disclaimed such political precociousness when he stated that he had not joined the revolutionary movement until his sixteenth year.[31] Yaroslavsky may also be improving on Stalin's own version of the Gospel when he reports G. Glurdzhidze's tale of the boy Comrade converting his friends to atheism at Gori. 'You know, they are fooling us, there is no God. . . . I'll lend you a book to read; it will show you that . . . all this talk about God is sheer nonsense.' The book turned out to be Darwin's *Origin of Species*.[32]

Another, more extravagant, fable relating to the period has Comrade Stalin and his Gori schoolmates forced to witness, in 1892, the public execution on three specially erected gibbets of peasant-highwaymen such as were all too common in the Caucasian mountains. Robin Hoods who robbed the rich and spared their fellow-peasants (according to the dubious evidence of one P. S. Kapanadze), these victims were made an object lesson in discipline, the boys of Gori school being compelled to witness the publicly staged ritual strangling ... and naturally finding it inconsistent with the Christian commandment 'Thou shall not kill'.[33] No doubt the twelve-year-old Comrade noted that, when human life is taken, a certain style is called for, and that a claim on the part of the slayer to be actuated by philanthropic motives does not come amiss. Here was a lesson which Real Stalin was to learn better than any other, whether or not the story of the Legend-Stalin's attendance at the hanging deserves credit.

Stalin's mother Keke was also duly woven into the Legend. In *Pravda* of 27 October 1935 we meet the dear little old lady as interviewed by a team of journalists from the Soviet news agency TASS in her modest quarters in the Tiflis viceregal palace, black-kerchiefed as she sits beneath a portrait of Lenin. At the mention of her son's name Keke's eyes glow with joy, affection and pride behind her horn-rimmed spectacles. It turns out that he has recently paid her one of his all too rare visits, arriving unexpectedly after being announced by 'our Lawrence': the future police overlord Lavrenty Beria, now Caucasian Party boss. Carefully and reverentially drinking in the slow speech of 'the one who has bestowed on the world the greatest of men', the awed journalists learn of Keke's own early struggles and of her efforts to obtain a good education for little Soso. There is much talk of his favourite walnut preserve before the 'deeply moved' interviewers leave the room of 'Her who has given the World the Great Leader of the Toilers of All Peoples'.[34]

In Keke's only other recorded interview, given in 1930, she told the American journalist H. R. Knickerbocker what a good little boy Soso had always been: she had never had to punish him.[35] As the comment suggests, Mrs Dzhugashvili was something of an amateur Legend-builder in her own right, for we have Stalin's own testimony – noted above – that his mother in fact *did* beat him as a child. We also learn from another source independent of Legend – Soso Iremashvili – that Soso Dzhugashvili was not at all the model little lad whom his mother has portrayed. In fact, he was the naughtiest boy in the school! He was punished almost daily, and was in the habit of organizing protests against authority. Such an upheaval occurred, for instance, on the occasion when he unleashed a mob of yelling, booing boys on a particularly unpopular master, who could be rescued only by the combined intervention of the entire teaching staff.[36]

What had especially incensed these fiery Georgian lads was the decision (enforced from 1890 onwards) to make Russian the official language of instruction at their school, along with all other Georgian teaching establishments. This affront to national pride derived from the russification policy imposed on the many non-Russian peoples of the Empire by the Tsar

Alexander III as part of a general programme of reactionary measures designed to counteract the reforms enacted by his father, Alexander II (the liberator of the serfs). So strictly was the new rule enforced that Soso and his friends did not merely receive all their formal instruction in Russian, but were even forbidden to converse in their native tongue out of class – and on penalty of incarceration for hours in the school lock-up. But though Soso was forced to learn Russian under such circumstances, which seemed ill-adapted to prejudice him in favour of the language and its speakers, he was eventually to become an outstanding Russian patriot by adoption. Not that he was ever to speak Russian like a Russian, for he retained a guttural Georgian burr throughout his life. On the other hand, he did handle the language effectively enough to manipulate millions of Russians into slaughtering each other: a fair index of linguistic competence.

Despite what Iremashvili has to tell us of Koba's pranks, he also confirms what Legend has to say of his academic prowess, describing him as the best pupil in the school. So well did the boy acquit himself that, when he left at the age of fourteen, he was awarded a scholarship to help pay for his further education.[37] A hitch must have occurred at some stage, though, because he had taken six years to complete a four-year course. Perhaps his street accident, or the blood-poisoning episode, was responsible for the delay? Or perhaps his apprenticeship at the boot factory, as enforced by his father, lasted longer than surviving evidence appears to indicate?

In any event Koba was accepted, in 1894, for transfer to the Tiflis Orthodox Theological Seminary as the next stage in his preparation for the priesthood in accordance with his mother's ambitions.

Seminarist

Quitting the comparatively easy-going elementary church school in his native Gori, after attending it as a day-boy for six years, Stalin boards at the Tiflis Orthodox Theological Seminary between 1894 and 1899, leaving or being expelled one year before completing his arduous course of studies.

Vary though they might in atmosphere, Imperial Russian church schools and seminaries were all part of an empire-wide standardized ecclesiastical educational network. Taken as a whole, the two courses – four years' elementary schooling (as at Gori) followed by six years' secondary schooling (as at Tiflis) – included all the basic elements of the exacting syllabus pursued at the secular classical *gimnazii* (grammar schools), and it involved a heavy concentration on three ancient languages: Old Church Slavonic, Greek and Latin. From the *gimnazii*, themselves no strangers to scriptural study, the ecclesiastical schools were distinguished by a heavier theological bias. Apart from this emphasis, Stalin followed at Gori and Tiflis a course similar to that pursued, for example, by Anton Chekhov at the Taganrog *gimnaziya* some twenty years earlier. As with Chekhov, study of the classical languages left little permanent imprint, though the dictator's daughter Svetlana has noted that her father remembered Greek in his old age.[1] On Stalin's rhetorical style, with its repetitive and ritualistic cadences, the liturgy of Orthodoxy and the rhythms of the stately Old Church Slavonic tongue were to leave a lasting stamp. This catechistic training also taught him to think of life as a series of problems to which all-sufficient answers, couched in exactly prescribed verbal formulae, were supplied by authority. But it was chiefly by bringing the boy into contact with revolutionaries that the seminary influenced his future career.

For the fourteen-year-old Soso the move to Tiflis marked a big upheaval. Hitherto free to explore the fields, hills, caves and medieval castles surrounding his home town, he now found himself in the chief city of Georgia – and not of Georgia alone, but of the Empire's Caucasian Viceroyalty as a whole. Tiflis was the administrative capital of the entire Caucasus: a diverse amalgam of ethnically varied communities embracing territory of Armenia and modern Azerbaijan as well as Georgia itself. The thriving Caucasian and Georgian metropolis now had some 150,000 inhabitants, Armenians outnumbering both Georgians and Russians. It offered a motley, picturesque spectacle, with squares and streets newly-built in the architectural style of Imperial Russia – but also with narrow, crooked alleys and bustling bazaars where Turkic, Persian and native Georgian influences were powerfully evident.

Though his move to a bustling city no doubt stimulated the adolescent Soso, the grim seminary blighted his morale. Old boys of that establishment have likened it to a barracks or prison. But though this was a boarding establishment, the pupils were not permanently confined to its forbidding neo-classical premises – they were at least free to roam abroad, unsupervised, between the hours of three and five in the afternoon. From the presiding Rector and Inspector downwards, the staff consisted largely of monks who maintained a harsh regimen, much of the day being taken up with protracted church services. Pupils were not allowed to read newspapers, and were even forbidden such secular literature as the novels of Tolstoy and Dostoyevsky; but they were ingenious in evading these regulations. In doing so they risked being sent to the solitary darkness of the seminary punishment cell.

Embedded in Legend material we find certain extracts from the seminary conduct book, and though they cannot be checked at first hand there is no reason to suspect their authenticity. These entries have Comrade Stalin repeatedly in trouble for reading banned books. In 1896 he is sentenced to the lock-up on account of Victor Hugo's novel *Ninety-Three;* in March of the following year Letourneau's *Literary Evolution of the Nations* is the offending text. The Comrade has been caught with this work on the chapel stairs: the thirteenth occasion on which he has been found with books illicitly borrowed from the local Cheap Library. In September 1898 he is again found infringing this ineffectually enforced regulation, having been detected reading aloud from banned books to a group of pupils in the dining hall. The scandal provokes a general search of all the students' belongings: a common occurrence in an establishment where the monkish masters regularly spy on their charges, ransacking their lockers in their absence and encouraging them to denounce each other.[2] That such an atmosphere of tyranny really did dominate the seminary is confirmed by an early anonymous source independent of Stalinist controls: the memoirs, dated 1907, of an unnamed Russian member of the staff.[3]

According to Stalin's statement to Emil Ludwig in 1931, this atmosphere of suspicion and tale-bearing was the main influence which turned him to Socialism. 'I joined the revolutionary movement when fifteen years old . . . in protest against the outrageous régime and jesuitical methods prevalent at the seminary.'[4] When Ludwig asked whether the Jesuits did not also have their good points, Stalin granted them persistence in pursuing sordid ends, adding that 'their principal method is spying, prying, worming their way into people's souls and outraging their feelings.'[5] Was it partly a desire to rival or outdo these so-called Jesuits, rather than revulsion from their methods, which placed its peculiar stamp on Socialism as interpreted by the mature Stalin?

Odious as such monkish prying was to its victims, it had not arisen accidentally, but from the authorities' well-founded fear of their own pupils. Though intended for the training of priests, Orthodox seminaries throughout the Empire had long fulfilled a second, unavowed function as breeding grounds for revolutionaries. Outstanding among famous earlier subversives had been Nikolay Chernyshevsky, a product of the Saratov Seminary; he had graduated to pen the influential novel *What is to be Done:* the Bible of the early Russian revolutionary movement, this provided a programme for constructing and inhabiting a Socialist Utopia. When Muscovite seminarists rioted in 1885 the city Metropolitan called in the police, after which the turbulent priests-in-embryo were reputedly castigated in his presence with rods which he had specially consecrated for the purpose. The seminarists of Voronezh had once tried to blow up their rector with a bomb placed in a stove.

In staging such protests volatile Tiflis was not disposed to lag behind its sluggish northern rivals, dislike of authority in general being reinforced, in this distant outpost of empire, by outraged national pride; for though Georgians were not quite treated as 'natives' by their Russian masters, they were made to feel their inferiority in many ways. As already noted, such resentment was further inflamed by the policy, intensified during Stalin's schooldays, of russifying the non-Russian periphery of the Empire. As in Gori, so too in Tiflis, the Russian language was imposed in educational institutions; it was a Russian, not a Georgian, who held the post of rector at the seminary. Such slights were bound to be resented in the Georgian capital – especially as the Georgian Church had been founded in about 330 AD, many centuries before the Russian Orthodox Church, having enjoyed independent status for a millennium and a half before being unceremoniously annexed to the Russian ecclesiastical establishment in 1811.

Under such smouldering conditions the Tiflis rectorship was no sinecure, as emerged in 1885 when the revolutionary seminarist Silvestr Dzhibladze publicly slapped his rector's face for making disdainful comments about Georgia; Dzhibladze was exiled to Siberia as the result of this exploit. Worse was to come in the following year, when the same unfortunate rector was assassinated by another pupil. Where schoolmasters risked their lives by failing to nip sedition in the bud, we can begin to understand why they found it necessary to spy on their charges, and why the Orthodox Russian monk Germogen (rector in Stalin's time) and his chief assistant, Inspector Abashidze (a Georgian subservient to the colonial power), behaved as such 'jesuitical' inquisitors. It was to Abashidze that pupil-informers went to lay information against Soso Dzhugashvili. But was Dzhugashvili only informed against? Did he not himself also inform against others? That he indeed did so, and that a number of his school-mates were expelled as the result of his denunciations, has been plausibly reported.[6] The seminary thus served Dzhugashvili as a laboratory in which he could study the mechanics of espionage and intrigue. One witness, P. Talakvadze, tells how the students were once sitting in Pushkin Square near the seminary after dinner when someone suddenly yelled out that Inspector Abashidze was searching Dzhugashvili's belongings. Rushing back, Talakvadze noticed that Abashidze had already concluded his investigation; having broken open the offender's locker and extracted various illicit books, he was proceeding to the second floor, carrying these trophies under his arm and accompanied by the erring Soso.[7]

As a relief from more sordid preoccupations, seminarist Dzhugashvili sought – to be more precise, may have sought – refuge in writing poetry. Six lyrics, later attributed to him, were published in Georgian periodicals in 1895-6. Signed 'I. Dzh-shvili' and (in one instance) 'Soselo', these verses were first ascribed to Stalin in 1939 in an article, 'The Young Stalin's Verses', published in a Tiflis newspaper.[8] This story of the Comrade's excursion into poetry has a suspicious ring, though – especially as a better accredited Georgian poet, conveniently called Ivan *Dzhavakishvili* (who had an ode to Stalin published in 1938) could equally well have been the 'I. Dzh-shvili' of 1895. Whether or not this rival -shvili had been induced to co-operate in a fraudulent Legend-building operation, Stalin must have decided in the end to discard his own poetic laurels: no verses are attributed to him in his *Works*, as published from 1946 onwards. By then he no longer wished to present himself as author of such effusions as the following, previously attributed to him:

> The rose opens her petals,
> And embraces the violet.
> The lily too has awakened.
> They bare their heads to the zephyrs.[9]

If such verses really are Stalin's they betray a sentimentality which seldom intrudes elsewhere in his stern career. They also contain the motif of Georgian patriotism, and even occasional invocations of the Almighty – thus suggesting an allegiance to ideologies which he early abjured or never accepted. Still, we also remember the young Soso being described as a passionate lover of Nature. Apart from vague references to the suffering peasantry, Stalin's alleged verses are innocent of revolutionary implications; it was, perhaps, for this reason that his authorship came to be officially forgotten.

The problem of seminarist Dzhugashvili's revolutionary activity has been obscured by the Legend-builders, who have exaggerated his subversive impact and antedated it. We have already watched Yaroslavsky unconvincingly portraying Soso as an agitator of peasants back in pre-seminary days. That he really did take an interest in revolutionary politics during his first year in Tiflis is, however, attested by the more credit-worthy Iremashvili. In 1894, this witness claims, he and Stalin joined a Marxist youth group organized by a senior pupil. There were secret meetings, and a six-year reading programme was evolved. But it appears that Stalin – already a rebel, even in the context of rebellion – broke up the group and formed a rival circle dominated by himself; his disciples 'repeated their little dictator's words like parrots.'[10] Even at this early stage, then, and on this trivial level, Stalin was following disruptive tactics such as he was to pursue so successfully in his later career. We also note that he was already impatient of political leadership proceeding from any source other than himself.

13

Among the various available revolutionary doctrines it is Marxism which continues to attract Comrade Stalin most. He and some other seminarists club together and hire a scribe to provide them with a manuscript copy of Karl Marx's *Das Kapital* – in Russian translation, presumably – of which there is only one specimen in Tiflis. The Comrade reads it twice and makes detailed notes.[11]

The year 1898 was a landmark in Russian revolutionary history, since it was then – at a conference in Minsk – that the Empire's Marxists first founded an empire-wide organization: the Russian Social Democratic Workers' Party, from which the present-day Communist Party of the Soviet Union has evolved. Though Russia's active revolutionaries – Marxist or non-Marxist – remained few in numbers, and though it is possible to exaggerate in speaking of the late 1890s as a period of 'revolutionary ferment', the majority of Russian intellectuals was at this time opposed in some degree to the Imperial government and to the Tsarist social and political system as a whole. To express views other than liberal or radical was, indeed, barely respectable in intellectual circles of the period. This feature of Moscow and St Petersburg was fully reflected by the provincial intelligentsia of Tiflis . . . where anti-government sentiment was, of course, further inflamed by Georgian nationalist passion.

It was in this context, and in the year 1898, that Stalin – still a seminarist – joined a local Georgian Marxist circle. It was called *Mesame Dasi* (Group Three), and was headed by the ex-seminarist Noy Zhordania. Many years later, as a Paris-based refugee from the Stalin terror, Zhordania was to recall his first meeting with Dzhugashvili, who had called to offer his services. So deep an impression had Zhordania's articles made on the youth (he politely explained) that he had decided to leave school at once and spend his time proselytizing workers. But though Zhordania welcomed Joseph's decision in principle – since the infant Social Democratic movement sorely needed its missionaries – he found the new recruit's knowledge of history, sociology and political economy woefully superficial. Joseph should return to the seminary, Zhordania advised, and pursue his studies more effectively;[12] and Joseph seems to have followed this advice, at least to the extent of staying on at school for one more year.

As a counterblast to this deflating account, published abroad in 1936, Stalin's propagandists have their legendary Soso abusing Zhordania in public. After breakfast one morning Comrade Stalin is found denouncing that distinguished Georgian Marxist to fellow-pupils in Pushkin Square. This informal seminar is disrupted by the school bell announcing the beginning of classes – but not before Comrade Stalin has praised an article by Lenin, adding: 'I must meet him at all costs.'[13] Spurious though this material sounds, it is important as first injecting into Stalin's biography the name of Lenin, who was to enjoy such great prestige after inspiring the October Revolution of 1917 that all his political colleagues seized every opportunity to emphasize and exaggerate the extent of their early association with him.

Seminarist Dzhugashvili's revolutionary activity included clandestine meetings with disaffected railway workers of the city. It was on such an outing that he met a political prisoner, one Ormotsadze, who had escaped from Siberia and who impressed him as a romantic symbol of revolt against the Tsars.[14] Perhaps the memory of such visits was in Stalin's mind when, in 1926, he recalled being put in charge of a circle of Tiflis railway workers.[15] Beria has Comrade Stalin running two such illegal circles – that is, political discussion groups – within the seminary itself.[16] What Beria does not say is that at least one of these groups had to be taken away from the wretched youth. 'The scoundrel! We give him a job agitating against the government and capitalists, and he turns out to be agitating against *us*!' Such was the complaint (as reported in memoirs published outside the Soviet Union and dated 1936) of Silvestr Dzhibladze – the former rector-slapper of the Tiflis Seminary and a pioneer Georgian Marxist of some standing – who soon came to regret his decision to put the quarrelsome Dzhugashvili in charge of propaganda work.[17]

In spring 1899 Dzhugashvili left the seminary, after completing only five years out of a six-year course. As is usual with key events in his biography, we are by no means clear about what happened and why. That his dissatisfaction with the institution was growing during his last year is evident. It is clear, too, that his relations with the staff were deteriorating, and that he was neglecting his work. Iremashvili speaks of Koba's conviction that serious study was useless; he gradually became the worst pupil in the seminary; he would answer the reproaches of his teachers with venomous and disdainful laughter.[18] This account is borne out by signs of increasing indiscipline as recorded in the conduct book. Once, when some of the pupils' belongings were being searched by the school authorities (presumably for the usual illicit literature) Koba protested, complaining that such searches were never made in other seminaries. 'Dzhugashvili [the report continues] is generally disrespectful and rude towards persons in authority and systematically refuses to bow to one of the masters.' For these offences the youth was put in the lock-up for five hours on the Rector's orders.[19] On another occasion Dzhugashvili studiously ignored a Father Dmitry when the latter entered his room. 'Don't you see who is standing before you?' the monk demanded. But Dzhugashvili rose, dabbing his eyes, and said that he could see nothing except a black spot.[20]

Under these conditions it is hardly surprising that Joseph left college prematurely. Iremashvili maintains that he went of his own accord because his school marks had sunk so low that there was no point in carrying on, besides which he had undermined his health through reading by candlelight the illicit literature for which the monks were constantly on the look-out.[21] But Iremashvili is the only authority to claim that Stalin left the seminary of his own free will. The dictator's mother confirms that the lad was suffering from ill-health – but herself took credit for removing him from school, having been advised by a doctor that her boy risked contracting tuberculosis. 'I took him home on account of his health. . . . I took him out. He was my only son.'[22] One may doubt the accuracy of this recollection, if only because the nineteen-year-old Stalin was hardly docile enough to be 'taken' about like some babe-in-arms, as his mother has implied. All other sources have Stalin expelled by the seminary authorities, thus bringing his career into line with the classic pattern for nineteenth-century Russian revolutionaries. For example, Dmitry Karakozov, who unsuccessfully tried to assassinate Alexander II in 1866, had been expelled from two universities, and the famous revolutionary plotter Zhelyabov had been sent down from Odessa University for hounding an unpopular professor. 'Propagating Marxism' was, according to Stalin's *Works*, the reason for his expulsion;[23] other authorities also quote political reasons such as 'holding dangerous views', 'leading a Social Democratic circle' and the somewhat feeble 'political unreliability'. The continued reading of forbidden books (an offence both political and disciplinary) is also invoked; other contributory causes, as quoted in the various sources, include failure to pay his fees, missing the end-of-term examinations (while failing to offer a good excuse for this) and lack of application.

By now Dzhugashvili and the seminary had clearly reached the parting of the ways on many counts, and he seems to have sailed out of the institution on a gale of fury. He took with him a ferocious hatred of the college administration, the bourgeoisie and everything connected with the concepts of Tsarism and authority.[24]

Commenting on Stalin's abandonment of a career in the priesthood, Isaac Deutscher has well said that: 'In the Church he would, at best, have become a second Abashidze.'[25] A second Abashidze is, however, what Stalin did become on a grander scale – when he eventually turned the whole of Russia into a Tiflis Seminary writ large: a community in which spying, denunciation and intrigue were institutionalized by one who had had the opportunity to study such phenomena at close quarters and in relatively mild form, during his most formative years. Among the various features of the seminary which he was to adopt, none was to be so creatively expanded and multiplied as the notorious school punishment cell or lock-up.

The oppressive atmosphere so distasteful to Stalin was, it may be added, specifically that of the Tiflis Seminary rather than that of Imperial Russia as a whole. The country was at this time a far less regimented community than is commonly realized. Despite intrigues and counter-intrigues (to which abundant reference will be made below) between a handful of gendarmes and revolutionaries, and despite even the activities of a literary censorship, life under the last two Tsars, Alexander III and Nicholas II, was arguably far freer for those intellectuals who remained uncommitted to extremist political action than it is in Great Britain or the United States in the late twentieth century. To read, for example, the voluminous and uninhibited correspondence of Anton Chekhov, penned in the 1880s and 1890s, to steep oneself in the lively memoirs of his (and Stalin's) many contemporaries ... this is to plunge oneself into anything but the Tsarist police state of popular imagination and Soviet propaganda.

Such, then, was the background – institutionalized repression in the seminary within a society still comparatively unregimented so far as intellectuals were concerned – against which Stalin completed his eleven years of formal education at Gori and Tiflis. For all its faults, the training was superior to that which the average Georgian shoemaker's son might expect. It equipped the future dictator with techniques which he firmly grasped, even though many years were to elapse before he could exploit them fully. Accustomed to receiving doctrinal material in the shape of revealed truths, and drilled to regurgitate these truths by rote in the form of ritual answers to ritual questions, Stalin was to emerge in due course as an arbiter of ultimate verity in his own right – and as one furnished by the seminary with a ready-made catechistic procedure for handing down revealed truths of his own.

The instructional devices of the Tiflis Seminary were far removed from the methods of free-ranging enquiry – methods which were in some degree temporarily assimilated by the other two premier Russian revolutionaries, Lenin and Trotsky ... who admittedly later discarded and suppressed them. Having studied at universities, and possessing a wider general culture than Stalin, these more self-consciously intellectual rebels – and many among their senior revolutionary colleagues – would never have considered Stalin their educational equal. Many of these figures travelled widely and resided outside Russia, while Stalin stayed at home; many, too, were fluent in western European languages, while Stalin was stuck with his Georgian, his Russian and the remnants of ancient tongues unwillingly studied at the seminary. It was less, then, in the breadth of his learning than in a phenomenal ability to exploit educational resources of a modest order that Stalin eventually demonstrated his superlative intelligence. Before he could do so, however, a long and obscure period of underground revolutionary activity had first to be lived through. This was to prove a more potent educational experience, in the widest sense, than anything absorbed on the school benches of Gori and Tiflis.

Escorting Stalin, now, into his adult life we note the paradox that this militant atheist – this hater of his neighbour, this mass smiter of others' cheeks, this future slaughterer of his fellow men – was the product of a Christian education of the most intensive and rigorous variety, dispensed in the bosom of one of the most ancient churches in Christendom.

2

Caucasian Rebel

Urban Guerrillero

ESCAPING from the bondage of the seminary on 29 May 1899, Joseph can at last switch his main energies to political conspiracy. During the 1900s he remains a local or provincial revolutionary, active or non-active in and out of jail in Tiflis, Batum, Baku and other parts of the Caucasus. Though occasionally travelling far outside his homeland, he keeps his Caucasian base during all these years; after which we shall find him – in the 1910s – operating on an empire-wide stage, and as an adoptive Russian revolutionary organizer rather than as a mere Georgian conspirator.

To consider Russian revolutionary history is to be amazed at the freedom allowed by the supposedly tyrannical authorities to individuals dedicated to the overthrow of the Imperial system. Throughout much of the late nineteenth and early twentieth centuries advocates of political violence – Anarchists, Marxists, Socialist Revolutionaries and lesser breeds – seem to enjoy unrestricted freedom of movement in Russia. They cross national and provincial frontiers with impunity, bearing inflammatory proclamations in the false bottoms of suitcases. Many avowedly revolutionary publications – the Russian translation of Karl Marx's *Das Kapital*, for instance – can appear in print with the blessing of the Imperial censorship; other subversive material pours from illicit presses which revolutionaries seem able to establish wherever they wish. There are occasional police raids and arrests. There is the occasional deportation to Siberia. But it is impossible to reconcile these conditions with the implacably ruthless Tsarist police state later evoked by Stalinist propaganda . . . and evoked in a community which Stalin himself had turned into just such a despotism as his apologists were retrospectively attributing to the last Tsar-Emperors of Russia.

To recall these conditions is not to deny that political repression of a sort was maintained in the years of the declining Empire. Between revolutionaries and Tsarist police a duel – often desultory, always liable to flare into violence – was in progress all the time. If repressive measures appear lax and half-hearted, this is partly because the Empire's police was by no means immune from the corruption, complacency and incompetence which cursed the Imperial administration as a whole. But there is also the point that – as a matter of policy – the Imperial police often allowed a known revolutionary to remain at liberty. If kept under surveillance rather than immediately arrested, he might reveal his associates, thus exposing a whole network. To give a suspect rope in this way is standard police practice everywhere, no matter whether criminal or political investigation is involved. There can therefore be nothing surprising in finding such procedures adopted in the Tiflis of the 1900s by the Imperial Russian political police. Known colloquially as the Okhrana, this included both plain-clothes officials and a uniformed force: the Corps of Gendarmes. It was this combined organization which chiefly menaced Stalin in the years 1899 to 1917.

By the end of the century the Okhrana had over-complicated its operations through its very success in infiltrating revolutionary organizations with police spies. Since the revolutionary organizations were simultaneously infiltrating the Okhrana with *their* spies, and since such spies easily became double agents – and then perhaps triple, quadruple or even more multiply enmeshed operatives – a situation of considerable complexity developed. Many policemen-revolutionaries or revolutionary policemen were unable, ultimately, to distinguish their own true allegiances. This might oscillate between devotion to the Emperor and devotion to revolution, or might hover in some limbo between these poles: a background offering much scope to a determined young man such as Joseph Dzhugashvili, who had no doubts about a revolutionary's paramount duty to his own ego.

As for Joseph's political allegiances, we suspect them to have been vaguer, at an early stage, than those attributed to him by Legend, which has him as a precocious wholehearted disciple of Lenin and Lenin's Bolshevik faction ... almost before the word Bolshevism had been coined. That Marxism, the creed to which Lenin imparted a Russian accent, attracted the young Stalin more than its main rivals – the Socialist Revolutionary and Anarchist doctrines – is confirmed by his above-mentioned adherence, in 1898, to the Georgian Marxist organization *Mesame Dasi*. Within this local grouping and within the Marxist movement as a whole – theoretically united as an All-Russian Social Democratic Party since 1898 – Stalin early distinguished himself by advocating extreme violence, as also by his quarrelsomeness. Accustomed from his schooldays to tolerate only such associates as would submit to his will, he carried this trait into his early adult life, systematically provoking dissension among revolutionaries who might otherwise have achieved unity. But even Stalin needed, in his early twenties, someone to whom he himself could, at least temporarily, submit. This was to become Lenin's role. Now fostering Russian revolution from bases in western Europe, Lenin fascinated the boy from Gori, who – like his master – seemed to discern in a discreetly calculated combination of violence, guile and ideological manipulation the fulcrum with which a world might be overturned. Stalin could not of course leave school as an adherent of Bolshevism, since that concept did not even come into being until August 1903, when the split in Social Democratic ranks created two warring factions within the Party: that of the (extremist) Bolsheviks and that of the (moderate) Mensheviks. But Stalin's extremism was turning him into a prospective Bolshevik even before the term gained currency, besides equipping him to see in Lenin the leader-hero to whom he might hitch his personal ambitions.

Unfortunately the activities of this young rebel can only be seen through a haze. Since, even in Imperial Russia, a political subversive had to cultivate some degree of caution – using aliases, hideouts, false beards and the like – and since Stalin was an efficient practical operator, it is not surprising if he contrived to conceal some of his doings from posterity as well as from the Tiflis gendarmerie. There is also the point – which we shall shortly consider in greater detail – that this early revolutionary activity (or lack of activity) was later to be processed as part of the vast Legend-creating operation designed to reshape the young Stalin's biography in a form suitable for a major hero of revolutionary myth.

In this context we shall expect to find Stalin's early life full of blank patches. One of these occurred immediately after his departure from the seminary in May 1899. We do not pick up his trail again until 28 December of the same year, when he takes a post as observer or clerk at the Tiflis Physical Observatory.[1] Stalin holds this appointment for the next fifteen months; it remains the only paid employment which he is ever known to have taken, if we exclude his later political offices as member of the Bolshevik Central Committee and Soviet Government. Dzhugashvili's salary was a miserable twenty roubles a month, but he was conveniently housed in the observatory building.[2] The main feature of his small, austere chamber was a large table piled high with books, including the works of Plekhanov and Lenin. Such secluded quarters formed a useful base for the young political conspirator whom Iremashvili remembers as wearing a black blouse, a red cravat and unpolished shoes:[3] a protest against conventional 'bourgeois' dress ? Elsewhere the Stalin of these years is improbably described as if he were some romantic artist from the cast of *La Bohème*.[4]

A few months after joining the observatory Legend-Stalin took notable political action by leading the first workers' May Day demonstration ever to take place in Georgia. Sergey Alliluyev obligingly confirms the claim that Joseph – his future son-in-law – was in charge of this affair. Alliluyev has Comrade Stalin helping to select a suitable site in the hills near the Salt Lake, about eight miles from the town. To this secret tryst workers make their way by night, in twos and threes, armed with lanterns and passwords until about five hundred are assembled. The Comrade has commissioned portable likenesses of Marx and Engels, together with slogans in Georgian, Russian and Armenian on a background of red bunting. As these banners are unfurled, the demonstrators sing the *Marseillaise*, which echoes from the surrounding crags. And it is the twenty-year-old Comrade Stalin who heads the list of speakers.[5] Though the text of his alleged speech has not survived, the occasion is important as the first on which the future dictator is recorded as haranguing a crowd: a craft at which he is never to become very adept. In August of the same year the Comrade begins to foment industrial troubles, according to Legend, which has him 'leading' a mass strike of Tiflis railway workers.[6]

That most of these details are exaggerated or invented we may suspect; and it is unlikely, now, that further evidence will ever be forthcoming.

On the night of 21-22 March 1901, the young man's career as a clerk is rudely shattered when the police suddenly raid his observatory as part of a general swoop on the hideouts of Social Democrats in Tiflis. For some reason, sinister or not, Dzhugashvili is one of the few among these suspects not to be arrested – though he has already been under police surveillance since January, according to an official report.[7] After the raid there can be no question of his returning to the observatory, and he is compelled to go into hiding, thus becoming a politically wanted man: an 'illegal', in the jargon of the period. An illegal he is to remain during all his spells of liberty over the next sixteen years: until the February Revolution of 1917.

Now that underground politics are to become Dzhugashvili's main concern for a decade and a half, Legend begins to make claims more extravagant than those relating to his juvenile years. Piloting the future revolutionary chieftain into young manhood and the early twentieth century, his official annalists assume accents increasingly devotional. No important development ever takes place in the early Georgian Social Democratic movement, one gathers, except 'on Comrade Stalin's personal initiative' or 'under Comrade Stalin's leadership': two characteristic phrases from the Hieratic argot developed by the dictator's creatures in the 1930s.

A stirring tale it is which Beria and the lesser apostles of Stalinism unfold as they describe the young man's defiance of Imperial Russia from 1900 onwards. Maintaining his secret agitational work in numerous ever-expanding workers' 'circles', as begun during his schooldays, Comrade Stalin is soon found leading these same workers and their mates in heroic clashes with authority as he organizes strikes; promotes labour unrest; inspires political demonstrations; and heads protest parades – himself their leading organizer, himself marching in the van of the indignant proletarians whom he has marshalled. Theoretician of subversion as well as man of action, the blazing-eyed Comrade drafts inflammatory manifestoes and proclamations, founding and managing the illicit presses on which they are printed. He establishes clandestine journals, he writes their leading articles. Pioneer administrator too, he sets up networks of secret revolutionary committees all over Transcaucasia, appearing in person from time to time to rally waverers, while 'mercilessly lashing' a wide variety of political opponents – among whom Mensheviks, opportunists, advocates of Caucasian federalism and local nationalists (Mussavatists, Dashnaktsutyunists and so on) are prominent. That these are all – like Dzhugashvili himself – dedicated opponents of Tsarism, the young man knows well enough; but he already understands that the worst political heretics are those who share or partly share one's own view while refusing to submit to one's orders.

Thus spoke Legend of the 1930s onwards with a myriad brazen tongues, among which that of Beria sounded loudest. At the core of the saga we may recognize four especially influential works. For the early 1900s Beria's *History of Transcaucasian Bolshevism* (1935) is pre-eminent. It is flanked by a second, no less portentous, official source, also deriving in part from Beria's authority: the so-called 'Biographical Chronicle' appended to each successive volume of Stalin's *Works*, as published in 1946-51. The contributions of two lesser apostles are also significant: Yaroslavsky's *Landmarks in the Life of Stalin* (1940), to which reference has already been made; and *Joseph Stalin: a Short Biography*, compiled by G. F. Aleksandrov and others in 1947. Drawing where necessary on the 'recollections' of alleged eyewitnesses, the Gospel according to Beria, Yaroslavsky, Aleksandrov and the 'Chronicle' is supplemented by many other mythopoeic compilations such as two dating from 1937: *Tales of Veteran Transcaucasian Workers about the Great Leader* and *The Batum Demonstration of 1902*. In these studies and in other anthologies of purported memoirs, numerous Georgian contemporaries of the dictator's vie in adding further heroic aprocrypha to the accumulating Legend. But though such material will occasionally be quoted in illustration, we shall base our exposition of the Legend largely on the Vulgate as contributed by Beria, Yaroslavsky, Aleksandrov and the 'Chronicle'. Except where otherwise indicated, this material will be treated as a composite whole – despite certain differences of detail between the individual Gospel versions.

How, even with the advantages of hindsight, can we check this corpus of advertising copy? That Stalin was not at all the hero-figure portrayed in Legend the unctuous tone of its Hieratically couched claims leads us to suspect. Are we then to go to the other extreme, deducing that he was a totally passive and obscure figure in this early period? Hardly, since to be praised by a Beria for doing something is not necessarily to be proved to have done nothing. Stalin surely made *some* contribution to the Transcaucasian revolutionary cause, even if a comparatively modest one? What was it?

Fortunately we can test the Legend against certain other material, which is flimsy by comparison with the great cult works sponsored by Beria ... but which has the advantage of having been recorded outside the reach of Beria's police. In discussing Stalin's childhood we have already used Iremashvili's memoirs in this way, and his evidence is fortunately available for the post-seminary period too. It supplements that of certain other Georgian Mensheviks as set down in emigration, among whom we have already met Zhordania; the names of Arsenidze and Uratadze, and that of the Socialist Revolutionary Vereshchak, will shortly be added. All these witnesses wrote their testimony on un-Kremlinized territory – but, unfortunately, long after the events which they describe. Taken as a whole, the evidence of these mostly Georgian anti-Stalinist political émigrés adds up to a useful body of Counter-Legend. So we may properly term it, since it is all hostile to Stalin – and we shall therefore beware of a bias contrary to that of the Legend.

With the May Day workers' demonstration of 1901 – by which time Koba had already been in hiding for a few weeks – we can begin our observations of the interplay of Legend and Counter-Legend as it affects the Stalin of the early post-seminary period. The 1901 May Day affair is more ambitious than the previous year's clandestine meeting near the Salt Lake, for now we find Legend-Stalin 'personally leading' some two thousand workers on a protest march through the very heart of Tiflis. Though it is known that the gendarmes have been tipped off, and that bloodshed is likely, the Comrade's preparations have gone ahead regardless. He advises those most exposed to reprisals to wear their thick winter overcoats and Caucasian sheepskin caps as protection against the *nagayki* (whips) of Cossack troops.[8] One of his main motives in organizing this affair is to provoke politically useful casualties among his worker supporters, and in this he is fairly successful. The main battle is joined in Soldiers' Bazaar in the centre of Tiflis after the demonstrators have duly sung revolutionary songs and called down chanted curses on the autocracy. The workers fight whips and sabres with sticks and stones; fourteen are wounded and over fifty arrested.[9]

Was Dzhugashvili indeed a leader of the 1901 Tiflis May Day demonstration? Was he even present in Soldiers' Bazaar? Independent confirmation is available from Iremashvili. Since leaving the seminary he had become a schoolmaster at Gori, and it was to Gori that his friend Joseph Dzhugashvili secretly proceeded after eluding the wave of arrests provoked by the Tiflis demonstration ... of which he had indeed been 'one of the leaders'.[10] Unable to visit his mother – the police would expect to find him at her home – Dzhugashvili went into hiding, visiting Iremashvili occasionally at night. Normally so taciturn, the more violent of the two Sosos could not stop talking about the May Day demonstration; as he warmed to his theme, Iremashvili noticed with alarm that his old chum seemed downright intoxicated by the blood which he had caused to flow in Soldiers' Bazaar. The more sanguinary the struggle, he had decided, the sooner the issue would be settled.[11] We note, though, that while the heroic Comrade Stalin had been 'in the forefront' of this affair, the cautious Dzhugashvili had – as usual – contrived to elude arrest and injury as suffered by so many others.

Though little is known about Dzhugashvili's comings and goings in late 1901, November of that year reportedly witnessed an event which (if it indeed occurred) forms a landmark in the career of one who was later to pioneer new ways of bureaucracy. It was on the eleventh of the month that the young rebel was elected to his first revolutionary committee: a body newly established, according to Legend. It represented the Tiflis Social Democrats' Leninist faction: that is, hard-liners such as were to be known as Bolsheviks after the official split in the Party in 1903. According to various evangelists, the conference had been called 'on the initiative of Comrade Stalin', and it consisted of twenty-five delegates.[12] One over-eager source (the Tiflis newspaper *Zarya vostoka* [Dawn of the East] of 24 April 1939) out-Berias Beria by having Stalin elected as the 'head' of this nine-man committee.[13] That he assuredly was not; and where, if ever, Legend touches truth in the above account can no longer be determined. An entirely different story emerges from the independent evidence published by Georgian Mensheviks in emigration. These witnesses are the memoirist G. Uratadze and the Paris-published Georgian journal *Brdzolis khma* (Echo of the Struggle). According to them, young Dzhugashvili was by no means elected to any allegedly influential body at this time. On the contrary, he was pitched out neck and crop with ignominy; far from becoming a Tiflis Social Democratic committeeman, he ceased to be a Tiflis Social Democrat altogether. Such, these inverted evangelists claim, was the decision of a Party Court of Honour called to consider Dzhugashvili's insistent blackguarding of Silvestr Dzhibladze, the actual chairman of its newly-constituted committee. Dzhugashvili was dismissed by a unanimous vote as an 'incorrigible intriguer'.[14] Since, however, the committee's jurisdiction did not extend beyond Tiflis – there being no general Caucasian Party organization at the time – Koba was able to start up his intrigues all over again in a different city: Batum. To Batum he proceeded in November 1901, having made the capital of the Caucasus too hot to hold him, and having – in effect – been 'run out of town' by revolutionary comrades incensed with his uncomradely behaviour. The Legend-builders, by contrast, have Comrade Stalin officially 'sent' to Batum by the Party in order to organize the local Social Democrats along more militant lines.[15]

Where the many ambiguous episodes of Dzhugashvili's life are concerned, the more indecorous interpretation so often appears the more plausible that one is inclined to accept the Georgian Mensheviks' version, though it must not be forgotten that these were Stalin's deadly political enemies. The indecorous version of Stalin's behaviour also receives confirmation from a much earlier account of the Transcaucasian labour movement: that of S. T. Arkomed (1910). Arkomed describes the activities, in autumn 1901, of a certain unnamed comrade whose features seem to become more and more familiar as the narrative proceeds. The unknown's behaviour was dictated by 'personal caprice and the striving for absolute power', and he had transferred his activities from Tiflis to Batum at this time; from his new base he was still intriguing against the Tiflis Party organization. During his Tiflis days the unknown had vigorously opposed a suggestion that working men should be co-opted to the Social Democratic committee, objecting that mere proletarians were too ill prepared, and too lacking in class consciousness, to serve alongside the intellectuals. That Arkomed's Unnamed Comrade was indeed Stalin is accepted by at least three of Stalin's biographers;[16] and it is certainly true that Arkomed's mystery conspirator seems to have Dzhugashvili written all over him.

Whether dishonourably expelled from his Tiflis Party organization or specially commissioned by Tiflis to revolutionize Batum, Dzhugashvili duly proceeds, in November 1901, to this Black Sea port and petroleum-refining centre: the most important Caucasian industrial area after Baku and Tiflis. Having failed to take over the Tiflis organization, he appears to have better luck in Batum, appealing directly to the workers over the heads of the local Social Democratic moderates. Still operating the policy which he had already applied in Tiflis, Comrade Stalin is busy organizing workers' circles: eleven, according to Beria.[17] He also establishes an illegal printing press and issues inflammatory manifestoes. In early February he organizes a strike at one Batum petroleum refinery, and by early March we find him 'leading' a strike committee at a second.[18]

No mere political thug, Dzhugashvili has arrived in Batum as a sophisticated theoretician of urban guerrilla warfare. He has already laid down its principles in an article of late 1901 contributed to the illegal Marxist journal *Brdzola* (Struggle): newly-founded on the initiative of Comrade Stalin, according to Legend.[19] Here Stalin – anonymously and in his native Georgian – propounds the tactics of the urban guerrillero as suited to the dawn of the new century. He argues in favour of street demonstrations at all costs. True, they are bound to provoke bloody reprisals – as had happened in Soldiers' Bazaar. But reprisals are welcome because they draw initially indifferent 'inquisitive' spectators into a revolutionary struggle from which they would otherwise have stood aside. The Cossack *nagayka*, as used to quell public disorders, is a great leveller; not differentiating between age, sex or social class, it is an impartial revolutionary recruiting agent. Every fighter who falls in the struggle, or is snatched from the ranks, raises up hundreds of new fighters. 'We are advancing under the blows of whips to sow the seeds of political agitation and Socialism.'[20]

Though Koba himself never appears to have felt the blows of Cossack *nagayki* or police sabres, he was far indeed from being the coward whom his biographer Payne portrays.[21] He was, rather, intellectually convinced of the unwisdom of hazarding property as patently valuable to the revolutionary cause as his own person; as he knew instinctively, reprisals are for the led, not for the Leader. This tactic reminds one of the custom whereby early Muscovite Grand Princes and Tsars would withdraw discreetly from a battlefield on occasions when defeat appeared imminent; even so bold a leader as Peter the Great had followed this proceeding at Narva in 1700.

Dzhugashvili's actions and arguments show a clear grasp of subversive tactics as deployed in later, less sanguinary clashes: those of the campus 'revolutions' in American and other universities during the late 1960s. The tactic is the same: outrageous behaviour by a few provocative manipulators provokes the authorities to reprisals which incense and thereby recruit to the subversive cause wider circles of 'inquisitive' but originally indifferent spectators. That Russian students contemporary to Dzhugashvili were already pioneering these techniques was recognized by that arch-manipulator himself when, in the article quoted above, he drew the appropriate practical lessons from the university disorders which had broken out in St Petersburg and other parts of the Empire in 1899-1901.[22]

So much for theory. What of Stalin's guerrilla tactics as applied on the streets of Batum? He does indeed seem to have fomented trouble along the lines foreshadowed in his article. On 7 March thirty-two strikers are arrested. On 8 March, Comrade Stalin leads a march of strikers to the jail, where they demand their imprisoned comrades' release. Then these demonstrators are themselves arrested, to the tune of three hundred. Accelerating so satisfactorily, the upheaval provides Stalin with an excuse to organize and lead a further, much larger, protest parade: the famous Batum Demonstration of 9 March. Now no less than six thousand workers rally to demand the release of those previously arrested. That this is to be no mere whip-and-sabre affair becomes clear when troops open fire with rifles. Fifteen demonstrators are killed, fifty-four are wounded and there are over five hundred new arrests. Thus the Battle of Soldiers' Bazaar is eclipsed, and Dzhugashvili-boosted violence begins to acquire its own momentum. Himself ever in the thick of the conflict, Comrade Stalin 'leads' yet another workers' demonstration when the martyrs of 9 March are buried three days later.[23]

Despite the prominent role later claimed for Comrade Stalin, and despite arrests eventually running into many hundreds, the hero of Soldiers' Bazaar was yet sufficiently adroit or lucky to elude the local police for a month after he began 'leading' Batum workers' demonstrations. Not until 5 April 1902 was he arrested – and for the first time – by the Okhrana. Such immunity is surprising if the demonstrating Comrade indeed went out of his way to present himself as a 'target' for the security forces, as is insisted by the alien – yet apparently Stalin-briefed – sycophant Henri Barbusse.[24] According to Zhordania, Dzhugashvili's arrest was a stroke of luck for him. It restored his prestige, for not all Batum workers had appreciated his heroism in persuading them to march into a hail of bullets.[25] So Dzhugashvili *was* prominent in the Batum affair, then, since even Zhordania concedes it! Zhordania further describes the youthful Koba as engaged in constant intrigues against his rivals within the revolutionary movement. He would accuse local leaders of cowardice and treachery towards the masses, appealing over their heads direct to the workers; and he had 'created inside the organization a *personal organization* exclusively subordinated to himself.'[26] Such was the technique pioneered in microcosm by Dzhugashvili in Tiflis and Batum: a *modus operandi* which he eventually applied on an empire-wide scale.

Dzhugashvili remained in Batum Jail for over a year, until 19 April 1903. He was then transferred to another prison about eighty miles away: in the inland town of Kutaisi, where he languished for several months before being deported to Siberian exile. From his cells in Batum and Kutaisi, Comrade Stalin is able to maintain contact with the Caucasian Social Democratic movement outside, and even to 'direct' its work.[27] 'With unflagging energy' he continues to control all the Party's activities throughout Georgia, while also conducting 'massive' political-educational operations among his incarcerated comrades. The 'unflagging energy' and the 'massive' are, of course, strictly devotional terms characteristic of Legend.[28]

Since Imperial Russia's control over her political prisoners was so remarkably lax, Dzhugashvili might indeed have been able to exercise such supervision over revolutionary activity both inside and outside the jail, had his status in his Party – and his Party's in the country – been that claimed for them by Legend. In fact, however, there was nothing 'massive', whether 'led' by Comrade Stalin or any other phantom, taking place under Social Democratic auspices in the Caucasus of 1903. Nor can we pick up more than the vaguest traces of communications between the imprisoned Koba and the outside world. There is a story about two notes which he supposedly tossed through the bars of his cell so that they could be picked up and delivered by unidentified couriers. One of these is addressed to Iremashvili, and requires that old schoolfriend to furnish Koba with an alibi for the period of the Batum troubles. According to a Trotsky-sponsored variant of this fable, Iremashvili is instructed in the same note to ask Mrs Keke Dzhugashvili to testify (if questioned by the police) that her son had been in Gori during the entire period of the Batum disturbances; Iremashvili is also required to confirm this by his own evidence. The note is delivered by two Batum workers, strangers, who inform Iremashvili that Koba had indeed organized the great demonstration in that town. But though Koba's old friend readily agrees to co-operate in supplying the required alibi, his testimony (if it was ever given) is of no avail to Koba, who stays where he is, in prison.[29]

The second note, also flung through Koba's prison bars in Batum on 21 April, is addressed to his political associate Elisabedashvili, and urges him to continue working for the revolutionary cause undeterred by police reprisals at Batum. Since Elisabedashvili – hitherto hunted in vain by the Okhrana – is arrested shortly after receiving this missive, and since instructions are also given for the police to search Iremashvili's quarters and to question Keke Dzhugashvili, it appears that the prison warders or gendarmes of Batum have somehow intercepted both Koba's messages. That Koba himself had all along been an *agent provocateur* – that he had, in fact, deliberately scattered these compromising notes about with the express intention of letting them fall into police hands, having himself already been recruited as an Okhrana spy – is certainly no 'inescapable conclusion', as has been argued.[30] A Comrade Stalin was, of course, perfectly capable of loosing the gendarmes on his own mother; but we have no proof whatever that he in fact did so. Surely Koba could have found some less roundabout way of getting his associates into trouble with the gendarmes.

Besides allegedly directing revolutionary work outside the jails of Batum and Kutaisi – ineptly enough if the history of his two carelessly broadcast notes is to be credited – Comrade Stalin conducts propaganda among his fellow-prisoners, advocating Leninist views. He is also active in 'unmasking the opportunism of the majority of *Mesame Dasi*';[31] which, being translated from Hieratic into ordinary secular speech, means that he was blackguarding those among Caucasian Marxists who held views more moderate than his own.

One such 'opportunist', Grigory Uratadze, happens to have spent part of 1903 in Kutaisi Jail, and has provided a valuable non-Legendary description of the twenty-three-year-old Dzhugashvili. Unprepossessingly pockmarked, bearded, with long hair combed back over his forehead, the young man stood out among those arrested over the Batum affair as the only intellectual in their number. When – later in life – Stalin moved to the centre of Russian revolutionary activities, he was frequently assessed as the only *non-intellectual* in such circles: which suggests that the other internees from Batum must have been 'uncultured' to an extreme degree. Uratadze further describes Koba as remarkable for his stealthy gait and short steps – often described as catlike – as also for his inability to laugh heartily, since nothing more than a carefully calculated smile was ever seen to crease his ill-favoured features. Koba's main trait was complete imperturbability. Never losing his temper, never shouting, never cursing, he was the very paragon of icy self-control.[32] For a Georgian such phlegm was astounding indeed, and it was to become a great asset as Stalin's later political career unrolled.

On 9 July 1903 Comrade Stalin is sentenced without trial to three years' exile in eastern Siberia under police supervision; he is one of sixteen revolutionaries listed in the same decree.[33] The 'Chronicle' has him arriving on 27 November at his distant destination, Novaya Uda:[34] a remote village in Irkutsk Province, some four thousand miles from Tiflis. Here Legend-Stalin dwells in the cottage, long since perished, of a dear old peasant granny who is devoted to him; here too he maintains or revives his seminary habit of intensive nocturnal reading by candlelight.[35] But Granny's devoted care is not enough to hold Comrade Stalin in this backwater. Barely established there, the Comrade is already planning to escape – and does so on 5 January 1904. On this dating the 'Chronicle' concurs with an official gendarme report on Dzhugashvili.[36] However, various other authorities suggest different dates for Comrade Stalin's escape, as they do for the date of his original departure from Batum to Siberia, also disagreeing about where he went immediately after somehow completing the long return journey. Was it to Batum or to Tiflis that he first betook himself?[37]

From this mass of discrepancies in the very Legend material bearing on Stalin's exile to Novaya Uda, as also from the travel conditions of the period (which would have made it difficult for him to cover so many thousands of miles even inside the widest span of dates indicated within the conflicting evidence), it has been argued that he never went anywhere near Siberia in 1903-04, but hid out somewhere locally under police protection. According to this interpretation, Dzhugashvili was now a secret Okhrana agent of some standing, having probably been recruited by the Tiflis gendarmerie in 1899. The spurious 'exile' to Siberia was, on this view, synthetically injected into the spy's dossier by the Okhrana in order to enhance his prestige within the revolutionary movement, thereby also enhancing his value as a police informant.[38] Thus, while the intrepid Comrade Stalin was slogging up to eastern Siberia and back, his other self – the crafty Dzhugashvili – was taking his ease in some Caucasian lair and gathering strength for further betrayals.

To the saga of his Siberian exile or non-exile Stalin himself, emerging as the creator of his own early Legend, added – in a speech of 1924 – a further detail which must surely be spurious. At the end of 1903 and while in Siberian exile, according to this unlikely story, he receives from Lenin (in European exile) a letter 'simple but full of profound content': a vintage Hieratic phrase. The letter laid down a programme for the Party's forthcoming work. 'I cannot forgive myself [Stalin continues] for having followed the practice of an old underground worker by consigning this letter of Lenin's ... to the flames.'[39]

How very convenient!

That no such letter was ever sent, or ever received at Novaya Uda – even if Real Stalin did sojourn there in 1903-04 – seems a safe speculation from the brevity of his alleged stay and the primitive condition of the postal services connecting western Europe and eastern Siberia. The 'letter' invoked in 1924 was, presumably, an invention designed to antedate Legend-Stalin's first contact with the founder of Bolshevism: part of a larger campaign to overthrow rivals – Trotsky, Zinovyev and Kamenev – who could look back to a more extensive and intimate early association with Lenin.

We know little about Stalin's first marriage, on which our information all comes from Iremashvili. The bride – Yekaterina Svanidze – was a traditionally pious Georgian girl devoted to the care and service of her husband, her home and her religion. It was by the rites of the Orthodox

Church, we infer, that her marriage to the former seminarist – and now militant atheist – Dzhugashvili, was celebrated. The wedding is described as taking place in 1903, in which event it must presumably have been solemnized in prison, either at Batum or at Kutaisi. In any case no official record of the occasion survives. Nor has Stalin ever been reported as alluding to the earlier of his two experiments in wedlock. The bride's main achievements were to look after her husband and their home – where that may have been located we simply do not know – while praying fervently that he might adopt some occupation less profane than that of peripatetic revolutionary agitator. She also presented Stalin with a son, Yakov, who later became a pupil of Iremashvili's; and who was eventually to perish – renounced by his father – in German captivity during World War Two.

Equality between the sexes – as officially advocated under militant Stalinism – played no part whatever in the married life of the young Dzhugashvilis,[40] which ended when Stalin's first wife died in 1907 after four years of domestic submission. Iremashvili had an opportunity to observe the young widower's comportment at the funeral; which, again, was celebrated according to the rites of the Orthodox Church. We read of his great sadness and pale face. Only in the impoverished home of his family had Stalin's unquiet spirit ever found love.

From the contempt with which he treated everyone, only his wife, his child and his mother were exempt. ... I knew that henceforward Koba was bereft of all moral restraint, and that from now onwards he would surrender himself entirely to his fantastic plans, which were dictated solely by ambition and revenge.

As the two young men entered the cemetery on their way to the burial, Stalin

pressed my arm harder, pointed to the coffin and said to me: 'This being softened my stony heart. She has died, and with her my last warm feelings for human beings have perished.' He laid his right hand on his breast: 'Everything is so hollow, so unspeakably empty in here.'

On that day, Iremashvili insists, Stalin lost the last remnants of human feeling, his heart being filled with terrible hatred for mankind. Pitiless towards himself, he became pitiless towards all other men as well.[41]

Stalin's melodramatic behaviour over his first wife's grave is out of keeping with his mature manner. One suspects that the story has gained something in the telling ... a quarter of a century after young Mrs Dzhugashvili's death.

Police Spy?

The greatest revolutionary ruler in history ... yet in youth a spy on the pay-roll of the very police state which he purportedly sought to overthrow?

True or false, this accusation is less far-fetched than it might seem to those unversed in the annals of the declining Russian Empire. In working for the Okhrana, Koba would have been only one among the many police infiltrators to whose activities we have already alluded. So extensively developed was this system that Lenin, for example, was surrounded, during his decade-and-a-half as an émigré revolutionary, by dozens of Okhrana spies masquerading as disciples.[1] The most notorious, Roman Malinovsky, was elected to the Duma (the parliament-in-embryo instituted in 1906), even heading its Bolshevik fraction. Such *agents provocateurs* penetrated Menshevik as well as Bolshevik groupings. Nor, of course, was the Social Democratic Party the only revolutionary organization to be riddled with Okhrana spies. The Socialist Revolutionaries' key Fighting Organization – the leading group of political assassins during this period – was headed by a police agent, Yevno Azef. Yet again, the assassin Bogrov was in police pay when (in 1911) he gunned down his ultimate employer, the Home Secretary and Prime Minister Stolypin at a gala performance in a Kiev theatre.

Was Bogrov's true allegiance to the revolution? Or to the police? Had he, indeed, *any* true allegiance? Or was he himself as muddled in his loyalties as a historian can easily become in trying to disentangle them? Again, was Azef's main fealty to the Okhrana, to the Socialist Revolutionaries. ... or to his personal advantage? Did the Okhrana effectively control the infiltrator Malinovsky's operations within the Bolshevik movement? Or was Malinovsky more of a Bolshevik agent infiltrating the Okhrana? Where spy so easily slipped into the role of counter-spy, ultimate allegiances tended to dissolve.

In a society which was throwing up its Malinovskys, Azefs and Bogrovs there would have been nothing unusual about a mere Soso Dzhugashvili joining the hundreds of police-controlled revolutionaries or pseudo-revolutionaries of the period. Such a role would have offered Soso certain advantages – and not least in the financial subsidies which the Okhrana paid to its most useful agents on a generous scale. It must be stressed in this connection that the young Stalin had no known source of income outside his fifteen months on the pay-roll of the Tiflis Observatory in 1899–1901 ... not, at least, until he began, several years later, to enjoy the fruits of robberies and extortions executed by the Party – and sometimes organized by him personally – as 'expropriations' designed to swell its funds. Another advantage offered to Koba by co-operation with the police would have been the chance to advance himself within the Social Democratic organization by denouncing inconvenient rival comrades, thus causing their arrest. In this way an active pseudo-revolutionary police spy could secure rapid promotion within his subversive organization – as also could a revolutionary sincerely opposed to the autocracy, but unscrupulous enough to exploit police connections to further personal ambitions. Promotions thus achieved were welcome to the Okhrana, for the higher their own man rose in revolutionary ranks the greater his usefulness to the security authorities.

Nothing in the Okhrana's traditions suggests that the organization would have jibbed at recruiting a Dzhugashvili among its countless *agents provocateurs*. That such an overture was once made, and by a Colonel of Gendarmes Zasypkin, the independent witness Arsenidze asserts,[2] though the outcome of this particular approach is not recorded. Would Dzhugashvili have been likely to accept such a proposition if he had seen some advantage to himself in collusion with the Okhrana? Or would moral scruples have deterred him? Nothing in the future dictator's devious and treacherous temperament suggests that he would have rejected Okhrana advances on principle. In view of the Okhrana's habit of recruiting school-children as spies, he may even have started his career of treachery while still a seminarist and not (as has been suggested) in mid-1899.[3] As mentioned above, it was widely believed that he denounced a group of school-fellows to the police.[4] So much for the beginning of Koba's putative collaboration with the Okhrana. When might it have ended? From 1908 onwards his periods of detention become too considerable to be reconciled with the role of Okhrana infiltrator enhancing his prestige within a revolutionary organization by adding samples of police persecution to his dossier. By 1908 the Okhrana must have wearied of collaborating with Dzhugashvili – if, that is, such collaboration ever took place at all.

The point must also be made that there were innumerable gradations between out-and-out police spy and out-and-out revolutionary. It was possible to hover between these two positions while keeping one's ultimate options open. Moreover, any collaboration by Koba with the Okhrana might – in a situation offering so many potential shades of involvement – have stopped well short of total commitment. At the lowest end of the scale, there was nothing to stop him sending the police an occasional anonymous tip-off indicating the whereabouts of wanted revolutionaries whose activities he found inconvenient to himself. On the other hand, he could conceivably have been a salaried secret agent pseudonymously entered on the Okhrana's books, and thus a junior colleague of Azef and Malinovsky.

Evidence establishing Stalin as a fully-fledged Okhrana agent has not yet come to light, and not for want of looking. Most painstaking detective of all, Edward Ellis Smith (author of *The Young Stalin*) has scoured the annals of the Leader's youth – including the archives of the Okhrana's Foreign Department now at Stanford, California – for such testimony . . . but has scoured in vain. Indeed, Smith resorts to such extremes of special pleading in his attempts to put Dzhugashvili on the Okhrana pay-roll that he damages his own case. Far from identifying Stalin as an Okhrana spy, Smith's researches go a long way towards establishing the impossibility of so identifying him. What *The Young Stalin* proves is not that Stalin was an *agent provocateur*, but that existing evidence permits us neither to assert nor to deny that he was guilty of such duplicity. This itself is a valuable achievement, though. It fully justifies Smith's detective work, even while running contrary to his conclusions.

Direct documentary evidence of complicity between Stalin and the Okhrana is restricted to a single much disputed letter dated 12 July 1913 and signed by a Colonel A. M. Yeryomin – head of the section which supervised police infiltrators within the revolutionary parties. Writing to another gendarme officer, Yeryomin states that Stalin had worked as a police informer and agent between 1906 and 1912. There are, however, numerous technical reasons for mistrusting this document. One authority has pronounced, after careful examination, that he found the marks of genuineness too strong to permit him to view it as totally fraudulent, and the marks of fraudulence too strong to permit him to view it as totally genuine.[5] Even Smith, so eager to place Koba on the Okhrana's pay-roll, shows similar reserve in his assessment of this particular clue.[6] In the last analysis, therefore, the Yeryomin letter does little either to substantiate or to refute the theory that Stalin may have been a police spy.

Though Stalin the Okhrana agent must be put into cold storage for lack of evidence, the dictator's early biography abounds in indications that the authorities were, for some reason or other, treating him as a protected person. There were the numerous occasions on which Koba mysteriously eluded arrest when many of his comrades were seized. Elusiveness was always one of his characteristics. We seek him here, we seek him there . . . but what of the gendarmes supposedly hot on his trail? They seem to have sought him practically nowhere. And even when Koba *is* arrested he receives mild sentences of two to three years' exile – such as that to Novaya Uda – from which he easily escapes, travelling many thousands of miles on railways policed by gendarmes and passing innumerable check points on the way. Nor, on frequent recapture by the police from 1908 onwards, is Koba ever penalized for his previous escapes.

On the other hand, Koba was by no means the only wanted revolutionary to tour the country unmolested. Nor was he the only 'illegal' to cross and recross the Russian national frontier with similar ease, as he did on several occasions from 1906 onwards. It was not only the Imperial authorities' undoubted inefficiency which rendered such exploits possible, but also their policy of deliberately turning a blind eye to certain subversive activities. We have already noted the Okhrana's custom of leaving a suspect at liberty while watching him in the hope of unearthing a network of associates. There were also occasions when the Okhrana decided against arresting the known members of a particular revolutionary organization in circumstances where such a body seemed likely, if liquidated, to be replaced by a successor-group impervious to penetration. It was to this consideration that Azef's Fighting Organization owed its long immunity.

There were also special reasons why the Bolshevik faction enjoyed more official indulgence than was extended to other revolutionary groupings. Though Lenin's followers were indeed dedicated to the ultimate overthrow of the State, their immediate passions were geared to the destruction of rival revolutionaries. They seemed more likely to undermine their own Social Democratic movement than to topple the Imperial Government. Leninists, moreover, not only attacked Mensheviks – the rival body within the Social Democratic organization – but were also prone to turn and rend non-Leninist fellow-Bolsheviks. All this made Lenin and his disciple Dzhugashvili seem useful assets to the Imperial authorities, who – if they *must* be threatened by a revolutionary movement – preferred to see the enemy split into as many competing factions as possible. The authorities may therefore have thought Stalin worth preserving simply because he was so effectively quarrelsome, being – in his small way – a greater nuisance to Caucasian fellow-revolutionaries than a whole squadron of gendarmes. This factor is probably sufficient to explain the freedom from persecution enjoyed by Stalin, without making it necessary to claim him as an outright agent of the Tsarist authorities.

If Stalin indeed was an Okhrana agent, then why (it may be asked) did none of his powerful political enemies or rivals ever make the damning revelation during the inner-party struggles of the 1920s? Would they not have had every opportunity to unearth and explode so gigantic a scandal? Many Okhrana files were captured intact in 1917 (though many had also been destroyed), and such archives by no means immediately fell into the hands of Stalin's minions. Had Trotsky, for example, possessed evidence of Stalin working for the Okhrana, would he not have used this knowledge to end his rival's career there and then? Yet Trotsky – Stalin's biographer and premier victim – has shown no signs of believing that his successful rival and future destroyer had ever been an Okhrana agent. May we not deduce, then, that no such evidence existed?

Perhaps ... but further consideration inclines one to doubt whether Trotsky or Stalin's other rivals could ever have brought themselves to raise this particular issue even if documentary evidence, establishing Stalin as an Okhrana spy beyond doubt, had chanced to come to their notice. Would any Bolshevik have dared to open a door behind which so many skeletons lay concealed? The question of the German money made available to Lenin during the First World War, the expropriations issue, the question of Okhrana-revolutionary interpenetration from the Malinovsky scandal downwards ... these were matters on which the ruling Bolsheviks maintained silence throughout the fierce controversies of the 1920s which preceded the Stalin dictatorship. The issue of Okhrana-Bolshevik relations had, by general agreement, become too hot to handle. On the failure of Stalin's rivals to pillory him as a former police agent we can, therefore, base no deduction whatever about the availability to these rivals of clinching documentary evidence revealing him as a police spy.

Some useful reflections on Koba as a suspected Okhrana collaborator – and on his early operating technique in general – have been contributed by his former Social Democratic comrade, the émigré Georgian Menshevik Arsenidze. This independent witness is the most valuable of the many Georgian émigrés who have supplied biographical details on the future dictator. Arsenidze first met Koba in Batum in early 1904, immediately after the latter's escape or pseudo-escape from Siberia. Koba remembered Batum as the scene of the demonstration of March 1902, and was now once more attempting a takeover of the local Social Democratic organization by appealing direct to the workers over the heads of their existing leaders. When this venture failed – his earlier following in the town, such as it was, had by now melted away – Koba left Batum with that sudden turn of speed which he usually showed when writing off a failure. But he was back again in early 1905. 'This time [says Arsenidze] Soso was a fully-fledged, orthodox, committed Leninist, repeating the arguments and thoughts of his Master like a gramophone.'[7] *This time!* Soso had, then, been something less than a hundred-per-cent Bolshevik at some earlier time: presumably that of his previous year's Batum visitation. Could Comrade Stalin even have been that most despised of creatures: a Menshevik? According to his Okhrana file he certainly could. A police report, dated March 1911, states that Dzhugashvili had been first a Menshevik and only later a Bolshevik.[8] There may not be much in this, since the rift between these two opposing factions of Social Democracy had not fully declared itself in Transcaucasia as early as 1904. Still, the very hint of

Menshevism on the police dossier of that scourge of Mensheviks Comrade Stalin . . . it was yet another motive for him to capture all sources of revolutionary history in the days of his prime, and to replace them with a Legend.

Unfortunately the hundred-per-cent Bolshevizing Soso, as observed by Arsenidze in Batum in 1905, was no more successful than the possibly Menshevizing Stalin of the previous year, for he managed to subvert only a dozen or so out of a thousand Batum Party adherents to the Leninist cause which he was now whole-heartedly advocating.

Arsenidze describes an underground political meeting chaired by himself at Tiflis in 1906. Koba, typically, tried to disrupt the proceedings by crude heckling. When Arsenidze rebuked such unseemliness from the chair, the barracker quipped that he was not aware of having removed his trousers, and that his behaviour had therefore remained within the bounds of propriety. Arsenidze countered by claiming that Koba less resembled a trouserless male than a whore offering her wares unencumbered – such was the local practice – by knickers. Undaunted by this uncultured sally, Koba merely twisted the left corner of his mouth in a crooked leer and left the meeting. Shortly after his departure the conclave was dispersed by whistles from the street: a signal previously arranged as their warning of an imminent police raid. When it turned out that there were no police in the area it became clear that the whistler had been Koba: his revenge for being bested in vulgar repartee at the meeting.[9]

Whatever the facts may be about direct collaboration between the whistler of Tiflis and the police, at least Koba's fellow-Bolsheviks were convinced that he was in the habit of informing on his comrades. It was, they believed, his practice to betray their hideouts by anonymous tip-offs, the denounced invariably being those who had somehow come into conflict with the suspected denouncer.[10] This claim is supported by the evidence of a leading Armenian Bolshevik, Stepan Shaumyan. During the revolutionary year 1905, a split developed among Caucasian Bolsheviks between the more strictly political element, led by Shaumyan, and those who favoured the gangsterlike methods sponsored by Koba. Then, when the feud was at its height, Shaumyan was suddenly arrested. That a tip-off by Koba had put the police on his track, the victim himself was certain: Koba, and only Koba, had known the address from which Shaumyan was operating.[11]

According to Arsenidze, the independent witness who knew him best during these years, Koba was an eccentric who resembled no one but Koba. A dry, heartless, soulless mechanism rather than a man, he lacked eloquence, always speaking roughly and brusquely, but with great force and drive. His sarcasms, his ironies, his sneers, his vulgar wisecracks often exceeded the limits of propriety. Repeatedly accusing his opponents of lying, of seeking to deceive others, he would maintain such attacks with relentless persistence. Never did he betray the faintest trace of embarrassment. When his use of bad language evoked protests from more genteel fellow-revolutionaries, Koba would retort that he was no aristocrat – that he spoke as a blunt, straightforward working man. Self-centred, lacking all moral restraint, Koba could not conceive human relations except in terms of subjection and submission. Already, in these early years, he would treat his associates like cattle to be exploited and sent to the slaughterhouse; and somehow nearly all his closest associates in the early Caucasian underground did contrive to perish in clashes with authority or were sent to Siberia. Notorious for his abject devotion to Lenin, Koba earned himself the nickname 'Lenin's Left Foot'.

All in all, it is not surprising that the name Koba became a term of abuse in these circles. To say of someone 'he's a regular Koba' was to accuse him of impropriety, foulmouthedness and lack of moral refinement.[12]

Journalist and Agitator

Stalin's early journalistic articles are less remarkable for any intrinsic interest or merit than for the characteristic processing to which they were subjected for many years after their first appearance by the creators of the author's Legend.

Such juvenilia help to fill the first volume of his collected *Works* in Russian, as published between 1946 and 1951 by the Marx-Engels-Lenin Institute in Moscow. But the thirteen volumes of this edition take the dictator's writings no further than January 1934. At that point publication was suspended in Moscow. It was taken up by the Hoover Institution at Stanford, California, which has given us the last three volumes – covering the period 1934-53 – in a format similar to that of the Moscow edition: a piquant and surely unique example of East-West textual coexistence.

Even with regard to the limited period which it embraces, the Moscow *Works* is far from comprehensive, since it includes only 480 out of a total of 895 titles which can be traced to Stalin in Soviet-published bibliographies and other sources. Such suppressions are particularly common in the earliest volumes, no less than 54 items out of a total of 110 traced to the dictator's Caucasian years (up to 1910) having been omitted.[1] Since the Moscow edition does not advertise itself as complete, such self-censorship cannot be faulted on purely scholarly grounds; after all, any author may assume the right – as, for example, Chekhov did – to exclude from a comprehensive collection of his writings early items which, on mature consideration, he happens to dislike. What puts the Moscow edition of Stalin beyond the pale, from a scholarly point of view, is the inclusion in it of numerous items falsely ascribed to the author: items originally produced by other revolutionary scribes toiling anonymously in the Caucasian political underworld.

This stricture applies with greatest force to the dictator's earliest writings, most of which were originally published in the Georgian language. We are, indeed, advised by Stalin's leading bibliographer, Robert H. McNeal, to accept as authentic only those items in the *Works* which are signed by an accepted pseudonym, such as 'Koba' or 'Besoshvili'.[2] And since no such authenticated pseudonym surfaces until 8 March 1906, when we first meet a 'Besoshvili', all eighteen items of 1901-05 included in the *Works* are potentially suspect. McNeal's warning has been confirmed by Arsenidze, who asserts roundly that 'a number' of other people's articles were unceremoniously appropriated by Stalin to his *Works* after the living witnesses had been disposed of, or had died a natural death. Among these plagiarisms Arsenidze specifies only one: the leading article from the first number of *Brdzola*, which appeared in September 1901 and is the first of Stalin's alleged works to figure in his alleged *Works*.[3]

Between the first appearance of these anonymously published articles, in obscure corners of darkest Transcaucasia, and their embalmment in the fraudulently canonical Kremlin-sponsored text of Stalin's collected writings, nearly half a century had passed. During so long an interval the dictator himself must, surely, have forgotten which of these pathetic items he had or had not composed. Original begetter or not, he felt sufficiently proprietorial towards them to make sizeable author's corrections, for the text of the printed Russian *Works* differs considerably from that of the long-forgotten Georgian originals.[4] Since, however, even the least dictatorial of scribes may be permitted to revise his writings for collective publication, this is another feature of the *Works* which cannot be faulted on scholarly grounds. No doubt such revision must seem all the more desirable after four decades or so have passed . . . and especially if the 'author' suspects or remembers that some of the material concerned had not been his in the first place! That Stalin took a keen personal interest in the editing of his own *Works*, not being content to delegate this to Beria or lesser sycophants, was directly stated in 1957 by an official of the Marx-Engels-Lenin Institute.[5] As an administrator with a vast appetite for detail and a keen eye for his own image, the dictator would indeed have been the last man to neglect such a chore.

As for the purpose behind these manoeuvres, the omission of certain items or passages elsewhere ascribed to Stalin is often due to the presence of what later became doctrinal heresies, while the appropriation and doctoring of other people's work may be ascribed to the need for ballast. Here was the mature Stalin challenging comparison with such revolutionary giants as Marx, Engels and Lenin: all prolific authors. Was their greatest heir to lack a *Works* suitably multi-voluminous? Hence the need to attribute alien contributions to himself, which could be done at will. What -shvili or -idze, originator of an obscure article published in the 1900s, would be so besotted by author's vanity as to risk arrest by defending his ravished copyright in the 1940s?

Since the early contents of Volume One of the *Works* are translations later edited, polished and reworked – besides including, in an unknown proportion, the work of pens other than Stalin's – it is difficult to pronounce on the dictator's quality as an apprentice journalist. Despite all editing, much of the work remains repetitive and clumsy. The extreme clarity which (despite the abuse of detractors) characterizes the mature dictator's writings, is often conspicuously absent in these juvenilia. Yet the authentic voice does ring through. The liturgical cadences, the constant emphasis on violence, the harping on 'organization' and 'power' ... such features help one to discern the future dictator in these earliest documents. As for their content, we have already noted Stalin's début (presuming it genuine) as a theoretician of urban guerrilla warfare, to which be added essays on the minority nationalities of the Russian Empire: discussions of inner-party controversies; and manifestoes issued under some such impersonal signature as 'The Tiflis Committee'.

The young Legend-Stalin is also active in founding illegal periodicals. He has these printed, together with a mass of political leaflets, pamphlets and proclamations, on various illicit presses set up or managed by himself. *Brdzola*, the first illegal Social Democratic newspaper in Georgia – which starts publication in September 1901 and carries a leading article later incorporated in Stalin's *Works* – is founded 'on the initiative of Stalin', and of his ally Lado Ketskhoveli.[6] In the same year Ketskhoveli sets up an illegal press in Baku, being supplied with type, plant and money from the Tiflis organization: this too 'on Comrade Stalin's initiative'.[7] When Comrade Stalin arrives in Batum in late 1901 he brings with him a portable printing press, and operates it in a suburb called the Swamp.[8] In June 1906 the Comrade 'directs' a newly-established Georgian newspaper, *Akhali tskhovreba* (New Life).[9]

Though these claims cannot be discounted, they are certainly exaggerated.

It was not Koba's initiative, but that of another and more influential Social Democrat of the period – Leonid Krasin – which founded the illicit Baku press in 1901, according to the voluminous Soviet-published material on Krasin's life brought out in 1928;[10] in this material Stalin's name does not figure at all. Nor does a recent investigator of Krasin find cause to mention Koba once in connection with illicit Baku printing initiatives at this time.[11]

Among the illegal printing operations of the period few were more ambitious than the great underground press established in the bowels of the earth and approached down a well shaft, at Avlabar, a suburb of Tiflis. Created in November 1903 – on the instructions of the imprisoned Comrade Stalin, according to the Legend –[12] this was possibly the largest illegal press in Russia at the time. It produced copious propaganda in Armenian, Georgian and Russian: a fount of subversion vainly sought for two years by the Okhrana until suddenly, in March 1906, a tip-off was received and the premises at Avlabar were put under surveillance. By now printing operations had ceased, but the underground stronghold was still in use as a bomb factory and training depot for political terrorists. On 15 April police swooped on Avlabar, also undertaking a raid on Tiflis subversives in general. Though twenty-five to thirty arrests are said to have followed,[13] Koba was not among those seized, for he was now attending the Fourth Party Congress in Stockholm.

Was Koba himself the mysterious informer who tipped off the police about the Avlabar press? Since the installation had recently come under the control of local Mensheviks – and since Stalin's hatred of Mensheviks greatly exceeded his hatred of the Imperial system which he was nominally undermining in alliance with Mensheviks – he would have had every motive for such treachery. It would explain the failure to publish details of the Avlabar affair until after his death.[14]

Similar confusion obscures Stalin's arrest or arrests in 1905-06. One police document contains the bald information that he 'was arrested in 1905 and escaped from prison.'[15] Trotsky has Koba arrested and released on 15 April 1906 in connection with the Avlabar raid – which cannot be accurate, as we have seen, since Koba was in Stockholm at the time.[16] But Arsenidze too speaks of an arrest in Tiflis: an event which he appears to relate to 1906 and which was followed by Koba's speedy release from the local gendarme office after the attempt (successful or unsuccessful) made by Colonel Zasypkin to recruit him as a police informer.[17] Whether such a detention indeed took place in 1905-06 we cannot say, for which reason the total of Stalin's arrests cannot be established with certainty. The minimum number is six.

Such, then, were some of Koba's activities during a period when the Russian Empire was occupied with two great conflicts: one external (the Russo-Japanese War of 1904-05) and the other internal (the abortive Russian Revolution of 1905). So far as Stalin's authenticated doings are concerned, these two crises might as well never have occurred at all. They made little impact on the future dictator, whose concerns at the time were more parochial. His real enemies were not the Tsar-Emperor Nicholas II and his temporarily threatened government, but such obscure local rivals as might challenge whatever ascendancy Koba could now and then precariously assert over some regional Caucasian revolutionary association.

It is not so much that Stalin was idle during the revolutionary year 1905 – when he travelled the length and breadth of the Caucasus, abusing Mensheviks and other rivals – as that his activities were unproductive. Attracting only a small personal following here and there in the course of his tours, he sought (says Arsenidze) to glorify these miserable handfuls of supporters with such grandiloquent titles as 'Committee of the Kutaisi-Imeretian Group in Guria'. Far from leading a single broad popular or social movement, or a single revolutionary strike, Koba was not even on the fringes of such activities. When a great rising broke out in Tiflis in December 1905, he was simply nowhere to be found,[18] having taken himself off to Finland.

So much for Counter-Legend on what Koba did in 1905. That the account is fairly accurate, and that Stalin was anything but the life and soul of the Caucasian 1905 revolution, is confirmed by the negative evidence of Soviet-published works issued in the pre-Cult and post-Cult periods. An official Party history (1925) of this first Russian Revolution breathes no word on any insurgent activity by Koba in the crucial year; nor does Makharadze's lengthy history (1927) of the upheaval number Koba even among its minor heroes.[19] Similarly, a post-Cult (1956) collection of documents on the year 1905 in Georgia runs to over eight hundred pages; yet mentions Stalin fewer than ten times.[20]

So obscure was Stalin's role in 1905 that even Legend can do little more than recite the titles of articles and manifestoes attributed – some, perhaps, fraudulently – to his pen. The very 'Biographical Chronicle' for 1905, as appended to Volume One of Stalin's *Works*, is a confession of the author's insignificance during that year. While others grapple with the Tsar's minions and sell their lives in street fighting, he can only issue brochures, speak at funerals and denounce other revolutionaries.[21] And from what we know of the 'Chronicle', even these feeble items may be the product of fantasy or exaggeration.

First Meetings with Lenin

Stalin's activities up to the end of 1905 have been exclusively confined to the Caucasus, except for his brief disputed excursion to Siberia in late 1903. Even within his Caucasian limits the future dictator has so far made little political headway. Perhaps he should test his talents on a broader stage? For instance, he might make an impression at one of the Party congresses or conferences where Social Democrats from all parts of the Empire met at irregular intervals to determine higher policy. By 1905 Koba had already missed three Party congresses. When the first of these gatherings founded the Party at Minsk in March 1898, he had still been a pupil of the Tiflis Seminary. During the Second, London, Congress of July-August 1903 – that which split the Party into Bolsheviks and Mensheviks – the future dictator had languished in Kutaisi Jail. From the Third Congress, held in London in April 1905, he had also been absent – probably because his position in the Caucasian Party was too obscure for him to be accepted or financed as a delegate.

It was with his arrival – however sponsored – at Tampere in Finland in December 1905 that Stalin first effectively emerged from the Caucasus. The Tampere gathering was no congress, but a mere conference: a body lacking policy-enforcing status. Nor was it an all-Social-Democratic affair, being a gathering of Bolsheviks only, from which members of the rival Menshevik faction were excluded. Nor yet did the Tampere Conference enjoy the status and convenience of foreign siting, as did all the pre-1917 Party congresses after the first. But though Finland was by no means foreign territory, having been part of the Russian Empire since 1809, it was not quite Russia either. As an Imperial Grand Duchy, this country-within-an-empire enjoyed local autonomy, remaining relatively immune from the operations of the Okhrana and offering Russian subversives a safer refuge than any other corner of the realm.

Another feature of the Tampere conference is the lack of any surviving transcript such as those which enable us to trace Koba's role at later gatherings. That his contribution was insignificant seems clear, however, from the modest part assigned to it even in Legend. Yaroslavsky, for example, is almost silent about Comrade Stalin's role at Tampere; so too is Aleksandrov, though referring to the Comrade – absurdly – as already 'one of the prominent leaders of the Party'.[1] Nadezhda Krupskaya, Lenin's wife, contrives to describe the conference in some detail without finding it necessary to mention Stalin's name at all.[2]

At the Tampere conference the disciple Stalin first set eyes on the master Lenin. Stalin himself has described the impact of this historic meeting.

He was struck by what at first seemed an anti-climax: Lenin's unassuming, ordinary quality. Knowing that he was about to see the Mountain Eagle of the Party, Koba had expected Lenin to contrive an impressive entrance artificially delayed in order to build up suspense. Instead of that the Mountain Eagle had arrived early and was twittering unassumingly in a corner with birds of less pretentious feather. 'I shall not conceal from you [Stalin adds in characteristic style] that this struck me at the time as being, rather, a violation of certain basic rules.'[3] Only later did Stalin realize that he himself could simulate modesty, such as appears to have been genuine in Lenin's case, and convert it into a form of self-advertisement more effective than overt posturings. Hence his later habit of wearing a plain, unadorned tunic as he moved quietly among the bemedalled marshals and blue-suited civilian officials menaced by his executioners, making himself, by his very inconspicuousness, the most conspicuous of all. Here Stalin was, consciously or not, aping a device of the dreaded Count Arakcheyev (*de facto* internal dictator under the Emperor Alexander I), who was accustomed to wear a simple, threadbare cloak when appearing before dazzling assemblages of the early 1800s – thereby striking universal terror as the one man who did not have to bother.

In the following year, 1906, Stalin first attended a major Social Democratic conclave: the Fourth Party Congress, which met in Stockholm between 10 and 25 April. During this excursion, his first outside the Russian Empire, he used the alias 'Ivanovich'. The avowed purpose of the Stockholm Congress was to forge unity in a Party split by the quarrels of Mensheviks and Bolsheviks. By now these bickerings were making the Party's intellectual leaders unpopular with the rank and file, until it had become necessary to patch up Bolshevik-Menshevik differences on pain of losing support in what was by no means a mass movement. To Stockholm the Mensheviks sent over sixty voting delegates, while the less numerous Bolsheviks had less than fifty, of whom Stalin was one. He was the sole Bolshevik representative from Tiflis, which fielded ten Mensheviks; and he represented, if anyone, only a small minority of the Social Democrats in the Menshevik-dominated Transcaucasian Party.

The published minutes of the Fourth Congress enable us to assess Stalin's contribution with some precision. His alias, 'Ivanovich', figures on 27 out of nearly 700 pages. As this indicates, the future dictator played a modest part at Stockholm, ill-equipped though he was to co-operate in a gathering which was intended to pursue harmony. He showed this by his first intervention: a personal attack on Plekhanov, the senior Marxist present, whom he criticized for introducing a jarring note into a meeting designed to forge agreement.[4] To begin by quarrelling with a senior colleague for being over-quarrelsome! One recognizes the Koba of Arsenidze's and Zhordania's reminiscences. But the young Georgian's contributions went beyond abuse. Their chief interest is that they show 'Ivanovich' as no slavish imitator of Lenin, whose admirer he had indeed become, but whose lead he failed to follow over three issues.

The first disagreement concerned the policy to be adopted, after any successful future revolution, towards the peasants of the Russian Empire. That land should be confiscated from the existing landlords and farmed by peasants – so much was common ground between all Social Democrats. But who was to be the legal owner of the confiscated acres? The State, said Lenin. But Stalin disagreed, recommending that the land should be bestowed on the peasants as their personal property.[5] His policy was better designed than Lenin's to gain support in the villages, since it offered the peasants a stake – such as Lenin's proposed nationalization of the land would have denied them – in the success of a coming revolution. And though a Marxist revolution must by definition be proletarian in inspiration, how could *any* Russian revolution hope to succeed without support from the peasants who still formed an overwhelming majority of the Empire's population? Stalin's far-sightedness – or long-term cynicism – over this issue was to be vindicated in 1917, when Lenin switched to the policy put forward by 'Ivanovich' at Stockholm eleven years earlier. By encouraging the peasantry to appropriate land in 1917, Lenin obtained the degree of temporary peasant support essential to his seizure of power. Then, twelve years after that, when Bolshevik rule had been consolidated – and when power had passed from the dead Lenin to Stalin – it became possible at last to nationalize (in effect) all the land in collective or state farms. Thus did the Stalin of 1929 implement the policy advocated by Lenin in 1906.

At Stockholm, Stalin also signalized his disagreement with Lenin over the State Duma, as first established in 1906. Should the Social Democrats participate in this institution, which appeared to enshrine – in rudimentary form – some of the principles of a Western parliament? Or should they ignore the Duma, boycotting the elections to that body which were taking place in Russia even as the Stockholm delegates sat in conclave? Lenin himself had vacillated over the boycott issue. Anti-boycott on arrival at Tampere, he had there swung to a boycottist position. Now, at Stockholm, he had switched back, and was again favouring Social Democratic participation in the Duma elections. Whether favouring or opposing a boycott at any given time, Lenin was of course solely interested in the Duma as an object for political exploitation: not as an instrument for achieving parliamentary democracy in Russia. So was Stalin. But while

Lenin was voting, at Stockholm, for participation in the Duma, Stalin was abstaining – thus once again failing to echo his master's voice.[6] Neither on the question of participation in the Duma, nor on that of peasant land tenure was Stalin's independent stance due to sudden whim: he had published articles in Georgian on each topic in March, forcefully stating the non-Leninist position which he was to take up in April at Stockholm.[7]

At Stockholm, Stalin also failed to follow Lenin's lead over another important matter. Though Menshevik-Bolshevik unity was indeed formally proclaimed by the delegates as a whole, Lenin yet issued a minority manifesto criticizing the Congress and reserving the right of the Bolshevik fraction to a measure of independence within the framework of the Party. Out of more than forty Bolshevik delegates, twenty-six signed this document; but Stalin failed to do so.[8]

Stalin was, accordingly, no blind and unquestioning follower of Lenin in 1906. Why should he be? It was far from clear, at this stage, that the Mountain Eagle would one day soar so high. For the moment the Stockholm Congress marked Lenin's temporary eclipse, especially when seven Mensheviks, but only three Bolsheviks (of whom Lenin himself was not even one), were elected to the new Central Committee: the Party's governing body between congresses. But Lenin, even in defeat, had dominated the Congress to a degree which no victorious Menshevik could achieve, as Stalin later noted. Defeat, says Stalin, transformed Lenin into a coil of energy; unabashed by all setbacks, he denounced manifestations of alarm and despondency among his fellow-Bolsheviks, and told them that there was to be 'no snivelling, Comrades, for we shall certainly win'.[9]

Among the issues debated at Stockholm, none was more vital to Stalin's career than that of expropriations: highway robberies and other criminal enterprises undertaken by revolutionaries with the aim of replenishing Party coffers. Politically motivated street hold-ups, muggings, robbery with violence from banks and other institutions, attacks on individuals, the extortion of political protection money . . . all these felonies had boomed during the revolutionary year 1905. And though the revolutionary upheaval was already subsiding by the time of the Stockholm Congress, such activities still continued, raising awkward questions about the nature of Russian Social Democracy. Could those who sanctioned such methods consider themselves a respectable political party? Or were they degenerating into a criminal gang? A majority of the delegates to Stockholm was for respectability, and passed a resolution condemning the expropriations. 'Criminals and the scum of the urban population [they fulminated] have always used revolutionary upheavals for their anti-social aims, and . . . the revolutionary

47

people has had to take stern measures against an orgy of theft and highway robbery.'[10] Though Lenin did not find it expedient to oppose this resolution at the time, and though he was theoretically bound by its terms, he secretly intended to defy it. Of the Party's continuing need for cash, however acquired, an illustration was provided as soon as the Stockholm Congress broke up: many delegates turned out unable to pay their fares home, and the Stockholm chief of police had to lend them money.[11]

By contrast with the Mensheviks and with the more squeamish among his fellow-Bolsheviks, Lenin was willing to use any instrument equipped to further a revolution sponsored by himself. Of his readiness to embrace criminal methods he openly testified in an article on partisan warfare of September 1906: 'When I hear Social Democrats declare proudly and smugly "We are not Anarchists, not thieves, not robbers, we are above it, we reject partisan warfare", then I ask: do these people understand what they are talking about ?'[12] Expropriations were a necessary evil from Lenin's point of view, simply because ordinary Party funds were inadequate to meet travelling and conference expenditure, the cost of publishing political literature and the living expenses of the full-time professional revolutionaries who formed the leadership. Despite many donations from wealthy sympathizers – and despite such other sources as the sale of contraceptives and the dowries of wealthy young women seduced by Bolsheviks – the Party treasury was never so full that the proceeds of robbery from the State and the bourgeoisie (with which Lenin considered himself at war) could come amiss.

Lenin simulated acquiescence in the Stockholm resolution against the expropriations, but immediately set up a Bolshevik Secret Centre in order to plan more seizures of funds earmarked exclusively for the use of his fraction. Illegal so far as the Party as a whole was concerned, the Centre was Lenin's instrument for mounting clandestine operations independent of the new Menshevik-dominated Central Committee. Other members of the Secret Centre, in addition to Lenin himself, were Bogdanov and Krasin.[13] Stalin has never been mentioned as a member in any formal sense, but seems to have acted as the Centre's Man in the Caucasus. Agreeing with Lenin over the expropriation issue, Koba was soon to gain repute – largely evil – in Bolshevik circles for the organization of armed hold-ups and other acts of violence in the Caucasus: in direct violation of Party discipline, but in accordance with Lenin's secret wishes. Thus Koba – undistinguished outside Legend as orator, debater, political theorist, journalist and editor – first earns a reputation within his Party as a political master-criminal or gangland boss.

Stalin is beginning to discover his true vocation.

In May 1907 Stalin attended the Fifth Congress of the Russian Social Democratic Party. At the Brotherhood Church in Whitechapel, London, some three hundred Social Democrats congregated, representing many parts of the Russian Empire and attracting the suspicions of the British press and police. Some of the women delegates were reported as performing pistol practice in front of mirrors. No less embarrassingly, the Russians – when invited to a banquet by certain English parlour Socialists – turned out to be travelling without such basic equipment as evening dress; besides, their everyday wear was hardly respectable, what with all those Caucasian fur caps and blue workers' blouses. Okhrana spies were naturally present in quantity, and included a Dr Zhitomirsky who was especially close to Lenin.[14] Such *agents provocateurs* were in turn trailed by English detectives impartially investigating both Russian revolutionaries and Okhrana infiltrators: an operation much assisted by the frequency with which both roles were simultaneously played by one and the same person.[15]

With sizeable delegations from three fraternal Socialist parties representing minorities within the Russian Empire (the Jewish Bund, the Polish and Latvian parties) the congressmen of 1907 formed a varied group. Jews were particularly numerous – and not only in the Bund, but also within the Menshevik fraction. Among the Bolsheviks they were less prominently represented. 'There was therefore something to be said for us Bolsheviks organizing a pogrom within the Party' . . . such was the quip of a Bolshevik jester, as repeated shortly afterwards by Dzhugashvili in one of his articles.[16] Here he was airing feelings which have led many observers, including his daughter, to regard the mature dictator as a militant anti-Semite. From Arsenidze we learn that the young Stalin was accustomed to sneer at Martov, Dan and Akselrod – Jews and Menshevik leaders all – as 'circumcised Yids'. He was already speaking of Jews as cowards who would not stand up and fight: a charge which he was to repeat nearly forty years later in conversation with the Polish General Anders. Yet Arsenidze expressly acquits Stalin of anti-Semitism; though entirely indifferent to the Jews as such, he was less keen on anti-Semitism for its own sake than as a commonly-held prejudice ripe for political exploitation.[17] As this acute comment indicates, the mature Stalin was not narrowly biased against any specific section of humanity, for his sympathies were broadly and generously anti-human in general. Rarely in his career shall we find him discriminating in favour of Jews or of anyone else.

Well might Dzhugashvili commemorate the London Congress with sneers against fellow-congressmen, for his own billing was confined to a

49

walking-on part...and even that proved a fiasco. No longer (as at Stockholm) an accredited delegate, he had presumably forfeited this rating through inability to muster sufficient local support. And though Lenin insisted on sponsoring the swarthy 'Ivanovich' (for Dzhugashvili was still travelling under this alias), it was not possible to offer him more than consultative status without voting rights. Even this modest proposal led to an exchange damaging to Stalin's later claim to have been the messiah of early Caucasian Bolshevism. At a session chaired by Lenin the Menshevik leader Martov objected to the nomination of 'Ivanovich', and of three other proposed consultative delegates. No one knew, said Martov, who 'these persons' were or where they came from.

'Quite true, *we don't know.*' Such was Lenin's devastating reply.[18]

Can he really have been ignorant, still, of the very existence of the man who would one day be hailed in Hieratic idiom as his closest Comrade-in-Arms? Hardly. We must assume, rather, that Lenin knew very well who 'Ivanovich' was, but found it impolitic to give him public recognition: perhaps because 'Ivanovich' was now heavily involved in Caucasian cloak-and-dagger work of which the less said the better.

Accepted, despite Martov's intervention, as a consultative delegate at London, Stalin had the right to speak at the Congress, but the official record shows that he did not once open his mouth. Small wonder, then, that commentators (Trotsky included) have been inclined to sense a hidden purpose behind Stalin's excursion to the British capital.[19] Perhaps Lenin was privily conferring with Stalin in his capacity as contact man between the Bolshevik Secret Centre and the local terrorists of the Caucasus.

As this reminds us, the Social Democrats' pious resolution against the expropriations (carried at their Stockholm Congress) had remained a dead letter ever since so far as Lenin's group was concerned. Far from obeying orders by refraining from terrorism, Krasin had gone to the opposite limit by busily co-operating, as head of the Leninist Secret Centre, with the ultra-terrorist wing of the rival Socialist Revolutionary Party. Krasin it was who furnished the explosives and weapons used by three doomed Socialist Revolutionaries in a sensational but unsuccessful attack on Prime Minister Stolypin at his island villa near St Petersburg in August 1906.[20] Krasin, too, helped to set up the notorious bank raid in Lantern Alley in St Petersburg, which netted for the Socialist Revolutionaries a large sum in roubles – from which the Bolshevik Secret Centre took its cut.[21]

Moneys such as these enabled Lenin to dominate the London Congress as he had been unable to dominate Stockholm, for the Bolsheviks could meet their delegates' expenses from the profits of expropriation, whereas the more scrupulous Mensheviks disposed of no comparable loot. Yet even among Bolsheviks there were many who deplored dependence on means normally regarded as criminal. They added their voices to those of Mensheviks and others opposed to the expropriations. The result was an overwhelming majority for a new resolution, passed against Lenin's opposition and condemning the expropriations in terms yet more forthright than had been agreed at Stockholm. There was no reason, though, why Lenin should pay any more attention to this pious resolution than he had to its predecessor. Defeated in the vote, he still held expropriated funds denied to his rivals, and was thus able to acquire, in London, the political weight which had eluded him in Stockholm. His victory was marked by his own election to the new Central Committee: one on which Leninists could now hope to control a majority.

Describing (in 1924) the conquering Lenin of 1907, Stalin stressed his leader's refusal to show complacency over this triumph. One should not be carried away by victory (Stalin quotes Lenin as saying), but should consolidate and crush one's opponents.[22] Among all the lessons imparted by the Russian revolutionary master, none was to be more thoroughly assimilated by his still insignificant Georgian disciple.

Expropriator

On 13 June 1907 the most notorious of all revolutionary expropriations – the Erivan Square hold-up – took place in Tiflis. Occurring barely two months after the Fifth Congress had condemned such activities, this outrage represented a defiance of Party authority by the Georgian Bolsheviks who staged it. They were led by a certain Semyon Ter-Petrosyan, known as Kamo. He was an Armenian, and also – like Stalin, who had once coached him for an army examination – a native of Gori. When tutoring Kamo, Stalin had argued against an officer's career, advising the prospective cadet to read Zola and helping to convert him to Socialism.[1] The very nickname Kamo – deriving from Ter-Petrosyan's mispronunciation of a common Russian word – was bestowed on him by the same political mentor, ill as it became Dzhugashvili of the comically staccato speech to criticize any fellow-Caucasian's Russian accent.

A grotesque desperado, connoisseur of disguise, bomb fabricator and terrorist, Kamo was an ideal tool in the hands of Lenin, to whom he was devoted. He also went in awe of Stalin, who was regarded by many Bolsheviks as their chief organizer of expropriations within the Caucasus. Operating in the shadows, as always, Stalin was well equipped to manipulate such a dangerous marionette as Kamo, thus gaining important early experience on the administrative side of political terrorism.

It was at about 11 a.m. on 13 June that Kamo – wearing Russian officer's uniform – led his gunmen and bomb-throwers into action in Erivan Square in the centre of Tiflis. As the city rocked to a series of explosions, the target might be seen as a phaeton heavily guarded and escorted by mounted Cossacks; it was occupied by two cashiers and was conveying a large sum in five-hundred-rouble notes from the Post Office to the State Bank. Seizing the swag amid scenes of horror and confusion, Kamo's men conveyed it to their leader, who stood in the centre of the square firing a revolver into the air: to show the other conspirators where he was, to create a diversion, or out of sheer high spirits. The area was already littered with the bodies of the dying and the wounded. In the end, though, this sanguinary coup petered out in fiasco: after the haul of about a quarter of a million roubles had been taken to Lenin in Finland,[2] it turned out that the serial numbers of the bank notes had been recorded by the Russian police. Banks all over the world were alerted, and secured the arrest of those Bolshevik agents who attempted to change the fatal currency. Kamo himself was imprisoned in Germany.

Typically enough, we cannot determine the exact degree of Stalin's involvement in Kamo's exploit on Erivan Square. Arsenidze has dismissed the claim, sometimes put forward, that Koba directly participated in this hold-up and other Caucasian expropriations of the period. He has Koba skulking in the Tiflis railway station at the time of the Erivan Square business: presumably in readiness to take the first train out of town should any hitch occur.[3] In any case Kamo would have refused to expose Stalin – his 'adored leader' – to the hazards of open combat. But the organizational and theoretical leadership of these expropriations was another matter. There Stalin's involvement was beyond all doubt, says Arsenidze, adding that the original decision to carry out the Erivan Square robbery was taken at a meeting of Bolshevik activists led by Koba.[4]

That Stalin did indeed supervise or organize Bolshevik expropriations in the Caucasus is also confirmed by one Tsintsadze, who himself takes credit – in memoirs antedating the Stalin Legend – for initiating such operations. Tsintsadze writes that he decided to start a Bolshevik 'club' for appropriating State funds.

Our advanced comrades, and particularly Koba-Stalin, approved my suggestion. In the middle of November 1906, the expropriators' club was organized and at the railway junction at Chiaturi we attacked a post office railway car, and took 21,000 roubles, of which 15,000 were sent to the Bolshevik fraction and the rest to our own group to provide for a series of expropriations later on.[5]

Another of Stalin's enterprises was to tunnel into the treasury department in his native Gori. Though we do not know whether this exploit succeeded, we do know that Stalin himself was not one of the shovel-wielders. Nor would he so much as inspect the tunnel when his diggers invited him in: he was afraid of it collapsing on top of him. From this the deduction – surely incorrect – has been made that he was a physical coward.[6]

Stalin's role in organizing such *coups* is further confirmed by his expulsion from the Caucasian party organization for defying the injunction, so recently imposed at the London Congress, to abstain from expropriations. The Bureau of the Transcaucasian Social Democratic Organization set up a special commission to investigate this matter; all organizers and participants, from Koba downwards, were expelled from the Party. But the Central Committee, now under Lenin's influence, appears to have let the matter drop.[7]

Over a decade later the expropriations issue led to further scandal when Martov, the Menshevik leader, ventilated the matter in a Menshevik newspaper which was still permitted to appear for a short time during 1918.

That the Caucasian Bolsheviks attached themselves to all sorts of daring enter- prises of an expropriatory nature should be well known [wrote Martov] to that same Citizen Stalin, who was expelled in his time from his Party Organization for having had something to do with expropriation.

Now newly-appointed Commissar for Nationalities in the Soviet Govern- ment, Stalin reacted as vigorously as he was able, in the mild atmosphere of 1918, by having Martov indicted for criminal libel. At the first hearing, before three Bolshevik judges, Stalin indignantly denied Martov's charges. 'Never in my life was I placed on trial before my Party or expelled. This is a vicious libel.... One has no right to come out with accusations like Martov's except with documents in one's hand. It is dishonest to throw mud on the basis of mere rumours.'[8]

The court granted an adjournment during which a political colleague of Martov's went to the Caucasus and obtained affidavits from local witnesses – only to find on his return that the case had collapsed because the record of the first hearing had mysteriously 'disappeared'. Martov was repri- manded by the court and the matter was dropped. This appears to be the earliest documented instance of Stalin deliberately suppressing details of his biography.

Another muffled echo of the Erivan Square explosions was heard when Kamo died in 1922. His end was suitably violent, but not in keeping with his spectacular career: he was run over while riding a bicycle in a Tiflis street. Stalin at once dispatched a special emissary who confiscated all the deceased's records and papers, taking them to Moscow. He feared that these documents might discredit his own revolutionary past: a fact revealed in the biography of Kamo by Bibineishvili. This book also 'disappeared' in its turn, and Bibineishvili himself was shot –[9] in an age when inside information about Stalin's past had become the most dangerous form of knowledge on earth.

An amusing gloss on these exploits is to be found in Emil Ludwig's account of his interview with the Soviet dictator in December 1931. Aware that Stalin had suppressed references to his early involvement in expropriations, the interviewer ventured to mention rumours concerning 'certain armed attacks which you are said to have organized in your youth to obtain money for the Party'. How much truth was there in these stories? Stalin laughed and handed over some pamphlet describing his career, presumably in Legendary terms: this would supply Ludwig with all the necessary indications, the dictator remarked with a malicious smile. The pamphlet, of course, contained no allusions whatever to Stalin's role in any armed robbery or other similar enterprise.[10]

The obliteration of Stalin's record as an expropriator had doubtless been carried out on policy grounds. To foment strikes, to organize workers' protest demonstrations, to found illicit printing presses . . . these were all perfectly respectable occupations for a revolutionary hero. Armed robbery was not. A craving for decorum, such as the mature Stalin carefully cultivated, is sufficient to explain the removal of his expropriatory role from the Legend. It is not necessary to invoke a more sinister explanation for this officially imposed silence: that the Erivan Square robbery had been organized on police instructions by Stalin in his capacity as an Okhrana agent.[11]

So much for the issue of expropriations. What of the associated charge: that Stalin also helped to organize political assassinations at this stage of his career? Tsintsadze states that Koba-Stalin recruited him as a reserve assassin for use against the hated General Gryaznov, who was in charge of measures against the Caucasian revolutionary movement. Tsintsadze was to proceed with Gryaznov's assassination only if an earlier attempt by someone else should fail; but in fact it succeeded.[12] Then, on 15 August 1907, Prince Chavchavadze – a leading Georgian nationalist and man of letters – was waylaid and shot dead near his country home. Iremashvili has charged Stalin with this crime: 'Koba was behind it; he was indirectly responsible for the murder.'[13] There is also a suggestion that Stalin was responsible for the attempted murder of a police informer at about the same time.[14]

What truth there is in these allegations we cannot say. However, since Stalin later became a mass murderer by proxy, any indications of his early involvement in assassination seem worth recording. If he was indeed stage-managing such outrages in the 1900s, he was already foreshadowing his later achievements as the liquidator of Trotsky and so many others. But he was also contravening established pre-revolutionary Social Democratic practice, for though the years 1904–07 were indeed the prime age of Russian political murder, such assassinations did not form part of the Social Democratic programme. It was, rather, the rival Socialist Revolutionaries who embraced that policy, being responsible for many hundreds of deaths. The Bolsheviks rejected it, as also did their moderate Social Democrat rivals, the Mensheviks: not, of course, because they were opposed to violence on principle, but because they did not number this particular form of violence among those which they considered politically expedient.

As for violence between Bolsheviks, though Stalin was more apt to provoke this than to take part in it personally, we do learn of a serious fist fight which developed between him and Filipp Makharadze, the later historian of the Caucasian revolutionary movement. The affray occurred on some unknown date in the Tiflis lodgings of Silvestr Dzhibladze – that other Georgian political rival of Stalin's – who had to separate the two. Once again, we are told, Stalin had to leave town as the result of a scandal.[15]

Prisoner and Exile

Having failed in his attempts to dominate the revolutionary underground of Tiflis and Batum, Dzhugashvili turned his attentions to Baku in summer 1907. As the hub of the Empire's booming oil industry, this city on the Caspian Sea was more of a working-class stronghold than any other Caucasian centre. It was therefore particularly suitable for capture by the champion of a militant, proletariat-orientated movement such as Bolshevism.

Koba was active in Baku for some eight months punctuated by occasional return trips to the Georgian capital, and possibly by an excursion to see Lenin in Germany.[1] In Baku his career continues to display familiar conflicting features. The Legend has Comrade Stalin assuming leadership of the Baku Bolsheviks with his usual dynamism, while dominating Caucasian Bolshevism as a whole. The Comrade organizes the subversive press, licit and illicit, himself publishing a number of articles; he intrepidly serves on a profusion of committees; he boldly leads a campaign to fight the election to the Third Duma while simultaneously seeking to discredit that body with the electorate. Now promoting a conference between workers and owners in the oil industry, now fomenting large-scale strikes, Comrade Stalin also recruits squads of vigilantes to protect the Reds of Baku against the local branch of a notorious right-wing hooligan organization, the Black Hundred. Comrade Stalin orates at the grave of one Sarafalyev, murdered by the agents of capitalism.[2] Under the leadership of Comrade Stalin the Mensheviks of Transcaucasia are crushed after the masks have been torn from their faces ... by Comrade Stalin. Baku becomes a fortress of Caucasian Stalinism.

Once again in accordance with long familiar pattern, sources independent of the Legend tell a very different tale. According to the memoirs of A. Stopani (as quoted by Trotsky), a prominent part was played in the activities of Baku trade unionists by someone entirely different: the 'irreplaceable' Alyosha Dzhaparidze. And Dzhugashvili? He took ... '*a lesser role*'![3] This seems confirmed by a recent, post-Cult, Soviet-published biography (1965) of Stepan Shaumyan: that old rival of Stalin's for ascendancy over Transcaucasian Bolshevism. The work contrives to describe Shaumyan's many Baku activities of 1907–08 while ignoring the Comrade Stalin once advertised as the very life and soul of Baku Bolshevism.[4] But this version too appears to be misleading, owing to the convention whereby the defunct dictator's role – once lauded to the skies, then discreetly disparaged – has since tended to be ignored entirely. According to other evidence, the Baku of 1907–08 became the arena for a renewed struggle between Stalin and Shaumyan. Stalin was believed to have denounced Shaumyan (for the second time) to the police; and there was a move to bring the Comrade before a Party tribunal (yet again) for committing the familiar offence of informing on other comrades.[5]

It was on 25 March 1908 that Koba was arrested in Baku under the most mellifluous of his many aliases: Gayoz Nizharadze. The event marks a swing in the balance of his pre-revolutionary life. Nine years had now passed since he had left the Tiflis Seminary to begin a revolutionary apprenticeship, and during those nine years he had spent a mere twenty-one months in detention. Now, from March 1908 onwards, this proportion is to be reversed in Koba's disfavour: out of the next nine years he is to spend only a year-and-a-half at liberty. During this later period he is arrested five times in all; he escapes four times; and he owes his eventual release to the February Revolution of 1917. And yet, despite restrictions so severe on his freedom, it is in this later period that the future dictator at last begins to make some headway within the revolutionary movement. In keeping with his rise in status the centre of his free activity will have moved, by 1912, from the Caucasus to St Petersburg.

During the six months between Koba's arrest of March 1908 and his departure for exile, in September of the same year, he was held in the Bailov Prison in Baku. Originally designed for four hundred inmates, this celebrated house of detention now housed nearly four times that number.

They were accommodated on the open principle, which allowed considerable freedom for social intercourse within the prison walls – as was more or less inevitable when many had to sleep in crowded corridors and on stairways. Bailov was thus one of those many Imperial Russian jails in which the detainees were able to conduct running seminars on revolutionary politics, besides which they also had excellent opportunities for observing each other at close range.

Of such opportunities one fellow-prisoner of Dzhugashvili's, the Socialist Revolutionary Semyon Vereshchak, made particularly good use.[6] Closeted with Koba for six months in Bailov Jail in 1908, and again in 1910, Vereshchak was also to share the future dictator's exile at Narym in Siberia in 1912. On arrival in prison, Koba first impressed Vereshchak by his pointed nose, small eyes and cat-like gait. He wore an unbelted blue blouse and a kind of hood flung over his shoulders. Cautious and uncommunicative, he showed steely self-control. Whenever condemned prisoners were taken out, amid groans and lamentations, to be hanged – as happened not infrequently – intolerable nervous strain naturally affected the prison population as a whole: but not Koba, who either slept through these horrors or continued his study of Esperanto. Having tried and failed to master German during an earlier incarceration, he had convinced himself that the simpler, synthetic tongue was the language of the future.[7] Koba betrayed no concern when obliged – as part of a collective punishment imposed for some unknown offence – to run the gauntlet of blows from soldiers' rifle butts. Undeterred by their buffets, he sauntered calmly through the double row of beaters, book in hand.[8] The same tale has been admirably retold in priestly argot by the evangelist Yaroslavsky: 'Stalin marched beneath the rain of blows with head erect, a volume of Marx in his hand, showing how a true Bolshevik, fearless of all persecution, and despite all obstacles, proudly and confidently carries forward the Marxian idea, convinced that its triumph is inevitable.'[9] On this purple passage, Trotsky – himself on occasion no mean wielder of Hieratic jargon – has well commented that: 'Marx's name is dragged in here for the same reason that a rose appears in the hands of the Virgin Mary. All of Soviet historiography is made up of such roses.'[10] Further evidence of Koba's phlegm was provided by the ferocious 'needling' sessions with which the prisoners were wont to amuse themselves. The pastime consisted of tongue-lashing some selected victim with insults, abuse and false accusations – none of which verbal bludgeoning ever caused Koba to bat an eyelid.

On certain occasions the jailed Koba successfully provoked violence by proxy. He secretly tipped off fellow-inmates that two of their number – a young Georgian and a Baku worker – were police spies. As a result both were assaulted. The Georgian was taken to hospital after a beating by a group of prisoners, while the Baku worker was stabbed to death by a cut-throat called Greek Mike. Only after some delay did Koba's role in these affairs emerge. No doubt mindful of previous affrays in Tiflis and Batum, he would also incite his fellow-prisoners to stage futile reprisal-provoking demonstrations. He showed great skill in prompting others to actions from which he himself remained aloof. 'This aptitude for striking secretly by the hands of others while staying in the background ... showed Koba as an astute intriguer, using all means to gain his end and escaping the penalties and the responsibility for the actions in question.'[11]

Koba frequently debated politics with his fellow-prisoners. During these wrangles he would clinch his arguments with formulae lifted from the Marxist scriptures: which much impressed the illiterate. Yet more significant, as a pointer to Koba's future, is Vereshchak's note on his preference for the society of common criminals whom other political detainees shunned. Blackmailers, gunmen, forgers, cut-throats and burglars ... these were his chosen cronies.[12] As this foreshadows, the mature Stalin often favoured individuals whom a superficial observer might have placed on a lower moral level than himself.

After sentence without trial to two years' exile, Koba was deported from Baku on 29 September 1908, but did not reach his eventual destination, Solvychegodsk, until five months later, having been detained in prison at Vologda and hospitalized with undulant fever at Vyatka. Nothing is known of his life at Solvychegodsk – an ancient fur-trading centre in northern European Russia – beyond a police report describing him as rude, insolent and disrespectful to the gendarmes of the region.[13] After a four-month stay the exile decided to escape, casually eluding the despised local gendarmes and making his way by train to St Petersburg early in July. His future father-in-law, Sergey Alliluyev, helped him to find refuge for about two weeks with a political sympathizer who lived in an outbuilding of the Horse Guards Barracks.[14] Then Koba returned to Baku.

During ten months of liberty between summer 1909 and spring 1910, Legend-Stalin's activities seem to reproduce those recorded two years earlier. Once again the Comrade makes Baku his main base, but pays flying visits to Tiflis. He flays and unmasks Mensheviks; he scourges Liquidators (those who wish to disband the Party's illegal activities); he reconstitutes the illicit Bolshevik press in Baku, himself writing articles for it; he helps to found a Bolshevik newspaper in Tiflis. He leads the work of restoring and consolidating the Party organs of Baku and Transcaucasia ... [15] but to so little effect that the Party organization of the great oil city now enters a period of decline. From early 1910 onwards, Party and trade union life in Baku is at a stand-still.[16] Not that this stagnation remains a direct concern of Koba's, for on 23 March 1910 – almost two years to the day after his previous arrest – he is again seized by the Baku gendarmes and again consigned to Bailov Prison. The wheel has come full circle. It continues to turn exactly as before. Despite a flattering recommendation by a Captain of Gendarmes – that Dzhugashvili should be treated with extra severity as an especially hardened subversive –[17] he is merely deported back to Solvychegodsk to serve out the unexpired portion of his exile. Not until October 1910 does he reach that remote outpost for the second time.

Since Stalin has left no memoirs and little personal correspondence, particular interest attaches to two letters which survive from his second period of exile in Solvychegodsk. These are the earliest of Stalin's few private letters – but are private only in the sense that they were not written for publication. The contents are entirely political, while the style betrays a jaunty element which is less prominent in works composed by Stalin for publication. Writing in Russian – his second language – he somewhat overdoes the racy colloquialisms, striving more anxiously than might a native speaker to demonstrate his familiarity with idiom.[18] Both letters are addressed to fellow-Bolsheviks, and in both Koba boasts that he is in a position to escape from his place of exile at will. Now, the missives in which he aired these boasts were not only liable – as he must have known – to interception by the Okhrana; they actually were intercepted and copied before being sent on to their destinations. But for this we might still remain ignorant of them, for it was the Okhrana's files which eventually yielded up the copies published to the world. And, incidentally, after boasting of his ability to escape from exile at will, Stalin eventually made good this intention by evading custody thrice in 1911–12. The fate of his earliest published correspondence thus illustrates the laxness of security precautions as practised by the revolutionary exile who so carelessly betrayed his intention to escape – and also by the authorities who learnt of this intention in advance but did nothing to thwart it.

The first letter is dated 31 December 1910, and signed 'K.S.'. Ultimately intending what he wrote for Lenin's eyes, Koba addressed himself to a 'Comrade Semyon': itself the alias of a Paris-based associate of Lenin's. The second letter, dated 24 January 1911 and signed 'Joseph', was sent to a group of Moscow Bolsheviks. Both letters mark a pathetic attempt by Koba to assert himself from his isolated lair. In the first he sends 'warm greetings to Lenin, Kamenev and Co.',[19] proceeding to call Lenin a 'canny operator'; Lenin 'knows where the crayfish spend the winter' (has his head screwed on tight) – witness his manoeuvres designed to split the

Menshevik leadership from its rank-and file support. Rival Social Democratic groupings are curtly dismissed: that of Trotsky as combining a 'sickly amalgam of heterogeneous principles' with 'a putrescent lack of principle'.[20] The remark has some interest as an early vituperative reference by Stalin to his greatest future political enemy and victim.

In both letters Stalin advertises his own credentials as a revolutionary who is based on Russia, and who is therefore more closely in touch with the mood of the Russian worker than the most eminent of émigré Social Democrats can hope to be. He recommends the establishment of a central, Russia-based organization to co-ordinate all the Party's legal, semi-legal and illegal activities in Russia herself; such a body is as necessary as air and bread, Koba maintains, clearly seeing himself in the directing role. His attempt to boost his own position as a revolutionary firmly based on the Empire's home territory, and to devalue the pretensions of the many émigré Social Democrats, becomes more explicit in the second letter. This is remarkable for Stalin's condescending tone in referring to the political dissensions of the émigrés ... by no means excluding Lenin. Loftily dismissing their historic bickerings as a 'storm in a teacup', he claims that the Russian workers are beginning to despise émigré political activity, even if they do – so far as he knows – prefer Lenin to his rivals. Let these foreign-based politicians prosecute their futile activities till they're black in the face![21] Anyone with the movement's true interests at heart will ignore them and get on with preparing the revolution. That, claimed Koba, was what the workers were saying. Perhaps they were. But how tactless of him to pose as an arbiter of proletarian moods superior to his more experienced, more sophisticated foreign-based colleagues! His impertinence did not go unnoticed – Lenin complained of Koba's inconsistency and immaturity as a Marxist, as revealed in 'nihilistic little jokes about a storm in a teacup'.[22]

There is, in these two letters, a distant anticipation of the massacre of voluble, much-travelled, polyglot, cosmopolitan, europeanized, university-trained Leninists which was one day to be organized by the obscure, seminary-drilled Georgian who now sought to draw attention to himself from the remote provinces in the depths of the Russian winter.

Since both letters were intercepted by the Okhrana, the possibility has been mooted that Stalin expressly designed them to be seized, hoping to remind the authorities of his continuing potential value as a police agent in touch with current trends in Bolshevik thinking.[23] If such were indeed Koba's motives the device was not successful, for on this occasion he served out the sentence restricting him to Solvychegodsk until it duly ended on 27 June 1911. He was then freed – but forbidden to go to the

Caucasus, and to all large cities and industrial centres. He therefore settled down in the nearest provincial capital, Vologda. Then, on 6 September, he simply took the train out of town – which was perfectly legal – and emerged from it (which was perfectly illegal) in St Petersburg.

The illicit resident enjoyed no more than a three-day sojourn at liberty in the Russian capital. After once more making contact with the Alliluyevs, he was arrested on 9 September and placed in the St Petersburg remand prison, where he received a sentence of three years' exile. Assigned to Vologda, so recently his temporary refuge, Koba began his latest period of exile in that town on Christmas Day 1911.

3
Northern Underground

Central Committeeman

WITHIN a few weeks of embarking on his new term of exile at Vologda, Stalin receives the important political promotion which first puts him on the map as a Bolshevik of standing, and which ends his period as a provincial revolutionary – as a local boy who has not even made good on a local level. Henceforward the capital city, St Petersburg – not Tiflis, Batum or Baku – is to be the focus of his operations during his brief periods of liberty. From now onwards he is a metropolitan, not a merely regional, revolutionary.

The event which accomplished this transformation occurred in January 1912. It was then that Stalin was unexpectedly made, in his absence, a member of the new Bolshevik Central Committee which emerged after a Party Conference held in Prague. By no means, however, was he 'elected' to this body, as is claimed in Legend.[1] On the contrary, he was brought in through the personal decision of Lenin, who had received from the conference the power to co-opt new Central Committee members at will. That such was Stalin's route to the Central Committee is worth stressing; indeed, it has been plausibly claimed – not with complete accuracy, for we shall meet certain exceptions – that he 'was never elected by *free* voters, in public or party, to any office on any occasion.'[2]

Momentous though this promotion was eventually to prove, it was not calculated to jolt the consciousness of the world. In January 1912 Lenin's name was not yet a household word, while the pseudonym Stalin had yet to see the light of day. Also unknown to the world at large, the Russian Social Democratic Party as a whole was passing through a period of grievous decline. A substantial reduction in membership had been accompanied by continuing factional rifts which had proceeded far beyond the original split into Bolsheviks and Mensheviks. Now both Bolsheviks and Mensheviks were themselves divided into competing segments. By early 1912, Lenin had decided to abandon all alliances with any of them, and to establish a small splinter group consisting essentially of those who owed personal allegiance to himself, and who represented a small minority of the Party's dwindling membership. While parting company with Social Democrats of all other complexions – including non-Leninist Bolsheviks – Lenin aimed to present his dissident group as the main core of the Party.[3]

When this context is remembered, Lenin's choice of Stalin as a co-opted central committeeman becomes less surprising than it might otherwise seem. None of the Party's 'big names' was willing to be associated with Lenin's Prague activities – Plekhanov, Trotsky, Martov and Bogdanov were all absent, for instance – and Lenin had to pick up his hard-core Leninists where he could find them. Consequently, none of the newly-elected central committeemen enjoyed great seniority within the Party. While some (Zinovyev and Ordzhonikidze) could claim greater prominence than Stalin, several of the others were yet more obscure. One among them, incidentally, was the Okhrana spy Malinovsky: by no means the only police infiltrator present at Prague. That the Prague Conference took place – as, in effect, it did – under the benevolent supervision of the Okhrana was not surprising in the developing political atmosphere, for though the ultimate aims of Lenin and the Imperial security police could hardly have been further apart – since each sought the other's total destruction – their short-term goals chanced to coincide exactly. Both aimed to foment dissension among Social Democrats; no matter, for the moment, that the Okhrana wished to crush the Party, Lenin to capture it.

The above considerations show why Stalin's modest position within the Party was no bar to his advancement, but do not explain why Lenin now chose to single him out from other seeming mediocrities. It is unlikely that Stalin's promotion represented recognition for his work in organizing the Erivan Square expropriation, as has been claimed,[4] since Lenin invariably based his actions on calculations of future political advantage – not on gratitude for services rendered. More probably he prized Stalin as one of those fairly rare Bolsheviks who possessed a respectably humble, if not fully proletarian, background. Man of action, too, Koba little resembled the more verbose type of Russian intellectual whom Lenin tended to dislike and mistrust. Stalin had a record of ruthlessness worthy of any out-and-out fanatic – yet was no mere blind executant of orders such as Kamo. Stalin had a mind of his own. He also possessed, as his mature career was to show, enormous latent organizational talent, and the plain fact is that Lenin had the wit to discern this when others could not. Finally, on a point of detail, Lenin may have been impressed by Koba's suggestion, mooted in the 'Comrade Semyon' letter of 31 December 1910, that the Party should establish a special Centre to co-ordinate its operations within the Empire. Whether influenced by Koba or not, the Prague Conference did resolve to set up precisely such a centre: the Russian Bureau of the Central Committee. According to Legend, Comrade Stalin was himself 'put in charge' of this Bureau,[5] but an authoritative post-Stalin Soviet source has him as only one of ten Bolsheviks who helped to co-ordinate the activities of local Party organizations within the Empire under Lenin's general direction.[6]

Koba was languishing in Vologda when he learnt of his promotion to the new Central Committee from another member of the same body – Ordzhonikidze, who visited him there and then wrote to inform Lenin how delighted the new central committeeman was with his promotion.[7] Not long afterwards Koba decided to celebrate by escaping from Vologda, as he did on 29 February 1912, in order to try his luck again in the political underworld – now, at last, as a figure of some slight consequence. This spell of liberty in March-April 1912 lasted only fifty-two days. Much of this time must have been spent on travelling, for he contrived to sandwich a Caucasian expedition between brief halts in St Petersburg.

During this period the pattern of claim and counter-claim by Legend and Counter-Legend remains unchanged. Legend has the new central committeeman implementing the decisions of the Prague Conference on pan-Caucasian level during personal visits to Tiflis and Baku; in the latter city he organizes a regional conference of his own. On 1 April, Comrade Stalin leaves the Caucasus for St Petersburg, pausing in Moscow to confer with Ordzhonikidze. The Comrade also attempts to negotiate the transfer to the Party of certain disputed funds held in trust by German Communists. Arriving in the capital on 10 April, he edits the Bolshevik periodical *Zvezda* (Star), himself writing six articles for it. He also takes a leading role in founding a more celebrated Bolshevik publication, the daily newspaper *Pravda* (Truth). But on 22 April, the very date of *Pravda*'s maiden issue, its intrepid chief organizer is picked up by the police on the streets of St Petersburg and flung into the city's remand prison: his fifth (or sixth) arrest.[8]

Again according to pattern, Counter-Legend and Non-Legend offer dimly discerned and less glorious variants. One witness suggests that Koba did not appear in Georgia at all during this period.[9] Another speaks of two meetings between himself and Koba in Baku, and also hints at Koba's responsibility for betraying to the Okhrana numerous members of the Party who were arrested in the wake of his visit.[10] Any editing of *Zvezda* by Stalin is ignored in both pre-Legend and post-Legend Soviet sources.[11] And though *Pravda* was founded 'on the initiative' of Comrade Stalin, according to Legend, the newspaper yet contrived – in a special fifteenth-anniversary issue of 1927 – to make no mention whatever of its chief initiator's name.[12] Nor does J. V. Stalin figure in the *Soviet Historical Encyclopaedia*'s article on *Pravda* (1968). Yet Stalin did, according to one non-Legend witness, produce a 'considerable effect' on the work of this infant newspaper; such is the testimony of the Bolshevik journalist Olminsky, himself a co-founder of *Pravda*. As an influence on early *Pravda*, this witness brackets Stalin with Yakov Sverdlov, who also appeared in St Petersburg at various times in the intervals between spells of exile.[13] As this evidence tends to confirm, the elusive truth about Stalin is often to be sought at some intermediate point between the total participation in politically approved enterprises claimed by Legend and the total non-participation so often asserted by Counter-Legend.

To the scant information on Koba's activities during March and April 1912 the hieratically ghosted reminiscences of his sister-in-law Anna Alliluyeva contribute what is at least a variant from the standard picture. She speaks of him taking the Alliluyev children – including his own ten-year-old future second wife Nadezhda – for a sledge drive in St Petersburg. On this trip the gay, laughing, boyishly joking Soso always sees the funny side of people and has everyone 'roaring with laughter' at his comic anecdotes. 'Every word makes us laugh. Soso laughs with us at everything.'[14]

To those who sought him here and sought him there at this time, a more illustrious name must be added. 'I have no news from Ivanovich [Lenin wrote on 28 March 1912, using Stalin's old alias]. What is he up to? Where is he? How is he?'[15] How aptly this first reference to Stalin in Lenin's correspondence emphasizes the vanishing Georgian's ability to cover his traces.

After his latest – fifth or sixth – arrest, on 22 April 1912, Koba is again taken out of circulation: on this occasion for a period of some twenty weeks. The first half of this spell is spent in the St Petersburg remand prison, where he receives a three-year sentence of administrative exile to Narym in western Siberia. He reaches that remote area in late July after a three-hundred-mile steamer trip down the Ob from Tomsk, and finds himself in the usual small colony of political exiles. Sharing the quarters of Sverdlov, now also in exile, Koba contrived by various devices to foist the bulk of household chores, such as lighting the stove and cleaning, on his hutmate. Sverdlov found him untidy and disorganized.[16]

After a few weeks at Narym, Comrade Stalin eludes the supervision of the local gendarmes on 1 September. Eleven days later he is back in St Petersburg.

Lenin's Man in St Petersburg?

Restored to circulation by his escape from Siberia, Stalin reaches St Petersburg on 12 September 1912, and enjoys a period of nearly six months' liberty – though hunted by the police – to indulge in intensive political activity: up to 23 February 1913, the date of his last arrest. During this half-year period the Russian capital remains his main base, but he also makes two excursions to the Austro-Hungarian Empire for discussions with Lenin.

Collaboration with Lenin is the key issue of this last and most significant spell of Koba's pre-revolutionary activity as a free man. Lenin shares Stalin's three main concerns of the period: the newspaper *Pravda*; Bolshevik participation in the Fourth Duma;[1] the nationalities issue.

Legend has Comrade Stalin operating as Lenin's Man in St Petersburg, controlling *Pravda*, directly managing the entire Bolshevik campaign for the Fourth Duma elections, 'guiding' the work of the six Bolshevik deputies elected as the result of his efforts,[2] and pioneering a new area of Bolshevik thinking on the nationalities question. Of these events Trotsky provides an ingenious interpretation as unfavourable to Stalin as Legend is favourable. According to Trotskyite Counter-Legend, Stalin does indeed control *Pravda*, but infuriates Lenin by allowing the paper to degenerate into rampant anti-Leninism. Under Stalin's leadership *Pravda* truckles to Mensheviks and other political enemies, also abetting anti-Leninist heresy among the six Bolsheviks on the Duma. As for the contribution made to Marxist theory by Stalin's article on the nationalities question, Trotsky does indeed admit that to be tremendous – but adds that all the credit is due to Lenin.[3]

From the available evidence, some of which has come to light since Trotsky's death, it seems likely that on these matters Legend – for once – offers a less inaccurate version of events than does Counter-Legend.

Before the issue is considered in detail we must recall Lenin's situation as it was developing from mid-1912. It was now that the Bolshevik leader, accompanied by his consort and amanuensis Nadezhda Krupskaya, moved his headquarters from Paris to the Polish city of Cracow: now belonging to Austria-Hungary, but conveniently situated near the Imperial Russian frontier. After their exile to Paris this seemed no more than semi-exile, for the Polish police – unlike the Parisian – tended to leave Russian revolutionaries alone. Newspapers from Russia took only three days to arrive in Cracow, and postal facilities were comparatively good.[4] But Lenin was in no position to exercise control over the Russia-based Bolshevik faction, which was far from having yet evolved into the disciplined political army which it later became. Lenin disposed of no chain of command; he could rely solely on personal prestige and powers of exhortation. He inundated his followers with impassioned rebukes, protests, suggestions and directives, but even with Cracow as his base the impact of these paper darts was much reduced by distance. Lenin's emissaries were liable to arrest; his letters were often lost in transit or intercepted by the Okhrana. For security reasons they were commonly written in invisible ink between the lines of some visible text of palpably innocent content. As a further precaution, cover-names were commonly used for institutions and individuals: Stalin features variously as 'Ivanovich', 'Vasilyev', 'Vasily' and 'Vaska'.

Bombarding his rarely seen Russia-based lieutenants with peremptory advice, Lenin sought to wean them from Conciliationism: that is, from seeking co-operation with Social Democrats who were not committed Leninists. Conciliationism – as is illustrated by letter after letter dispatched from Cracow – proved particularly difficult to stamp out among the Russia-based Social Democrats; for, despite differences of political emphasis, these all tended to cultivate solidarity in the face of shared dangers and a common enemy: the Imperial State.

Lenin attached great importance to *Pravda*, but was far from controlling it. Founder of the newspaper only in the sense of having approved (at the Prague Conference) the original proposal to bring out a new Bolshevik daily, he was horrified when he saw its first leading article, published on the first date of issue: 22 April 1912. What was this but blatant Conciliationism, calling as it did for unity among all Social Democrats of all complexions ? The article, anonymously published at its first appearance, was later ascribed by Legend to Stalin, and consequently appears in his *Works*.[5] This attribution presents him as flagrantly at odds with Lenin: and on what Lenin considered the central political issue of the day. Here is a point at which the Legend-building editors of Stalin's *Works* have preferred to stress the Comrade's significance (as author of *Pravda's* first leading article) even at the expense of spoiling his record as Lenin's unswerving disciple. In fact, of course, Stalin may have had no part whatever in drafting the offending leader; or it may have been a joint effort to which he contributed.

Between late April and mid-September 1912 (when Stalin was in prison and exile) Lenin was so far from exercising direct control over *Pravda* that the newspaper even rejected articles submitted by him. Spurning Lenin's pen, the editors – of whom Poletayev was chief – also lost or failed to return such items; alternatively, they subjected Lenin's words to their own censorship, removing all references to Liquidators. This was the disparaging term which Lenin applied to those Mensheviks whom he could not hope to influence; but it was *Pravda*'s editorial policy to cultivate Social Democratic harmony, and therefore to avoid the very mention of such issues: much to Lenin's disgust. Also complaining that the articles submitted by Lenin were boring, the editors introduced a criterion all too rarely invoked in Marxist polemics.[6]

The months went by. Stalin returned to St Petersburg from exile. Lenin's complaints against *Pravda* grew more and more savage: the Conciliationist rag was riddled with misprints; copies were not dispatched to Cracow with adequate regularity; Lenin did not always receive the fees due for his articles – fees on which he was now dependent for his living expenses.

But though Lenin does indeed complain of all these matters, conducting a running feud with the early *Pravda*, it by no means follows automatically that he held Stalin responsible for the newspaper's misdemeanours, as Counter-Legend maintains. Nor was a desire to wrest *Pravda* from Stalin's clutches Lenin's main reason for luring his Georgian protégé to Cracow in late 1912.[7] Far from it, for nowhere does Lenin accuse or rebuke Stalin in person. It is others whom Lenin blames: Poletayev, in effect *Pravda*'s first chief editor; and the paper's secretary, Vyacheslav Molotov – Stalin's future chief henchman.

Figures such as these, or the editorial board in general, incur Lenin's wrath: for the crime of passivity towards the Duma elections; for failure to elicit and publicize the required polemical statements by Bolshevik Duma deputies, for the appalling financial mess into which the paper has fallen. This led Stalin to warn Lenin that the management of its affairs was a scandal;[8] he also told Lenin that these difficulties made it necessary to suspend the honorarium which the Cracow-based leader was receiving from *Pravda*. But so far was Lenin from blaming Stalin for this state of affairs that he expressly called upon Stalin to purge *Pravda*, and to stage – in effect – a *coup d'état* by snatching the paper out of Poletayev's clutches. It was on Stalin, too, that Lenin depended to seize control of *Pravda*'s all-important financial resources. Particularly eloquent is Lenin's letter to Stalin of 16 December 1912 in which he gives the following instructions: 'In the name of all that is holy, do take the most energetic measures to get W. [*Pravda*] out of Krass's [Poletayev's] hands . . . and especially to get hold of the funds and the subscription money. Without that we're sunk.'[9] By early 1913 Stalin had carried out these measures.

One of the tasks performed by Stalin as Lenin's Man in St Petersburg was the supervision of the six Bolshevik deputies elected to the Fourth and last Duma, which began its deliberations in November 1912. Though Lenin despised the Duma as an institution, calling it a 'black parliament', he had come to appreciate its considerable nuisance value. Far from advocating a boycott of the Duma, as on occasion in earlier years, he had therefore urged his Russia-based supporters to contest the latest election with all possible vigour. It was from this campaign that the six Bolshevik deputies emerged. All could boast proletarian origin, as could Stalin himself to some extent; but, unlike Stalin, the six were also proletarians in the sense of having worked in factories. Malinovsky (the Okhrana spy who headed the six) was an articulate and intelligent individual capable of serving Lenin and the Police Department simultaneously, while contriving for a time to satisfy both masters. But the other five were relatively unenterprising figures of whom Lenin tended to speak as if they were robots or marionettes. They needed to have their speeches written for them and to be kept informed of the political postures which they were from time to time required to assume. This was the task assigned by Lenin to Stalin.

The ultimate fate of the Bolshevik deputies to the Fourth Duma has a certain interest, since none of them perished in Stalin's Great Terror of the late 1930s, when so many other veterans were liquidated. Four of these old-timers (Badayev, M. K. Muranov, Petrovsky and Samoylov) lived on into the 1950s, and two of them even survived Stalin himself: perhaps owing such immunity to their political insignificance in the post-revolutionary period rather than to clemency shown by Stalin for old times' sake.

Far from supporting Trotsky's version of events, the evidence of Lenin's correspondence suggests that he did indeed regard Stalin as his Man in St Petersburg. He appears to have viewed Stalin as one of the most dependable among the various Russia-based lieutenants on whom he relied for organizational purposes. As for the general tone of Lenin's letters and references to Stalin, these are not at all the missives of Superman haranguing some minion or moron, but are practical, businesslike communications addressed by one colleague to another whose competence is patently taken for granted.[10]

So much for Lenin's attitude to Stalin. What of Stalin's attitude to Lenin? This remains more a matter for speculation. The fact that Lenin did not blame Stalin for *Pravda*'s misdemeanours does not mean that Stalin was free from guilt. One of his articles in particular, published in *Pravda* of 1 December 1912, carries the taint of advanced Conciliationism: which presumably explains its omission from the *Works*. There is therefore no reason to reject Trotsky's contention that Koba was permanently open to deals with the non-Leninist forces of Social Democracy. That it was not Stalin's nature to commit himself unreservedly to Lenin or any other human being seems, in any case, adequately established by his general record: it was ever Stalin's nature to hedge, to seek the middle way, to keep all his options open. But it does not follow from this that Lenin was fully aware of Stalin's potentialities for duplicity: still less that he failed to set a high value on Stalin's services.

Among the landmarks of this period is Dzhugashvili's adoption of the revolutionary pseudonym under which he was to become known to the world at large. The name Stalin first appears as the byline to the above-mentioned Conciliationist *Pravda* article of 1 December 1912. Forming his *nom de guerre* from the Russian word for 'steel', Koba was adopting the symbolism of durables as cultivated by his colleagues Molotov and Kamenev, whose names – also pseudonymous – derive from the words for 'mallet' and 'stone' respectively. We may contrast the less truculent-sounding pseudonym of Lenin (Ulyanov), which may have originated in the name of a river.

The Austrian Episode

In mid-November 1912, Stalin went to Cracow, where he conferred with Lenin and attended his first Central Committee meeting. In late December he was back again, also visiting Vienna and remaining on Austro-Hungarian territory until mid-February 1913: the longest sojourn which he ever made on foreign soil.

As Stalin's two Austrian excursions illustrate, there was still little difficulty in crossing the Russian border illegally. For such crossings Stalin would use a Finnish passport or a so-called half-passport: the travel document issued to commuting locals in Austrian Galicia.[1] To the saga of these excursions Stalin has himself contributed certain details. He was once guided over the frontier by a kindly Polish shoemaker; as a sign of solidarity between cobbler-victims of Tsarist oppression, this sturdy proletarian refused all payment.[2] It was, presumably, just before this encounter that Stalin had rejected the proffered services of certain villainous-looking Jews whose intention of delivering him direct into the clutches of the Russian gendarmes he could see written all over their rapacious features.[3] Such, at any rate, is the tale which he told the Polish General Anders thirty years later, perhaps seeking to elicit an anti-Semitic reaction rather than to parade one of his own. On another occasion the young Koba was enraged by poor service received at a Polish railway buffet on the Austrian side of the frontier: the waiter deliberately delayed serving a bowl of piping hot soup until the moment when the traveller's train was just about to leave. Pouring the steaming fluid over his table in disgust, Stalin remained unaware (until Lenin later explained the incident to him) that the Polish waiter was protesting against having to serve a meal ordered in the hated Russian tongue.[4]

After attending his second Central Committee meeting and conferring with Lenin in Cracow in late December 1912, Stalin proceeded to Vienna to carry out research for his article on Marxism and the Nationalities Question: the most important of his pre-revolutionary writings.

That the Russian people constituted only a minority of about 43 per cent within the Russian Empire, Lenin himself had repeatedly pointed out. But, he had not yet formulated any clear-cut policy for dealing with the numerous non-Russian subjects of Russia. Besides the relatively numerous Ukrainians, Belorussians, Poles, Balts, Jews, Caucasians and Tatars, these included many other peoples, and totalled about two hundred nationalities or tribes in all. What was the proper role of these various peoples in the revolutionary struggle? What was their status to be in the revolutionary State which Lenin sought to establish in place of the Russian Empire? Two conflicting factors had to be reconciled in Bolshevik thinking. On the one hand, anti-Russian nationalist fervour within the Empire had been an important factor in the 1905 Revolution, and remained a potent force which Lenin could not afford to neglect – even the Socialists among the minority peoples tended to dislike Russian rule less because it was based on capitalism than because it was based on Russians. But could Lenin, on the other hand, afford to support local nationalist sentiment to the limit? No – for in doing so he would risk seeing a Bolshevik-toppled Empire collapse into a collection of autonomous nations which might or might not call themselves Socialist, but were in any case likely to prove lamentably and uncontrollably un-Leninist.

Stalin's hidden task in defining Bolshevik policy towards the minority nationalities was, accordingly, to mask the above conflict of interest in order to encourage non-Russian Socialists of the Russian Empire to give Lenin full support in his struggle for power. Hence the emphasis in Stalin's article on the sovereign rights of nations. He concedes that individual nationalities will be entitled to secede from any larger political unit after the coming Socialist revolution. They will be entirely free to assert either complete independence, or some form of local autonomy; should they wish they may even return to their pre-revolutionary ways.[5] But Stalin adds an important *caveat:* the Social Democrats retain *their* sovereign right: to struggle and agitate against all 'harmful institutions' and 'inexpedient demands'.[6]

What criterion is to determine where harmfulness and inexpediency begin? By whom is it to be applied? What degree of violence is admissible in such struggles? The skill of Stalin's argument lies in by-passing these crucial questions. By such omissions, more than by anything else in his analysis, he helped to define the principles on which he was eventually to sponsor, as People's Commissar for Nationalities, the establishment of a Union of Soviet Socialist Republics. Each republic was indeed to enjoy legalized freedom to secede from Bolshevik Moscow; but Moscow – which happened to possess preponderant military, political and economic strength – was to be equally, and more than equally, free to struggle against such harmful moves by whatever means might seem expedient.

In seeking to thwart secessionist tendencies within the minority Social Democratic organizations of the Russian Empire, Lenin was conforming with the supra-national traditions of Marxism, which had always asserted the primacy of the class struggle over national origin as a factor determining the structure of society. But however authentically Marxist this posture might be, it could all too easily appear as that of a Russian chauvinist. How advantageous, therefore, to have seemingly russocentric sentiments expressed by a tame 'native' from an alien corner of the Empire – himself the representative of a minority nationality, but one who had long abandoned any lingering romantic Georgian patriotism of his youth and was becoming a Russian nationalist by adoption. In 1913 a Dzhugashvili from Gori could voice views on the nationalities question which might have been suspect had they come from an Ulyanov of Simbirsk.

Viewed with historical hindsight and shorn of Marxist jargon, Lenin's and Stalin's pre-revolutionary views on the nationalities question seem deceptively simple. The minority peoples are to be led gently down the garden path. First they are to be gulled – by promises of freedom, independence and the right to secede – into supporting a Bolshevik revolution. Then, when the new revolutionary State is established and consolidated, these minorities will find it impossible to exercise their rights in practice: a Central Committee resolution of later 1913 states outright that the post-revolutionary decision to secede must rest in each individual case with the Social Democratic Party.[7] Lenin and Stalin both seem to have shown foresight and flexibility when they framed in terms of solemnly worded Marxist ideology what – to non-Marxists – may look like the crudest of confidence tricks. But it by no means follows that their handling of the nationalities problem was, at this early stage, consciously conceived as a diabolical conspiracy against the rights of the minority peoples. After all, the truly effective politician is he whose manoeuvres delude even himself.

Among the various nationalities discussed in Stalin's article the Jews appear to obsess him more than any other. There are no less than 185 references to Jews in the text, not one of them favourable.[8] On the Jewish question Stalin was, again, closely following Lenin's lead – as expressed, for example, in a letter of 20 December 1912. Here Lenin deplores a decision by the Social Democratic Duma members, both Mensheviks and Bolsheviks, to support a demand for cultural autonomy put forward by nationalistic Jewish revolutionaries. *Pravda* must protest against this line, Lenin insists; otherwise the Jewish Marxists 'will have us by the short hairs.'[9] Here Lenin shows antagonism to Jewish solidarity as a source of power independent of his control: not to the Jewish people as such. By contrast, Stalin's attitude, throughout his career, has laid him open to charges of anti-Semitism.

That Stalin's approach to the nationalities question was approved by Lenin is confirmed in the most celebrated single reference to the early Stalin in Lenin's writings: his letter to Maxim Gorky of February 1913 in which he says that 'a certain *marvellous Georgian* has settled down here to write a long article ... after collecting all the Austrian and other materials.'[10] Marvellous though the Georgian might be, one notes that even one as well versed in Social Democratic affairs as Gorky was still presumed unaware of his identity. This letter and other approving references show that Lenin endorsed Stalin's early approach to the nationalities question, but do not solve the problem of Lenin's personal participation in writing Stalin's article. On this Trotsky states baldly that Stalin's work 'was wholly inspired by Lenin, written under his unremitting supervision and edited by him line by line.' Regarding 'Marxism and the Nationalities Problem' as 'undoubtedly Stalin's most important – rather his one and only – theoretical work', Trotsky cannot agree that a mind so limited could have produced such a masterpiece, especially as the plodding Caucasian's ignorance of German allegedly precluded him from handling much of the source material.[11]

On all these counts Trotsky erred. True, Stalin's knowledge of German was sketchy or minimal, but the fact is that the bulk of the source material was available to him in Russian translation. Stylistic analysis also favours Stalin's authorship, as do certain points of detail, including the contention that North America was still known as 'New England' in the early nineteenth century: a sample of ignorance too gross to be associated with Lenin.[12] Nor is this article the masterpiece which Trotsky believes it, for there are many flaws in the argument and presentation. However, if it is not a masterpiece, neither is it a catastrophic failure, being clearly and forcefully written. Neither an exercise in stylistics not a scholarly essay, it should be judged for what it is: a political instrument. As an excursion in concept-juggling suitable for enlisting nationalist sentiment to the Leninist cause without compromising Lenin's ultimate control over the non-Russian peoples of the Empire, the work is well conceived.

One particular paragraph in Stalin's article has acquired a strongly ironical flavour if read with historical hindsight. Rejecting a contention made by certain Austrian Social Democrats – that national peculiarities should be preserved and developed – Stalin asks sardonically whether it is necessary to maintain such localized quirks as the self-flagellation of Caucasian Tatars, practised during one of their national festivals. Is one also to develop such Georgian national characteristics as the blood feud ?[13] Though self-flagellation by festive Azerbaijanis may indeed have declined under Stalin's rule, the same claim can certainly not be made for the Georgian vendetta, which was to flourish far beyond any flight of fantasy conceivable in 1913.

Koba's Viennese trip of early 1913 brought him into brief but memorable contact with Trotsky, premier victim among so many later sacrificed to the Georgian blood feud writ large. According to a memoir never published by Trotsky and written in the last year of his life, the haggard, pockmarked Dzhugashvili burst without knocking into some Viennese room where Trotsky was conferring with a colleague over a samovar, uttered a guttural growl which might have been intended as a greeting, filled a glass with tea and left without a word. Trotsky was struck by his future destroyer's appearance, dim but not commonplace, by the morose concentration of his face and by the fixed hostility of his yellow eyes.[14] At about the time of this wordless clash, Stalin was denouncing Trotsky – in an article on the Duma elections in St Petersburg – for attempting to reconcile warring factions within Social Democratic ranks. Stalin described Trotsky as a paper tiger: literally, 'a vociferous champion with false muscles'.[15]

Final Exile

Returning to St Petersburg in mid-February 1913, Comrade Stalin helps to reorganize *Pravda* in accordance with Lenin's instructions.[1] But Lenin is now beginning to show concern about his marvellous Georgian. On 23 February he writes to Malinovsky asking why there is no news of Stalin: 'What is the matter with him ? We're worried.'[2] Two days later Lenin urges that very good care should be taken of Stalin, continuing: 'He is clearly shaky and very ill.' *Shaky* and *ill* were code expressions denoting the danger of imminent arrest, and Lenin continues in terms which show the undiminished value which he placed on Stalin: he writes of the need to organize, harmonize and systematize, with Stalin's help, the daily work of *Pravda* and the six Duma Bolsheviks.[3] So much, again, for Trotsky's contention that Lenin blamed Stalin for handling the early *Pravda* incorrectly.

23 February, the date on which Lenin wrote to ask the police spy Malinovsky about Stalin's whereabouts, chanced to be the very day on which Stalin was once again arrested in St Petersburg, having been betrayed by . . . Malinovsky. The event took place at a musical evening held in aid of Party funds. According to one account, Malinovsky actually witnessed the arrest; he followed Stalin out as he was removed by the police, uttering protests and seeking to convey the impression of one about to campaign for the victim's release.[4] Stalin is now taken to the St Petersburg remand prison for the third time, embarking on his last and longest period under restraint. After three months he leaves to serve four years of exile in the Turukhansk Region on the northern reaches of the River Yenisey in central Siberia. This is the longest of the periods of banishment imposed on Stalin, and to the remotest area. A month's journey takes him to southern Turukhansk by 10 August. Seven months after that he is deported yet further into the tundra: to the tiny settlement of Kureyka near the Arctic Circle.

While enjoying some freedom to travel within the grim, frozen, swampy wastes of the area, the exile found himself unable to escape from this last place of banishment. It was the most monotonous and empty period of his life, reflecting the bleakness of the local tundra 'with its endless snow horizons, and the frozen rivers where the sturdy, good-humoured natives sit for hours on end at an ice-hole, fishing.' Such were Stalin's own reminiscences, as later retailed to the Alliluyevs. For a time he lived in a fisherman's hut and was taught to fish by Ostyak tribesmen of the region; but soon he was pioneering new angling techniques which gained him a local reputation for possessing occult powers. Once he was nearly killed – caught by a storm when fishing on one of the local rivers.[5] Trapper and huntsman too, Stalin had a favourite dog called Tikhon Stepanovich, his faithful hunting companion; this creature was apt to figure in the dictator's occasional sentimental reminiscences in later life, by which time he had lost the habit of friendly contacts of any kind and no longer even kept a dog. Stalin also kept a local peasant woman during one of his Siberian exiles – according to information given to Svetlana Alliluyeva by her aunts – and engendered a bastard son whom he never acknowledged.[6]

In this grim outpost Stalin remained in good health. His strength was not undermined by the experience; unlike certain weaker brethren among political exiles to Siberia, he did not become mentally unbalanced by the monotony of life in the tundra. Parcels of food and clothing from the Alliluyevs helped to maintain his morale. The same friends also sent him a hundred roubles – which led the authorities to suspend the official subsistence allowance of fifteen roubles a month, as paid to exiles lacking other resources.[7]

Though Stalin later rewarded the Alliluyevs' kindness by driving one of the daughters (Nadezhda) to suicide after marrying her, subsequently imprisoning her sister Anna, he was more gracious at the time. Anna Alliluyeva has recorded a letter of thanks received from the great Siberia-based friend of the family. For a long time (before the publication of Stalin's notes to his daughter Svetlana) this remained the only private non-political letter of the dictator's on record. Stalin thanks the Alliluyevs, but begs them not to spend on him money which they can ill afford. He will be content, he says, 'if you will occasionally send me some postcards with views of nature and so on. In this accursed region nature is stark and ugly: the river in summer, the snow in winter. . . . That's all the scenery there is round here. So I have an idiotic longing to see some landscape, if only on paper.'[8] Thus, from the frozen northern plains, does the marooned southerner distantly echo that 'passionate love of nature' which he had once briefly displayed in early youth.

Sverdlov was once again Stalin's companion in exile, sharing his quarters at Kureyka. Dzhugashvili was a good chap, Sverdlov recalled, but added that the Georgian was 'too much of an individualist in everyday life, while I at least believe in a semblance of order.' The trouble was that Stalin liked to leave his hunting, trapping and fishing gear littered about the place, apart from which the natives, including children, made the lives of both exiles a misery by their incessant social calls. They had no paraffin for lamps and hardly any books. Such is the account given in Sverdlov's correspondence, as published in the post-Legend year 1957; writing under the shadow of Beria, another witness bolsters the Legend by describing Comrade Stalin's table as piled high with the books and newspapers obligatory in devotional literature.[9]

Other events in the bald saga of Kureyka include the removal by the authorities of a local guard after Stalin had complained about the man's rudeness: an episode which well points the differing standards of penal rigour maintained in the Imperial and the Soviet empires. So amiable did the ousted guard's successor, one Merzlyakov, show himself that Stalin gave him a testimonial (in 1930) absolving him from suspicion of having behaved with 'typical policeman's zeal' in Kureyka. Armed with this document, the ex-gendarme was able to appeal against a decision excluding him from membership of one of the newly-established collective farms.[10]

Under these conditions contact between Lenin and Stalin was much restricted, but not entirely suspended. After the outbreak of hostilities in Europe – the Germans sent an ultimatum to Russia on 18 July 1914 (31 July according to the western European calendar) – Stalin somehow obtained a copy of Lenin's 'War Theses', and read them aloud to a circle of exiled sympathizers.[11] To Lenin he also penned a jaunty letter – dated 27 February 1915 – in which he refers to the Anarchist Kropotkin as an 'old fool', calls Plekhanov 'an impossible old gossip', and adds that the Liquidators all 'need a good hiding'.[12] Finally, Lenin's correspondence of autumn 1915 (published in 1931) contains an apparently damaging reference to his marvellous Georgian. It turns out that Lenin has forgotten Stalin's name! 'Find out [he asks his correspondent] the last name of Koba . . . Joseph Dzh . . . ?? We have forgotten. Very important!!'[13] In the Soviet-published material of the dictator's heyday there is no reference more harmful to the Legend of Stalin as Lenin's closest collaborator. Even after ten years of what was to become the most highly publicized political alliance on record, one partner cannot even remember what the other is called! In fact, of course, Lenin must have remembered Stalin himself well enough; that the little used legal surname Dzhugashvili should have eluded him is less significant than it may seem.

Summer 1915 finds Stalin in Monastyrskoye, a village accessible from his assigned place of exile, where he takes part in a political meeting of an unusual kind. It is attended by four exiled Bolshevik central committeemen and five exiled Duma Bolsheviks. The Duma quintet having been sentenced for anti-war propaganda, the main debate at the Monastyrskoye meeting centres round this activity and Kamenev's part in it. Kamenev – also exiled, also present at the meeting – had previously succeeded to the post of handler to the Duma Bolsheviks: the task carried out by Stalin before his most recent arrest. But Kamenev had committed what, for a wartime Bolshevik, was a grave political error: that of failing, at the time of the deputies' trial, to endorse their action in opposing Russia's participation in the war. It was for this that he now found himself under fire in the tundra.

What part did Stalin take in this unofficial court-martial of his future victim? Did he indeed 'unmask the capitulationist, anti-Bolshevik, traitorous position of Kamenev and brand with shame his conduct at the trial'? Thus Samoylov (one of the Bolshevik Duma members present at the Monastyrskoye meeting) has claimed in priestly idiom.[14] Or did Stalin hear out the proceedings in total silence – thus weakening the case against Kamenev – and then leave abruptly for Kureyka without helping to draft a resolution condemning the culprit? Such is the claim of Sverdlov's widow.[15]

The last lap of Stalin's last exile began in October 1916, when the Imperial authorities decided to recruit all able-bodied men – including those exiled to remote Turukhansk – into the armed forces now sorely pressed on the Russian western fronts. Summoned to face a draft board, Stalin made the difficult two-month journey of nearly a thousand miles from the far north by sledge to Krasnoyarsk, situated on the Trans-Siberian Railway: but in vain so far as any future military] laurels were concerned, since he was not accepted for the army. According to Legend, the rejection was due to official fears of Comrade Stalin's political influence; but from his sister-in-law Anna we learn that it was based – less gloriously – on the malformation of the future Generalissimo's left arm.[16]

Spurned by the army, Koba now received permission to serve out the few remaining months of his sentence in Achinsk: a large village west of Krasnoyarsk and conveniently close to the railway. Here other Bolshevik exiles were also congregating. They included Kamenev and Kamenev's wife Olga, an attractive but fussy creature who protested in vain against Stalin's infuriating habit of puffing at a foul pipe. Such is the evidence of one Baykalov, who wrote a book on Stalin in emigration. In this work, published in 1940, Baykalov describes Stalin as of low intellectual standard, narrow-minded, ill-educated, fanatical, coarse, rude, repellent, cynical and lacking in charm. He claims that the taciturn, morose Stalin was invariably snubbed by Kamenev on the rare occasions when he ventured some guttural intervention in the conversation, speaking in poor, halting Russian with a strong Georgian accent. To chat with Kamenev was, by contrast, an intellectual delight.[17]

It was in Achinsk that these Bolsheviks learnt of the sudden and totally unexpected February Revolution which led to the abdication of the Tsar-Emperor Nicholas II on 2 March 1917. Suddenly freed from exile by the political amnesty which immediately followed, Stalin entrained in Achinsk on 8 March along with many another exulting liberated revolutionary, and began the four-day journey back to the capital city. Gleeful crowds greeted the returning exiles at the the stations through which they passed. From Perm a telegram of congratulations was sent to Lenin in Switzerland; but this document was later expunged from Stalinist record because it contained the unperson Kamenev's signature as well as Stalin's.[18]

4

Nineteen Seventeen

March and April

HAVING been arrested in the peacetime St Petersburg of 1913, Stalin returns four years later to the same city – which has acquired the new name of Petrograd, and is now the capital of a nation at war. Arriving a few days after the February Revolution has overthrown the three-hundred-year-old Romanov dynasty, the returning exile makes as usual for the Alliluyevs' home, where he regales members of the family with comic imitations of the revolutionary orators who had spoken during whistle-stop meetings on the way back from Siberia.[1]

Such is the exhilaration of the unknown future that everyone in the Russian capital seems to have forgotten the greatest war in the Empire's history, which is still being fought a few hundred miles away, having by no means miraculously ended with the abdication of the last Autocrat. Not that the Germans and their allies were concerned to intensify military activity on their Russian front, which was to remain quiet during much of 1917. What need, in that hectic year, for Germany to seek the destruction of an enemy who already seemed intoxicated with the notion of destroying himself?

Between the collapse of the Imperial system in late February and the seizure of power by the Bolsheviks in late October, Russia experienced the only period of political freedom in her history. During these eight months Russians were at last able to speak, write and associate as they wished, unhampered by the Imperial apparatus of repression – which collapsed along with the autocracy. Prisons were flung open and disgorged tens of thousands of captives, including both political and criminal offenders. Now released from detention or exile, each was at liberty to promote his personal ambition, whether this involved the takeover of the State or of his neighbour's pocket-book. Riots, mutinies, lootings, street muggings, roof-top snipings, strikes, denunciations, shrieking orators . . . all these things seemed to herald the dawn of a new age, and combined to form a crescendo of mounting violence, anarchy and chaos. As for the Georgian future master of that Brave New World, he was little in the public eye in 1917, but was active behind the scenes as a senior officer in the small but fast-growing Bolshevik party which, at first, seemed only one among many competing factions.

So far as the formal exercise of power was concerned, Russia was ruled between March and October 1917 by a Provisional Government consisting at first largely of Liberals who had been prominent in the Fourth Duma: a body which ceased to function along with the Imperial Government. Enjoying no legal title to rule, the provisional régime claimed to hold the government in trust until a Constituent Assembly, elected by a free vote of the nation at large, should establish a permanent administration. In May the Provisional Government became a coalition containing several Socialist ministers as well as Liberals. Further coalitions followed. In July the Socialist Aleksandr Kerensky became Prime Minister.

From the outset the activities of the Provisional Government were paralleled and frustrated by those of a rival body which was also newly-constituted and which shared the same headquarters: the Taurida Palace. This was the 'Soviet' or 'Soviets'. The notoriously elusive term covered a network of loosely-constituted, characteristically revolutionary assemblages set up by factory workers, soldiers and peasants – unsystematically, but on a nationwide scale. Soviets were representative councils inspired by memories of 1905, when such bodies had originally come into being; 'sprung up' is the usual, unhelpful term. It is not, however, the many regional Soviets, but the large, cumbrous, Petrograd Soviet, its sizeable Executive Committee and that Committee's Presidium or inner ring which we chiefly have in mind when we speak of the 1917 Soviet or Soviets as a thorn in the flesh of the Provisional Government. The All-Russian Congress of Soviets and its Central Executive Committee also come into the picture – taking nominal precedence over the Petrograd Soviet, but meeting less frequently.

Supported by the Petrograd workers and by the numerous military reservists stationed in the capital – that is, by those whose riots and mutinies had overthrown the Emperor in February – the Soviet was potentially more powerful than the Provisional Government. But this assembly of Socialists was not at first willing to wrest control from the Provisional Government's nerveless fingers. The main factions in the Soviet believed that a bourgeois administration – as established by the supposedly bourgeois revolution of February and vested in the Provisional Government – must precede an eventual takeover by the Left. Of the two main parties represented on the Soviet, the Mensheviks clung more pedantically to this taboo, but the less doctrinaire Socialist Revolutionaries were prepared to follow suit.

Both in representation on the Soviet and in general popularity the Bolshevik Party to which Stalin belonged was only a minor group in March 1917. It seemed to have little chance of dominating and destroying the more powerful socialist parties. The total number of Bolsheviks at the time of the February Revolution has been estimated at over forty thousand: a figure which must be exaggerated. Still, there were factors favouring rapid Bolshevik growth, and by August their over-all strength could be put at about two hundred and forty thousand.[2] The Bolsheviks had the advantage of standing further to the Left than any other political grouping except the Anarchists, and could thus capitalize on a general leftward movement by the population as a whole. This itch found expression in the mass seizure of land by peasants; widespread desertions from the army; the lynching of officers; contempt for all authority. Moreover, small though Bolshevik membership remained, the Party was far more dangerous than mere statistics suggest since its support was concentrated in the areas most vital to a *coup d'état*: the factory workers of the capital; the soldiers and sailors stationed in or near it.

Like everyone else, the Bolsheviks had been caught unawares by the February Revolution. When the Emperor abdicated on 2 March, no leading Bolshevik was even present in the capital. Lenin and Zinovyev were in Zürich; Bukharin was in New York, as also was Trotsky (not yet a Bolshevik). At Achinsk, in Siberia, Stalin and Kamenev were nearly as far removed from the Russian capital as these exiles to America.

On the Bolshevik movement – as on all rival revolutionary factions – the February upheaval suddenly conferred the status of officially sanctioned political party free to organize, proselytize and pursue its objectives openly. The first reaction of the leaders, from Lenin downwards, was to make their way to Petrograd as fast as wartime conditions permitted. Meanwhile certain lesser Bolsheviks, already resident in the capital at the time of the monarchy's collapse, were making their presence felt. The least insignificant Party members available in Petrograd on 2 March were Molotov, Shlyapnikov and a certain Zalutsky. This trio formed the rump of the Russian Bureau of the Party's Central Committee. Its first major act was to put Molotov in charge of reconstituting *Pravda*: the Bolshevik daily which had been closed down in 1914, on the outbreak of war.

Under Molotov's leadership the revived *Pravda* took an extreme leftist line close to that of Lenin, now chafing in Switzerland and seeking a means of returning to Russia. In particular, Molotov's *Pravda* preached sound Leninist doctrine on two major issues facing the Bolsheviks: the war and the Provisional Government. Co-operation with the Provisional Government was rejected, and a demand was made for an immediate end to the imperialist war against Germany which that government was pledged to continue. Meanwhile the Bolshevik Russian Bureau was swiftly expanded until it contained about a dozen members.

Such was the situation when, on 12 March, Stalin reached the capital from Achinsk after a four-day train journey; such was the general background against which his activities were to be deployed between March and October. As for the later conversion of those activities into Legend, that was to proceed along lines familiar from earlier material. The Comrade Stalin of ripe, Beria-sponsored myth faithfully collaborates with Lenin . . . until, in October 1917, Legend-Stalin becomes the main individual responsible for the Bolshevik *coup*: '*he had direct charge of all the preparations for the insurrection.*'[3] In sharp contrast with such fairy tales is the Counter-Legend promoted by Trotsky, which presents Stalin as a dim, bungling, vacillating, provincial bumpkin vaguely tagging along in the tail of great events which he can neither dominate nor understand. Somewhere between these extremes we discern the true Stalin of 1917: a cautious figure intensely active in the background as he experiments in the techniques of political manipulation. Apt to antagonize colleagues by his tactlessness, he is yet entrusted with a wide variety of organizational tasks, earning their respect as a competent administrator.

This is the picture which emerges from various Party minutes, suppressed in the Soviet Union under Stalin but made available in quantity during the period of destalinization under Khrushchev or later. Though published as part of a campaign to discredit the defunct dictator, these documents yet help to redeem his reputation from the slurs cast upon it by Trotsky. They are of great value in giving a truer picture of Stalin as he was in 1917 . . . but with one major reservation. Enthusiastic in promoting destalinization, these publications of the Khrushchev era staunchly refuse to *deleninize*. We therefore find the fallible Stalin repeatedly unmasked for failing to follow Lenin's guidance, the unspoken premiss behind such accounts being that the faintest deviation from Lenin's lightest whim then constituted – as it still constitutes – an act of blackest political perfidy. Could any assumption be more remote from the realities of the revolutionary year, when Lenin's word carried anything but total authority – when Lenin still had to fight for the acceptance of his policies by his closest associates? Dominated and fascinated by Lenin though the Party was, it had not yet become the monolithic hierarchy, centred on the worship of a charismatic leader, into which Lenin and Stalin were eventually to convert it. Nor did the Party's various organs work in harmony in 1917, when four leading Petrograd-based bodies in particular – the Central Committee, the Russian Bureau, the 'Petersburg Committee' and the Military Organization – were often at odds with each other. The notional supremacy of the Central Committee over the other three bodies did not prevent them from asserting autonomy such as would later become unthinkable within the Party of Lenin and Stalin.

With Stalin's arrival in Petrograd, the Russian Bureau's early dispositions were rudely disrupted, as was Molotov's editorship of *Pravda*. Having been a Central Committee member since 1912, Stalin was senior to Molotov, Shlyapnikov and any other Bolshevik yet to be found in Petrograd. So were two of his travelling companions: Kamenev, long one of Lenin's closest associates in emigration; and M. K. Muranov, leader of the five Duma Bolsheviks exiled to Siberia in 1915. But however important these three returning chieftains might feel, the Russian Bureau by no means welcomed them with open arms. Though Muranov aroused no objections, and was made a full Bureau member, Stalin was snubbed.

With regard to Stalin [the minute of the 12 March Bureau meeting reads] it was reported that he had been an agent of the Central Committee in 1912, and that it would therefore be desirable to have him as a member of the Bureau. . . . But in view of *certain personal characteristics peculiar to him* . . .

the Bureau decided to grant him only consultative status. The characteristics in question were, presumably, Stalin's well-known tactlessness, rudeness and habit of rubbing people up the wrong way. As for Kamenev – less obstreperous, but compromised (as we have seen) by his failure to take a militant anti-war stance in 1915 – he received yet harsher treatment, being excluded from the Bureau altogether.[4]

This attempt to repress Kamenev and Stalin was unsuccessful. Undaunted by the pygmies of the Bureau, they simply took over *Pravda*. Of this event Shlyapnikov has written that Stalin, Kamenev and Muranov carried out an editorial *putsch*, having decided to seize *Pravda* and run it their own way.[5] By 15 March the newspaper was fully in their hands, Kamenev still being the pacemaker, as emerges from a complaint issued by the Bureau two days later: 'In protest against the strongarm methods used to install Kamenev in *Pravda*, the Bureau refers the matter of his conduct to the next Party conference.'[6] The resolution in effect conceded victory to Kamenev.

In the takeover of *Pravda*, as in his general posture during the six weeks following the February Revolution, Stalin played second fiddle to Kamenev. Here was the caution of a superior tactician who preferred to lurk in Kamenev's shadow while Kamenev exposed himself. This was not evident at the time, however, and it is unlikely that the thirty-seven-year-old Stalin could himself yet sense his ultimate potential. During these weeks he helped Kamenev with *Pravda*, and joined him in imposing an abrupt swing to the Right. Far from denouncing Russia's participation in the war, far from trying to throw out the Provisional Government neck and crop (as Lenin advocated), Kamenev and his shadow Stalin were in effect recognizing and legitimizing that government when they tried to put pressure on it to open peace negotiations. Stalin also stressed the need to strengthen the Soviets, while saying nothing about the need for the Soviets to take power in place of the Provisional Government, as Lenin was now urging.[7] Kamenev and Stalin were also pursuing an anti-Leninist line by seeking common ground with Mensheviks and other revolutionary rivals. Insignificant though the Bolsheviks still remained, this sudden swing – from hard to soft policies, from Left to Right, from intransigence to Conciliationism, from Leninism to anti-Leninism – set the corridors of the Taurida Palace buzzing. The news astounded representatives of the whole political spectrum, from businessmen on the Right to the firebrands of the Soviet's Executive Committee.[8]

Meanwhile Lenin – marooned in Zürich, hampered in attempts to communicate with Russia – had set forth his views in *Letters from Afar*, written in early March. But the Kamenev-dominated *Pravda* would only publish (possibly only received) one of these five letters – and that with considerable cuts.[9] Once again, as in late 1912, Lenin found his contributions to *Pravda* censored by Conciliationist colleagues, Stalin being jointly responsible for this outrage. So much for Legend's claim that Stalin consistently followed a Leninist line from the February Revolution onwards! Some years later Stalin himself admitted – in a pre-Cult (1924) statement – that he had erred through failure to promote Leninist policies in March-April 1917, confessing his failure to oppose the Provisional Government adequately and to advocate the transfer of power to the Soviets. 'This erroneous position I shared at that time with other Party comrades, and I only renounced it completely in mid-April when I accepted Lenin's theses.'[10]

At a caucus of Bolshevik delegates from all parts of Russia, meeting between 27 March and 2 April, Stalin continued to argue the moderate, Kamenev-sponsored line of limited and temporary support for the Provisional Government, which he described as 'consolidating the achievements of the revolutionary people'.[11] At the same conference Stalin also carried a Conciliationist proposal: to negotiate with the Menshevik leaders a joint Bolshevik-Menshevik congress; and he became member of a commission appointed to pursue such negotiations.[12]

Such were the moderate, anti-Leninist views embraced by Stalin and other Petrograd-based Bolsheviks on the eve of Lenin's return to the capital. This occurred on 3 April after Lenin, with other Russian émigrés presumed dangerous to Russia's war-waging capacity, had received permission from Berlin to approach Russia across Germany. No sooner had Lenin completed his complicated journey and climbed down on to the platform of Petrograd's Finland Station than he was already flaying the political heresies promoted during his absence. He snubbed the Menshevik Chkheidze, Chairman of the Petrograd Soviet and leader of a delegation from that body which came to welcome him at the station. He also rebuked Kamenev sharply for the erroneous line taken by *Pravda*. 'We saw a few numbers and cursed you heartily.'[13]   No similar rebuke was meted out to Stalin on this occasion, for he was not even a member of the small welcoming band of Bolsheviks which accompanied Kamenev to the Finland Station. 'That little fact [Trotsky later pointed out] shows better than anything else that there was nothing even remotely resembling personal intimacy between him and Lenin.'[14] That Stalin was not on the platform to greet Lenin, Legend agrees. . .but explains that the Comrade had already joined Lenin's train down the line at Beloostrov![15]

At Party meetings on the following day Lenin reaffirmed his uncompromising hostility to the Provisional Government and to the Russian war effort. He also declared his continued opposition to co-operation with the Mensheviks. These seemed to be the views of a single forceful eccentric who openly threatened to 'go it alone' if no one else would support him – as for a time seemed likely. It is therefore difficult to accept Trotsky's thesis that Stalin had been 'humiliated before the entire Party' by the revelation that his political stance was not shared by the newly-arrived Lenin.[16] In any case Stalin was not alone in his humiliation, for the majority of leading Bolsheviks was also rejecting – for the time being – Lenin's policies. Nor, we repeat, was it yet evident that Lenin's approval and disapproval would one day come to be accepted within the Party as the sole, simple, automatic criterion of right and wrong.

Such was Lenin's prestige that his aberrant views could not be dismissed out of hand, but they made few immediate converts. On 6 April they were attacked by Kamenev as reducing the Party to a mere collection of propagandists. Stalin, still backing Kamenev, called Lenin's theses unsatisfactory abstractions unsupported by facts.[17] Two days later the Party's Petersburg Committee decisively rejected Lenin's line.[18] By mid-April, though, Lenin's impassioned arguments were beginning to make headway. Stalin's earlier hostility had given way to thoughtful silence by then, veering into open support of Lenin at the Seventh Party Conference, held in Petrograd on 24-29 April.[19]

Kamenev's continued obstinacy did not prevent his election to the new Central Committee which emerged from the Seventh Party Conference. But he obtained less support than Stalin, who yielded only to Lenin and Zinovyev in the number of votes cast in his favour, and could therefore congratulate himself on being the Party's third most popular figure.[20] This appears to have been the first occasion on which Stalin was ever elected by a free vote to any office in the movement to which he had belonged for nearly twenty years. He was now becoming rather more than the oafish provincial whom Trotsky describes as 'forced by the trend of the times to assume the Marxist tinge',[21] tempting though it may be to accept Trotsky's portrait on the rebound from the obvious absurdities of Legend-Stalin the undeviating Leninist. Nor was it accurate to describe him as a 'grey blur, looming up now and then dimly and not leaving any trace': Sukhanov's celebrated comment on the Stalin of 1917.[22]

Attempting to relate Sukhanov's and Trotsky's assessments of Stalin to the elusive realities of 1917, we are struck by the failure of both witnesses to allow for the oafish blur's talent as a late developer. The moderate, Kamenev-dominated Stalin of March and early April 1917 does admittedly seem to resemble the vague, puzzled mediocrity portrayed by Trotsky and Sukhanov. It is also true that Stalin's published articles of March-April 1917 are fumbling, hesitant contributions which indeed do come over as the work of a clumsy provincial. But Trotsky tended to confuse the Stalin of March with the very different Stalin of July.

The turning point comes in late April 1917 with Stalin's abandonment of Kamenev-sponsored moderation and with his adherence to Lenin's radical line. Feeding Stalin's hidden appetite for power, Lenin's militant leadership helped to supply an element which the Georgian had previously sought in vain until, by the summer of 1917, we find in him an authority and confidence such as seem lacking in his earlier career. That Stalin was no rabble-rousing orator, no intellectual, no builder of ideological systems, no flamboyant personality – either in 1917 or at any other time – remains true. But Trotsky, who possessed all these talents or defects, failed to sense that they were less valuable in the power struggle than persistence, organizational drive and caution, combined with a talent for gauging one's associates' strengths, weaknesses, usefulness and nuisance value.

June and July

By mid-1917 popular disorders in Petrograd were facing the Bolsheviks with an urgent dilemma: should they support or restrain the rioting workers, soldiers and sailors who at times surged out by their tens or hundreds of thousands to threaten the Provisional Government on the streets of its capital?

Whichever decision the Bolsheviks might take, certain disadvantages were likely to follow so long as the Government remained capable of asserting its authority. If an abortive Bolshevik-sponsored rising were to take place, and if it were to be followed by governmental repression, the Bolsheviks would suffer a serious setback. But what if the Party should now refuse its leadership to would-be rioters who wished to thrust leadership upon it? To fail them was to risk loss of popularity; besides, these very expressions of general discontent had been inflamed by intensive Bolshevik propaganda. If the Bolsheviks were now to refuse leadership to the demonstrating mobs, other rabble-rousers – especially the Anarchists – would step into the breach. And though Anarchism remained a useful ally in undermining what was left of authority, the Bolsheviks rejected that creed on principle, as Stalin reminded them in an article of 14 June 1917.[1]

This dilemma first became serious in late May, when disaffected soldiers stationed in Petrograd – and anxious above all to avoid being posted to the front – expressed a desire to stage mass protests on the streets. On 1 June the Bolshevik Military Organization – one of the Party's more militant leading bodies – agreed to sponsor a march by sixty thousand men. A few days later the project was discussed in the Party's Petersburg Committee; Stalin spoke in support.[2] How far he had travelled since March the tone of his discourse well illustrates. Where he had formerly talked of bringing pressure to bear on the Provisional Government, he now wanted to send the masses into battle against it; and he boasted that the Petrograd bourgeois would go into hiding once they saw armed soldiers demonstrating in the streets. Stalin also wrote a leaflet calling for an armed demonstration.[3]

Meanwhile other, less militant, Bolsheviks – Zinovyev and Kamenev among them – wanted to call off the proposed demonstration. The same view was taken by the First All-Russian Congress of Soviets: a composite leftist body on which the Bolsheviks enjoyed minority representation, and which came out firmly against the proposal to demonstrate. This ruling was accepted by the Bolshevik Central Committee, with the result that the march was countermanded: a change of policy which stung Stalin into offering his resignation from the Committee.[4] Such proffered resignations are a common feature of Bolshevik history; like others by Lenin and Kamenev, this came to nothing.

Having induced the Bolsheviks to cancel their protest march, the Congress of Soviets decided to sponsor one of its own: a more general anti-government demonstration which would embrace left-wing forces as a whole. This took place on 18 June. It was a triumph for Lenin's followers, since the slogans chosen by the marchers turned out overwhelmingly Bolshevik in content. The main manifesto, addressed to all the capital's workers and soldiers, was that originally composed by Stalin for 10 June.[5]

Some two weeks later the same problem recurred in more acute form. In planning a new, bigger protest demonstration for early July, men of the First Machine-Gun Regiment were prime movers. They were supported by other Petrograd-stationed troops still fearful of transfer to the fronts, as also by Kronstadt sailors who dreaded a return to the harsh disciplinary conditions of the Imperial Russian Navy. These disaffected fighting men found allies among factory workers incensed by the activities of food speculators and by the failure of wages to keep pace with inflation.

Bolshevik policy towards the July demonstration developed along lines opposite to those of early June. Then the Party had begun by deciding to sponsor a protest march, only to withdraw at the last moment. Now the Bolsheviks began by opposing the demonstration. They did not want to be blamed for undermining resistance to the Germans at a time when a massive Russian offensive in Galicia looked like ending in disaster.[6] There was also the continuing danger of exposing the Party to unpopularity through inciting riots destined to be suppressed by the authorities and followed by reprisals.

Stalin played a leading but not a publicly exposed part in the build-up to this latest drama. On the afternoon of 3 July he led a Bolshevik delegation to the Soviet Central Executive Committee, of which he himself had been a member since 20 June. Formally proclaiming to that committee a clear-cut Bolshevik decision not to participate in the new demonstration – which was even then gathering strength in the streets outside – Stalin asked that this decision should be written into the official minutes, and quitted the meeting somewhat hurriedly. It all looked rather suspicious. Could the Bolsheviks be simultaneously attempting a *coup d'état* and trying to insure against possible failure by publishing a declaration that nothing could have been further from their minds? As one witness sardonically commented, those who have genuinely peaceful intentions do not need to ask for their peaceful intentions to be entered in official minutes.[7]

The non-Bolshevik Socialist parties now believed themselves faced with a Bolshevik conspiracy to seize power. Was this indeed the case? If so it seems strange that Lenin himself was out of town on 3 July and took little part in the affair, though he did come to Petrograd on the next day. But the developments of early July were so complex – and so difficult is it to assess the collective intentions of a body of politicians as divided as the

Bolsheviks still remained – that no clear ruling can be given on their attitude to the riots. The official Bolshevik version of these events, as retailed by Stalin himself, was that the Party had definitely decided not to back the July demonstration. But then – when it became clear that a demonstration was going to take place in any case – the Bolsheviks went into reverse. They took charge of the affair with the intention of imparting an organized, peaceful character to what might otherwise have become – actually did become – a violent and chaotic business.[8] But we cannot accept this contention of Stalin's that the Party was making a united effort to restrain the inflamed masses. As the Bolsheviks themselves were well aware, it was their propaganda which had helped to whip up the rabble to demonstration pitch in the first place. And though the leaders collectively expressed opposition to the proposed marches, many individual Bolsheviks continued to favour these disturbances all along.[9]

Of this ambivalent position, as it affected Stalin personally, the well-known Bolshevik versifier Demyan Bedny has borne witness. Bedny chanced to be with Stalin in the offices of *Pravda* when would-be sailor demonstrators from Kronstadt rang up to ask for instructions. They intended to demonstrate in any case, and the only question was: should they bring their rifles to Petrograd? Or should they march unarmed? The query was embarrassing to Stalin. As an enthusiastic disrupter of the existing semi-order, he of course preferred armed to pacific protesters any day. But it might prove awkward for him later if it could be shown that his instructions had brought rifle-bearing Kronstadt sailors to Petrograd. After all, even under the Provisional Government incitement to armed insurrection was a punishable offence. Here was a delicate diplomatic problem which called into play both Stalin's sense of irony and his natural caution. Screwing up his face in an expression crafty in the ultimate degree and stroking his moustache with his free hand, he spoke his Delphic reply into the telephone: 'Rifles, eh? You're the best judges of that, Comrades. We scribblers always take our own weapon – the pencil – along with us. As for what you do with your weapons, you can judge that best yourselves.' Hearing this deft riposte, Bedny over-reacted by rolling about on the sofa in frantic delight. In the event the Kronstadt sailors did, of course, bring their 'pencils' with them.[10]

Despite Bedny's ill-bred cachinnations, the July Days were no laughing matter. By evening on the third the atmosphere was taut with the threat of violence menacing the very Bolshevik leaders. At 7 p.m. mobs of rowdy soldiers were milling about outside Bolshevik headquarters in the Kshesinsky Mansion, once the property of a prima ballerina and mistress of the last Tsar. The crowd demanded that Bolshevik speakers should address them from the balcony. That Stalin himself – never a mob orator – was not among those deputed to reason with the rabble need cause no surprise. Others spoke – only to be booed when they called for an end to the disturbances in accordance with Bolshevik policy. It was this episode, and this atmosphere, which caused the Bolshevik leaders to reverse their policy – again at the last moment – by suddenly attempting to take charge of a movement which no words of theirs could halt.

How wise the Bolsheviks had been to discourage the July demonstration became clear within forty-eight hours as the affair developed into an orgy of looting, window-smashing, tram-bashing and shooting. Several hundred persons were killed or wounded. So far so good. But then troops loyal to the Government imposed order, whereupon the Bolsheviks did indeed find themselves blamed for causing the disorders in the first place, and for attempting a *coup d'état*. On the night of 4-5 July *Pravda* was closed down by loyalist forces. The Bolsheviks also learnt of a government move to expel them from the Kshesinsky Mansion, and Stalin undertook to forestall this by tackling the Menshevik Minister Tsereteli. He tried to bully Tsereteli into leaving the Bolshevik headquarters alone, threatening that it would be defended by force of arms. In fact, though, the Party was unable to offer serious resistance, as Tsereteli well knew. He called Stalin's bluff, and when loyalist troops moved against the Kshesinsky Mansion the Bolsheviks had pulled out.[11]

The Party was now forced into general retreat, Stalin himself helping to restore the *status quo* by persuading sailors in occupation of the Peter and Paul Fortress in Petrograd to evacuate that historic stronghold peacefully.[12]

Lodger and Orator

Besides occupying Bolshevik headquarters, closing down *Pravda* and smashing the Party's printing presses, the Provisional Government also issued warrants for the arrest of leading Bolsheviks considered guilty of aiding the German enemy by incitement to armed insurrection during the July Days. Stalin was not among them. Lenin and Zinovyev – for whom warrants were issued – managed to elude capture. They hid in the apartment of Stalin's future relatives by marriage, the Alliluyevs, at 10 Rozhdestvensky street in Petrograd: the same Alliluyevs who had so often furnished Stalin with a between-exiles *pied-à-terre*.

According to Anna Alliluyeva, Stalin visited Lenin almost daily during his brief sojourn in their house. She has Lenin and Stalin tenderly fussing about each other's welfare, each anxiously enquiring whether the other was getting enough to eat: a passage in which one again recognizes the familiar heartbeats of Hieratic prose. When Lenin decided to leave the Alliluyevs' flat, on 11 July, it was Stalin who personally shaved off the Party leader's beard in order to disguise his appearance ... says Anna Alliluyeva, writing in 1946.[1] When Lenin left the capital, Legend-Stalin went to see him off at the suburban station where he caught the train for the near-by village of Razliv.[2] Here Lenin was able to hide safely in the dwelling of a workman called Yemelyanov, whom Stalin later consigned to a concentration camp, presumably because the man's recollections of Lenin's activities at this time did not harmonize with the picture of the Lenin-Stalin axis as enshrined in Legend.[3]

In the anti-Bolshevik reaction which swept Petrograd after the July Days, Lenin was widely rumoured to be an agent of the Germans. But though the Party certainly was in receipt of funds ultimately emanating from the German Government, that did not make the Bolshevik leader an 'agent', in any meaningful sense, of the Wilhelmstrasse. Whatever the exact nature of Lenin's involvement with the Germans may have been, the scandal caused the Bolshevik Central Committee much embarrassment. Acting on behalf of that body, Stalin attempted to have certain 'slanderous' material – accusing Lenin of treasonable relations with Germany – suppressed through intervention by the Soviet, but was unsuccessful.[4]

After Lenin had quitted No. 10 Rozhdestvensky Street, Stalin began to make sporadic use of the spare room which the Alliluyevs kept available for him. There was no knowing when he might arrive or leave, since considerations of personal security and the duties of a senior Party official combined to make his movements irregular. Nor could so busy a revolutionary find time to attend to his personal appearance; noting the shabbiness of Joseph's raiment, his future mother-in-law went out and bought him a more becoming suit off the peg. Such spare time as Stalin had was, perhaps surprisingly, devoted to reading the works of Chekhov and Pushkin.[5] Of three works by Chekhov which are reported as having aroused the lodger's interest, the early *Chameleon* and *Corporal Prishibeyev* were well calculated to attract a militant revolutionary because of the outspoken, somewhat crude satire of Imperial Russian *moeurs* which they contain. Chekhov's later *Angel* (much admired by Tolstoy) is a different proposition, since it lacks all political implications and portrays the unsophisticated love of a simple, uneducated woman for a succession of nondescript husbands and a small, adopted, kitten-chasing son. Perhaps this story touched the future tyrant's well-buried sentimental streak, of which an occasional hint emerges in his daughter's memoirs.

Always bubbling over with fun, according to Anna Alliluyeva's somewhat improbable recollection, Stalin the sporadic lodger of summer and autumn

1917 was for ever cracking jokes and mimicking people, sometimes good-humouredly and sometimes maliciously. It was an exhausting life – the weary mimic once dozed off while smoking his pipe and set fire to a blanket.[6]

The Sixth Party Congress, held between 26 July and 3 August, marks a landmark in Stalin's career. Ten years had elapsed since the previous congress had taken place in London. That – the Fifth Congress – had been a combined Bolshevik-Menshevik affair, whereas the Sixth was exclusively Bolshevik: the first real Bolshevik congress, in effect. The occasion was marred by Lenin's enforced absence. But Lenin was well used to directing his followers from a greater distance than the series of hideouts which he maintained in or near Finland between July and October 1917. Through letters, manifestoes, articles, through word-of-mouth messages conveyed by emissaries, he kept his Petrograd-based colleagues under a fierce bombardment of exhortation and advice. In addition to other material, which has survived, Lenin also prepared certain detailed 'July Theses', which have been lost. Stalin allegedly held the only copy of this document: presumably the leader's blueprint for the conduct of the Sixth Congress.[7] Also absent from the Sixth Congress were Zinovyev (Lenin's companion in hiding) and those in police custody, who included Kamenev and Trotsky. It was, incidentally, at the Sixth Congress that Trotsky, still under arrest, and his followers at last joined the Bolshevik Party.

The absence of so many prominent colleagues proved Stalin's great opportunity. He it was who presented the main report on behalf of the Central Committee. He also made speeches summing up proceedings on 27 and 31 July, besides dealing in detail with criticisms from the floor. Could there be any greater contrast with the Stalin of the Fifth Congress, held ten years earlier in 1907? As we remember, he had barely contrived to gain admittance to that gathering – and then only with consultative status after Lenin had publicly conceded that he had no idea who this obscure provincial 'Ivanovich' might be. Now, at the Sixth Congress, Stalin's speeches and interventions reveal authority and lucidity such as are scantily represented in his utterances preceding mid-1917. By July 1917 he has accumulated a formidable stock of political experience and confidence, though we should not forget that his speeches to the Congress, as enshrined in his *Works*, owe something to later editing.[8]

Amongst other material Stalin gave the Congress a blow-by-blow account of the July Days. He also expounded Lenin's contention that the slogan 'All Power to the Soviets' had become obsolete, since the Soviets were now a force on the side of counter-revolution; in other words, the non-Bolshevik component of the Soviets had become more actively hostile to Bolshevism than before. The peaceful period of the revolution was now over, Stalin stressed. He called for the transfer of power, not to the Soviets now disgraced in Bolshevik eyes, but to the revolutionary proletariat and poor peasants combined. What this might mean in practical terms was difficult to picture, but Stalin spelled it out to some extent. Admitting that counter-revolution (i.e. forces hostile to Bolshevism) had scored a temporary triumph, he called for a new revolution. He was really asking for a Bolshevik *coup d'état*, though the Congress took no specific decisions on the precise form which such an upheaval should take.

At the Sixth Congress Stalin came close to advocating, briefly, Socialism in One Country: the policy most closely associated with his name, and which he was to sponsor with such effect in the following decade. To insist that Russia should postpone Socialist measures until the rest of Europe was ready to embark upon similar steps . . . such a policy would be the height of pedantry, Stalin claimed. Might not backward Russia conceivably turn out to be the pioneer of world Socialism, enjoying as she did greater political freedom in wartime than any other belligerent nation? Bolsheviks should abandon the old idea that only Europe could show them the way. Though such a thesis might seem un-Marxist – contradicting, as it apparently did, Marx's claim that a revolution termed Socialist would first break out in countries more advanced than Russia – Stalin was equipped with a typical formula for refuting such criticism. There were two kinds of Marxism, said he: the dogmatic and the creative. And he was for the creative brand –[9] a neat way of saying that he proposed to follow strict Marxist doctrine only as and when he might find it expedient to do so.

Though the Sixth Congress does indeed mark an increase in Stalin's prestige and authority, he did not receive as many votes as he may have expected in the elections to the new and expanded Central Committee of twenty-one members and ten candidates which emerged from the conclave. After previously gaining the third largest number of votes, at the Party Conference of April 1917, he now came only seventh in the poll.[10]

Meeting after the Congress, the newly-elected Central Committee voted itself a salary of five hundred roubles for married members and four hundred for unmarried,[11] thus providing Stalin with an identifiable source of income for the first time since his hasty departure from the Tiflis observatory in March 1901. The meeting also elected Stalin to an inner ring of eleven members empowered to conduct day-to-day business.[12]

After the Congress was over, Kamenev – now released from custody – was denounced in the press as a former agent of the Okhrana. When he demanded an investigation, the Central Committee instructed Stalin to form a commission of enquiry. Leaping to his slandered colleague's defence, Stalin described the campaign against Kamenev as a bacchanalia of lies ... shameless deception, forgery and falsification unprecedented in history.[13] The episode retains an ironic flavour: firstly because of the unproven possibility that Stalin himself may have been an Okhrana agent; and secondly because of the bacchanalia of Stalin-sponsored lies which were eventually to sweep the wretched Kamenev to his doom.

In mid-August, Stalin clashed with the Party's Military Organization. The Central Committee had decided to take over the Organization's newspaper *Soldat* (Soldier), to rename it *Proletary* (Proletarian), and to make it the official party newspaper in succession to the banned *Pravda*. Instructed to implement this decision, Stalin descended on a meeting of the Military Organization's Central Bureau to announce the takeover. He refused even to discuss this high-handed decision, stating flatly that once the Central Committee had passed a resolution it must be implemented without more ado. The Bureau members resented Stalin's manner and undemocratic behaviour, and made an official protest to the Central Committee, complaining that such nuisances had increased since the Sixth Congress.[14] The episode provides continuing evidence of Stalin's tendency to rub people up the wrong way, reminding one of the *certain personal traits peculiar to him* which had led to an attempt to exclude him from inner Party counsels on his return from Siberia in March.

October

Late August 1917 saw a change in the political tide, which now began to run strongly in favour of Bolshevism.

We have seen the Bolsheviks accused of attempting a *coup d'état* in July, and we have seen them suffering setbacks in consequence. At the end of August it was the turn of rightist forces to incur similar forfeits after the army Commander-in-Chief, General Kornilov, had unsuccessfully attempted to march on Petrograd and take control of that harassed city. Ending with Kornilov's arrest on 1 September, this bid to assert authority from the Right rallied previously disunited leftists. Non-Bolshevik Socialists dropped their hostility to Bolshevism, accepting Lenin's party as their ally. The arrested Bolshevik leaders were released, and the Party was able to recruit and drill openly the armed workers known as Red Guards. In the atmosphere of solidarity generated by Kornilov's threat, these no longer seemed to constitute a Bolshevik private army directed against all other factions.

Swept forward on this new wave of popularity, the Bolsheviks notably increased their leverage as key Soviets began to fall under their control.

On 31 August the Petrograd Soviet first adopted a Bolshevik resolution, the Moscow Soviet following suit five days later. On 9 September the Petrograd Soviet reaffirmed its pro-Bolshevik position and its Chairman, Chkheidze, resigned: to be succeeded by Trotsky.

Observing these events from his latest hideout in Helsinki, Lenin decided that the hour was ripe for a Bolshevik seizure of power. There was no time to lose, since the much-postponed elections to the Constituent Assembly could not be put off for ever. When this long-heralded body should eventually be set up the Bolsheviks were certain to find themselves in a minority, for the electorate as a whole consisted overwhelmingly of peasants who favoured the Socialist Revolutionaries. The prospect of such a peasant-orientated conclave was particularly unwelcome to the Bolsheviks in view of the nationwide authority – transcending that of any possible combination of Soviets – which the Constituent Assembly might be expected to enjoy. Now, therefore, was the time to strike, while Bolshevik domination of the key Soviets offered an opportunity to grasp power in the name of those organizations – but before the Constituent Assembly could rob them, and the Bolsheviks who dominated them, of most of their authority. What made it especially necessary to act quickly – before any Constituent Assembly could be elected and convened – was the fact that the Bolsheviks had gone out of their way to commit themselves fully in favour of that institution. Should it ever come into being, therefore, they would be particularly ill-placed to defy its dispositions.

It was against this confused and hectic background that Lenin, on 12 and 14 September, sent to the Central Committee from his hideout in Helsinki two long, highly secret letters calling for an immediate Bolshevik seizure of power. But the Central Committee remained unconvinced – deciding to use its influence in the opposite direction, and voting to restrain outbreaks of disorder in factories and barracks. Kamenev was particularly forthright in condemning Lenin's policies, while Stalin – typically – sat on the fence. Proposing that Lenin's letters should be circulated – but without endorsement by the Central Committee – for discussion by the most important Party organizations, he implied something less than full acceptance of them ... yet contrived not to state any open objection.[1] That a contrary, pro-Leninist interpretation can be put on this intervention of Stalin's is one more tribute to his skill in balancing between two conflicting positions.[2]

Another source of friction between Bolshevik moderates and Bolshevik radicals was the proposal, on which the other Socialist groups were more or less agreed, to set up a so-called Pre-Parliament. To this body, it was

hoped, the Provisional Government – hitherto a cabinet lacking responsibility to any larger assemblage – might become answerable until such time
as the arrangement should be superseded by the Constituent Assembly.[3]
Ought the Bolsheviks to support the Pre-Parliament, thus making common
cause with the non-Bolshevik Socialist parties? The more moderate
Bolsheviks were in favour, while the radicals (spurred on by Lenin) were
against. Now following Lenin's line – while remaining poised to join the
moderates if necessary – Stalin sided with Trotsky in advocating a boycott
of the Pre-Parliament.[4] The first real political contact between these two
arch-rivals thus has them operating as allies. When, on 7 October, Trotsky
demonstratively led a Bolshevik walk-out from the Pre-Parliament's inaugural session – after delivering a characteristically bombastic harangue –
he was implementing a policy concerted with Stalin.

As conditions in Russia became increasingly chaotic, and as the country
moved ever closer to her second revolution of 1917, so Lenin – still a
fugitive – was moving ever closer to the hub of events, proceeding in
due course to an apartment in the Vyborg District of Petrograd: a working-
class area and traditional Bolshevik stronghold. He briefly emerged from
this lair on 10 October to take part in a historic session of the Central
Committee. This was the gathering which at last adopted, by ten votes
to two, a resolution in favour of an armed Bolshevik uprising. To be more
precise, the decision was that such an uprising had now become inevitable,
and that 'the Party's organizations should be guided by this consideration.'[5]
This marked an important step towards meeting Lenin's demands, but
fell well short of a concrete plan to seize power by specified means on a
named date. Stalin was present on this occasion. The skimpy surviving
minutes do not record him as contributing to the debate, but he did vote
in favour of the resolution. The two who voted against were Zinovyev
and Kamenev.

At the same meeting a decision was taken to set up a seven-man Political
Bureau, of which Stalin and Trotsky both became members. So too did
Zinovyev and Kamenev – which is puzzling in view of their opposition to
the proposed uprising.[6] In any case this 'Politburo' of October 1917 never
met or functioned, being one of those innumerable bureaux, centres,
committees, commissions and the like which so readily 'sprang into being'
in 1917, only to lapse into immediate oblivion. With the later, true,
Politburo – set up in 1919 and eventually to become a major power base
for Stalin the emerging dictator – its namesake of October 1917 has
nothing in common except the title.

Similarly abortive was another organ of the Central Committee set
up on 16 October: a five-man Military Revolutionary Centre.[7] There is

no record of this impressive-sounding body meeting or performing any function – not, at least, until 1924. In that year Stalin's membership of the non-operative Centre was resurrected as 'proof' that he had been in the thick of preparations for the October *coup* during the crucial preceding days. The long-forgotten Centre had been discovered in the archives by a Committee on Party History, and to the delight of Stalin's Secretariat. 'They are going to wind something around that bobbin,' Trotsky was told on enquiring into the matter.[8] Indeed they were: the 'something' was the Legend of Stalin the major architect of the October Revolution. Confusion, favourable to Stalin, on the origins of the October upheaval, could the more easily be created since the armed *coup* was to some extent directed by a body which happened to bear a title similar to that of the phantom Centre. This was the Military Revolutionary *Committee*: an organization of the Petrograd Soviet set up under Trotsky's chairmanship, but one on which Stalin played no part at all.

Stalin's contribution to the burning issue – to rise or not to rise – as further discussed at the Central Committee meeting of 16 October, remained characteristically non-committal. Vaguely advocating Russian and world revolution, he accused Zinovyev and Kamenev of permitting counter-revolution to rally its forces. But Stalin made no positive contribution to setting the date for a Bolshevik rising when he sagely stated that this should be timed with regard to expediency –[9] that none of those present was prepared to argue in favour of an inexpedient date is hardly surprising. Once again we find Stalin covering himself against charges which might have arisen later had the *coup* failed; in that event fellow-Bolsheviks would have been unable to accuse him of leading the Party into disaster.

As a Bolshevik radical, but a radical who insisted on keeping a toehold in the moderate camp, Stalin clashed with the less cautious radicals Trotsky and Lenin in mid-October over the disciplining of Zinovyev and Kamenev. Kamenev had disobligingly published a statement in the press openly betraying the Bolshevik intention of staging an armed uprising, and Lenin was now demanding his expulsion from the Party and that of his associate Zinovyev.[10] On 19 October Lenin violently attacked the two 'blacklegs' in *Rabochy put* (Workers' Way): the Party's official organ which had succeeded the banned *Pravda*, and of which Stalin was editor. As such he attempted to reconcile the conflicting sides by publishing a brief riposte to Lenin from Zinovyev on 20 October, and by appending an editorial note of his own. In this unsigned item Stalin expressed the hope that the quarrel between Lenin and the offending moderates might now be forgotten. 'The harshness of Comrade Lenin's tone [Stalin added] does not alter the fact that we remain basically in agreement.' But Trotsky was neither prepared to let this matter rest nor to ignore the slight offered to Lenin by Stalin on the pages of the Party's leading organ. At the Central Committee meeting of 20 October, Trotsky described the situation created by *Rabochy put*'s editor as intolerable and called Stalin's editorial note unacceptable. The result of this first political clash between Stalin and his greatest rival was that Stalin offered to resign from the editorship of *Rabochy put*: one of the many unaccepted resignations which punctuate his career.[11] At the same meeting Stalin – still counselling moderation – also expressed the view that Zinovyev and Kamenev should not be expelled from the Party outright, or from its Central Committee, but should merely be compelled, in the interests of Party unity, to submit to Central Committee decisions.[12]

The Bolshevik takeover of 24–26 October appears to have proceeded without any initiative of Stalin's. Nor was Lenin himself directly involved – not at least before midnight of 24–25 October, by which time the *coup* had already been launched – though his importance as the inspirer of these events can hardly be exaggerated. As for the Central Committee, that body too played little part in directing the confused operations which resulted in the overthrow of the Provisional Government by 2 a.m. on 26 October. A main architect of the *coup d'état* was Trotsky in his capacity as Chairman of the Petrograd Soviet's Military Revolutionary Committee; but that body itself – including, as it did, non-Bolshevik members – was a cloak for the Bolshevik Military Organization.

Supervised by the Military Revolutionary Committee (headed by Trotsky), the Bolshevik Military Organization (headed by Podvoysky) was able to exercise uncertain control over sections among the 150,000 troops stationed in Petrograd, who were still swayed by the determination to avoid being posted to the front. Some of these, including cadet forces and Cossacks, were likely to support the Provisional Government, while others appeared amenable to Bolshevik or Soviet control. But the day-to-day allegiance and likely moves of individual units remained uncertain. Greater reliance could be placed by the Bolsheviks on the militantly leftist sailors stationed in Petrograd, Kronstadt and Helsinki – as also on the Bolshevik-organized armed factory workers known as Red Guards, who now amounted to about 15,000 men.[13]

Not until the last moment does any specific time and date appear to have been fixed for the rising. Lenin himself had been arguing for weeks that the Bolshevik *coup* should precede the inaugural session of the Second All-Russian Congress of Soviets: first fixed for 20 October, and then postponed until the 25th. Since that body seemed likely to produce, for the first time, a Bolshevik majority in the nationwide Soviet organization, its opening session offered the prospect of a peaceful transfer of power to Lenin's party. But it was characteristic of Lenin's extreme militancy that, given the choice, he preferred to obtain power by force rather than wait for it to come to him by non-violent means. In the event the Bolshevik coup was concentrated – more or less by coincidence – around the very day on which the Congress first forgathered: 25 October.

The sequence of events culminating in the takeover had begun three days earlier, when Trotsky instructed military units to execute no orders unless countersigned by a member of the Military Revolutionary Committee. On the next day Bolshevik-controlled commissars were sent to individual units to see Trotsky's instructions implemented. To this attempted takeover of the armed forces Kerensky's administration reacted with half-hearted measures which included outlawing the Military Revolutionary Committee; the renewal of warrants for the arrest of Bolshevik leaders; and the drafting of the Women's Battalion of Death to defend the Winter Palace, now governmental headquarters. The Government also ordered the seizure of the Bolshevik printing plant in Horse Guards Street: an event which took place at 5.30 a.m. on 24 October, even as copies of the Stalin-edited *Rabochy put* were coming off the press. Copies already printed were confiscated, type was broken up and the premises were put under guard; but the Bolsheviks managed to recapture their plant and to have *Rabochy put* rolling again by 11 a.m. The issue contained an unsigned leading article by Stalin claiming that the Second All-Russian Congress of Soviets, due to forgather on the following day, [would take power peacefully if only the citizenry could present a sufficiently solid front in favour of such a move.[14] Thus Stalin is found advocating a non-violent transfer of power just as his party was moving into armed insurrection. Even at this late hour, then, he was still hedging his bets; but it is also true that, as *Rabochy put*'s editor, he was well advised to put a pacific gloss on even the most militant of Bolshevik acts.

Here we find Stalin wielding his preferred weapon, the pen, as the first skirmishes of the October Revolution were beginning to break out around him. They included tussles between insurrectionists and loyalists for control of the bridges over the River Neva. On the night of 24–25 October pro-Bolshevik forces took over key buildings and installations in the capital: the postal and telegraph offices, the railway stations. With the capture of the Winter Palace, and with the arrest of the Provisional Government in the small hours of 26 October, the most portentous *coup* in history was completed: a muddled, casual, unheroic affair in many of its aspects, and one involving – so far – little bloodshed.

Stalin's whereabouts and activities during these crucial hours remain a mystery. On 24 October, at a Central Committee meeting in the Smolny Institute – now Bolshevik headquarters – Kamenev carried a motion forbidding members of the Committee to leave the premises without special dispensation.[15] Stalin, though, was not even present at the session to which this motion was put. Very possibly – since the outcome of the insurrection could not be predicted – he judged it prudent not to expose himself to the reprisals which an unsuccessful *coup* would have provoked. Such evasiveness would be typical of Stalin's caution, and would accord with his general pattern of behaviour as a practising revolutionary from earliest times. As we remember, young Dzhugashvili had always been adept at melting away from political demonstrations provoked by himself – and at leaving comrades more expendable to face the fury of Cossacks and gendarmes. But neither the Stalin of those early days nor the Stalin of 1917 can seriously be described as cowardly, even when his actions coincided with those which one might expect a coward to take. That much Trotsky himself admits after describing how his Georgian rival simply dropped out of the picture as the October Revolution was surging to its climax. Stalin 'was waiting to see how the insurrection turned out before committing himself [Trotsky explains]. In the event of failure he could tell Lenin and me . . . "It's all your fault." '[16]

For what her Legend-promoting memoirs may be worth, Anna Alliluyeva does something to locate Stalin during these crucial days. She has him surfacing at her family home 'on the eve of the Revolution': presumably on 24 October. He drank some tea with her father, and calmly stated that all was ready for the next day's *putsch*. After the seizure of power, Stalin returned to the Alliluyevs, 'as calm as ever', to give an eyewitness account of the capture of the Petrograd telephone exchange by sailors of the Baltic Fleet. Anna Alliluyeva also claims to have encountered Stalin 'surrounded by comrades', in the Smolny Square in the small hours of 26 October when he nodded to her and told her that the Winter Palace had just fallen.[17] Such is the picture of an all-powerful revolutionary chieftain benignly presiding over the majestic unrolling of great events, as conjured up in Legend.

Since the evolution of the Stalin Legend was a slow and complex process, it need cause no surprise that early pre-Legend Stalin is found generously praising his enemy Trotsky as the main architect of the October Revolution. In a speech of 1918 commemorating the first anniversary of that upheaval, Stalin paid the following tribute:

All the work of practical organization of the insurrection was conducted under the direct leadership of the Chairman of the Petrograd Soviet, Comrade Trotsky.

It is Comrade Trotsky, one may confidently assert, whom the Party has chiefly and principally to thank for the fact that the troops so quickly transferred their allegiance to the Soviet; as also for his skilful handling of the Military Revolutionary Committee's work.[18]

From the text of Stalin's *Works*, as published in 1947, this passage has been omitted.[19] By then the demon Trotsky had become a fanatical opponent of the October Revolution as 'directed' by Lenin and Legend-Stalin.

5
Civil Warlord

First Taste of Power

ON 26 October 1917 the victorious revolutionary party proclaimed a new, all-Bolshevik government consisting of fifteen ministers called People's Commissars. Known collectively as *Sovnarkom* (Council of People's Commissars), this cabinet had Lenin as Chairman and, in effect, Prime Minister. The fifteenth and last-listed member of the government was J. V. Dzhugashvili, who received the appointment of People's Commissar for Nationalities.

Having played some part in imposing Bolshevik rule on Russia, Dzhugashvili-Stalin now embarks on a new phase which is to span the dozen years following the October take-over: the imposition of Stalinist rule on Bolsheviks. But before this process can be considered in detail we must briefly review its background in the earliest days of Bolshevik rule, and in the years which followed.

One obvious feature of the new Soviet Government was its extreme precariousness: it seemed, at first, just as 'provisional' as the Provisional Government swept aside in October. As noted above, that takeover had owed less to widespread active support for Bolsheviks among the masses than to localized disaffection among troops and workers in the sensitive Petrograd area. Yet Lenin's new government was at least strong enough to brush aside such opposition as its enemies could muster in immediate reaction to the Bolshevik *coup*. An attempt by the deposed Prime Minister Kerensky to retake the capital – with Cossacks under General Krasnov – quickly petered out. Krasnov himself was taken prisoner. Released on parole, he escaped to the Don region in the south-east of European Russia: the first centre of armed opposition to Bolshevik rule which was to develop into outright civil war by the early summer of 1918. Many years later Stalin was to quote Krasnov's perfidy as an act justifying the Bolshevik terror in all its ramifications.[1]

The Bolsheviks met serious resistance only in Moscow, where a week's hard fighting preceded the city's capture. In the provinces power was generally transferred without violence. Within Petrograd a revolt by army cadets collapsed. So too did attempts by the Menshevik-dominated railway union to paralyse communications by a nationwide strike. Nor did the Bolsheviks suffer long from a strike by civil servants summarily assigned to commissariats in place of the ministries where they had once served the Imperial and Provisional Governments. The hostility of such permanent officials did not disrupt Stalin's Commissariat for Nationalities, since that was a new department for which no precedent existed in previous Russian administrations.

Long after Kerensky's flight and the collapse of the civil servants' strike, Lenin's government still remained vulnerable. The Bolsheviks – whose total membership was probably nowhere near the quarter of a million which they claimed – seemed too few to dominate a community outnumbering them more than fiftyfold. And though they could expect to poll far more votes in a nationwide election than the total of their membership, they enjoyed nothing approaching majority support. It was awkward, then, that Lenin should still be pledged to hold elections to a Constituent Assembly, for so long as that prospect impended his new administration remained a mere caretaker government. It was apparently doomed to step down as soon as delegates freely chosen by the nation at large should forgather and create a constitution: the focus of Russian liberal and democratic hopes for more than a century. That the Bolsheviks would not obtain a majority in the Constituent Assembly remained certain owing to the widespread support still enjoyed – after the October takeover as before it – by the Socialist Revolutionaries. For this reason the convocation of a Constituent Assembly still seemed to threaten Bolshevism with relegation to a minor position. Yet Lenin did not dare cancel the elections, which the previous régime had arranged to begin on 12 November: repeated Bolshevik denunciations of the Provisional Government – and for postponing this very poll – were too fresh in popular memory to permit an act so dictatorial, so liable to provoke Bolshevism's many opponents into staging a counter-*coup*.

Unable though Lenin was to countermand the inconvenient election, he could and did grasp many levers of control before the Constituent Assembly was ready to meet. He sanctioned the arrest of *Kadet* (Liberal) leaders, and silenced much of the non-Bolshevik press, including organs representing Socialist parties other than his own. Early December saw the establishment of the Cheka: a political police force created as a successor to the Okhrana and destined soon to outdo the atrocities, so often denounced by Bolsheviks, of that earlier organ. Instituting such measures, Lenin was treading a tightrope. He must develop sufficient severity to contain initial opposition to Bolshevik control; yet he must not rule so harshly as to provoke effective resistance to his administration, since it still remained highly unstable.

Such were the initial symptoms of the creeping Soviet authoritarianism which was to gather strength throughout the years – partly through Lenin's preference for dictatorial methods, partly through political exigencies. It was, above all, Lenin's determination – not shared by all leading Bolsheviks – to hold a monopoly of power, while yet lacking adequate popular support, which dictated the need to rely heavily on repressive measures from the outset. This need for discipline, imposed first on enemies and finally on friends and colleagues, was further reinforced by the war against the Central Powers inherited by the Soviet Government: a conflict which was to merge into a cruel Civil War between the Bolsheviks and their White opponents. Through such pressures Lenin's followers, many of whom felt sincere in professing democratic sentiments, were pushed ever further towards absolutist tyranny. One who needed least pushing was, of course, Stalin, whose temperament – still prudently concealed – was yet more authoritarian than Lenin's, and who was destined to supersede Lenin as architect-in-chief of Soviet totalitarianism.

As first fostered by Lenin and then accelerated by Stalin, the growth of Soviet totalitarianism was distinguished by two important features which were in evidence from the earliest days of Bolshevik rule, becoming increasingly prominent with the passage of time.

The first was the Party's predominance over the Government: a development obscured by the common practice of appointing the same individual to simultaneous high office in both hierarchies. Subordination of Government to Party therefore became completely evident only when – as happened with the Foreign Commissariat from May 1918 onwards – the post of People's Commissar was held by an official who was not a member of the Party's Central Committee: it was not People's Commissar Chicherin, but the Central Committee which determined foreign policy. But no such subordinate role fell to Stalin in his capacity as Nationalities Commissar, since he happened to be a senior Central Committee member. High standing in the Party, not ministerial appointments, became the main source of Stalin's power from the earliest days of Soviet rule.

Stalin's power, and that of competing Bolshevik leaders, was also enhanced by the second underlying trend distinguishing the onset of Soviet totalitarianism: that whereby small sub-committees came to control the larger bodies by which they were nominally elected, and to which they were nominally responsible. The tendency was evident in both the governmental and in the Party hierarchies. In government the nominally sovereign Congress of Soviets elected an All-Russian Central Executive Committee (*Vtsik*), which in turn elected *Sovnarkom*. But the two larger bodies soon lost any lingering power to control the smaller. Similarly, within the Party hierarchy, the large annual Congresses elected and nominally controlled the Central Committee, which in turn elected (from 1919 onwards) the smaller Politburo as an executive body responsible to itself. As time passed, however, residual power filtered out of the Party Congresses to the Central Committee, then to the Politburo, Orgburo and Secretariat . . . and finally to the one man who sat on all three bodies and who eventually succeeded in manipulating both them and the larger organizations which they had dominated.

For the post of Nationalities Commissar – which involved responsibility for the non-Russian peoples of the former Russian Empire – Stalin had been an obvious choice. He happened to be the leading non-Russian Bolshevik on the Central Committee: unless, that is, one should choose to consider the russified Jews Trotsky, Zinovyev and Kamenev to be non-Russians. Stalin had, moreover, long specialized on the Empire's minority peoples. His article of 1913, 'Marxism and the Nationalities Question', was merely the best known among his many speeches and writings on this topic, which Lenin considered second in difficulty only to the peasant problem.

The problems posed by the non-Russian nationalities were reduced after the October Revolution by the drastic loss of Russian territory under the Peace of Brest-Litovsk. Regions such as Poland, Lithuania, Latvia, Estonia and Finland could not weigh heavily on their newly-appointed Georgian supervisor since they were under German occupation when he assumed office – or in any case acquired their independence shortly afterwards. Stalin's native Caucasus, too, remained or became largely independent of Soviet control between 1917 and 1920–1, thus falling outside the direct jurisdiction of the Nationalities Commissar during the early years of the Bolshevik régime. So also, to an extent varying with the fortunes of the Civil War, did the Ukraine (with the largest population of all the minority areas), Belorussia and Turkestan. For the time being, then, the Nationalities Commissar seemed to be presiding over the liquidation of the Russian Empire, reduced as it was – at the lowest ebb of Bolshevik fortunes during the Civil war – to an ethnically Great Russian area roughly coinciding with that ruled by the Muscovite Grand Prince Ivan III at the end of the fifteenth century. For this Lenin-controlled area the name Russia – tainted with bourgeois associations – was no longer officially used, the term Russian Soviet Federated Socialist Republic (RSFSR) being employed instead. Not until the end of 1922 were other Soviet republics to join the giant RSFSR (which came to include all Siberia) and form the USSR or Soviet Union: a process in which – as will be seen – Stalin himself took the leading part.

That *Sovnarkom* and the Bolsheviks might one day preside over such a Soviet-reconstituted Russian Empire would have seemed unlikely to anyone observing Lenin's first steps from late October 1917 onwards. Now it was that revolutionaries, hitherto versed only in the techniques of overthrowing governments, were suddenly faced with establishing their own government. And though much attention had, over the years, been devoted to the politico-ideological problems likely to face a victorious revolutionary régime, surprisingly little thought had been given to practical techniques of administration. It was partly for this reason that Lenin found himself confronted by chaos during his first few days of power: everything had to be improvised out of the wreckage of the Imperial and Provisional régimes.

Of these improvisations Stalin's first steps as Nationalities Commissar were typical. Lacking premises and funds, he was taken in tow by a Communist of Polish origin, Pestkovsky, who was seeking useful employment. Pestkovsky offered to set up the new commissariat, obtained an authorization from Stalin and began to search the Smolny Institute for suitable accommodation. He found a single empty table in a large room where several committees were sitting, moved it against a wall and pinned up a hand-written notice:

PEOPLE'S COMMISSARIAT FOR NATIONALITIES.

Introduced to his new premises, Stalin characteristically muttered something indeterminate and disappeared. Pestkovsky soon spent his available funds on stationery and rubber stamps, and had to apply to Stalin for more money: an acute problem to all the commissariats at a time when anti-Bolshevik civil servants still dared refuse their new masters access to State funds. But Stalin knew that Trotsky (now Foreign Commissar) had 'found' some cash in the former Foreign Ministry. He was thus able to borrow three thousand roubles from Trotsky with which to launch the Nationalities Commissariat.[2]

Pestkovsky's account suggests that Stalin had little time for his new commissariat during his first few days of office. Nor, indeed, at any period could Soviet Russia's one and only Nationalities Commissar devote himself exclusively to his department, since he was discharging so wide a variety of other tasks as well. These included, on the governmental side, membership of *Vtsik* and – later – charge of another commissariat. More

Above: Legend–Stalin in boyhood, 1880s, a painting by D. Volgin

Below: Stalin (top, centre): Gori Ecclesiastical School, *c.* 1888

Above: Stalin (top, centre): Kutaisi Prison, summer 1903

Right: Stalin's first wife, Yekaterina Svanidze, *c.* 1905

Above: Legend–Stalin receives Lenin's 'letter' while in exile at Novaya Uda, Siberia, 1903; 'The Shining Light', a painting by M. Maryash

Below: Legend–Stalin first meets Lenin: during the Party Conference of December 1905 at Tampere; painting by I. Vepkhavadze

Opposite: Legend-Stalin as Lenin's closest comrade-in-arms at the First All-Russian Congress of Soviets, June 1917; painting by Kibrik

Above: A larger-than-life Stalin addresses railway workers: Tiflis, 8 June 1926; painting by M. Toidze

Left: Stalin 'at the front', 1941; drawing by K. Finogenov

Opposite top: Dzhugashvili's (Stalin's) police record; St Petersburg Okhrana files, *c.* 1913

Right: Dzhugashvili: 'mug shot' from Okhrana files, *c.* 1910

Far right: Stalin at Kureyka, central Siberia, during his last period of exile (1913–17)

Top: Stalin (right) and Trotsky (second from left), October 1917

Left: Stalin as People's Commissar for Nationalities, from 1917

Above: Voroshilov, Mikoyan, Molotov, Stalin and Dimitrov help to carry Lenin's coffin, 27 January 1924

important, though, were the future dictator's Party offices: first as continuing member of the Central Committee, then as member of the various powerful sub-committees which were to evolve out of the Central Committee and to usurp its power: the Politburo, the Orgburo, the Secretariat and so on. Some of these offices were to develop their full potential only after Lenin's death.

During the Civil War Stalin's most important role was to be that of combined trouble-shooter and factotum to Lenin: a strong-arm man switched from crisis to crisis in the certainty that he would make an impact. Whether these were Party or governmental assignments was not always clear owing to the loose method of administration evolved by Lenin, who was operating in effect through personal emissaries responsible to himself. However briefed and authorized, Stalin often behaved tactlessly and brutally; but he also had the knack of wading into a trouble spot, summing up its practical implications and solving them with laconic orders and minimal fuss. Skilled, too, in lubricating command with the mythopoeic political patter of the period, Stalin had the further advantage of not being bemused by his own propaganda. These were rare characteristics among Lenin's other colleagues, all of whom were to prove less flexible, determined, single-minded and efficient than the seminarist from Tiflis.

Any friendliness which might have developed between Stalin and Trotsky was soon scotched by a trivial incident which preceded the first meeting of *Sovnarkom*. Arriving early, Trotsky and Stalin chanced to overhear one end of a highly unofficial telephone conversation. The speaker – his voice emerged from behind a wooden partition – was Dybenko, the Navy Commissar. This black-bearded giant sailor was engaged in amorous chat with his current mistress, Central Committee member Aleksandra Kollontay: a woman of upper-class origin and long a celebrated 'hot number', both as a revolutionary and as a proselytizer of free love. Kollontay's liaison with the Navy Commissar had become the talk of the Party. Trotsky was shocked, though, by Stalin's indelicate reaction to Dybenko's erotic telephoned badinage: crossing the room with an unexpectedly jaunty air, the Nationalities Commissar jerked a shoulder towards the partition, smirking and gesticulating in a manner intolerably vulgar. When Trotsky failed to give the knowing wink which the 'marvellous Georgian' may have hoped to elicit, but indicated curtly that relations between Dybenko and Kollontay were strictly their own affair, Stalin's expression suddenly changed. Now, for the second time, Trotsky noticed in those yellow eyes that same hostile glint which had impressed him during their first encounter in Vienna in 1913. Henceforward, Trotsky notes, Stalin never again spoke to him on personal matters.[3]

This recollection reflects the fastidious dislike which the cultivated Russian-Jewish intellectual Trotsky felt for the appalling crudity of Stalin's manners . . . as he interpreted them. We make this reservation because of other evidence that Stalin – later in life, at least – dispensed considerable social charm on the not infrequent occasions when he chose to exercise it. Dismissing Stalin as intolerably vulgar, Trotsky was betraying certain genteel class prejudices of his own. What Trotsky rejected was less any essential coarseness in Stalin, as it might be objectively assessed, than the unfashionable-looking Georgian's failure to accept or ape the elaborate social taboos, gesticulations and grimaces of a typical Russian intellectual such as Trotsky and many another leading revolutionary was or wished to present himself.

Within a week of the October Revolution Stalin became embroiled in an internal Bolshevik quarrel between Leninist hard-liners and Zinovyevite moderates. This was a continuation of disagreements preceding the Bolshevik takeover. Then the moderates had opposed the seizure of power; now they opposed its retention as a Bolshevik monopoly. The moderates opened negotiations with other Socialist parties, being willing to admit non-Bolsheviks to a proposed coalition government – and even to exclude the firebrands Lenin and Trotsky from such a coalition. One reason for this readiness to contemplate a Lenin-free coalition was the realization that an exclusively Bolshevik government could be kept in power only by political terror. Lenin thought so too. But Lenin did not shrink from terror. Believing it necessary – desirable, rather, for its own sake – he reacted vigorously to the attempted revolt. On 2 November he persuaded the Central Committee to demand the moderates' expulsion from the Party. Among the ten signatures to this ultimatum that of Stalin occurs after those of Lenin and Trotsky.[4] Several moderates now resigned from the Central Committee and from *Sovnarkom*, but the revolt petered out when they recanted shortly afterwards and accepted Party discipline. One result was that certain Left Socialist Revolutionaries joined *Sovnarkom*, thereby creating a coalition government after all – until their resignation in the following March. While doing little to curb the Bolshevik power monopoly the admission of these temporary allies fostered the illusion that power was being shared with another party.

Stalin's involvement in military affairs began shortly after the Bolshevik *coup*. He was at Lenin's side (with War Commissar Krylenko) in the small hours of 9 November when this trio of *Sovnarkom* representatives took part in a historic exchange of teleprinted messages with General Dukhonin, Commander-in-Chief of the Russian armed forces. Replying from GHQ at Mogilyov, Dukhonin refused to recognize the new government or to

open immediate armistice negotiations with the Germans, and thus provoked a signal dismissing him from his post. Signed 'LENIN, STALIN,
KRYLENKO', the message replaced Dukhonin with the last-named
signatory.[5] A few days later Krylenko arrived in Mogilyov and began
negotiations leading to an armistice with the Germans, and eventually to
the Peace of Brest-Litovsk. Thus Stalin, himself a future generalissimo,
began his martial career on a suitably exalted level by helping to dismiss a
commander-in-chief.

As is confirmed by Stalin's participation in dismissing the supreme
commander, his status was higher than that of a mere minister for minority
affairs. His special role in the régime's early days can only be understood
in the light of his party's attitude to political leadership. The Bolsheviks
attached great importance to democratic forms, and were thus – if only
in theory – opposed to the leadership principle as later enshrined in Fascist
doctrine. Authoritarian though many of his policies were, Lenin cultivated
a style more modest than was to be adopted by the three premier dictators
of the 1930s: Hitler, Stalin and Mussolini. As the dominant political
leader in Soviet Russia from October 1917 until his incapacitating illness
of May 1922 onwards, Lenin never did cultivate the posture of an absolute
dictator ruling by fiat. He neither sought, nor – such was his prestige –
needed to seek such a position. He therefore avoided issuing decrees in
his own name alone, preferring to consult some senior colleague who
might be conveniently at hand, and whose signature could appear alongside his own. For this purpose Stalin was especially useful; as commissar
for the nationalities which were rapidly throwing off Russian rule, he was
freer than other leading Bolsheviks to act as Lenin's 'clerk'. This ungracious
interpretation of Stalin's role is Trotsky's.[6] But a study of the surviving
documents as a whole shows that Stalin's role was far closer to that of
Lenin's 'right-hand-man' than Trotsky would allow. Lenin valued Stalin's
judgement, and was now treating him – even more than in pre-revolutionary
days – as a trusted colleague with whom he could deal on terms of equality.
Stalin and Lenin were inseparable at this time. Even Trotsky admits that
'Lenin could not get along without Stalin even for a single day.' Lenin
was always sending for Stalin, and would spend most of the day with him.[7]

At the end of November 1917 an attempt was made to systematize control,
so far as the ruling Party was concerned, by setting up a four-man Bureau
of the Central Committee. Consisting of Lenin, Stalin, Trotsky and Sverdlov, this quartet was empowered to take decisions on all urgent matters, but
was also obliged to call in any other members of the Central Committee
who might be available at Party headquarters when such decisions were
under review.[8] Despite this last qualification, the formation of the Bureau was

a step towards that concentration of power which eventually led to the emergence of a single dictator. Among the quadrumvirs of 1917 Stalin was the only one who 'really had no definite duties', according to Trotsky,[9] whereas Trotsky himself was active as Foreign Commissar and then Commissar for War; Sverdlov was the busy Party manager; and Lenin headed the Government as Chairman of *Sovnarkom*. The Bureau established in November 1917 was short-lived, but may be seen as a forerunner of the Politburo through which Stalin was to develop much of his power during the next decades.

At Helsinki, on 14 November 1917, Stalin made his first public speech as Nationalities Commissar. Addressing a Congress of the Finnish Social Democratic Party, he redefined Bolshevik policy towards the minorities of the former Russian Empire as conceding full self-determination, including the right of seceding from Russian overlordship. Stalin confirmed that the Soviet Government meant to grant Finland her independence: a promise fulfilled in December. The concession was made to a Finland now ruled by a bourgeois (non-Communist) government, and Stalin admitted at the time that *Sovnarkom* had acted unwillingly in giving freedom to the Finnish bourgeoisie, but not to the Finnish people. Equating a local *people* with local Communists, in accordance with Bolshevik practice, Stalin ascribed this 'tragedy' to the wavering and cowardice of the Finnish Communists in failing to assert themselves.[10]

The Bolsheviks were to preach national self-determination throughout the Civil War, profiting greatly from the White generals' tactlessness in avowedly seeking to restore to a Russia united and undivided her old Imperial boundaries. Such a policy did not appeal to the newly independent Finns. Nor did it attract the Poles, whose independence was also recognized by the Soviet Government shortly after the October Revolution; it cost nothing – Poland was under German occupation at the time. Nor was White imperialism calculated to win support among any of the other nationalities, great and small, who had once been ruled by the Russian Tsar-Emperors.

To Stalin, with his authoritarian, empire-building and centralizing temperament, the policy of self-determination was to grow ever more irksome as increasing Soviet strength conferred the power to pull peripheral non-Russian peoples into the Soviet Russian orbit whether they liked it or not. In a speech of December 1917 the Nationalities Commissar is already seeking a formula for withdrawing the liberal concessions of official policy. Addressing Ukrainian Communists, he reaffirms self-determination as the continuing policy of the Soviet Government; but he goes on to say that the Government is ready to recognize any national region of Russia as a republic should the *working population* of that region so wish. The Soviet Government was also ready to recognize a federal system – once again if the *toiling populations* of the various local areas should so desire.[11] Returning to this theme in a speech of 15 January 1918, Stalin spoke of the 'need to limit the principle of self-determination': it should be bestowed, not on the bourgeoisie, but on the *toiling masses* of a given nation.[12] Since the wishes of no toiler or worker could, in Bolshevik minds, have any existence whatever except as interpreted by Bolsheviks, the formula contained expansionist potentialities such as became manifest only at a later date.

On this point Stalin, always a centralizer at heart, was to clash with Lenin, who remained closely attached to the original professions of liberalism undiluted by formulae such as could be invoked to sanction Bolshevik empire-building. In the event both Lenin's and Stalin's formulae, however sincerely intended in the early stages, were to be revealed as illusory, since none of the incorporated minority nationalities was to enjoy the *de facto* right to secede once a central Soviet Government was solidly established. Though the minorities have always retained a nominal right to independence, this has proved valueless owing to Moscow's monopoly of another, conflicting right: that of exclusively arbitrating the validity of any and all secessionist claims which might arise within the minority peoples; of equating all such urges with treason; and – in the last resort – of imposing its rulings by armed force.

As 1917 drew to a close the problem of the Constituent Assembly remained unsolved. At the elections held in November, Lenin's party had, as predicted, polled only a minority – under a quarter – of the votes, and their elected delegates, 175 in number, were greatly outnumbered by the Socialist Revolutionaries, who had 410 representatives. The retention of political power still remained Lenin's overriding aim, however, and he was not to be deterred by the expressed preference of an electorate committed indeed to Socialism – but to Socialism of non-Bolshevik varieties. With his government now less vulnerable after more than two months of rule, Lenin was no longer obliged to pose as a champion of the Assembly, which still remained unconvened as 1917 drew to a close. Lenin was also able to impugn the credentials of the Socialist Revolutionary delegates who formed the majority among those elected to the Assembly. As noted above, the Socialist Revolutionary Party had split into an opposing Left (pro-Lenin) and Right (anti-Lenin) faction. And since this split had been formalized only a few days before the elections, doubt could conveniently be thrown over the intentions of that substantial majority of the electorate which had voted the Socialist Revolutionary ticket. Nominally only 40 out of over

410 elected Socialist Revolutionary representatives were classified as belonging to the Left persuasion, but there were reasons for claiming that so low a figure might be misleading. Reinforced by such arguments, as also by his control over the Cheka and such armed forces as Petrograd could now boast, Lenin judged himself sufficiently well poised to deal with the Constituent Assembly by force. The Bolsheviks and their allies walked out of its one and only session, on 5–6 January 1918, after which it was prevented from reassembling by Red Guards – and never met again. Lenin had skilfully played for time until he felt strong enough to destroy a dangerous competitor.

Stalin's policy towards the Constituent Assembly seems to have shown less creative flexibility than his leader's. On 12 December 1917 Stalin had been appointed to yet another *ad hoc* 'bureau' – one charged with guiding the Bolshevik delegates to the Constituent Assembly. Whatever Stalin's personal role may have been, this bureau as a whole took a capitulationist line over the Constituent Assembly, proposing to transfer power to it in accordance with the policy to which the Bolsheviks had nominally committed themselves. On Lenin's proposal the offending bureau was accordingly voted out of existence. Stalin's participation in this short-lived rightist heresy was, naturally enough, concealed during the period of the Legend – and after.[13] The episode bears out other indications to the effect that Lenin was Stalin's original tutor in the strong-arm methods which the younger leader was eventually to develop so extensively.

Among the Bolsheviks' many problems that of peace with Germany was proving especially troublesome. Lenin's promise to end the war had helped to win popular support for the October *coup d'état*. But could such a promise be implemented on acceptable terms?

So demoralized was the Russian army by late 1917 – partly by Bolshevik anti-war propaganda – that its very capacity to fight on was in doubt. But the Bolshevik leaders were slow to draw the obvious conclusion: that they must accept whatever terms the Germans might impose. Far from being willing to capitulate, they believed the Germans and other 'imperialists' to be menaced by the imminent prospect of a world revolution destined to break out as part of a chain reaction sparked off by the Russian October upheaval. On this view the military situation was far from favourable to Germany. Russia (it was believed) had only to declare a 'holy' revolutionary war against her imperialist enemies for the conflict between nations to be transformed overnight into a frontier-transcending clash of classes in which the German worker would rally to the side of his Russian comrade.

No disbeliever in world revolution, Lenin yet took the realistic view that it was not, at this particular moment, on the point of erupting swiftly enough to save Russia from the Germans. In the hope of securing a breathing space for his régime he therefore urged his colleagues to accept the best terms which Berlin would offer. It was better (Lenin suggested) to lose Poland, Lithuania, Courland and so on than to lose the Socialist revolution in Russia.[14] That this was sound common sense is now evident; but if ever common sense was in short supply it was in the blissful dawn of early revolutionary Russia.

A practical man, a realist, Stalin gave Lenin's peace policy valuable support. By mid-January he had abandoned any illusions about the imminence of a world revolution destined to rescue Russian Bolshevism from German imperialist encroachments. To preach a revolutionary war against Germany was to pander to imperialism, Stalin told the Central Committee on 11 January. There *was* no revolutionary movement in the West. There were no facts. There was only a potentiality. In October 'we spoke of a holy war because we were told that the mere word "peace" would start a revolution in the West. But this has not been justified.' Replying to this intervention, Lenin refused to countenance, even from this close supporter of his peace policy, quite so blatant a rejection of the possibilities for revolution in the West; so far, Lenin admitted, no Western revolution had begun; but it would be treachery to international Socialism to dismiss the very prospect as chimerical.[15]

On 18 February the Germans – irritated by Bolshevik delays over peace negotiations – resumed hostilities and began advancing rapidly further into Russia. On the same date Stalin once more urged common sense on the Central Committee. 'The Germans are advancing. We have no forces. It is time to state outright that we must renew negotiations.... Five minutes of intensive bombardment would leave not a single Russian soldier at the front. This muddle must be ended.' As for Trotsky's wildly unrealistic view – that Russia could, as it were, turn her back on the whole situation by refusing to fight while yet refusing to sign a peace treaty – that, sneered Stalin, was the way a question might be posed 'in literature'.[16]

After hard bargaining within Party and government – after threatening to resign – Lenin had his way in the end, and German terms were accepted. By the Brest-Litovsk Treaty, Russia lost a quarter of her population and railways, three-quarters of her iron and steel, a third of her crop-producing lands. The Ukraine and Poland were no longer to be ruled by Russia. Nor were Finland and the other Baltic countries. But the Russian heartland, now named the RSFSR, did at least remain in Bolshevik hands as a base from which they might hope to recover, eventually, all the former imperial dependencies now abandoned.

In March 1918 Stalin moved his commissariat to Moscow as part of a general transfer of government to that ancient city, which thus became – for the second time, after an interval of over two centuries – the capital of Russia.

The Soviet administration still retained an air of frantic improvisation, and to this the Nationalities Commissariat formed no exception. It consisted of a Chairman (Stalin), a Deputy Chairman (Pestkovsky) and a Collegium, besides which individual sub-commissariats were formed to deal with the problems of individual nationalities: Belorussians, Latvians, Estonians, Poles, Tatars and so on.[17] In Moscow these sub-departments were scattered among former private houses, with the result that Stalin could not keep an eye on everyone. Wishing to concentrate his department, he decided to take over the Great Siberian Hotel, in Zlatoustensky Lane, which happened to have been allotted to the Supreme Council for National Economy. He told Nadezhda Alliluyeva – his future wife, now his secretary – to type out several copies of a notice: THESE QUARTERS OCCUPIED BY PEOPLE'S COMMISSARIAT OF NATIONALITIES. Then he broke into the Great Siberian by a back entrance with a posse of underlings. Groping around in the dark with the aid of matches – since the electricity was not working – the Commissar affixed his requisition notices to a number of doors at random. But this attempted *coup* failed, the building being later reclaimed through proper channels by the Economic Council.[18]

Few of Stalin's other early initiatives within his commissariat were more successful than this. In April 1918 he was chosen to represent the Soviet Government in peace negotiations with the Ukrainian Rada, the 'bourgeois' government then in control at Kiev – but just in time to see the Rada deposed by the occupying Germans in favour of their own puppet administration. Then Stalin helped to set up a Tatar-Bashkir Republic . . . which soon fell to the White forces in the developing Civil War. Apart from such fiascos, Stalin was also reputedly at odds with most members of his own commissariat. These ultra-leftist centralists favoured strong-arm tactics towards the minority peoples, rejecting the policy of voluntary federalism and concessions to the nationalities as ostentatiously proclaimed by Lenin and (less eagerly) by Stalin.[19]

For the period from 1917 onwards we must note a change in the conditions governing the manufacture of the Stalin Legend as concocted – in the 1930s and later – many years after the events which it purports to describe. In its impact on the period from 1917 onwards the Legend ceases to be as prominent a concern as hitherto. Stalin is now a public man in the public eye. His doings are, therefore, very largely a matter of public record. This record could of course be – and repeatedly was – fudged, distorted and selectively presented. But there was a limit, from now on, to the degree in which Comrade Stalin could be credited with feats wholly legendary. Nor – now that he had genuine achievements to his credit – was there any longer so great a need to fabricate for him a fairy-tale biography. From this point, accordingly, we shall have less and less need to refer to the Legend. However, we shall find it fairly actively reshaping the material of the Civil War, and crediting Stalin with heroic achievements in excess of his real contribution. After that we shall find it promoting the continued myth of Stalin as closer to Lenin than anyone else . . . but during a period when the two men were in fact involved in a bitter political and personal quarrel.

The general effect of these factors is that the Legend dwindles between 1917 and 1923 . . . until, a few years later, its subject-matter begins to be replaced (as a major factor in Stalin's biography) by the story of its fabrication.

Military Trouble-Shooter

The Russian Civil War of 1918–20 did much to promote Stalin's early development as a leader.

The war was a struggle for the survival of Bolshevism. Based on central European Russia, the Reds faced attack from White armies on the periphery of the huge surrounding territory and from almost all points of the compass. But however menacing these enemies might seem, they were united by little more than opposition to Bolshevism. Lacking a common platform and effective over-all leadership, they presented a wide political spectrum, ranging from diehard ex-officers of the Imperial Russian army to Socialists professing different brands of the creed from Lenin's. Not that such intense political involvement affected more than a small minority of the troops on either side. The bulk consisted of peasants innocent of ideological urges and conscripted at gun point to fight for Whites or Reds according to the fortunes of war. Other factions – variously termed Greens, bandits or Anarchists, and owing allegiance to neither major camp – further complicate the Civil War picture.

Appalling atrocities committed by Reds, Whites and lesser factions added to the casualties of war widespread gratuitous bloodshed such as had not disfigured the early months of the revolutionary régime. A further factor was the intervention on the White side of Britain, France, the USA, Japan and other powers anxious to preserve their assets in Russia or prevent the spread of world revolution. Foreign intervention was too weak to affect the issue of the Civil War, yet powerful enough to arouse Russian resentment; in the end it became a disadvantage to the Whites.

As conducted by participants of all shades, the war had an improvised, haphazard character. The Reds enjoyed central lines and centralized control, but their military dispositions were unsystematic. The over-all direction remained with Lenin in Moscow, where he governed as Chairman of *Sovnarkom* – and without cultivating the style of a military dictator. Direct control of military affairs was exercised by Trotsky: People's Commissar for War and creator of the Red Army. A dashing figure who toured the fronts in a special armoured train, he sneered at the dim Stalin as one who could never appear before a regiment under the open sky.[1]

The role of Stalin, as of the other very senior Bolsheviks, tended to be intermediate between that of Lenin and that of Trotsky. Often active at the Centre, Stalin was also frequently employed as a mobile troubleshooter who could be switched to any endangered front. Such emissaries would take over some crisis point at short notice, superseding less trusted local commanders: a typical feature of a situation in which traditional lines of subordination had lapsed and new traditions had yet to crystallize. Like other mobile trouble-shooters, Stalin was often temporarily seconded to one or other of the three-man Revolutionary Military Councils which controlled each war theatre, and which generally consisted of a military specialist together with a government and a Party representative. Operations were thus conducted less by individual commanders than by small committees, or – at a lower level – by two leaders working in tandem: a military specialist and a political commissar. Military organization as a whole came under the Revolutionary Military Council of the Republic, chaired by Trotsky. But attempts to maintain unified control from this or any other centre were often hampered by recriminations and complaints; by orders countermanded or disputed; by insubordination up and down the hierarchies.

On 6 June 1918 the first and most celebrated of Stalin's war duty tours brought him to Tsaritsyn on the lower Volga with a detachment of Red Guards and two armoured trains. From this base he maintained the four months of intensive activity which he later sought to immortalize by arranging for the city to be named Stalingrad. Stalin's original assignment to Tsaritsyn was unmilitary, for he arrived as Director-General of provisioning operations in south Russia. This was a key assignment: the area north of the Caucasus for which he was responsible – seriously threatened by the Whites – was the sole major food source for the industrial Centre now that the Ukraine was under German occupation. That this was no minor chore was clear from the authorization vesting Stalin with extraordinary powers and calling on all local authorities, civilian and military, to obey him.[2]

Established in Tsaritsyn, Stalin tackles his new duties with gusto. At last he is operating in his chosen element. Such is the impression created by his numerous dispatches to the Centre. Many of these were published in a special collection of material brought out in 1942, and therefore automatically suspect as belonging to the period of fully developed Legend.[3] The wholesale concoction of spurious historical documents does not, however, appear to have been a feature of the Legend-building process. One suspects, of course, that Stalin's published dispatches represent a carefully vetted selection from an even larger collection containing material less edifying. Be that as it may, the collection convincingly presents a man who has found his vocation in coping with wartime muddle and crises. As is also evident, Stalin lost no opportunity to turn himself into a local dictator over the whole North Caucasian Military District centred on Tsaritsyn.

Not having been written for publication, Stalin's dispatches are refreshingly free from the Hieratic style which he judged suitable for public utterance. 'I'm chasing up and bawling out whoever requires it . . .' he informed Lenin on 7 July. 'We shall spare no one, ourselves or others, you may rest assured. And we'll send you the food.'[4] Within twenty-four hours of his arrival in Tsaritsyn, Stalin has fixed food prices and introduced rationing. He has also unearthed a cache of railway trains; it had escaped the notice of his predecessors, who – need one say? – come over as unbelievably inefficient in his presentation.[5] Soon firmly established in his new satrapy, he bombards Moscow with demand after demand. He requires railway engineers and maintenance gangs; seventy-five million roubles in small notes; a vast array of manufactured goods; forty more trains. Still fighting speculators, he sets up a check point on the line between Tsaritsyn and Moscow, and hijacks black-market food consignments on behalf of the State. He salts and stores meat in bulk. Sniffing out two million poods of fish stock-piled in Saratov, he sends a posse to commandeer it.[6]

Stalin demands ever greater powers, ever more authorizations. He requires an order putting the merchant fleets of the Volga and the Caspian under his jurisdiction. Finding it impossible – in this front-line area – to confine his activities to matters civilian, he is soon clamouring for military authority as well. On 7 July he asks Lenin to 'grant *someone or me* special military powers in southern Russia so that emergency measures can be taken before it's too late.'[7] Three days later he complains that this request has gone unanswered. 'All right then,' he tells Lenin.' I shall myself dismiss out of hand the army commanders and commissars who are wrecking things.'[8] Officially granted in due course the extra powers thus usurped, Stalin has practically appointed himself a general overnight. In the military sphere too his desires are insatiable. Now he requires from Moscow a thousand trained soldiers, now an extra division to re-establish the front. An enthusiast for combined operations, he demands four aeroplanes; a few torpedo-boats; a couple of submarines.[9] All this was valuable training for the military leadership which, in World War Two, Marshal Stalin was to exercise in the area of supplies, reinforcements and general economic control.

Stalin of Tsaritsyn does not confine himself to desk work. Irritated by the unwillingness of one local commander to resist White Cossack raids on the railway line to Moscow, the Commissar commandeers a special train and steams off in person, like a second Trotsky, to the threatened area. After slugging it out with the Cossacks for half a day, he drives them off the line and restores communications.[10] But such occasional excursions barely interrupt the flood of complaints with which he inundates Moscow: complaints of wholesale incompetence; of deliberate sabotage; of dire treachery on all hands. That muddle and chaos tend to dominate all military business – even so regimented an affair as a peace-time drill parade, let alone a Civil War in a demoralized and desperate semi-primitive country – he seems not to suspect. Everything must be the fault of some-one or other: someone punishable. Then, as time goes on, one particular burden becomes especially obsessive: Stalin's irritation with the military specialists active within his fief. These were former officers of the Imperial Russian army whose martial talents had been enlisted on the Bolshevik side – though many were anything but Red, politically – at a time when few Communists were competent to command troops in battle. The policy of recruiting specialists was Trotsky's; only, indeed, through his establish-ment of such an officer corps was the Red Army quickly made into an effective fighting organization. So intensively were the specialists enlisted that there were soon thirty thousand of them: about three-quarters of the Red officer *corps* as a whole.[11] The disadvantage lay in their suspect affiliations, and it was for this reason that commissars were appointed to supervise each specialist commander and countersign his orders. The practice of holding the specialists' wives and children hostage also helped to discourage – but could not eliminate – desertion and treachery.

Treachery and desertion by the specialists – together with innumerable cases of mismanagement, sabotage or undercover pro-White activity – gave Stalin a convenient weapon in the intrigues which he was now con-ducting against Trotsky. 'If our military specialists – the bunglers! – had not been so lazy and idle, the line would not have been broken,' Stalin tells Lenin on 7 July. 'And if the line *is* restored it won't be thanks to the military, but in spite of them.'[12] 'Not having a piece of paper from Trotsky isn't going to stop me,' thunders Stalin when announcing a unilateral decision to assume supreme military powers in Tsaritsyn.[13] In such comments the Georgian confirms Trotsky's contention that he had turned the North Caucasus District into a private empire. 'I only want to restore Tsaritsyn to Soviet Russia' ... such was Trotsky's mild remonstrance during one meeting between the two rivals.[14]

As part of the empire-building process, and as a counter-weight to Trotsky's military specialists, Stalin began to collect protégés of his own: the 'Tsaritsyn Clique'. By contrast with the specialist ex-officers, these tended to be former NCOs of the Imperial Army. Two of them were to become particularly well-known, and were to outlive Stalin's Great Terror, the Second World War and Stalin himself: Voroshilov (in 1918 Commander of Tenth Army); the cavalry leader Budyonny, commander of First Cavalry Army – Stalin's favourite military formation. Of all Stalin's protégés, it was Voroshilov who most irritated Trotsky. He once informed the outraged Commissar for War of his intention to ignore all orders from the Centre unless he himself happened to consider them correct.[15] Nor would Voroshilov obey Sytin, a former colonel of the Imperial Army whom Trotsky appointed as his superior. Only gradually, though, did Trotsky realize that the trouble in Tsaritsyn really stemmed from Stalin, who was encouraging Voroshilov's insubordination while himself feigning a posture less unco-operative.

During the Civil War most of the Caucasus remained independent of Soviet rule, being partly under German, Turkish and British occupation. But Bolshevik governments did briefly control two eastern regions between spring and autumn 1918: the period of Stalin's satrapy in Tsaritsyn. From Vladikavkaz his close ally Ordzhonikidze headed the turbulent Republic of the Terek, pioneering strong-arm methods and intensive Chekist repressions, possibly under Stalin's direction and surely with his approval.[1] More important strategically was the Bolshevik government of Baku, headed by Stepan Shaumyan, who was now receiving orders from Stalin: his old rival from the days of the pre-revolutionary Caucasian underground. One of Stalin's directives permitted Shaumyan to nationalize the Baku oil concerns: a policy soon revealed as leftist heresy when Lenin tried to countermand it. Eventually, in July, there was a move in Baku to invite British military occupation in order to avert a threatened Turkish invasion and an attendant massacre of Armenians. But Stalin categorically forbade the enlistment of British aid. 'Inform Shaumyan ...' he fulminated by telegram, 'that I, Stalin, am in the south and shall soon be in the Northern Caucasus.'[17] Scouting this empty boast, Baku went ahead and asked in the British; whereupon Shaumyan and his colleagues – far from being rescued by Stalin – took flight across the Caspian, fell into White hands, and were shot in the wilds of Transcaspia. For the martyrdom of these 'Twenty-Six Baku Commissars' Soviet propaganda still blames the British interventionists, as it did from the outset – Stalin himself being one of the first to denounce these imperialist cannibals. Yet Stalin was also to be the ultimate chief beneficiary of a massacre which removed from the scene his old enemy Shaumyan and other Caucasian Bolsheviks; it was useful to have these people out of the way, since all of them were far too well informed about the young Dzhugashvili's heroic or unheroic pre-revolutionary activities or non-activities in and around his native Georgia. That Caucasian atrocities should not be one-sided Stalin himself had ensured – instructing his underlings to show absolute ruthlessness by burning villages in reprisal for local guerrilla attacks on grain-carrying trains.[18]

It was in Tsaritsyn that Stalin first exercised, on a modest scale, the arts of mass repression. He had the Cheka operating intensively in the city, also maintaining a prison barge in the middle of the Volga. To this first Stalinist terror added stimulus was provided through the abortive anti-Bolshevik revolt staged by Left Socialist Revolutionaries in Moscow on 6 July 1918: an event which provoked savage reprisals against their party as a whole. The 'merciless crushing of these pathetic and hysterical adventurers' was demanded by Lenin in a message to Stalin.[19] 'Be sure our hand will not tremble,' the laconic Stalin replied. 'We shall treat enemies as enemies deserve.'[20] One sequel to the abortive rebellion, and to the wave of terror which it unleashed, was an important event with which Stalin was not directly concerned: the slaughter – ordered by Lenin – [21] of the ex-Emperor Nicholas II and his family, at Yekaterinburg in the Urals on the night of 16–17 July 1918. As these and other examples show, the use of mass terror by Stalin during the years of his unchallenged power did not – as is often implied – represent a deviation from gentler methods pioneered by Lenin. Lenin was, rather, Stalin's original tutor and inspirer in the arts of political repression.

Further intensification of the Red Terror was provoked by events of 30 August 1918 in Moscow and Petrograd. On this date a Socialist Revolutionary attempted to assassinate Lenin and succeeded in wounding him. This, together with the assassination on the same day of the Petrograd Cheka boss Uritsky (also by a Socialist Revolutionary), provoked reprisals yet more savage than any so far imposed. They included the execution, in Petrograd, of several hundred hostages, largely taken from available bourgeois who were held responsible for the outrages on the characteristic ground that they might have approved of them in advance, had they known that such things were about to occur. Thus the fully developed Red Terror at last swung into action. That it should operate effectively in Tsaritsyn, Stalin's presence ensured. He made this clear in a telegram stating his intentions in impeccable Hieratic:

Having learnt of the dastardly attempt by hirelings of the bourgeoisie on the life of the World's Greatest Revolutionary – the Experienced Leader and Teacher of the Proletariat, Comrade Lenin – the Military Council of the North Caucasian Military District is replying to this base, hole-in-the-corner attack by organizing overt, systematic mass terror against the bourgeoisie and its agents.[22]

And terror meant, in effect, mass indiscriminate arrests and shootings, often conducted by casually recruited, drunken, drugged or insane Chekist executioners.

Ordained by Lenin, such unseemly occurrences in the cellars of his secret police neither disrupted that Leader's imperturbability nor impaired his usual genteel courtesy towards his closest colleagues. When, in October 1918, Stalin was eventually recalled (on Trotsky's insistence) from Tsaritsyn, Lenin softened this blow to the Georgian's *amour propre* by asking Trotsky to have a talk with him and soothe his ruffled feelings.[23] As this face-saving device indicates, Lenin was not so lavishly equipped with competent subordinates that he could afford to have them feuding with each other. He did all he could to suppress the quarrel between Stalin and Trotsky, but could not prevent it from smouldering and flaring throughout the Civil War and beyond.

The armistice of 11 November 1918 between the Germans and the Allies brought many changes to the Russian situation: not least by releasing the Ukraine from the German occupation which had followed the Treaty of Brest-Litovsk. As the largest, by far, of the former Empire's minorities, the Ukrainians had special claims on the attentions of Stalin's Nationalities Commissariat. Elected, in October 1918, to the Central Committee of the Communist Party of the Ukraine, the Nationalities Commissar had already been variously involved in the complex evolution of that troubled province or country: a saga so intricate that its chief city, Kiev, changed hands seventeen times during the Civil War period as a whole. On 1 December 1918, Stalin celebrated German withdrawal from the Ukraine with an article, 'The Ukraine is Freed'. But in implying, here, that the region might now immediately come under a government acceptable to Moscow, he turned out to be mistaken. The Ukraine was to remain one of the most hotly disputed Civil War theatres, fought over again and again by Whites, Reds, Anarchists, Poles and others. Only in late 1920, and with the defeat of Wrangel's armies, did the Nationality Commissar's most populous nationality finally come under complete Soviet control.

In late 1918 Stalin was appointed to two influential committees charged with directing the over-all conduct of the war: the Revolutionary Military Council of the Republic (chaired by Trotsky); and the Council of Workers' and Peasants' Defence (chaired by Lenin). The latter body took precedence over the former; it was conveniently compact, consisting only of Lenin, Stalin, Trotsky and three others. Trotsky claims to have suggested Stalin's candidature to both these organs in the hope of flushing his disgruntled rival into the open and forcing him to criticize Trotskyite policies overtly instead of sulkily intriguing against them in private. The manoeuvre was ineffectual, for Stalin played little or no part on either body, but continued to intrigue against Trotsky outside them.[24]

In January 1919 the Central Committee rushed Stalin to the eastern front, where he and the Cheka chief Dzerzhinsky conducted an inquiry into the disastrous fall of Perm (about eight hundred miles east of Moscow) in the previous month. Arriving at the front, Stalin sent back an emergency demand for immediate reinforcements needed to rally the Soviet Third Army; so demoralized had this formation become by its recent rout, he explained, that groups of men had collapsed in the snow and asked their commissars to shoot them.[25] But valuable though this mission was in helping to restore a catastrophic military situation,[26] Stalin never forgot that he was fighting a war on two fronts: against Trotsky as well as against the Whites. Striking at many aspects of military policy in his report on the Perm affair, he criticized Trotsky and Trotsky's protégé, the Commander-in-Chief Vatsetis. He said that one reason for the collapse of Third Army's morale had been inadequate political screening at the recruiting stage, when too many socially hostile elements had been unwisely admitted. There had also been large-scale desertions by various military specialists: a term which Stalin had converted into a deadly insult. Trotsky's Revolutionary Military Council had disorganized the whole front by its inept orders. Investigation had shown that lack of co-ordination between Second and Third Armies was due to lack of contact with the Revolutionary Military Council, as also to the lack of thought in the Commander-in-Chief's directives.[27]

Stalin's return from the eastern front was followed by his appointment to various new civilian offices in Moscow. It was now, at the Eighth Party Congress of March 1919, that the Central Committee's Politburo was established: in name a revival of the non-operative Politburo set up in October 1917. Nominally subordinate to and elected by the Central Committee, the new body was empowered to take immediate decisions on urgent matters such as the unwieldy parent organ could not keep under review. Stalin was one of the five original Politburo members of 1919, all of whom remained in office throughout the Civil War; the others were Lenin, Trotsky, Kamenev and Krestinsky. Since attempts to safeguard the Central Committee from domination by the Politburo proved ineffective from the outset, Stalin's membership of the new body immediately provided him with a fresh injection of power.

Nor did Stalin scorn membership of the Organization Bureau (Orgburo), newly established simultaneously with the Politburo and also nominally subordinated to the Central Committee. The Orgburo's status was comparatively low and was defined by Lenin as follows: 'The Orgburo allocates forces while the Politburo decides policy.'[28] As first constituted, the Orgburo too contained only five full members, Stalin being one of the two (Krestinsky was the other) who sat on the Politburo as well. Both bodies were to remain an important part of Stalin's power base for many years. As these developments suggest, he was already discovering within himself the lusts of a bureaucrat by instinct – in contrast with many of his rivals. Such organizational posts as these were scorned by more 'brilliant' and ideologically militant colleagues from Trotsky downwards, who as yet saw no danger to themselves in the laconic, allegedly plodding and uncouth Georgian's patient accumulation of offices. Stalin's promotions of 1919 also owed much to a fortunate accident. On 16 March Sverdlov, hitherto main Party manager and secretary, died of a chill combined with overwork.[29] The passing of so efficient an organizer left a gap, and Stalin was the chief beneficiary. As the episode reminds us, he always tended to be lucky in the deaths of colleagues and potential rivals, even when he was not able to make his own arrangements for their removal.

Though Soviet bureaucratic elephantiasis was by no means fully developed in 1919, steps to counter proliferating red tape were already beginning to seem necessary. To combat such abuses a new commissariat, that of State Control, was set up in March 1919. Its first commissar was Stalin. He held the post simultaneously with his continuing office of Nationalities Commissar. That a body like this – expressly designed to cut out bureaucratic absurdities, and by subjecting the administration as a whole to the democratic criticism of ordinary workers and peasants – only promoted the further proliferation of precisely such excrescences as it had been designed to check . . . such a paradox will surprise no one. And that the arch-bureaucrat Stalin should have headed such an organization only intensified the paradox: it was like setting a wolf to guard sheep. Empowered as he was through this and his other new offices to interfere in all governmental and Party matters, the 'marvellous Georgian' was to make extensive use of such increased scope for self-promotion. In early 1919 Stalin also attended the First, founding Conference of the Comintern: the international organization of Moscow-dominated Communist parties throughout the world.

Busy as he was, Stalin yet found time during the Civil War to take a second wife, Nadezhda Alliluyeva: his typist in the Nationalities Commissariat and daughter of the family which had so often sheltered and helped him during his years as a revolutionary hunted by the Tsarist police. Unsubstantiated rumour has Nadezhda seduced before her marriage at some orgy in Moscow where much Georgian wine was drunk, and where she supposedly 'surrendered her innocence' to the new People's Commissar for State Control.[30]

Stalin's next major exploit occurred in May 1919 when he helped to organize the defence of Petrograd, now threatened by Estonia-based Whites under Yudenich. Though this White advance did indeed threaten Petrograd, it was less menacing than was to be claimed by the Legend of later years, when Comrade Stalin was to be presented as a miracle-working saviour of the old capital in its hour of direst peril. In offering this version the Legend-builders blurred the lines between two separate campaigns against Petrograd: both by Yudenich's forces, both in 1919. That repelled in May and June under Stalin's supervision was a comparatively trivial affair. The more serious push took place in October, and was thrown back by Trotsky. At the time even Stalin admitted that the Whites had employed only light forces against Petrograd in the earlier campaign; he claimed that they were encouraged in such impudence by treachery behind Red lines, including a plot to seize the naval base of Kronstadt.[31]

At Tsaritsyn and Perm, Stalin had interpreted military situations too exclusively in terms of pro-White conspiracies behind Red lines, and he continued to do so on the Western front. On 18 June he had sixty-seven Kronstadt officers executed for disloyalty: partly - it seems - to stress the seriousness of the crisis which he was engaged in combating. 'He created the situation himself, and then had the satisfaction of clearing it up.'[32] Stalin also arrested foreign diplomats, some of whom were still based on the old capital, and gave orders for their embassies to be searched. His men found machine-guns and even - in the Rumanian legation - an artillery piece. A swoop on the bourgeois district of Petrograd yielded four thousand rifles and several hundred bombs.[33]

In imposing harsh repressive measures, Stalin was still responding to urgent promptings from on high. On 27 May Lenin had emphasized the likelihood of organized treachery at Petrograd, asking Stalin to take urgent steps to uncover the plots in question.[34] And since treachery, in this context, need mean no more than a preference for living under non-Bolshevik rule, it was indeed rife on the Petrograd front, as in all other theatres of war. What is a civil war, after all, but a conflict between forces each of which regards the other as treacherous? Even without Lenin's encouragement the atmosphere was fitted to nurture the paranoid suspiciousness later to become so salient a feature of Stalin's character.

During his mission to the Western Front Stalin continues his attacks on Trotsky's military specialists. He does so with especial vigour in his report to Lenin on the capture of Krasnaya Gorka: a Red naval fort (on the southern Baltic shore) which had mutinied and gone over to the Whites.

Naval specialists claim that the capture of Krasnaya Gorka from the sea stands naval science on its head. So much the worse, then, for so-called naval science. Our swift seizure of Krasnaya Gorka was due to the most blatant intervention in operational matters by myself and the civilians in general . . . intervention which did not shrink from cancelling orders on land and sea and imposing my own. . . . I consider it my duty to announce that I intend to act like this in future too, despite all my reverence for science.[35]

In planning the attack on Krasnaya Gorka, Stalin perhaps had in mind a common slogan of the period: 'There are no strongholds which the Bolsheviks cannot take.' Habitually so cautious, he was already showing a flair for overturning established proceedings and pioneering spectacularly unconventional methods.

Besides revealing originality, persistence and vindictiveness, Stalin's Petrograd policies of summer 1919 also show a typical practical grasp. More significantly, perhaps, they reveal a concern, transcending personal ambition, for the Red cause as a whole. On 18 June, for example, he refrains from asking Lenin for reinforcements in more than divisional strength, much though he needs them, since he considers the threat posed by Admiral Kolchak's forces – far away on the eastern front – to deserve priority as more serious than any danger from Yudenich. Writing of Kolchak, Stalin employs the crisp, laconic style habitual when he is dealing with practical matters untainted by political mythopoea. He describes the Admiral as Soviet Russia's most serious enemy because he has enough space to retreat; enough manpower for his army; a well-provisioned rear. Yudenich's forces lack all these advantages.[36]

Kolchak's forces did indeed seriously threaten the eastern front at the time of Stalin's secondment to Petrograd. Advancing from Siberia far into European Russia, the eastern Whites made gains of over two hundred miles along a seven-hundred-mile front. But their lines were over-extended, and by June 1919 Red counter-attacks were everywhere hurling them back. This sorely-needed success led to further conflicts between Stalin and Trotsky. Trotsky and his protégé Vatsetis (supreme Commander-in-Chief) favoured caution in following up Kolchak's routed armies, while Stalin and *his* protégé S. S. Kamenev (Commander-in-Chief of the Soviet eastern armies) advocated hot pursuit of the retreating Admiral. The more adventurous policy advocated by Stalin carried the day, and was vindicated by success in the field. Here was a grievous blow to Trotsky's prestige. Not only did his military judgement seem discredited by events, but he also saw his ally Vatsetis dismissed from supreme command. Then, to make matters worse, Vatsetis was replaced by Trotsky's *bête noire* – S. S. Kamenev (whom Trotsky had recently attempted to dismiss). Trotsky now offered to give up all his major offices, but on Lenin's insistence his resignation was rejected, steps being taken to mollify his wounded ego.[37]

The rout of Kolchak in the east was followed by the most serious threat of the entire Civil War: from the advancing southern White armies under Denikin. By late June 1919 they controlled Kharkov and the Crimea; on 2 July Denikin's men, led by Wrangel, entered Tsaritsyn – a bitter blow to Stalin, who had invested so much energy in its earlier defence. But Denikin's most serious threat was to Moscow itself, after Oryol had fallen to the Whites on 13 October. Stalin was now engaged in this area, having been appointed to the staff of Army Group South. Comrade Stalin it was (according to Legend) who evolved the plan which speedily routed a Denikin now as dangerously over-extended as Kolchak had been some six months earlier.[38] Trotsky, though, maintains that this defeat was due to *his* plans, taken over and carried out by others in his absence.[39] For Trotsky had now switched places with Stalin, becoming the Kremlin's man in Petrograd. He had been rushed there to organize its defences against the second and more serious of Yudenich's campaigns: that which took his forward elements within sight of the city on 20 October. So perilous was the situation that Lenin at one time even proposed to abandon Petrograd. But Stalin argued against such a retreat, taking Trotsky's side against Lenin: a stand soon vindicated by Trotsky's successful defence of the old capital.[40]

The episode has a scarcity value for two reasons. Firstly, Stalin successfully opposes Lenin and is proved right. Secondly, he does not allow jealousy to prevent him from agreeing with Trotsky over a matter affecting the safety of the Republic. Crude and ham-handed though Stalin's methods might be, he was genuinely and effectively committed to the Red cause in the Civil War. He was not, at this stage, so corroded by ambition – or by the urge to protect himself at all costs – as to take risks comparable to those involved in his slaughter of the Red Army's High Command in the late 1930s, whereby he was to lay the Soviet Union wide open to attack by Hitler.

By January 1920 the Whites were everywhere in retreat. Admiral Kolchak was a prisoner facing execution in Siberia; Denikin was losing his last footing in the Ukraine: a catastrophe accelerated by bitter quarrels with his leading general, Wrangel. This feud more than counter-balanced any damage done to the Red cause by the differences between Stalin and Trotsky. As a member of the Revolutionary Military Council of Army Group South, Stalin had played his part in the defeat of Denikin. And with the clearing of the Ukraine a new assignment came his way: the organization of the so-called Ukrainian Labour Army. This was one among several Labour Armies newly established under Trotsky's direction. The intention was to transfer military units to civilian work *en masse* now that the problems of war were giving way to the no less acute problems of peace and reconstruction. Meanwhile, however, in mid-January 1920 a resurgent Denikin began to menace the Ukraine again, operating from bases in the northern Caucasus. He gained several local victories, almost recapturing Rostov-on-Don. In response Lenin urgently instructed Stalin to remilitarize certain formations of his Ukrainian Labour Army and to dispatch them to the Caucasian front. Stalin refused. 'I don't see why *I* should be singled out to cope with Army Group Caucasus. . . . Reinforcement of the Caucasian theatre is the job of the Revolutionary Military Council of the Republic, whose members are in excellent health so far as I'm aware. This isn't a job for Stalin, who is overworked already.'[41] Lenin retorted that Stalin was expected to make himself generally useful not to raise demarcational quibbles.[42]

Reinforced by a now pliant Stalin, Soviet forces in the North Caucasus routed Denikin, capturing the key port of Novorossiysk, whence the Whites were hastily evacuated to the Crimea: their sole remaining stronghold. Here, on 4 April 1920, Wrangel succeeded the discredited Denikin as White Commander-in-Chief. In June (to anticipate events) Wrangel's armies burst out of the Crimea and gained some successes in the southern Ukraine, only to be flung back at the end of the year and forced to evacuate through Crimean ports: a great Soviet victory which virtually ended the Civil War after nearly three years of fighting.

Poland and the Caucasus

Among Stalin's military involvements of this period none was to become more controversial than his role in the Soviet-Polish War of April-September 1920. This was not, strictly speaking, part of the Russian Civil War, since the enemy was a sovereign foreign state – albeit recently a dependency of the Russian Empire. But the Soviet authorities could not consider the Polish War in isolation from the struggle with the Whites, especially as the last major White effort – under Wrangel – coincided with the Polish campaign. When Wrangel burst out of the Crimea in June and began campaigning north of the Perikop Isthmus, he threatened the left flank of the Red forces embroiled with Poland. This was one of many factors behind the military fiasco into which the Polish War developed for the Bolsheviks.

The Polish-Soviet campaign fell into three main phases: the initial attack by Pilsudski's forces in April, leading to the fall of Kiev on 6 May; the Soviet counter-attack in June, which took the Red Army within sight of Warsaw's suburbs by 10 August; the Polish counter-attack, launched on 16 August, which flung the Soviet forces back from Warsaw in headlong rout and led to a peace disadvantageous to Moscow.

The question which concerns us is the extent to which Stalin (as alleged by Trotsky) contributed to this defeat through pursuing private ambitions in defiance of orders.

One major cause of the Soviet rout was the dissipation of the Red Army's efforts between two imperfectly co-ordinated army groups. In the northern sector Tukhachevsky's Army Group West took Warsaw as its objective, while in the south Yegorov's Army Group South-West – of which Stalin was the Political Member, and therefore in a sense joint commander – had its sights on Lwow. Since the axis of advance of the former group was west-north-west, and that of the latter west-south-west, it followed that the further each penetrated into Polish territory the greater must be the gap between the two. This was, in effect, the reverse of the more familiar pincer movement, being a tactic so inept that even military science seems to have no term to cover it; it is to be explained by the presence of extensive swamps between the two formations.

No less calamitous was the dissipation of effort within Yegorov's (and Stalin's) Army Group South-West. Only part of this formation was committed to the hinterland of southern Poland, for its left flank (one might almost say its rear) was menaced by the talented Wrangel. So successfully did his incursion develop that he had become, by the beginning of August, a 'colossal danger'.[1] The words are Lenin's in a telegram of 2 August to Stalin. Only now had the Politburo at last decided to create a separate southern command for operations against the Crimea, and to hive off the forces committed against Poland, bringing them under unified control. Henceforward Stalin was to busy himself with Wrangel alone, Lenin told him. But Stalin cabled back from the Ukraine to say that the Politburo should not waste its time over such 'trifles' as the disposition of the fronts! The remark appears less insubordinate – though not less foolish – when one remembers that Stalin was, after all, himself a member of the directing Politburo ... as well as one of its subordinates in the field. Now evidently battle-weary, he added that he was capable of only another fortnight's work on the fronts anyway, that he needed a holiday ... and that his job should be given to someone else. For once Stalin was showing signs of strain, but when Lenin shrewdly asked him to recommend a replacement for himself he failed to submit any name. On 4 August, Lenin – unruffled by this display of pique – asked Stalin for a considered appreciation of the situation on both the Polish and the Crimean fronts to assist an impending Central Committee meeting. 'The most important political decisions may depend on your conclusion,' Lenin added.[2] The sentence fairly reflects the weight generally given to Stalin's views by Lenin. Trotsky's claim that Stalin was a mere clerk, executant or 'stooge' is once again refuted by the evidence.

As part of the reallocation of Soviet forces ordained in early August it was decided to switch two formations of Army Group South-West (Twelfth Army and First Cavalry Army) to Tukhachevsky's command. He was in great need of such reinforcements, for by now his drive against Warsaw had spent itself and he was threatened with a powerful Polish counter-blow. The order for the transfer of the two formations went out from the Commander-in-Chief, S. S. Kamenev – on 10 August. But it was not implemented in time to strengthen Tukhachevsky's resistance to the Polish counter-attack which began six days later and rolled his armies back from Warsaw in headlong flight. According to Trotsky, this disaster was due to Stalin's unco-operativeness. Jealous of the glory which Warsaw's fall seemed likely to bring Tukhachevsky, the ambitious Georgian had allegedly set his heart on bringing off at all costs a comparable *coup*: the capture of Lwow. It was for this reason that he supposedly insisted on 'waging his own war', and refused to surrender the two formations which General Headquarters was attempting to switch to the Warsaw front.[3]

Thus Trotsky accused Stalin of preventing the capture of Warsaw by trying to capture Lwow, a charge to which Stalin's propagandists of the mid-1930s retorted by blaming the traitor Trotsky's policies – chiefly executed by Tukhachevsky – for preventing the capture of Lwow by concentrating on the capture of Warsaw. Neither accusation was effectively sustained. So far as Stalin's culpability is concerned, Trotsky's version ignores the degree of chaos – unusual even by military standards – attendant upon the Red Army's Polish operations of 1920. There were endless delays in transmitting signals between the two army groups. Then again, road-rail communications in the heart of Soviet-occupied Poland were so primitive as to cast doubt on the possibility of either First Cavalry Army or Twelfth Army participating decisively in the Warsaw battle – even if the order for their transfer had been executed without quibble. That First Cavalry Army was committed to action at the time when the crucial order was received, and that it could not be extricated, was another contention.

There is also the more elusive problem of Stalin's whereabouts during the crucial period. According to Legend, which by no means always lies, he was nowhere near Poland in mid-August, but divided his time between the Ukraine and Moscow.[4] We know that he was exhausted and war-weary at the time, and that barely two weeks had passed since Lenin had instructed him to concern himself exclusively with Wrangel. This in itself would not have prevented Stalin from sending messages encouraging his cronies Budyonny and Voroshilov (not for the first time) to ignore orders. But the evidence is too confused to bear out Trotsky's assertion that Stalin's ambitions and intrigues were a major factor in causing the catastrophe. That Stalin was capable of acting insubordinately and trying to fight a private war, we already know from his behaviour at Tsaritsyn. The question is, though, whether he actually did so during the Soviet-Polish War. It remains unresolved.

If blame for the failure of the Polish campaign falls on any one individual, that individual is surely Lenin. It was Lenin's over-optimistic forecast of a Polish workers' revolution which had led him to sanction Tukhachevsky's all-out drive on Warsaw in the first place. At that stage both Trotsky and Stalin (though not in concert) had shown caution in approaching the Polish problem.[5] For failure to regularize the Soviet order of battle until it was too late, Lenin must also bear responsibility as the most influential member of the Politburo: as a member, moreover, permanently stationed at the Centre, which Stalin and Trotsky were not. Lenin was also culpable through his continued sanctioning of so anarchic a command structure. How on earth could any rational direction of the campaign be expected from the so-called Supreme Soviet Commander-in-Chief, S. S. Kamenev, so long as Stalin was – simultaneously – his subordinate as peripatetic Commissar to various Army Groups engaged on the fronts, and his superior officer as one of the main political leaders responsible for the conduct of the war ?

One result of the Polish campaign was to strengthen the solidarity be-between Stalin and his favourite military formation, the newly established

First Cavalry Army commanded by Budyonny. The Cavalry Army also had Voroshilov – Stalin's ally against Trotsky from Tsaritsyn days – on its Revolutionary Military Council. As this indicates, Stalin's Tsaritsyn clique was still very much in the saddle. And so it was to remain. When, in 1935, Stalin created the rank of Marshal of the Soviet Union, these two old friends were among the first five officers promoted to the new grade.

Both as Soviet Russia's most influential Caucasian and as her Nationalities Commissar, Stalin retained a keen interest in the Caucasus during the Civil War period, when possession of this complex region was disputed between Reds, Whites, Mensheviks, sundry local nationalists, foreign interventionists and others. By early 1920 the position began to clarify: White defeats had brought the Red Army to the borders of Azerbaijan, while the recent rapprochement between Moscow and Kemalist Turkey left all the Caucasian peoples – small and disunited as they were – at the evident mercy of the Kremlin.

In the armed Bolshevik seizure of Caucasia, which was spread over the twelve months between April 1920 and March 1921, Stalin took a leading part. He thus blatantly abandoned the firm stand in favour of self-determination for minority peoples which he had so often adopted in print. Only a minor role was assigned, in the takeover of Caucasia, to local Communist parties, which were chiefly useful as focuses of unrest and in providing the pretext for annexation. The operation as a whole was planned by a specially established Caucasian Bureau appointed in Moscow and headed by Stalin's close ally Ordzhonikidze. That Stalin was instrumental in securing this Georgian associate's appointment seems likely, though it cannot be confirmed. In any case the new bureau soon went into action. On 27 April the independent Azerbaijan Government capitulated to an ultimatum presented through local Communist organizations, after which Ordzhonikidze moved in and instituted a reign of terror in Baku, imprisoning and shooting nationalist leaders. He was thereby introducing a new phase in Bolshevik policy, which had hitherto treated local nationalists with comparative leniency. Thus Ordzhonikidze showed himself a zealous pioneer of Stalinism, as he also did in welcoming Stalin himself during his first visit to the Caucasus for years. Stalin reached Vladikavkaz on 21 October 1920, and proceeded to Baku, where he spent two weeks. It was there that Ordzhonikidze greeted him. Referring to the Beloved Leader's and Seasoned Proletarian Champion's exceptional selflessness, energy, vigour, experience of revolutionary tactics and modesty,[6] this gifted linguist was revealing a notable flair for early Stalinist Hieratic locutions, and a degree of servility such as others were unable to acquire in a decade's hard study.

On 27 November 1920, shortly after returning to Moscow, Stalin telephoned Ordzhonikidze, ordering him to proceed with the annexation of Armenia, which was duly carried out by the end of the year.

Finally, on 16 February 1921, the Red Army invaded Stalin's native Georgia, enforcing the capitulation of its independent Menshevik government within five weeks. Over the rape of Georgia there was no such harmony in higher Bolshevik councils as had attended the ravishment of Azerbaijan and Armenia. Lenin, in particular, was opposed to the use of force against Tiflis, partly because he realized that such a policy must antagonize the Western European powers whom he had recently decided to conciliate. According to one somewhat wild report, Stalin and Ordzhonikidze deliberately defied Lenin over Georgia by going ahead with the annexation on their own initiative; the incensed Lenin even ordered the abandonment of the invasion and the trial of its promoters.[7] Exaggerated this version may be, but there is at least 'considerable evidence that Lenin at first hesitated to approve of the invasion of Georgia advocated by some of his colleagues, especially Ordzhonikidze and Stalin.'[8] Reconciled later to the accomplished event, he sought vainly to induce Ordzhonikidze, as reigning Caucasian satrap, to adopt a conciliatory policy towards the local population. Already, then, in 1921 Georgia had become a bone of contention between the cautious Lenin and the empire-building Stalin, thus foreshadowing the violent clash which was to take place between them in the following years.

6

Shadow over Lenin

Peace Breaks Out

BY early 1921 the Civil War was almost over and Soviet-ruled citizens
could hope for a relaxation of discipline: a hope shared by many a Party
member. But Lenin and his immediate colleagues were otherwise minded.
After winning the war they continued to strengthen their political monopoly, totally suppressing the non-Bolshevik Socialist parties – the Menshevik and the Socialist Revolutionary – which had maintained sporadic,
barely tolerated political activity since 1917.

The end of White resistance did not solve all the ruling Party's problems.
Nor did it end suffering and danger for the population at large. A shattered
economy had to be rebuilt, food supplies and transport being in especially
parlous condition after six years of war against enemies foreign and
domestic. A great famine, that of 1921-2, was impending, while a connected
phenomenon – guerrilla resistance by anti-Bolshevik peasant bands –
demanded large-scale campaigning by the Red Army. So too, briefly,
did the revolt by sailors and civilians which exploded in early March
1921 in the island naval base of Kronstadt near Petrograd. The most
ominous feature of the affair was the extensive participation of local
Bolsheviks: and that in a centre famed as a traditional bulwark of their
movement. Though the Kronstadt rising was ruthlessly crushed within
three weeks, the episode was a blow to the leadership – especially as strikes
and workers' demonstrations had preceded it in Petrograd, an even
more celebrated Bolshevik stronghold. One notable sequel was Lenin's
New Economic System (NEP), introduced in March 1921. This restored
a measure of private trade – banned under the rigours of the Soviet wartime
economy – and was designed to conciliate the mutinous peasantry, thereby assisting the flow of food to the mutinous and hungry proletariat.
NEP was to last seven years, its end (in 1928) ushering in the attainment
of absolute power by Stalin.

Neither in introducing NEP, nor in suppressing the Kronstadt revolt, did Stalin take a prominent part – except as a member of the policy-making group around Lenin. But he assumed a leading role in crushing other dissident movements within the Party, thus helping to pioneer a new phase in its history. Hitherto active in destroying rival political parties, Bolsheviks of all ranks were now finding themselves under attack from their own organization. Once they had robbed others of freedom. Now it was their turn to be enslaved: first by a small controlling Centre, and finally by a single individual. That Stalin emerged as this omnipotent individual was due to a flair for political manoeuvre; for knowing when to efface himself and when to strike boldly. Painstaking preparation – through the assiduous planting of supporters in Party and Government – played a crucial role. So did a fair measure of luck. The process was one of discreetly persistent self-promotion combined with the out-manoeuvering of rivals, among whom Trotsky was the chief.

In the developing Trotsky-Stalin feud the crushing of the 'Workers' Opposition' played a part. These dissident Bolsheviks championed the proletarians in whose name the Party claimed to rule, but who seemed to be deriving no practical benefits whatever from their notional political ascendancy. The Workers' Opposition was led by Shlyapnikov, who had been a worker himself – unlike Stalin and so many other Bolshevik leaders; another main figure was that genteel pioneer of sexual emancipation Aleksandra Kollontay. Their aim was greater independence for Soviet trade unionists in determining industrial policy and electing representatives to union office. They were thus seeking to reverse the system – already vigorously promoted by Stalin – whereby officials of all kinds were increasingly appointed by nomination from above instead of being democratically elected from below.

Since the Workers' Opposition had the entire Central Committee against it, its defeat was a foregone conclusion. On strategy, though, the Central Committee was seriously divided. Trotsky – creator of the Labour Armies of 1920–now advocated the regimentation of the labour force. This authoritarian stance had not previously been opposed by Lenin – or by Stalin, who had so recently headed, in the Ukraine, one of the Trotsky-sponsored Labour Armies. Now, however, both Lenin and Stalin rejected Trotsky's severe line. Not that Lenin was any less eager than Trotsky to subject the trade unions to increased Party control; nor was he less hostile, ultimately, to the Workers' Opposition. But he thought it expedient to disguise his long-term intentions in milder language. Where Trotsky stressed compulsion, Lenin preferred to emphasize persuasion.

This affair stimulated a lively debate in the press and at meetings from December 1920 onwards. It was the last occasion on which a major political issue was argued in public so strenuously, and without the guide-lines having been predetermined by authority. Stalin's role combined modesty, caution, slyness and calculation. Siding firmly with Lenin, he made only one public intervention – publishing a *Pravda* article on Trotsky's errors. He accused Trotsky of ignoring differences between the army and the working class, and of importing military methods into the trade unions.[1] Stalin was also intriguing against Trotsky behind the scenes over this issue;[2] but he was careful to leave a more prominent role in the campaign to the vociferous Zinovyev – thus projecting himself as the one reasonable man among Lenin's over-exuberant lieutenants.

At the Tenth Party Congress of March 1921, the trade union controversy was settled in Trotsky's disfavour along the milder-sounding lines advocated by Lenin, Zinovyev and Stalin. In handling the Workers' Oppositionists, Lenin was less gentle. Accusing them of *deviating*, he introduced a term which was to play a malignant role in future Stalinist witch-hunts.[3] It was now, too, that Lenin introduced his momentous decree on Party unity. Designed to foil future deviations in every shape and form, this forbade members to enter 'fractions' advocating policies differing from those of the established leadership. For fractionalism the penalty was fixed, under a secret clause, as expulsion from the Party. The same clause also provided that such expulsion could be imposed on Central Committee members only by a two-thirds majority of the Committee sitting jointly with the Party's Central Control Commission:[4] a body newly constituted to ensure the maintenance of political discipline. This provision infringed the rights – already much eroded – of the nominally sovereign annual Party congresses to control the composition of the Central Committees which they 'elected'.

By outlawing rank-and-file opposition, and by introducing NEP, the Tenth Congress became one of the most influential in Party history. To Stalin the ban on fractionalism was to prove especially useful. No less important was the continuing infiltration of Stalinists into key positions – a process promoted by the Tenth, as by succeeding congresses. Among the members of the 1921 Central Committee there were a dozen newly elected figures whose records already identified them as Stalin's creatures.[5] By now the ability to control appointments on all levels was a highly potent weapon in the future dictator's hands. In 1920 the Stalin-dominated Orgburo had received power to appoint and transfer Party officials – excluding those in the central Apparatus – without reference to the Politburo.[6] In the next year appointments to provincial Party secretaryships were made subject to confirmation by the highest authority.[7] This meant that provincial secretaries were to be nominated by the Centre, not elected locally. 'Orgburo', 'Centre', 'highest authority' . . . these concepts were all gradually becoming synonyms for Stalin.

Stalin was also acquiring the power to dismiss or transfer hostile officials. Of this the Tenth Party Congress witnessed an instructive example: all three secretaries of the Central Committee – Krestinsky, Preobrazhensky and Serebryakov – were replaced, and by a trio more congenial to the Georgian. Among these Molotov – Stalin's chief subordinate of future years – received the special status of Responsible Secretary, while a certain Mikhaylov and that outstanding future Stalinist Yaroslavsky became secretaries pure and simple. At this time, too, another instrument of Stalin's power – the Central Control Commission originally set up in 1920 – was strengthened as a body responsible for Party discipline.[8]

In contrast with later practice, the Party's disciplinary powers were used sparingly in these early years. Admittedly, late 1921 saw an extensive 'purge': the first systematic purge in Party history, and thus an event of historic importance. It involved the expulsion of nearly a quarter of the membership, which reduced the over-all number from about 650,000 to less than half a million. But *purging* still involved no consequences more painful than loss of one's Party card; the term had not yet acquired the sinister flavour which Stalin was later to impart.[9] Nor was fractionalism severely chastised at this stage. The first Bolshevik of consequence to incur the charge, G. Myasnikov, did so for a crime which would later seem unthinkably heinous: seeking to establish freedom of speech . . . freedom even for non-Bolsheviks. Yet Myasnikov was merely expelled from the Party for twelve months. Similarly, when the trade union chief Tomsky proved remiss – by failing to dragoon the Bolshevik caucus at the Fourth All-Russian Trade Union Congress of May 1921 – he received only a reprimand for lack of zeal. But it is significant that the commission which issued this rebuke was headed by Stalin. When the screw needed tightening, his was increasingly the hand which seemed best adapted for the task.

So mild did Bolshevik disciplinary practice yet remain that the newly excommunicated Workers' Opposition continued its activities into 1922, when a score of its members took the extreme step of appealing against Soviet Party authority to the Comintern. They were predictably rebuffed by that recently established yet already Moscow-dominated body of international Communists, but the very appeal dealt Bolshevik prestige a blow in the eyes of the world. To investigate their insubordination a disciplinary commission was appointed, with Stalin – again – as one of the members. But when this body duly recommended that the three leading Workers' Oppositionists – Shlyapnikov, Kollontay and Medvedev – should be expelled from the Party, it came up against determined opposition from the Eleventh Congress to which it was responsible, and which rejected these proposed key expulsions.[10] This was the last occasion on which a Party congress was to prove so disobedient.

Hence, perhaps, the decision, taken on 3 April 1922 – the most momentous of the Eleventh Congress – to appoint Stalin Secretary-General of the Central Committee.

Stalin thus acquired the most useful of his various power bases. It was to stress the exceptional significance of his appointment that the honorific *General* was added to the title Secretary. The partly discredited Molotov stayed on as secretary junior to Stalin, while Kuybyshev was elected to the third secretaryship. Thus a Stalinist triumvirate stood poised to make the Secretariat an implement in further enslaving the Party as a whole to the top leadership. Meanwhile yet more Stalinists were brought on to the Central Committee. Significant, too, was the continuing expansion of that body, which grew steadily in numbers as each Congress elected it anew. Only the innocent could interpret such expansion as a strengthening of the Committee. It was, rather, part of the continuing process whereby all Party and governmental bodies were being gradually emasculated through a progressive increase in their membership and a consequent loss of power. Each enlargement of the Central Committee strengthened its supposedly subordinate organs – Politburo, Orgburo and Secretariat – from which, in turn, power was passing into the hands of a single individual.

Viewed purely in organizational terms, Stalin's power base was already stronger than that of Lenin, Trotsky or any other Party leader. But it does not follow that Stalin's prestige yet equalled the latent capacity for mischief which he was so rapidly acquiring. Though his standing was improving all the time, he continued to lag behind Zinovyev and Kamenev in general esteem, not to mention Trotsky – while Lenin, of course, still eclipsed all others.

Among the many colleagues, allies and rivals whom Stalin was eventually to liquidate, the growth of his personal ascendancy caused little alarm at this time. Only one future victim is recorded as protesting openly against the Secretary-General's accumulation of offices. This was Preobrazhensky. Himself ousted from the Secretariat in the previous year, he dared to criticize Stalin by name at the Eleventh Congress. 'Is it thinkable,' Preobrazhensky asked, 'that the man can take on two commissariats, besides work on the Politburo, Orgburo and a dozen Central Committee commissions?'[11] But Lenin rose to defend Stalin against these aspersions. There was no one better qualified to deal with the complications of nationality affairs, he claimed. As for Stalin's other commissariat (*Rabkrin:*

the Workers' and Peasants' Inspectorate, successor to the Commissariat for State Control) ... that must have someone really authoritative in charge: 'Otherwise we shall sink and drown in petty intrigues.'[12]

Such protests as Preobrazhensky's are so rare as to suggest that Stalin was skilfully dissembling his awesome ambitions, or was not yet aware of his own potential. To many colleagues he still seemed harmless and useful: a plodder who did his stint uncomplainingly on committees, while other, 'brilliant' operators handled policy, doctrine, ideology and global strategy. Such is Trotsky's picture. To him Stalin always remained a mediocrity, though by no means a nonentity. It was not, on this view, personal merit which had thrown the marvellous Georgian into prominence, but the accident of typifying the new Soviet ruling bureaucratic class. Against Trotsky's view that the bureaucracy created Stalin we may set the more plausible contention that it was Stalin who created the bureaucracy. Sensing that his mastery of the bureaucratic machine would defeat more showy rivals in the end, he went on patiently perfecting its organization – thus stooping (Trotsky absurdly implies) to methods which were not quite fair.

It is hard to measure the exact weight which Stalin carried at this time. That the new Secretary-General was not yet widely feared is a consideration supporting Trotsky's attempt to establish lustreless obscurity as Stalin's leading characteristic: one does not fear a mediocrity or a 'grey blur'. The main point, though, is that the avoidance of flamboyant postures *à la* Trotsky was simply part of Stalin's operating style – by no means a clue to his innate capacities. It was a grave – a fatal – error to interpret his self-effacement and apparent lack of panache as indexes of inferior intelligence.

As a counterweight to Trotsky's disparagement of Stalin we may quote a little known source: the report, dated 1921, of the Emmott Committee to Collect Information on Russia appointed by the British Government. With infinitely less opportunity for observing Stalin than Trotsky, and at so early a stage, this body yet noted the Georgian's reputation for 'remarkable force of character and considerable ability'. On one point, though, the Emmott Committee was wrong: 'There is reason to believe that as an organizer and a man of action Stalin is second . . . to Trotsky.'[13]

With Party intrigues Stalin contrived to combine work within the State Apparatus as head of his two commissariats: those of Nationalities and the Workers' and Peasants' Inspectorate (*Rabkrin*). The latter body had been established by a decree of 7 February 1920 in succession to the Stalin-headed Commissariat of State Control, while Stalin stayed on as Commissar. Here he steered a course typical of Soviet institutions in combining strident democratic pretensions with bureaucratic elephantiasis and centralized control. The avowed purpose of the inspectorate was to check official corruption and abuses within the entire State machine through the activity of rotating amateur snoopers elected by rank-and-file workers and peasants. That 'ordinary workers from the bench' could by their mere presence mystically infuse into Soviet officialdom higher standards of integrity and rationality was an obsession of Lenin's, his phenomenal political flair being shot through with many such a naïve streak. But it was Lenin, too, who objected when it turned out – all too predictably – that *Rabkrin* had become yet another bureaucratic Empire. It had more than twelve thousand officials by 1922, and there was little to show for all that activity.[14]

Since *Rabkrin*'s brief sanctioned unlimited interference within the governmental machine, its operations suited Stalin, but were unpopular with his colleagues. In spring 1922 Trotsky made a violent attack on *Rabkrin*'s record,[15] and Stalin relinquished his nominal control over this commissariat shortly after becoming Secretary-General. It was an unaccustomed step backwards for so remorselessly advancing a politician, but he still retained considerable influence over the inspectorate's Apparatus. As for the Nationalities Commissariat, Stalin had no intention of quitting that yet. During his absence at the fronts the organization had done little more than tick over. In mid-1920, however, he began the process which soon transformed the commissariat 'from one of the minor ministries ... into a federal government of the autonomous regions and republics of the RSFSR'.[16] By 1923 Stalin had set up no less than seventeen such regions and republics to cater for minority peoples within the giant RSFSR. Maintaining branch offices of the Nationalities Commissariat within the minority areas, he also claimed rights of supervision over other commissariats in so far as these became involved in nationality affairs.

So much for the ethnic minorities of the RSFSR. But there was also the larger problem of uniting the giant RSFSR as a whole with the other, smaller, non-Russian Soviet republics which still nominally lay outside its jurisdiction. There were now three of these: the Ukraine, Belorussia and Transcaucasia, this last consisting of the forcibly federated Azerbaijan, Armenia and Georgia. On 6 October 1922 Stalin was named as chairman of a commission appointed to merge the four republics. Since the RSFSR Party and Government already exercised from Moscow considerable *de facto* control over the Ukraine, Belorussia and Transcaucasia, the task was easier than it might have been. Still, Stalin scored a personal triumph when, on 30 December 1922, the four republics duly ratified an agreement which had been drafted by him, and which combined them in the Union of Soviet Socialist Republics (USSR).

Thus Stalin became the chief architect of the Soviet Union. In doing so he had, so to speak, worked himself out of a job, for it was decided that the newly-federated state did not require any People's Commissariat for Nationalities. Stalin's commissarship accordingly lapsed in 1923. Not until May 1941, when he promoted himself prime minister, did Russia's one and only Nationalities Commissar hold governmental office again.

Lenin Thwarted

Never was Stalin's post-revolutionary career more gravely imperilled than during the crisis of Lenin's last illness: a crisis which coincided with the development of a serious quarrel between the two leaders. At no phase of Stalin's life was the Legend of Stalin as Lenin's closest comrade-in-arms more at variance with the facts as divulged after both men had long been dead. It was on 25 May 1922 that the already ailing Lenin first became seriously incapacitated by a cerebral stroke. Only on 2 October did he return to work, but with reduced and varying control over his faculties. Then, on 10 March 1923, a further stroke deprived him of the capacity to speak and ended his political life; after which he lingered on for nearly ten months.

To Stalin and his rivals Lenin's illness posed acute problems. They had long known a Lenin all-powerful within the party which he ruled by moral force rather than dictatorial fiat. But now they had to adjust to a Lenin partly paralysed and rendered sporadically ineffective by a disease of which the course could not be predicted. To grasp for power prematurely under these conditions was to risk one's career; but there were hazards, too, in abandoning all initiative at a time when each rival contender had his eyes secretly fixed on the succession.

For Stalin the greatest dangers arising from Lenin's illness were to be concentrated in early 1923: in January, February and the first days of March. But storm signals were already accumulating somewhat earlier. The first hint of a serious rift arose from disagreements over commercial policy. By early 1922 Stalin and other Politburo members were favouring some relaxation of the strict monopoly over foreign trade hitherto exercised by the Soviet Government. Lenin strongly disagreed, advocating the maintenance of the monopoly. But though he pressed his case as vigorously as health permitted, the Central Committee overruled his wishes in October 1922 by enacting the relaxations which he so strongly deplored. Too ill to attend, Lenin immediately determined to have the October decision reversed at the next, December, meeting. Meanwhile he was deploying all his considerable influence from his sickbed. To the Politburo he addressed a note urgently condemning the new trade policy: a document to which Stalin appended the comment that Lenin's intervention had not changed *his* mind.[1] But Stalin did agree to sanction reconsideration of the trade issue.

Struck by further serious attacks on 13 December, Lenin could not attend the Central Committee meeting at which the trade question was to be reopened. But he had found a fellow-spirit in the most prominent colleague who shared his views on commercial policy: Trotsky. On 15 December, Lenin informed Stalin of this rapprochement between himself and the Secretary-General's most dangerous rival, adding that Trotsky would defend his, Lenin's, views as well as he could himself.[2] Thereupon Stalin decided to back down over the trade issue, as was his common practice when he found himself dangerously exposed. He had the disappointment of seeing Trotsky restore the much-ventilated trade monopoly. On 21 December the delighted Lenin sent Trotsky warmest congratulations for 'capturing the position' without firing a shot, also suggesting that he and Trotsky should continue their successful joint campaign.[3]

So far relations between Lenin and Stalin had conformed with traditional Party manners, which – within a general framework of petty bourgeois gentility – still permitted the plain speaking on which Bolsheviks prided themselves. But in late December these taboos began to be disrupted. So far Lenin had merely sided with Trotsky. Now he was to turn against Stalin, until he was conducting an outright destalinization campaign. From the country and the Party at large this feud remained concealed; and, fortunately for Stalin, the details were to leak out piecemeal, to restricted audiences, over a long period of time. Some items did not receive Soviet-backed confirmation until after Stalin's death: in Khrushchev's 'revelations' of late 1956; in post-Stalinist publications of Lenin's works; in the memoirs and notes of Lenin's secretaries.

As can now be seen, the background was one of multiple dramatic irony. Incapacitated and partly paralysed, Lenin languishes in his small Kremlin apartment surrounded by doctors and women. The devoted and efficient female circle includes the dying man's wife Krupskaya, his sister Mariya and several secretaries. These are his only channel of communication with the outside world. Besides, the patient's scope for communicating is hampered by more than physical weakness, since the Central Committee has ordered him to conform strictly with the severe but varying medical regimen prescribed by his doctors. And the Central Committee has even appointed one of its own senior members to police the sick-room by enforcing a ban – sporadically imposed and sporadically evaded – on Lenin's access to official papers and right to engage in correspondence.

Lenin's supervisor – or jailor, as he may well have felt – was appointed on 18 December: Stalin.[4]

Thus Stalin – once Lenin's creature, raised by him from obscurity – now stood guard over his incapacitated master on the eve of a feud which was to render the expiring leader ever more determined to destroy his custodian's political influence. But though Stalin could – and did – bully the women around the sickbed, he could not prevent them from recording the painfully delivered dictation which Lenin insisted on giving. Nor could the Secretary-General prevent them from communicating to the press, or from preserving in sealed envelopes, certain deadly attacks by Lenin on himself which were eventually to see the light of day. While Stalin sought to silence Lenin, Lenin was seeking to silence Stalin, with Lenin's fluctuating health as the most crucial factor bearing on the outcome of this tug of war.

Barely had Stalin succeeded to the office of Lenin's warder when he was already committing one of his few gross tactical errors. So incensed was he by the discovery of one letter of Lenin's (composed on 21 December and mentioned above as clinching a close political alliance with Trotsky) that he angrily picked up the telephone and subjected Krupskaya to an abusive tirade for having permitted her husband to give dictation contrary to doctors' orders. Stalin also threatened to have Lenin's wife investigated by the Party's Central Control Commission.[5] Such 'uncultured' behaviour flagrantly infringed the code of petty bourgeois manners which Bolshevik intellectuals continued to cultivate in their relations with each other ... continued to cultivate even as their drunken or cocaine-crazed executioners were exterminating non-Bolsheviks in the cellars and courtyards of the Cheka and its successor, the OGPU. Never during her thirty years of political activity had anyone taken this sort of tone with Krupskaya, she informed Kamenev. Lenin himself was no less shocked when he learned of the incident: perhaps not immediately, for it would have been Krupskaya's desire to shield him from such an emotional upheaval, but certainly before 5 March 1923. On that date Lenin was to make Stalin's offensive outburst the subject for the last and most forthright of all his attacks.[6]

This grievance was not yet rankling severely in Lenin's mind on 24 December, when he dictated his so-called Testament: a document of capital importance in the Stalin dossier.[7] Here Lenin singles out six Bolshevik leaders by name, briefly discussing their merits and demerits with the evident intention of guiding the Party's efforts to resolve the leadership crisis posed by his illness. One is struck by the prominence accorded to Stalin. He is mentioned first, being bracketed as equal or almost equal with Trotsky, while four other named leaders (Zinovyev,

Kamenev, Bukharin and Pyatakov) receive obscurer billing. Lenin points
to the unlimited authority which Stalin has already acquired as Secretary-
General. But Lenin is not sure that Stalin will always use that authority
with sufficient caution. The remark shows considerable insight, since – to
a superficial view – *excess of caution* might have seemed Stalin's most
noteworthy feature, so often had he hedged his bets or climbed delicately
down from over-exposed positions. Evidently Lenin sensed in Stalin what
was not obvious to others: the willingness to go to any lengths which he
was to display in the years of collectivization and terror long after Lenin's
death.

In the Testament, Trotsky receives a report more favourable than Stalin's,
but only marginally so. Trotsky, says Lenin, is perhaps the most capable
man in the present Central Committee. But Trotsky also suffers from
excessive self-confidence, besides being 'over-preoccupied with the purely
administrative side of things': addicted, that is – as the word 'administrative had come to be used – to high-handed and over-dictatorial methods
In so far, therefore, as Lenin was attempting to bequeath a successor to
the Party he was grooming Trotsky for the senior role on 24 December
1922 – but with Stalin as a potent second-in-command. By that date,
accordingly, disagreements between Lenin and Stalin have not yet hardened
into a feud.

One week later, though, we find Lenin taking a much harsher attitude
to Stalin, as witness certain notes 'On the Nationalities Question' dictated
by the sick man on 30 and 31 December 1922.[8] As these remind us, the
local Georgian Communist Party had been protesting against Moscow's
high-handed methods ever since the invasion of Georgia in February 1921.
A bitter quarrel had sprung up between the Tiflis-based Georgian Communists (led by Mdivani and Makharadze) and the Kremlin-based or
Kremlin-instructed Georgians (Stalin and Ordzhonikidze) whom Bolshevik
compatriots in their homeland increasingly regarded as foreign conquerors
rather than as political allies and fellow-countrymen. Even the original
intention to invade Georgia had not been communicated to the local
Communists in advance, the Mdivani group complained. As for Ordzhonikidze – in effect Stalin's proconsul in Georgia – he was ruling by fiat
without consulting local Party interests. In thus throwing his weight about,
Ordzhonikidze was ignoring a warning from Lenin to behave tactfully.[9]

Ordzhonikidze – and Stalin through Ordzhonikidze – were imposing
flagrantly centrist and authoritarian policies on a small country which had
long wearied of its role as an outpost of empire in Tsarist times. Especially
unpopular was Stalin's decision to group Georgia with Azerbaijan and
Armenia in a Transcaucasian Federation destined for incorporation as a

single unit in the USSR. The Georgian Communists wished to retain their republic as an integral entity, but their numerous complaints to Moscow did little to curb Stalin's empire-building urges. In October 1922 the majority of the Georgian Central Committee resigned – but to no effect, for Ordzhonikidze simply appointed a substitute Central Committee of pliant conformists.[10]

In October 1922 Stalin's dragooning of Georgia still enjoyed the support of Lenin, who curtly dismissed complaints from the local Communists. But by December Lenin's views on Georgia were being rapidly revised. A trivial incident fostered the change of heart: it turned out that the swaggering Ordzhonikidze had so far forgotten himself as to slap or punch some local Georgian Communist! This breach of genteel etiquette preyed on Lenin's mind, as his 'Notes on the Nationalities Question' show. Who but Lenin or a Leninist (one is tempted to ask) would have attributed such importance to a mere slap in the face delivered in a country now ravaged by famine, Cheka-controlled massacre and arbitrary arrest? But Lenin describes the episode as symptomatic of 'the swamp in which we have landed'. For behaving like a bullying, fist-swinging Great Russian colonizer of Tsarist times, Ordzhonikidze deserved exemplary punishment (said Lenin). But the truly disastrous role had been played by Stalin's precipitate haste; by Stalin's rancour against local nationalist urges; by Stalin's excess of administrative zeal: his tendency to adopt dictatorial methods. Aided by Dzerzhinsky (who had visited Georgia on a commission of inquiry which had whitewashed Muscovite policies), the Soviet Nationalities Commissar had furthered brutal Great Russian nationalist expansion, Lenin said. No matter that neither the Pole Dzerzhinsky nor the Georgian Stalin could possibly claim to be a Russian. 'It is well known [Lenin observes, using a notorious Stalinist phrase] that russified aliens always overdo things when they try to show themselves authentic Russians by adoption.'[11]

As these features reveal, the Stalin of 30 December 1922 was already, in Lenin's mind, a very different figure from the Stalin of the Testament dictated a week earlier. By 4 January 1923 Lenin's hostility to Stalin has further hardened. Now it is that Lenin dictates a Postscript to the original Testament, choosing words calculated to damage Stalin's career and to dislodge him from the chief among his many power bases:

Stalin is too rude [*gruby*] – a defect wholly acceptable in our milieu and in dealings between us Communists, but intolerable in a Secretary-General. I therefore propose to our comrades to consider a means of removing Stalin from this post and appointing someone else who differs from Stalin in one weighty respect: being more tolerant, more loyal, more polite, more considerate of his comrades, less capricious and so on.[12]

Besides rudeness, Great Russian chauvinism and obstreperousness over the foreign trade monopoly, Stalin was guilty of yet another sin in Lenin's eyes: promoting the over-bureaucratization from which the Party and governmental apparatuses now so notoriously suffered. At the end of 1922 Lenin had proposed to form with Trotsky a joint bloc 'against bureaucracy in general and the Organizational Bureau [the Orgburo, i.e., Stalin] in particular'.[13] In February 1923 Lenin returned to this theme with a blistering attack on *Rabkrin:* the Inspectorate headed by Stalin until the previous May,[14] and still regarded as very much his business. Entitled 'Better Less, but Better', Lenin's article – his last – was dictated on 6 February.[15] In it he denounces the proliferation of red tape in Party and Government. Though Lenin does not mention Stalin by name, that multiple office-holder in Party and Government was unmistakably his target – so much so that the Politburo made strenuous efforts to stop the publication of the 'Better Less' article. When Lenin, through Krupskaya, continued to press for publication, Kuybyshev showed his mettle as a Stalinist by suggesting that a special dummy issue of *Pravda*, containing the article, should be printed for Lenin's eyes only.[16] In the end the article did appear, after a month's delay, on 4 March: on the eve of further attacks by Lenin on the Secretary-General.

It was now, on 5–6 March 1923, that the enfeebled Lenin girded himself for his final, most forthright bid to destroy Stalin's political influence, producing three short letters. They are the last which he is known to have dictated.

In the most strongly worded missive of the three, Lenin harks back to an incident of the previous December: the occasion when the Secretary-General had savagely abused Krupskaya over the telephone. Lenin addresses Stalin directly, copies of his letter being sent to Zinovyev and Kamenev.

> Dear Comrade Stalin,
> You were sufficiently ill-bred to call my wife to the telephone and abuse her. Though she has informed you of her willingness to forget what was said, the fact has nevertheless become known to Zinovyev and Kamenev through her. I do not intend to forget so easily what has been done against me. And I need hardly say that I consider what has been done against my wife to have been also directed against myself. I must therefore ask you to consider whether you are ready to take back your words and apologize or whether you prefer the rupture of relations between us.[17]

On the same day Lenin wrote to Trotsky asking him to defend the Georgian Communist Party now under 'persecution' by Stalin and Dzerzhinsky, on whose impartiality (Lenin said) no reliance could be placed.

Trotsky replied that he could not accept this assignment because of illness.[18] Still incensed with Stalin over the Georgian affair, Lenin addressed his last brief letter, dictated on 6 March, directly to the leading local Georgian Communists Mdivani and Makharadze. He promised them his support, stressing his continued indignation about Ordzhonikidze's rudeness as abetted by Stalin and Dzerzhinsky.[19]

Thus Lenin, in his last recorded words, was guilty of 'fractionalism' such as he had so forthrightly excommunicated at the Tenth Party Congress of 1921. Flagrantly deviant in his last political act, the failing leader suffered yet another stroke on 10 March. It robbed him of speech and kept him hovering between life and death for a further ten months. During most of this period the invalid resided at his country retreat at Gorki, about twenty miles south of Moscow. That the acutest stage of Lenin's malady coincided with the acutest stage of his campaign to dethrone Stalin was a piece of luck for the Secretary-General. It had indeed been a close-run thing. Not surprisingly, the suspicion has arisen that Stalin may have hastened Lenin's end artificially. The main accuser is Trotsky, who recalls an occasion in February 1923 when Stalin told him, Zinovyev and Kamenev that Lenin was asking for poison with which to end sufferings now grown intolerable. Trotsky points out that Lenin considered Stalin the only person qualified to supply him with the means for suicide, since Stalin alone had an interest in doing so. Trotsky also quotes the testimony of one of Lenin's doctors: that the sick man's prospects had been better than the course which his disease actually took. From Stalin's bloody later career Trotsky adduces ample evidence to show that moral scruples would not have deterred him from murdering the Founding Father of Bolshevism – or from helping Lenin to commit suicide, had such a service been requested.[20] But whatever the presumptive value of these indications, they come nowhere near to establishing Stalin's guilt.

This further crux must therefore be relegated to the vast flotsam of unsolved problems which the Secretary-General's career has left in its wake.

With Lenin's incapacitation we leave the phase of Stalin's life which has obliged us to make frequent references to the Stalin Legend. As has so often been indicated above, this Legend did not come to be concocted until well after the events which it describes, since it did not evolve in any notable degree until (in 1929) the Stalin Cult began to get well and truly under way. The middle and late 1920s therefore represent a limbo between the period *covered by the Legend* and the period *of the Legend's fabrication*. In this interim phase Stalin is not yet strong enough to foist on the Soviet public a creatively spurious picture of his early life. But he has already been strong enough – since the October Revolution – to suppress certain information, inconvenient to him, about those early years. Moreover, so far as his current doings of the middle and late 1920s are concerned, his mastery of Soviet communications is already such that he can generally arrange for these actions to be portrayed, even as he performs them, in a highly favourable light: a light sufficiently favourable, moreover, to exempt his future Legend-builders from the need to refurbish, retrospectively, his activities of 1923 onwards to the extent which came to be judged necessary in respect of his activities as deployed before that year.

We are thus entering, now, the limbo between Stalin's early life and the period when it begins to be recreated in Legend.

Around Lenin's Death-Bed

During Lenin's last ten months of life – the period of total withdrawal from politics which begins with his incapacitating stroke of March 1923 – Stalin continues to consolidate his position within the Party. He now ranks roughly fifth in the hierarchy – after Lenin, Trotsky, Zinovyev and Kamenev. Within a year he will be the most powerful individual in the country – with Lenin dead and Trotsky smarting from a major defeat, and with Zinovyev and Kamenev in decline. Yet Stalin will still be far from having established a personal dictatorship at the time of Lenin's death.

During Lenin's last months of life three issues in particular dominated the struggles of those who were competing with each other around his sick-bed: the unsatisfactory development of industry under NEP; resistance to Muscovite domination within the national minority parties and hankerings for independence within the Party as a whole. It was on the second and third of these problems that Stalin chiefly concentrated; both hinged on the question of power, involving as they did the Party's ability to keep its members in order. Meanwhile it was equally characteristic of Trotsky to be stressing matters economic. But grave though the industrial crisis might be, he was unwise to immerse himself in it so thoroughly while neglecting the levers of control which were being quietly captured by his main rival.

As this difference of approach illustrates, Stalin was more keenly attuned to the dynastic situation than Trotsky. Not that Trotsky lacked the appetite for personal ascendancy. What he lacked, rather, was the readiness to work for it. He would counter Stalin's intrigues only with a monumental faith in his own admittedly considerable abilities, believing these to be so great as to entitle him to automatic pre-eminence. If others could not see this, so much the worse for them. Contemplating this attitude, one may wish (with Isaac Deutscher) to praise the nobility of Trotsky's lofty character in disdaining petty subterfuges such as those of his pedestrian Georgian rival;[1] alternatively, one may feel – with E. H. Carr – that Trotsky's failure to make a determined bid for the succession to Lenin was due to a lack of political sense and acumen.[2] In any case Stalin owed his victory in part to Trotsky's decision not to fight at a time when he might still, conceivably, have won. Yet this very decision was itself an index of Trotsky's inferior calibre as a politician by comparison with Stalin, who emerges as the wiser, the cleverer and the more professional operator of the two.

The Stalin-Trotsky duel, as conducted in 1923–4, passed through three phases: armed truce (March to September); active skirmishing (September to December); all-out war (December to January).

In April 1923 the Twelfth Party Congress took place: the first since 1917 to be held in Lenin's absence. By now Stalin had formed an unofficial alliance with Zinovyev and Kamenev, the two other leaders who most feared an assumption of Lenin's mantle by Trotsky. For the time being this trio had nothing to gain from plunging into battle, and a deal was therefore arranged with their enemy Trotsky. The major Central Committee report to the Congress (as normally delivered by Lenin) was assigned to Zinovyev, while Trotsky was allowed a free hand with industrial policy – delivering the main economic speech, and framing sweeping proposals for comprehensive planning. Trotsky also refrained from exploiting Lenin's campaign to designate him, in effect, heir apparent; nor did he attempt to make capital out of Lenin's destalinizing utterances on the nationalities question and other matters.

By now Lenin's Stalin-disparaging statements had reached varying stages of disclosure. The attack on Stalin's direction of *Rabkrin* was common knowledge – it had appeared openly in the Party press. At the other end of the scale, Lenin's Testament (with its damning Postscript) was still effectively concealed; Stalin himself may not yet have known of its existence. As for Lenin's anti-Stalinist 'Notes on the Nationalities', they occupied an intermediary position, having been communicated to the Politburo and extensively leaked. But delegates were unable to use them from the congress floor, since the information had been given in confidence. In any case, no one but Trotsky could have exploited it with full effect, and it was in failing to do so that he revealed his chivalry or folly. Trotsky was also flouting Lenin's strongly expressed last political wish: that he should champion the persecuted Mdivani-Makharadze group among the Georgian Communists. Whatever its motives, such reticence was either a lucky bonus for Stalin – or a triumph for his secret diplomacy in persuading Trotsky to hold fire.

Even if Trotsky had challenged the triumvirs at this favourable stage, he might well have lost. Though Stalin would not, or could not, indulge in Trotskyite verbal fireworks, his less obtrusive methods of debate were formidable. Essentially a patient and repetitious debater, he by no means lacked polemical finesse. Few politicians have shown greater skill in selecting from a welter of complexities some potent over-simplified non-issue, whittling it to a sharp point, dipping it in poison, and thrusting it into an adversary with a deadly twist. Though Stalin increasingly enjoyed the support of a rowdy claque on these occasions, he was well able to look after himself without that aid to debate.

At the Twelfth Congress the Secretary-General had little scope for employing his offensive armoury. Highly vulnerable because of Lenin's known strictures on Stalinist red tape and chauvinism, he protected himself from this criticism by blandly admitting its validity. Using just such language as Lenin had once used against him, he denounced the growth of Party bureaucracy,[3] and also the evils of Great Russian chauvinism. Still, even a Stalin in apparent retreat needed watching carefully. In no area did he make concessions of substance. Assaults by the Georgian Communists foundered on his tough, flexible defence based on conceding most of their case. Reiterating the principle of self-determination as the corner-stone of the Soviet nationalities policy,[4] and denouncing Great Russian chauvinism in forthright terms, he went on to argue that chauvinism was by no means confined to representatives of the Centre. The sinister disease could also arise within a sizeable minority area which itself contained minorities of its own. There was, for example, local Georgian chauvinism as directed by . . . the Mdivani-Makharadze group against such minority elements within Georgia as the Armenians, the Osetins, the Adzhars and the Abkhazians! One reason for overthrowing Great Russian chauvinism was precisely because its destruction would also involve 'overthrowing nine-tenths of that nationalism which has survived or is developing in the individual republics'.[5] Through such twists the Secretary-General out-manoeuvred Mdivani and Makharadze. They were in a difficult position in any case, agreeing as they did with Stalin that the Party should enjoy a power monopoly within Georgia, and differing only in thinking that this monopoly should be theirs rather than his.

One novelty of the Twelfth Congress was the devotional language used by Zinovyev and others about the ailing Lenin, while Stalin – later an extreme promoter of the Lenin cult – was not yet ready to indulge in this ritual.[6] He respectfully alluded to Lenin as his teacher, but in decent, restrained terms, thus making – as so often – the comforting impression of the reasonable man who is never carried away by emotion.

On this subdued level the Twelfth Congress was a minor triumph for the Secretary-General. True, the conclave witnessed many vigorous attacks on the leadership, but such sallies were never allowed to develop collective impetus. Unity behind a united leadership was, rather, the general impression created, all the Central Committee's official resolutions being passed unanimously. It was a tribute to Stalin's success as an organizer; well might he, in his concluding address, boast that the assembly was welded together and inspired by a single idea. He even permitted himself one of those little jokes of which the full irony can only be evident to posterity: 'I am sorry that Comrade Lenin is not here.'[7] Had Lenin indeed been present it is unlikely that Stalin would have remained a Secretary-General, let alone a Secretary-General triumphant. As it was, he entered the Congress as a figure junior in status to Zinovyev and Kamenev, but left it on more or less equal terms with these elder statesmen. Meanwhile Trotsky – though still a towering figure, still a potential menace to the triumvirs – had few grounds for satisfaction. His sponsorship of industrial planning had won him little support; his refusal to assert himself had discouraged potential backers.

The elections conducted by the Congress further strengthened Stalin's leverage. The usual enlargement of the Central Committee – from twenty-seven to forty full members – brought in yet more officials whose careers depended on the Secretariat. And the decision to hold joint plenums of the Central Committee and the Central Control Commission (now enlarged to fifty) further enhanced the increased power which any manipulator enjoys when the body which he controls is expanded. That such bureaucratizing measures were presented as blows against bureaucracy was yet another irony which Stalin no doubt savoured. Thus improving his position on the Central Committee, Stalin was automatically able to improve his leverage on the Politburo as newly elected by that Central Committee. Of the four new candidate members now introduced (Kalinin, Molotov, Rudzutak and Bukharin) the first three were all Stalin's men. So, too, was Kuybyshev, the new Chairman of the Central Control Commission. It had been a useful week's work.

The summer of 1923 is a quiet period in the annals of the Stalin-Trotsky feud. In June a minor clash occurred when it turned out that the Secretary-General's clerks had omitted certain amendments, agreed by the Politburo, from a diplomatic note addressed to Great Britain – whereupon Trotsky wrote to all members of the Politburo individually, denouncing Stalin and Stalin's clerical staff. But if this was indeed part of a deep-laid attack against Stalin's Apparatus, as has been suggested,[8] it was a singularly feeble one. Stalin reacted with aggressive rudeness, but gave way a little later, dismissing the two offending clerks and replacing them with one Boris Bazhanov: an undercover anti-Bolshevik agent whose reports on Politburo proceedings afford a valuable glimpse into the Kremlin's secrets of 1923-4.

Another feeble assault on Stalin came from his temporary ally Zinovyev, who must already have begun to sense danger in the Secretary-General's accumulation of powers. During the holiday season Zinovyev called an informal meeting, attended by Bukharin and Voroshilov amongst others, in a cave near the Caucasian spa of Kislovodsk, and there broached a plan designed to curb Stalin's powers.[9] These touring conspirators sent Stalin a letter expressing concern at the Secretariat's operations, whereupon he went to Kislovodsk in person and explained that such fears were groundless. In order to allay them he now invited Zinovyev, Trotsky and Bukharin to attend meetings of the Orgburo, where they could scrutinize Stalinist organizational procedures from the inside. When it came to the point, though, his critics did not bother to attend – apart from Zinovyev, who turned up once or twice. No doubt they were bored by the details of the personnel-shuffling process.

Another feature of summer 1923 was the new practice of arresting Party members for political indiscipline. At first these arrests were on a small scale, the culprits being released after brief periods in custody. Among them were members of the Workers' Group and Workers' Truth: associations which sought to re-establish democracy within the Party, and to protect the toiling masses against the dictatorship 'of' the proletariat increasingly imposed *on* the proletariat by the inner leadership. Some of these dissidents were briefly detained by the OGPU, as the Soviet political police (formerly the Cheka) was now known; others suffered no more than expulsion from the Party.[10]

The most significant act of disciplining was that of Sultan-Galiyev, in which Stalin took a keen interest. Sultan-Galiyev was a Tatar from Kazan and a former protégé of Stalin's, having worked within the Nationalities Commissariat. Enjoying great influence among his fellow-Tatars, as also within the extensive Muslim areas of the USSR as a whole, he had become disillusioned with the form of Communism dispensed from Moscow. In his view the Soviet provinces were suffering from colonialist exploitation little different from that practised under the Tsars. Attempting to rally resistance against these encroachments, he was expressing a regional protest against Kremlinite oppression: a position akin to that simultaneously adopted by the Mdivani-Makharadze group in Tiflis. But Stalin decided to treat Sultan-Galiyev more severely than those two Georgian recalcitrants. Sultan-Galiyev accordingly goes down in history as the first Party member whose arrest is known to have been ordained by the Secretary-General in person; for this momentous step Stalin had obtained the consent of Zinovyev and Kamenev.[11]

In June Stalin staged a Central Committee conference to discuss the Sultan-Galiyev affair. As so often, the Secretary-General sought to pose as a moderate by defining his attitude as intermediate between the extremes of Right and Left. The rightists were those who gave undue encouragement to local nationalist urges, while the leftists went to the opposite extreme by riding roughshod over local customs – they forgot that the struggle against nationalism need not necessarily involve opposing everything national. How restrained and reasonable – one is invited to infer – must be the leader who veers to neither extreme, but arbitrates their differences with statesmanlike wisdom. Such was the benign illusion fostered by the Secretary-General as a means of imposing his personal dictatorship on the country. Stalin went on to berate individual representatives of the minorities as guilty of 'Sultan-Galiyevism'; he also claimed that Sultan-Galiyev – who was not present to defend himself – had confessed his errors.[12] These were the ponderous means still required, in 1923, to secure the expulsion of a single individual from the Party – for such, it appears, was the only penalty suffered by the victim at the time. (Six years later he was arrested again, and condemned to death.)[13]

In autumn 1923 the armed truce between Trotsky and the Zinovyev-Kamenev-Stalin triumvirate gave way to active skirmishing. An attempt was made to weaken Trotsky's control over the armed forces by bringing anti-Trotskyites into the Revolutionary Military Committee of which he had been Chairman since its establishment in 1918. Stalin was one of various figures hostile to Trotsky who were now proposed for membership. Violently resenting this attempt to undermine his control of the Red Army, Trotsky told the Central Committee that he was willing to resign all his offices there and then. Let him serve as a humble soldier in the German revolution now in progress! At this suggestion Zinovyev jumped to his feet. He too would leave and become a humble fighter for the German revolution! With two such prima donnas competing for attention the self-effacing Secretary-General could only appear to advantage. Reasonable as ever, he said that the Central Committee could ill afford to risk two lives so precious. In the end Trotsky could bear the farce no longer, and strode out of the debating chamber; but when he tried to slam the door behind him even that gesture failed, for the heavy timbers resisted his efforts.[14]

Such manoeuvres were exasperating Trotsky more and more – to the point where he was found reading French novels at Politburo meetings, and would feign surprise should anyone choose to address him.[15] Nor was his temper improved by malaria contracted while duck-shooting in the swamps during that autumn.[16] Thus hampered, he swung belatedly into action against the triumvirate on 8 October. He then wrote to the Central Committee a letter in which he denounced the dictatorship of Orgburo and Secretariat – thereby fixing Stalin in the centre of his sights – and called for the replacement of Secretariat-dominated bureaucracy by Party democracy.[17] But the sensational aspect of his letter lay less in such criticisms – which had been levelled again and again by lesser figures during the previous two years – than in the fact that Trotsky himself had spoken at last; that he had at last thrown off restraints hitherto accepted in the name of Party discipline. To Trotsky's strictures the triumvirate replied by refusing to yield to *his* dictatorship. They accused him of absenting himself from *Sovnarkom* meetings and of refusing Lenin's invitations – repeatedly extended in 1922 – to become Deputy Chairman of that body.[18] Trotsky retaliated by dredging up – at long last – the disagreements between Lenin and Stalin over the Georgian question and *Rabkrin*; but though these might have imperilled the Secretary-General in the early months of the year, the time had passed when Trotsky could hope to win an outright victory with such weapons.

On 25 October the triumvirs struck again – at a joint plenum of the Central Committee and the Central Control Commission – by formally condemning Trotsky (now absent through illness) for encouraging fractionalism. At the same time a characteristic verbal concession was made: the principle of democracy was solemnly reaffirmed. As a further earnest of good faith, the columns of *Pravda* were thrown open for free discussion of controversial issues. That this would prove the last occasion on which the Party newspaper would ever serve as a forum for open debate, some of the controversialists must already have suspected.

Meanwhile Trotsky had by no means spent his great political influence, for which reason the triumvirs were not ready to mount an all-out attack on him. Rather were they anxious to prevent him from putting himself at the head of all the motley forces within the Party which disapproved of dictatorship from the Centre, and which Trotsky alone could hope to unite effectively. Far from doing anything of the sort, though, Trotsky was now persuaded to form a concordat with the triumvirs, joining them on 5 December in a Politburo declaration which attempted to blur the differences between the two sides. But then, with the ink barely dry on this scrap of paper, Trotsky suddenly declared war on the triumvirs. In a broadside dated 8 December he repeated familiar denunciations of bureaucratic degeneration and dictatorship by the Secretariat, also criticizing the practice of making appointments from above instead of permitting free elections. And he called on younger members of the Party – with whom he was personally popular – to save the Bolshevik Old Guard from the degeneration threatening it.[19] In reply Stalin sneered at Trotsky for trying to pass himself off as an Old Bolshevik. Everyone knew that Trotsky had not joined the Bolsheviks until July 1917, and everyone could therefore savour the characteristic sarcasms with which Stalin embellished his theme.

Trotsky evidently ... regards himself as one of the Bolshevik Old Guard, thus showing his willingness to shoulder charges which may fall on the Old Guard should it really embark on the path of degeneration. No doubt this readiness to sacrifice oneself constitutes a sign of nobility. But I must defend Comrade Trotsky from Comrade Trotsky – since (for understandable reasons) he neither can nor should bear responsibility for the potential degeneration of the basic cadres of the Bolshevik Old Guard.[20]

As part of an all-out campaign mounted from mid-December 1923 onwards, local Party meetings rigged by Stalin's Apparatus condemned Trotsky by overwhelming majorities. Zinovyev, too, played his part, wielding the newly-coined opprobrious term 'Trotskyism'.[21] Meanwhile *Pravda* had been called to order, its columns being closed to oppositionists; they were opened to a serialized treatise in which Bukharin anonymously analysed the many occasions on which Trotsky had disagreed with a Lenin whose lightest recorded word was fast acquiring the force of Holy Writ even as he himself lay speechless and dying.[22]

At the Thirteenth Party Conference of January 1924 the campaign continued with vigour unabated. Once again Stalin took the lead in hounding Trotsky, deploying his accusations under six headings. Trotsky was behaving like a superman who had set himself above his colleagues; Trotsky's position was ambiguous: was he for the Central Committee or the Opposition? Trotsky sought to set the Party at loggerheads with the Apparatus; he wanted to drive a wedge between youth and age within the Party; he relied on students and intellectuals instead of the proletariat. Finally, Trotsky was trying to legalize fractions within the Party: the practice so strongly condemned by Lenin.[23] Stalin went on to sponsor a sweeping resolution denouncing Trotsky as head of the Opposition. At the same time the Secretary-General also brandished two threats against political opposition in general. Firstly, he made public the secret clause of the 1921 resolution which prescribed expulsion from the Party as the penalty for fractionalism.[24] Secondly, severe measures were threatened against anyone circulating confidential documents; the insistence on this makes it likely that Stalin was now aware of Lenin's Testament with the deadly Postscript proposing his own removal as Secretary-General – and that he was taking steps to prevent its disclosure.

Trotsky was not present to hear the anathema pronounced against him at the Thirteenth Conference. After publishing his views in a pamphlet which at last made him appear as would-be head of all Party opposition, he took the train for the Caucasus. Declared unfit by his doctors, he was continuing to infringe the cardinal law of politics: never be ill.

Lenin died on 21 January 1924 – from disseminated arteriosclerosis of the brain, according to the medical bulletin –[25] at his country villa at Gorki near Moscow. Arrangements were made to stage obsequies suitably ceremonious, and on the same night Stalin and the other triumvirs sleighed out to pay their last respects. Lenin's death was happily timed for them, being ripe for exploitation in the campaign to consolidate their victory over Trotsky. As it happened, that disgraced leader was still in transit through the Caucasus when he received the news of Lenin's death – wired to him by Stalin. At once Trotsky asked to be informed of the date of the funeral, but received (he says) a mendacious reply indicating that the ceremony would be over before he could hope to complete the four-day journey back from Tiflis to Moscow.[26] Thus was Trotsky tricked into missing Lenin's funeral: an omission which further damaged his standing in the Party.

Meanwhile Stalin was making the most of Lenin's death. In his fallen leader's memory he pronounced, on the eve of the funeral, a grotesque Hieratic oration.[27] As was clear from its extravagantly devotional cadences, the Secretary-General was now promoting an all-out cult of Lenin such as he had been slow to take up a few months earlier. Intoning in his guttural Georgian accent the liturgical Russian drummed into him at the Tiflis Seminary, the aspiring arch-priest of Marxism-Leninism punctuated his solemn litany with the multiply-repeated hypnotic formula which is suitably dignified with capitals in the relevant passage of the *Works*:

LEAVING US, COMRADE LENIN ENJOINED ON US . . .

. . . WE VOW TO THEE, COMRADE LENIN, THAT

WE SHALL HONOURABLY DISCHARGE THIS THY

COMMANDMENT.

Encapsulated within this reiterated formula was a sequence of relatively prosaic injunctions: to preserve Party unity; to consolidate the Dictatorship of the Proletariat; to reinforce the alliance between workers and peasants; to strengthen the USSR; to show loyalty to the Comintern.

On 27 January, the day of the funeral, Stalin was discreetly prominent among other leaders in bearing Lenin's coffin from the Trade Union House in Moscow. In the afternoon he helped to lower it into a vault by the Kremlin wall: a preliminary to housing the embalmed remains in a specially erected sepulchre on the Red Square ... which the Secretary-General himself was one day to share temporarily. Lenin's successors further celebrated his death by giving to Petrograd the new name of Leningrad: a devotional act which the living Lenin would not have permitted. Nor, indeed, would he have sanctioned other aspects of the Lenin Cult which was to serve as the prelude to the yet more extravagant cult of Stalin. That began to emerge when, in 1924-5, the place names Yuzovka, Yuzovo and Tsaritsyn became Stalino, Stalinsk and Stalingrad respectively. And lest the Secretary-General should seem to be having it all his own way, there was also – briefly – a Zinovyevsk.[28]

7
More Equal than Others

Trotsky Extruded

IMMEDIATELY after Lenin's death, Stalin's control over the Party was further tightened by the massive enrolment of new members, over 200,000 recruits being inducted within a few months. Consisting largely of workers, they were docile by comparison with such veterans of pre-revolutionary Bolshevism as were still expressing independent views. By a special dispensation the new recruits – still only probationary members – were permitted to vote for delegates to the impending Thirteenth Party Congress; the Secretary-General's ability to pack that conclave with his nominees was thus further increased.

On 22 May 1924, just before the Congress was due to open, a grotesque scene took place when the Central Committee met to discuss a startling revelation sprung by Krupskaya: Lenin's Testament, including the Postscript stressing the need to remove Stalin from the secretary-generalship. Krupskaya now demanded that this damning material should be put before the Congress. Such, she insisted, had been Lenin's own express desire.[1] Such could not, however, be the wish of the triumvirs. Among them Stalin was most threatened by the Testament and Postscript; but Kamenev and Zinovyev were also slighted by the junior status attributed to them in that document – as also by Lenin's reference to their failure to support his *coup* of October 1917. Were Lenin's Testament indeed to be recited before the Congress, Trotsky alone would benefit. This soon be-became evident when – amid general dismay – Kamenev read out the explosive text at the eve-of-congress discussion. For all his customary self-control, even Stalin looked tense as he sat on one of the tribunal steps, clearly aware that his fate hung in the balance. But then, when Kamenev had finished, Zinovyev rose to champion the Secretary-General. That 'every work of Lenin possesses for us the force of law', Zinovyev piously conceded; in the present instance, though, Lenin's fears had happily proved unfounded, as Stalin's recent record proved. Kamenev then added his voice to Zinovyev's in urging the meeting to keep Stalin on as Secretary-General. The meeting also decided that Lenin's Testament should not – as Krupskaya had urged – be read out in congress; instead its contents would be communicated confidentially to heads of delegations.[2] Stalin could breathe again. As for the fastidious Trotsky, he sat through this ignoble pantomime in silence, showing his contempt by expressive grimaces and gestures.[3]

When the Congress convened on the following day, Zinovyev opened a new chapter in Party history by asserting that Bolsheviks guilty of political opposition should make confession of their errors from the platform.[4] Though he did not name Trotsky, it was clearly Trotsky whom he was requiring to perform such an act of public recantation. But Trotsky refused to recant in full. He was prepared to submit to Party discipline, and to do so abjectly; but he would not simulate compunction for having been in the wrong when he was perfectly certain that he had been in the right. For this failure to assume the required posture he was abused by Stalin and Zinovyev. A resolution was passed denouncing Trotskyite opposition as a petty bourgeois heresy. And yet – despite so outright a condemnation – the Congress did re-elect Trotsky to the Central Committee, if only by a narrow margin. Trotsky also retained his Politburo seat, despite pressure from Zinovyev and Kamenev for his exclusion. It was Stalin who now championed the retention of Trotsky in the Politburo,[5] such a posture being consistent with the Georgian's moderate style and wish to preserve a balance between rivals actual or potential.

The Congress had a dramatic sequel when, at the first Central Committee plenum following it, Stalin offered (so he says) to resign from the secretary-generalship in view of the attack made on him in Lenin's Testament. Stalin claims that this offer was unanimously rejected. 'Stalin,' says Stalin, 'was *compelled* to remain at his post.' Among those who insisted on this were Zinovyev, Kamenev and Trotsky.[6]

Of Stalin's behaviour at Politburo meetings during the struggle between the triumvirs and Trotsky, Bazhanov's memoirs provide a valuable eye-witness account. It was the young man's duty to attend these conclaves as Stalin's personal assistant: a post which he held for eighteen months from August 1923. But Bazhanov was far less impressed by his employer Stalin than by Trotsky, who seemed to outshine all other Politburo members – he treated them with unconcealed contempt. As for Stalin, that uncouth Caucasian was (Bazhanov claims) ignorant of finance and economics; had no real interest in affairs of state; read little; understood little; spoke little. When he did speak he never expressed his innermost thoughts. Stalin was endowed with peasant shrewdness, not with real intelligence. Here was a Secretary-General barely capable of uttering a generalization. He was uncivilized, vengeful, given to wine-bibbing (though not in excess); he was dominated by a passion for power, but not for its trappings, since he insisted on living modestly in a simple two-room apartment. His only distraction was listening to Verdi's *Aida*.[7] No one could have behaved less like a tyrant or dictator than did Stalin at Politburo meetings. He always seemed to follow others, never to direct them. Silent during debates, he would eventually intervene to support the majority view – hence giving the impression of one whose will always prevailed in the end. Never did he preside at meetings; he would sit smoking his pipe or pace the room with his hands behind his back. Already, though, one could sense that he was the man in charge.[8]

As such details indicate, Politburo deliberations were less formal than would appear from the solemnity of members' published speeches and articles. Many were the merry quips exchanged between the Secretary-General and his future victims. They would guffaw lustily over the British Prime Minister Ramsay MacDonald, whose strenuous attempts to please Moscow earned him nothing but derision in the Kremlin. In MacDonald the Party now had it is own Man in London, Bukharin sneered – but added that this well-meaning Scot was unfortunately too stupid even for the post of British Premier. Stalin and others accordingly drew up and signed a formal resolution which solemnly appointed Ramsay MacDonald Communist Party Secretary at Kyshtym: a proverbially stagnant backwater in the Urals. To the vacancy at Ten Downing Street, London, the Soviet trade union chief, future victim of Stalinist persecution and future suicide – Misha ('Mike') Tomsky was, amid general cachinnation, assigned.[9] Such were the amusements of those who were later to co-operate so intricately with Stalin in compassing each other's violent doom.

After the usual summer truce, the autumn of 1924 finds Trotsky seized by a seasonal itch to assert himself. With a hard-hitting article, 'Lessons of October', he violently assails Kamenev and Zinovyev, but without mentioning Stalin's name. Perhaps Trotsky was trying to split the triumvirs, perhaps he still did not think it worth wasting ammunition on so despised a foe as the Secretary-General. In any case Stalin's habitual caution had kept his record fairly free of the political sins which Trotsky now set himself to flay, and which centred on the revolutionary year 1917. Kamenev had been at odds with Lenin throughout that year, as Trotsky now pointed out; in October both Kamenev and Zinovyev had opposed the Bolshevik *coup*; then they had cravenly resigned from the Central Committee in November. That a similar lack of revolutionary panache had contributed to the collapse of the abortive German revolution in October 1923 was also Trotsky's contention: a blow at Zinovyev as head of the Comintern.[10]

To Trotsky's assault the triumvirs replied with a massive counterattack, eliciting anti-Trotskyite resolutions from the Party faithful in Leningrad, Kharkov and elsewhere. Kamenev combed the history of Bolshevism from earliest days, and made a speech cataloguing the many occasions on which Trotsky had been at odds with Lenin. By now, as this reminds us, the cult of Lenin had reached formidable proportions. On 1 August 1924 the Red Square sepulchre containing the Messiah's embalmed corpse had been opened to the public. But in no sphere did the cult have a more deadening effect than in political controversy. The convention was quickly established whereby quotations from Lenin's voluminous and self-contradictory writings were deemed conclusive argument-clinchers against which no appeal was possible save by counter-quotation from these same scriptures. To be shown as having differed by a hair's breadth from Lenin at any point in the Party's chequered history – as every prominent Bolshevik had differed repeatedly over the years – was to be proved guilty, in effect, of mortal sin.

In the anti-Trotskyite winter war of 1924, Stalin too reveals himself no mean bigot. But his contributions transcend the mere itemizing of the occasions on which Trotsky has sinned against Lenin, for now the Secretary-General pioneers a new technique quintessentially Stalinist, while also launching a new, peculiarly Stalinist, doctrine. Neither innovation attracted much attention at the time; their significance was to become evident later in the decade.

The first of these contributions is embedded in a speech of 19 November at a point where Stalin is belittling Trotsky's role in October 1917. The time had not yet arrived when the Secretary-General could portray Trotsky as the fully-fledged traitor to Bolshevism which he was to become in later demonology. But Stalin could and did assert that Trotsky's role in 1917 had been grossly exaggerated. Why, Trotsky had not even been a member of the five-man 'Practical Centre' elected by the Central Committee on 16 October 1917 to direct the takeover! As noted on an earlier page, such a centre had indeed been voted into notional existence and Stalin had indeed been elected a member of it, whereas Trotsky had not. But there is no record of the Practical Centre ever meeting, no record of it ever performing any function, practical or other – let alone of it having 'organized the leadership of the revolution', as Stalin now claimed.[11] Like the 1917 'Politburo' and many another committee of that busy year, the Practical Centre was still-born ... until Stalin resurrected the corpse in 1924, endowing it with a life which it had never possessed. In this modest fashion did the Stalinist rewriting of history begin.

Then, on 17 December 1924, the Secretary-General first propounded his celebrated theory of Socialism in One Country by asserting that the Soviet Union could build a Socialist economy by her own unaided efforts, and without waiting for revolution to break out in other lands.[12] For the moment the new doctrine seemed no more significant than a hundred others in Stalin's speeches. But it was a convenient hook on which to impale the error (attributed to Trotsky) of relying excessively on a world revolution to rescue the infant Soviet state from its innumerable troubles. Stalin also denounced a misleadingly named, out-dated doctrine of Trotsky's, that of Permanent Revolution, which could the more easily be pilloried now that it was possible to suppress the texts in which it had been elaborated. Here we note yet another characteristic Stalinist practice: that of unmasking heretical views before an audience denied all access to those views as originally expressed by the alleged heretic.

To the latest avalanche of abuse Trotsky made no reply, but again succumbed to illness. On 15 January 1925, he wrote to the Central Committee apologizing for inability to attend the impending meeting which was to review his misdemeanours. In this letter he still falls short of abject recantation, but does offer to give up the War Commissariat –[13] where his influence has already been undermined.

When the Central Committee met on 17 January, Stalin indicated (without expressing any preference of his own) that Trotsky might be handled in one of three ways. He might be expelled from the Party outright; he might be removed from both Politburo *and* War Commissariat; he might be deprived of the War Commissariat only.[14] It was the third and mildest solution which the Committee adopted. Trotsky accordingly gave up responsibility for the Red Army which he had created in 1918. His departure at least relieved him from the long-standing suspicion of promoting a military *coup*. Though there is no evidence that he ever contemplated such a move, fear of his staging a 'Bonapartist' takeover had helped to forge the triumvirs' anti-Trotskyite alliance in the first place.

Now that one phase of the struggle against Trotsky was over, the Secretary-General was the only contestant to emerge with prestige heightened – once again through adopting a reasonable posture contrasting with the other controversialists' excesses. While Zinovyev and Kamenev were urging the removal of Trotsky from the Politburo,

we did not agree [says Stalin] with Zinovyev and Kamenev because we knew that a policy of decapitation is pregnant with great dangers for the Party; we know that the method of axing and blood-letting – for blood is what they were demanding – is dangerous and infectious. Today you cut off one man, tomorrow another, the day after tomorrow a third . . . and what shall we have left of the Party then?[15]

When making this statement amid general applause Stalin could not know that he would one day have his main adversary axed – literally – to death; that he would have his present allies Zinovyev and Kamenev shot; or that he would slaughter an overwhelming majority among those who were applauding these very words. The scope which he was to enjoy, a decade later, to massacre these acolytes derived in no small measure from the reasonable, sensible pose which he was assuming or feigning in these earlier years. Presenting himself as a respectable public servant surrounded by fanatics and firebrands, Stalin seemed the one leader whose power menaced nobody. Notable, too, was his correctness in calling Trotsky 'Comrade' long after Zinovyev and Kamenev had ceased to accord their falling enemy that courtesy.[16] Nor are we necessarily justified in suggesting that Stalin was always playing a part when he behaved in this modest, companionable fashion. Despite his tendency to be rude, he was, by many accounts, a very decent sort of fellow; it is his decisions and policies, not his social manners, which have earned him the title of the 'most ferocious human tiger ever to walk the earth'.[17]

Less unassumingly affable than the Georgian, Zinovyev and Kamenev would openly parade their personal dislike of Trotsky – at the first Politburo meeting which he attended, Bazhanov was struck by Zinovyev's rudeness in ignoring Trotsky's presence, while Kamenev would give him no more than a perfunctory salute. But Stalin greeted his arch-rival with every sign of friendship, ostentatiously shaking his hand across the table. Yet Stalin was Trotsky's most implacable enemy among the triumvirs.[18]

We need not mourn Trotsky's defeat in this, the greatest personal political duel of the twentieth century. A dictatorship by Trotsky would not necessarily have proved less disastrous for the average citizen than that of Stalin. What use, precisely, a Trotsky victorious over Stalin would have made of autocratic powers such as his rival was to enjoy in 1929–53 we naturally cannot say. But we do at least have certain pointers to Trotsky's potential as a totalitarian administrator: the lines along which he actually did employ the considerable leverage available to him during the Civil War of 1918–21 and its immediate aftermath.

As People's Commissar for War active on many of the far-flung fronts, Trotsky behaved with brutality which became a by-word at the time. He issued orders to shoot the commissars and commanders of Red Army regiments which showed cowardice in face of the enemy, also reviving the old Roman custom of decimation (executing one man in ten) for retreating privates.[19] Impressing ex-officers of the Russian Imperial forces into the Red Army as military specialists, he terrorized them – as we have seen above – by holding their families hostage. Though such severities might seem excused by the exigencies of war, the advent of peace saw no softening in Trotsky's general attitude. Rather did he remain prominent as a leading disciplinarian: now of the very working class in the name of which the October Revolution had originally been made. We have already noted his policy of converting military formations into uniformed labour armies, as also his eagerness to impose on non-militarized workers an extreme degree of regimentation designed to rob them of trade union organizations devoted, even nominally, to protecting their interests.

In his handling of the Kronstadt Rising of March 1921, Trotsky had again shown himself an advocate of extreme regimentation and iron discipline. Trotsky it was who sent the harsh ultimatum of 5 March to the insurgent sailor-and-worker Bolsheviks – formerly his own most ardent supporters – of this island fortress. Urging and implementing the suppression of the Kronstadt revolt with maximum brutality, and even sanctioning the use of poison gas (though the incident ended before this could be employed), Trotsky was denounced as a 'murderer' and a 'bloody field-marshal' by the mutineers.[20]

Though Trotsky himself and his apologist Isaac Deutscher have attempted to tone down or explain away such episodes,[21] Trotsky's record as a leader of considerable ruthlessness remains. Whether or not a Trotsky endowed with supreme power would, in the end, have had recourse to measures quite as bizarre and barbaric as Stalin's show trials of 1936–8 must remain a matter for speculation. But there are indications of leanings in that direction in the man's imperious temper and approach, and not least in his habit of personifying in his speeches and writings the forces of Revolution and History: forces (in his presentation) of the utmost virulence and malignancy . . . forces independent of non-Trotskyite human control, forces with which he closely identified his own person, forces before which individual men and women were as ants before a flamethrower. These considerations suggest that a dictating Trotsky would at least have made his mark as a tyrant of impressive stature. There is certainly no reason why he should benefit posthumously from the common assumption that, if a notoriously cruel despot (Stalin) can be proved to have had a deadly enemy (Trotsky), then the latter is thereby shown to be endowed with tolerance, compassion and forbearance such as the former conspicuously lacks.

As for Trotsky's well-founded claims to be regarded as a person of greater intellectual distinction than Stalin, some victims of a Trotskyite Great Terror (had such a holocaust occurred) would no doubt have gone to their doom comforted by this consideration. Others might well have taken the contrary view. If there was indeed no alternative to persecution by one or other of these rampaging fanatics, one might well choose the

oppressor who lacked such intellectual trimmings as a university education
and a talent for the sophisticated discussion of literature and philosophy.
As for the warm humanity attributed to Trotsky by his biographer Deutscher, one is reminded that the same quality was repeatedly ascribed to
Stalin by Stalinist minions.

Kamenev and Zinovyev Quelled

Ousted from the War Commissariat in January 1925, Trotsky submitted
to Party discipline by avoiding controversial political activity for over two
years. So docile had he become that, on the demand of the Politburo, he
even put his name to a statement of which the precise terms were dictated
to him and which denied the very existence of any political Testament
left by Lenin.[1] This was one of the most damaging among Trotsky's many
self-inflicted wounds, and made it virtually impossible that he should ever
lay claim to the succession to Lenin.

The Zinovyev-Kamenev-Stalin alliance did not long survive Trotsky's
defeat – as was inevitable, since only fear of Trotsky had forged the links
between the triumvirs. Yet the triple combination at least held together
during the greater part of 1925: that is, for several months after Trotsky's
withdrawal as a serious contender for power. At the time of Trotsky's
withdrawal Zinovyev and Kamenev still retained certain advantages over
Stalin. Both had longer, more distinguished records; both could claim closer
association with Lenin. As Chairman of the Comintern's Executive Committee, Zinovyev arguably enjoyed greater supranational prestige than any
other living Communist. His influence had, however, been weakened by the
failure of revolution in Germany in October 1923, since when Stalinist
intrigues had begun to make headway within the Comintern. Zinovyev
also retained an influential base on Soviet soil, since he controlled the
powerful Leningrad Party organization, while his ally Kamenev directed the
local Party machine in Moscow – as opposed to the central, all-Union Party
machine: Moscow-based too, but dominated by Stalin.

As 1925 was to demonstrate, the local fiefs of Moscow and Leningrad
were less firmly in the grip of Kamenev and Zinovyev than they thought.
At some stage during the year the Moscow Party Secretary Uglanov went
over to Stalin. With this defection Kamenev was robbed of his organizational base in Moscow. Henceforward he had only his voice, and no power
lever whatever, to lend to Zinovyev's aid in the struggle against Stalin.
Meanwhile Zinovyev still held a seemingly firm grip on the Leningrad
party. He was able to exploit the local patriotism of Leningraders, whose
city – as Petrograd – had so recently been the Russian capital and the very

hub of Bolshevik revolution. Inheriting a contempt for Moscow rooted deep in their Imperial past, Leningraders now added to traditional anti-Muscovite grudges the jealousy of metropolitans recently converted into provincials. They made determined attempts to assert local independence for the Leningrad Party, thus promoting the last significant regionally based schismatic movement to arise within Soviet Communism.

Though skirmishing between Zinovyevite Leningrad and the Stalin-controlled Kremlin continued periodically throughout 1925, it was contained within the limits of propriety during most of the year. In April the Fourteenth Party Conference passed off fairly harmoniously, provoking no strong differences of opinion on the issue of the hour: the treatment of the peasants. These still remained surprisingly untouched in their habits and attitudes by the great revolution which had already destroyed so many by violence and famine. Despite such sufferings, small-scale private farming yet continued much as it had under the Tsars, posing an acute problem to the Party. Should concessions be made to the peasantry in the hope of founding a prosperous economy on a prosperous countryside? That might be expedient from the point of view of economics, but was it politically sound? Who, after all, was less Bolshevik-minded than a success-ful small farmer – or 'kulak', as the more prosperous were termed? But the contrary policy associated with Trotsky – the rigorous exploitation of the peasantry as a basis for constructing a powerful planned industry – also had its dangers. The exploited peasants might rebel, as they had in Tambov Province and elsewhere in 1921. More recently, in August 1924, rural dissatisfaction had helped to provide a brief and savagely repressed revolt in Stalin's native Georgia: an event from which Stalin himself had deduced the need to persist with his policy of conciliating the peasants.[2]

During early 1925 something approaching harmony ruled on this crucial question. Trotsky – that great would-be industrializer and peasant-ex-ploiter – having now been quelled, Stalin, Zinovyev and Kamenev were all agreed on a policy of limited concessions, in terms of tax reductions and other relaxations, to the agricultural population. They differed only in their emphasis. Stalin was less conciliation-minded than his fellow-trium-virs. His reluctance to go too far in favouring the peasants also contrasted with the zeal of Bukharin – soon to be his new ally against Kamenev and Zinovyev. When Bukharin promoted a slogan calling on the peasants to enrich themselves by exploiting the extensive facilities for private enter-prise extended under NEP, Stalin was careful to dissociate himself from this message – which almost seemed to advocate a return to capitalism.[3]

In late October 1925 Stalin's triumphal progress was further assisted in a small way by the mysterious death of Mikhail Frunze, the leading

Bolshevik Civil War commander, who had succeeded Trotsky as War Commissar. Suffering from a stomach complaint, Frunze died after a surgical operation imposed on him by a convocation of doctors acting under instruction from the Secretary-General. The operation was undertaken against the advice of the War Commissar's own doctors, who claimed that his weak heart made it inadvisable to put him under chloroform. So, at any rate, Trotsky alleges when virtually accusing Stalin of arranging for Frunze to be murdered by medical means.[4] Shortly after Frunze's death a similar allegation was levelled against Stalin by the author Boris Pilnyak in a work of fiction, *Tale of the Unextinguished Moon*, a publication which was quickly confiscated by authority. Whether Frunze was or was not eased out of this life on Stalin's instructions remains uncertain. All we know is that a mysterious death had occurred – and under circumstances favourable to Stalin, for Frunze was no cowed minion of the Secretary-General's. Trotsky claims that Frunze had been supporting Zinovyev and Kamenev against Stalin, besides being opposed to increasing OGPU interference in the Red Army.[5] His replacement by the more pliant – though not yet fully Stalinized – Voroshilov therefore helped to increase Stalin's power leverage on the eve of the vital Fourteenth Party Congress.

Whatever the true facts may be, the episode is important in foreshadowing a pattern frequently repeated in Stalin's career: a prominent political figure perishes mysteriously under circumstances which seem to point suspicion at the Secretary-General, who in any case benefits politically from the death. As has been noted above, Trotsky attempted to insinuate Lenin's name into this roll of possible murder victims of the grim Caucasian. Later developments were to add Kirov, Kuybyshev, Gorky, Ordzhonikidze and others whose passing was – as Frunze's – ostentatiously mourned by the Secretary-General even as he was presumably gloating in secret over the attendant political gains.

In September 1925 signs of a breach between Stalin and the Zinovyev-Kamenev combination begin to accumulate. From the policy of increasing concessions to the peasantry this doomed pair has now swung to advocating intensive industrialization at the expense of the peasantry. When Zinovyev writes an article denouncing Bukharin – the main advocate of concessions – Stalin has the article extensively mangled before publication, removing Bukharin's name altogether. To this declaration of war Zinovyev counters by publishing a volume on Leninism attacking Bukharin and Stalin without naming either.[6] Zinovyev and Kamenev attempt to form, with Krupskaya, a bloc against Stalin, but this comes to nothing. By the end of the year a violent slanging match has developed between Zinovyev-dominated Leningrad on the one hand and the Stalin-dominated Party as a whole.

In this battle of words and resolutions Uglanov's local Moscow Party plays a prominent part on Stalin's side. To avoid unseemly squabbling at the impending Fourteenth Party Congress, Stalin offers Zinovyev a truce; but Zinovyev refuses to accept Stalin's stiff terms, which he regards as equivalent to capitulation. He insists on claiming his right to present the Congress with a dissentient report.

In the climate of late 1925 such defiance by Zinovyev could be only a gesture, his defeat being a foregone conclusion when the Congress opened on 18 December. It duly ended thirteen days later with a decisive victory by Stalin over Kamenev, over Zinovyev and over the Leningrad-based opposition as a whole. Ostensibly the position of the peasantry remained the chief point at issue. Stalin, who now delivered the main political report (previously Lenin's and then Zinovyev's privilege), was still cautiously in favour of concessions towards the countryside. The *volte face* on this issue executed by Zinovyev and Kamenev owed little to convictions of principle, having been adopted for tactical reasons, and in order to provide an issue on which they could challenge official Stalin-backed policy. How little consistency of policy towards the peasantry mattered in what was essentially a power struggle was to be further illustrated in Stalin's subsequent career, when the peasant-favourer of 1925 became the peasant-destroyer of 1929 onwards.

Stalin also took advantage of the Fourteenth Congress to consolidate Socialism in One Country, the doctrine which he had first put forward twelve months earlier, as a basic plank in official policy. Those who opposed this doctrine – as Zinovyev and Kamenev now did – were accused by Stalin of weariness and lack of faith in the revolution's present and future achievements.[7] However, the real conflict between Stalin and the opposition hinged neither on Socialism in One Country nor on any other principle or slogan, but on the question of power. Was opposition to Stalin to be tolerated in any degree whatever? That was the main point at issue. To ensure that it was settled decisively in Stalin's favour, his followers among Congress delegates – who greatly outnumbered the dissidents – heckled opposition spokesmen, making it difficult for them to obtain a hearing. Even Krupskaya's status as Lenin's widow did not protect her from storms of protest when she attempted to mobilize opinion against Stalin.

Kamenev proved better equipped than Lenin's consort to deal with these hecklers, challenging them to state openly whether or not they had been given instructions to interrupt him. With the Stalinist claque thus temporarily quelled, he launched into the most forthright and courageous speech of his career. Flinging an outright challenge at the Secretary-General,

Kamenev proclaimed himself unalterably opposed to the idea of a single individual – whether Stalin or anyone else – enjoying the status of supreme Party leader.

We are against creating the theory of a leader. We are against making a Leader. We are against having the Secretariat combining in practice both politics and organization and placing itself above the political organ.[8]

But eloquently though Kamenev spoke, his onslaught only provoked an ovation in favour of Stalin, who later modestly informed the Congress that the Party did indeed require collective leadership.[9]

The conclave eventually adopted a mildly worded resolution confirming official policy without explicitly condemning the opposition. How decisive Stalin's latest victory had been the sequel showed. A team of Stalinists headed by Molotov went to Leningrad, where the Zinovyevites were purged or won over, Zinovyev himself being ousted from the local party in favour of Stalin's ally Kirov. Zinovyev now had leisure to reflect on the justice of a jeer uttered at the Fourteenth Congress by the emerging Stalinist Mikoyan: 'When Zinovyev is in the majority he is for iron discipline. . . . When he lacks a majority, even for a moment, he is against it.'[10] This reproach falls not only on Zinovyev, but also on Trotsky, Kamenev and almost all other oppositionists of whatever persuasion.

The organizational changes following the Fourteenth Congress included the usual expansion of the Central Committee, which was now yet further Stalinized. The Politburo was expanded to include nine full members instead of seven, Kamenev (but not yet Zinovyev) being downgraded to the status of candidate, while the Stalinists Voroshilov, Kalinin and Molotov were elevated to full membership.

The Route to the Summit

Stalin's struggle for supreme power was spread over some eight years, being one of the most remarkable examples of self-assertion on record, and it is natural to pause in mid-narrative to review the techniques of power-gathering which he was perfecting as he went along.

By early 1926 the Secretary-General has completed the third act of the five-act struggle which is carrying him to the position of unchallenged dictator. Among those who have potentially threatened him, Lenin has been removed by the good fortune of his paralysing illness and premature death; Trotsky has been temporarily neutralized by his withdrawal from the War Commissariat; Zinovyev and Kamenev have wilted under the Secretary-General's hammer blows. With these victories behind him Stalin is ready for the two final campaigns of the decade: that of 1926–7 in which he will destroy the United Opposition of Trotsky, Zinovyev and Kamenev; and that of 1928–9 in which he will crush the Right Opposition represented by Bukharin, Rykov and Tomsky.

In all these contests Stalin enjoyed or exploited the advantage of a central position. In debate he would either adopt an intermediate posture for tactical reasons, or else artificially create it by positing two more or less imaginary deviationist extremes between which he himself occupied middle ground as the most reasonable among the contenders. Posing as the one cool head among the Party leaders, Stalin still exuded an air of harmless dependability congenial to those who feared the extremism of such zealots as Trotsky and Zinovyev.

To what extent was the Stalin of the 1920s already a monster-in-embryo? Tough, ruthless, sly and unscrupulous though he had always been, he resembled in these qualities many another historical figure who has not – when exalted to supreme power – proved so persistent a slaughterer of his fellows. For the moment he was no more than an unusually clever, quietly determined power-seeking politician – one who was prepared to go to all lengths, and to use all means, in strengthening his position.

Stalin's great sequence of political victories cannot be attributed solely to superior ruthlessness combined with a capacity for seeming harmless. His greatest advantage over all other contenders was, surely, his ability to learn from experience. Here he showed flexibility which might seem surprising in one whose behaviour pattern was so militantly anti-intellectual. Learning from his own mistakes, solving each successive problem as it came along, this modest empiricist eventually plodded his way into the excesses of the Great Terror. And yet, though all this remains true, Stalin's achievement was, paradoxically, far more creative than has been allowed by any of his biographers. Derided by Trotsky and others as – in effect – no more than the biggest wheel in a mighty bureaucratic machine, Stalin deserves more credit, or discredit, than he has received for helping to design, build, fuel and fire that machine in the first place. In the new, unprecedented and chaotic situation of revolutionary Russia, where old traditions had been overthrown, where new practices were slow to take their place – a situation which baffled colleagues more intellectual, erudite, cultured and ideologically-minded – Stalin instinctively sensed the real possibilities. Far from being the accidental product of blind bureaucratic forces proceeding by some mysterious momentum of their own, he was himself responsible, to a greater extent than has been conceded, for setting those forces in motion in the first place. If Stalin sensed the mysterious rules of the new game better than any rival, this was partly due to his greater subtlety and sensitivity. But it was also due to his skill in inventing and imposing the very rules of the game even as he played it. Nor should we forget that the newly created Soviet bureaucracy, through which Stalin worked, consisted almost exclusively of individuals lacking practical experience of any genuinely democratic process, just as they were unconversant with democratic political theory.

There is, therefore, no reason to deny to the Great Stalin the title of genius so lavishly and sycophantically conferred on him in the heyday of his cult – though we must add that his genius was of quite a different order from that claimed for him by Stalinist propaganda. Nor, we must remind ourselves, was genius alone enough to turn this phenomenal late developer into the most powerful individual known to history. He also had, and needed, a great deal of luck.

When, in 1922, Lenin had referred to the 'boundless power' accumulated by Stalin during his first months at the Secretariat, the statement had been prophetic rather than strictly accurate. But by 1926 Lenin's claim no longer seemed fanciful, so successful had the Secretary-General been in insinuating his nominees into innumerable intermeshing committees, sub-committees, cells, commissions, bureaux and other bodies in Party, government and elsewhere. Ever tightening his grip on the highest organs, Stalin constantly increased his ability to determine appointments at lower levels too; and since these lower appointments, in turn, carried the right to vote members into higher office, the presence of obedient minions in all strata had created a vast structure of self-perpetuating vested interest. Shuttling his supporters up the hierarchies, while his opponents were shuttled down or out, Stalin was constantly strengthening his own position. The process could not be hidden from his adversaries, but they were fatally slow to realize how dangerous a Stalinist bureaucracy might become to themselves. They could resist only by initiating attacks on the Secretary-General – who himself had no need to pick such quarrels, since he was winning in any case. He could afford to sit back and wait for his enemies to come to him. It was they, therefore, who tended to figure as the aggressors while Stalin seemed a man of peace reluctantly involved in controversy by the importunities of quarrelsome self-seekers.

Though Stalin's shuffling of Party, government, trade union, Comintern, *Komsomol* and other appointments cannot be scrutinized in detail here, it is worth looking more closely at the general framework of his expanding operations inside the most important hierarchy of all: the central Party Apparatus. Within that Apparatus significant promotion began with candidate membership of the Central Committee: it continued with full membership of that Committee, and was followed by further elevation to such bodies as Orgburo, Secretariat and Central Control Commission,

Especially important was appointment to the Politburo, first as candidate and then as full member. The removal of senior rivals naturally proceeded in the opposite direction as these undesirables were successively ousted from full, and then from candidate membership, of the Politburo; after which they would lose full and then candidate membership of the Central Committee, this being followed and consummated by the ultimate sanction of expulsion from the Party. On their way down the ladder individuals often skipped a rung or two – while Stalin showed unflagging patience, and an acute sense of timing in provoking each successive fall. Neither precipitate nor over-cautious, he dealt with his opponents piecemeal, easing first Kamenev, then Zinovyev and then Trotsky down by one or two stages at a time in such a way that no sudden mass onslaught developed. Sometimes, as noted above, Stalin found it politic to delay the process of degrading individual enemies, urging restraint even as his minions were clamouring for their blood. Only at a late stage, when the Secretary-General at last had his rivals on the run, would he suddenly accelerate the progress of their ruin – overwhelming them with an avalanche of blows, himself ostentatiously wielding the whip.

This complex process evolved within the structure of democratic symbols originally created and ingeniously manipulated by Lenin, and further perverted by Stalin to the purposes of personal tyranny. Yet, however skilfully the Secretary-General might exploit liberal-sounding formulae, the Party's democratic or pseudo-democratic traditions continued to offer a serious potential threat to his position long after he appeared firmly established as supreme autocratic ruler. Taking its decisions by consensus or majority vote, the Politburo might have induced the Central Committee to deprive Stalin of the secretary-generalship and other key offices at any time during the 1920s and beyond, had its members possessed the desire and will-power to insist on such a demotion. Against this possibility Stalin was, of course, increasingly insuring himself by introducing supporters of proven docility. On occasion he would also neutralize potential opposition within the Politburo by appealing over its head to the Central Committee, for there were times when this larger and theoretically senior organization could be called in to redress a worrying imbalance within the smaller. Similar pressures could be exerted laterally or downwards through and on the other central organizations – the Orgburo and the Central Control Commission – below which a nationwide network of provincial and district Party committees was (as already described) subjected to remorseless Stalinization. Positions in the other hierarchies – of government, trade unions, Comintern, *Komsomol* and so on – were also held by Party members subject to the same filtering process which was everywhere replacing independent-minded Bolsheviks with officials responsive to the Secretary-General's whim.

Of the various arenas in which the great conflict was staged the Party congresses remained the most august, and – in view of the large number of participants – the most difficult for Stalin to manipulate. Second in significance were the Party conferences which alternated with the congresses but carried less authority, each type of major conclave being an annual event from 1919 until 1925. 1926, however, saw a new departure: for the first time since 1917 the Party held no annual congress, contenting itself with a mere conference (the Fifteenth) and postponing the Fifteenth *Congress* until the end of 1927. This tendency to space out meetings of the chief Party assembly was characteristic of maturing Stalinism, until over thirteen years are found elapsing between the Eighteenth (1939) and Nineteenth (1952) Congresses.

Successive Central Committees (as elected by each successive congress to serve until the next congress) continued throughout the 1920s and beyond to reflect Stalin's growing influence on their composition. In size, too, the Central Committee continued to grow, each newly elected body being larger than its predecessor ... and thus more malleable. From the mid-1920s the Central Committee was regularly meeting in concert with the full Central Control Commission in joint plenums attended by numbers progressively increasing and already well over a hundred, since candidates were present as well as full members. It was to such joint plenums that Party statutes had assigned the right to expel Party members by a two-thirds majority. Meeting at irregular but ever rarer intervals – about twice a month between congresses and conferences – the Central Committee also determined appointments and dismissals favourable to Stalin within the organs nominally subject to itself: the Politburo, the Orgburo and the Secretariat.

While exploiting the nominally democratic Party organization to further his ambitions, Stalin was also acquiring increasing influence within the OGPU. Only after expulsion from the Party did a Bolshevik become liable to arrest by this secular arm of Stalinism: a procedure which had been firmly established by the end of the 1920s; when, however, it still continued to be used sparingly by comparison with the Terror of the following decade. Banishment also became a useful method of dealing with oppositionists. Some were put out of harm's way by assignment to diplomatic posts abroad, as was Kamenev when he became, briefly in 1927, Soviet ambassador to Rome. Some were administratively exiled to the Soviet provinces: a fate which was to befall Trotsky – and, in milder degree, Zinovyev and Kamenev too – at the beginning of 1928.

The decade also witnessed the growth of violence and intimidation within Party meetings. Provincial and local gatherings were increasingly induced to vote virulent unanimous denunciations of the opposition, while oppositionist representatives were violently assailed – though only verbally at first – whenever they attempted to speak, by increasingly boisterous Stalin-briefed hecklers who hooted them down, shrieking abuse, and later hurled inkpots, tumblers, heavy bound volumes or other convenient missiles. Oppositionist meetings were broken up by persons variously described as hooligans or police: a distinction which was becoming more and more difficult to draw.

The growth of such gangsterlike methods throughout the late 1920s has done much to obscure the considerable forensic skill which Stalin was simultaneously deploying to his opponents' discomfiture. Though it is true that he could – and did – easily arrange for a Trotsky, a Zinovyev or a Kamenev to be shouted down by hooligans, it by no means follows that the Secretary-General was himself unable to stand up to these giants of debate, or that he could not take them on with their own weapons and beat them. Less showy, less coruscating, less intellectual in his methods, Stalin commanded a brutal finesse which often had his enemies smarting from his rapier thrusts even as they quailed before the verbal sledgehammer which also formed part of his armoury. Less hampered than his rivals by allegiance to principle, Stalin could give all his attention to the elaboration of debating ploys.

Socialism in One Country

Among the various weapons in Stalin's arsenal one had already begun to show itself particularly deadly: his new doctrine of Socialism in One Country. By the end of 1925 this was beginning to prove its value as a major bulwark of Stalinism against which the attacks of the Secretary-General's adversaries spent themselves in vain. To colleagues more ideologically inclined the successful launching of a new doctrine by the Secretary-General came as a shock, for Stalin's weakness as a political theorist had long been proverbial. His previous excursions into ideology had aroused only general contempt. 'Stop it, Koba, don't make a fool of yourself,' the learned Marxist Ryazanov had implored him on one occasion. 'Everybody knows that theory is not exactly your field.'[1] But now, by early 1926, the Ryazanovs were being forced to think again. Never, admittedly, would those Marxist thinkers who regarded doctrine as an art form, constructing ideologies for ideology's sake, have cause to regard the Secretary-General as a fellow-spirit. To Stalin, who subordinated his every word and deed to practical purposes, the erection of theoretical structures could never be an end in itself. Rather was ideology, in Stalin's eyes, yet another weapon in the battle for power: a weapon to be used discriminatingly and with a calculation of its practical effects, just as he used the rigging of appointments, the intimidation of opponents, bombardment by unanimous resolutions and the like.

Viewed from this point of view, Socialism in One Country was already beginning to justify itself beyond all expectations. If Stalin indeed stumbled on it 'unwittingly', as one historian has claimed,[2] we can only admire the political instincts which enabled him to blunder creatively in the dark, so many advantages did the new doctrine turn out to possess. Both in domestic and in foreign policy it served admirably to confound the Secretary-General's enemies. At home those who denied the possibility of building Socialism in One Country could be accused of having lost faith in the very revolutionary régime which they had helped to create, since they made its survival contingent on the eruption of other revolutions elsewhere – and this at a time when no such upheaval seemed to be in prospect. By opposing Socialism in One Country, Zinovyev and Kamenev therefore appeared to cast doubt on the wisdom of carrying out the original Bolshevik *coup* of October 1917 – an accusation jibing neatly with their notorious failure to back Lenin's seizure of power at that time. Even Trotsky, who had supported Lenin up to the hilt in October, found himself caught in the same logical trap. He, too, could be derided as hypercautious, pessimistic and lacking in self-reliance by comparison with the solidly confident Stalin, who firmly asserted that Bolshevism – despite NEP, despite the slow progress of industrialization – was essentially on the right road. Even when Stalin executed a complete *volte face* later in the decade, embracing a policy of militant industrialization and intensive collectivization similar to – but far outstripping – that of Trotsky . . . even then Socialism in One Country still served to bolster the Secretary-General and despite his abrupt change of course; for now Stalin was clearly engaged in building a Socialist society by the efforts of that society alone – as deployed independently of the prospects for further revolutions in other parts of the world.

Socialism in One Country also served Stalin as a stick to beat his opponents' policies towards the other Socialist parties of the world. Relying, in their foreign policy, on global revolution, these rivals appeared guilty of an error diametrically opposed to the hyper-caution and pessimism which they allegedly showed on the domestic front. In this area Stalin could portray them as rashly eager to provoke hostile capitalist states by attempting to foment workers' revolutions within them, thereby hazarding all

174

the Soviet Union's gains at home in the interests of a quixotic and unrealistic foreign policy. As this accusation illustrates, the arguments of each side had become polarized, as is common with political controversy, all their differences being exaggerated in consequence. Despite the concentration of Stalin's main efforts on the extension of his own power within the Soviet Union, he had by no means abandoned all hope of an ultimate world revolution, as his opponents asserted. Nor, on the home front, did those opponents wish to dismantle the Soviet régime by cravenly relinquishing power: the logical conclusion of their policies, according to the sneering accusations levelled against them by Stalin. Somehow, though, whenever the welkin rang with such jeers, Socialism in One Country always seemed to give Stalin a debating edge over his adversaries. And yet, however prominently this formula might figure as the central issue in controversy – one on which all the many arguments over Soviet economic and foreign policy seemed in the end to turn – its chief value remained that of a decoy. For Socialism in One Country was by no means the most important political question of the decade, being all the more useful to Stalin because it distracted attention from an issue which mattered infinitely more: who, in the end, would wield how much power in the Soviet Union? The longer Stalin's opponents and supporters could be bamboozled into arguing the secondary issues centring on Socialism in One Country, the more effectively could Stalin strengthen his hidden levers while their attention was thus diverted.

Socialism in One Country also served to clinch the personal allegiance of Stalin's minions. Of what might or might not happen in foreign climes members of his faction on the whole knew little and cared less. Even less than Stalin were they citizens of the world, such as many Old Bolsheviks of Lenin's entourage could claim to be, having resided abroad for years or decades as political émigrés. Stalin, who had spent only a few fleeting weeks outside the Russian and Soviet Empire, was – like his growing mass of henchmen – far less of a European than Trotsky, Zinovyev, Kamenev and hundreds of other former political émigrés. Knowing no western European language – if we except the Latin which he had studied at the Seminary – the Secretary-General represented a home-based tradition founded on Russian patriotism (as adopted by a Georgian) rather than on internationalism. To the Party's rough-hewn practical organizers and managers Socialism in One Country also appealed because of its optimistic message. It told them that their efforts were not in vain: that they were building something positive, something which would last irrespective of developments in foreign parts... whereas the contrary Trotskyite-Zinovyevite creed seemed to cast doubt on the very essence of Soviet achievement, making the ultimate impact of the Russian revolution dependent on events which might or might not take place beyond the Bolsheviks' control in faraway countries of which they knew nothing.

To this bond must be added yet another which further united Stalin with his following, and which further estranged the Secretary-General's faction from Bolsheviks of more cosmopolitan colouring: militant anti-intellectualism. When Stalin invoked, as he repeatedly did, the image of whining, pathetic Party intellectuals alienated from life, from the workers, and from the revolution, he struck a particularly responsive chord in his followers. These were, like their leader, rough, not particularly well-educated men. They had not attended university and they disliked theoretical argument. Bolsheviks of this stamp could identify themselves far more easily with Stalin than with his better educated, more europeanized, more intellectual rivals. They preferred Stalin because they saw him as a man of action like themselves, not a man of words. This was something of an illusion, for Stalin too split words by the hundred thousand in the course of the inner-party struggle. But his words were simpler and sharper, his sentences shorter and more telling than those of his rivals. The vaguer, obscurer, more verbose – but not necessarily subtler – formulations of those rivals might well be superior as samples of the orator's art to the bludgeoning repetitive speech in which Stalin denounced and mocked them. But the rough, homespun Stalinists did not think so. They preferred their leader's style as well as the contents of his message; they liked his bluff sense of humour; they cheered the sarcasms and jibes which he directed at the Old Bolshevik intellectuals. Here was a practical man, an organizer, whom other practical men could understand and follow. For such a seemingly straightforward, realistic, non-intellectual, anti-ideological leader the plain man's no-nonsense doctrine of Socialism in One Country proved ideally suited.

Stalin's pet doctrine received a more elaborate formulation in an important essay of January 1926: 'On Questions of Leninism'. Still polemicizing with his opponents, and chiefly with the defeated Zinovyev, the Secretary-General here repeats yet again that the building of Socialism *is* possible – and fully possible – in a single country. It does not depend on the sympathetic outbreak of revolution elsewhere. Nor is Russia's admitted technological backwardness any unsurmountable deterrent to the achievement of Socialism, as is sometimes suggested. But the new Socialist structure cannot – and this is the Secretary-General's sole reservation – be fully guaranteed against foreign intervention so long as capitalism continues to exist in the advanced countries of the world.

Henceforward Socialism in One Country, as expounded in this latest and most considered definition, is to form the main theoretical plank in Stalin's political platform. Publishing, in book form in February 1926, an anthology of his theoretical work – to which he gave the title *Problems of Leninism,* adapted from that of his January essay – the Secretary-General was now asserting a place in the line of thinkers which had run from Marx and Engels through Lenin. *Problems of Leninism* was eventually issued in a succession of eleven editions spaced over the remaining years of the author's life, important new pronouncements being added to it in course of time, while some of the less significant were periodically removed in order to keep the work within the scope of a single volume. The tome became, in its various recensions, an authoritative repository of the gospel according to Stalin. What he lacked in other respects by comparison with the founding fathers of Marxism, the Secretary-General made up for in clarity. At least one could always understand just what lesson he was ostensibly hammering home at any given moment, even if the hidden connection between that crystalline message and his ultimate political purposes was often elusive in the extreme.

The United Opposition Vanquished

The United Opposition to Stalin appears to have been founded in April 1926. Trotsky now revived his former militancy and joined his previous antagonists Zinovyev and Kamenev in an alliance rendered uneasy by memories of much scurrilous mutual abuse.[1] To Trotskyites and Zinovyevites were added the rumps of other former oppositionist movements such as the Democratic Centralists and the Workers' Opposition – and also Lenin's widow Krupskaya. They formed a loose association of anti-Stalinists said to have been between four and eight thousand strong.[2]

The first clash between Stalin and the United Oppositionists took place at a Central Committee plenum of July 1926 after the Opposition had issued a manifesto denouncing Party bureaucracy. Criticizing concessions made by the ruling Stalinist faction to the richer peasants termed 'kulaks', the oppositionists now proposed to collectivize agriculture and promote intensive industrialization: the very programme which Stalin himself was to steal from them two years later. In the sphere of foreign affairs the oppositionists attacked Stalin's common front with Socialists outside the USSR – denouncing, for example the Anglo-Soviet Council, which was based on an agreement between the trade unions of the two countries. When Trotsky attacked this policy, Stalin leapt to its defence, accusing Trotsky of adventurism and favouring the politics of the 'dramatic gesture'. And when the Opposition once again harped on Lenin's Testament, Stalin showed his growing strength by blandly promising to ask permission from the next Party Congress to publish it; he further flaunted his self-confidence by reading out to the Central Committee another statement of Lenin's almost equally damaging to his reputation: the anti-Stalinist notes 'On the Nationalities Question' of December 1922.[3]

Stalin went on to attack the Opposition for fractionalism, and he accused Zinovyev of turning the Comintern into a hotbed of anti-Leninism. Despite the formidable debating team fielded by the Secretary-General's opponents, the Central Committee upheld him on all counts and voted for Zinovyev's dismissal from the Politburo. The vacant place went to a prominent Stalinist, Rudzutak, while candidate membership of the Politburo was simultaneously conferred on a quintet of other rising Stalinists: Andreyev, Kaganovich, Kirov, Mikoyan, Ordzhonikidze. Meanwhile Stalin allowed Trotsky to retain his Politburo membership for the time being. By this gesture – for Trotsky's participation in Politburo meetings had in practice long been curtailed – and by handling the Trotskyites of the United Opposition more gently than the Zinovyevites, the Secretary-General helped to plant dissension between these uneasy, newly allied partners.

Thus blocked in the Central Committee, the oppositionists could hope to defeat Stalin only by appealing directly to the Party rank and file. They therefore sent missionaries into the provinces, hoping somehow to build up Union-wide support. In late September 1926 they were haranguing Party cells in a number of factories, but were severely harassed by Stalinists briefed to shout them down. Soon realizing that they were making no headway, the Opposition leaders went back to Stalin, and asked – in effect – for a truce. They agreed to treat all Central Committee decisions as binding, and to abjure fractionalism. Stalin also compelled them to disavow their supporters: a manoeuvre calculated to impair their popularity within their own faction. As a further device for prying Zinovyev, Kamenev and Trotsky loose from their following, the Secretary-General left the top stratum of the Opposition relatively immune, while increasingly imposing on humbler Trotskyites and Zinovyevites the disciplines of banishment, transfer to distant parts, dismissal from office, loss of Party membership . . . and, eventually, arrest. The oppositionist rank and file thus received an opportunity to ponder both the perfidy of their leadership in renouncing its followers and its weakness in being unable to protect them.

Incensed with the Secretary-General's tactics, Trotsky accused him, at a Politburo meeting held on 23 October, of 'offering his candidature for the post of gravedigger to the Revolution'; whereupon the normally phlegmatic Stalin blenched and rushed out, slamming the door.[4] A few days later he took his revenge in the Theses which he presented to the

Fifteenth Party Conference, and in two long, superbly cynical, sarcastic harangues delivered to that conclave.[5] He invoked Trotsky's abuse of Zinovyev and Kamenev, and their abuse of Trotsky, while lavishly quoting the Leninist scriptures to prove all three guilty of direst heresy. Himself no mean niggler over the minutiae of Party dogma, Stalin accused Trotsky of juggling with Leninist phrases, and pronounced a sermon on the need to develop Marx and Engels creatively while renouncing dogmatic attachment to the dead letter of texts written fifty or sixty years earlier. That Stalin was secretly savouring the irony of these condescending homilies is evident from the flavour of his text.

The Secretary-General also wielded with relish his favourite slogan: Socialism in One Country. The Oppositionists' rejection of this doctrine was (he jeered) a symptom of weariness, vacillation, defeatism and despondency alien to the proletariat; while their zeal in attempting to promote world revolution was a sign of ultra-leftist self-deception and revolutionary adventurism. The Opposition's policy was hostile to the peasantry; it sought to break the bond between Soviet peasant and Soviet worker; it disparaged the leading role of the Party Apparatus. Small wonder that the Opposition was praised abroad – and by such riff-raff as émigré Russian Socialist Revolutionaries, Mensheviks and Kadets! As for Trotsky's newly forged alliance with his former enemies Kamenev and Zinovyev, this had only led to their mutual castration. It was a union of eunuchs! Stalin also taunted them with the recent defection of an influential, though somewhat embarrassing adherent: Krupskaya, who had recently been induced to abandon their cause ... perhaps through a threat which Stalin is believed to have made: that the Party would 'appoint someone else as Lenin's widow'.[6]

The oppositionists did their best to hit back from the conference floor. Not for the first time Kamenev showed himself especially bold, but sadly out of touch with the emerging epoch: 'We are not living in the Middle Ages; witch trials cannot be staged now; you can't burn us at the stake.'[7] Trotsky and Zinovyev also spoke, hampered by uncouth yells such as had become an established feature of protocol on these occasions. A pack of Stalinists, among whom Bukharin was outstanding, vied in maligning the Opposition in terms yet more virulent than those used by Stalin himself: a service which did not save such leading officials as Chubar, Gamarnik, Syrtsov and Uglanov from being driven to their death in the following decade, any more than it prevented the judicial murder of Bukharin. Meanwhile Bukharin's intemperate words at the Fifteenth Conference drew a bluff word of praise from his master: 'Good old Bukharin; he wields a knife, not a tongue.'[8]

The Fifteenth Conference set the seal on Stalin's victory over the United

Opposition. On the eve of the Conference the Central Committee had deprived Trotsky of his Politburo membership and Kamenev of his candidate-membership. Zinovyev was dismissed from the Comintern's Executive Committee: a prelude to his total elimination from the Comintern as confirmed a few weeks later by a plenum of that committee. Here a pungent address was delivered by a Stalin whom even foreigners as well as Soviet citizens must now recognize as the most powerful man in Russia. Foreign politicians, including the British Foreign Secretary Austen Chamberlain, greeted with relief the advent of so statesmanlike, so moderate, so restrained a figure after the world had so long been intimidated yet amused by the revolutionary threats of his toppled rivals.[9]

After a seasonal lull in early 1927 the battle between Stalin and the United Opposition flared up again. On 12 April the Chinese nationalist leader Chiang Kai-shek took a step which suddenly discredited Stalin's foreign policy. The Chinese Communists had, much against their will, been compelled by the Secretary-General to form an alliance with Chiang Kai-shek's Kuomintang. But now, in Shanghai, the Kuomintang leader suddenly massacred these reluctant allies by their tens of thousands, thereby signalizing the collapse of Stalin's policies in China and giving the Soviet Opposition a weapon which might have been more effective a year or two earlier. But such was Stalin's grip by 1927 that he could already afford even major mistakes. Another such error became manifest, again in the area of foreign affairs, when the British Government broke off relations with the Soviet Union in May 1927: the sequel to a police raid which produced evidence that the Soviet trade mission's premises in London had been operating as a centre for espionage and subversion. But though Stalin's policy of commercial rapprochement with the British now stood in ruins alongside his Chinese policy, he yet derived some profit from this rupture by inflating his disagreement with Britain into a war scare; this put a premium on unity within the Party, making it possible for him to pillory dissident members as potential traitors.

Difficult as their position had become, the oppositionists renewed their attack on Stalin in May 1927, when his vulnerable Chinese policy was denounced to the Comintern by Trotsky. China also figured in an anti-Stalinist declaration signed by eighty-three dissidents and dated 26 May. The signatories repeated a familiar demand that they should be permitted to publish a political manifesto. Among Stalin's countermeasures was the transfer or banishment – it was not clear which – of the prominent oppositionist Smilga to eastern Siberia. This provoked, in mid-June, an impromptu political demonstration by Party members against the current Party line – an event unprecedented in Soviet annals – the offenders being oppositionists who had gathered at a Moscow railway station to speed Smilga on his way. Trotsky and Zinovyev both made speeches, and though the political contents were fairly inoffensive, the very holding of such a meeting was an act of indiscipline. Shortly afterwards the offenders were brought before the Party's inquisition – its Central Control Commission – to answer for this misdemeanour. Trotsky defied his judges. Until he was physically gagged (he said) he intended to go on criticizing the Stalin régime, which would otherwise undermine all the achievements of the October Revolution, besides being useless, unstable, ideologically weak, superficial and shortsighted. Deriding Stalin's minions, Trotsky mocked their habit of recording unanimous votes at the Secretary-General's behest. Today they were covering Trotsky and Zinovyev with abuse such as, tomorrow, they would pour on Stalin's current allies Bukharin and Rykov: a prophecy soon to be abundantly fulfilled. No less prophetically barbed was the derisive rhetorical question which Trotsky posed when he inquired at what stage the victorious Stalinists intended to begin shooting oppositionists.[10]

In the following month Trotsky and Zinovyev again appeared before the Party inquisition. Defiant as ever, Trotsky concluded another fighting speech with the words: 'For a Socialist fatherland? Yes. For the Stalin line? No.'[11] Despite such outspokenness these two senior offenders received no more than a severe reprimand.

In September 1927 the oppositionists again attempted to appeal to the Party rank and file against the Stalin-dominated Central Committee. They set up a secret printing press to reproduce their officially banned political programme – thus reviving a practice familiar from Tsarist times – but soon learnt that they were pitting themselves against a force more powerful than the Imperial Okhrana. Barely had their illicit press begun operations when the OGPU swooped, acting on information from an *agent provocateur*. Several organizers of the press were expelled from the Party, and one (Mrachkovsky) was arrested; he was the most prominent Bolshevik yet to be imprisoned for political misbehaviour.

The futility of this conspiracy was amply demonstrated at the next Central Committee plenum, that of 21-23 October 1927. It was yet another triumph for Stalin, who now attacked the Opposition more venomously and effectively than ever before. Trotsky had ill-advisedly tried to frighten him yet again with the bogy of Lenin's Testament, claiming – correctly – that this document had been concealed from the Party. Rejecting the accusation as a slander, the Secretary-General went on to quote at length, and with devastating effect, Trotsky's own statement of two years previously: that in which he had falsely denied (and to please Stalin) the very existence of any such Testament! Now here was Stalin sneeringly conceding that the document *did* exist after all . . . and showing himself no whit perturbed over the matter. He did not even shrink from invoking the seemingly deadly Postscript in which his own removal from the secretary-generalship had been proposed on grounds of his toughness, roughness, crudeness or rudeness – the word *gruby*, in the original, conveys all these flavours. With superb effrontery Stalin continued as follows:

> It is said that Lenin's Testament invited the [Twelfth] Congress to consider Stalin's replacement as Secretary-General by another comrade in view of Stalin's 'toughness'. *This is perfectly true.* Yes, Comrades, I *am* tough – tough with those who crudely and perfidiously destroy and split the Party. I did not conceal it then; I do not conceal it now. Very possibly the Party schismatics do require kid-glove treatment here; but that isn't my line of country.'

In any case, Stalin continued, Lenin's Testament had not so much as hinted at any *political* mistakes made by himself; for 'toughness', however regrettable, was no political defect such as those with which Lenin had charged Stalin's rivals.[12] That Lenin had violently disparaged members of the present Opposition Stalin was unlikely to let anyone forget; he now emphasized as much by having *Pravda* publish, with facsimiles, the letters of 18 and 19 October 1917 in which Lenin had proposed to exclude Zinovyev and Kamenev from the party as political blacklegs or 'strikebreakers of the Revolution'.[13]

Turning to the accusation that dissident Bolsheviks were being imprisoned on an increasing scale, Stalin again showed that the best form of defence is attack. 'Yes, we *are* arresting them. And we mean to go on doing so unless they stop undermining the Party and the Soviet Government.' Such incarcerations (said Stalin) were by no means as unprecedented as the Opposition alleged. What about the Myasnikov Group and adherents of Workers' Truth imprisoned back in 1923? Those arrests had been expressly approved by Trotsky, Zinovyev and Kamenev. If one could arrest Bolsheviks then, why not now?[14] To this just reproach neither Trotsky nor Zinovyev nor Kamenev would ever be able to find any telling riposte. Having created, approved and administered political repression, first outside and then inside the Party, they were in no position to claim themselves mysteriously exempted from the very sanctions which they had so enthusiastically endorsed in the first place.

In the same speech Stalin at last made a firm demand for the expulsion of Trotsky and Zinovyev – not as yet from the Party, but from its Central Committee. Previously the Secretary-General had pleaded – as he now reminded his audience – for leniency towards Trotsky and Zinovyev. Many had cursed him for this, said Stalin, evoking a characteristic response from his claque: 'Yes, and we still do curse you for it.'[15] The effect of this little pantomime was, once again, to present the Secretary-General as an easy-going, decent fellow, who needed to be recalled to the stern path of recti-tude by the voices of 'honest' Bolsheviks . . . no doubt carefully briefed with their responses in advance.

When necessary, Stalin could operate unsupported by his claque. He showed as much on 5 November 1927 during a six-hour discussion with eighty delegates from workers' parties in Germany, France, South America, China and other regions of the world. Here he adroitly parried awkward queries which showed how little subject his guests were to Soviet-type pol-itical disciplines. Why, they asked, was there no freedom of the press in the USSR? But there was, said Stalin. It was not, of course, freedom for the bourgeoisie, but for the proletariat: a term which increasingly tended, in the Secretary-General's mouth, to serve as a synonym for the first person singu-lar pronoun. Why were Mensheviks still languishing in Soviet jails, the foreign Socialists asked. But the Mensheviks had even tried to arrest the great Lenin in summer 1917, Stalin told them; what else could they expect? Further taxed with the excesses of the OGPU, and with the growing Soviet vogue for arbitrary political arrests, Stalin blandly admitted that such things did occur. To the bourgeoisie they were naturally abhorrent. But the Soviet worker respected the OGPU as a faithful defender of revolution; and there was something wrong with any foreign Socialist who might feel differently on the subject.[16] To one barbed question – were the Comintern and the Russian Party indeed betraying the workers to counter-revolution? – Stalin replied in a passage typical of his personal style in a moment of self-indulgence. The imputation was only too well founded, he confirmed. Yes, of course the Comintern and Russian Party were busily betraying the work-ing class to counter-revolutionaries all over the world. Nor was that all, for the Party now proposed to permit émigré capitalists and landlords to return to Russia, and to repossess their factories and estates. The Party had also decided that Bolsheviks should eat human flesh; nationalize women; em-bark on the systematic rape of their own sisters! This sally ended amid 'general laughter'.[17]

Meanwhile the United Opposition was attempting to carry the struggle against Stalin into the streets. On 7 November 1927, the tenth anniversary of the Bolshevik *coup*, they staged dissident demonstrations in Leningrad and Moscow. But such was their fear of sinning by fractionalism that they marched under harmless-seeming slogans which conveyed little to the mas-ses, being distinguishable as subversive only by experts in political analysis. In any case Stalin's police and 'honest' loyalist hooligans soon moved in, dispersing the demonstrators and tearing down the offending banners.

This pathetic enterprise only made it easier for the Secretary-General to complete the rout of the United Opposition. A week after the anniversary demonstrations, Trotsky and Zinovyev were both expelled from the Party. Now, at last, as the Fifteenth Congress assembled on 2 December 1927, Stalin was ready to celebrate total victory. Securing from the ejected Zinovyev and Kamenev a complete recantation of their political sins, the Secretary-General forced them to castigate themselves as anti-Leninist. Then, having compelled them to grovel, he contemptuously refused to have them back in the Party, granting them only the right to apply for readmission after a six-month interval. By now the United Opposition was united no longer; the Zinovyevites had parted company from the more recalcitrant Trotskyites, who took their cue from their disgraced but still defiant leader, refusing to perform ritual self-abasement in full.

Trotsky did not himself attend the Fifteenth Congress – which was just as well, for never had the rowdiness of Stalin-briefed hecklers been so outrageously deployed at a major conclave. By now the Secretary-General and his creatures had elaborated a complex technique of antiphonal responses between Leader and Chorus, of which the following passage (taken from the Secretary-General's main political report) is an example.

STALIN: The Opposition is said to be intending to present Congress with some statement or other about its submitting, now and in future, to all Party decisions –

A VOICE: *Isn't this October 1926 all over again?*

STALIN: – and about dissolving its fraction –

VOICE: *We've heard that twice before!*

STALIN: – and about defending its views, which it does not renounce –

VOICES: *Not likely! We'd far better dissolve them ourselves!*

STALIN: – within the framework of the Party statutes –

VOICES: *Yes, with all sorts of little reservations! Our framework ain't elastic!*[18]

As this exchange illustrates, some passages in the Secretary-General's *Works* might form the basis for a musical comedy script, while also recalling those exchanges in ancient Greek drama known as stichomythia.

The Fifteenth Congress saw seventy-five prominent Trotskyite-Zinovyevites expelled from the Party; to these were added fifteen Democratic Centralists. Further expulsions followed among the Party rank and file, to the tune of about fifteen hundred members; others (some 2,500) hastened to file their recantations.[19] In January 1928 the OGPU carried off – literally – the passively protesting Trotsky and deposited him in Alma Ata near the distant frontier of Soviet Central Asia. In all, thirty leading Trotskyites were banished at this time, while Zinovyev and Kamenev were sent only as far as Kaluga, a mere eight hundred miles from Moscow. This concession was earned by the abject recantations which they had made and which Trotsky had spurned. Such was the present fate of those whom Stalin described – by no means fancifully – as petty bourgeois intellectuals cut off from Life, from the Revolution, from the Party and from the Workers.[20]

The Stalin of the Fifteenth Congress showed continuing skill in exploiting the vocabulary of democracy – as Lenin had taught him – to attack such remnants of liberty, equality and fraternity as might yet lurk within odd crannies of the Party:

> Only the blind can fail to see [a typical formula] that our inner-party democracy, real inner-party democracy . . . is growing and developing. People babble of democracy. But what *is* Party democracy? Democracy for whom? If democracy means freedom for a couple of intellectuals alienated from the Revolution to chatter endlessly, to have their own press organ and so on, then we don't need such 'democracy', because it is only democracy for an insignificant minority which seeks to break the will of the overwhelming majority. But if by democracy we mean freedom for the Party masses to solve the problems of construction; if we mean an increase in the Party masses' activity; if we mean bringing them into the Party leadership; if we mean developing in them a feeling that they are masters of the Party . . . then such a democracy we do have. We need it. Come what may, we shall develop it unswervingly.[21]

Alongside true democracy, true collective leadership was also flourishing, the emerging absolute ruler no less unjustifiably averred.

> The solution of our most vital problems is being increasingly transferred from a narrow élite to a broad Centre closely linked with all branches of construction and with all regions of our boundless land. Is that not a fact?[22]

It was not. But what whimperer or unstable element dare say as much after the Fifteenth Congress had deprived Party members of any lingering freedom to express independent opinions? Within a decade or so most oppositionists would also have been deprived of their lives. But so, too, would a majority among those creatures of the Secretary-General who were now so zealously hounding miserable, whimpering petty bourgeois oppositionist intellectuals, blissfully unaware that their own turn for political and physical extinction would come round in due course.

Bukharin Overwhelmed

By the beginning of 1928 Stalin had unquestionably become the most powerful individual in the Soviet Union. Yet he was still no more than the first among near-equals. In the newly elected nine-man Politburo he could count on a majority for the moment. But could he count on retaining it? By no means everyone took his continuing ascendancy for granted;

for example, Trotsky was inclined to predict the victory of Bukharin, whose right-wing views he abominated.[1]

This new stage in Stalin's career coincided with a spectacular policy switch. Now it was that he dropped the cautious programme associated with Bukharin and NEP in favour of intensive industrialization and farm collectivization. So far-reaching were the effects that a new and yet more drastic revolution seemed to be taking place from 1929 onwards. But a change may be sweeping without necessarily occurring abruptly. It was by many barely perceptible touches on the helm that the Secretary-General gradually accomplished a complete reversal of course, while pretending to steam ahead in a straight line. Thus did Stalin apply the very policy – rapid industrialization combined with exploitation of the peasantry – for which he had long condemned Trotsky . . . and for which he, of course, continued to condemn Trotsky all the more ferociously even as he himself was becoming an unacknowledged super-Trotskyite. Increasingly a leftist deviant from the Party line of pre-1928 years, Stalin also contrived to pillory Bukharin and other former allies of his own for the crime of rightist deviation. All that meant was that they had failed to wheel to the left along with Stalin.

The years 1928–9 also witnessed the further development of Stalinism as a control system. Long familiar techniques – rigged elections within the hierarchies, prearranged 'spontaneous' unanimous resolutions, intimidatory heckling, censorship, the suppression of information and the like – were intensified, as also was the activity of the OGPU: now deployed on an ever-increasing scale to imprison and banish political offenders. The same two-year period also sees the first Stalinist show trial and the first execution of a Party member for a political offence: precedents ominous in the extreme.

Just when did Stalin decide to change course? It is hard to be sure. So opposed had he been to intensive industrialization back in April 1926 that he had even denounced the Dnieper Dam which was one day to become the prime symbol of industrializing Stalinism. The Soviet Union simply could not afford the big dam, he had sneered when it was in the planning stage – this was like a peasant buying a gramophone with money needed to mend his plough or renew his stock.[2] Had Stalin already decided on his new leftist course at the Fifteenth Party Congress of December 1927? Without abandoning NEP – the economic system introduced in 1921, whereby small-scale capitalism was permitted to operate within a general framework of State control – that conclave had yet passed resolutions approving collectivization and industrialization: resolutions cautious in their terms, but sufficient to serve the Secretary-General later as a pretext for maintaining that his new course had been laid down in advance by a Party congress.

Even as he was steering the country towards headlong collectivization and industrialization, Stalin continued to pay lip-service to NEP as the basis of Soviet economic policy. No less typically, he was still praising individual husbandry as a necessary concomitant to collective agriculture even as he embarked on the wholesale destruction of small-scale peasant farming. That deep-laid cunning lay behind these pronouncements cannot be doubted; but it does not follow that every move was planned as part of a diabolical conspiracy. Solving each problem pragmatically, with his personal status always an overriding consideration, the Secretary-General moved sure-footedly from one crisis to another as each stage carried him further towards absolute personal despotism.

What of Stalin's motives? Was he a power-crazed tyrant obsessed by a need to assert himself? A paranoiac fighting off an infinitude of imaginary enemies? Or a fanatical Marxist dedicated to strengthening the one country in which Socialism so far held sway? Was total industrialization chiefly important to Stalin as a tool to destroy Bukharin? As a means of foisting totalitarian controls on the country at large? Or was the power struggle more important to him as a grotesque multi-dimensional chess game involving countless expendable pieces?

The rout of the United Opposition coincided with a threatened food shortage. One cause was grain hoarding by peasants who were waiting for a better price – or preferred to turn their surplus stocks into home-brewed spirits. Must the State, then, be held to ransom by the many millions of small farmers who produced its basic foodstuffs; who still formed, with their families, a majority of the population? Not if Stalin could help it! There were two possible long-term solutions. The mild ('rightist') approach was to offer the peasant greater incentives: better prices, better consumer goods. The harsher ('leftist') solution was intensive collectivization: the wholesale dispossession of individual small-holders, combined with their enserfment in collective and state farms which would produce and deliver to order. The former was Bukharin's solution. It was Stalin's too until 1928.

In January 1928 it was still the short-term problem which most concerned the Secretary-General: how to make the peasants disgorge existing stocks. As a leading sponsor of grain extraction by force, he spent three weeks of January-February 1928 inspecting the crop-producing areas of western Siberia. He visited Novosibirsk, Barnaul and Omsk – haranguing local authorities, threatening direst penalties. Denouncing the hoarding kulaks as responsible for the emergency, the Secretary-General also attacked local Party officials for failing to squeeze these socially hostile elements. He threatened grain-hoarders with criminal proceedings as speculators, and he brow-beat officials of the local judiciary for laxness in enforcing this provision. Offering a quarter of any newly discovered grain stocks to poor peasants at concessionary rates,[3] Stalin was bribing the more indigent villagers to inform on their richer neighbours (few of whom were affluent by non-Soviet standards). This kulak-baiting policy was designed to pay off economically – by making more grain available – but later played an increasing political role. Where a gap could be created or widened between poor and less poor villagers, the Soviet peasantry was deterred from offering united resistance to the terrible onslaught which Stalin was soon to launch.

Stalin's Siberian expedition of early 1928 is the only recorded occasion on which he came near to dirtying his boots with the proverbial mud – now frozen – of the Russian village, as was stressed by Khrushchev in 1956:

> Stalin separated himself from the people and never went anywhere. This lasted for decades. The last time he visited a village was in January 1928 when he visited Siberia in connection with grain deliveries.[4]

Among auguries of future Stalin-sponsored disasters no episode of the 1920s was more ominous than the so-called Shakhty Trial. This affair was staged in May-July 1928, being the Secretary-General's first notable enterprise as a special kind of theatrical impresario. Here, as often, he was reviving a tradition established under Lenin: the only previous Soviet show trial of any importance had been that of certain Socialist Revolutionaries in Moscow in 1922. Like this predecessor, the Shakhty affair was a disciplinary and educative pageant designed to drill the Soviet people in the postures of servility.

The charges were based on information laid by an OGPU official, Ye. G. Yevdokimov, who also happened to be a drinking crony of the Secretary-General's.[5] When Yevdokimov charged mining engineers in the Donbass township of Shakhty with sabotaging coal production at the behest of foreign capitalists, we may suspect – though we do not know – that Stalin had put him up to make these accusations in the first place. The charges seemed far-fetched: flooding pits; breaking machinery; causing explosions; arson. Even the OGPU chief Menzhinsky rejected them; indeed, he offered to prosecute Yevdokimov for sabotage, since his accusations threatened to damage the economy by removing valued experts. But Yevdokimov appealed to Stalin, who sanctioned the prosecution against the protests of Politburo colleagues.[6]

That the Shakhty Trial was chiefly a macabre public relations exercise soon became clear. A two-month press campaign preceded lavishly advertised court proceedings which were staged before an audience including diplomats and foreign newspaper correspondents. No evidence other than their own confessions was offered against the fifty-two accused, who – to judge from Eugene Lyons's eyewitness account of the trial – had been intimidated and tortured in custody by the OGPU until they were ready to repeat a prearranged script before the arc-lights.[7] At these barbarous proceedings the question of guilt was irrelevant, the trial being a didactic pageant, not a legal process. No detail more typifies emerging Stalinism than the role of the twelve-year-old son of Andrey Kolodub, one of the accused. Kolodub Junior was quoted in *Pravda* as denouncing his father; as clamouring for the death sentence; as wishing to change his surname from the tainted Kolodub to the ludicrous Shakhtin.[8] This was the first notable instance of the denunciation of traitor-parent by loyalist child: later a staple feature of Stalin's drive to disrupt all associations, including family relationships, which remained uncontrolled by his machine.

With the Shakhty Trial, directed against technicians outside the Party, Stalin ended the ten-year alliance between the Soviet régime and the bourgeois specialists who had been prepared to serve the workers' state without adopting its ideology. Ultimately, of course, the Soviet state must train its 'own' specialists – it could not depend for ever on those bequeathed by the pre-revolutionary régime. Indeed, the process of creating Soviet technical cadres had already begun, and was now proceeding under the forceful sponsorship of Stalin himself. But technologists were still in woefully short supply, and the Secretary-General's decision to attack them is an early foretaste of that recklessness which was to mark his later career. Judged by later standards, the Shakhty Trial was a primitive affair – it lasted longer, and had more defendants than necessary, while the OGPU's confession-extracting techniques were still in their infancy. Still, the affair led to five executions, and thus heightened the atmosphere of crisis in which accelerating Stalinism flourished. The trial also provided Stalin with a reservoir of scapegoats – the bourgeois specialists – on whom to blame economic disasters such as would inevitably occur during the campaign of rapid industrialization which he was about to launch. The use to which Stalin could put the Shakhty Trial, long after it was over, is well illustrated in a speech of 1929.

It is impossible to regard as accidental [Stalin stated, using a characteristic paranoid formulation] the so-called Shakhty affair. 'Shakhtyites' are now lurking in all branches of our industry. Many – though far from all – have been caught. Wrecking by bourgeois professional men is one of the most dangerous forms of opposition to developing Socialism. Wrecking is all the more dangerous because it is linked with international capital. Bourgeois wrecking is an indubitable sign that capitalist elements have by no means laid down their arms, and that they are gathering strength for new attacks on the Soviet Union.[9]

Thus Stalin made the Shakhty affair serve one of his many developing theses of the late 1920s and the 1930s: that class antagonism – and hence the need to intensify repressive measures – increases in proportion to the progress made in constructing a Socialist society. As is broadly hinted in the passage quoted above, the Shakhty affair was to be only the first in a chain of increasingly scandalous Stalinist show trials.

Stalin's defeat of the Right Opposition follows a pattern unprecedented in the saga of his political triumphs, owing to the secrecy preserved during the active period of the conflict. By mid-1928 the struggle had already begun – but behind the scenes. Not until August 1929 – by which time the Opposition had been routed – did a frenzied press campaign suddenly reveal what had long been privily rumoured: that Stalin's supposed ally Bukharin had become his Political Enemy Number One.

When, in mid-1928, the conflict first began to smoulder, Stalin's leftwards swerve was already taking him away from the line which he had so far pursued in alliance with the Right (Bukharin, Rykov and Tomsky) against the Left (Trotsky, Zinovyev and Kamenev). But the Secretary-General could not yet afford to clash openly with the Right: firstly because the rank and file of his supporters needed time to accept the *volte face* which their master was executing; and secondly because Stalin's position within the Politburo remained potentially somewhat precarious. Of that organ's nine full members (elected at the Fifteenth Congress) only Kuybyshev, Molotov and Rudzutak were out-and-out Stalinists. With Bukharin, Rykov and Tomsky being gradually isolated in the opposite camp, two waverers – Kalinin and Voroshilov – for a time held the balance of power. Stalin was busily converting both into obedient instruments, using – it has often been hinted – blackmail based on shady aspects of their past; but no details of such extortion have come to light, except that some leverage may have been presented by Voroshilov's service as a volunteer in the Imperial Russian army during the First World War.[10] In any case Stalin appears to have secured the provisional allegiance of Kalinin and Voroshilov by mid-1928. Though not yet ready for an open breach with the Bukharin group, he was already foreshadowing a severer policy towards the peasants in a speech to the Central Committee, and basing this on a claim that general economic expansion must be paid for by 'tribute' exacted from agriculture.[11] Stalin also redefined NEP as an aggressively anti-capitalist policy rather than as the retreat – however limited – towards capitalism which it had commonly been considered. However, when it came to agreeing a policy resolution to put before the Committee, Stalin consented to a compromise which – since it purported to halt the current leftwards swing – appeared to represent victory for the Bukharin group.[12]

Realizing that this was no concession of substance, feeling anything but triumphant, and terrified of Stalin now forming an alliance with the defeated Left – whose policies he was in process of adopting – Bukharin sought to forestall such a development by secretly parleying with his former enemy Kamenev: newly restored to Party membership after a period of probationary penitence. On the morning of 11 July, Bukharin – lips twitching, manner excited and distraught – harangued Kamenev for an hour. During this rambling and ill-recorded discourse the rightist chief described Stalin as a Genghis Khan who intended to 'cut our throats'. That, said Bukharin, was why he and his allies Rykov and Tomsky would now like to make a deal with their old enemies Zinovyev and Kamenev.[13] In other words, the rightist trio had belatedly become aware that Stalin constituted a danger transcending all conceivable differences among his colleagues, and that it was desirable to form a common front in self-defence. Among recruits whose support might now become available to the cause of anti-Stalinism, Bukharin told Kamenev of two high OGPU officials, Yagoda and Trilisser. Bukharin's reliance on disaffection among the OGPU chiefs was, however, to prove unfounded – in strong contrast with his other statements to Kamenev: that Stalin's policy was ruinous; that he was an unscrupulous intriguer; that his programme would inevitably culminate in wholesale political terror, civil war and bloodshed. All very true. But unfortunately Bukharin's harangue was no call to battle; it sounded more like the bleat of some sacrificial sheep.

Far from achieving any new united front of rightist and leftist anti-Stalinists, Bukharin and his allies helped to compass their own destruction by co-operating with Stalin's policy: that of hushing up differences within the Politburo and presenting a front of simulated harmony to Party and nation. Bukharin even went out of his way to denounce, in public, the very Right Opposition which he himself secretly headed. Such folly was giving Stalin time to undermine the Bukharin group in areas of his own choosing.

Rather than begin by attacking Bukharin, Rykov and Tomsky in the Central Committee, Stalin – following his usual strategy – opened his campaign outside the Central Party Apparatus: in the Comintern, in the Moscow provincial Party and in the trade unions. At the sixth Comintern Congress (Moscow, July–September 1928) Bukharin took a major role, having succeeded Zinovyev as Comintern chairman. But he was publicly humiliated when his very theses, as presented to the Congress, were amended no less than twenty times by Russian colleagues to whom (Stalin later claimed) Bukharin had high-handedly failed to submit his text in advance; besides which a whispering campaign was being conducted against the new Comintern chief in the Congress corridors.[14] Bukharin was also forced to give public support to the new leftist international line now promoted by Stalin. This involved abandoning the earlier Stalinist policy of rapprochement with certain foreign non-Communist parties (the Chinese Kuomintang, the British Labour Party and so on) in order to exploit – exclusively through Kremlinized resources – a great new revolutionary upsurge allegedly taking place within the capitalist world at large. Bukharin would have preferred a continuing broad alliance of the Left directed against emergent Fascism in Europe, but conformed with Party discipline by loyally defending the new militant Stalinist line according to which international Communism had no enemies more deadly than Socialist or nationalist forces independent of Stalin's control.

By now Stalin had condemned his own former Comintern policy as criminally deviant; had labelled it rightist; and had induced Bukharin (as the prime heretic) to simulate abhorrence of these same rightist views – to which he, Bukharin, remained privately committed. The time had therefore come when anti-Bukharinist operations could begin nearer home. The Secretary-General removed *Pravda* and the Party journal *Bolshevik* from Bukharin's sphere of influence, after which a *Pravda* article obediently pronounced – and for the first time – that rightist deviation (as already denounced in the international arena) was also a major problem within Russia itself.[15] Still, in mid-October, avoiding conflict in the Party's central organs, Stalin hunted down a nest of rightists in the Moscow provincial Party. This was still headed by Uglanov: once a scourge of Zinovyev and Kamenev, once a protégé of Stalin's.

In attacking such second-grade tycoons as Uglanov, the Secretary-General made adroit use of 'democratic' pressures. He provoked Uglanov's subordinates to denounce – with every justification – their boss's dictatorial methods, but blandly pretended not to know that these very methods had been evolved at his own express behest and within the over-all dictatorial framework imposed by himself. Persistently advocating 'control from below', 'Party democracy' and 'self-criticism', Stalin was disciplining recalcitrant little Stalins by invoking libertarian symbols which his victims had helped him to pervert and exploit in the first place . . . and which they could hardly abjure at this late stage. For such tactics Uglanov proved no match, finding himself no longer able to rig appointments within his own organization now that lower-ranking officials had received the signal from

Stalin to elect – democratically! – anti-Uglanovites within the Moscow machine. How far Uglanov had slipped became clear when he found himself addressing a mid-October Committee of the Moscow Party unapplauded; worse still, his underlings and former sycophants now ventured to disparage him openly. But how could poor Uglanov hit back when that would have been to stifle 'criticism from below'? Then, on 19 October, Stalin appeared in person before the Moscow Party Committee to denounce the rightist deviation. A month later he evoked laughter at the Moscow leader's expense – and conjured up the spectre of his downfall – by solemnly reminding the Central Committee of the Party's democratic right to elect new secretaries in place of old.[16] What could the out-manoeuvred Uglanov possibly say now? That he himself had helped Stalin to rob the Party of such democratic rights over the past few years? That he had zealously worked to replace them with such pseudo-democratic verbiage as Stalin was now using to discomfort him?

Stalin also reminded the Moscow Party organization that the conflict might spread into spheres more exalted when he conceded that the very Central Committee contained . . . nothing so sinister as deviating rightists, but 'certain admittedly highly insignificant symptoms of a tendency to tolerate the rightist danger'. As for the Politburo, that included neither rightists nor leftists – nor yet those who would tolerate either. 'This must be said here as categorically as possible; it is time to abandon gossip spread by the Party's ill-wishers and all kinds of oppositionists about the existence of a right deviation or a conciliatory attitude towards it in the Politburo.'[17] His use of the Leninist term *conciliationism* – to pillory tolerance of a deviation as a crime barely less heinous than the original deviation – is worth noting as an element in his evolving technique. As this refinement made clear, Party members could no longer expect to keep out of trouble by the mere avoidance of error. That was simply not good enough any more, since they could now escape being pilloried for heresy and conciliationism only by coming out with forthright denunciations of heretics and conciliators. We are reminded that failure to denounce treason had, in seventeenth-century Russian law, been equated with treason itself. But Stalin also threw in the 'conciliation of conciliators': another, yet subtler, brand of political misdemeanour which might have been beyond the comprehension of the Muscovite Tsars.

Autumn 1928 finds Bukharin making determined but futile attempts to hit back at Stalin. On 30 September he publishes in *Pravda* the long article 'An Economist's Notes': a rightist manifesto stressing the peasantry's central role in the economy and the dangers of excessive planning. Ignoring this, the planner and peasant-persecutor Stalin seeks to impose his radical economic policies on the Politburo during Bukharin's absence on holiday in the Caucasus. But Bukharin suspects what is afoot; he attempts to fly back to Moscow at once; is grounded, reportedly, by the OGPU on Stalin's orders. Arriving in due course by slow train (there were no others) Bukharin makes an angry scene, threatening to resign as Comintern Chairman and editor of *Pravda*, while Rykov and Tomsky also propose to abandon their posts: as *Sovnarkom* Chairman and trade union chief respectively. Not yet prepared for an open breach, Stalin blenches; trembles; offers various concessions; persuades his rivals to withdraw their resignations; has them sign yet another unanimous declaration stating that the Politburo is politically united.[18]

On 19 November 1928 Stalin delivers a long harangue to the Central Committee on the twin themes of industrialization and deviationism. Emphasizing production of the means of production as a major goal, while proposing to boost agriculture through mechanization, the Secretary-General launches the slogan – ultimately deriving from Lenin – of catching up and overtaking the capitalist countries in economics and technology. But the Secretary-General was not yet advocating extreme measures. While stressing the need to collectivize agriculture, he also spoke of increasing the productivity of the individual farms which he was virtually to abolish when collectivization later gained full momentum. Nor, as Stalin took up the theme of deviation, was he yet openly gunning for Bukharin, Rykov and Tomsky. It was on one Frumkin that he concentrated his fire – a comparatively minor figure whose rightist views were close to Bukharin's, but whose junior status made it possible to attack him in the Central Committee without scandal.

Even as Stalin maintained his drive to impose policies once considered heretically leftist, he was still pretending – as usual – to occupy a central area between the two unacceptable extremes of Left and Right. By now, indeed, he had almost acquired a prescriptive right to such a middle-of-the-road position; for however extreme or eccentric the policy which he might be advocating at a given moment, that policy automatically became – by virtue of his advocacy alone – the orthodox, central Party line, any divergence from which automatically constituted a deviation.

Discussing the emergency measures now directed against the peasantry, Stalin regaled the Central Committee with a display of forensic ingenuity. The Right was (he indicated) in error in rejecting these measures out of hand; the Left's error consisted in wishing to make them permanent. The Right wanted to take pressure off the kulak; the Left would pressurize not only the kulak, but the 'middle' (moderately prosperous) peasant as well. The Right would refrain from launching such ambitious industrial undertakings as the Dnieper Dam, now under construction in the Ukraine; the Left would build a Dnieper Dam every year.

'We are faced with difficulties,' says the Right '. . . and therefore we must call a halt'; 'we are faced with difficulties,' says the Left '. . . and therefore we must push ahead regardless.'

Between each set of poles lies the path of reason and good sense followed by Stalin . . . Stalin infers.[19] And yet, despite all seeming differences between Left and Right (he proceeds to argue) the two deviations are in essence identical. What, after all, are leftists but rightists trying to conceal their true political essence by the use of leftist phraseology? Both deviations are in practice assisting the restoration of capitalism in Russia: both have their petty bourgeois social roots.

To this and much other logic-chopping Bukharin, Rykov and Tomsky were compelled to listen in silence, bound by their latest declaration on Politburo solidarity, until Stalin concluded with a characteristic plea for tolerance of the – still unnamed – chief deviants of the hour. Claiming to detect a prophetic grin on the faces of certain Central Committee members who now foresaw a political massacre of rightists, the Secretary-General peaceably asserted that the time was not yet ripe for measures so drastic. As for Trotskyites, that they were suffering repressions Stalin admitted, justifying such severity by their decision to form a new Party and foment anti-Soviet demonstrations.[20]

At the end of 1928 Stalin turned his baleful gaze on the rightist trade-union chief, Tomsky. Tomsky found himself under attack within his own private empire, and by the same methods which had toppled Uglanov. Since July – when Tomsky had first combined with Bukharin and Rykov against Stalin's new, radical course – official references to undemocratic practices within the trade union hierarchy had sounded the note of impending doom. At the Eighth Trade Union Congress in December, Tomsky's fall from power within his organization was duly engineered. By that time Stalin had taken over the trade union newspaper, and had packed the key Bolshevik fractions within the unions with his own nominees. It thus became possible for Stalinists to push through the trade union Congress an anti-rightist resolution in favour of all-out industrialization – Tomsky being powerless to resist, since he no longer controlled his own subordinates. In a gathering which he had been accustomed to dominate he now found himself heavily voted down. The Congress ended with the election of five Stalinists – including the militant industrializer Kaganovich – to the Trade Union Council. Tomsky attempted to resign; and when this resignation was contemptuously rejected, he simply withdrew from what had so recently been his feudal domain.[21] Tomsky's departure – and his replacement by a submissive Stalinist – was an inevitable prelude to all-out industrialization. Under the Five Year Plans the trade unions were to be deprived of even such limited power to protect the workers as they had retained under Tomsky, being converted in effect into a factory police.

Chiefly occupied, in 1928, with battling against the Right, Stalin had by no means forgotten the deviant Left: the United Oppositionists whom he had routed at the end of the preceding year. Among these vanquished opponents the two premier recanters, Zinovyev and Kamenev, had been readmitted to the Party in June 1928 – though not restored to high office. But Trotsky continued defiant in Alma Ata. When the OGPU had kidnapped him in January 1928, removing him to an undisclosed destination without medicine or change of linen, Trotsky had considered such treatment more outrageous than any which he had ever received from a capitalist police force;[22] that the OGPU was capable of worse atrocities than the confiscation of clean underwear, the great exile did not yet suspect. At Alma Ata he was permitted to live in moderate comfort; to hunt; to receive a lorry-load of books and papers; even to correspond with political supporters now banished to various parts of Russia.

As the year proceeded – and as it became obvious that Stalin was increasingly appropriating Trotskyite policies which he had once venomously denounced – many followers of the sage of Alma Ata began to reconsider their opposition to the triumphant Georgian. Stalin was, after all, only putting into effect what they themselves had long been urging in vain. Sundry Trotskyites therefore recanted and were readmitted to the Party; the most notable was Pyatakov, who became a major architect of industrialization under the early Five Year Plans – and, a few years later, a major show trial victim. But there were also Trotskyite irreconcileables, with Trotsky himself at their head. These the Secretary-General victimized until, by the end of the year, some six to eight thousand left oppositionists had been exiled or imprisoned.[23] Trotsky himself also came under increasing pressure. His mail was censored; a senior OGPU officer turned up in Alma Ata and ordered him to abstain from counter-revolutionary activity: a demand which was contemptuously rejected.[24] Finally, in January 1929, Stalin secured the sanction of the Politburo – against the futile protests of Bukharin, Rykov and Tomsky – for the expulsion of Trotsky from the USSR. On 10 February 1929 Stalin's greatest rival sailed from Odessa for Turkey, beginning an exile which was to continue in France, Norway and Mexico.

The decision to expel Trotsky perhaps shows lack of foresight by Stalin, since his chief adversary would have made a choice victim for judicial murder a few years later. Could there ever be better show trial material than a Trotsky, assuming that he might have been adequately softened up? Still, as matters developed, even a Trotsky removed from the OGPU's immediate grasp was to prove an asset to Stalin over the years. Trotsky's unremitting anti-Stalinist activity on foreign soil in 1929–40; his foundation of a Fourth, anti-Stalinist, International; his publication of the anti-Stalinist *Bulletin of the Opposition*; his contributions – also anti-Stalinist – to the capitalist press . . . these operations, taken as a whole, proved less disadvantageous to the Secretary-General than might seem. In the 1930s, far more than in the 1920s, the deified Stalin needed a bogyman who could easily be identified as the fount of all evil, and who could be invoked in all denunciations of political sin. Representing no real threat to Stalin's power, the exiled Trotsky was to function as a valuable hate focus, playing an important part in Stalinist demonology. In course of time, however, the menace of Trotskyism came to outweigh any value which Stalin may have attached to it – until he eventually gave the orders which led to Trotsky's assassination in 1940.

In late 1929, Yakov Blyumkin – a dissident OGPU official – was arrested and shot in Russia after returning from Constantinople, where he had been in contact with Trotsky. Blyumkin thus became the first Party member to be executed for an inner-party offence.[25] Among the many precedents set in 1928–9 none was more ominous than this.

Early 1929 sees a new phase in the conflict between Stalin and the Bukharin group. The controversy now bursts out of the Politburo and rages on a wider arena until – in August – the rightist trio is suddenly unmasked before the entire nation. The first round opens in January–February 1929 at a joint inquisitorial session of the Politburo and the Presidium of the Central Control Commission. By now Bukharin's secret discussions with Kamenev – of which Stalin has no doubt been informed all along – have been publicized by members of the former opposition, and it is for this act of sinful intercourse of the previous July that Bukharin is called to account. Not denying contact with Kamenev, Bukharin counter-attacks; he denounces the Party's anti-democratic régime; points out that all policy decisions are now taken by one individual; berates the accelerating collectivization drive as involving the military-feudal exploitation of the peasant. Stalin counters by abusing the Bukharin group for wanting to slow down industrialization and reverse collectivization. He castigates them for right deviationism; for treating with Kamenev; for capitulationism; for wantonly threatening to resign their posts. The Party had assumed that they had renounced their errors – after all, they had twice signed solemn declarations affirming Politburo unity. Yet here they were still persisting in sin. Could one wonder that Lenin had once (in 1916) referred to Bukharin as 'devilishly unstable' in his politics?[26] To this the rightist trio retorted by condemning Stalin's exploitation of the peasantry; his use of bureaucratic methods; his emasculation of the Comintern. Calling for a reduction in industrialization tempos and for the restoration of a free market, the rightists also clamoured for the restoration of democracy within the Party: that predictable demand of Bolshevik losers. There the matter rested for the moment, since the Party inquisition did not impose concrete sanctions, merely denouncing oppositionist sins in a forthright resolution.[27]

In April 1929, Bukharin, Rykov and Tomsky were attacked by Stalin at a Central Committee plenum. It was the Secretary-General's longest and most outspoken assault on the group. Refusing to spare these old comrades, he pointed out that Bolsheviks were not members of a cosy family circle, but of a working-class political party which could not afford sentiment. He accused the trio of deviating from the Party line; forming a fraction; ignoring the progressive exacerbation of the class conflict attendant – according to Stalinist dogma – on success in the building of Socialism; not seeing beyond their own navels; living in the past; being unable to distinguish pro-Bolshevik peasants from kulaks. In answer to Bukharin's criticism of the word 'tribute', as used by Stalin to describe the peasantry's enforced contributions to industrialization, the Secretary-General neatly turned the accusation by brandishing a quotation from Lenin where 'tribute' appears in a similar sense. Stalin also raked up Bukharin's numerous differences with Lenin. In 1916 Lenin had accused Bukharin of semi-anarchistic error. Then, in 1918, Bukharin had plotted to arrest Lenin at the time of their disagreement over the Brest-Litovsk Treaty. And had not Lenin – in his Testament – denounced Bukharin's claims to be regarded as a leading theoretician? No wonder, either, since the immodest Bukharin had sought to usurp Lenin's theory of the state. Such, sneered Stalin, was 'the hypertrophied pretentiousness of a half-baked theoretician'.[28]

Stalin now enforced Bukharin's dismissal from the Comintern and formally ejected Tomsky from the trade union organization whence he had in practice already withdrawn. But Rykov was left as Chairman of *Sovnarkom* for the time being. The dismissals were kept out of the press, being finally publicized in August as part of an overt campaign suddenly unleashed against the rightists by then wholly discredited. Eventually, in November, all three defeated rightist leaders confessed their political sins and Bukharin was dismissed from the Politburo.

Quinquagenarian

By the end of 1929 Stalin had fully imposed his left-about-turn in economic strategy. In two years he had swung from an unadventurous NEP-based policy of watered down Bukharinism to headlong industrialization similar to that long advocated by Trotsky ... except that Stalin secretly stood poised to carry this policy beyond what the most rabid rival leftist may ever have plotted. Yoked with industrialization was the drive to collectivize agriculture on the basis of plant to be provided by newly booming Soviet industry.

There was a marked contrast between the violence with which this policy was eventually implemented and the gradual tempo of its introduction in 1928–9. During those years repression of the peasantry, arrests of recalcitrant villagers, grain confiscations, rural riots and the like were steadily gaining momentum. As a parallel process intensified industrialization was being imposed. The State Planning Commission, which was working out an industrialization programme on comparatively orthodox economic lines, suddenly found itself bypassed by the rival Supreme Economic Council – headed by the then Stalinist Kuybyshev. In May 1928, Kuybyshev sprang a proposal to increase productivity by 130 per cent in five years; but even this was dismissed as insufficient, a yet more ambitious project being accepted by the Central Committee in November 1928. This – the First Five Year Plan – was formally adopted in April–May 1929; it was then declared retrospectively operative since October 1928.

So extravagant were the aims, so brutal the methods of the combined industrialization and collectivization campaigns that we are now about to register no mere change in policy, but rather a change of mentality, on Stalin's part. Such boldness, such a capacity for transcending the apparent limits of the possible, must have been latent in his character before 1928. As noted above, however, qualities of an entirely opposite order – caution, reliability, a preference for the middle of the road – had appeared dominant in the dictator during his steady rise to power. But now that he at last had the power, now that he had crushed the last systematic opposition movement – Bukharin's – ever to rear its head within the Party during his reign, he was prepared to go to extreme lengths, unimpeded by moral restraints or humanitarian considerations ... and impeded least of all by the dictates of that solid common sense which had hitherto seemed so comforting an element in his nature. Suddenly the plodding Georgian emerges as a reckless pioneer who pushes the manipulation of humanity by terror into a new experimental area which – but for him – might for ever have remained happily unexplored. As for the new Stalin's attitude to economics, it was well expressed by one of his leading economists, S. G. Shumilin:

> Our task is not to study economics, but to change it. We are bound by no laws. There are no fortresses which the Bolsheviks cannot storm. The question of tempo is subject to decision by human beings.[1]

Of such miracles the future course of Stalinism was to provide many examples as the dictator forged ahead, his commands imposed by maximized exhortation and violence. Meanwhile Stalinist apologists would be hastening, pen in hand, to provide the rationale for a continuing chain of decisions which would come to embrace their own liquidation and replacement by further, equally doomed, relays of servile scribes. This process was already to be observed in embryo at the end of the 1920s, when a controversy broke out in the world of economics between the Geneticists (who believed that industrialization, however intensive, must remain within the bounds of the possible) and the Teleologists, who inferred that the human will could overcome all obstacles – including, of course, the laws of cause and effect. It was, naturally, to this latter school, that Stalin lent his support now that his policies depended increasingly on magic. And it was, naturally, the cautious Geneticists who were purged . . . first! That the Teleologists, too, were crushed shortly afterwards, and despite their pro-Stalinist postures, will surprise no one who is attuned to the emerging pattern of Stalinism.

A similar controversy broke out in philosophy between the Mechanists and the Dialecticians, who differed on the extent to which a law of cause and effect could be regarded as limiting human conduct. The temporarily successful Dialecticians (who inclined to magical, fact-transcending, Stalinist claims) saw their more pedestrian rivals purged, only to fall into disgrace themselves shortly afterwards . . for the Dialecticians, too, had been guilty of thought processes claiming some degree of originality; and by now all mental activity – even that exercised in Stalin's own interests – was becoming suspect. In such ways the foundations of Stalinist thought control were being laid.

If there is a single date to which we can attach the establishment of Stalin's power as absolute dictator, it is that of his fiftieth birthday on 21 December 1929. From this occasion, too, may be dated the extravagant Stalin Cult which far outdid the deification of certain Roman Emperors, as practised many centuries earlier – for that was decently confined, in many of its more extreme manifestations, to the provinces. No such decentralization was practised in Russia, where the Kremlin became the centre of compulsory emperor worship embracing a large part of two continents. Banner headlines, a press campaign lasting several weeks, endless telegraphed dithyrambs from organizations high and low, mass-produced icons and graven images of the quinquagenarian genius . . . these were only a few features of a campaign which was to surge through the 1930s and beyond, lauding the courage, dedication, industry, wisdom, foresight, insight and hindsight of one commemorated by an increasing number of new place names: Stalingrad, Stalinabad, Stalin-Aul, Staliniri, Stalinissi, Stalino, Stalinogorsk, Stalinsk; the suffixes varied according to local linguistic peculiarities, but the root was common. Not merely towns, but also collective farms, barracks, schools, factories and power stations came to bear the sacred name, as did the highest peak in the Pamirs, Mount Stalin.[2]

Such was the explosion of controlled mass sycophancy on and around 21 December 1929 that adulation of Stalin seemed to have attained an unsurpassable zenith. But future developments would reveal such a view to be mistaken, as praise ever more extravagant was lavished on the Man of Steel, the Bolshevik of Granite, the Brass-hard Leninist, the Soldier of Iron and the Universal Genius. Successively liquidated and increasingly abject relays of Legend-creators were to forge a mendacious biography of the Leader until he had been transformed into the main architect of the Bolshevik Revolution, the chief victor in the Russian Civil War, a cult figure of towering stature besides whom even Lenin – though never, of course, discredited – would fade into insignificance.

One element in the Cult bears, more than any other, the authentic Stalin touch: the inevitable stress on the *modesty* of the Leader who inspired this atrocious bombast even as he affected to – and genuinely did – deprecate it. That the Cult in fact privately disgusted the pockmarked god, even as he continued to promote it for reasons of expediency, his daughter has borne witness.

8

The Dictator Emerges

Peasant and Worker Regimented

BESIDES marking the genesis of the Stalin Cult and the associated Legend, the attainment of the dictator's half century also signalizes the end of all organized opposition within the Party. At last the Secretary-General emerges as dictator in all but name. Already his ascendancy is greater than that of any autocrat in previous Russian history. And yet his achievement still falls short of his hidden ambitions. On the threshold of nearly a quarter of a century's sway as totalitarian ruler, he stands poised to expand the bounds of his control ever wider in the four major operations which are to occupy his remaining career. In 1929-33 intensive industrialization and agricultural collectivization are to be his main achievements. Then, from late 1934 onwards, his attack switches to the Soviet élite, including the interlinked structures of Party Apparatus, political police, government, industrial management and armed forces: an offensive which culminates in the Terror of 1937-8, directed against all sections of the community. From the events of 1939-45, Stalin emerges as a national leader victorious in the greatest war known to history. Finally, in his declining years, the ageing despot presides supreme over a mighty empire which has now engulfed numerous satellite Stalinist states.

The onset of the dictator's sixth decade marks the end of a relatively passive phase. Great as is the tactical ingenuity displayed by Stalin in the 1920s, he has not so much been creating policy during that period as reacting to complex external stimuli. Policy, so far, has been something very largely imposed on him by events outside his control – whereas, from 1930 onwards, it is he who imposes his own pattern on the community. Henceforward, until his death in 1953, almost everything Soviet happens at the will of Stalin: either positively, because this industrious bureaucrat interferes in so many spheres; or negatively, in the sense that whatever occurs independently of Stalin comes within an area which he is liable to invade at any moment. His shadow lies over the entire community.

Both at home and abroad the dominant feature in Stalinism of the early 1930s is the maintenance of the extreme leftist position signalized by the overthrow of the Bukharin group. In foreign affairs this policy results in instructions given by Stalin, through the Comintern, for foreign Communist parties to abandon all alliances with the non-Stalinized Left in their own countries, and to treat these as their political enemies. Throughout the world a Stalinist anathema is now, accordingly, pronounced on all Socialists other than those taking their orders from the Kremlin. The policy leads to especially disastrous results in Germany, where it splits working-class opposition to Hitler during the period of his swiftly growing influence from 1930 onwards. Whether the German National Socialists would have obtained power in 1933 without Stalin's aid we cannot say. Certainly they would have found it more difficult to do so had Stalin permitted the German Communist Party to confront them with resolute opposition. 'Without Stalin there would have been no Hitler' – this comment on the Austrian dictator's rise to power was frequently made by Germans of the non-Stalinized Left,[1] and they may well have been justified in saying so. It is certain that Stalin underestimated Hitler's potentialities as a totalitarian ruler who would one day come near to destroying Russia. Far from sensing this menace, and the need to concert opposition to it, the Soviet Leader continued in the early 1930s to act on a principle which he had enunciated in 1924: that foreign Social Democrats (by which he meant un-Kremlinized Socialists) were not the enemies of Fascism, but its allies. The two movements were, he said, 'not antipodes but twins'. [2] The analysis was faulty, and its consequences were disastrous in permitting or at least facilitating Hitler's rise to power. This misreading of German National-Socialism up to 1941 (when he was at last forced to face reality) remains the single most colossal blunder of Stalin's entire career. He was the more easily betrayed into it through the relatively insignificant part played in his thinking by foreign affairs during the phase when his main energies were concentrated on the early building of Stalinism in One Country.

It was, then, at home, through headlong industrialization and through the enforced collectivization of agriculture, that Stalin made his greatest impact in 1930-3. Collectivization radically changed the lives of a particularly large section of Soviet citizens by nationalizing – in effect – about twenty-five million small holdings. Almost at a stroke it sought to convert this multitude of small farmers, together with their families, into socialized employees of state or collective farms (a reservoir from which a proportion was syphoned off into the industrial labour force). This was the transformation which Stalin himself later described as a revolution from above –[3] and justly so, in view of the scale and violence of the collectivization process.

If Stalin's 'revolution' of 1929 onwards is compared with the Lenin-sponsored revolution which began twelve years earlier, certain significant differences emerge. Lenin's revolution was also responsible – if only partially and indirectly – for causing the death of millions of peasants. But this earlier upheaval had not greatly changed the peasant's way of life, only his way of death. At the end of the NEP period, Russian rural conditions were closer in many ways to those of the nineteenth-century Tsarist Russian countryside than to the life of the Stalinized countryside as it was to emerge in the 1930s.

Both revolutions, Lenin's and Stalin's, bore hard on the peasant, involving as each did many millions of fatalities. But there is a difference in the extent to which these catastrophes can be attributed to the policies of Lenin and Stalin respectively. Lenin's peasants died largely through military action, disease and starvation: through civil war and the appalling conditions which it created. It is true, of course, that many a peasant was executed by the Cheka; but such victims did at least succumb to a campaign of terror evolved in an emergency by a government which many of its subjects found more acceptable than White or interventionist rule. In Stalin's revolution, by contrast, Stalin's subjects *were* the enemy! Here was a war declared by one man on the largest social class within his realm. The peasant fatalities attending both revolutions elude precise reckoning, and must be counted in millions. But whereas those of the Lenin era were to a large extent incidental, Stalin's victims were gratuitously sacrificed by Stalin. This becomes especially clear if we compare the two great famines – that of 1921 and that of 1932 – which attended the two successive revolutions. Coming in the wake of the Civil War and provoked in considerable degree by Bolshevik policies, the earlier disaster was assuredly not willed from on high. But the second catastrophe was very much Stalin's personal handiwork; it has been called 'perhaps the only case in history of a purely man-made famine'.[4] Not that even Stalin had expressly set out to starve his peasantry in the first place. Once mass starvation had broken out, however, he callously refused to alleviate it, maintaining the bulk export of Soviet-produced foodstuffs which might have saved hundreds of thousands of lives at home. Here was the Secretary-General's revenge on Soviet peasants for resisting collectivization. Nor was Stalin-imposed famine the only item in a catalogue of brutality which included wholesale execution and mass deportation to concentration camp or exile: all on a scale which dwarfs Leninist persecution of the peasantry.

The most significant date marking the speed-up of collectivization is 27 December 1929. It was then, within a week of his fiftieth birthday, that the Secretary-General propounded a new policy: that of *liquidating the kulaks as a class.* 'We now have the opportunity to mount a decisive offensive against the kulaks, to break their resistance, to liquidate them as a class, and to replace kulak production with production by collective and state farms.'[5] This statement marks the transition from acute harassment to extermination, and from the imposition of severe 'extraordinary measures' against the wealthier peasantry – which had been in operation for two years – to outright massacre and mass deportation. It also marks the extent to which the earlier campaign of enforced grain collection was being replaced by a policy of outright dispossession and collectivization. Already, between October and December 1929, the total of collectivized households had doubled, moving from about $7\frac{1}{2}$ per cent of the whole to about 15 per cent. That was fast enough in all conscience. But for the Secretary-General even such a tempo was too slow: in January and February 1930 he – literally – redoubled the pace of collectivization, converting the process into an avalanche. At the end of that period 60 per cent of peasant households had been collectivized, at least on paper.[6]

By the end of February such confusion reigned in the Russian village that Stalin was forced to repudiate his own policies – as he did in 'Dizziness from Success', a *Pravda* article of 2 March. That he was personally to blame he did not, of course, admit. It was all the fault of over-zealous subordinates, he explained: such people easily grew intoxicated by their own successes; they became dizzy; they abandoned all sense of measure; they lost touch with reality in their eagerness to overestimate their own strength and underestimate the strength of their opponents; they irresponsibly sought to solve all problems of Socialist construction in two ticks. 'One cannot implant collective farms by violence; that would be stupid and reactionary.'[7] Thus did the Secretary-General blatantly disavow a procedure of which he himself had been chief promoter – and which he intended to resume at the first opportunity.

Stalin's retreat of March 1930 relieved the pressure on the countryside for a while. Peasants trooped out of the collective farms in droves until about a half had denationalized themselves within a few weeks.[8] So delighted were they that some carried pictures of Stalin in procession – confusing him, perhaps, with a saint of the Orthodox Church. But prayers to the moustachioed icon proved unavailing, for Stalin resumed intensive collectivization within a few months. By 1934 some three-quarters of peasant households had been incorporated in collective or state farms. Six years later the percentage collectivized had risen to 96·9 per cent.[9]

It has been claimed that collectivization was imposed 'by force alone'.[10] Nor can it be denied that extreme violence was employed, all manner of Soviet agencies being involved. As in every major Stalinist initiative, the

Party Apparatus played a key role. It was backed by local government, by the militia (non-political police) – and in extreme cases by the regular army, which employed artillery, tanks and aircraft in instances where peasant resistance proved particularly stubborn. Workers from the cities and other 'activists', including students, were drafted to the villages by their tens of thousands to add verbal exhortation to force and threat of force. But the impassioned arguments of such intruders were ill fitted to sway the canny muzhik, couched as they were in the unintelligible Stalinist Hieratic tongue; besides, any farmer could see at a glance that these townee agitators did not know one end of a plough from another. Still, it was as well to listen politely to the urgings of such touring 'plenipotentiaries', on pain of being categorized as a kulak and consigned to exile or concentration camp.

In imposing sanctions on the reluctant villagers Stalin's OGPU was more prominent than any other agency. Methods ranged from summary execution to 'dekulakization': the eviction of peasants from their homes, together with their wives and children, to be transported – often many thousands of miles – to north European Russia, to Siberia or to Central Asia. There they swelled the fast growing concentration camp population or – if more fortunate – scratched out a meagre existence as exiles under nominally free conditions. Reliable casualty figures are unobtainable, however. We neither know how many peasants were shot out of hand nor how many were killed in local skirmishes with authority; nor yet can we tell how many were dispatched to exile and concentration camps. Relegation to a camp was, for the majority, only a slower and more painful form of execution; it might drag on for decades in the case of the hardier victims, but also caused many swifter deaths in transit by unheated freight car in the depths of the Russian winter. According to one authority, about ten or eleven million peasants were forcibly removed from the Russian villages through Stalin's dekulakization policies, one third of the total being accounted for by concentration camp inmates; one third by forced exile without actual incarceration; and one third by death through execution and other causes.[11] Though not all the above victims necessarily perished, these figures leave out of account the famine fatalities of 1932-3, which have been put at over five million.[12] The number of peasants whose death was caused or hastened by Stalin's collectivization drive may therefore stand at ten million or more. For what it is worth, that figure coincides with information given by the dictator to Winston Churchill in Moscow in August 1942. It was then that Stalin, for once, unbent sufficiently to confide in his English guest that collectivization had been a terrible struggle. 'Ten millions,' Stalin said, holding up his hands and alluding to the number of peasants *dealt with*. 'It was fearful. Four years it lasted. It was absolutely necessary for Russia.'[13]

So enormous were the casualties, so brutal were the methods of collectivization that we risk ignoring the ingenuity which also distinguished the operation. To say that collectivization was accomplished 'by force alone' is to do the Secretary-General less than justice, since results so far-reaching could not have been obtained by force unaccompanied by double-talk. With persistent guile the dictator continued to exploit the term 'kulak' to disguise an onslaught on the peasantry as a whole by pretending that the target was only a small, universally execrated section of that class. No precise meaning had ever been attached to the word kulak – originally applied to village usurers or such otherwise tight-fisted peasants as ill-treated their poorer neighbours. Technically, in so far as the word retained any exact meaning in Soviet times, it still applied to the more prosperous peasants – who might own more than one cow or hire the labour of others. Attempts were made to define the term while categorizing the kulaks on a scale of ascending perniciousness, ranging from passive resisters to rabid counter-revolutionaries. The aim of such concept-shuffling was to ease the campaign against the Russian countryside by exploiting within each village grudges such as the poorer peasants might feel, or be induced to conceive, against their less indigent neighbours.

When kulak families – however arbitrarily defined – were dispossessed, it was customary for non-kulaks from the same village to plunder the victims' possessions, seizing their clothing and drinking their liquor. 'Eat; drink, it's all ours' . . . such was the slogan commonly uttered as this looting took place under the benevolent eye of Stalinist authority well aware that, while peasants were quarrelling with each other, they were less likely to quarrel with those who were manipulating them. Though official attempts were made to regularize the process of dispossession by requiring a dossier on each 'dekulakized' (dispossessed) family, such endeavours only added a veneer of bureaucratic verbiage to a nationwide battery of anarchic assaults carried out by one section within each village against another. Not that the drive to set villagers at each others' throats was an unqualified success, for it often foundered on peasant solidarity in the face of the common enemy: Soviet authority.[14]

As the campaign proceeded the term 'kulak' acquired clearer outlines, this deadly label being increasingly applied to any villager who – whatever his financial status might be – opposed collectivization actively. It was in this way that 'liquidation of the kulaks as a class' became the cloak for an onslaught on the peasantry as a whole. And the portentous term 'liquidation' – hardly less vague in its way than 'kulak' – greatly enhanced the potentialities for mischief-making built into the slogan. To *liquidate* could mean to massacre; but it could also mean to render ineffectual in some comparatively painless manner, while the addition of the phrase 'as a class' imparted an air even more remote. There was a quasi-clinical, abstract flavour about 'liquidating as a class', and it was easy to forget the potential implications in terms of human suffering. Not necessarily all brutes, Stalin's officials thus found their co-operation enlisted by the dictator on terms which masked the savagery of the operation. Ready and willing to liquidate kulaks as a class, they might have hesitated if invited to shoot, starve, imprison and freeze large numbers of Vanyas, Annas, Yeroshkas and Pelageyas as individuals. By the time when they realized that this was exactly what they were doing, many of them had become too corrupt and vicious to care.

This was the over-all framework within which Stalin juggled his concepts and sub-concepts. Having long ago learnt from Lenin to divide the villagers into poor peasants, middle peasants and kulaks, he then split the kulaks into three sub-categories. He also propagated the sinister term *podkulachnik* ('sub-kulakizer') to smear those peasants whose hostility to collectivization made them ripe for liquidation, but whose circumstances were so devastatingly humble that they could not conceivably be relegated even to the lowest stratum of prosperous villager.

Prone to reinforce success, and to plunge further when an initial plunge had proved effective, Stalin continued to hound the kulaks even after the collectivized peasantry had ceased to offer active resistance. Now the dictator began to claim that the seemingly peaceful collective farms had become a haven for crypto-kulak counter-revolutionaries: they were quietly undermining collectivization while pretending to support it. Having branded, such 'pseudo-co-operation' with collectivization as a new form of crime, the Secretary-General went on to legislate against yet another even more involuted category of political offence: *connivance in or toleration of pseudo-co-operation*.[15] It was a quintessentially Stalinist concept. As we are reminded, Stalin's campaign against the peasants combined two seemingly irreconcilable qualities: ingenuity and crudity. One does not know which to admire the more: the subtlety of his so-called dialectic or the keen instinct which told him that, in politics, the most unsubtle form of chicanery can often be the most effective.

Peasant resistance could not stave off collectivization, but it could and did render the campaign an economic disaster. Faced with dispossession and confiscation, villagers continued to hoard their grain; they converted it into home-brewed spirits or otherwise consumed it; they refused to sow their lands; they burnt their crops; they slaughtered their livestock; they murdered the Secretary-General's emissaries; and they adopted many other desperate procedures which might have defeated even a Stalin, had the peasantry managed to co-ordinate its activities on an all-Union scale. As it was, production declined drastically, particularly in stock-breeding, until over-all holdings in cattle, horses and other farm animals stood at about half the pre-collectivization total. Nor could Machine Tractor Stations, newly established to provide the collective farms with a pool of agricultural machinery, at first make good the deficiency of draught animals caused by the slaughter or starvation of many millions of horses.

In 1932 famine erupted in the main grain-producing areas: not as the result of a disastrous harvest (for the crop was only slightly below average), but through Stalin's policy of confiscating the peasants' grain stocks by force. The dictator's fortunes were now at a low ebb: his extravagant policies seemed discredited, and it was at this period, if ever during his long career, that he came near to falling from power – not because any political opposition remained, but because the country seemed to be dissolving in chaos. He was saved, to some extent, by the very scale of the disaster which he had provoked, and by having involved so vast a corps of officials who – like their Leader – had a strong vested interest in proclaiming that everything had gone according to plan. Stalin was also sustained by the stolid courage which enabled him to sweat out the crisis until 1933, when a better harvest helped to rescue him – particularly as there were now considerably fewer peasants who needed to be fed! By now he was drawing dividends from 'thinking big' even in error – and also from organizing the country in such a way that he could afford to make all the mistakes, knowing that others would pay all the penalties. By 1933 collectivized agriculture seemed to have established itself as the pattern for the future, while manpower was migrating or was being drafted on a satisfactory scale from the terrorized countryside to the towns as yet somewhat less terrorized, thus swelling the industrial labour force. But the real profit was political, not economic. By conscripting the peasantry, Stalin had foisted totalitarian controls on the largest and most conservative class in Russian society.

Imposing collectivization, Stalin was successfully disguising as an economic reform what was essentially a political campaign, and the same pretence was present in his industrializing operations. These, too, were presented to the world as an economic exercise, whereas their prime function was to subject Soviet industry – no less than the Soviet peasantry – to the dictator's unchallenged command. The industrialization programme was ruthlessly enforced, but with less cruelty than the collectivization campaign, and also enlisted enthusiasm which was conspicuously absent among the collectivized peasantry. Moreover, the industrial drive was more successful in attaining its economic objectives. Already, in June 1930, Stalin felt able to announce that the Soviet Union was on the eve of changing from an agrarian into an industrial society.[16] The boast was premature, but far from absurd.

To survey the transformation of the USSR into a modern industrialized society is to run into a hurricane of Stalinist statistics purporting to chart Soviet performance, past, present and future. For ever publicizing percentages and tonnages relating to what allegedly had been, was being, should be, would be, could be, might have been produced in the way of coal, oil, pig iron, steel, tractors, combine harvesters, factories, hydro-electric stations and the like, the director invested with an air of spurious exactitude pronouncements essentially magical and liturgical. His statistics were not, to put it mildly, designed for checking by independent observers; they were prayer formulae laden with emotions quasi-religious, not a precise record of performance. Hence the element of portentous elusiveness so characteristic of the Five Year Plans from the first onwards. No date, no target, no percentage ever seemed to solidify, even the period within which the First Five Year Plan operated being subject to Stalinist prestidigitation. Formally adopted in mid-1929, as noted above, the Plan was simultaneously back-dated to the previous October, in which month it was retrospectively deemed to have begun. Then, in January 1933, Stalin triumphantly announced that the Five Year Plan had already been fulfilled: not in five years but in four and a quarter.[17] The dates, the percentages, the tonnages with which he supported this claim remained unverifiable.

All this occurred against a background of extreme tension and confusion. Production targets, deceptively termed norms, were subject to periodical unheralded upwards revision; nor were they in any real sense targets: they were not intended to be hit, but to be overshot – if possible to a spectacular degree – through maximal over-fulfilment. Straining to maximize the production of individual enterprises, while failing adequately to coordinate production as a whole, the Stalinized economy was far indeed from presenting the model of exemplary planning which its promoters sought to advertise by publicizing production figures designed to function as a collective intoxicant. To increase the general mood of exaltation and bewilderment, members of the Stalinist priestly caste intoned phrases such as 'full steam ahead' or 'at full tilt', while drawing lavishly on military vocabulary to describe successes on the Industrial Front. Meanwhile waste and inefficiency were to be observed on all sides: breakdowns; accidents; lack of safety precautions; vital machinery left to rust and moulder unused after being delivered to the wrong place; valuable plant accidentally ruined by unskilled operators. To criticize such fiascos was to utter anti-Soviet propaganda, while to fail to denounce them was to connive at sabotage! Moreover, the more deeply Stalin became involved in his economic revolution, the more did he sense – or pretend to sense – all around him the presence of traitors, counter-revolutionaries, capitalist spies and innumerable other brands of enemy. Now that collectivization and the Plan were causing fiascos on an ever increasing scale, and hence creating an ever greater need for scapegoats, this long familiar demonology had become more necessary to him than ever.

Despite excess of zeal, lack of food, primitive conditions, despite innumerable errors and miscalculations, substantial progress was yet achieved under the First and succeeding Five Year Plans. While older industrial enterprises were reinforced and expanded, new projects also came into being. They included the great Dnieper Hydro-electrical Station, the largest in Europe, which (as we remember) Stalin had deprecated when it was in the blue-print stage, but which was opened with Hieratic fanfares in 1932. There were the Stalingrad Tractor Factory; the iron and steel plant at Magnitogorsk in the Urals; the vastly expanded coal fields of the Kuznetsk Basin in southern Siberia. There was the new canal linking the Baltic with the White Sea; and there was a host of other enterprises, great and small. Some, including the White Sea Canal, were built by the labour of political prisoners. Others were the work of free labourers who found their liberties progressively restricted as the Plan moved into top gear, bringing with it harsh new labour laws.

Once permitted to change his employment at will, the 'free' Soviet worker now found himself tied to his job. A new law made absentees liable to severe penalties. Piecework was introduced – despite Marxist doctrine deploring it as exploitation of the workers. Factories were managed on authoritarian lines by a single boss vulnerable to harassment by Party and police – but in no degree by the workers, who had no say in management. The internal passport – a compulsory identity card carried by all town-dwellers, and once abominated as a symbol of Imperial Russian police control – was reintroduced. Differential pay scales created between privileged and unprivileged citizens a gap so wide that no trace remained of Communist egalitarianism. Fervently opposed to any such levelling policy, Stalin lost no opportunity of saying so. Meanwhile his trade unions were more than ever operating as a factory police, spurring on the workers to over-shoot their targets, but omitting to defend their rights and interests. Thus did the Soviet worker of the early 1930s find himself converted into a cog in the machinery of totalitarianism – as, on an even humbler level, did his rustic cousins.

If one seeks, as any student of Stalin must, to assess the over-all impact of his industrialization-collectivization drive, the ultimate verdict must depend on the standard of judgement which is applied. Viewed exclusively as a technique of imposing totalitarian political controls and of concentrating power in the hands of a single individual, Stalinism was a spectacular success. If, on the other hand, the individual liberty and personal prosperity of the governed are to be accepted as the main criteria, then Stalinism must be judged an equally resounding failure. We can therefore expect no unanimity on the degree of credit due to Stalin the wholesale industrializer. According to Deutscher: 'Those who still view the political fortunes of countries in terms of national ambitions and prestige cannot but accord to Stalin the foremost place among all those rulers who, through the ages, were engaged in building up Russia's power.'[18] This assessment is less favourable than may at first appear, however, since the records of the principal earlier Russian power-builders – Ivan III, Ivan the Terrible, Catherine the Great and Peter the Great – were marred, as was that of the Secretary-General, by elements of gross wastefulness and brutality.

Taking control of a huge but backward nation at the end of the 1920s, Stalin was to leave it nearly a quarter of a century later as a mighty force in international affairs. By the time of his death he had made the USSR second in strength and influence to the United States alone. Here was a major achievement, calling for unusual qualities of insight, persistence and cruelty; yet it was anything but an unqualified triumph. Ruthlessness such as Stalin's is no index of extreme competence, as is commonly assumed, but rather the reverse. Despite its ultimate effectiveness in creating a great industrial and military complex, Stalinism was all along a slipshod and messy process. Nor can one contention of the dictator's apologists be accepted: that Stalinism and Stalinism alone could have achieved comparable results under Russian conditions. Given stable government, almost any imaginable system would have promoted modernization . . . and not necessarily less effectively than the Secretary-General's. Even so inept an administrator as the last Tsar, Nicholas II – had he survived and somehow miraculously regained control of the country – would almost certainly have presided over a rapidly industrializing Russia . . . as, incidentally, he already had been presiding in the 1890s and 1900s. It has been well said, with reference to Stalin's record in this area, that: 'At least the same degree of industrial development could have been achieved by 1941 with less drastic means.'[19] It has also been admirably said that: 'Stalinism is one way of attaining industrialization, just as cannibalism is one way of attaining a high protein diet.'[20]

Heavily though Stalin depended on terroristic methods – which indeed did provoke cases of cannibalism in the famine areas – he also owed much of his success in modernizing Russia to his ability to elicit a sincere patriotic response from his subjects. Nowhere did he do so more eloquently than in one celebrated statement which occurs in a speech of February 1931. Contradicting those who would retard the headlong modernization of the Soviet Union, the dictator points out, in typical style, that:

To slow down means to lag behind. To be backward means to be beaten. But we don't want to be beaten! We certainly do not! Actually, the history of the old Russia has consisted in being beaten again and again because she was backward. She was beaten by Mongol Khans, beaten by Turkish beys, beaten by Swedish feudalists. She was beaten by Polish-Lithuanian gentry. She was beaten by Anglo-French capitalists. She was beaten by Japanese barons. All have beaten her – because of her backwardness: military backwardness, cultural backwardness, governmental backwardness, industrial backwardness, agricultural backwardness. She was beaten because to beat her has paid off, and because people have been able to get away with it. . . . Such is the law of exploiters: to beat up the backward and weak. Such is the jungle law of capitalism. If you are backward and weak, then you are in the wrong, and you may be beaten and enslaved. But if you are powerful you are *ipso facto* in the right and people must beware of you.

That is why we must lag behind no longer.[21]

This inspiring call to action helped to mobilize the Soviet Union behind Stalin until, by the end of his life, fears of foreign exploitation had been very largely allayed. By then it was foreign countries which increasingly feared, or already suffered, exploitation and domination by Russia . . . just as many another easily forgotten foreign country and people (including Stalin's own Georgian motherland) had feared and been absorbed by Muscovite and Imperial Russia in earlier centuries.

As for being 'beaten up' by foreigners, Stalin's subjects had good cause from 1930 onwards to reflect with patriotic pride that neither Anglo-French capitalists, nor Polish-Lithuanian gentry, nor Swedish feudalists, nor yet Turkish beys had ever inflicted punishment on Russia remotely comparable to that which their own latest autocratic ruler – engendered within the Russian Empire – had come to dispense. Among the catalogue of oppressors listed in Stalin's oration of 1931 only the Mongol-Tatar heirs of Genghis Khan – those burners, enslavers and slaughterers of ancient Russia – could claim parity, as liquidators of Slavs, with the Georgian universal genius.

Patterns of Oppression

No institution was more characteristic of rampant Stalinism than the Soviet concentration camp empire as it flourished from 1930 onwards.

So-called concentration camps had been maintained on a modest scale since the first years of Lenin's rule. The prisoners, who had then numbered mere thousands or tens of thousands, had consisted to a significant degree of genuine ideological dissidents, and their treatment had been marked by leniency which was to become a dim memory under all-out Stalinism. With mass collectivization, camp conditions grew harsher and the total of inmates increased until it was numbered in millions. The new influx mostly comprised freshly 'dekulakized' muzhiks. Then, towards the end of the decade, the Great Terror took a heavy toll from the educated sections of the community. During and after the Second World War the camps came to be newly stocked by Soviet prisoners 'released' from German captivity; by non-approved foreigners from the satellite states; and by members of inconvenient Soviet minority nationalities.

Unless OGPU and later security police archives should be opened, exact statistics will continue to elude investigators. But numerous indications make it unlikely that the total camp population ever sank below ten million during the last two decades of the dictatorship, and it may have far exceeded that figure at times.

[Owing to the high mortality rates, massive waves of new arrests were necessary to replace wastage through starvation, exposure, ill treatment, overwork and disease. Hence the constant search for new categories of prisoner, since the camp system was not merely the chief buttress of Stalin's political terror apparatus, but also had an economic role. Prisoners were harnessed to the Five Year Plans, being employed on lumbering, coal mining, gold extraction and the construction of transport undertakings: canals, railroads, highways and airports. Vast areas of northern Russia, Siberia and Central Asia became, in effect, concentration camp provinces ruled by the OGPU. In some of the more populous areas, gangs of slave labourers were hired out to Soviet industrial agencies, most of which suffered from a manpower famine; here too conditions ensured that many a ganger died on the job.]

Since Stalin always veiled the seamier aspects of his régime in mystery the very existence of Soviet concentration camps was a state secret. But it was a truly Stalinist secret in that the truth was widely known or suspected, while never being openly admitted. Nor was it in Stalin's interests that his subjects should be unaware of these institutions to which they might never allude; for how, in that case, could the camp empire serve its purpose as a terrorizing agency and means of ensuring political discipline? Thus uncamps containing untold millions of unpersons were relegated by Stalinist thought control to the vast memory hole of topics known but unmentionable. Nor did the Stalinist machine ever publicize the camp empire to the world outside the Soviet Union. Though evidence of so widespread an abuse inevitably did filter abroad, foreign public opinion was persuaded by its Stalinist manipulators to dismiss such tales as figments of bourgeois propaganda. A similar campaign of secrecy had done much to hush up the great Soviet famine of 1932-3 – thus confirming Stalin's hunch that humanity's collective political brain is infinitely gullible, and that there is no need to be over-subtle in feeding it with spurious data.

Not content with exploiting its victims, Stalinism also mocked them in characteristic idiom. After the completion, in August 1933, of the White Sea Canal – a slave labour project which had caused the death of many (perhaps a third) among the three-hundred-thousand-strong labour force –[1] Stalin's propagandists issued a lavish publicity hand-out sponsored by the 'Great Humanist' Maxim Gorky, and disguising this monument to conscripted misery as a triumph of Socialist construction achieved by the enthusiastic efforts of free men. Jointly authored by thirty-seven pliant scribes in all, this glossy publication mendaciously stresses the allegedly lavish welfare aspects of the murderous enterprise, including the libraries and brass bands purportedly made available to the enthusiastic toilers. Photographs of eager workers queuing for hot pies emphasize the talent for adding insult to mortal injury which typifies fully-fledged Stalinism.[2]

Though the peasantry was the prime target for the repressions of the early 1930s, and though Stalin's terror was not to strike the Soviet élite with full fury until 1937-8, it would be an error to conclude that the upper crust of Soviet society remained immune from the dictator's malign attentions in the preceding period. Managers, technicians, engineers and officials were already coming under attack earlier in the decade – the campaign being principally directed, at this stage, against those who remained outside the Party. Such repression of non-Party professional men received its most spectacular expression through three show trials resembling the Shakhty affair of mid-1928, as described above.

In November-December 1930 certain alleged members of a so-called Industrial Party, purportedly headed by a Professor Ramzin, were subjected to this special form of judicial processing, while a great hate campaign echoed through the Soviet Union. For 'scientifically inflated sensationalism and for the transparency of its make-believe', this affair outdid even the later Moscow show trials of 1936-7.[3] According to the indictment, numerous engineers and planners had, since 1925, been systematically wrecking Soviet industry at the behest of Raymond Poincaré, Sir Henry Deterding, Lawrence of Arabia and other alien mischief-makers. In accordance with Communist protocol, the guilt of the eight Soviet accused was extensively proclaimed long before their trial, and resolutions demanding the death penalty were carried on a nationwide scale. Among bodies clamouring for the execution of these saboteurs was the Soviet Academy of Sciences: an index of the extent to which Stalinism had already contaminated the most exalted areas. As for the righteously indignant masses, over half a million 'workers' trudged past the court-room as the trial was in process, screaming 'Death! Death! Death!'[4] Meanwhile similar rigged explosions of the people's wrath were 'spontaneously' erupting all over the Soviet Union. Once again the son of an indicted wrecker dutifully filed a demand for his father to be shot as a class enemy.

Such was the atmosphere as eight mild, scholarly-looking arch-villains were submitted to elaborately staged pseudo-judicial processing. Fifty-six blazing chandeliers, seventy-five reporters (Soviet and alien) and numerous diplomats witnessed the ritual humiliation of the accused, as each intoned the long self-condemning litany drilled into him under OGPU supervision. Here, as in other Stalinist show trials, no evidence was offered other than the confessions of the accused men, including their mutual implication of each other. But though proceedings were duly interrupted by devotional shrieks ('Death to the wreckers!') from the body of the court, and though five of the eight were indeed condemned to execution, these capital sentences were commuted to imprisonment; shortly afterwards Ramzin and his accomplices were reported back at their desks working away as if nothing out of the ordinary had ever happened to them.

The two other main show trials of the period – the Menshevik trial of March 1931 and that of the Metro-Vickers engineers in April 1933 – followed the same pattern, but were less elaborately stage-managed. Once again the charges had an international flavour deriving from alleged collusion with émigré Mensheviks in the one case, and from the presence of six British citizens among the victims of the other. As usual, the confessions of the accused formed the sole evidence offered against them. The question therefore arose once again: why were they so eager to admit to crimes which they had every motive to disavow even if they were guilty? As is now evident, these results were obtained by exploiting all means of pressure and trickery while the accused were undergoing preliminary 'investigation' in captivity. Torture and threat of torture in the cellars of the OGPU were only the most lurid among the devices employed. Others included menaces to the families of the accused and promises of leniency in return for the undertaking to recite one's lines correctly. From the British Metro-Vickers engineers Stalin's court obtained only limited co-operation; one of the accused, for instance, denounced the entire proceedings as 'a frame-up based on the evidence of terrorized prisoners'.[5]

Though this and other early show trials did indeed fall short of perfect stage-management, they at least furnished more scapegoats for the innumerable breakdowns attending Stalin's industrialization and collectivization drive. Hungry, exhausted, ill-housed, ill-clothed and surrounded by broken or neglected machinery, the Soviet citizen was supplied – in the persons of Professor Ramzin and Engineer MacDonald – with a focus for hatred which might otherwise have been directed against the Secretary-General. More important was the trials' function in justifying intensified general repression throughout the Soviet Union. Only in an atmosphere of crisis, witch-hunt and exaggerated tension could the population be panicked into accepting the ever-increasing severities which Stalin had in store. Last and by no means least, the framing of non-party and foreign engineers helped to build up a body of judicial or anti-judicial precedent which would one day enable Stalin to turn the show trial weapon against bigger game: his leading enemies within the Party, from Zinovyev and Kamenev downwards.

Among professional men repressed in the early 1930s, show-trial victims represented only the minority selected to attract maximum publicity. More frequently proceedings took place *in camera*: for example, trials of bacteriologists; trials of state farm officials; trials of officials from the commissariats of finance and agriculture. It made little difference to the victims whether they were secretly tried or – as also happened extensively – simply executed out of hand. That was the fate of forty-eight alleged saboteurs of the meat supply, as also of alleged adherents of a dissident 'peasant party', such victims being scapegoats for the failures of collectivized agriculture. Physicists, too, were privily arraigned. There was also a secret trial of historians; it followed a stridently dogmatic article of 1931 – in the form of a letter to the historical journal *Proletarskaya revolyutsiya* (Proletarian Revolution) – in which Stalin is found personally rewriting early Bolshevik history to conform with his developing Legend.[6] But not all the victims of these persecutions were shot, not all disappeared in captivity. One expert in energetics was successively condemned to death, pardoned, sent to a concentration camp, released, rehabilitated and decorated: all in the space of twenty months.[7] The case was by no means exceptional.

Not least among the period's atrocities was the forcible extraction of foreign currency, as also of gold, silver and jewellery which could be sold to provide much-needed funds. Those suspected of possessing such valuables were confined in small, hot, crowded chambers known as sweat-rooms or louse-pits: treatment which led to madness or death in some cases. It was sometimes varied with the 'conveyor': a system which involved the non-stop screaming interrogation of suspects denied sleep. Blows, abuse and racial insults – the term *zhid* ('yid') being applied to the many Jews subjected to this process – were now a commonplace among procedures which had deteriorated from the unedifying level of the 1920s, as the OGPU fought to meet the demands of accelerated Stalinism.[8]

Continuing the saga of increasing repressiveness, we come to the one area in which the dictator met significant resistance in the early 1930s: that of the ruling Party. Although, as we have noted, open Communist opposition to Stalin had ended with the defeat of Bukharin, the years 1930–2 yet witnessed at least three attempts by Party members of some standing to discredit the Secretary-General behind the scenes. And though these offenders were indeed punished, they at least escaped summary execution as increasingly meted out to non-party undesirables.

In 1930 two hitherto loyal Stalinists – Syrtsov (a Politburo candidate) and Lominadze (a Central Committee member) – challenged the newly established dictatorship. Syrtsov jeered at the First Five Year Plan, referring to it as 'eyewash', and comparing the new tractor factory at Stalingrad with a Potemkin village: that is, a fraudulent show-piece designed to deceive the eye of casually inspecting authority. Lominadze accused the authorities of taking a lordly, feudal attitude to the peasant. Both were expelled from the Central Committee.[9]

More ominous was the Ryutin Case of late 1932. Ryutin was a former rightist who had circulated a two-hundred-page clandestine manifesto containing an outspoken denunciation of Stalin. Though the text has never been released, Ryutin is known to have harped on the dictator's role as the vindictive, power-crazed evil genius of the Russian revolution, claiming that he must be removed if Soviet society was not to collapse.[10] The appearance of this outburst coincided with the lowest ebb of Stalin's political fortunes: the time when breakneck collectivization and industrialization both seemed discredited; when the standard of living was falling; when food rationing had been introduced; and when the future seemed black. As the leader responsible for such disasters, Stalin should be dismissed from high office, Ryutin argued; but he does not appear to have called for Stalin's assassination, as Stalin himself tried to claim.[11]

Why did Stalin thus exaggerate Ryutin's offence? Why did he make such strenuous efforts to have Ryutin shot? The great attraction was Ryutin's status as a Party member of some prominence, though he was by no means one of the top leaders. Hitherto far too few Bolsheviks had been shot for political reasons, the only case of importance being that of the Trotskyite Blyumkin in 1929. But Blyumkin had not been shot for opposing Stalin; nor was he a veteran Bolshevik. In spite of that and other cases, the taboo against the execution of Party members still held firm in 1932. It was high time to break it by shooting someone of Ryutin's seniority. Such an execution would establish a valuable precedent, bringing the dictator closer to what we now know to have been his goal: the right to consign to death without question, let or hindrance, any Communist or expelled Communist, from the most senior downwards.

No wonder, then, that Stalin could neither persuade the Central Control Commission to sanction Ryutin's execution in 1932 nor induce the OGPU to carry it out on the quiet. Instead of that the Secretary-General was compelled to debate the Ryutin affair in the Politburo. For once he found himself in a minority, since even his most abject colleagues could assess the danger to themselves personally. Stalin tried to win the Politburo over, pointing to an alleged wave of political terrorism directed against the régime and claiming this to be especially prevalent among young Communists. Surely Ryutin deserved shooting as the inspirer of such activities? But other Politburo members, headed by Sergey Kirov, urged leniency. Stalin had to withdraw, and Ryutin was merely sentenced to confinement in an isolator: the special type of Stalinist prison in which important political offenders were held.[12] He was also expelled from the Party as a degenerate, traitorous would-be restorer of capitalism.[13] Others who had known of Ryutin's manifesto, but had not reported the matter, were also persecuted – among them being Zinovyev and Kamenev, who were now expelled from the Party for the second time and exiled to the Urals.

Rallying in 1933 from the decline of the previous year, Stalin had less to fear from an attack such as Ryutin's. But the affair continued to rankle. It was still rankling when, on 25 September 1936 (to anticipate our narrative), the dictator dispatched the famous telegram replacing the NKVD (OGPU) chief Yagoda with Yezhov, and thus launching the Great Terror. Recommending this change at the head of his political police, Stalin stated that the OGPU was now *four years behind* in dealing with the 'Trotskyite-Zinovyevite bloc'.[14] As has frequently been noted, precisely four years had passed since the Ryutin scandal of autumn 1932; and though Stalin made no explicit reference to this affair in his telegram of 1936, there can be little doubt that he had it in mind. Association with Ryutin was also to figure prominently among the charges put forward at the great Moscow show trials of 1936–8.

Patron of Literature and Interviewee

The fate of literature is a valuable index to the progress made by galloping Stalinization.

Considerable licence had been permitted to Soviet writers of the 1920s, provided that they had been willing to avoid open criticism of the régime and its ideology; and even that restriction had been successfully defied by certain satirists. By the end of the decade, however, the Stalinist control system was engulfing literature too – first regimenting and intimidating Soviet writers, then terrorizing and liquidating them. For the previous, negative obligation (not to abuse the régime) Stalin substituted the positive duty to produce publicity material – whether novels, stories, poems or criticism – designed to boost the Five Year Plan and other aspects of his system. For a time he permitted RAPP – an association of 'proletarian writers' and the most militant among many competing literary associations of the period – to dragoon and bully rival groupings; then he liquidated RAPP, many of its spokesmen being destined to perish in the Terror. In 1932 a new and purportedly liberal Soviet Writers' Union was set up, superseding all other authors' groupings. But this was merely one more temporary retreat enabling the dictator to pounce yet more ferociously after a brief recoil. The Writers' Union soon became more restrictive than RAPP, successfully imposing greater regimentation through a newly promoted and compulsorily imposed literary method: Socialist Realism. Stripped of a Hieratic coating designed to deceive the simple-minded, Socialist Realism was simply a device for completing the conversion of Soviet authors into advertising copywriters hired to 'sell' Stalin and his system.

The enlistment of Maxim Gorky as a sponsor of Socialist Realism and Chairman of the Writers' Union – and thus as an apparent all-out propagandist of Stalinism – was a triumph for the dictator. But though it is tempting to dismiss the ageing Gorky as a mere creature of Stalin's, his attitude remained ambivalent, as it had always been. After openly criticizing the authoritarianism of early Bolshevik rule, and after being silenced by Lenin's censorship in July 1918, Gorky had withdrawn to Italy, where he had lived in exile during most of the 1920s. By luring the Great Writer and Humanist back to his homeland – first to celebrate his sixtieth birthday on 16 March 1928, then as a permanent resident from 1931 onwards – Stalin scored heavily, for he could now parade the most celebrated living Russian author as an admirer of his system. Vulnerable to flattery, Gorky received an Order of Lenin; a major city, Nizhny Novgorod, was named Gorky; Moscow's chief thoroughfare became Gorky Street; and there were innumerable other widely publicized marks of esteem. Gorky, according to the émigré Russian poet Khodasevich, had finally sold out:

Not for money, but to preserve the principal illusion of his life. . . . no matter how the Revolution had turned out, it was the only thing that could guarantee his reputation during his lifetime as the great proletarian writer and leader and after his death assure him of a niche for his ashes in the Kremlin wall. In exchange for that, the Revolution required of him, as it requires of everyone, not honest service but slavishness and sycophancy. He became a slave and sycophant.

So instead of being a writer and friend of writers, he was transformed into a superintendent of writers.[1]

Thus the service which Gorky might expect to receive from Stalin was exactly that which Stalin hoped to receive from Gorky: powerful assistance in selling his image to the world and to posterity.

Though gross flattery and double-talk might manipulate Gorky into temporary postures of servility, he had an awkward tendency to spring briefly erect, thus representing a danger as well as an asset to Stalin. That the Great Writer required careful handling, Stalin well understood. His *Works* include a letter to Gorky couched in the rare, excruciatingly jaunty style which passed with him as friendly badinage between equals; here the Secretary-General rebuts criticisms levelled by the Great Writer against various features of developing Stalinism.[2] Redomiciled in Russia, Gorky sought to mediate between Stalin and the defeated oppositionists, even contriving to arrange a meeting to reconcile Stalin and Kamenev. Bukharin has said that Gorky exercised great influence on Stalin and that the Soviet Union had Gorky to thank for the relaxed atmosphere of 1934, when Stalin 'suddenly became milder, more affable, more yielding; he took pleasure in the society of writers, artists and painters, in listening to their conversation and in stimulating them to frank discussion.'[3]

One much-publicized episode of the Gorky-Stalin honeymoon occurred when the dictator inscribed the Great Writer's verse tale *Death and the Maiden* with the words: 'this . . . is more powerful than Goethe's *Faust*.' A tribute from the one-time lyricist of Tiflis to another equally inept versifier, this widely advertised comment came to the ears of Osip Mandelstam, the most sensitive Russian bard of the era; it led him straight to a poet's conclusion, which was to be borne out by events: 'We are finished.'[4]

The eventual fate of Mandelstam, Gorky and other writers must be considered below. Meanwhile we note that contact with Stalin was not yet – in the early 1930s – proving fatal to the authors concerned, and that there were instances of writers, and others, who dared to oppose the dictator and yet outlived the terror of the later decade. The novelist Mikhail Sholokhov protested to Stalin about the evils of collectivization in his native Don Cossack countryside, but survived a rebuke (for 'one-sidedness')[5] to continue publication of his multi-tier masterpiece *The Quiet Don*: a work which flouts the canons of Socialist Realism. Yevgeny Zamyatin – an ex-Bolshevik, and an outspoken satirist of the Soviet system since its early period – wrote to Stalin in June 1931 complaining that publication of his works had been banned, and that he had become the victim of a systematic campaign of abuse in the press. Zamyatin asked permission to emigrate from the Soviet

Union . . . and lived to use an exit visa obtained through Gorky's intercession. Such episodes reflect the dictator's erratic responses to individuals. Exacting abject obedience while despising those who fawned on him, he liked a man who could look him in the eye and speak to him as an equal. Not that such boldness was any guarantee of immunity, for one can be safe from a Stalin only by remaining outside his orbit entirely. Zamyatin and Sholokhov were lucky to survive.

From 1930 onwards Stalin – who had so far kept himself proverbially inaccessible – began to grant interviews to favoured foreigners: journalists and travellers from England, Germany and the USA. First to obtain such a scoop was Eugene Lyons, an American press correspondent, who interviewed the dictator on 23 November 1930. The scene was Stalin's office in the Central Committee's headquarters on Moscow's Old Square: a six-storey building not far from the Kremlin. Lyons was astonished to find an atmosphere of austerity. Here was no emphasis on the trappings of power, only on 'power naked, clean and serene in its strength'.[6] The room had a high ceiling and was simply furnished; there were framed portraits of Marx, Engels and Lenin – but none of Stalin himself, which meant that this was probably the only office in the empire to lack such an embellishment. Stalin wore his familiar garb, consisting of a high-collared olive-drab jacket, belted at the waist, with trousers tucked into black jack-boots. He seemed vigorous and there was no trace of grey in his hair. His smile was shy; he resembled anything but the scowling, self-important dictator of popular imagination; he was relaxed and completely at ease; he had an air of immense, highly disciplined power in reserve. The despot coolly parried Lyons's question ('Are you a dictator?') by reference to the Soviet system of government which, said he, excluded the very possibility of one-man rule. In the Soviet Union, Stalin blandly explained, decisions were made by the Party and acted upon by its chosen organs, the Central Committee and the Politburo. Though Lyons was neither an admirer of Stalinism nor one of those many naïve foreigners who took the Secretary-General at his own valuation, he found Stalin personally likeable: an impression which he retained thereafter, even when the actions of Stalin's régime seemed most detestable.[7]

Such was a common reaction to the Georgian, whose occasional diffidence of manner, talent for listening and sporadic but impressive courtesy gained him much personal sympathy. The English travel-writer Rosita Forbes was under few illusions about the excesses of the Stalin régime, yet could not bring herself to think of its creator as personally cruel. 'I have seen him smiling at children, pleased by the flattery of panic-stricken comrades, cherishing a dog, teasing factory-girls with a blunt and amiable humour which appealed to them.'[8] One is reminded of the American diplomat's wife who described the Secretary-General as 'dreamy',[9] and of other testimonials to the social or sexual charm exerted by the tyrant.

On 13 December 1931 the German author Emil Ludwig – romantic biographer of Napoleon and Bismarck, and interviewer of Mussolini – plied Stalin with questions in an attempt to probe beneath the surface of the Secretary-General's methods.[10] Did Stalin regard himself as the heir of Peter the Great? What was the role of great men in history? How was one to understand the excessive cruelty of Bolshevik methods? Why did he govern by fear? What – once again – was the meaning of one-man dictatorial rule in the Soviet Union? With the ease of a consummate politician, Stalin parried all these thrusts. Did Ludwig really believe that the Bolsheviks could have held power for fourteen years by fear alone? There was no dictatorship, for the Russian worker would never have tolerated the concentration of power in one man's hands – as Trotsky and Plekhanov had once found to their cost, despite the exalted position which they had once occupied within the Party. All decisions were taken collectively, power being vested in the Party's seventy-man Central Committee. Stalin called this 'our Areopagus'; the parallel was closer than he perhaps realized in so far as the Athenian Council of the Areopagus ceased to be elective during the fifth century BC, losing its real power (apart from the function of judging homicide cases) but retaining certain religious responsibilities.[11] As for Peter the Great, Stalin disclaimed any comparison, professing himself merely the humble pupil of Lenin and asserting that all his efforts were devoted to improving the conditions of the working class, whereas the Great Tsar had been a scourge of the enserfed peasantry. As for the theory that history is made by 'great men', Stalin was prepared to agree; the idea was not, as commonly thought, counter-Marxist. But, said Stalin, a great man must operate within the context of his epoch; otherwise he would become a mere Don Quixote. Nor did Russian Marxists believe, as often supposed, in the vulgar egalitarianism which would reduce all citizens to a common denominator. Throughout the interview Stalin maintained the fiction of Bolshevik bluntness and straight dealing. 'If we had said one thing and done another we should have lost our authority with the popular masses.'[12] The claim has an appeal for the connoisseur, since it was by the endless, hypnotic repetition of such soothing lies that the popular masses had been reduced to a huddle of Stalin-dominated material.

Describing his interview, Ludwig praises the shoemaker's son from the Caucasus who had spoken so trenchantly that his every word could be published just as it stood in the stenographic report.[13] Here, of course, the dictator had an advantage over most politicians, since his every word automatically became official policy solely by virtue of the fact that he, Stalin, had enunciated it. One should not, however, underestimate the formidable skill employed by Stalin when challenged by Ludwig: an experienced if somewhat facile observer not subject to OGPU jurisdiction.

In 1931 Stalin's knowledge of the 'bourgeois' world was further enriched through a visit paid to Moscow by the author George Bernard Shaw and Lady Astor, the British Member of Parliament of American origin. Their tour has claims to be regarded as the most frivolous episode in recorded history. Celebrating his seventy-fifth birthday in the former Gentry Club in Moscow – scene of Stalin's show trials – Shaw ridiculed the idea that the USSR might, in this famine year, be faced by food shortages; he based his assessment of Soviet food resources on the menu in the Metropole Hotel. The prankish veteran also had himself photographed astride the great cannon in the Kremlin, impishly regurgitating everywhere the Soviet hand-out material with which he was constantly fed, his every word snapped up by an attendant posse of journalists.[14]

That such base clowning should not seem the exclusive prerogative of the male sex was the concern of that redoubtable feminist Lady Astor. On one memorable public occasion she went down on bended knee to present a petition 'as in days of yore' on behalf of a persecuted Russian family. Her protégés were the wife and children of a certain émigré Russian professor, for whom the rich and titled suppliant now sought Soviet exit visas to enable them to join the head of the family in America. Though the petition was politely received, the only effect was – or so it seems likely from enquiries later pursued by Eugene Lyons – to consign its intended beneficiaries to the clutches of the OGPU.[15]

In due course these eminent persons were received in audience by Stalin, who impressed Shaw as a cross between a pope and a field-marshal, resembling the illegitimate soldier son of a cardinal. The dictator's manners would have been perfect 'if only he had been able to conceal the fact that we amused him enormously'. Once again Lady Astor grasped the initiative, asking Stalin: 'How long are you going to go on killing people?' When this had at last been unwillingly translated on the dictator's insistence by a Soviet interpreter scared out of his wits, Stalin coolly replied that the process would continue as long as was necessary; some slaughter was inevitable before a Communist state could be established under conditions so disrupted. Lady Astor then criticized the bringing up of Soviet children, asking Stalin to send 'a good sensible woman' to her in London: 'I will take care of her and show her how children of five should be handled.' Unabashed by such officiousness, Stalin duly noted his guest's London address and saw to it that she was visited by a troop of 'sensible' Soviet women emissaries whom she was thus compelled to entertain. 'She must have felt that Uncle Joe had got a bit of his own back,' was Shaw's comment on this episode.[16]

Shaw's view of Stalin remained highly favourable throughout the following years, being an outstanding example of the admiration which extreme brutality so easily arouses in the fashionable intellectual, and reminding one of the benevolence with which the same observer also regarded Hitler and Mussolini. In a pamphlet of 1941, Shaw very properly protests against the tendency to view Stalin exclusively as a bloodstained monster whose sole occupation and delight is the shooting of his political opponents. But in assessing Stalin's positive achievements Shaw ignores – perhaps, even, relishes ? – their cost in suffering. Stalin has solved the agricultural problem by collectivization: a problem which our own 'chosen fainéant Prime Ministers failed so dangerously to solve.' Stalin has been 'founding new cities and colonies in two continents much faster than we can get a private bill through Parliament for a new tramline. We could not even put a bridge across the Severn while he was irrigating deserts and digging two or three Severns.'[17] As will be noted below, Hitler was to praise Stalin in terms very similar, deriding German inefficiency as allegedly shown up by alleged Stalinist efficiency.

H. G. Wells was another notable bourgeois interviewer of Stalin during these years. In 1934, Wells flew into Moscow full of prejudices against the Soviet dictator as a self-centred fanatic; as a despot without vices; as a monopolizer of power; as 'a sort of Bluebeard at the centre of Russian affairs'. Shortly afterwards the same observer was flying home again with an entirely different and even more misleading set of misconceptions. Stalin in the flesh had not borne out Wells's apprehensions. Here was no dour, sinister 'Highlander', but a diffident, gentlemanly fellow who courteously asked permission to smoke his pipe! As was his practice during such conversations, Stalin avoided looking directly at his guest: 'he looked past me rather than at me, but not evasively.' Soon Wells had plumbed his host's personality as that of an exceptionally unsubtle Georgian. 'I have never met a man more candid, fair and honest, and to these qualities it is, and to nothing occult and sinister, that he owes his tremendous undisputed ascendancy in Russia. I had thought before I saw him that he might be where he was because men were afraid of him, but I realize that he owes his position to the fact that no one is afraid of him and everybody trusts him.'[18] As such comments remind us, absolute power can corrupt its beholder no less effectively than its holder.

Never the rude, bungling oaf portrayed by Trotsky, the cobbler's son from Gori was now – when he chose – the very model of courteous and gentlemanly consideration. It must be added, though, that the milder-seeming Stalin tended to be reserved for potentially gullible foreign visitors – and also for his domestic servants, who adored him; his notorious 'roughness' could still surface easily enough when he was dealing with senior subordinates. Thus Stalin, a monster of cruelty in his policies, could be mild, affable and gentle in private. Should such a combination be thought surprising? Why is it often assumed that a tyrant's ruthlessness must be reflected in his personal manner? Not every despot rants and splutters like a Hitler, for style and impact are not necessarily correlated in this way. In the long run humanity has far more to fear from the quieter Georgian fanatic (whose system survives him) than from the extinct Austrian carpet-chewer.

Though Stalin might make himself available to a Wells, a Shaw or a Lady Astor, he often denied interviews to better qualified observers. One of these was Lord Chilston, British Ambassador to Moscow. Undeterred by lack of personal contact, this competent professional submitted a confidential report to London in which he dismissed the views of both Shaw and Wells – and in language admirably undiplomatic – as 'absurd'. Far from being a kindly man (the Ambassador reports), Stalin was loathed and feared by millions of his subjects. As for a claim made by Shaw, that Stalin could be dismissed from office at a moment's notice – nothing short of natural death, assassination, a military *coup* or a palace plot could remove him. Chilston explains why none of these procedures is likely to succeed; he stresses the security precautions surrounding the Leader and the availability of OGPU troops (independent of military command) to counter a possible army *coup*. As for other potential risks to Stalin, the OGPU head Yagoda lacks the weight for such an intrigue, as do all other members of the dictator's entourage with the doubtful exception of Kaganovich. When the author of this objective, realistic assessment claims Stalin as more human, sociable and friendly with people than would be expected, his words command respect, and we can forgive him the overrating of Kaganovich. Chilston also notes 'the calm assurance and strength in the Georgian and somewhat oriental face', together with Stalin's administrative ability and driving power.[19]

Family Man

In November 1932 the suicide of Stalin's second wife Nadezhda breaks suddenly into a career unusually free from domestic entanglement. So successfully had the Leader shielded his family life from publicity that many Soviet citizens discovered him to have been a husband only at the point when they learnt from the press that he had become a widower.

Unlike Stalin's first spouse – the pious Yekaterina Svanidze, who had perished some twenty-five years earlier – Nadezhda was no submissive oriental consort, and she rejected the humble role for which the Secretary-General (an 'Asiatic' in his domestic habits) attempted to cast her. Husband and wife were constantly quarrelling, and in 1926 Nadezhda decided to return to her parental home in Leningrad. She left Moscow with the two small children – the boy Vasily and the baby daughter Svetlana – abandoning a husband then involved in his struggle with the United Opposition. Stalin telephoned and persuaded her to return,[1] but relations remained strained: not least owing to his insistence on using foul language when entertaining guests in her presence. Herself a Party member who took her civic duties seriously, Nadezhda was determined to be more than a housewife. She followed a course in industrial chemistry, specializing in synthetic fibres. Stalin accepted this with reluctance, arranging for his wife's identity to be concealed from her fellow-students – which suited her well since she disliked the role of Soviet first lady. He also had her watched by his secret police.

By fellow-students (unaware of her exalted status) Stalin's wife was initiated into the horrors of Stalinism. She was appalled by the hardships of which she was told, and especially by cases of cannibalism reported in the starving villages. Nadezhda also learnt of the mass executions; the deportations; the gangs of starving, orphaned children who scoured and terrorized the countryside. She taxed her husband with these atrocities, only to be abused in obscene terms and accused of collecting Trotskyite rumours. Stalin ordered the arrest of her informants, also instituting a general persecution of the students who had helped his collectivization drive.[2]

At a party given on 7 November 1932 – the fifteenth anniversary of the October Revolution – Stalin and his wife had their last quarrel, during which Nadezhda protested before witnesses against Joseph's brutal treatment of the peasantry, provoking another stream of obscenities in reply.[3] Nadezhda left the party in great distress; poured out her resentment to Molotov's wife Polina; went home to the Kremlin apartment which she shared with Stalin; and shot herself with a Walther revolver presented to her by her brother, Pavel Alliluyev. Such was Pavel's version, confirmed through the account independently given to Stalin's daughter Svetlana by her old nurse.[4] Another, more spectacular narrative appears in Lermolo's suspect memoirs, and has Stalin himself attempting to strangle Nadezhda, also implying that his may have been the finger which pressed the trigger of the revolver;[5] but though this version agrees with widespread rumours portraying the dictator as his wife's murderer, it is almost certainly untrue.

The death of Stalin's second wife affected him profoundly. It provoked recurrent fits of rage, inspired in part by a reproachful suicide note in which she made political accusations for which the dictator's black record provided so ample a basis. Stalin was always harping on the tragedy of his second wife's death, especially when its anniversary came round each year, coinciding with that of the October Revolution. Someone must be guilty. And that someone must, of course, be someone other than Stalin himself. At first the dictator blamed Michael Arlen: best-selling novelist of the period and author of *The Green Hat*, which Nadezhda had been reading shortly before her death;[6] it was fortunate indeed for Arlen that he had long separated himself geographically from his Armenian origins to become the chronicler of London's Mayfair. Brooding on his wife's death over the years, the increasingly paranoid dictator began to reach out for victims closer to hand, finding them in her surviving confidantes: her sister Anna and her sister-in-law Yevgeniya (Pavel's widow); her friend Polina Molotova; all three were to be arrested some sixteen years after the suicide for 'knowing too much' about the death of Stalin's second wife.[7]

These arrests illustrate a fascinating trait in Stalin's developing personality. As the sum of his crimes increased, so did the need to fix the guilt on others. Hence, perhaps, the self-perpetuating character of the terror. For every relay of victims among the dictator's multi-million sacrifices a new relay of fresh victims must, in due course, take on the guilt and pay. Stalin's daughter's evidence brings out the crucial role played in this evolution by Nadezhda's suicide. 'I believe that my mother's death, which he had taken as a personal betrayal, deprived his soul of the last vestiges of human warmth.'[8] According to this theory, the impact of Nadezhda's passing on Stalin would resemble that of the Tsaritsa Anastasiya's decease on Ivan the Terrible in the year 1560. That event too had become the prelude to an orgy of atrocities: the only episode in Russian history comparable to the Stalin terror in the number (proportionate to the total population) of victims exterminated at the whim of a single tyrant. The point should not be pressed too strongly, however. Stalin's potentialities as a sponsor of atrocities had already claimed millions of victims – through the collectivization campaign – during the last three years of Nadezhda's life. He did not need a wife's death to inspire him to massacre. Moreover, the death of Stalin's first wife Yekaterina, back in 1907, had – as noted above – called forth comments uncannily similar to those made by his daughter some sixty years later: 'On the day when he buried his wife [his schoolfriend Iremashvili had written of this earlier tragedy] Stalin lost the last vestiges of human feeling.'[9]

Nadezhda's death coincided with the lowest ebb in Stalin's fortunes as established dictator: the end of 1932, when famine stalked the Soviet countryside; when industrialization still seemed to hang in the balance; when Ryutin's memorandum was still fresh in the memory of all who had read that clarion call to dismiss the Secretary-General. At this point Stalin is reported as tendering his resignation from the Politburo. Perhaps (he said) he had become an obstacle to unity within the Party? If so he was ready to efface himself. An embarrassed silence followed as each of Stalin's Politburo colleagues waited to see whether any of the others would risk endorsing his retirement. In the end Molotov closed the incident by telling Stalin: 'Come, come! You have the confidence of the Party.'[10] The episode may reflect a genuine moment of self-doubt on Stalin's part, or may represent an attempt to trap and compromise waverers. As will be remembered, threatened resignations had long been a favourite move in the Bolshevik power game.

Had Stalin been a faithful husband? Rumour has attributed to him an active extra-marital sex life and the fathering of various bastards,[11] but hard evidence is characteristically elusive. The name which occurs most persistently in this context is that of Roza Kaganovich: sister of Lazar Kaganovich, hardest of Stalinist hard-liners on the Politburo. Roza was (according to Lermolo) a vivacious brunette – witty, sophisticated and so striking in appearance that even the alluring Nadezhda paled by comparison. Roza aimed her charms at Stalin and conquered him completely.[12] Unconvincing as this account sounds, a reported marriage of Stalin's to a sister of Kaganovich is mentioned by a more reliable witness, Alexander Barmine.[13] Yet Stalin's daughter Svetlana asserts that there was never any Roza Kaganovich at all. She indicates that her father could not conceivably have taken to wife a Jewish woman, such as Roza (if she existed) must have been – so violent were his anti-Semitic prejudices. Any such possibility was (Svetlana claims) absolutely excluded from the life of a father who, generally speaking, 'paid little attention to women'.[14] These are not, however, matters on which a young daughter – Svetlana was only six years old at the time of her mother's death – qualifies as the best possible observer.

Further obscurity is shed on Stalin's domestic arrangements by a passage in Rosita Forbes's memoirs. She claims to have met a wife of Stalin's in 1933. This was 'a young woman in a crumpled blouse straining away from a black skirt shining with wear ... pale, with wisps of hair falling round her neck'. She is reported as having been a factory worker and a teacher.[15] It hardly sounds like the dashing Roza. Miss Forbes goes on to provide a rare picture of Stalin's domestic environment, referring to a suburban dwelling where Stalin's wife lived amid a perpetual smell of cabbage-soup, strong soap, mouldering papers and stale water flavoured with tea. 'It was half-villa, half-cottage, small, cramped and inconvenient. One of the glaring electric bulbs, hanging by dusty wires in unsuitable places, had a shade surrounded by highly coloured bobbles. This struck me as pathetic – as also did the electric saucepan in which scraps of meals were cooked on the living room table.' In this unpromising setting Rosita Forbes and Stalin discoursed on global politics, but the whereabouts of the suburban residence remains as mysterious as the identity of the pale-faced 'wife'.[16]

Whatever Stalin's sexual arrangements may have been after his second wife's death, her passing brought changes for the worse in his ménage. The household now came under strict control by the security police, the maids, housekeeper, gardeners and so on all being recruited, trained and appointed by the OGPU.[17] In keeping with these increasing rigours, the quinquagenarian dictator's love life may well have lapsed with Nadezhda's death. Perhaps it finally expired through an episode promoted by Avel Yenukidze, an old crony and future victim of Stalin's. This joking, club-bable extrovert once tried to act as a pimp for his master by introducing him to a beautiful librarian called Zoya Nikitina. That the seductive Zoya was bent on assassinating the dictator soon transpired when she turned out to be carrying a pistol under her cape.[18] The incident is probably apocryphal. But there is no doubt that Stalin did fear assassination, or at least soberly reckoned it a likely prospect in a realm where so many had cause to hate him. Moreover, as many a historical parallel shows, there is no area more difficult to police than a bedroom. This consideration may have combined with the continuing concentration of his passions on politics to wean the tyrant from sexual activity.

If the Leader did indeed embrace celibacy during the last two decades of his life, this would be consistent with his expressed views on sex. No prude, the Secretary-General once described love-making as a natural, healthy occupation necessary for the procreation of children; but added that people ought to forgo it during a national emergency such as the First Five Year Plan! A man's true emotional bond should be with his class and people, not with his woman. Confronted with a certain publication devoted to sexual perversions, Stalin once enquired: 'Do people really do this sort of thing?' As for the 'glass-of-water' theory – that one takes one's sex when one needs it, as a thirsty man takes a drink – Stalin's comment was: 'Who wants to drink dirty water?'[19]

Turning to the Leader's record as a father, we find a unique streak of tenderness in his relations with his little daughter Svetlana. By contrast with Nadezhda (the stricter parent), Stalin indulged Svetlana, especially as a small child: an aspect of his life which would have remained for ever buried in obscurity had it not been for her enterprise in emigrating from the Soviet Union after his death. Adopting her mother's surname, Alliluyeva, Stalin's daughter has done more than any other individual, through writings published in emigration, to shed light on her family's long obscured domestic life.

Stalin appears to have lavished more affection on Svetlana than on any other human being. Early infancy left her with a memory of his loud, moist kisses and habit of carrying her about in his arms. The indulgent father once comforted Svetlana after she had been slapped by her undemonstrative but adored mother for mutilating a tablecloth with a pair of scissors. Though Stalin's concentration camps had swallowed countless children of 'enemies of the people', and though his infamous law of March 1935 was to make even twelve-year-olds liable to execution, he yet could not bear the sound of a weeping infant at close quarters.[20] He was always ready to comfort little Svetlana in her tears. He invented pet names for her, calling her Setanka (from her childish mispronunciation of her own name), and alluded to her as his 'little fly', his 'little sparrow', his 'housekeeper'. A score of letters from dictator to daughter are reproduced in her memoirs, bearing out her claim that: 'I loved him tenderly, as he loved me.'[21] But, while spoiling his daughter, Stalin yet played the traditional Georgian heavy father by prudishly interfering with her way of dressing. He would not allow her to wear skirts which showed her knees, and objected to tight sweaters.[22] He often used foul language in her presence, and once he slapped her face. But at least he was not subject to fits of ungovernable rage, his grossness being 'limited in essence to his tongue':[23] a comment which again reminds us that violence by proxy was Stalin's speciality, and that he rarely stooped to administering it in person.

As might have been predicted, Stalin was less indulgent towards his two sons, being cold and distant towards Svetlana's half-brother Yakov (born to Yekaterina Svanidze) and full brother Vasily (born to Nadezhda Alliluyeva).

Towards his first-born, Yakov Dzhugashvili, the Secretary-General showed himself especially unsympathetic. The peaceable, inoffensive, meek young man exasperated his exacting father, who felt more at home with males of extrovert, hooligan or semi-criminal temperament. For a time Yakov lived in the Stalins' Kremlin apartment, being on excellent terms with his step-mother, but his father ill-treated and even beat him, eventually ordering him to keep out of Moscow.[24] Stalin despised Yakov. His harshness provoked the young man to attempt suicide in 1928 or 1929. He shot himself in the kitchen of the Stalins' Kremlin apartment, but merely inflicted a non-lethal wound – whereupon Stalin took to sneering at him as a weakling who couldn't even shoot straight. Stalin also disapproved of Yakov's marriage to a Jewish girl, which took place in the late 1930s.[25]

Eventually, as will be described below, both Stalin's sons came to a bad end.

The Seventeenth Congress

The Seventeenth Party Congress met in Moscow between 26 January and 10 February 1934.

Of nearly two thousand delegates who now basked in an atmosphere of mutual congratulation, well over half were soon to be arrested for counter-revolutionary crimes in the course of Stalin's Great Terror.[1] For the moment, though, they were calling themselves the Congress of Victors: a term which hindsight renders singularly inappropriate. So united did the Party now seem that even disgraced oppositionists, including leading future show trial victims from Zinovyev to Bukharin, were permitted to address the assembly without evoking the usual jeers and cat-calls. 'There is nothing left to prove, and, perhaps, no one left to beat': such was Stalin's own genial appreciation of the situation.[2]

The dictator indeed had some reasons for satisfaction. In the country-side the situation now seemed stable after the shock of collectivization: for good or ill the peasantry had been socialized; the war in the villages was over; the great famine of 1931–2 had been succeeded by the plentiful harvest of 1933. Though Stalin admitted to the Congress that there had been no rapid rise in agricultural productivity since collectivization – which was to put it mildly, since livestock had been reduced by about a half – he could, or at least did, claim that preconditions for such a rise had been established. With industrial production he was on less shaky ground, asserting that it had doubled within the last four years, even if metallurgy had failed to achieve its goals. Extensive new cadres of managers and technical experts had been trained. The achievement of a ninety-per-cent literacy rate was gratifying too. That the newly literate masses could obtain access only to such reading matter as Stalin chose to put before them, he naturally failed to point out.

Turning to foreign affairs, Stalin contrasted the slumps and unemployment of the effete West with the booming Soviet economy backed by full (he might have said excessive) use of the labour force. Ever fearful of capitalist encirclement, the dictator warned alien powers that attempted aggression would meet a rebuff which would teach them 'not to stick their pigs' snouts into our Soviet vegetable garden'.[3] But the spectre of war need not frighten the Soviet Union, since any conflict involving capitalist states might bring further revolutions in its trail. These foreign policy statements contain one declaration which would have repaid particularly close study at the time: Stalin asserted that the Soviet Union would never be swayed by alliances with this or that foreign power, be it France, Poland or Germany, but would always base her policy on self-interest. As for German National Socialism, while denying that Hitler's system was Socialist, the Soviet dictator yet indicated a readiness to deal with Berlin: 'Of course we are very far from enthusiastic about the Fascist régime in Germany. But Fascism is beside the point – if only because Fascism in Italy, for example, has not prevented the USSR from establishing excellent relations with that country.'[4]

Referring to internal problems, Stalin sounded a more ominous note. He warned the Party against awaiting a future classless Utopia in a complacent trance. Besides pillorying the kind of easy-going Communist boss who was content to sit back and enjoy the perquisites of office, he also drew laughs by deriding certain well-meaning chatterboxes who made the mouthing of current political catch-words a substitute for action. He went on to denounce the theory that Soviet citizens should be equal in pay and privileges. 'To conclude that . . . the Marxist plan requires everyone to go around in identical clothes and eat the same dishes in the same quantity . . . this is to utter banalities and to slander Marxism.'[5]

Though this address to the Congress duly ended with a standing ovation, thunderous cheers, choruses of 'Long Live Stalin' and the singing of the Internationale, the Leader also had certain reasons for dissatisfaction. He had by no means had everything his own way. True, the newly elected Central Committee consisted largely of out-and-out Stalinists; but the election of the repentant Trotskyite Pyatakov, as also (but only as candidates) of the rightists Bukharin, Rykov and Tomsky, represented minor defeats. Moreover, the Politburo of ten members and five candidates, as newly elected by the new Central Committee, was essentially the same as that which had been chosen four years previously; it was, indeed, the very Politburo which had refused to allow Stalin to execute Ryutin and shoot leading Communists at will. After the Seventeenth Congress, as before it, the dictator was still confronted by certain Politburo members (Kirov, Kuybyshev and Ordzhonikidze) who were shaping as 'moderates' opposed to his more extreme policies.

Kirov was now causing particular concern. Among those who still dared hope for Stalin's dismissal, there were some who thought Kirov the best qualified successor. Though Kirov had fully supported collectivization and the persecution of Party oppositionists, he had begun to display generosity towards the defeated heretics now that those battles had been won. No colonial upstart, but a pure-blooded Russian, Kirov also enjoyed other advantages over Stalin: he was younger; better-looking; more eloquent; more popular. Nor should it be forgotten that Kirov's satrapy was Leningrad: always a focus for Stalin's suspicions. Why had the Leningrad contingent welcomed Kirov's appearance at the Congress with applause so frenetic as to rival that accorded to Stalin himself? Could this former Zinovyevite fief be relapsing into delusions of grandeur and independence such as Stalin had already quelled more than once? And what of Kirov's new promotion, as voted in the post-Congress elections? These not only re-established him in the Politburo, but also put him on the very Secretariat – a body no less influential – where he now joined Stalin, Zhdanov and Kaganovich.

This fillip to Kirov was accompanied by a corresponding slight to Stalin, who had held the title of Secretary-General since his original appointment to the Secretariat in 1922. But now, in the announcement of his re-election, he was listed as a mere 'secretary'! Only a secretary . . . in no way distinguished by title from his three colleagues on the same body! That this represented an attempt to reduce the Leader's influence seems certain, for such alterations of style do not occur by accident in a Soviet context.[6] Sensitive to the most trivial slights behind his façade of benign indifference, the dictator must have resented the humiliation bitterly – or dispassionately assessed it as an acute danger signal – and was soon to arrange for the massacre of more than two thirds of the Central Committee which had treated him so shabbily.[7]

Before launching the sudden pounces which periodically knocked his colleagues off balance, Stalin liked to make painstaking secret advance preparation, and traces of such dispositions may be found in the months preceding and following the Congress. In 1933 the show trial impresario Vyshinsky was promoted Deputy Prosecutor-General, while the hitherto obscure Yezhov – future architect of Stalin's greatest terror campaign – also received significant promotions. Meanwhile another shadowy figure, Poskryobyshev, was continuing to build up Stalin's *private* Secretariat: private, as opposed to the Secretariat of the Central Committee which Stalin had headed as Secretary-General since 1922. The Private Secretariat was now becoming one of the dictator's main power centres. It was here that the various Apparatuses of Party, Army and Government were played off against each other; it was here that the purges were organized.[8] And it was through this private machine that Stalin maintained surveillance over the very secret police, working through an inner and even more clandestine body: the Special Secret Political Department of State Security.[9]

Left: Voroshilov and Budyonny during the Polish campaign, 1920

Below: Stalin with Rykov, Zinovyev and Bukharin, early 1920s

Bottom: Stalin with Mikoyan (left) and Ordzhonikidze: Tiflis, 1926

Above: Stalin and Kirov: Leningrad, 1926

Top left: Trotsky in exile with his wife and son: Alma Ata, 1928

Middle left: Stalin and his second wife, Nadezhda Alliluyeva, picnicking with the Voroshilovs: Sochi, 1929

Bottom left: Stalin and Gorky

Opposite top: Industrial Party Trial (Moscow, 1931); the chief defendant (Professor Ramzin) is on the extreme left, the chief prosecutor (Krylenko) on the extreme right

Opposite middle: Industrial Party Trial; the accused hear the death sentence (later commuted)

Opposite bottom: Kalinin, Stalin, Voroshilov and (far right) Molotov follow Kirov's coffin, December 1934

Above: Soviet leaders in the early 1930s; left to right: Kaganovich, Ordzhonikidze, Stalin, Voroshilov, Kirov

Left: The agricultural front; collectivized Uzbek farmworkers present mattocks, early 1930s

Heads of the Secret Police: Dzerzhinsky (1917–26)   Yagoda (1934–6)

Yezhov (1936–8)   Beria (from 1938)

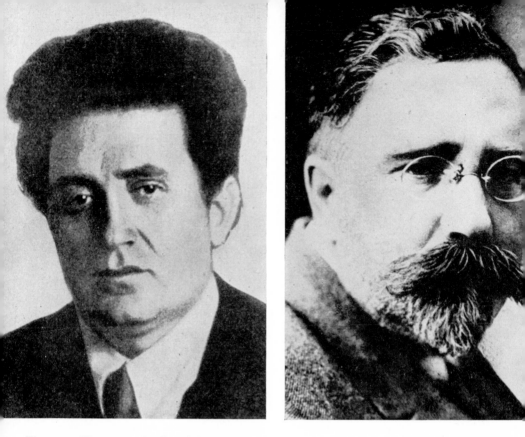

Zinovyev; Kamenev: leading defendants at the first great Moscow purge trial, August 1936

Pyatakov; Radek: leading defendants at the second great Moscow purge trial, January 1937

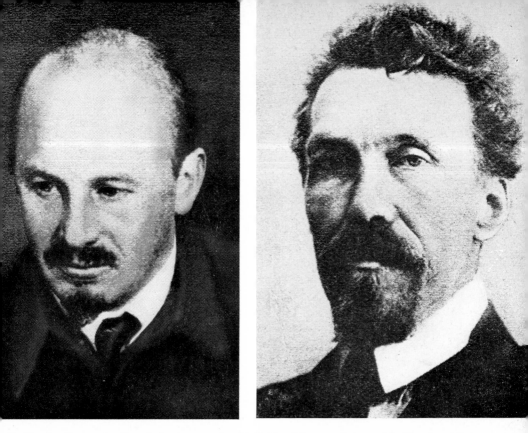

Bukharin; Rykov: leading defendants at the third great Moscow purge trial, March 1938

Tomsky (d. 1936, by suicide)   Ordzhonikidze (d. 1937, reputedly by suicide)

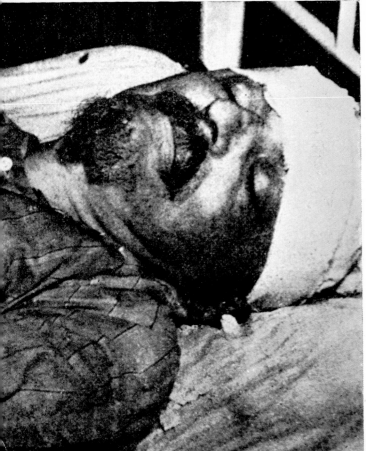

Above: Soviet leaders
review a May Day Parade
preceding the military
purge: Red Square,
Moscow
Stalin (top) and other
civilian leaders; below, left
to right: Marshal
Tukhachevsky, General
Belyov, Commissar
Voroshilov, Marshals
Yegorov and Budyonny

Left: Trotsky on his death-
bed: Mexico City, 1940

The nine months following the Seventeenth Congress proceeded in the atmosphere of harmony so loudly advertised at that gathering. Engineers and managers were no longer indiscriminately prosecuted;[10] bread rationing was abolished; peasants received increased rights to cultivate the small private plots which they retained within socialized agriculture.[11] On 10 July 1934 the most spectacular concession of all seemed to have been made when the OGPU was abolished, responsibility for political security being now vested in the People's Commissariat of the Interior. The Russian initials of this body, NKVD, seemed free of sinister implications at the time when the change occurred; for a few months, therefore, the illusion was created that the powers of the security police had been effectively trimmed. These concessions were paralleled by anti-totalitarian moves on the international board. 1934 witnessed the formation of the Popular Front directed against Hitlerite Fascism, as also the negotiations towards the Soviet-French Pact which was to be concluded in the following year. The Soviet Union joined the League of Nations and entered into diplomatic relations with the United States, the last major power to recognize revolutionary Russia.

Foreign affairs were also marked by an event less edifying, which may have influenced Stalin more than any of the above. In Germany, on the night of 30 June 1934, Hitler massacred the dissident Roehm group within his National Socialist Party. The details were unsavoury in the extreme, but the tally of those slaughtered on this Night of Long Knives was modest – barely topping the thousand mark.[12] Still, it may have been Hitler's miniature holocaust which sowed the seed of a great idea in Stalin's receptive brain.

The exhibition of ruthless brutality against Party comrades evidently made a profound impression upon Stalin. Alone among his leading associates he is said to have insisted that this act would strengthen, not weaken, the Nazi régime. He was, I am sure, filled with admiration. From now on, there was no stopping him.[13]

Only now, moreover, did Stalin – who had once done so much to foster Hitler's rise to power by instructing German Communists not to offer him serious resistance – belatedly begin to realize that the German dictator was fully in control of Germany, and that he represented a serious menace to the Soviet Union.[14]

9

Licence to Kill

Kirov Assassinated

THERE are few dates more significant in Stalin's biography than 1 December 1934, when his friend and colleague Sergey Kirov, Politburo member and Leningrad Party boss, was shot dead by an assassin at 4.30 in the afternoon. The murder occurred in a corridor of the Smolny Institute, Kirov's Leningrad headquarters.

Not until twenty-one months later did the full purport of the assassination become apparent, when Zinovyev, Kamenev and certain associates were executed after being sentenced to death at a Moscow show trial of Communist leaders – the first of three such major spectacles – on charges which included the murder of Kirov. As is now clear beyond doubt, the Zinovyev Trial was an act of murder performed by Stalin: an act advertised in advance and carried out by judicial means before the eyes of the world. The same may be said of the two succeeding trials at which Pyatakov and Bukharin were the main defendants, and which also pivoted on the assassination of Kirov. Stalin's motive in staging these three great pageants was to set precedents calculated to extend his freedom of action yet further. Once he had demonstrated that he could openly exterminate Lenin's closest political allies, he would be free to repress all remaining rivals, however exalted. Kirov's murder accordingly helped to make possible the judicial extermination of Zinovyev and Kamenev, as later of Pyatakov and Bukharin – thus equipping Stalin with what he had so long sought: unlimited licence to kill. Though the slaughter of Kirov removed only one political rival, it therefore paved the way for removing all other rivals, actual or potential, numbering several million, in the Great Terror of 1937-8.

During these appalling years members of the Party Apparatus, from the highest to the lowest, were to qualify for liquidation. The Terror was also to destroy the Soviet administrative, managerial, governmental, military, trade union, *Komsomol* and cultural élites: a campaign so devastating that it may be considered yet another revolution, the second to be carried out

236

by Stalin since Lenin's death. We have already observed the Secretary-General forcibly collectivizing and industrializing a backward country, from 1929 onwards, through the earlier of these upheavals. Now the second Stalinist revolution, inaugurated by Kirov's murder, will see the dictator turning his fury against those very seasoned Stalinists who have helped him to accomplish the previous transformation. That vast numbers of politically neutral citizens will also be caught up in the maelstrom need hardly be said.

Such, eventually, was to be the outcome of Kirov's murder. But what of the crime's origin? Was Stalin, who later openly paraded himself as the liquidator of Zinovyev and Kamenev, also the real, secret, assassin of Kirov?

It was not, of course, Stalin who discharged the murder weapon; there is no record of his ever performing so humble a chore. Leonid Nikolayev it was (a disgruntled, recently expelled minor member of the Leningrad Party) who fired a Nagan revolver at Kirov on the fateful December afternoon. But what was Nikolayev's motive? More important, who put him up to it? Who removed – who ordered the removal of – the bodyguards and security apparatus surrounding the victim? One account has the assassin as a jealous husband avenging himself on the notorious lecher Kirov, whom he once chanced to surprise in bed with the attractive Milda Nikolayeva.[1] But could a mere cuckold, unaided by accomplices within Party and police, so easily have penetrated the heavily guarded Smolny building? How was it that the murderer had not been detained while making two previous attempts to approach Kirov on the same premises: the one some six weeks before the successful assault, the other a few days previously? That Nikolayev – a dismissed Party member, and one known to be nursing a grievance at that – had even been searched on one of these occasions, that he had been caught with a revolver and an incriminating notebook, yet was merely sent about his business without suffering detailed investigation . . .[2] these and other details suggested that the assassin had not been acting on his own, but that members of the Leningrad NKVD had afforded him every facility short of actually pressing the trigger.

The officer immediately responsible for relaxing security measures in the Smolny was Zaporozhets, second-in-command of the Leningrad NKVD. He in turn had been briefed by Yagoda (head of security police from 1934 until 1936), according to the official Stalinist version of the episode as developed at the Bukharin Trial.[3] But who set in motion the chain leading from Yagoda through Zaporozhets to Nikolayev? Was this instigator indeed, as also stated at the Bukharin trial, the Leader's former crony Yenukidze,[4] who had since been conveniently liquidated? Or should we look further back? Even if Yenukidze *was* involved, may he not have been yet another go-between? Was the prime mover indeed Stalin himself?

The dictator's complicity has been accepted with varying degrees of conviction by leading Western authorities,[5] also receiving confirmation by innuendo in certain statements made by Khrushchev. 'There are reasons for the suspicion [Khrushchev stated in 1956] that the killer of Kirov, Nikolayev, was assisted by *someone* from among the people whose duty it was to protect the person of Kirov.'[6] Khrushchev returned to the theme again in 1961, pointing out that Kirov's main bodyguard (whose name was Borisov) had been murdered by NKVD agents in a fake traffic accident on the day following the assassination ... murdered just as he was being taken to an interrogation which threatened to reveal too much about the real origins of the Kirov killing, as also about Borisov's mysterious absence from the scene and failure to protect his master. Then Borisov's killers had been exterminated in their turn; evidently '*someone* needed to have them killed in order to cover up all traces.'[7] Since three such 'someones' (Zaporozhets, Yagoda, Yenukidze) had already been clearly identified at the Bukharin Trial, Khrushchev was now transparently hinting – in the language of one who longs to wound, yet fears to strike – at a fourth, previously unidentified, hand behind these murky proceedings: that of Stalin himself.

Another theory has also been put forward: that the assassination was indeed staged on Stalin's orders, but that it was all along intended as a fake attempt expressly designed to be 'narrowly averted' at the last moment, thus providing the dictator with the excuse to introduce severe emergency measures while yet leaving his old friend Kirov intact.[8] Such a bogus assassination would have been a delicate affair indeed, and some last-minute failure in co-ordination might easily have led on to the real thing. In the absence of evidence for or against this version, one can only say that it is hard to square with Stalin's usual *modus operandi*. Rarely, if ever, do we find him seeking to be more subtle than the practical exigencies of his situation required.

The fact is that we simply do not know exactly how Kirov's murder came about, and we are still in no position to assess the degree of Stalin's complicity with any certainty. To state outright, as Robert Conquest does,[9] that the dictator had decided in advance to murder Kirov is to go beyond the evidence which the Stalinist machine was so remorselessly engaged in destroying. Nor, in the light of Stalin's thoroughness as a suppressor of inconvenient information, are we ever likely to tap any new, mysteriously surviving source which might clear up this affair once and for all. We can merely speculate in the dark on the basis of the scanty evidence and of Stalin's known character, opportunities and motives.

That one who was to accomplish so many publicly flaunted judicial murders – those of Zinovyev, Kamenev and many another old comrade – that such a man would not have been deterred by mere scruple from ordering the earlier, secret extermination of his friend and colleague Kirov, need hardly be stated. There is no evidence that Stalin was ever influenced by considerations of morality or of loyalty to his associates, either in late 1934 or during any other phase of his march to supremacy. The dictator's opportunities for accomplishing such villainy undetected were considerable, too, owing to his total mastery of Soviet communications, not to mention the elaborately intermeshing security police organs which he maintained: all operating in secret, yet none being sufficiently close to the dictator to be certain that it was not itself under surveillance by some other body of custodians yet more clandestine.

So much for Stalin's opportunities. With regard to his possible motives, we have already identified one of them, and the most significant in the long term, as the search for a general licence to kill. Kirov's popularity, his claims to be considered a potential alternative Number One, his grip on the Leningrad Party machine . . . these, too, have already been mentioned as features likely to have embarrassed the dictator. To them must be added Kirov's inconvenient posture as a focus for 'moderate' opinion – opposed to Stalin's extremism – within a Politburo consisting, before the assassination, of ten full members. Two other Politburo moderates were Kuybyshev and Ordzhonikidze, who had recently allied themselves with Kirov in urging a retreat from out-and-out pro-Stalinist positions.[10] With regard to these so-called moderates, we should add that all three of them had long been prepared to sanction extreme mass violence so long as this had been applied to other people. They were 'liberals' in the highly restricted sense of seeking means to curb government by massacre only at the point where their own persons appeared to be threatened. Since other members of the Politburo have also been rumoured as vacillating in their support for Stalin, the importance of removing from the ten-man ruling caucus the three most disaffected among potential hostile voters can hardly be exaggerated. Every such individual removal increased Stalin's leverage within so small a body.

The murder of Kirov also provided the dictator with an excuse for decreeing an immediate state of emergency throughout the USSR. To combat political terrorism as exemplified by this assassination possibly or probably ordained by Stalin, it was arguably expedient to employ counter-terrorist Terror most certainly ordained by Stalin. On receiving the news of Kirov's death, the dictator accordingly leapt into sudden action, hastening to extend his persecutions to fellow-Bolsheviks hitherto immune. Without waiting for the Politburo's approval he at once issued a decree accelerating the investigation of terrorism and ordering the immediate execution, without right of appeal, of those found guilty.[11] This new directive helped to provide the rationale for the coming tidal wave of Stalinist atrocities.

After promulgating these measures, Stalin immediately left Moscow for Leningrad by train. He descended on the former capital at dawn on 2 December, taking over a floor of the Smolny Institute and personally assuming control of the 'investigation' into the murder.[12] The main object of this inquiry was to exploit the case politically, while ensuring that the dictator's own involvement (great or small) should be buried deep with the bodies of any who might have inside knowledge of the background. The assassin Nikolayev was 'tried' *in camera* and then shot on 29 December, taking with him to the grave any information compromising higher authority which he may have possessed. The Leningrad NKVD chiefs were also arrested and sent to concentration camps, but under privileged conditions and with relatively short sentences; later, in 1937, when a few extra shootings could no longer attract attention, they were quietly liquidated.[13]

These minor police officials were not particularly important to Stalin, and were presumably exterminated because they knew too much. Nor need we waste time puzzling over the hundred-odd alleged White supporters shot in Leningrad and Moscow soon after Kirov's murder,[14] in accordance with an early official version of the outrage: that it was the work of anti-Soviet emissaries from abroad. Nor yet need we make more than passing reference to the forty-thousand-odd Leningraders deported to Siberia and the Arctic after Kirov's murder.[15] The dictator's real targets were Zinovyev and Kamenev – as became evident barely a fortnight after Kirov's death, when these two senior victims-designate were arrested. In the following month they were secretly tried, for giving encouragement to the terrorist 'centre' supposedly responsible for Nikolayev's crime; they were persuaded to admit moral culpability, but received only prison sentences of ten and five years.[16]

Though this was the 'first occasion (apart from the case of Sultan-Galiyev in 1923) . . . on which political opposition by Communists . . . was made the subject of an open criminal charge',[17] and as such was a minor milestone in Stalin's career, measures so half-hearted were of little use to him at this stage. He had, one must suspect, already set his heart on exterminating Lenin's former comrades-in-arms, and nothing less would do. If, as seems likely, the dictator was already pressing hard for the physical annihilation of Zinovyev and Kamenev, he must have been thwarted by temporarily effective opposition within the Politburo. How convenient, therefore, when Kuybyshev died of a 'heart attack' within two months of Kirov's even more convenient demise. The police overlord Yagoda and various doctors were later to stand accused of murdering Kuybyshev – more strictly, of hastening his death by deliberately failing to give him correct medical treatment. But if Yagoda did indeed do away with Kuybyshev somehow or other, he may well have been acting on Stalin's orders ... especially as the Leader is actually known to have been responsible, between 1934 and 1940, for the death of at least sixteen other persons who had been, at one time or another, members of the Politburo.[18] We must also remember that, at the time of Kirov's and Kuybyshev's deaths, Stalin still had no means of removing Politburo members other than discreetly camouflaged murder. In any case the main point was that the disappearance, contrived or accidental, of every such 'moderate' brought the Leader one step nearer to the kind of Politburo which he needed: one with a dependable majority consisting of obedient flunkeys.

Stalin used more gradual methods to oust the genial Yenukidze, the old crony and fellow-Georgian who was eventually to be charged posthumously with ultimate responsibility for Kirov's murder. As a veteran Georgian Bolshevik, Yenukidze was guilty of one particularly heinous offence: that of knowing too much about Stalin's past as a member of the Caucasian Bolshevik underground. In particular, Yenukidze was all too well aware that the youthful Dzhugashvili's role in early Party history had been obscure and inglorious. Though Yenukidze had since tried to atone for this by writing mendacious accounts of the Leader's heroic youth, he had never managed to catch up with the fast developing Legend, and his own contributions to Stalin's fictitious biography were soon to be eclipsed by the yet more thorough-paced fabrications of Beria. As first mooted, Yenukidze's public disgrace revolved about this very point: he admitted in *Pravda* of 16 January 1935 that he had been guilty of errors in describing early Bolshevik history in the Caucasus. Within a month or two he had been deprived of his various offices as a prelude to liquidation and posthumous vilification at the Bukharin Trial.

Signs also began to appear that the 'great' writer and humanist Maxim Gorky, who had done so much to bolster Stalin's reputation, was also in trouble. On 28 January *Pravda* published an attack on Gorky, who had hitherto been sacrosanct. Gorky was to die in June 1936, and since he too is known to have been a moderate, urging Stalin to be reconciled with Kamenev and other political enemies,[19] the suspicion has arisen that he too may have been murdered. This was to be expressly asserted at the Bukharin Trial, at which Gorky figured as one victim in the series of medical homicides allegedly engineered by Yagoda. That Stalin had Gorky killed seems all too possible.

While disposing of various moderates, whether by murder or not, Stalin was also quietly moving his trusty hatchet men into key positions. Chief among these was Nikolay Yezhov, the future NKVD chief, who became a Secretary of the Central Committee in February 1935. In the same month Nikita Khrushchev first emerges into the limelight with his appointment as Moscow Party boss. Georgy Malenkov moves up to take a position under Yezhov in the Central Committee Apparatus, while Vyshinsky is promoted Prosecutor-General. These figures, together with the mysterious Poskryobyshev – head of Stalin's personal secretariat – are ready to act as the dictator's general staff in administering the mass liquidation of Party stalwarts which he now contemplates.

In mid-1935, as a foretaste of measures more drastic, Stalin proceeds to dissolve two societies of veteran revolutionaries: the 'Old Bolsheviks' and the 'Former Political Prisoners and Exiles'. Such revolutionary veterans were soon to discover that a record of persecution under the Tsars could easily become a passport to repressions far more severe under the Tsars' heir-in-chief. For though Stalin did indeed view all groupings – even those dominated by his own creatures – with mistrust, his deepest misgivings were reserved for combinations formed by revolutionaries old enough to remember the Great Leader from his days as a comparative nonentity or 'grey blur'.

As a parallel measure, Party documents became subject to 'verification' in May 1935, and again to further checking in December of that year: all this despite the intensive purges already conducted in earlier years. The offence of flight from the Soviet Union was made subject to the death penalty, relatives of such offenders being rendered liable to imprisonment, whether or not they had been aware of the original intention to defect. The hostage system, already widely employed to enforce political docility, was further strengthened through an enactment severe even by Stalinist standards: that extending all penalties, including capital punishment, to children down to the age of twelve. This was to prove useful later as a means of blackmailing selected trial victims, who were induced to confess by the threat of sharing the dock, and cross-examination by the thin-lipped Vyshinsky, with their own offspring.

Thus the dictator was already forging and sharpening his weapons. Nor did he neglect the vital art of camouflage. Amid the tribulations of the immediate post-Kirov era, a commission was instituted to prepare a new and more democratic constitution. The main drafter was Bukharin, who was ripening for liquidation even as he framed the liberal terms of a document guaranteeing the populace widespread civil rights. Never translated into practice, the Constitution well served its purpose as a syrup designed for those who were just about to swallow the bitter pill of the Great Terror.

As mention of the Stalin Constitution reminds us, the dictator was far more than a devious manipulator behind the scenes, for he could also show himself no less devious a manipulator in the full glare of global publicity. A consummate actor, he was increasingly presenting himself to the world as a modest, good-humoured, relaxed, genial, jocular servant of his people and Party: and, indeed, of humanity at large. In an interview with an American journalist, the benign tyrant claims to be building a society which will enjoy 'real personal freedom, freedom without inverted commas'.[20] From governmental inefficiency – Stalin claims on the eve of the Great Terror – the Soviet population will soon be protected by general, equal, direct and secret elections under the new constitution which the public will be able to use as a 'whip' to scourge inefficient administrators.[21] On another occasion Stalin sententiously remarks that: 'We should cherish human beings as carefully and attentively as a gardener cherishes his favourite fruit tree.'[22]

Wearing, as always, a public air of dignified benevolence, Stalin is found opening the newly constructed Moscow underground railway on 14 May 1935 and uttering homely wisecracks to a chorus of laughter, cheers and thunderous applause.[23] On 17 November of the same year he makes a long speech to a conference of Stakhanovites: followers of the coalminer Stakhanov. This quintessentially Stalinist campaign involved creating for selected and highly publicized workers conditions exceptionally favourable to the achievement of misleadingly spectacular production results, these being later used as a pretext for imposing higher production targets on other toilers. Some Stakhanovites were murdered by incensed workmates, and the movement was eventually exposed as spurious. At first, however, it seemed to promise a steep rise in general productivity, and the Leader's speech of 17 November helped to stoke the fires of 'spontaneous' enthusiasm with which Stakhanovism was officially launched.

Stalin also gave jovial addresses, or sent messages of encouragement, to recipients as various as Soviet gold-miners; the French Communist newspaper *Humanité*; female shock-workers in sugar beet production; the pioneer of space travel Tsiolkovsky; combine-harvest operators of both sexes; the collective farmers of Tadzhikistan and Turkmenistan; and the doomed Marshal Yegorov on the occasion of his fiftieth birthday.

Now at last, it seemed, the genial Leader could look back at the struggles of the past with a tolerant smile. He could even make the occasional bluff reference to such early troubles in his speeches. On 4 May 1935 he told Red Army cadets of the obstacles which it had been necessary to overcome, adding that: 'We admittedly had to *rough up one or two comrades* on our way. . . . *I must confess that I took a hand in this.*'[24] In the phrases here italicized we recognize the jolly irony of the tough master in a relaxed moment. In similar style Stalin sneered at certain railway administrators who had fallen short of the challenge of the hour and had been dismissed: 'We obviously had to *bash in the teeth of these distinguished persons* a bit. They had to be *politely escorted* out of the central apparatus of the Transport Commissariat.'[25]

Such minor inconveniences apart, claimed Stalin: 'Life has become better, Comrades, life has become happier.'[26]

Zinovyev Framed

Baulked, by mid-1935, in his attempts to obtain Politburo sanction for the judicial murder of Zinovyev and Kamenev behind the scenes, Stalin decided to change his methods. Hitherto he seems to have been pressing his senior colleagues to approve the victims' condemnation at secret trials. But now that those trials had given such disappointing results, leading to mere prison sentences, the Leader resolved to make ultra-secret preparations for public inquisitions. He was determined, in other words, to revive the technique of the show trial as directed against mining engineers, Mensheviks and others in 1928-33. Though the weapon was not new, there was spectacular originality in aiming it at members of the Party – the highest-placed members at that. And there were to be no half-measures on this occasion. Zinovyev and Kamenev would be forced to make grovelling confessions in court, sentenced to death and shot. From the outset the rigging of the Zinovyev Trial was closely planned by Stalin in person, aided by Yezhov, while Yagoda and his minions acted as their executives. So acute was the Leader's interest in the trial-rigging process that not a single day passed without his inquiring personally into the state of the investigation. 'All the accusations were fabricated to the minutest details by Stalin himself and . . . he personally revised the testimony obtained from them.'[1]

Having decided on a show trial, Stalin wasted no time making any immediate frontal assault on the captive Zinovyev and Kamenev. They were left to simmer for many months, while pains were taken to implicate them by bogus confessions of conspiracy extracted from smaller fry. With this in view the dictator gave orders for about three hundred former oppositionists to be brought under arrest to Moscow; he calculated that about one fifth of them could be broken down to sign any required testimony.[2] In practice, a mere quartet of such forced junior collaborators proved sufficient, especially as the 'evidence' extracted from them was backed by that of four *agents provocateurs* from the junior ranks of the NKVD itself. These were simply ordered, as part of their official duties, to sign certain spurious confessions and to parade as trial defendants on the understanding that their lives would be spared once the proceedings were concluded.[3]

With the aid of these eight minor defendants, consisting of low-grade police officials and insignificant oppositionists, Stalin's henchmen proceeded to build a case implicating the eight major figures who were his real object of attack: four Zinovyevites, headed by Zinovyev and Kamenev, and four Trotskyites, headed by I. N. Smirnov. By the time when the case came up for trial, on 19 August 1936, all sixteen victims, major and minor, were ready – with trifling exceptions – to confirm the charges against themselves and each other in elaborate detail. They accordingly confessed to conspiring, under Trotsky's direction, to seize power by terrorist means; to murdering Kirov; and to plotting the assassination of Stalin and other Soviet leaders. That the defendants should reveal such eagerness to co-operate with the prosecution seemed odd, but not entirely surprising in view of previous Stalinist show trials, at which the accused had regularly been condemned on the exclusive basis of their own confessions. Once again, it seemed, the accused at the Zinovyev Trial might have escaped entirely had they but chosen to remain silent. Yet, far from doing so, they made humiliating admissions which seemed especially baffling in the mouths of figures once so exalted. How, then, did Stalin induce Zinovyev, Kamenev and other former power-wielders to make circumstantial confessions to charges which are now universally agreed to have been faked from start to finish?

The false accusations of underlings and stooges, to which reference has already been made, were weapons – but only minor weapons – in the dictator's confession-extracting arsenal. As Stalin's victims soon discovered, he had many other ways of making them talk. Held in isolation for months or even years on end, deprived of sleep, periodically harangued, cajoled or browbeaten night and day by relays of frenzied tormentors (themselves in peril of similar treatment in the event of failure), the defendants-elect were usually more than half broken already when confronted with the signed confessions of associates previously brain-washed, or had to face their whimpered bogus accusations at skilfully timed confrontations. Physical intimidation and torture were widely and increasingly used, but in many cases such extreme methods were not even necessary, for threats and promises – affecting the victims' families as well as themselves – were often sufficient. There was also the device of appealing to Party loyalty by presenting confession to charges admittedly false as one last service which the defendants could still make to the cause to which they had dedicated their lives. If they could do nothing else, they could at least bolster up the Party which was now united, for good or ill, under Stalin's leadership. Then again, if all else failed, stubborn non-confessors – apart from the very few star performers – could always be shot on the side while the heat was turned on potential substitutes, of whom a large reservoir existed.

Mighty as Stalin's confession-extracting machinery was, the breaking of Zinovyev and Kamenev yet proved a difficult assignment. For many months they, and some of the lesser defendants, refused to bear false witness against themselves. On learning of his victims' continued refusal to sign the confessions required of them, the Leader would 'turn green with fury'. He would shout in his guttural, Georgian-accented Russian that Zinovyev and Kamenev were to be 'given the works' until they came crawling . . . on their bellies with confessions in their teeth.[4] On Stalin's determination to push through this affair one episode provides an especially illuminating commentary. When Mironov – the NKVD official in charge of Kamenev's case – appeared to be making little progress, Stalin asked him to say how much the entire Soviet state weighed, with all its factories, machines, army, armaments and navy. Neither Kamenev nor any other individual could withstand that astronomical weight, Stalin argued in all seriousness, and Mironov was not to return until he had Kamenev's confession in his brief-case; Mironov was also instructed to tell Kamenev that his son, still a child, would be tried in his place if he continued to refuse to co-operate, and that evidence would be produced to show that the boy had been trailing Stalin and Voroshilov by car as a prelude to an assassination attempt.[5]

Zinovyev, too, was influenced by threats to his family, being also subjected to the physical ordeal of a cell deliberately overheated in the height of summer, which was additionally irksome in view of his poor health. As for promises, those cost nothing, and many of the accused were assured that their lives would be spared if only they would sign what was required of them. In the end Zinovyev and Kamenev agreed to consider such a deal. But knowing by now how worthless Stalin's undertakings were, they would not accept the arrangement unless he would repeat his offer to spare their lives in the presence of the entire Politburo. Taken to this proposed confrontation, the two defendants-in-chief found only two Politburo members present: Stalin and Voroshilov, who described themselves as a Politburo commission appointed for the purpose. This meeting provided the occasion for yet another of the dictator's jests, when Kamenev asked what guarantee there could possibly be that Stalin would not have them shot despite his promise.

'A guarantee ?' Stalin sneered. 'What guarantee can there be? Perhaps you want an official treaty certified by the League of Nations ?'

The dictator did, however, give his personal word, on behalf of the Politburo, that neither Zinovyev nor Kamenev, nor any other Old Bolshevik, would be executed if they would stand trial on his terms.[6] It was on the basis of this lying assurance that the two chief victims finally went to their doom.

Astonished by the lavishness of the confessions extracted by Stalin, world public opinion was also shocked by the severity of the ensuing sentences – and even more by the promptness of the executions, which were reported as taking place within twenty-four hours of the trial's end. All sixteen accused were shot, from Zinovyev and Kamenev down to those minor NKVD employees who had merely repeated the lines scripted for them by the trial-riggers. Secure in the assurance that their lives were safe, some of these wretches had made their depositions in jaunty, self-confident style,[7] only to find in the end that they had failed to grasp Stalin's logic: once their usefulness had expired they had no way of compelling him to keep his agreement to spare their lives. These underlings had not been alone in expecting the sentences to be commuted . . . especially as judicial appeal machinery, suspended on the day following Kirov's assassination, had been restored shortly before the Zinovyev trial.[8] The restoration may now be seen as a device of Stalin's designed to persuade the accused that there was no intention of executing them. That he had been privily resolved on their extermination all along now seems clear. Nor could anyone concerned in the affair easily bring any last-minute pressure to bear on the tyrant in person, for he had taken the precaution of removing himself from Moscow during the period of the trial; holidaying on the Black Sea coast, he was secure in the knowledge that the wheels had been set in motion and that none dare countermand his instructions.

As we have seen, Stalin had to put in several years of careful preparation before he could compass the execution of Zinovyev and Kamenev. Once their trial had been successfully concluded, howevev, he suddenly accelerated, ordering Yagoda to execute five thousand former oppositionists who were already under arrest. It was the first occasion – but the first of many – in the history of the USSR on which Party members were executed *en masse* without having formal charges brought against them.[9] This manoeuvre accomplished, Stalin turned to attack his chief executioner, whose dismissal was ordered in a telegram from Sochi to the Politburo on 25 September 1936. 'We deem it absolutely necessary and urgent that Comrade

Yezhov be nominated to the post of People's Commissar for Internal Affairs. Yagoda has definitely proved himself to be incapable of unmasking the Trotskyite-Zinovyevite bloc. The OGPU is four years behind in this matter.'[10] As mentioned above, the reference to 'four years behind' was a specific allusion to the year 1932, when it had proved impossible to secure the execution of Ryutin after the attempt to remove Stalin from the secretary-generalship of the Party.

A reluctance on Yagoda's part to press political persecution to the limit, either in Ryutin's day or later, may indeed have been a major factor in leading Stalin to ordain the NKVD chief's disgrace. By now Yagoda must have come to realize only too well how easily the techniques of trial-rigging, so thoroughly taught to him by Stalin, could be turned against himself. Besides, Yagoda was in the awkward position of knowing more than almost anyone else about the dictator's methods. Yagoda was also, presumably, the victim of a recurrent itch which every absolutist ruler must feel from time to time: to rid himself of his security police chief of the moment. However docile such an officer may seem, the office itself is too intimately linked with the supreme ruler's person to be long entrusted to a single individual, offering as it does special facilities for mounting a *coup d'état*. For these or other reasons the liquidation of Yagoda had by now become imperative.

Yagoda's replacement by Yezhov anticipated a large-scale purge of the police machine . . . but anticipated it by several months, for again Stalin moved warily. The new chief of political police had already been busy recruiting – outside the ranks of Yagoda's commissariat – a shadow security administration consisting of some two or three hundred officers who stood poised to take over the the key posts in the NKVD.[11] These men were introduced into political police headquarters in the Lubyanka so that they could understudy Yagoda's top administrators, by now privily earmarked for liquidation. Yezhov's own career had been with the Party Apparatus, and the same was true of many of the understudies whom he brought with him into the NKVD. The episode is therefore a classic example of Stalin's use of one institution potentially dangerous to himself (the Party Apparatus) to discipline another (the Security police). That he was equally capable of going into reverse and unleashing the police on the Party, the events of 1937 were also to show.

Of Stalin's relations with his security police chiefs during the early months of Yezhov's rule one anecdote provides a fascinating glimpse. On 20 December 1936 the dictator celebrated the nineteenth anniversary of the foundation of the Cheka, the first Soviet political police organization – by holding one of those drinking orgies which afforded him a regular form of relaxation throughout the years. Among the roistering security chiefs, regaled at the genial Leader's table on this inauspicious occasion, were Yezhov and K. V. Pauker. The latter was an official of Hungarian-Jewish extraction who had once been dresser to a Budapest opera company before learning to preside over Sicilian Vespers of his own as a security police chief in Moscow. Here he had become a department head in the NKVD, being responsible for the personal safety of Stalin and the other leaders. As this indicates, the dictator had once reposed great trust in Pauker. The Hungarian was the only person permitted to shave Stalin, apart from which one source even refers to a homosexual relationship between the two men: 'Pauker means to Stalin more than you think, more than a friend . . . and more than a brother,' an NKVD informant is quoted as stating with emphasis and 'a meaningful hint'.[12]

Pauker, a talented mimic, rendered Stalin's NKVD jubilee supper memorable by giving an impromptu imitation of Zinovyev's last moments on earth. Dragged along for execution, Pauker-Zinovyev moaned and cast fear-crazed glances in all directions before falling on his knees in the middle of the room, embracing the boots of a 'warder' and uttering a last plea: 'For God's sake, Comrade, call up Joseph Vissarionovich!' Then, in an encore demanded by the delighted audience of security tycoons, the mock Zinovyev introduced an additional variant. Raising his hands to heaven, he screamed: 'Hear, Israel, our God is the one God!' Stalin laughed so much at this that he almost choked, and had to make signs for the Kremlin's Demon Barber to stop the performance.[13] For Pauker, however, the joke had only just begun, since he was liquidated shortly afterwards as a German spy. Thus the atheist Jew Zinovyev was derided, and for cravenly reverting to the faith of his fathers during his last seconds of life, by a police chief who was himself Jewish . . . yet, as was later to be 'disclosed' at the Bukharin Trial, had all along been a Gestapo agent.

Successful though the Zinovyev Trial had been, Stalin still found himself lacking the unlimited licence to kill which he craved. He had already – or so he believed – neatly trapped the two rightist leaders Bukharin and Rykov as future show-trial victims by ensuring that they were named in the proceedings against Zinovyev among various suspects requiring investigation. But then, on 10 September 1936, a brief *Pravda* announcement revealed that the inquisition into these two rightist leaders had been discontinued for lack of evidence. Attempting to force the pace in framing them, Stalin had – according to Bukharin's own testimony – come up against unexpectedly stubborn opposition from Politburo colleagues who still retained some power to thwart his designs.[14]

Pyatakov, Plenum and Police Disciplined

Robbed for the moment of bigger prey – Bukharin and Rykov – the Leader launched the second of the great Moscow show trials on 23 January 1937 with an array of lesser victims. The chief martyr, Pyatakov, was a mere Deputy Commissar for Heavy Industry, and was not even a candidate member of the Politburo. Yet he was a far from negligible figure, having been sufficiently prominent in 1922 to gain favourable mention in Lenin's Testament: itself a capital offence to Stalin. Pyatakov had been a Trotsky-ite before recanting and becoming the prime mover behind the industrializa-tion programme; he ranked as Russia's leading technocrat, and his nominal superior – Sergo Ordzhonikidze, the Commissar for Heavy Industry – deferred to him in technical matters.

Among the motives for framing Pyatakov, a wish to undermine Ordzhoni-kidze may have been prominent. As we remember, Ordzhonikidze was a Stalinist hard-liner of many years' standing, and was a fellow-Georgian. He still retained the bluff, hearty manner of former days, continuing to call Stalin by his old revolutionary nickname 'Koba'. But, as noted previously, Ordzhonikidze had recently become one of the reputed Politburo moder-ates ... together with the late Kirov and the late Kuybyshev. Now sole survivor of that trio, the flamboyant Sergo was vigorously opposing the extreme measures enforced by Stalin. 'He protested to Stalin, created stormy scenes at Politburo meetings, fought like a tiger with the NKVD.'[1] That Ordzhonikidze was indeed no Stalinized robot-bureaucrat is illus-trated by his reaction on an occasion when he learnt that one of his sub-ordinates had been arrested. He rang up Yezhov and shouted: 'You little snotnose, you filthy lickspittle, how dare you!' Clamouring for the relevant documents, Ordzhonikidze telephoned Stalin, demanding to know why the NKVD was allowed to arrest his men without his being informed. 'I demand that this authoritarianism cease!' Ordzhonikidze shouted before slamming down the receiver. 'I'm still a member of the Politburo! I'm going to raise hell, Koba, if it's the last thing I do before I die!'[2] It was, more or less. It may also have been the last occasion on which anyone ever addressed Stalin in such terms.

As a full Politburo member, Ordzhonikidze was less vulnerable to attack than lesser comrades. But he could be assailed, as was regular Stalinist practice, through the persecution of his underlings. Hence, perhaps, the choice of his deputy Pyatakov as chief victim in the second of the great Moscow show trials. Comprising seventeen defendants in all, the newly arraigned group was presented as an Anti-Soviet Trotskyite Centre, and to

the extent that the victims were all former supporters of Trotsky the indictment bore a trace of truth. Besides being charged with political terrorism –
a theme already familiar from the Zinovyev Trial – the seventeen were also
accused of offences which made the frame-up of August 1936 seem feeble
by comparison. These included the deliberate wholesale wrecking of Soviet
industry, which some of the defendants – especially Pyatakov – had given
much of their energy to building; their alleged sabotage was presented as
part of a sinister grand design, inspired by the exiled Trotsky, to secure
the abandonment of collectivization and planned industrialization in favour of restored capitalism. The campaign was said to be backed by Germany and Japan – countries which were to be recompensed with territory
in the Ukraine and Siberia. It was alleged that the accused had been systematically wrecking Soviet mines, chemical works and railways, another of
their motives being to discredit the Government with the workers. Far-
fetched though these charges were, they helped to provide new scapegoats
for the many breakdowns which were occurring in an economy so recklessly
expanded. But Stalin's most important motive in framing the seventeen
was to increase the momentum of the Terror by enforcing public acceptance
of fabrications yet more outrageous than those foisted on the Zinovyev
group.

Lasting eight days – nearly twice as long as the arraignment of Zinovyev
– the Pyatakov Trial was embellished with much complex technical detail
calculated to confuse any reader who might attempt to digest the nearly
six hundred pages of intermeshed mendacity contained in the official report.
Other special features included the notably feeble participation of defence
counsel 'assisting' three of the accused, and the fact that only thirteen of
the seventeen were sentenced to be shot, though all were found guilty.
Such clemency may have been designed to lend credibility to promises
dangled before the next batch of trial victims to be incriminated: the
Bukharin group.

With two major show trials now safely out of the way, Stalin could
reflect with satisfaction on his skill in ensuring the elaborately rigged proceedings against unforeseen disruption. There was little danger of this in a
courtroom – the October Hall in the Moscow House of Unions – selected
because it was fairly small and could be packed with minor NKVD
officials primed to create a disturbance if proceedings threatened to deviate
from their predetermined course. Should any of the accused depart significantly from his script an uproar would ensue, giving the Chairman of the
Court an excuse to adjourn and the NKVD a chance to 'persuade' the recalcitrant during the interval. A few foreign newspaper correspondents were
also admitted, for the trials were designed by Stalin to echo on a global

scale. When his underlings told him that foreigners would never believe in the authenticity of the proceedings, the dictator was apt to remark – with ripe political wisdom – that they would swallow anything.[3] Though this claim was slightly exaggerated, the authenticity of the trials at least became a basis for controversy among foreigners. And that, for Stalin, was quite enough.

So far as domestic consumption was concerned, the very implausibility of the proceedings had an important part to play in disciplining the Soviet population. Had the despot presented his subjects with pageants less outrageously bizarre, there would always have been a danger of the people swallowing his assertions on the grounds of their apparent credibility: not – as was essential for purposes of control – because the dictator himself had propounded them. The less a given individual might sincerely believe in the culpability of a Zinovyev or a Kamenev, the more valuable his capitulation when he was compelled to affirm his belief in their guilt at public meetings called to condemn these imperialist mad dogs. Such explosions of induced hatred gained in usefulness through the presence of NKVD minions. Themselves potentially suspect of deficient vigilance, they scanned the screaming hordes for the odd deviant physiognomy expressing 'face-crime': failure to simulate effectively the emotion appropriate to a given political context.

Against this lurid background even the most patent fabrications of the trials had a part to play. When one defendant, at the Zinovyev Trial, testified that he had met Trotsky's son at the Hotel Bristol in Copenhagen in 1932, it was felt by some foreign observers that the trial-riggers had committed a grave error: the hotel in question turned out to have been pulled down fifteen years before the alleged rendezvous. This was duly pointed out in the foreign press, and there was even some attempt on the Soviet side to cover up by claiming, belatedly, that the meeting had taken place at a *Café* Bristol.[4] There was no need, however, for such self-exculpation by the riggers of a trial expressly designed to ensure, not only that injustice should be done . . . but also that it should manifestly be seen to be done. Nor, at the Trial of the Seventeen, could Stalin's position be seriously shaken when it was similarly proved (abroad and by reference to airport records) that Pyatakov could not in fact have met Trotsky in Oslo on 12 December 1935, as he had confessed in court.[5] From such apparent blunders the dictator could only gain, since one function of the trials was to mount an assault, almost metaphysical in character, on truth itself. It was as part of such a process that large sections of the population were compelled to affirm propositions which the very affirmers knew to be spurious at the time of making their obeisance.

As all these details indicate, the Moscow trials were in no sense judicial proceedings. Rather did they constitute what can now be seen – in the light of recent developments in the theatre – as a stage performance of a peculiar type. Like any other effective dramatic or fictional production, they were designed to create an illusion sustaining the qualified suspension of disbelief in the minds of an audience which was simultaneously aware, with another part of its brain – no less than the audience at a performance of *Hamlet* – that the entire proceedings were the concoction of a powerfully inventive and creative intellect. Far in advance of their time, the three big Moscow trials strikingly anticipated the later Theatre of the Absurd. They were a gigantic Happening which went far beyond the mere audience-participation of those present in the October Hall to embrace the population as a whole in one great dance of death. If the dramatist's function is to bring human emotions fully into play, and to make his audience in the widest sense an integral part of the performance, then Stalin's great trilogy leaves even the *Oresteia* of Aeschylus (its nearest previous rival) in the shade, for it set up convulsions more than dionysiac among millions who were not even present at the original spectacle.

Such was the sheer scale of Stalin's dramatic vision that he was compelled to delegate much of the script-writing to lesser authors, among whom were Vyshinsky and the NKVD interrogators. Some scope for ad-libbing by individual defendants was also admitted – another daring modernist device. We also have evidence of individual lines concocted by the dictator himself. For example, he inserted the following sentences in Kamenev's evidence: 'Stalin's leadership is made up of too hard a granite to expect that it would split of itself. Therefore, the leadership will have to be split.' Stalin also caused Zinovyev to be quoted as saying that Stalin's underlings must be assassinated along with Stalin and as adding that: 'It is not enough to fell the oak; all the young oaks growing around it must be felled too.'[6]

Always an economical artist, Stalin gained many minor incidental advantages from his manipulation of trial material. One such intervention concerned Molotov, now Chairman of *Sovnarkom* as well as a leading Politburo member. Molotov had originally been scheduled for mention in the Zinovyev Trial – along with Stalin himself and all other leading Politburo members – as the object of alleged assassination plans, selection as a purported assassination target being the highest distinction which the dictator could bestow. At some stage, however, Stalin personally removed Molotov's name from this roll of honour.[7] The inference is that Molotov may have expressed disapproval of the proposed frame-up. If so he must have changed his mind later – by the time of the Pyatakov Trial, Molotov had recovered sufficient standing to figure at length as the alleged object of an elaborate murder bid faked to look like a car accident. Thus did Stalin use the show trials to discipline even his closest colleagues.

If Stalin had indeed conceived the Pyatakov Trial as an indirect assault on Ordzhonikidze, that rumbustious Georgian was the last man to take such treatment lying down. What finally turned him into an all-out last-minute opponent of the Terror was, perhaps, Stalin's duplicity in having Pyatakov shot after first promising to spare his life.[8] Soon after this valued deputy had been executed in defiance of the dictator's solemn undertaking, Ordzhonikidze himself mysteriously perished. After delivering an ultimatum to Stalin demanding the end of the Terror, he was visited by several security men who handed him a revolver, offering him the alternative of shooting himself in his own flat or dying in the cellars of the NKVD. Ordzhonikidze said good-bye to his wife and shot himself in the presence of the secret policemen – whereupon a doctor, who was conveniently waiting in attendance, certified that death was due to heart failure.[9] Such is one among many conflicting versions of the Industrial Commissar's death. Another has him poisoned by Dr Levin, one of the four doctors who signed the official death certificate.[10] The suicide version is confirmed by Khrushchev, while the murder theory is supported by evidence from Ordzhonikidze's widow.[11] Whatever the truth may be, a natural death must surely be ruled out.

With Ordzhonikidze perished the last of the Politburo 'moderates'. Henceforward Stalin was absolute and undisputed master of that body. No longer, after February 1937, was it so necessary for him to stage for his most senior colleagues the kind of thriller-mystery death possibly or probably meted out by him to Kirov, Kuybyshev and Ordzhonikidze. From that month onwards the Leader could simply have these people arrested and shot at will.

It was the Central Committee plenum of 23 February to 5 March 1937 which finally granted Stalin the unlimited licence to kill which he had so long sought in vain. Now at last the committeemen – themselves doomed to perish, for the most part, as the result of this folly – sanctioned the arrest, and processing as show trial material, of the two most celebrated residual oppositionists: Bukharin and Rykov. Stalin had these shabby and exhausted figures paraded before the plenum of nearly a hundred and forty members. But though Bukharin wept, pleading with his old comrades and protesting that he had never plotted against Stalin or the Government, he made no headway. 'If you are innocent, you can prove it in a prison cell!' Stalin snapped. The pliant claque of Stalinists then began shouting: 'Shoot the traitor! Back to jail with him!' Broken and sobbing, Bukharin and Rykov were removed by their guards.[12]

This was to prove the last occasion on which Stalin needed to seek the

Central Committee's sanction – in accordance with Party statutes – for the expulsion and arrest of its own members. It is not surprising, therefore, that the same fatal plenum also witnessed attempts to halt the Stalinist terror before it was too late. The leader of this gallant last stand against the tyrant was Postyshev, a candidate member of the Politburo. He was supported by three other Politburo candidates: Chubar, Eykhe and Rudzutak.[13] In the end, however, the attempted mutiny broke against the solidarity of Stalin's henchmen. All the rebels mentioned above were liquidated in due course. So too, of course, were most of the henchmen.

The same plenum marked the further disgrace of the former police chief Yagoda, now languishing in pre-liquidation limbo as Commissar of Posts and Communications. Still at liberty, but only just, Yagoda listened in silence while his methods were attacked by Stalin. Once the dictator had finished worrying Yagoda, who was now a political corpse, a pack of lesser predators pounced, asking why the former NKVD head had coddled 'Trotskyite reptiles'. Why had he harboured traitors on his staff? After listening in silence for a time, Yagoda gave his answer in an undertone: 'What a pity I didn't arrest all of you before, when I had the power.' His words were drowned in a wave of jeering.[14]

Though no transcript of the plenum as a whole has been published, two speeches by Stalin do survive. These show him celebrating his victory in especially macabre terms as he propounds the sinister doctrine which is sometimes regarded as his own special contribution to Marxist theory: that the greater the success in achieving Socialism in the USSR the greater the need for the vigilant repression of enemies.[15] No longer did Stalin describe these foes as confined to the oft-invoked hostile ring of capitalist states, or to the spies allegedly infiltrated from abroad at the malign behest of Trotsky. The very Party was now, it transpired, eaten out by treachery, harbouring numerous wreckers and diversionaries who were seeking to hide behind their membership cards.[16] Stalin further attacked the practice whereby local Party bosses were accustomed to acquire personal retainers whom they were liable to move with them *en bloc* when transferred to a new posting. 'In selecting . . . people personally devoted to them [Stalin complained] these comrades apparently wanted to create for themselves an atmosphere of some independence, both in relation to the local people and in relation to the Central Committee.'[17] With these words the dictator let slip one of his main motives for mounting the great purge: a resolve to crush all corporate loyalties, together with all urges towards independence, within every Soviet institution and association down to the individual family.

While strengthening his grip on the Party at the fateful February-March plenum, Stalin was not neglecting the Security Police. He was now engaged in purging that organization through new executives drafted from the Party Apparatus, in preparation for the day when the purged police should be fit, in turn, to purge . . . the Party Apparatus! In mounting this double-edged attack and a myriad other linked assaults, the dictator intended to rely heavily on Yezhov, the new head of the NKVD. It was Yezhov whom the dictator had chosen to preside over the Great Terror of 1937–8, which has since been identified with his name and is colloquially termed the *Yezhov-shchina* or the Time of Yezhov. To celebrate Yezhov's new prominence, Stalin created a special title for him: that of Commissar-General of State Security.[18] Commissar-*General*! The new rank was a brutal reminder to the Party of its folly in stripping Stalin of the title Secretary-*General* back in 1934, when he had become a mere Secretary undistinguished by any embellishing honorific. As will be recalled, a shadow team of Yezhov men had been understudying the main roles in the NKVD administration for some months. With the Pyatakov trial safely out of the way, the time had come for this new team to take over and liquidate the old. All NKVD veterans of any seniority were guilty of knowing too much about Stalin's methods, besides which some of them still retained lingering vestiges of squeamishness in the processing of their victims. It was time for them to go. As Yezhov's net grew tighter around the NKVD Old Guard, many of the superseded security officials cheated the executioner by defenestrating themselves from the upper floors of the Lubyanka; to judge from one account, the flying bodies of suiciding persecutors must almost have become a traffic hazard in that part of Moscow.[19] Other leaders of the old NKVD were removed by an adroit stratagem of the new Commissar-General's. They were dispatched simultaneously to different parts of the country, purportedly to investigate regional political misdemeanours, but in fact in order to convey them from Moscow to points on the railway line where they could be arrested without fuss. At the same time Yezhov – fearing reprisals – barricaded himself in a specially protected wing of the Lubyanka, to which access could only be obtained by a devious, heavily guarded route.[20]

On 18 March 1937 Yezhov celebrated the success of these tactics by summoning surviving NKVD leaders to their club-room in a Lubyanka annexe and unleashing a vicious verbal attack on Yagoda. The deposed police tycoon was accused of having been an agent of the Tsarist Secret Police (the Okhrana) since 1907, at which time he had been only ten years old. This was, however, not such an impossibility as might be thought, owing to the Okhrana's practice of recruiting school-children as informants: a practice by no means abandoned by the Soviet political police. Yagoda was also accused of having been a German agent since 1917.[21] Other departmental chiefs of the NKVD were also executed as Nazi spies. They included Stalin's talented barber 'friend' Pauker. From the Centre the NKVD purge spread to the provinces, with the result that three thousand police operatives were executed in the year 1937 alone.[22]

The purging of the secret police was accompanied by a similar process in the procuracy, as Vyshinsky presided over the liquidation of prosecutors ill adapted to the new methods: to the tune of ninety per cent in the provinces, according to one assertion.[23] With the simultaneous removal of moderates from the Commissariat of Justice the entire apparatus of repression – police, procuracy and judiciary – was ready to strike blows yet more deadly than those already inflicted.

The Generals Shot

Having at last obtained absolute mastery over the Party through the unlimited licence to kill extorted from the doomed Central Committee of early 1937, and having adequately retuned his secret police by late spring of that year, Stalin was poised to intensify still further the repressions which were already engulfing all sections of the Soviet élite. In this co-ordinated campaign a crucial role was played by the dictator's attack on the officers of his armed forces. The curtain was raised on the assault with the announcement, published on 11 June, that eight very senior generals, including various army and corps commanders, had been arrested. Most distinguished among them was Marshal Tukhachevsky: a Civil War hero, an old adversary of Stalin's from the Soviet-Polish War of 1920, a pioneering military thinker and Deputy Defence Commissar.

An important element in the Terror as a whole, the military purge was to rage for eighteen months and more, until it had destroyed or eliminated about half of Stalin's officers, amounting to some thirty thousand victims.[1] If we ask how many of these purged officers were physically exterminated, we shall have the usual difficulty in attaining precision, since 'purging' implied dismissal at least and summary execution at most, with prison and concentration camp as intermediary stages which, though not necessarily lethal, were more likely than not to prove so in the end. That the number of fatalities among officers ran well into five figures seems certain. The more senior the individual the greater his peril, for among colonels and generals the proportion of victims was to reach the fantastic total of 80 and 90 per cent respectively.[2] 'Never did the officer [corps] of any army suffer such great losses in any war as the Soviet Army suffered in this time of peace,' as Stalin's Soviet-based (but not Soviet-published) biographer Roy

Medvedev points out, also quoting Hitler as congratulating himself (in 1941) on facing a Soviet military machine deprived of its best brains by Stalin's persecution of 1937.[3]

What can have possessed Stalin to mount this assault on his armed forces at a time when he claimed the Soviet Union to be seriously menaced by hostile capitalist states ? One would have thought that he already had the military establishment thoroughly subordinated to his will long before the question of arresting Tukhachevsky ever arose. A variety of controls, introduced soon after the Revolution and specifically designed to forestall any military takeover, had later been strengthened and rendered yet more sophisticated under the Stalin dictatorship until, by the mid-1930s, the Red Army's structure had become intimately enmeshed both with that of the Party and that of the Political Police.

To study these links, even in brief outline, is to receive useful insights into the intricacies of the Stalinist bureaucracy. Most army officers, including virtually all those of high rank, were card-holding Communists, and as such subject to Party discipline. An additional element of control was supplied by the army's Political Administration, which possessed a hierarchy independent of the military and directly responsible to the Party Central Committee.[4] The Administration supplied the political assistants or military commissars who operated in all units and formations, thus saturating the army with independently-based supervision. With regard to police controls over the army, the OGPU/NKVD maintained special branches in all army units above battalion level. Like the Political Administration, the police-within-the-army had its own independent hierarchy; it was responsible for checking individuals' political reliability at all levels, for which purpose it recruited within the armed forces spies who were persuaded or bullied into reporting on their comrades-in-arms. Then again, as if all this were not enough, the NKVD had its own independent army, or series of armies. Consisting of frontier, escort, special duty and other troops, and numbering in all perhaps as many as a million men, these disposed of their own artillery, armour and aircraft. Nor must it be forgotten that the police, whether in their independently based units, or in independently controlled special branches attached to army units and formations, consisted largely of Party members. Thus the complex of controls over the régime's three main pillars – Army, Party and Security Police – formed a tight ring with meshes so intricately interwoven that the opportunity for independent action by any of these institutions seemed effectively thwarted in advance.

With so many checks and inbuilt safeguards any ruler other than Stalin might have felt sufficiently insured against the possibility of a *coup d'état*. Yet the fact still remains that a reckless and determined officer might conceivably have been able to seize the Kremlin, at the head of a handful of troops, exploiting the special vulnerability of a system so over-centralized: so hard, yet potentially so brittle. The ever-suspicious Stalin could never be absolutely certain that the military was innocent of such intentions. And in any case it was always his way to make assurance doubly sure. Has any other ruler in history ever practised so ruthlessly the policy of pre-emptive overkill, whereby whole categories of persons who might be innocent of any conspiratorial design – but who could conceivably become dangerous at some point in the future – were picked out in advance and destroyed? And remote though the danger of a military *putsch* might seem, the Red Army's very cohesion – its excellent morale and discipline – could not fail to alarm Stalin. In the mid-1930s practically all regimental and divisional command-ers consisted of Civil War veterans,[5] whose memories reached back to the days when Communists had spoken to each other as equals. Subservient these soldiers had since become, but by the standards of the emerging slave-state they were still inadequately servile.

Hyper-sensitive to the potential dangers (however remote) which mili-tary independent-mindedness (however limited) might present to his own position, Stalin had carefully lulled his future officer-victims into a sense of false security during the period preceding the Tukhachevsky Trial. The army had suffered less than other sections of the community from the various earlier, comparatively bloodless purges of the decade. In terms of concessionary housing and other perquisites army officers enjoyed advan-tages over the population as a whole, while those of a certain seniority had even been granted immunity from arrest.

How valueless this last concession might prove, close observers could already detect on 5 July 1936 – nearly a year before Tukhachevsky's exe-cution – when the first significant military arrest occurred: that of Divis-ional Commander (in effect, Major-General) Dmitry Shmidt. A dashing cavalry commander of the Civil War, Shmidt had sided with the Trotsky-ites in 1925-7. But it was presumably a personal grudge which weighed most heavily with the Leader when he chose Shmidt as the earliest of many senior army victims. Back in 1927, at the time of the Sixteenth Party Con-gress, Shmidt had chanced to clash with Stalin near the Kremlin. Resplen-dent in huge black Caucasian riding cloak, belt with jangling silver orna-ments, with his fur cap cocked over one ear and his great curved sabre, the swashbuckling cavalryman had abused the small, pockmarked Secre-tary-General in barrack-room language which had to be heard to be believed. Then he made a gesture as if to draw his sabre and threatened to lop off the future Generalissimo's ears! Stalin heard the harangue out in total silence, tight-lipped and white-faced.[6] Nine years later he gave his reply by granting Shmidt priority in arrest, torture and execution over the highest-ranking officers in the army.

That Stalin was gunning for bigger game than Shmidt became evident when the first public hints of Tukhachevsky's imminent disgrace were dropped, the Marshal's name being invoked a dozen times at the Pyatakov Trial. Not that these references, as such, reflected discredit on Tukhachevsky, whom one witness went out of his way to describe as absolutely devoted to Party and Government. But the mere occurrence of Tukhachevsky's name in the script – even in a favourable context – was immediately recognized by connoisseurs of Stalinism as a code signal indicating that the Marshal was approaching the abyss.[7] Further hints of trouble for the High Command were dropped at the February-March Central Committee plenum of 1937, where Stalin drew attention to the dangers presented by a few spies in the army, while Molotov accused the military of softness towards enemies of the people.[8] Several high-ranking officers, including future purge victims, were present as Central Committee members, and it seems possible that some of them had the courage to oppose Stalin over the arrest of Bukharin.[9]

Within a few weeks even the public could see that the lights were dimming for Tukhachevsky and his colleagues. Zombie-like, hands in pockets, the Marshal turned up for the May Day Parade of 1937 in the Red Square, but did not bother to salute his colleagues; in the middle of the proceedings he strolled moodily away, hands still in pockets, though Stalin himself was presiding. As has been remarked of Tukhachevsky and the other doomed generals on this occasion: 'Each knew he was a prisoner, destined for death, enjoying a reprieve by the grace of a despotic master.'[10] Further signs of Tukhachevsky's impending fate soon followed. On 4 May it was announced that he would not be attending the coronation of King George VI in London, as previously arranged. Then army officers were officially warned to show greater vigilance: always a danger signal. On 10 May Tukhachevsky was dismissed as Deputy Defence Commissar; so, too, was Yan Gamarnik, head of the Army Political Administration. Tukhachevsky was posted to an obscure command on the Volga, while another earmarked victim, Army Commander Yakir, was assigned from Kiev to Leningrad. Stalin's purpose in decreeing these pre-purge postings was to remove the officers concerned from local power bases where they might conceivably have attempted to resist arrest, and to isolate them so that they could be picked off at leisure.

Despite such signs of imminent disaster the wider public was taken by surprise when Stalin's major attack on his officer corps was at last openly and decisively launched on 11 June 1937 with *Pravda*'s announcement of Tukhachevsky's arrest, and that of the seven other senior officers. They were accused of passing military intelligence to a foreign power (Germany by implication); of sabotaging the Red Army; and of promoting the restoration of capitalism in the USSR. All were said to have pleaded guilty. Twenty-four hours later came the grim proclamation that they had already been tried, condemned and executed. Among various conflicting accounts of their end, one has them shot in a Lubyanka courtyard to the sound of revved-up lorries.[11]

Thus, through an alleged trial reported as taking place *in camera* – as opposed to a blatantly advertised show trial – did Stalin dispose of his first major military victims by a 'most delicate piece of surgery'.[12] One speaks of an *alleged* trial because there is little evidence – apart from assertions made in Stalin-controlled media – to indicate that any court proceedings actually took place on 11 June. The court was described, officially, as comprising nine named persons, of whom Ulrich – already blooded as senior judge in the show trials – was President, while the rest were themselves senior generals. Thus the eight 'mad dogs' were sentenced by an equal number of their peers, and the impression was created that the Army was judging itself. It is doubtful whether many of the judges suffered from that illusion; indeed, some of them may well have been relieved to discover, on entering the court room, that they were to be placed on the bench and not in the dock ... not yet, that is. A majority of the court-martiallers, including Marshal Blyukher, did eventually fall at later stages of the military purge.

While the generals were thus hustled to their death a blare of pre-scripted spontaneous execration arose from factory workers, poets, academicians, polar explorers and numerous other representatives of Soviet society who were still demanding the death penalty for all such traitors, mad dogs and filthy spies as Tukhachevsky long after the victims' bodies had grown cold in their unknown resting place.

Three days after the execution a manifesto signed by Defence Commissar Voroshilov repeated and expanded the charges against the generals to include contact with Trotsky and plotting the assassination of Soviet leaders. The charge of planning a military *coup* against Stalin was to follow at the Bukharin Trial, as was that of intending to 'open the front' (offer no serious resistance) to German armies invading the Soviet Union. That these accusations were all baseless is now generally conceded, in the Soviet Union no less than in the West, Tukhachevsky and other leading victims having been rehabilitated posthumously and accorded martyr status in their native land. No evidence of any *coup* planned by them has ever come to light. Nor has any evidence of collusion with the Germans surfaced, either in the Nuremberg Trial documents or in the mass of Nazi secret archives.

After the slaughter of his first eight military victims, Stalin lost little time in exploiting his breakthrough. In Moscow alone about twenty more generals were promptly executed, some hundreds of other senior officers also being arrested.[13] The assault took in provincial commands as well. In Kiev over six hundred senior officers of the Ukrainian Military District were arrested, tainted as they were by association with their executed commander, Yakir. Civilian repercussions included the liquidation of certain radio station directors for broadcasting a funeral march on the day of the Tukhachevsky shooting, while a cinema manager was arrested for failing to cut a newsreel featuring that offending Marshal.[14] Similar horrors and absurdities raged in Minsk – involving the large-scale extermination of the executed Uborevich's officers in the Belorussian Military District – and soon spread to most other parts of the country. As in civilian life, so too within the forces, the many arrests much improved promotion prospects, but junior officers who stepped into the shoes of liquidated seniors often found themselves liquidated in turn. Promotion became almost synonymous with arrest, and the only way of improving one's chances of survival lay in being posted to some particularly obscure backwater.

After a brief lull in late 1937 the military purge flared up again in February 1938 with the dismissal of Marshal Yegorov. His arrest, followed by his death (variously reported as occurring in 1939 or 1941)[15] broke the pattern of immunity hitherto extended to those senior military colleagues whom the dictator remembered from his days as Political Commissar to the South-Western Front (Yegorov's old command) during the Soviet-Polish War of 1920. Failure to give Stalin political support over Bukharin's arrest, insufficient zeal in blackguarding his murdered brother officers, face-crime or mere whim ... any of these could have caused Yegorov's downfall. Among other notable victims of the second-wave military purge was Vatsetis, who had been the first Commander-in-Chief of the Red Army, and Army Commander Dybenko, the giant former sailor whose love life had once provoked from Stalin a coarse reaction offensive to the delicate sensibilities of Trotsky.[16]

The military purge was slow in spreading to far eastern Siberia: Marshal Blyukher's command. After acting as one of Tukhachevsky's judges, and perhaps also as commander of the very firing-squad, Blyukher had returned to the far east; here the immense distance between himself and the Kremlin, combined with a developing military threat from the Japanese, bought him and his forces comparative immunity lasting about twelve months. But then, in May 1938, the full Terror burst on Blyukher's command. Recalled from Siberia, he himself was allowed to cool his heels on the Black Sea coast before being arrested on Stalin's personal orders and tortured to death while refusing to confess that he had been a Japanese spy since 1921.[17] With Blyukher were crushed all the military and other establishments of the far east.

Besides the Red Army proper, two other leading martial institutions – the Navy and the Army's Political Administration – also contributed their share of victims. The liquidated naval commander-in-chief, Admiral Orlov, and the alleged suicide Gamarnik (head of the army's Political Administration) were each escorted or followed to disgrace or death by a majority of their subordinates.

The military purge ran true to Stalinist pattern by also taking in the widows, orphans and other relatives of the slaughtered officers. Two widows of Marshal Tukhachevsky – who had been blessed with a profusion of family ties – were sent to a special camp for wives and sisters of 'enemies of the people', where fellow-prisoners included the sister of the deposed police tycoon Yagoda.[18] The purge also swept up the victims' children, among whom Pyotr Yakir was arrested at the age of fourteen; after many years in camps and prisons he emerged to edit a book of memoirs on his – now rehabilitated – father Iona, and to fall foul of Soviet authority in 1972 through his participation in post-Khrushchevite political opposition. Other children were sent to NKVD orphanages, from one of which Tukhachevsky's daughter Svetlana graduated to a camp sentence of five years as a 'socially dangerous' element.[19] Once again Stalin was practising pre-emptive quarantine, perhaps mindful of the bloody record of young girls in Russian political life: a member of the gentler sex had, after all, led the successful bomb attack on Alexander II in 1881, while a female Socialist Revolutionary had once wounded Lenin.

There could be no act of Stalin's so outrageous that Western observers were not found to explain it away, thus adding their own characteristic 'bourgeois' extension to the excesses of the Terror. With minor qualifications Joseph E. Davies, United States Ambassador to the Soviet Union in 1936-8, accepted the official Stalinist version of the generals' guilt. He also believed that the extermination of the generals was not Stalin's doing at all: 'the responsibility is generally attributed to the "action of the party" through its party leaders.' Faced with a serious threat from the army, they 'hit first . . . with great speed and ruthless severity.'[20] One telling minor feature of the Ambassador's reactions is the subtle change wrought by the executions in his personal attitude to the victims. Having entertained Tukhachevsky and other generals to dinner back in March 1937 – when he could not suspect what Stalin had in store for them – Roosevelt's envoy had been 'impressed by the fine appearance of these men – strong, healthy and with fine faces'.[21] But once Tukhachevsky had been shot this image underwent a startling metamorphosis in Ambassador Davies's mind. Tukhachevsky 'did not impress me very much. He . . . was rather overweight for his size, and looked like a man who enjoyed good living.'[22] How different from Stalin himself, who remained, in Mr Davies's unforgettable words 'a clean-living, modest, retiring, single-purposed man'![23] To be one of life's losers was, obviously, no recommendation to the American Ambassador.

Even within his own embassy Mr Davies's words carried little conviction at the time. On 23 June 1937 Loy Henderson, the US *chargé d'affaires*, reported that 'not one diplomatic mission here, nor a single foreign observer in Moscow whose opinion bears weight, believed that the executed Red officers were guilty of the crimes attributed to them.' Nor had George F. Kennan and Charles E. Bohlen (then secretaries at the American Embassy) accepted the guilt of the generals.[24] Isaac Deutscher's biography of Stalin bears further witness to the success with which the truth about the generals' guilt has been distorted. In the first (1949) edition of that work we read that '*all non-Stalinist versions concur in the following:* the generals did indeed plan a *coup d'état*.'[25] However, by the time when Deutscher's book reached its second edition, in 1967, the Soviet authorities themselves had pronounced the generals guiltless, posthumously rehabilitating Tukhachevsky and his brother officers, while leaving the biographer in an uncomfortably exposed position. He responded by amending the above-quoted sentence to read: '*quite a few non-Stalinist sources maintain that* the generals did indeed plan a *coup d'état*.'[26] But deutero-Deutscher was almost as out of date as proto-Deutscher, for there has long been virtual unanimity, shared by authorities in East and West alike, that the generals had been plotting no *putsch*.[27]

To what extent was Stalin himself guilty of the very offence for which he framed the Tukhachevsky group? While accusing Tukhachevsky of collusion with Nazi Germany, and of an intention to offer no resistance in the event of a Hitlerite attack on the Soviet Union,[28] the dictator had himself already been attempting for some time to do a highly secret political deal with Hitler through certain undercover emissaries to Berlin. It was precisely the crime of which Tukhachevsky stood accused! Nor was this by any means all, for Stalin also commissioned – in effect – from the Germans an elaborate forged document purporting to give evidence of treasonable contact between Tukhachevsky and certain Hitlerite generals. In the end, though, the Leader decided not to make public use of this sinister forgery, which was concocted by the Nazi secret police at his behest, transmitted via the versatile Paris-based Russian émigré General Skoblin: a combined NKVD and Gestapo agent.[29]

In the light of these circumstances – obscure in their tedious ramifications,

but well established in their general outline – Stalin's framing of Tukhachevsky for collusion with the Nazis acquires a special piquancy of its own.
It fits into the recurring pattern whereby the dictator apparently sought to
saddle others with crimes which may have been commissioned by himself:
the Kirov murder, the death of Gorky, Kuybyshev's 'heart attack' and
the like.

When we recall that Stalin also had Tukhachevsky accused of *undermining the Red Army's fighting capacity*, we are tempted to see the same guilt-
transfer mechanism operating again. Who, after all, had done most to
weaken Soviet defences in this period? Not Tukhachevsky, but rather the
man who was engaged in shattering the Soviet High Command and the
entire officer corps of the Red Army at a time when the USSR was first
seriously menaced by Hitlerite expansionism. And who ever came nearer than
Stalin was to come, in 1941, to 'opening the front' to the German invader?
As these considerations suggest, the Soviet military purge does indeed
throw a lurid light on Stalin's scale of priorities. That the dictator indeed
was, as often claimed, a militant Russian patriot-by-adoption we shall
not attempt to deny, only pointing out that this great patriotic drive related exclusively to a Russia wholly dominated by himself. When it came
to the point, the dictator did not hesitate to put his country in grave peril
of defeat rather than take the faintest risk of seeing his own power overthrown by the Soviet military establishment.

The Party Smashed

Assaulting the governmental, technical, managerial, cultural and other
élites, the Great Terror could not but take a high toll within the Party,
since so high a proportion among the most prominent members of the
various Soviet establishments consisted of card-holding Communists. Nor
did the Party's inner core of full-time functionaries – the *apparatchiki* –
escape Stalin's fury.

In Moscow, in Leningrad, at provincial centres within the RSFSR,
as also in the Ukraine, Belorussia, the Caucasus and Central Asia . . . everywhere the Terror struck. While higher officials sought to cover up or buy
time by zeal in liquidating lesser fry, these juniors themselves strove to
forestall their fate by feverishly denouncing high-ups to still higher authority: all in vain. None, at any level, could count on immunity, though
danger was fairly closely correlated with seniority. Thus the way was
opened, as in the Army, for the rapid promotion of juniors. But such beneficiaries were, more often than not, soon dismissed and shot in their turn,
to be succeeded by further doomed relays. Such was the general picture

throughout Stalin's slave empire at this period, though many variations are recorded from one area to another: in timing: in the identity of the main purgers; in severity of impact; in the extent of our knowledge.

We are best informed of all on the purge in the province of Smolensk, owing to the chance which has made the Party archives of that area generally available.[1] But the Muscovite Terror has been obscured, as has that of the Ukraine, by the fact that Khrushchev was proconsul in both areas during the purge years, and that he later came to control all Soviet sources on the subject. In 1956-64 – the years of Khrushchev's ascendancy and also the years of disclosures damaging to the reputation of Stalin and Stalinists – revelations implicating Beria, Malenkov, Molotov and Kaganovich were naturally dispensed more freely than material compromising the controller of this information.

The full impact of the Terror was somewhat delayed in far eastern Siberia, as noted above, partly owing to the increased military threat from the Japanese in that area. In the Ukraine, too, the hurricane struck comparatively late, owing to the unwillingness of the Ukrainian Party bosses to co-operate in destroying each other. Some of them had to be lured to Moscow for a 'conference' so that they could be conveniently arrested; in August 1937 a trio of top purgers (Molotov, Khrushchev and Yezhov) descended on the Ukraine to carry out the slaughter at which Kosior, and other squeamish locals, had jibbed.[2] Soon the Ukraine could boast a bloodier record than that of any other republic in the Union. No less severe were the tribulations of Leningrad, always a special object of the dictator's rancour. Here Zhdanov – successor to the slaughtered Kirov – held sway, and to such effect that only two out of one hundred and fifty-four Leningrad delegates to the Seventeenth Party Congress survived to be re-elected to the Eighteenth.[3] From the junior ranks of the multi-purged former capital, Aleksey Kosygin somehow emerged, as did Leonid Brezhnev from the shattered Ukrainian Apparatus, to rise to highest office almost three decades later.

Zhdanov-controlled Leningrad and Beria-controlled Transcaucasia were the only two provincial areas in which Stalin already maintained a resident purger who was prepared to butcher his neighbours with adequate zeal. Beria was even allowed the special privilege of staging his own local trials: trials publicized, but not public. One of these swept away the veteran Georgian Bolshevik Mdivani. Coiner of many a quip at Stalin's expense, Mdivani is said to have remarked, when facing execution, that Stalin, whom he had known for thirty years: 'won't rest until he has butchered all of us, beginning with the unweaned baby and ending with the blind great-grandmother.'[4] At the Centre Stalin himself kept a firm grip on high-level purging, with Yezhov as his right-hand man, while in many outlying areas of the Union the slaughter of top Communists was directed by touring purge-masters specially dispatched from Moscow. Among these missionaries Kaganovich was prominent – he it was who destroyed the Smolensk Apparatus, also devastating those of Ivanovo and the Kuban. Malenkov's attacks embraced Belorussia and Armenia.[5] Among the various purgers of Central Asia, A. A. Andreyev helped to administer the terror in Tashkent.[6]

How, in these chaotic circumstances, could any individual hope to preserve a whole skin? Certainly not by protesting to Stalin about the excesses of the Terror, for there was no quicker passport to liquidation. Nor might immunity even be guaranteed by excess of zeal in exterminating one's colleagues, since such arch-exterminators automatically qualified as convenient scapegoats against the inevitable day when Stalin should decide to pose as the advocate of restraint. Nor yet could the cultivation of passive unobtrusiveness – an attitude no less conspicuous, in this grotesque age, than any other – be relied upon to deflect the sword of injustice. Amid the raging Terror only one tiny group of persons retained immunity: Stalin's half dozen senior colleagues among full Politburo members: Andreyev, Kaganovich, Kalinin, Mikoyan, Molotov and Voroshilov. To them must be added three top-échelon touring purgers, slightly junior in Party rank, but soon to achieve Politburo candidate membership: Khrushchev, Malenkov and Beria. With these must be contrasted the ten Politburo members or candidate members, elected in 1934 or later, who fell by the wayside during the following years: the Kirov-Kuybyshev-Ordzhonikidze trio, early removed by murder or good luck; four Ukrainian Party chiefs (Postyshev, Kosior, Chubar and Petrovsky); the two Latvians Rudzutak and Eykhe; and – in the end – the chief author (under Stalin) of the Great Terror, Yezhov.

The two Politburo Latvians figure among those posthumously accorded martyr status by Khrushchev, who speaks of a secret trial of Rudzutak at which the latter denounced a conspiratorial centre 'as yet not liquidated . . . which is craftily manufacturing cases, and which forces innocent persons to confess'.[7] Aware or not that he was denouncing Stalin himself with these words, Rudzutak was shot, his last accusation remaining buried for nearly twenty years in the archives. Eykhe, the other Politburo Latvian, was among the many physically tortured by NKVD officers; they exploited the knowledge that his 'broken ribs had not properly mended and were causing me great pain.'[8] Physical torture was sanctioned by Stalin in the summer of 1937, and had been widely applied before that. Administered with extreme brutality, it was yet employed unsystematically on the whole, and in accordance with the individual NKVD interrogator's inspiration of the moment.

All in all, as many as a million Party members or former members may have perished in the Great Terror.[9] Even so they probably contributed no more than 10 per cent of the grand total of fatalities, which – as will be discussed below – may well have exceeded ten million.[10] Forming so small a proportion among the totality of martyrs, card-holding Soviet Communists surely remain, among all Stalin's victims, those whose passing has least claim on the regrets of posterity. By whatever combination – of gullibility, misplaced idealism, careerism, corruption, conceit in trying to build a Utopia on their contemporaries' bones – each slaughtered Party man had in some degree contributed to his butcher's professional advancement. 'He that diggeth a pit shall fall into it.'[11]

Stalinism Exported

Foreign Communists – Polish, German, Hungarian, Italian, Bulgarian and others – qualified for slaughter during the *Yezhovshchina* no less than Russian Party members. Already present in Moscow or lured from abroad on some pretext, members of these non-Soviet Parties were concentrated in the Hotel Luxe, where the amenities included that of being picked off by the NKVD in nightly raids. Members of the Comintern leadership were prominent among such victims.

Stalin's destructive suspicions also extended to Soviet and Comintern agents operating on foreign soil. He saw no reason why such spies should enjoy immunity, and began to summon them home for unobtrusive purging – also attempting to lull their fears by delaying the purge of the NKVD's Foreign Department (which controlled them) and of its chief, Slutsky. Scenting what was in the wind, some of these earmarked victims took the momentous decision to defect and seek asylum abroad: to which indiscipline Stalin responded by forming mobile squads of assassins charged with tracking down and exterminating such renegades.[1] One noteworthy victim was the NKVD's defecting Polish spymaster Ignace Reiss, who took his wife and child to a secret refuge in Switzerland, but was traced by Stalin's agents. Reiss's bullet-ridden corpse was found in a road near Lausanne on 4 September 1937; his widow survived to describe the episode many years later.[2] In October of the same year Reiss's colleague Walter Krivitsky, head of Soviet military intelligence in Western Europe, was summoned to Moscow from France, but defied orders – removing himself, wife and child to America. After three years of hunted existence his corpse was found in a fifth-floor room of a Washington hotel on 10 February 1941.

A bullet had been fired at contact range into the right temple; the weapon itself lay near his right hand; he had left three notes indicating an intention to commit suicide; the door of the room was locked. Not doubting that he had indeed killed himself, his widow claimed that he had been forced to do so by Stalinist agents who had threatened to murder her and their child should her husband fail to co-operate.[3] In the meantime Krivitsky had managed to publish his book *I Was Stalin's Agent*, which contains much information on the dictator's life.

Wiser than Krivitsky, another defecting Soviet intelligence chief of the period, Alexander Orlov, took the precaution of lodging an account of Stalin's various crimes with his lawyer. He sent a copy to the dictator, warning that this black record would be made public immediately in the event of his own death by violence: a device which appears to have saved its author from the NKVD's roving thugs. At any rate Orlov survived to see his *Secret History of Stalin's Crimes* published after Stalin's death.

Less fortunate than Orlov was the defecting Ukrainian nationalist Evhen Konovalec: blown up in a Rotterdam street in May 1938 while carrying a bomb-parcel foisted on him by a political 'sympathizer'. Two months later Rudolf Klement – a former secretary of Trotsky's – disappeared; his headless corpse was eventually recovered from the River Marne. Another martyr to Stalin's travelling assassins may have been Trotsky's son, Lyov Sedov, who perished mysteriously in a Paris nursing home at about the same time; Trotsky accused the GPU of employing White Russian émigré agents to poison the young man.[4] These and many other deaths appear to confirm that Stalin did indeed maintain in France 'a body of assassins directed by the GPU, backed by the resources of an entire state machine, supported by the diplomatic representatives of that State, and with its activities smoke-screened by Communist Party propaganda'.[5]

Meanwhile, back in Moscow, the affable Slutsky (head of the NKVD's Foreign Department) had exhausted his usefulness by February 1938, when he died of a 'heart attack' brought on by a dose of cyanide administered to him in his own office.[6]

The Spanish Civil War was prominent among Stalin's foreign preoccupations during the years of the Terror. Beginning in July 1936, and ending in March 1939, the conflict straddled the period of the *Yezhovshchina*. With his policies towards Spain, Stalin showed himself anxious not to become closely involved in a struggle which threatened to develop into a world war for which the Soviet Union was ill prepared. On the other hand, so professedly left-wing a government as the Soviet could not remain entirely aloof now that Spanish Left and Spanish Right were locked in combat before the eyes of the world. It was therefore necessary to simulate commitment to the struggle, while remembering that the all-out victory of neither side was desirable. A Francoite success would – and eventually did – weaken France, thus freeing the avowedly anti-Communist Hitler to concentrate on aggression in the east; as for the prospect of a Republican victory, that would certainly produce a left-wing Spanish government, but one imperfectly responsive to Kremlinite control: the last kind of régime which the Soviet Leader ever wished to see established anywhere. Even the emergence of a wholly Stalinized Spain would only have given him a weak ally at the other end of Europe – and that at the expense of antagonizing his existing allies, Britain and France. The dictator's general attitude to the Spanish war was, therefore, that he would not help the Republic to win, but would not permit it to lose: a policy which he did not, however, promote with sufficient vigour to forestall Franco's eventual victory. Meanwhile, though, 'the mere continuance of the war would keep him [Stalin] free to act in any way. It might even make possible a world war in which France, Britain, Germany and Italy would destroy themselves with Russia, the arbiter, staying outside.'[7]

It was in keeping with this policy of calculated caution that Soviet military aid did not begin to reach the Republicans until October 1936.[8] Always limited in scope and subject to many restrictions, Soviet assistance to Spain was channelled through the Comintern, not given directly by Moscow. Nor were Soviet fighting units ever sent to Spain – by contrast with the German and Italian 'volunteers' drafted to Francoite service. Instead of dispatching Red Army forces, Stalin sponsored International Brigades manned by anti-Francoite volunteers. Arms, food and medical supplies were also shipped to the Republicans in quantity, but Stalin ensured – and with characteristic unsentimentality – that the Soviet Union should not be the loser in the deal by laying hands on most of the Republicans' gold reserves. This Spanish gold, valued at some sixty million pounds sterling, was shipped from Cartagena to Odessa, and Stalin celebrated its arrival – in nearly eight thousand boxes – with a banquet; he also boasted, using a common Russian idiom, that the Spaniards would never see their gold again, 'any more than they will see their own ears'.[9] While keeping Soviet fighting units away from Spain, Stalin did send Soviet pilots, flying instructors and tank experts. Certain senior Red Army officers were also posted to Spain as advisers, but were strictly enjoined to stay out of artillery range.[10] To them were added various diplomats, journalists, financial experts and Comintern representatives.

Towards Spain, Stalin pursued a dual policy analogous to that symbolized at home by the New Constitution on the one hand and the *Yezhovshchina* on

the other: a façade of sweet reasonableness masked covert, or at least unacknowledged, political terror. The reasonableness was expressed in Soviet
adherence to the international non-intervention agreement in August
1936, and in a letter sent to the Spanish Prime Minister Largo Caballero
on 21 December 1936. In this remarkable missive the Spanish Republicans
were urged by revolutionary Moscow to follow policies anything but
revolutionary: to base themselves on the parliamentary method; to respect
the property rights of foreigners and peasants; to spare the bourgeoisie.[11]
As this indicates, Stalin's main hostility was not directed against class
enemies on the Republican side, nor yet against Franco himself. It was,
rather, Spanish Republicans nominally closer to the Soviet position who
felt the full brunt of the Soviet leader's fury: leftists, including Marxists
not fully amenable to Kremlinite discipline, and Anarchists. As previously
illustrated, this animus against under-Stalinized leftists was a permanent
and ineradicable feature in the dictator's outlook throughout his career.

In conformity with this mentality, a strong NKVD contingent was
drafted to Spain, and launched a pogrom against Anarchists and against
'Trotskyites': a term which embraced most leftists imperfectly subservient
to the Kremlin, whether or not the persons concerned happened to be
followers of Trotsky. The Soviet police razzia struck Catalonia most
severely, an intention openly proclaimed on the pages of *Pravda*: 'So far as
Catalonia is concerned, the purge of Trotskyites and Anarchists has begun,
and it will be carried out with the same energy as in the USSR.'[12] In parts
of Republican Spain the NKVD enjoyed almost as much latitude as in
its native habitat to arrest, interrogate under torture and assassinate victims
who included individuals of many other nationalities in addition to the
Spanish and Soviet. Dissidence and violence within the Republican forces
inevitably weakened the general effort against Franco, but that mattered
little to Stalin. For him the Spanish Civil War remained an open sore
which should be kept running as long as possible. On this point his policy
conformed closely with that of Hitler.[13] But it was Hitler's (not Stalin's)
Spanish protégés who eventually triumphed with Franco's victory of March
1939; now contemplating a rapprochement with Hitler, Stalin had decided
to leave the Spanish Republic to its fate.

Eventually – again in conformity with normal Stalinist practice – the
very instruments of Stalin's Spanish terror were recalled and purged in
their turn. It has been claimed that 'Spain was a bad posting for all Soviet
personnel',[14] and so it was, of course; but so too was every other kind of
posting! Many of the Soviet and non-Soviet military, diplomatic, police and
Comintern officials accredited to Madrid or Barcelona were indeed
liquidated after returning to Moscow. But there were also some notable

survivors, at least among senior Red Army officers; they included Konev and Malinovsky, later to be promoted Marshals. The writer Ilya Ehrenburg also survived his Spanish experiences.

Bukharin Agonistes

Bukharin and twenty associates were tried in Moscow between 2 and 13 March 1938. This, the last drama in Stalin's grand trilogy, involved a larger number of defendants, and was yet more grotesque in content than its predecessors. Since the dictator had already enjoyed twelve months of absolute power over life and death, as conferred on him by the first two show trials of the Terror, we may wonder what reasons induced him to stage this third and most extravagant pageant of all. Was he, for once, indulging in art for art's sake? Or mounting a victory parade? Or was he chiefly concerned to pursue his personal vendetta against Bukharin to its final solution? Long politically disgraced, Bukharin had yet been allowed to visit western Europe as late as the spring of 1936, and had there held long confidential conversations with certain émigré Mensheviks whom Lenin had permitted to leave Soviet Russia in 1922: Boris Nikolayevsky; Fyodor and Lidiya Dan. The substance of these talks was later published, forming an especially valuable comment on the Terror and its author.[1] When Bukharin told the Dans about Stalin, his usually good-natured features were completely distorted by fear and anger. Stalin, said he,

suffers because he can't persuade everyone, including himself, that he is greater than everybody, and this suffering is probably the most human thing about him; perhaps it is his only human trait. But there is something diabolical and inhuman about his compulsion to take vengeance for this same suffering on everybody, especially on those who are in some way higher and better than he.... If anybody speaks better than Stalin, his doom is sealed. . . . Such a man is a constant reminder to him that he is not the first, not the best. If anybody writes better, so much the worse for him, because *he*, Stalin, and only he should be the first Russian writer. . . . This is a small, vicious man: no, not a man but a devil.[2]

Knowing Stalin's vindictiveness so well, Bukharin had nevertheless not hesitated to return to Moscow and face the terrible fate which awaited him. Among others degraded in March 1938 was Rykov, with whom Bukharin had (in 1928-9) been recently allied in a rightist bloc directed against Stalin's collectivization policies. One of the motives for discrediting Bukharin and Rykov – as for mounting the Great Terror as a whole – was, perhaps, to prove that collectivization had justified itself, when it had so signally failed to do so: a view which Pasternak allows one of his characters to express in *Doctor Zhivago*.[3]

Another senior defendant, Yagoda, provides the connoisseur of Stalin-ism with an especially fascinating spectacle. The first and only Soviet security overlord ever to be tried in public, Yagoda was in a particularly sensitive position, having collaborated so closely with Stalin in staging previous judicial assassinations. Yagoda knew more about the dictator's crimes than any other show-trial defendant. Hence the bitter irony of his appearance in court, for he was now intoning precisely the kind of script which he himself had so often forced others to learn by rote; and he showed himself well aware of this paradoxical situation when he departed from his lines in court on more than one cautious ad-libbing excursion. As a further ironical twist, some of the crimes to which Yagoda now confessed may even have been committed by him. But if he indeed did (as he testified at his trial) procure the slaughter of Kirov, Kuybyshev and Gorky, he very likely did so at the behest of the dictator himself . . . and, if so, his present Stalin-extorted self-incriminating testimony must have carried an especially pungent taste for him.

At the Bukharin trial themes mooted at earlier judicial pageants were merged in a great crescendo. Four diplomat-defendants were paraded to confirm the usual collusion with foreign powers, especially Germany, and the usual links with the absent Trotsky. Then a second quartet, consisting of economic managers, confessed to promoting large-scale sabotage, diver-sion and wrecking: in order to weaken the economy and discredit the govern-ment as a prelude to overthrowing Stalin by a military *coup d'état* with foreign assistance. Yet another quartet of defendants consisted of offenders drawn – and for the first time in a major show trial – from various non-Russian republics of the USSR: Uzbekistan, the Ukraine and Belorussia. They supplied the hitherto neglected ingredient of nationalist deviation.

An even more bizarre element was supplied by the remaining defend-ants: a trio of secretaries and a trio of doctors. The three secretaries – of Gorky, Kuybyshev and Yagoda – confirmed that Gorky and Kuybyshev had indeed been murdered on Yagoda's orders, while the three doctors pre-sented themselves as the self-confessed instruments of those orders. Besides medically exterminating Gorky and Kuybyshev, they had done away with Gorky's son, and had also disposed of Menzhinsky: the NKVD head who had preceded Yagoda. But the murder techniques admitted by these demon-medicos turned out curiously vague and half-hearted. Gorky had been exposed to bonfire smoke – to weaken his tubercular lungs – before being brought into fatal contact with grandchildren suffering from head colds; Gorky's son had been left lying on a garden bench when drunk so that he should perish of exposure; Kuybyshev had been incorrectly treated for a heart complaint; Menzhinsky had been dosed with some drug of dubious and disputed properties. Among the three doctor-defendants the elderly Professor Pletnyov was the most distinguished. His testimony had originally been extorted by framing him on a charge of 'sadistic rape': an NKVD girl had been put up to accuse him of biting her on the breast. Behind this and other gruesome absurdities seems to lurk an obsessive determination by Stalin to degrade the Soviet medical profession, which may well have irritated him by displaying *esprit de corps* such as he everywhere sought to destroy.

Alleged medical murders formed only part of the elaborate terrorist sub-plot structure deployed at the Bukharin trial. Once a pharmacist by profession, Yagoda now also confessed to the attempted murder of Yezhov by having a solution of mercury sprayed on the curtains and carpet of his office. It was now, too, that Yagoda confessed to the most notorious of all Soviet political murders – that of Kirov – asserting that this assassination had been arranged at the behest of Stalin's former crony, the since executed Yenukidze. That Yagoda had been ultimately responsible for the Kirov murder, but on Stalin's instructions – and that Yenukidze had thus become a code equivalent for Stalin himself – is, as stated above, a plausible assumption which is unlikely ever to be finally proved or disproved.

As usual, Stalin himself was quoted as the senior object for unsuccessful assassination attempts against leading Soviet statesmen. These attempts, it was now claimed, had formed part of an over-all plan to seize control of the government by a military *coup d'état* in which the army leaders Tukhachevsky and Gamarnik were to have played leading roles.

The Bukharin trial saw a new and greater degree of indiscipline – with a corresponding tendency to ad-lib – among members of the cast. Most defiant was the former leading Trotskyite Krestinsky, who pleaded not guilty to all charges on the first day, perhaps in the hope of leading a revolt by the defendants as a whole. However, a night of 'persuasion' by the NKVD was sufficient to restore the mutineer to his original place in the scenario, after he had reputedly been tortured by the dislocation of his shoulder.[4] Yagoda also attempted to fudge his lines, as already noted, and was particularly effective when denying charges of espionage; he pointed out that, had he really been a spy, dozens of foreign intelligence establishments would have had to close down –[5] their agents' work having presumably been rendered superfluous by the superior intelligence flowing from the head of the Soviet security forces. However, Yagoda too was induced to co-operate more decorously in later appearances.

As befitted the leading Party intellectual, Bukharin tried to stage an unobtrusive play-within-the-play while feigning full co-operation with the prosecutor. He pleaded guilty to the charges in vague general terms, but denied all responsibility on an individual concrete level. He would neither admit to spying nor to plotting Lenin's assassination in 1918. But though he was evidently seeking to discredit the trial from the dock, his methods were over-intellectual and too subtle for so crude a context.

The structure of mendacity erected by Stalin was now beginning to congeal in a self-supporting amalgam. When Krestinsky disavowed in court confessions previously extracted from him during preliminary investigation, a minor defendant – Bessonov – was at once produced in order to refute Krestinsky's disavowal. It then turned out that Bessonov's own capitulation had originally been obtained by confronting him during *his* preliminary investigation with the very false 'confession' by Krestinsky which the latter now sought to abjure in court.[6] Similarly, pressure appears to have been put on the captive Bukharin by arranging for him to stumble 'by chance' on a copy of Lion Feuchtwanger's newly-published book on the Pyatakov trial, *Moscow 1937*. In this work – which has been called 'perhaps the most nauseating of the Western apologies for the Moscow trials' –[7] Feuchtwanger states that 'there was no justification of any sort for imagining that there was anything manufactured or artificial about the trial proceedings.'[8] This gratuitous endorsement of Stalin's fabrications – and by a supposedly independent foreign observer – may well have played its part in inducing Bukharin to give up hope and produce a confession adequate for Stalin's purpose.

During this, the third and most elaborate of the Great Terror show trials, the Maestro himself took a close but unobtrusive personal interest in the proceedings: 'At one stage . . . a clumsily-directed arc-light dramatically revealed to attentive members of the audience the familiar features and heavy, drooping moustache peering out from behind the black glass of a small window, high under the ceiling of the courtroom.'[9]

The accused were found guilty on all counts. Eighteen were sentenced to be shot; three received prison sentences.

Man of Letters, Home Lover and Commuter

Worshipped as a god, acclaimed as a universal genius, the dictator busily monitored, personally and through his minions, a vast range of activities great and small in the sphere of science, culture and the arts.

The grand total of his victims and occasional favourites accordingly came to include errant or patronized philosophers, historians, jurists, geneticists, philologists, composers of music, actors, physicians, physicists and theatrical producers, together with practitioners in most other branches of human endeavour. Arrested on the denunciation of colleagues or roving busybodies, such victim-specialists were subjected in custody to 'persuasion', mental and physical, calculated to extract from them further denunciations implicating in political heresy others still at liberty. Meanwhile especially favoured protégés were able to establish minor Stalinist empires in various fields of activity. Such a dominion was that of the bogus geneticist, agricultural charlatan and hounder of orthodox scientists, Trofim Lysenko; another such fief formed in the world of Soviet linguistics around the eccentric philologian N. Ya. Marr, perpetuating itself long after his death in 1934.

As a dictator over the former Tsarist Empire, Stalin was bound to take a particularly keen interest in literature, now established for well over a century as the senior Russian art form and that which the Imperial state bureaucracy had most persistently attempted to tame since long before the birth of Joseph Dzhugashvili. But never in Russian history has the weight of official regimentation borne more heavily on Russian writers than during the quarter of a century of Stalin's supreme rule. Proudly conscious of his achievement as the greatest builder of fantasy structures in the Soviet State, the dictator did not intend to see this monopoly challenged by image-mongers less substantial. According to one author-victim, the survivor of a decade's incarceration, over six hundred writers were sent to prisons and camps; from these many – perhaps the majority – never returned. The same authority, Aleksandr Solzhenitsyn, adds that these maligned scribes were guilty of no crime;[1] but that of course does nothing to differentiate them from the mass of non-literary victims.

Apt to invoke Chekhov or Dostoyevsky in his cups, Stalin clearly felt more closely involved with literature than with any other specialist cultural field, and it also happens that we know more about his contacts with writers. It may therefore be instructive to select from the great mass of literary evidence the fate of six authors who all clashed with the dictator in one way or another, and of whom three perished and three survived. The three most celebrated author-martyrs of the Terror – Pilnyak, Babel and Mandelstam – had all given specific personal offence to Stalin. In an age when death struck apparently at random, they formed an exception in having all baited the Secretary-General in the days before he had fully developed into the Slaughterer-General.

Pilnyak's main offence had been his authorship, as noted above, of *Tale of the Unextinguished Moon*, in which he had virtually accused Stalin of responsibility for the murder, in 1925, of War Commissar Frunze. More than a dozen years later Pilnyak was shot as a Japanese spy,[2] for which accusation a recent visit to Tokyo had conveniently matured him.

The offence of Isaac Babel, perhaps Soviet Russia's most original prose writer, had been to publish (in 1924) a collection of short stories based on his service in Budyonny's Cavalry Army in 1920. As will be remembered, First Cavalry Army was Stalin's favourite military formation; he regularly sent formal salutations to this crack formation, promoting its officers – including Budyonny himself – to top commands. Describing the heroic but often barbarous feats of the First Cavalry with his own inimitable irony, Babel had irritated the bluff Budyonny . . . and hence, presumably, Budyonny's protector-in-chief. It also chanced that Babel had known Yezhov's wife before her marriage, and he had rashly taken to visiting her in the hope of solving the mystery posed by the *Yezhovshchina*. From these hazardous consultations Babel had correctly concluded that Yezhov was not the main instigator of the Terror: 'he does his best, but he's not the one behind it.'[3] By very largely suspending the publication of new work during the 1930s, and by claiming to have discovered a new genre (that of 'silence'),[4] Babel had further courted disaster in an age when merely to refrain from expressing subversive views was not enough, but when positive affirmations of loyalty were required from one and all. Babel is also recorded as having risked some 'rash joke' about the Secretary-General.[5] When arrested in the writers' colony of Peredelkino, near Moscow, in May 1938, he was clearly overripe for liquidation, and is reported as having died in custody three years later.[6]

Particularly gross offence was offered to Stalin by the poet Osip Mandelstam. He had penned, in November 1933, a short verse lampoon on the dictator. This was not published, of course, but somehow fell into the hands of the police; indeed, the NKVD chief Yagoda was so taken with it that he actually learnt it by heart. In this lyric, Mandelstam calls Stalin a 'murderer and peasant-slaughterer', which epithets – combined with references to the dictator's 'cockroach-whiskers', 'fingers, fat as grubs' and general blood lust – made this a document dangerous indeed for anyone who even knew that it existed, let alone for its only begetter. Still, 1933 was not 1937, and Mandelstam suffered no immediate penalty more severe than exile in the provinces. A few months later this affair provoked one of those terrible telephone calls with which Stalin was liable to strike out of the blue, the recipient being Pasternak: a friend of Mandelstam's and a comparably distinguished fellow-poet. Stalin rang up to say that Mandelstam would be 'all right', but then proceeded to chide Pasternak for not championing his friend in his troubles. 'If I were a poet,' Stalin claimed, presumably forgetting the early Tiflis-published verses attributed to himself, 'and if a poet friend of mine were in trouble, I would do anything to help him.'[7] The dictator also inquired whether or not Mandelstam was to be considered a genius: to which Pasternak wisely made an evasive reply, aware as he surely was that there was no longer room for more than one genius in the Soviet Union. Being, like so many others, 'morbidly curious about the recluse in the Kremlin', Pasternak asked for an opportunity to meet Stalin in order to discuss life and death: a request which those who have met the poet will recognize as typical of his conversational style. But Stalin merely rang off, leaving word with a secretary that Pasternak was free to quote the contents of their discussion as much as he liked. 'Everyone could see what miracles Stalin was capable of, and it was to Pasternak that the honour had fallen . . . of spreading the good tidings [of Mandelstam's reprieve] all over Moscow. . . . The aim of the miracle was thus achieved: attention was diverted from the victim to the miracle-worker.'[8]

After returning to Moscow, Mandelstam was rearrested in May 1938, and perished pitiably in a prison transit camp at Vladivostok in a condition approaching insanity.[9]

Among the three literary survivors of Stalinism whose stories are most instructive, Pasternak was particularly lucky to escape, having taken the serious risk of refusing to sign a document approving the execution of Tukhachevsky. The poet was saved from Stalin's wrath on this occasion by the caution of colleagues who did not dare report this insubordination to higher authority.[10] Another, earlier episode in Pasternak's relations with Stalin concerns a personal message which the poet had appended, in his own name alone, to a joint letter of condolence sent by Soviet writers on the occasion of the death of Stalin's second wife in 1932. In this postscript Pasternak wrote that he had been thinking about Stalin during the entire day preceding his wife's death, and that he had felt as deeply moved on reading of that tragedy as if he had been a witness to it.[11] This comment of Pasternak's has been said to reveal 'a human, and non-political good-will which may, by its very naïveté have been one of the factors which turned the scale when the General Secretary was bloodily purging the cultural world, and have disarmed him when it came to any idea of liquidating Pasternak.'[12] Perhaps.

Another remarkable survivor, whose life ended with a painful but natural death in 1940, was the playwright and novelist Mikhail Bulgakov. In the late 1920s Bulgakov found himself deprived of his livelihood when his plays were banned and his books allowed to go out of print. He therefore took the extreme step of addressing a letter to Stalin personally, asking for permission to leave the Soviet Union on the grounds that he was neither a Communist nor a fellow-traveller capable of writing pro-Communist works. A similar request made by another writer, Zamyatin, was granted by Stalin, we remember. Bulgakov was less fortunate. But his uncompromising message did at least evoke a sympathetic response such as a bold direct approach to Stalin occasionally stimulated, while always remaining a hazardous procedure. Though Bulgakov did not receive permission to emigrate, he was at least granted the right (over the telephone) to resume his interrupted career within the Moscow Art Theatre. An astonishing sequel followed in January 1932, when the dictator suddenly ordered that theatre to arrange, at very short notice and for himself as sole audience, a special showing of Bulgakov's best-known play: *The Days of the Turbins*, which had been banned since 1928. Despite a favourable attitude towards the Whites expressed through a plot set in the Russian Civil War, Stalin approved the text, allowing the Art Theatre to restore it to the repertoire. So taken was the Leader with this play that he eventually witnessed fifteen performances, as Moscow Art Theatre records show.[13] Cultivating Bulgakov's company, and addressing him in familiar fashion as Misha (Mike), the dictator protected his favourite playwright throughout the Great Terror.[14] The reason was possibly admiration for Bulgakov's rare courage in refusing to simulate the faintest degree of political conformity; there is also the point that Stalin, himself author-in-chief of the show trial scripts, may have craved the occasional company of a brother artist.

Another surprising survivor was Ilya Ehrenburg. An advocate of artistic 'modernism', as anathematized by Socialist Realists, Ehrenburg spent many years in western Europe, acquiring a wide international range of intellectual and cultural contacts; he visited Republican Spain during the Civil War; he was a dedicated opponent of Fascism; he was a Jew; he was even, for a time, a sincere political supporter of Stalin's.[15] These data should have spelled out liquidation many times over. And yet Ehrenburg survived: a living monument to the dictator's unpredictability. Ehrenburg himself could not explain it, except as a lucky accident in this epoch when human life resembled, not a game of chess, but a lottery.[16] The fact was (as Ehrenburg has well noted), that 'Stalin was a complex human being, and the accounts of those who have met him contradict each other.'[17]

Ehrenburg first set eyes on Stalin at a Moscow conference in November 1935. When the Leader appeared before the packed audience through a side-door, an orgasm of clapping and cheering broke out, lasting for ten or fifteen minutes. Stalin himself joined in. When everyone had at last sat down, a voice shrieked 'Glory to Stalin!' The audience then stood up and started applauding again until Ehrenburg's hands hurt. Somehow Stalin's appearance – the low forehead, the black hair, the gleaming eyes – fascinated Ehrenburg so much that he paid little attention to what the dictator said, but noticed that he exercised the same fascination on all other members of the audience.[18] Like everyone else, Ehrenburg himself always referred to Stalin as *khozyain* (the Boss), fearing to pronounce his real name, just as the ancient Hebrews never spoke the name of Jehovah. But, as Ehrenburg notes, the deification of Stalin was no natural, organic process. It did not spring from the people, but was systematically constructed by the dictator himself. It was at Stalin's own behest that his biography was re-written to conform with the fictitious heroic Legend; it was at his orders, too, that artists painted huge canvases inaccurately showing him at Lenin's side on major occasions in Bolshevik history.[19]

And yet, as other evidence confirms, no one could show himself more opposed to the Stalin Cult than Stalin himself . . . in certain moods. On 16 February 1938 he addressed a letter to a Soviet publishing house which had requested his permission to issue a volume entitled *Tales of Stalin's Childhood*. Stalin found that the text abounded in factual error, distortion, exaggeration and unmerited praise. Above all, said he, the book tended 'to implant in the consciousness of the Soviet people, and of humanity at large, a Cult of Personalities, of Leaders, of Knights in Shining Armour; this is both dangerous and harmful.'[20] Stigmatizing such adulation as alien to Bolshevik practice, the dictator ends by recommending that the book should be burnt. Thus does Stalin explicitly denounce the Cult of Stalin nearly twenty years before Khrushchev made history by purporting to pioneer such denunciation in the Secret Speech. But though this particular text may indeed have been burnt after Stalin's outburst, there was no lack of other gospel material to take its place. It is tempting to dismiss this intervention by the dictator as hypocritical, but we happen to know from his daughter's evidence that such adulation could indeed be acutely distasteful to him.

While exterminating numerous authors during the Terror, Stalin was himself engaged in composing the era's most notable single work of fiction: *A History of the All-Union Communist Party (of Bolsheviks): A Short Course*. To be more precise, only part of Chapter Four ('On Dialectical and Historical Materialism') of this publication is now recognized as the dictator's undiluted personal contribution, the rest being the work of a Central Committee commission.[21] Distributed in many millions of copies, and enshrining the Stalin Legend in canonical form, the *Short Course* became the object of widespread compulsory study and devotional exercise within the Communist orbit from 1938, the year of its first publication. That Stalin himself took this brain-child seriously is suggested by his sentimental gesture in presenting his daughter with the first copy to emerge from the press. What can have possessed him – nothing less than blind creator's pride, surely – to offer this turgid and mendacious clap-trap to a twelve-year-old girl, and even attempt to insist on her reading it? Not surprisingly, Svetlana never did read the *Short Course*, being perhaps the only literate person in Stalin's empire who escaped the ordeal. She simply found the book too boring. Seeing his masterpiece so undervalued – and by the person dearest to him – Stalin was furious.[22] The episode is useful as a warning against attributing Stalin's activities too exclusively to that callous, cynical calculation which certainly was a basic part of his make-up; we are also reminded once again of the elusiveness – as noted by Ehrenburg – of the dictator's personality.

While horrors multiplied around him, the widowed Stalin led the life of a modest professional man: modest in his tastes and habits, yet surrounded by luxuries such as he barely noticed. Wishing to cut himself off from painful memories of his wife's death, he had a new bungalow built in 1934 at Kuntsevo, about seven miles west of Moscow. This idyllic retreat, set among woods and flowers, was the creation of one Merzhanov, who in effect became the dictator's court architect, also building him numerous sumptuous homes elsewhere: two more in the Moscow area, several on or near the Black Sea Coast and in the Caucasian mountains, one near Novgorod. These Stalin rarely visited, but they were kept ready staffed with servants permanently poised for panic should news arrive that the master's whim was bearing him in their direction.[23]

Spurning, except on rare occasions, this chain of luxury residences, the ruler of the worst-housed industrial nation in the world did not even make full use of his base at Kuntsevo, where he worked, ate and slept – on a sofa – in a single room. Still, Kuntsevo was home of a sort, or at least the nearest thing to it which the bereaved tyrant could create.[24] It was from Kuntsevo that the world's most extravagant commuter was regularly conveyed to his office near the Kremlin, for he made little use of the small flat which he also maintained in the Kremlin itself.[25] Like his senior colleagues, Stalin was accustomed to travel in a bullet-proof Packard with green windows, which sped, sirens screeching, preceded and followed by police gunmen in Lincolns, along the Mozhaysk Highway leading east out of Moscow. Other traffic was kept off the route, which was guarded by thousands of plain-clothes men, 'their right hands on their revolvers ready for the draw'.[26] According to the suspect *Khrushchev Memoirs*, the commuting Stalin regularly imposed last-minute changes of route, ordering his driver to make unexpected détours along side-streets. These variations he himself worked out on a street plan of Moscow, without even informing his bodyguard in advance. The dictator's bungalow was protected by a varying array of bolts, locks, barricades, electrical alarms and other security devices –[27] all very natural precautions for one who perhaps suspected himself to be the most hated man on earth.

Reaching Kuntsevo safely, Stalin could (hour and season permitting) play with his young daughter on the flat roof of the bungalow. This was continually being rebuilt, receiving a second storey in 1948: an extension which was used once only, to entertain a visiting Chinese delegation.[28] But whether he was in Kuntsevo or Moscow, Stalin rarely relaxed. In the evenings he continued to enjoy working supper parties, generally attended by available Politburo members whom he could ply with liquor and goad into quarrelling with each other.

As for the dictator's office hours, these were notoriously exacting and eccentric. Kravchenko says that Stalin would work from about 11 a.m. to 4 or 5 p.m. and then again from about 10.30 p.m. until 3 or 4 a.m. or even later.[29] Since all the Soviet empire's myriad officials were expected to conform with the Leader's programme and to be on call whenever he might want them, they were practically compelled to live at their desks, fatigue combining with the Terror and the secret police to ensure the survival of only a small proportion among the fittest.

Post-Mortem

After raging with unabated fury throughout the first half of 1938, the Great Terror first began to show signs of petering out in July of that year. In a context where failure to betray one's associates was equated with treason, as also was the failure to act on denunciations, individuals had become involved in a frenzy of collective self-annihilation. This trend was aggravated by certain arrested persons who exploited to the full invitations, forcibly extended to them in custody, to denounce others; some showed especial zeal in implicating loyal Stalinists, believing that this was the only possible means of bringing the whole system into disrepute.

Excessive zeal in betraying one's associates, but also failure to betray them; excessive activity, but also excessive sloth; zeal in lying, but also zeal in telling the truth; sycophancy, but also independent-mindedness ... now that all these extremes, and all intermediate points between them, had become equally hazardous, there can be little wonder if general locomotor ataxia began to supervene. By mid-1938, it has been said, even the NKVD had begun to tire of the purge;[1] but it is doubtful whether the NKVD as such had ever felt much enthusiasm for an operation which had all along menaced its own members as much as those of any other hierarchy.

The decline of mass terror coincided with the dismissal of the security police chief Yezhov, who was made People's Commissar for Water Transport in the summer of 1938, while yet lingering on as nominal NKVD Commissar until December. In January 1939 he received his last public mention under Stalin, before vanishing from the scene. Rumour has spoken of his insanity and suicide. Not until 1966 was any semi-official version of his death published, when Stalin was revealed as having admitted (in 1940) that Yezhov had been executed for killing many innocent people.[2]

In July 1938 the Georgian Lavrenty Beria was appointed deputy NKVD head, nominally understudying the doomed Yezhov for a few months before taking over as fully-fledged Commissar at the end of the year. As already noted, Beria had first made his name as Stalin's proconsul and senior terror-master in the Caucasus. After nearly a decade of service with the local security police, he had risen to head the Transcaucasian GPU by 1931, then being transferred to Party office – first as head of the Georgian, and later of the entire Transcaucasian Apparatus. Beria seems to have had a special knack of worming his way into Stalin's confidence while cultivating a humble and inconspicuous front. Stalin's relatives by marriage, the Alliluyevs, all hated the new police boss, perhaps foreseeing that he would later play a part in persuading the dictator to sanction their arrest. Stalin's second wife Nadezhda had particularly disliked Beria, and had tried to deny him access to her home on the ground that he was a scoundrel: a criterion which, if consistently applied, might have rendered the Stalins' already meagre social life entirely non-existent. But Stalin told her to go to hell, and after her death in 1932 there was no one else to resist the encroachments of the bespectacled Beria, who ingratiated himself with the supreme master by methods of oriental flattery.[3] In 1935 Beria scored a notable success with his major contribution to the falsification of Stalin's biography, as first put forward in a lecture given in Tiflis. It was then published in *Pravda*, and later as a book: *On the History of Bolshevik Organizations in Transcaucasia*. Issued in nine editions between 1936 and 1952, this work established new norms in the distortion of Stalin's early biography. As is noted in an earlier chapter, it attributes to the youthful Dzhugashvili a yet more glorious, yet more outrageously fabricated role than any previous faker of early revolutionary history had ever ventured to purvey.

During the Great Terror, Beria had emerged as one of the few top-level purgers on whom Stalin could rely to administer his own local repressions with adequate gusto and without the need for control from the Centre. It was after thus performing as the Yezhov of Transcaucasia that Beria was translated to Moscow to supersede and liquidate his nominal master. Just as Yezhov had, in his time, introduced a new wave of senior subordinates to understudy and exterminate Yagoda's minions, so Beria now brought in an entourage of senior Georgians (whose native speech was unintelligible to most of their new subordinates) to oust and liquidate the Yezhov stratum of security bosses.

Beria's assumption of the NKVD commissarship was accompanied by an unpublicized decrease in mass arrests, as also by the widely advertised dropping of certain cases under investigation. Publicity was given to various obscure provincial prosecutors and NKVD officials who were now charged with having processed 'innocent people' for liquidation. But there was no significant release of concentration-camp prisoners, who continued to toil and die by their millions under Beria, as they had under Yagoda and Yezhov. Now terror went underground. Institutionalized, consolidated and erected into a permanent system of government under the new Commissar, the NKVD and its successor bodies operated more by stealth during the remainder of Stalin's reign than had been the custom in the days of Yagoda and Yezhov. But it was still business as usual, until Stalin's death and beyond, in the great concentration camp empires of the far east, of the far north, of Central Asia and elsewhere.

How accurately can we measure the results of the Great Terror in terms of suffering and death? Neither for the period 1937-8 nor for any other phase of the Stalin dictatorship are precise mortality statistics available, except in odd accidental areas of detail. Nor, in the nature of things, can one expect to compute the exact impact of persecutions which involved so many grades of severity from summary execution at one end of the scale to total immunity at the other. Since, however, even the most fortunate, in that hazardous age, could by no means avoid fear and demoralization, it may be argued that only infants, half-wits and some of the clinically insane escaped entirely unscathed. Suffering, in the widest sense, may accordingly be said to have penetrated every nook and cranny of the Soviet Union during the Terror. As for the range of fates intermediate between execution and immunity, consignment to concentration camps such as Stalin's was becoming increasingly equated with sentence to a lingering death.

Without attempting to break new ground in assessing the mortality statistics of the period, we can estimate these very crudely at a million executed out of hand, to which must be added a further loss of a million or more a year through the lethal conditions in the concentration camps. These held their mean total of inmates at around the ten million mark, give or take the odd million or two either way, among whom a proportion rising from about 10 to about 20 per cent was perishing annually. Since surviving captives of 1937-8 were continuing to perish in captivity throughout the following years, and since releases never took place on any significant scale, the *Yezhovshchina* was continuing to fulfil its norm of fatalities long after Yezhov himself had become one of them. Very crudely, then, the fatalities caused by the Terror of 1937-8 may be quantitatively equated with those of collectivization in 1929-32, if we include among the latter the victims of Stalin-induced famine as well as the victims of his bullets and his camps. We can guess that both casualty lists may have exceeded ten million dead.[4]

Since the victims of the *Yezhovshchina* included a high proportion of intellectuals – who had been left comparatively unaffected by the horrors of collectivization – historians and other members of the intelligentsia have been inclined to regard the second of these reigns of terror as more calamitous than the first. In fact, though, there was not very much to choose, in terms of rigour, between collectivization and the *Yezhovshchina*. Yet it must also be admitted that the *Yezhovshchina* – as compared with the collectivization campaign – presented two especially nightmarish features of its own: the increased insistence on extracting circumstantial confessions of political sin, and an even greater element of seemingly lunatic irrationality.

With regard to the extraction of confessions, it must be repeated that innumerable victims were held in prison, under interrogation and torture or threat of torture, for months or even years before merciful release through execution or to concentration camp. During this period the captives were harangued, bullied, terrorized and tormented into implicating themselves and their associates in elaborately framed charges of political heresy: from Trotskyism, Zinovyevism and Bukharinism to espionage, wrecking and sabotage, to name but a few of these felonies. This long agony gave the Terror an especially Stalinist flavour which distinguishes it from the persecutions ordained by a Lenin, a Hitler or a Genghis Khan.

Why did the dictator insist on this orgy of self-accusation? Did he himself, by now, feel in the depths of his consciousness a burden of guilt so overwhelming that he could no longer tolerate existence unless perpetually surrounded by the self-accusing wails of millions insisting in elaborate detail and billions of words that it was they – they and not the great moustachioed Humanist – who had brought down so many calamities on themselves and their country?

The other feature differentiating the horrors of the *Yezhovshchina* was the element of yet greater irrationality. Brutal as the earlier persecution had been, it could be defended – if only by those grossly insensitive to the sufferings of others and personally uninvolved in the consequences – as an essential prerequisite to the modernization of a backward country. Though such a view is emphatically rejected on these pages, it is recognized that a case of a kind can at least be argued. But what of the new situation as we find it in 1937-8? Collectivization is now more or less fulfilling its basic role, albeit wastefully and inefficiently, while the associated industrialization drive is far more of a going concern. Now, surely, is the time to build upon this foundation, not to menace and demolish it through the extermination of its constructors! Stalin has erected a viable system which enjoys a measure of public acceptance, and himself stands virtually unchallenged at its peak. Why, then, destroy so large a part of his own work? Why savage all the hierarchies on which his system depends? Why undermine that which he himself has so cunningly and patiently constructed over so many years?

The question was asked, again and again, by Stalin's myriad victims in their chronicled or unchronicled agonies, unable as they were to understand why innocents – why 'honest Communists', as they were apt to term themselves – should be used so cruelly: without Stalin's knowledge or approval, many incorrectly believed. No fully satisfactory answer has ever been offered. Nor, given the mystery of human personality, need one feel that an ultimately adequate explanation must necessarily be attainable, even in theory, however closely the dictator's psychology may be scrutinized. We can, however, at least hope to speculate creatively around this perennially tantalizing enigma.

Power, it may be suggested, nearly always wears, in the eyes of its holder, an aspect less impressive and formidable than that which it presents to those who merely behold it from below or afar. To the dictator's subjects, near-absolutist controls – as riveted on the country by the mid-1930s – already appeared to strain the limits of the rigorous; but to Stalin himself they still seemed inadequate. And perhaps Stalin, and only Stalin, was fully equipped to assess the hazards of an ascendancy vulnerable in so many ways: vulnerable to an assassin's bullet; to a daring military *coup*; to an unfavourable vote, such as always remained a theoretical possibility in Politburo or Central Committee. Driven by an inner urge to make certainty doubly certain, and to maximize dominion which had long seemed total to all save himself, while insuring against all possible threats to his person and system, the dictator could never rest easy so long as there remained, in the length and breadth of his realm, any established and cohesive institution – however thoroughly Stalinized – which might conceivably turn against its creator. Reconstructing, refreshing and reforming successive hierarchies in order to destroy existing vested interests, he found himself constantly impelled to turn and rend each newly arising organization even as it appeared to attain some degree of cohesion. From the Politburo down to the individual family all human associations must be prevented from acquiring stability and *esprit de corps*.

One outcome of these successive onslaughts – an outcome highly satisfactory to Stalin – was the progressive reduction which they effected in the role of Communist idealism. Once a potent force under Lenin, this commodity had long aroused the deepest distrust of Lenin's chief heir. By killing or corrupting successive waves of idealists, the dictator was leaving himself with a residue of those superlatively hardbitten and cynical executives on whom he felt able to rely at least temporarily: those who had proved criminally self-seeking in their willingness to betray their fellows; those who could be bought by cash and other perquisites; those, in the end, who were not even tainted with that most suspect of all loyalties – loyalty to Stalin himself. Just as the youthful Koba had often cultivated, in jail, the company of common criminals in preference to that of intellectual prisoners of conscience, so now, at the height of his power, he preferred to surround himself with the debased, the acquisitive and the corrupt rather than with those who retained some vestiges of integrity. One can perhaps understand his choice if one remembers how little his idealism-tainted associates had to recommend them. They held a record second only to Stalin's own for condoning widespread massacre in the interests of humanity at large, and for benignly contemplating mass slaughter sanctified by political dogma. It was also comforting, no doubt, for one with Stalin's appalling record to surround himself with individuals arguably more reprehensible and criminal than himself.

By now all Stalin's leading associates, whether low-principled or high-principled, had been deeply initiated into political criminality; but it was the high-principled who constituted more of a potential nuisance to a dictator so eager to extend to its ultimate limits his freedom to determine policy. In particular, he could hardly hope to carry through a deal with Hitler – such as he was now contemplating – so long as he was surrounded by Communists sufficiently ideology-lumbered to adopt a strong anti-Fascist stance on grounds of conviction. But the suggestion that the dictator organized the Terror exclusively in order to be free to negotiate with Hitler is misleading.[5] It was not a single aspect of foreign policy, however important, but the entire depth and range of decision-taking which Stalin wished to clear for action untrammeled by the qualms of others. Hence the need to surround himself exclusively with those who had given tangible proof of their emancipation from all ties of political and other morality.

To sum up – tentatively, as we must in so elusive a context – the main drive behind the Great Terror was to increase yet further political powers which, to all except the holder himself, had long ago seemed to reach the limits of the attainable. It may well be felt that Stalin had no objective need for domination so total; that the degree of control obtained by 1935 was already sufficient for any sane ruler; and that one should therefore seek the motivation for the Terror in the mental unbalance of its sponsor. One hesitates, however, to press such an argument too hard against the political judgement of Stalin himself, since this was so triumphantly justified in practical terms by his unrivalled success as power-seeker, power-holder and power-extender over a quarter of a century. In the field of political power Stalin must be respected as one who backed his judgement and saw it vindicated again and again. On the other hand, even Stalin could stumble – as witness his error in reposing trust in Hitler in 1939–41. Perhaps the Great Terror represents a similar blunder on the grand scale. And yet, despite the damage which it inflicted on the country, it undoubtedly did carry Stalin further towards his goal of ruling unchallenged: unchallenged above all by those whose commitment to ideology or idealism made them especially unpredictable – and also especially dangerous to one who liked to see his orders carried out quickly, ruthlessly and without question.

The Eighteenth Congress

In March 1939 the Eighteenth Party Congress took place after an interval of five eventful years since the preceding Seventeenth 'Congress of Victors'. Of the so-called victors of 1934 only a few – under sixty out of nearly two thousand – were now present as delegates, the majority of the remainder having fallen to the Terror.[1]

Rising before this audience of tiros to deliver the main Congress address (on the work of the outgoing Central Committee), Stalin found himself in a situation potentially embarrassing to a lesser man, since 70 per cent of the members of that expiring Committee had been arrested and shot as the result of his policies.[2] But Stalin simply ignored this aspect of the Committee's activities during the previous five years, merely referring casually to measures taken to strengthen the Soviet Union internally. In the following quintessentially Stalinist passage he even permitted himself to speak of a *purge*: 'We shall certainly not be compelled to resort to methods of mass purging in future. But the purge of 1933–6 was inevitable all the same, and in general it produced positive results.'[3] What the dictator was promising not to repeat, we note, was the comparatively bloodless purge of 1933–6: largely based on checking documents and expulsions from the Party. As his hearers were no doubt quick to observe, he gave no undertaking whatever not to repeat the *Yezhovshchina*, but passed over that nightmare in total silence.

Stalin also warned against a tendency to anticipate the so-called 'withering-away of the State', once proclaimed as their ultimate goal by the founding fathers of Marxism-Leninism. So far the Stalinist state had done anything but wither away. Nor could it be expected to dwindle in the future, Stalin now proclaimed: not, at least, until there should be an end to capitalist encirclement of the USSR.[4]

While speaking of foreign affairs, the dictator was – as not uncommonly – less devious than in dealing with domestic matters. The period since the previous Congress had seen the intensification of Japanese aggression against China, the Italian conquest of Abyssinia and the victory of Franco in Spain. Nearer home these years had also witnessed Hitler's triumphs in occupying the Rhineland, annexing Austria and extorting territory from Czechoslovakia under the Munich agreement. Stalin accordingly grouped the three anti-Comintern powers – Germany, Italy and Japan – together as an aggressive bloc among the capitalist states, contrasting them with the non-aggressive Britain, France and USA. But even as he stressed this distinction, the dictator also made it clear that he had no sentimental preference for either bloc: he would base his foreign policy, as always, on calculations of national self-interest. The non-aggressive powers, in his view, constituted at least as great a potential menace to the Soviet Union as did the aggressors; for they were playing a sly waiting game, hoping for an attack by the aggressors on the Soviet Union and planning to intervene from strength once the main contestants should have exhausted themselves.[5] Stalin also claimed that Britain and France had only conceded Czechoslovak territory to Hitler as a bribe to induce Germany to attack Russia.[6]

Thus the dictator reserved an equal measure of suspicion for all foreign non-Communist powers, totalitarian or non-totalitarian, aggressive or passive. That he held himself ready to do a deal with either side, guided solely by the interests of the Soviet Union and unswayed by ideology, his speech to the Eighteenth Congress makes clear, as had his corresponding speech to the Seventeenth Congress five years earlier. If world war was to come, Stalin preferred that it should rage between competing capitalist powers: Fascist versus anti-Fascist. Meanwhile the Soviet Union would stand on the side-lines, ready to fulfil the very ambition (of intervening from strength when other competitors should be exhausted) which the dictator had correctly or incorrectly attributed to the non-aggressive powers, Britain, France and the USA.

At the Eighteenth Party Congress a virtually new Central Committee was elected, but the 'new' nine-man Politburo, as elected in turn by that committee, consisted largely of familiar figures. One was, of course, Stalin himself, while others were veteran henchmen whose Politburo membership went back to 1930 or beyond: Andreyev, Kaganovich, Kalinin, Mikoyan,

289

Molotov and Voroshilov. As for Politburo promotions, two candidate members who had won their spurs in the Terror – Khrushchev and Zhdanov – were now elevated to full membership, while the new security chief Beria became a candidate. This team of veterans could be relied upon to implement the dictator's orders without interference from the new Central Committee or from anyone else.

10

Hitler's Friend

Prelude to a Pact

IN 1939 we enter a new phase in the Soviet dictator's career. Henceforward foreign affairs loom more prominently than before, internal policies being pushed into the background. It is now that Stalin acquires, in his German opposite number Hitler, first an ally and then an arch-enemy admirably qualified to fill the vacuum left in 1940 by the assassination of the prime hate-object Trotsky. During the six years 1939–45 Hitler and Hitler-linked problems remain Stalin's main concern. In August 1939 the German and the Soviet dictator unexpectedly form an alliance which they maintain, with various ups and downs, for nearly two years until the embattled Fuehrer pounces on his apparently helpless and floundering ally on 22 June 1941, and comes close to overthrowing the Stalinist system by armed force. At Stalingrad in late 1942 the hinge of fate begins to swing in the opposite direction until, in May 1945, Hitler collapses amid the ruins of his empire.

During the years of the Soviet-Nazi Pact and of the Soviet-Nazi War, Stalin comes into repeated contact with politicians and officials of many different nationalities: German, Polish, British, American and others. Many of these foreign witnesses have left accounts of their dealings with him, providing an impressive volume of evidence recorded independently of Kremlinite control. There is thus a greater corpus of reliable direct information on the dictator as he was between 1939 and 1945 than is available for any other phase of his life. The fog surrounding Stalin is slightly dispersed during these years, and we discern more of his movements.

Long before either Hitler or Stalin assumed dictatorial power the eventual clash between the two totalitarian chieftains had been foreshadowed. Laying down, in the mid-1920s, a programme for German expansion in his *Mein Kampf*, the future Fuehrer had stated that Germany needed new territory in the east: Russia and the vassal states on her border, a 'colossal empire in the east . . . ripe for dissolution'.[1] During the years when he was taking over and consolidating at home, Hitler did not forget his ultimate intention of incorporating Soviet lands in a Greater Germany. Between his assumption of power in 1933 and the Soviet-Nazi Pact of 1939, Germany and the Soviet Union were, or pretended to be, on the worst of possible terms. They assailed each other with abusive material stressing the ideological incompatibility of Communism and National Socialism, while studiously ignoring the obvious similarities between the two systems when considered as techniques of dragooning large populations by mingled deceit, fear and exhortation.

And yet, as we have seen, this antagonism did not prevent Stalin from trying to keep open the possibility of a deal with Berlin. We have even observed him inserting hints of such a *détente* into widely publicized statements made to two Party Congresses. Meanwhile, behind the scenes, his secret emissaries were attempting – for several years in vain – to elicit some helpful response from the Hitler régime. The first such messenger was Yevgeny Gnedin, press attaché at the Soviet Embassy in Berlin from May 1935. In two interviews with an influential Nazi official, Gnedin revealed that he had arrived with direct instructions to foster an improvement in German-Soviet relations. Stalin did not care (Gnedin indicated) what measures the Germans might take against Communists in their own country; that was their own affair; the *Realpolitik* of the USSR had nothing to do with the Comintern.[2] Such was Stalin's message to Hitler in 1935–6. But though Gnedin achieved nothing, and though other secret Soviet-German negotiations of the same period – held in Geneva – also proved fruitless,[3] the wooing of the Germans by the Soviet leader still continued. Stalin was now operating through a fellow-Georgian, Davyd Kandelaki: reputedly an old school-friend. As Soviet trade representative in Berlin, Kandelaki approached Hitler's Finance Minister, Schacht, apparently attempting to make commercial negotiations the opening for some kind of political settlement. Though Kandelaki's mission was no more successful than Gnedin's, it is significant and typical that Stalin kept all these overtures secret: not only from the world at large, but also from Soviet government departments, including the very Foreign Commissariat under Litvinov.[4] Meanwhile, as already indicated, the Soviet dictator was engaged in framing his generals – and with the aid of forgeries commissioned from Berlin – for carrying on precisely such secret negotiations with the Germans as Gnedin and Kandelaki were all along energetically pursuing on his own secret instructions.

Among Stalin's muted public overtures to Hitler, some contained in a speech of 10 March 1939 to the Eighteenth Party Congress have already been mentioned. It was then, too, that the Soviet Leader indicated – in a phrase much bandied about during the period – that the USSR did not intend to 'pull anyone else's chestnuts out of the fire'.[5] By this he implied an unwillingness to take part in the war which he now believed the Western Powers – and especially the hated British – to be provoking between the Soviet Union and Germany. With this speech Stalin signalled to Hitler his readiness to abandon the policy of collective security – hitherto pursued in alignment with those 'capitalist' powers which Stalin himself termed non-aggressive – and to negotiate an agreement with Berlin. That Hitler received the message and clearly understood Stalin's purport has since been confirmed.[6] Within a week the Fuehrer gave a reply which was peculiarly his own: he annexed the Bohemian and Moravian provinces of Czechoslovakia, while turning Slovakia into a German puppet state. This was a step on which the German dictator might not have ventured but for the assurance, conveyed by Stalin's speech to the Eighteenth Party Congress, that the USSR was not threatening Germany with a war on two fronts.

Another consideration was that a Stalin unsecured against Hitler himself faced a potential war on two fronts at this time, owing to the continuing menace of Japan's armies on his far eastern frontiers. Among the factors predisposing the Soviet dictator to make his pact with Hitler, the Japanese threat to Siberia may well have played a larger part than is commonly realized.

On 3 May, Stalin gave further encouragement to Hitler by dismissing his Commissar for Foreign Affairs, Litvinov, and by appointing in his place the veteran hard-liner Molotov, who already held – and did not now relinquish – the premiership. Since Litvinov was known as a champion of collective resistance to Fascism – since Litvinov also happened to be a Jew, and as such would have been a negotiator unacceptable to Hitler – this signal was easily decoded in Berlin. It was Litvinov's dismissal, as Hitler later told Mussolini, which made fully evident the Kremlin's wish to effect a transformation of its relations with Germany.[7] Then, on 30 May 1939, Hitler at last responded more directly to Stalin's wooing when the German Foreign Office informed its Moscow Embassy that Berlin wished to make 'a certain degree of contact' with the Kremlin,[8] thus beginning the process consummated by the Soviet-Nazi pact of 23 August 1939. That this apparent *volte face* should have surprised the British and French – with whom the Soviet Government was openly conducting parallel negotiations – is an index of the extent to which totalitarian politics remained incomprehensible to statesmen schooled in a more traditional approach.

Though Stalin played a prominent part in Soviet negotiations with the Germans, he possessed no nominal status which entitled him to do so since he held no governmental office at this time. Yet it was he who took all the initiative on the Soviet side, he who made all the detailed decisions; the combined Foreign Commissar and Premier Molotov was merely an exceptionally faithful echo of his master's voice, as German participants in the negotiations could easily discern.[9] It was Stalin, too, who signed – nominally on the 'instructions' of the Soviet Government – the key telegram of 21 August inviting Ribbentrop to Moscow. By now Hitler's readiness to deal with Stalin had been transformed into feverish eagerness, since he needed the assurance of a pact with the Soviet Union before he could feel free to launch the invasion of Poland on which he had set his heart. With the campaigning season already far advanced, Hitler's notorious impatience was fast approaching bursting point. When, at last, Stalin's invitation reached the Nazi dictator he drummed both fists against the wall, exclaiming: 'Now I have the world in my pocket.'[10] This reaction well underlines the difference in temperament between the rabid Austrian and the coldly calculating, warily cynical Georgian who was his senior in years by a decade and correspondingly superior as the builder of a durable empire.

When Ribbentrop reached Moscow on 23 August, he was surprised to find himself negotiating with the Soviet dictator personally, but discussions proceeded smoothly. Stalin was affability itself, his jocular manner occasionally alternating with frigidity as he rapped out some order or question to a senior subordinate.[11] The Soviet-Nazi agreement was signed that night. It consisted of an openly avowed non-aggression pact accompanied by a secret protocol of which the contents did not become known until after the war. This partitioned eastern Europe between the signatories in advance of the invasion of Poland for which Hitler was now, as it were, receiving Stalin's permission; Finland, Estonia, Latvia and the Rumanian province of Bessarabia were assigned to the Soviet sphere of influence, together with eastern Poland. When the terms of pact and protocol had been agreed, Ribbentrop showed Stalin the text of a grandiloquent communiqué, proposing that the two governments should issue it jointly on the following day. But Stalin insisted on rewording this draft in less bombastic style, pointing out that Germany and the Soviet Union had been pouring 'buckets of slops' over each others' heads for years, and insisting that public opinion must be prepared gradually.[12] A more modestly worded statement was therefore agreed.

Having arranged, with many expressions of cordiality and mutual esteem, that the Second World War could now duly commence, the grinning principals proceeded to celebrate with champagne, and with one of those unsavoury feasts which had long been Stalin's main form of relaxation. It was on this occasion that the Georgian ruler of Russia proposed his notorious toast to the Austrian ruler of Germany; he said that he knew 'how much the German people loves its Fuehrer.' Not to be outdone, Ribbentrop replied by retailing a jest which was said to be much admired in Berlin: that Stalin himself was now ready to join the Anti-Comintern Pact![13] There is no record that Stalin was amused by this display of Teutonic humour. Not to be outdone in the general exchange of witticisms, he drew the German Foreign Minister aside and told him that the Soviet Government took the new pact most seriously; he personally could guarantee, on his word of honour, that the Soviet Union would not betray its partner.[14]

Honeymoon and Disillusion

Events moved rapidly in September 1939. At dawn on the first of the month the Germans attacked Poland. Two days later Britain and France declared war on Germany in accordance with their treaty obligations – but were powerless to help their Polish ally, whose resistance was quickly crushed by the invader. The Germans urged the Soviet Government to attack Poland from the east, but Stalin stalled for a time. Shaken by the pace of the *Blitzkrieg* in Poland, he suspected his ally's intentions. Would Hitler's armies indeed retire behind the Soviet-German demarcation line, as secretly laid down in the pact between the two countries? Obtaining assurances on this point, Stalin duly committed the Red Army on 17 September, quickly occupying eastern Poland and meeting little resistance from a defence system already shattered by the Germans. When it was proposed to publish a joint Soviet-German communiqué to excuse the double rape of Poland, Stalin found the German draft insufficiently devious. He composed a version of his own, which he compelled the Germans to accept. This elegantly defined the combined Soviet-German aim: restoring to Poland peace and order as destroyed by the disintegration of the Polish State, and helping the Polish people to establish new conditions for its political life.[1]

After the fall of Poland, Stalin proposed a change in the partitioning arrangements and Ribbentrop accordingly reappeared in Moscow for further negotiations. It was agreed to add Lithuania (formerly allotted to Germany) to the Soviet sphere of influence, while compensating Germany with additional Polish territory. Also agreeing to concert measures against any independence movements within a partitioned Poland, the two totalitarian powers now supplemented their pact of the previous month with a Frontier and Friendship Treaty dated 28 September 1939. These negotiations yet again show Stalin as a skilled communiqué-drafter. He modestly drew attention to his expertise in this field when he told a German diplomat that the ancient Romans did not go into battle naked, but were accustomed to cover themselves with shields: 'Today correctly worded political communiqués play the role of such shields.' When the two versions of the communiqué – the pre-Stalinist and the Stalinist – were submitted to Hitler (who had not previously been informed that one was Stalin's work), the Fuehrer immediately chose the Stalinist draft as far the better; and he asked: 'By the way, who wrote it ?'[2]

The signature of the latest Soviet-Nazi treaty was celebrated by further junketings in Moscow, Stalin himself being the life and soul of the party. Pressing alcohol on the company – which included several Politburo members as well as Ribbentrop's party – the Soviet Leader drank little himself. One of the German revellers comments that though Stalin had once been known to imbibe very heavily, he had now begun to go more carefully on doctors' orders.[3] But he had not given up his long-standing practice of plying minions and enemies with liquor while he soberly monitored their unguarded chat. Whether applied to Germans or Russians, this technique was always helpful when an individual's usefulness or nuisance potential came to be assessed in the cold light of morning by the one man who, drunk or sober, never let down his guard. As for the roistering Ribbentrop, he later claimed to have been just as much at his ease in the Kremlin as he was accustomed to feel among his old Nazi cronies.[4] One can well believe it.

After the collapse of Poland, Stalin began to extend his control over the Soviet sphere of influence as laid down in the agreement with Hitler. In September and October the Soviet Government signed 'mutual assistance' treaties with Estonia, Latvia and Lithuania after the Foreign Ministers concerned had been summoned to Moscow in turn. All three Baltic countries were forced to concede bases to the USSR while accepting sizeable Soviet garrisons on their territory. They thus became, in effect, Soviet protectorates which could easily be annexed outright at any moment. Stalin personally negotiated with – or rather dictated to – these three states in turn, pointing out that he was free to use force against them now that they had been allotted to the Soviet sphere behind their backs. Germany would not help them. 'As far as Germany is concerned, we could occupy you,' Stalin bluntly told the Latvian Foreign Minister. He openly excused his encroachments by referring to the possibility of a German attack on the Soviet Union. For six years, he pointed out, German Fascists and Soviet Communists had cursed each other. Now an unexpected turn had taken place: 'That happens in the course of history. But one cannot rely upon it. We must be prepared in time. Others who were not ready paid the price.'[5]

Having half-swallowed Estonia, Latvia and Lithuania, Stalin turned his attention to Finland. Finnish representatives were duly summoned to Moscow and subjected to the courteous but relentless bullying in which the

Soviet leader specialized; and, deplorable though this seemed to its victims, the performance was at least more 'cultured' than that of Hitler when he chose to inflict his tantrums on the emissaries of small foreign powers. Moreover, while bringing pressure to bear on the Balts, Stalin could effectively contrast the mildness of his own territorial demands with the rapacity of the Fuehrer – not to mention the various Russian Tsar-Emperors who had long ago annexed all the Baltic States, Finland included, to their empire. The reasonable Stalin, by contrast, was merely trying to move the Finnish frontier a little further from Leningrad; as things stood, the city could be bombarded by long-range artillery sited in Finland. On this point the Finns were open to compromise. It was Stalin's demand for a naval base on the peninsula of Hangö, further to the west, which most troubled them. When they refused to abandon sovereignty over this slice of mainland Finland, Stalin showed a typically flexible approach: he would cut a canal and convert Hangö into an island! Anyway, Hangö was 'nothing really. Look at Hitler. The Poznan frontier was too close to Berlin for him, and he took an extra three hundred miles.' The reason for Soviet interest in Hangö (Stalin explained) was the need to deny a potential enemy access to the Gulf of Finland by siting Soviet coastal artillery there. As for the identity of this potential enemy, throughout the negotiations the Finns 'sensed that it was Germany they feared.'[6]

When the Finns refused to yield Hangö after nearly two months of tough negotiations, Stalin ordered the invasion of Finland in response to alleged border incidents. In fabricating this pretext he was copying Hitler's technique of attacking Poland in response to Polish 'frontier provocations'. The Soviet-Finnish War began with a Soviet attack on 30 November 1939 and ended with Soviet victory as signalized by a dictated peace treaty on 12 March 1940. Though the result was a foregone conclusion, this 'Winter War' was not one of Stalin's more successful exploits, for the Red dinosaur required nearly four months to crush its miniature enemy – despite a forty-fold superiority in manpower. December 1939 was disastrous for the Russians, and saw their main thrust halted on the Mannerheim Line which ran across the Karelian Isthmus. As operations everywhere emphasized, Finnish morale, equipment and tactical leadership were immensely superior to the Russian. Nor did the Russian cause gain from the device of setting up a puppet Finnish 'government' on Soviet-held territory.

Stalin's sixtieth birthday occurred during the Soviet-Finnish War, and evoked an exchange of courtesies with Hitler, who sent his best wishes. Replying in Hieratic, Stalin stated that the friendship between the peoples of the Soviet Union and Germany, 'cemented by blood', had every reason to be solid and lasting.[7] Meanwhile the Great Friend of the Finnish People

(Stalin himself, as described in Soviet propaganda) was still held up at the Mannerheim Line. Not until February 1940 were Soviet forces at last ready to make a more effective assault on that obstacle. By early March, Finnish resistance had at last collapsed. Imposing terms, Stalin refrained from annexing the country as a whole; nor did he occupy Helsinki. But he did exact territorial concessions well in excess of those which he had sought before the war, annexing about one tenth of Finnish territory in all, including the Karelian Isthmus. Though these conditions were naturally regarded as harsh by the Finns, as also by Finland's many international sympathizers, they were mild compared with the impositions which were about to be foisted on the other three Baltic countries. In the case of Finland, Stalin may have been deterred by the strong anti-Soviet feeling which his invasion had aroused throughout the world. Not yet forced into alliance with the West by the German attack on Russia, the Soviet dictator nevertheless wished to keep his ultimate options open, and to minimize the many disadvantages resulting from Soviet aggression. One of these – the expulsion of the USSR from the League of Nations – was not a major blow to his policies. More serious by far was the damage inflicted on Soviet military prestige by the Red Army's poor showing against its tiny Finnish opponent before, in the end, sheer weight of numbers told. Though Stalin had eventually attained his objectives in Finland, he had done so in a way which cast doubt on the Soviet Union's ability to wage a large-scale war anywhere else: a lesson which Hitler was quick – too quick – to learn.

For the initial failure of Russian arms in Finland a recently published Soviet history of the Soviet-Finnish War roundly blames J. V. Stalin.[8] According to this authority, the Leader intervened in advance of operations to disparage an invasion plan put forward by the Chief of Staff, Marshal Shaposhnikov, whom he rebuked for overestimating the Finns while underestimating the Red Army. It was a new plan, worked out on Stalin's orders and confirmed by him, which led to the fiasco of the Soviet defeats by the Finns . . . until, in the end, Shaposhnikov had to take over and remedy the situation created by his master. How fortunate for the dictator that his military purge, and other measures of the *Yezhovshchina*, had put him in a position so impregnable that he could afford such a blow to his reputation!

During the twenty-two-month period of the Stalin-Hitler Axis the two parties worked together fairly harmoniously, especially in the early phase. On the political side Stalin swung the weight of international Communist agitation behind the peace campaign mounted by Hitler immediately after the defeat of Poland, when he tried to induce Britain and France to accept the *fait accompli* and negotiate terms. When these overtures were ignored, Soviet propaganda abused the French and British as imperialist aggressors who must bear full responsibility for the continuation of the war: a theme which was obediently taken up by the British, French and other Communist parties.

Stalin further assisted Hitler's war policies by enabling Germany to evade the British economic blockade. Supplying the Reich with grain, oil and cotton in quantity, as also with timber, manganese, chromium and other vital goods, the Soviet Union obtained in return industrial machinery and weapons of war which included an uncompleted cruiser. The USSR also acted as Germany's purchasing agent, buying such strategic essentials as rubber and copper from other countries and freighting them to Germany over the Soviet railway system. Stalin took an active personal part in trade negotiations with the Germans, showing a formidable grasp of detail; he was a tough bargainer, who could not be deceived or bluffed,[9] but he was not so much on his dignity that he hesitated to deal in person with subordinate German officials.[10] As one of these has recorded, Stalin combined supreme decision-taking power with much expert knowledge; he kept all the threads in his grasp, and was the only Soviet official who could lift the embargo on certain items which especially interested the Germans.[11] Under Stalin's direction the Soviet Union punctiliously fulfilled her side of the economic agreements, delivering goods to Germany right up to the eve of Hitler's attack on Russia, while the Germans were considerably laxer in keeping their part of the bargain. On the military side, Stalin's chief contribution to Hitler's ambitions was the freedom conferred by the Pact to transfer German divisions to the west, leaving a mere skeleton force in Poland. Stalin sent Hitler best wishes for the success of German arms in Norway and the Netherlands; he also granted Germany refuelling and repair facilities for ships, including submarines, in the Soviet Arctic. As these details indicate, Hitler derived far more in the way of tangible benefits from the Pact than did Stalin, and Stalin seems to have been well satisfied that this should be so. The least trusting of individuals, the Soviet dictator for some reason showed a greater degree of confidence in his Nazi opposite number than he ever reposed in any other individual.

As for Hitler's attitude to Stalin – whom he was never to meet face to face – this was not only respectful and admiring during the period of the Soviet-Nazi Pact, but was even to remain so during the Soviet-Nazi war which followed. On the eve of Ribbentrop's first journey to Moscow, Hitler told his military leaders that he and Stalin were the only two men capable of anticipating the future. Ribbentrop has borne witness to Hitler's great admiration for Stalin, saying that the Fuehrer's only fear was lest

Stalin be replaced as Russian leader by some 'extremist'. Hitler was convinced, Ribbentrop said, that Stalin would strictly adhere to the terms of the Soviet-Nazi Pact;[12] there were occasions, though, when he expressed a more cynical view. That Bolshevism had materially changed its nature under Stalin was the common belief of Hitler and Mussolini. Mussolini once flatly asserted that Bolshevism was dead, having been succeeded by 'a kind of Slavonic Fascism'.[13] Hitler informed Mussolini in 1940 that Stalin was introducing 'a sort of Slavonic-Muscovite nationalism', and was steering Russia away from Bolshevism of the Jewish-international variety.[14]

From many references in Hitler's *Table Talk* we know that the Fuehrer retained 'unconditional respect' for his Soviet opposite number. He once described Stalin as 'a hell of a fellow', and as one who knew 'his models, Genghis Khan and the others' very well. Stalin was, according to Hitler, one of the most extraordinary figures in world history; but he was also a kind of petty official who governed through a terrorized bureaucracy. Stalin was indispensable, Hitler said. Should anything happen to Stalin, Russia would collapse at once.[15] In 1942, when Stalin still had more than a decade of rule to run, Hitler remarked that Russia would become the mightiest power in the world if the Soviet leader should be granted ten to fifteen more years of power. Stalin had raised Soviet living standards and had abolished hunger, Hitler incorrectly claimed. More accurately, Hitler also stated that Stalin had built factories as large as the Hermann Goering Works; he had constructed railways which were not even on German maps. And he had done so (the Fuehrer continued, lapsing into romanticism again) with more than Teutonic efficiency, finishing the job at a time when mere Germans would still be arguing about the price of the tickets. Hitler said that he had read a book on Stalin (he did not say which); he claimed to regard the Soviet leader as a tremendous personality and as an ascetic who had taken the whole of his gigantic country in an iron grasp. Only Hitler's own rise to power had (he claimed) saved Europe from being overwhelmed by a new wave of Stalin-led Huns. Even Hitler's few apparently unfavourable references to Stalin seem sympathetic. When Hitler called anybody an arch-blackmailer, as he called Stalin ('look at the way he tried to extort things from us'), he was paying tribute to what, in his view, was one of the most valuable skills with which a totalitarian dictator could be blessed. When Hitler called Stalin a 'beast', he hastened to add that he was a beast 'on a grand scale'.[16] As these romantic musings show, Hitler appears to have regarded Stalin as a species of Wagnerian monster; a mixture of Fafner and Loge, perhaps, engaged on constructing some Slavonic Valhalla.

By contrast, Stalin's view of Hitler – expressed by the Soviet dictator in conversations with Eden, and then with Roosevelt – was characteristically down-to-earth. Stalin thought Hitler able, but superficial. Hitler 'lacked culture': a reference to his spluttering speech habits? Hitler was primitive in his approach, being excessively greedy and unduly influenced by considerations of prestige. Stalin did not accept Roosevelt's view that Hitler was mentally unbalanced, though he implied that the Fuehrer had been stupid in throwing away the fruits of all his victories by attacking the Soviet Union.[17]

Neither the painful triumph of Russian arms in Finland in March 1940, nor the swift German occupation of Denmark and Norway in April, brought any great change to the continuing idyll of Stalin-Hitler collaboration. It was the full-scale German offensive in the west (beginning on 10 May 1940 and leading to the Compiègne Armistice with defeated France on 21 June) which dealt the Pact the first serious blow. By swiftly defeating the French army, together with its British, Dutch and Belgian allies, Hitler demonstrated that the German *Blitzkrieg* could be fatal to a major military combination. What hope could the Red Army possibly have – and after sustaining such a mauling from its diminutive Finnish enemy – if it should be attacked by this awesome military machine? And what need had Hitler of any Soviet ally now that he had knocked metropolitan France out of the war? He could easily attack Russia without involving himself in the war on two fronts from which the Soviet-Nazi Pact had hitherto protected him.

Stalin's immediate reaction to German victory in the west was, accordingly, to cash his outstanding cheques under the Pact as quickly as possible before Hitler could move to cancel them. On 14 June, the date of the German entry into Paris, the Soviet Government sent an ultimatum to Lithuania, which was occupied by the Red Army on the following day, as also were Latvia and Estonia within a few days. In July, Soviet-rigged elections were staged in all three Baltic states, which were formally embodied in the USSR as separate Union Republics in early August after their newly elected 'parliaments' had voted for this incorporation in accordance with a Kremlin-dictated script. As a further reaction to Hitler's triumphs in the west, Stalin ordered the annexation, in late June 1940, of two Rumanian provinces. One of these, Bessarabia, had been assigned to the Soviet sphere of influence by the Soviet-Nazi Pact, but the other – Northern Bukovina – had not; nor (unlike Bessarabia) had Bukovina ever formed part of the territory of Imperial Russia. Thus did Stalin first push the bounds of the Soviet Empire beyond the frontiers set by the Tsar-Emperors who preceded him. Accomplishing these acts of blatant aggression or territorial readjustment, he kept his own personality in the background, by contrast with the prominent role which he had played in brow-beating the four Baltic states in late 1939. The latest diplomatic manoeuvres were executed by Molotov, while trusted underlings were assigned to supervise the takeover of Lithuania, Latvia and Estonia.

These encroachments annoyed Hitler, putting the first serious strain on the Soviet-Nazi Pact. Stalin, for his part, sought to conciliate Berlin by ostentatiously turning a deaf ear to overtures reaching the Kremlin from Winston Churchill, the new British Prime Minister. In early July 1940, the British Ambassador Cripps obtained an audience with Stalin, to whom he stressed the German threat to Moscow, and sought a military alliance between Britain and the USSR. But Stalin coldly denied that German victories in the West menaced the Soviet Union, insisting that the Soviet-Nazi Pact was in the fundamental interests of the two countries. Not content with rejecting these British overtures, Stalin also instructed Molotov to give Berlin a memorandum of his discussion with Cripps.[18] But this attempt by Stalin to reassure Hitler was a signal failure, for it was at a secret conference with German military leaders held on 31 July 1940 – within three weeks of receiving Stalin's account of Cripps's intervention – that Hitler first declared to his leading generals a firm intention of attacking Russia.[19] If Russia could be destroyed, the Fuehrer argued, Britain's last hopes would be shattered. The sooner Russia was smashed the better. Hitler added that he intended to annex the Ukraine, Belorussia and the Baltic states outright. With this historic meeting German plans to attack the Soviet Union in the following year were set in motion.

During the six months following the fall of France three issues in particular bedevilled Soviet-Nazi relations: Rumania, Finland and the Tripartite Pact.

It was now Hitler's turn to intervene further in eastern Europe. Fearing that Stalin might seize the Rumanian oilfields, the Fuehrer in effect turned Rumania – apart from the two provinces annexed by Stalin – into a German protectorate. With Finland he concluded an agreement permitting the transit of German troops destined for Norway. Finally, the Tripartite Pact, signed between Germany, Italy and Japan on 27 September 1940, created a military alliance which could easily be turned against the Soviet Union. When Soviet protests against these developments proved unavailing, Stalin sent Molotov to extract assurances from Hitler. At a meeting held in Berlin, Hitler and Ribbentrop did their best to divert the Soviet Foreign Commissar from the Balkans and to turn Soviet expansionist aims towards the Persian Gulf, at the expense of the British Empire. But though not averse to including these vaguely defined regions in a theoretical Soviet sphere of influence, Molotov steadfastly refused to be sidetracked. Explaining that he was following a precise brief laid down by Stalin, who had given him exact instructions in Moscow, the 'stone-bottomed' visitor politely put the highly-strung Fuehrer in his place; Hitler's interpreter Schmidt had never heard any foreign visitor speak to Hitler in such terms before.[20]

Though Molotov's visit had ended in apparent deadlock, Stalin decided shortly afterwards that he would be prepared to join the Tripartite Pact on certain conditions. They included the assignment of Bulgaria to the Soviet sphere of influence; Soviet control of the Turkish Straits; the withdrawal of German troops from Finland. Stalin offered these terms to Hitler in a letter of 26 November, but received no reply. Meanwhile, though, Hitler was secretly reacting in his own way. He told his generals shortly afterwards that Russia must be 'brought to her knees with all possible speed'. On 18 December he issued his famous directive on Operation Barbarossa: the lightning campaign through which he intended to destroy the Soviet Union. Preparations were to be completed by 15 May of the following year.[21]

Infringements of Socialist Legality

During the period of his alliance with Hitler, as during that of his alliance with Yagoda and Yezhov, Stalin remained an outstanding pioneer of twentieth-century totalitarian bureaucratic terrorism. Though the NKVD was no longer crating, freighting and dumping concentration camp victims from the pre-1939 territories of the Soviet Union on the same scale as before, existing prisoners were not released to any notable degree and great shoals of freshly netted martyrs were being trawled out of the newly annexed territories in the west. The total of individuals, including prisoners of war, deported from Poland, Rumania and the Baltic states may have approached the two million mark;[1] they were assigned to camps or places of exile in remote areas of the Soviet Union.

A typically Stalinist variant to this practice was the treatment meted out to those of his own troops who had been captured by the Finns during the Winter War, and who were then released after the Soviet victory of March 1940. Under a triumphal arch, with bands playing and streamers flying a welcoming legend (THE FATHERLAND GREETS ITS HEROES), these happy Red Army warriors were marched through Leningrad; marched straight on through to sidings outside the city, where cattle trucks were awaiting to take them to the slave camps![2] As this episode reminds us, and as the Soviet-German war was to illustrate on so vast a scale, to be taken prisoner in action was a crime in Soviet military law. The ruthlessness of the procedure in general, but also the style of the hero-convicts' triumphant march through Leningrad . . . both bear the authentic brush-marks of the Leader. So, too, does his exchange of political undesirables with Hitler: a feature of Soviet-Nazi collaboration which resulted in several hundred German nationals – including Communists and Jews – being handed over to the Gestapo after they had sought refuge from Hitlerite persecution in the USSR.[3]

To this period also belongs the massacre by the NKVD, in the spring of 1940, of some fifteen thousand Polish prisoners of war: about one third of them at Katyn near Smolensk. The action was small by totalitarian standards, but large enough for Stalin's personal complicity to seem likely. According to a leading authority on Katyn, the order to execute the prisoners 'was given, in all probability, by Stalin through Beria . . . or by Beria himself with Stalin's approval.'[4] The Soviet authorities still deny Soviet responsibility for the Katyn operation, which remains surrounded by mystery, as also does the yet obscurer fate of the other Poles – some ten thousand in number – who simultaneously disappeared from Soviet concentration camps at Starobelsk and Ostashkov, and who must also be presumed massacred. One explanation of these horrors depends on nothing more solid than word-of-mouth rumour, but is worth quoting if only because it would, if true, offer so characteristic an example of Stalinist (and pre-revolutionary) Russian administrative practice, in which a certain casual nonchalance was a traditional element. This version has the Poles executed as the result of a purely verbal misunderstanding: Stalin asked Beria to *liquidate* the three camps in which they were held, and Beria chanced to give the word 'liquidate' the more severe of its two possible interpretations, applying it to the persons of the prisoners rather than confining himself merely to closing down their places of imprisonment.[5] Be that as it may, no evidence – other than presumptive – of the dictator's personal complicity has come to light. Whatever the degree of his involvement, it is abundantly clear that no moral scruples can have deterred him. Would he shrink from slaughtering forty-five per cent of an alien officer corps so soon after destroying a comparable proportion of his own?

And yet, technically speaking, the Katyn affair contains certain features untypical of Stalinist procedure. Stalin's minions starved and froze prisoners of war, also working them to death by the hundred thousand. But what other instance do we know of their being shot *en masse*? It is therefore by no means inconceivable that, in thus executing the imprisoned Poles, the NKVD was acting at the urgent suggestion of the Gestapo – with which contacts were close during this period of Soviet-Nazi collaboration, and which was simultaneously engaged in liquidating the Polish professional classes in German-occupied Poland.[6] As will be noted below,

Katyn was to erupt into the world's headlines three years after the shootings, and developed into one of those scandals which will not lie down. Whatever the true apportionment of guilt may be, Stalin eventually drew considerable political benefits from the massacre, exploiting its aftermath as part of his campaign to secure control over post-war Poland.

The activities of Stalin's killer squads on foreign soil continued during the years of the Soviet-Nazi Pact. To this period belongs the assassination of Krivitsky, mentioned above. These years also witnessed the most spectacular of all Stalin's political murders: that of his arch-rival of many years' standing, Trotsky. Since his expulsion from the Soviet Union in 1929, Trotsky had been the main focus of international Communist resistance to Stalin. Offering to world Communism an alternative approach, or at least an alternative leader, Stalin's chief opponent provided a rival Mecca to Moscow, thus plaguing the Kremlin with the spectre of Marxist polycentrism, which became so grave a problem after the defection of Tito in 1948. In Stalin – always concerned to maintain a monolithic power structure such as Trotsky was busily undermining – his enemy-in-chief evoked a characteristically obsessive vengeful drive. The Leader's desire to remove this offending competitor became yet more urgent when the news leaked out, at the end of the 1930s, that Trotsky was working on a biography of Stalin in which he intended to publish the Secretary-General's crimes to the world. To Stalin, engaged as he was in enforcing the wholesale rewriting of history with himself in the role of Jehovah, this intervention on the part of Satan seemed uncalled for indeed.

Stalin had consistently hounded his arch-enemy in exile. In 1932, Trotsky and members of his family were deprived of their Soviet citizenship. The great political émigré and his organization came under secret surveillance by a series of Stalinist spies as Trotsky moved from his first foreign refuge in Turkey to France, and then proceeded to Norway. There his freedom to engage in political activity was hampered by the authorities, and he was eventually deported as the result of Soviet diplomatic representation.[7] It was in Coyoacan, a residential suburb of Mexico City which he reached in early 1937, that Trotsky found his last haven. Meanwhile he was being pilloried in all three Moscow show trials as plotter-in-chief against the Stalinist state, and was declared liable to legal proceedings in the Soviet Union. But he continued to maintain, with the aid of sympathizers throughout the world, a rival political centre: the Fourth International.

When Stalin's roving assassins went to work in the late 1930s, Trotsky was their prime victim-designate. On 7 November 1936 Stalin's agents stole the archive which the exile had built up at his Paris headquarters.[8] As already noted, the death of Trotsky's son and political ally, Lyov Sedov, was the work of Stalin's killers, according to the bereaved father. Stalin's agents also liquidated at least two of Trotsky's former secretaries. But despite these embarrassments Trotsky was able to continue his Mexican operation for over three years before his fate finally overtook him. Meanwhile a vast Trotsky dossier had been compiled at NKVD headquarters in Moscow – so large that it is said to have occupied three floors.[9] A team of Kremlin-directed killers, whose experience had been gained while liquidating anti-Stalinists in Spain, proceeded to America.

Trotsky, being well aware of his danger, had his villa fortified with double steel doors, bomb nets, bullet-proof towers manned by machine-gunners, electrical alarm systems and the like, while the Trotsky-influenced American Teamsters' Union supplied bodyguards to maintain a twenty-four-hour guard over the Coyoacan hideout.[10] The need for such precautions was demonstrated at about 4 a.m. on 24 May 1940 when a score of gunmen, headed by the Stalinist Mexican painter David Siqueiros, shot their way into the exile's stronghold and raked his bedroom with automatic fire. Miraculously Trotsky and his wife escaped unhurt in an area later discovered to be perforated by seventy-three bullet holes.[11]

After this Trotsky's security precautions were yet further tightened, and it was through other methods that he eventually fell, when an infiltrating pseudo-sympathizer smashed in his skull with a cut-down ice-axe on 20 August 1940. The assassin was a young Spanish Stalinist whose name proved to be Ramon Mercader. He was detained by Trotsky's guards, handed over to the Mexican police, tried and sentenced to twenty years' imprisonment. At no time did Mercader admit his true identity or mission, but claimed himself a former Trotskyite; he said that he had turned against his leader when required to go to the Soviet Union and assassinate Stalin: a typical Stalinist cover story. But Mercader's status as a Kremlin-directed killer was never in doubt. According to one authority, he was even awarded the Order of Hero of the Soviet Union, in his absence, by Stalin, who also decorated the killer's mother with the Order of Lenin.[12]

Actively engaged on his remarkable unfinished biography of Stalin at the time of his death, Trotsky had left the Introduction to this work unfinished – and at a particularly dramatic point – when his head was split open. His last words read: 'Stalin's first qualification was a contemptuous attitude towards ideas. The idea had . . .'[13] Seldom has any last message ever tailed off in more eloquently symbolic style; it reminds one that, as Trotsky stated elsewhere, Stalin 'seeks to strike, not at the ideas of his opponent, but at his skull.'[14]

For all Trotsky's attempts, as conveyed in his biography of Stalin and other voluminous writings, to show himself cleverer than his great rival, it may be doubted whether posterity will maintain this verdict. As noted above, Trotsky's contempt for Stalin's lack of intelligence probably arose from a dislike of Stalin's inability or unwillingness to adopt the mannerisms and life-style of a typical member of the Russian revolutionary intelligentsia. In other words, Trotsky tried to show that Stalin was not intelligent, and merely succeeded in showing that he was not an intellectual.[15] But Trotsky's unfinished polemical biography of Stalin remains, however perversely argued, a magnificent literary monument; nor is it surprising that Bernard Shaw should once have said of Trotsky that 'when he cuts off his opponent's head, he holds it up to show that there are no brains in it.'[16]

Trotsky, like Shaw, was apt to speak in metaphors of this kind. It took a Stalin to act them out, by scattering Trotsky's brains – in the strictly literal sense – over the unfinished manuscript of his murderer's biography.

Have we Really Deserved This?

During the pre-war months of 1941 Hitler treats the Soviet Union with ever decreasing consideration, while Stalin persistently attempts to appease the German dictator and to deflect – or at least to postpone – the attack on Russia which looms ever more menacingly on the horizon.

On 25 March, Yugoslavia signs the Tripartite Pact – thus adhering to the German sphere of influence; but then, two days later, a *coup d'état* establishes a Yugoslav government hostile to the Axis. Hitler thereupon decides to avenge himself on the Yugoslavs for their *volte face*, and to do so regardless of the consequences to his timetable for the invasion of Russia. The Germans accordingly attack Yugoslavia on 6 April: the very day on which Stalin is signing a treaty of friendship and non-aggression with Belgrade – a gesture intended to stimulate Yugoslav resistance to the Germans. To such feeble shifts was the Soviet leader now reduced.

The German campaign against Yugoslavia triumphed to the extent of occupying Belgrade within a matter of days. Successful, too, was Hitler's simultaneous assault on Greece, which had repelled an Italian invasion launched six months earlier. The *Wehrmacht* was thus demonstrating its ability to achieve lightning victories – now in an area uncomfortably close to Stalin's frontiers. But though this display of Teutonic military strength threw the Soviet dictator into a yet greater flurry of appeasement, Hitler's decision to indulge in a brief Balkan war may well have made a major contribution to Germany's eventual defeat. Inspired by personal spite, the attack on Yugoslavia imposed a delay of five weeks in the launching of Operation Barbarossa, which had to be postponed from 15 May to 22 June.

Had it not been for this Balkan adventure in April ('probably the most catastrophical single decision in Hitler's career')[1] the Germans might well have captured Moscow before becoming bogged down in the mud of the Russian autumn.

On 13 April, Stalin signed a neutrality pact with Japan, thus relieving himself of the need to maintain a large military presence in far eastern Siberia. When the Japanese Foreign Minister left Moscow after signing the pact, the dictator took the unusual step of seeing his guest off at the railway station, beaming with skilfully projected good will. He also demonstrated ostentatious affability towards the German Ambassador, who was present on the platform; throwing his arm round that envoy's shoulder, Stalin told him that 'we must remain friends and you must do everything to that effect.'[2] By now his attempts to conciliate Hitler were sinking, almost, to the level of sympathetic magic.

On 6 May, Stalin took a step of considerable symbolic importance by assuming the Soviet premiership – that is, the chairmanship of *Sovnarkom* – in place of Molotov (who retained the Foreign Commissariat). Thus did the dictator reassume high governmental office after an interval of eighteen years since he had ceased to be Nationalities Commissar in 1923. By appointing himself Prime Minister, he no doubt hoped to rally the country at a time of grave crisis. He may also have aimed to reassure Hitler by making it plain that an enthusiastic conciliator of Germans was fully in control of Soviet policy. Like other Stalinist measures of the time, the assumption of the premiership was probably designed to avert the danger of war breaking out through a failure by Hitler to appreciate the Kremlin's truly pacific intentions.[3] That the German dictator was bent on war irrespectively of Soviet intentions, Stalin presumably could not bring himself to believe.

On the night of 10-11 May, Stalin acquired a new source of anxiety with the sudden, dramatic flight of Hitler's deputy, Hess, to Scotland. Hess had in fact travelled on his own initiative to propose that Britain and Germany should make peace, thereby freeing Germany's hands in Europe. The proposal was ignored, the proposer promptly interned. But Stalin, in his usual suspicious way, took the flight as evidence of a plot against the Soviet Union; he remained convinced of this when Churchill discussed the matter with him during the war.[4] Thus was the Soviet dictator obsessed with fear of a malevolent Britain, while simulating or feeling comparative unconcern about the mounting danger from Hitler. Not that Stalin showed himself wholly unmindful of the Hitlerite menace, but his countermeasures lacked bite. On 24 April, for example, he encouraged Ilya Ehrenburg to publish Part Three of his anti-Nazi novel, *The Fall of Paris*. This had seemed likely to be banned by the Soviet censorship as part of a general taboo, enforced during the period of the Pact, on material thought wounding to German susceptibilities. Ehrenburg himself interpreted Stalin's sudden encouragement to publish, conveyed to him over the telephone, as a sign that war was about to break out.[5] Not long afterwards Stalin directly conceded the likelihood of war with Germany: in a confidential address of 5 May 1941 to newly commissioned Red Army officers. He even admitted, for once, that Soviet defences were in a poor way – but added that things should be better by 1942; and it was not until then that he expected war to break out.[6]

Despite this exceptional admission, Stalin continued to act as if war with Germany were unthinkable. Of the colossal German military build-up which was taking place near his western frontiers he appeared unaware, also ignoring much available information on Hitler's proposed invasion strategy. Throughout pre-war 1941 such intelligence was increasingly flooding the Kremlin from various sources, among which were Winston Churchill, the American State Department, Soviet military attachés, Soviet frontier troops, Soviet Military District headquarters and German army deserters. Nor were Stalin's spies caught unawares; the most successful of them, Richard Sorge, was even able to report – from Tokyo on 15 May – the exact date of the impending German invasion together with details of Hitler's plans.[7]

All in all, Stalin received 'more and better information on the approaching general danger, even on specific details of date and hour of invasion, than has any other leadership of an attacked country in the history of modern warfare.'[8] All this the dictator chose to overlook – also ignoring the increasingly blatant infiltration of German espionage agents into Soviet territory, and the many overflights of German reconnaissance planes into Soviet air space. During the last months of peace these aerial trespassers had been immune from attack by Soviet anti-aircraft units, which were categorically forbidden to open fire;[9] and even when the intruders were compelled to land on Soviet territory the crews were released without fuss. Stalin reacted in a similar spirit on receiving, shortly before the outbreak of war, an urgent report from General Kirponos – commander of Kiev Special Military District – to the effect that German forces were massing behind the Bug, apparently intent on invasion. Kirponos requested permission to evacuate 300,000 people from the area, while setting up strong points, anti-tank ditches and trenches; to which Stalin replied that such measures would be provocative, and that the Germans should be given no excuse for military action.[10]

In his last-minute dealings with Germany, Stalin carried attempted appeasement to ever greater lengths, offering in effect to buy Hitler off by vastly increased grain deliveries. Such overtures met with no response. Nor did the Fuehrer vouchsafe any reaction to the notorious statement – this can only have been drafted by Stalin personally, and was issued by the Soviet news agency TASS on 14 June – in which rumours of German aggressive intentions were discounted as 'completely without foundation'.[11] The main effect of this ill-conceived communiqué was to lull the Soviet public and armed forces into a state of false security. Stalin was still pursuing similar tactics on 21 June, literally on the eve of war, when his ambassador to Berlin handed a note to the German Government containing a Soviet offer to 'discuss' Soviet-German relations . . . even as Hitler's troops were creeping silently up to their start lines.

This refusal to face reality persisted into and beyond zero hour. Not until 00.30 on the morning of 22 June – a mere three hours before the German attack – did the order go out from Moscow placing the Soviet armies on Stalin's western frontier in a state of alert. Poor communications ensured that many units and formations did not receive even that much warning, but discovered that war had broken out only when German bombs and shells were already bursting around them. Much confusion was created on the fronts when Moscow denied early reports of the German attack, attributing them to the initiative of deviant German generals. Typical of this situation was a telephone conversation between General Boldin of the Soviet Army Group West and Defence Commissar Timoshenko. When Boldin reported that the Germans were advancing into the Soviet Union, strafing troops and civilians from the air, Timoshenko reminded him that no action was to be taken without Moscow's consent. Boldin protested that Soviet troops were being forced to retreat, cities were burning and people were dying, but was told that: 'Joseph Vissarionovich [Stalin] thinks these may possibly be provocations on the part of some German generals.'[12] Of Moscow's refusal to accept reality another, better known, exchange was also characteristic. According to German radio intercepts, a certain Soviet front-line unit signalled its headquarters: 'We are being fired on. What shall we do?' – only to receive the grotesque answer: 'You must be insane. And why is your message not in code?'[13] Similarly, Stalin and his henchmen simply refused to believe the naval authorities in the port of Sevastopol when they telephoned Moscow to report that they were undergoing a German air raid.[14]

Not until 7.15 a.m., nearly four hours after the initial onslaught, did the Soviet Defence Commissariat give the order to attack and destroy the enemy; even then, however, Soviet troops were forbidden to cross their frontier into enemy territory without express authorization. By the evening of 22 June this order had been superseded by another requiring the Red Army to launch a counter-offensive *into* enemy territory: instructions already rendered farcical by spectacular German successes in penetrating the thousand-mile front. The Soviet air force also received permission to attack enemy targets – up to a hundred miles beyond the border – but by the time when this order was received a sizeable proportion of Soviet aircraft had already been put out of action by the enemy.[15]

As for more public responses to the invasion, while German planes and tanks were screaming into action in the forenoon of 22 June, Radio Moscow blandly ignored these irrelevancies for several hours – continuing to broadcast a routine programme on physical training, and cataloguing the 'achievements' of Soviet workers in normal peacetime style. Not until midday was news of the German attack broadcast, and even then the solemn announcement was made by Molotov, not Stalin. Denouncing Moscow's allies of the previous day, now suddenly revealed as a 'bloodthirsty clique', the Soviet Foreign Commissar spoke of treachery unparalleled in the annals of civilized nations, and pointed out that the German attack had been unprovoked. Unprovoked? Certainly.... But unexpected? Since September 1939, Hitler had launched devastating surprise attacks on eight countries, beginning with Poland and ending with Greece. How could the ultra-suspicious Stalin place such reliance on solidarity between totalitarian states – even if he had not been overwhelmed for months by intelligence reports betraying Hitler's intentions in detail? As for Molotov's famous earlier comment on receiving the official declaration of war from the German ambassador to Moscow – 'have we really deserved this?' – it has been well described as the epitome of that 'weird hypocrisy' by which Russo-German relations were bedevilled throughout.[16]

It is hard indeed to believe that the shrewd Stalin can really have been so blinded by faith in Germany's pacific intentions as his record of pre-war 1941 suggests. Nor does it seem likely that the Soviet dictator was as unaware as he often allowed it to appear of the extreme military vulnerability of the USSR at this time. What seems more probable is that the Leader – normally hyper-cautious, yet capable of the occasional reckless gamble – had banked too heavily, in 1939, on embroiling all his potential capitalist enemies in an orgy of mutual destruction. Unleashing Hitler on Poland and the West through the Soviet-Nazi Pact, Stalin must all along have reckoned with the eventual possibility of an invasion of the Soviet Union by a victorious *Wehrmacht*. What he had failed to foresee was the sheer pace of events, since he had grossly overestimated Western military strength, being perhaps as much astonished by the speed of Hitler's victories in 1940 as was world opinion in general. Here was an embattled Germany ready to take on her greatest eastern rival at a time when, by rights, her armies should still have been bogged down in the mud of France. Nothing could have been more unfair. Ill-prepared to meet the onslaught, Stalin could only attempt to stave it off by diplomatic means until 1942 at least. By that time Soviet defences might indeed have been put in a more adequate state of readiness.

The more closely 22 June approached the more certain did it appear that Stalin's gamble had failed. But in view of Soviet short-term military weakness there seemed to be nothing which the Leader could do except attempt to buy Hitler off at the last moment by conciliating him to an extent never attempted by that notorious appeaser Neville Chamberlain. Some such considerations may help to explain – but assuredly do not excuse – the fatal miscalculations for which as usual Stalin's subjects, not Stalin personally, were to pay with their lives.

II

Back to Stalingrad

The Lessons of 22 June

LAUNCHING their attack at first light on 22 June, German armies flung the Soviet defenders violently back from their thousand-mile frontier between the Baltic and the Black Sea, achieving complete tactical surprise.

Many Soviet troops were on leave, or in their barracks, or in training areas – anywhere but in the front line. Not that much of a 'front line' could be traced during the first weeks of an invasion which employed techniques previously pioneered in Poland, France and elsewhere: massed German tanks surged rapidly forward into Russia with heavy air support, maintaining carefully selected thrust-lines, while the consolidating infantry followed in their wake.

Lacking protection from the air – twelve hundred Soviet planes had been put out of action, largely on the ground, by the *Luftwaffe* by noon on the first day of war –[1] the ineptly deployed Soviet artillery and anti-tank units would have had difficulty in moving to their battle stations even if it had been clearer to them where these might be located. They were further endangered by ill-conceived orders obliging them to travel by day as well as by night, and were accordingly put out of action in their turn, leaving the Soviet infantry a helpless prey to German armour and planes.

One may search Stalin's biography in vain for any setback comparably disastrous. All the signs were that he and his system would collapse before the Germans in a matter of months, if not of weeks. How, then, did the Leader react as his whole life's work seemed to be crashing about his ears? According to Khrushchev, he fell into despair, lamenting 'all that Lenin created we have lost forever.' For a long time Stalin did not direct military operations at all. Indeed, he ceased to do anything whatever, reassuming active leadership only when some Politburo members told him that certain steps must be taken immediately to remedy the situation at the front. Even then Stalin acted with nervousness and hysteria, interfering in military operations and causing serious damage to the armies.[2] Khrushchev's

313

description receives some confirmation from Ivan Maysky, Soviet Ambassador to London at the time, who has reported that Stalin locked himself up in his study from the moment of the German attack onwards, and took no part in deciding matters of state: hence the total failure by Moscow to brief its ambassadors at this time of crisis.[3] By contrast with Khrushchev's and Maysky's evidence, Marshal Zhukov refers to Stalin as being no more than 'somewhat depressed' at dawn on 22 June; after which date, and throughout the war, he firmly governed the country.[4]

That Stalin was indeed demoralized by the first shock of total war – and that the destalinizing Khrushchev's account is probably nearer the mark than that of the restalinizing Zhukov – appears to be confirmed by the remarkable eleven-day silence preserved by the Soviet dictator after the first news of the German onslaught reached him. Not until 3 July did Stalin react publicly to the disaster.[5] When he did so, in his celebrated radio broadcast of that day, he made history and dumbfounded his hearers by calling them 'brothers and sisters', and 'my friends', in addition to the conventional 'comrades' – as if his Marxist faith had suddenly become tainted with some Quaker or Baptist pollution. In this grim call for national unity, Stalin admitted the enormous extent of German advances into the Soviet Union, while claiming that only on Soviet territory had the German *Blitzkrieg* ever encountered serious resistance; and he prophesied that Hitler's armies would meet a fate like that of Napoleon's. Stalin, who had been bombarded for months with full and accurate intelligence on Hitler's preparations, now ascribed early German successes to the factor of surprise! A hundred and seventy Hitlerite divisions had fallen on a peaceful Red Army deployed far from the frontiers. As for his pact with the aggressors (now suddenly promoted to 'monsters and cannibals'), Stalin defended that agreement as gaining time for the Soviet Union; but he failed to explain why so little use had been made of the time so expensively gained. He also stated that any non-aggression pact was defensible provided that it did not infringe, directly or indirectly, on the territorial integrity of a peace-loving state: '*As is well known*, the non-aggression pact between Germany and the Soviet Union is precisely such a pact.'[6] Students of Stalin's prose style will be familiar with the formula 'as is well known' – commonly employed, as here, to lubricate a sentence in which the level of mendacity rises above that of the context in which it occurs.

In the same speech Stalin also claimed – accurately, as is now confirmed from German records – that Hitler intended to turn Soviet citizens into slaves. He called for a merciless war against the Germans, but also against domestic deserters, panic-spreaders, rumour-mongers, spies and diversionaries. He required his retreating subjects to rescue all railway rolling stock, not abandoning it to the enemy; and he called for the formation of partisan detachments in the German rear. Stalin also thanked Churchill for his declaration, broadcast on the day of Hitler's invasion of Russia, that Britain was ready to help the Soviet Union in alliance against their common enemy.

According to one listener, Stalin's broadcast of this, his first wartime message to his people, was hardly calculated to inspire confidence. He

spoke in a sort of hollow, colourless voice, halting and breathing heavily; once or twice during the speech there was a clink from the glass out of which he was drinking water. Stalin seemed ill, seemed to be speaking with an effort. This was no way to raise his listeners' morale and enthusiasm.[7]

By contrast, numerous other Soviet sources have claimed that Stalin's speech of 3 July 1941 *was* effective in raising morale.[8]

By the time of Stalin's first wartime broadcast his attempt to excuse the Nazi-Soviet Pact – as providing the USSR with a vital breathing-space – had already been openly discredited by twelve days of total war. Soviet expansion under the terms of the Pact had indeed put a new belt of Stalin-controlled territory, a hundred to two hundred miles wide, between the USSR's pre-1939 frontiers and the Germans. But so rapidly were Hitler's armies overrunning these recently annexed territories (Soviet-occupied Lithuania, Latvia, Estonia, Poland and Rumania) that they appeared to be serving less as a buffer than as a corridor. The swift loss of the newly Stalinized lands was made even swifter by inexcusable neglect. By the outbreak of war the once formidable defences of the *pre-war* Soviet frontiers had been dismantled, and were in some cases being used as vegetable dumps by local collective farmers; yet no effective new defence line had been constructed behind the *new* frontiers. Work had begun here and there, but had been partly abandoned. The rapid German initial advance was also assisted by the seizure of Soviet ammunition dumps deliberately sited near the new frontiers in accordance with the doctrine that any future war would be fought on enemy territory.[9] And yet, by a peculiarly unhappy combination of errors, other no less vital explosives – those required to destroy bridges in the path of the invader – were often not available where they were needed. As a further example of Soviet unpreparedness, coastal artillery sited in Estonia had not been co-ordinated with batteries in the newly annexed Finnish peninsula of Hangö; yet Stalin had fought a calamitous minor war against Finland, losing scores of thousands of men, precisely in order to make such co-ordination possible.

Having assumed total responsibility for every department of Soviet life, Stalin also bears responsibility for the state of Soviet armaments production at the outbreak of war. Here the situation was no means as hopeless as the dictator was to pretend when he complained that the Germans en-enjoyed great numerical superiority in tanks and aircraft.[10] In fact the Soviet Union enjoyed overwhelming numerical superiority in both tanks and aircraft at the outbreak of war: a preponderance of about seven to one, and four or five to one, respectively.[11] Admittedly a high proportion of Soviet planes and tanks consisted of obsolete types, for in June 1941 mass production of new models still lagged behind. Even so, modern models – such as the T-34 and KV tanks – were plentiful enough to have given a far better account of themselves, and to have repelled the invader at an early stage, had they been less ineffectively deployed and handled.

Another difficulty sprang from the incomplete restoration of a specialized tank corps as established a few years earlier but then dissolved by an order of Stalin's given in 1939. By June 1941 this provision had been reversed, but the redeployment had been incompletely implemented, with the result that massed tank formations were not yet available and Soviet armour was therefore not able to mount effective counterattacks in bulk against German armour. In isolation, though, the Soviet T-34 and KV tanks proved them-selves more than a match for the German armour from the beginning.[12] As for Soviet planes, Hitler's success in knocking these out on the ground had been assisted by inadequate Soviet airfield facilities. There were too few airfields near the frontier, and those too crowded. Sixty-six fields were attacked on the first day, and with such success that Soviet troops were often compelled to destroy even the aircraft which remained intact; for the run-ways were often so badly damaged by German bombs that even unscathed Soviet planes could not take off, and were thus liable to be captured by advancing German ground troops.

To these colossal blunders must be added others in the area of personnel management and technology. The dictator's sabotage of the pre-war Soviet defence establishment had by no means been confined to the extermination of senior officers, but had also embraced military designers, inventors and technicians. When, in summer 1940, a certain disgruntled aircraft designer wrote to the Central Committee complaining that his plan for a new military plane was bound to be shelved by his seniors, Stalin summoned the chief of these, the top aircraft designer A. S. Yakovlev, and lectured him on the need to pay attention to such 'criticism from below'. Stalin then gave orders, against Yakovlev's advice, to proceed with the newly designed model, which crashed during its first flight and had to be abandoned after a large sum of money had been wasted to gratify the dictator's whim.[13] Again, Stalin once intervened to impose the exclusive manufacture of a 107 mm. tank gun against his experts' advice, having al-legedly confused this weapon with a different gun of the same calibre which he happened to remember from the First World War.[14] On the Leader's order two existing weapons – the useful 45 mm. and 76 mm. tank guns – were taken out of production; the larger-calibre weapon was adopted, but proved ineffective. Then again, Stalin shut down the only Soviet mortar design office in 1936, and jailed his mortar expert B. I. Shavyrin.[15] He also imprisoned the armaments expert B. L. Vannikov in June 1941, only to have him released from solitary confinement in the following month – when, by a change of fortune supremely typical of Stalinism – the captive was suddenly reinstated in his former office of People's Commissar for Armaments.[16] As for the navy, Stalin happened to like battleships and heavy cruisers, and to dislike aircraft carriers:[17] which was enough to determine naval construction policy in an age when serious criticism – inspired by the highest patriotic motives – of the dictator's plans was equated with sabotage and treachery.

Theoreticians of warfare were no more immune from persecution than its technicians, and in one flagrant instance a far-sighted analysis of military doctrine proved an immediate passport to the concentration camps. In 1940, the head of a department in the General Staff Academy, G. Isserson, published a book, *New Forms of Conflict*, on the military lessons of Spain and Poland. Contrary to official Soviet military doctrine of the day, Isserson asserted the need to concentrate on offensive, mobile warfare; he considered positional, static methods obsolete; he also stressed the importance of not allowing the Soviet air force to be destroyed on the ground. Having committed the supreme indiscretion of being proved right where Stalin was proved wrong, the offending strategist languished behind barbed wire until 1956.[18]

Nor had Stalin's assault on the uniformed ranks by any means ceased in 1938, when the military purge merely became less severe, but was not called off entirely, despite the release from concentration camps of certain high-ranking victims – including Generals Meretskov, Gorbatov and Rokossovky – who were permitted to rejoin the colours. But Stalin still continued to have others shot in captivity. A former head of the Air Force, Smushkevich, is reported as executed only a fortnight before – or four months after – the outbreak of war.[19] Then, a week after the German attack, Stalin had a further batch of generals shot for 'treachery' under fire: in other words, for finding themselves in a hopeless position due to pre-war dispositions depending ultimately on the dictator himself.

The chief victim of this affair was D. G. Pavlov, Commander of Army Group West. Pavlov's command happened to straddle the chief enemy thrust-line: that of von Bock's Army Group Centre. Unfortunately for the Soviet commander, the outbreak of war caught many of his troops deployed deep inside the Bialystok pocket which bulged into German-held Poland in such a way that the Russians were already more than half surrounded before a single shot was fired. Within six days the Germans were able to engulf and cut off the bulk of Pavlov's troops, amounting to several hundred thousand men. Pavlov himself was recalled by Stalin to Moscow with his Chief of Staff and other high-ranking officers: to be promptly court-martial-led and shot. Though Stalin's propagandists attempted to present the liqui-dated officers as traitors, the episode was more calculated to demoralize their brothers-in-arms than to encourage them. Even before shooting Pavlov, Stalin had of course long established a situation similar to that created by Hitler within the German Army, in that Soviet generals were far more frightened of their own dictator, and later Commander-in-Chief, than they were of the enemy. As for the secret police, the NKVD inspired greater fear in Soviet generals than did the Gestapo on the opposite side: 'the experienced Soviet officer, who would not normally lose his self-control in the most difficult combat conditions, became totally demoralized when men wearing the green caps of Beria's organization entered his office.'[20]

The Pavlov case remained unique, in that no more senior generals appear to have been shot with members of their staff – hot from the front and on grounds of treachery under fire. But the shooting, on Stalin's orders, of already imprisoned Soviet officers seems to have continued after the out-break of hostilities: there was one batch of such reported executions in October 1941, and another in July 1942.[21] These were moments of acute crisis when Stalin was concerned to ensure himself against a *coup* which might conceivably have freed such enemies and given them high military or political office in a destalinized Russia.

Having long ago done his best to ensure by domestic terror that no alternative leadership could ever arise – a danger liable to become especi-ally acute in war-time – Stalin was following his usual practice of continuing to make assurance doubly sure during hostilities. It was presumably as a result of his direct orders, as it was certainly consistent with his methods, that political prisoners in areas threatened by the German advance were massacred by the NKVD, so that they might not fall into German hands alive.[22] As for the great slave camp networks of the hinterland, these were rigorously harnessed to the Soviet war economy, their contribution being somewhat impaired by the need to detach potential front-line troops for guard duties.

As these details show, no amount of special pleading can absolve Stalin from responsibility for the appalling defeats inflicted on the Soviet Union in the early stages of the invasion. On this point Khrushchev's revelations in the Secret Speech of 1956 agree with the assessment of the Soviet-published (but later officially disavowed) military historian Nekrich, as also with the post-war denunciation of one of the dictator's own generals, Grigorenko, who was able to publish only outside the USSR. Even post-Khrushchevite memoirs of the discreetly restalinizing Brezhnevite period cannot absolve Stalin from guilt, though they often attempt to do so by the device of ascribing all Soviet defeats to General Headquarters, while crediting all victories to Stalin by name. Still, we also find such memoirists stressing the dominant role of the dictator in determining pre-war military policy: the policy which, after all, made things so easy for Hitler in the early stages of his invasion. 'Not a single military or military-economic problem . . . was decided without the direct participation of the Secretary-General', the one-time Chief of Staff Meretskov reports. He adds that Stalin often used to attend pre-war meetings of the General Staff, also inviting its members, together with Military District Commanders, to supper for intimate discussions of strategic affairs lasting far into the night.[23]

Frequent though such consultations may have been, we have seen how little fruit they bore in the shape of wise policies. In almost every branch of pre-war politico-military administration the dictator made catastrophic mistakes such as would have earned him many a bullet in the neck, had his own standards of discipline been applied to himself. As we have seen, these mistakes embraced military doctrine, international diplomacy, arms production, troop deployment and innumerable other matters great and small. Having canalized all responsibility through his own person, and having arrogated to himself the sole right to take decisions – while so frequently obliterating initiative in others – the dictator had created a situation in which no one else could have caused such widespread disaster even if he had tried, and in which few of his underlings dared to tell him anything except what he might be supposed willing to hear. So catastrophic were the ensuing calamities, so directly did they stem from Stalin's decisions and policies, that he could hardly have rendered Hitler better service had he been an agent in German pay all along.

It must be stressed, however, that such strictures apply most particularly to Stalin's failure to prepare an adequate Soviet defence system during the immediate pre-war years. It is on his pre-war record, but also for his management of affairs during the first few hours and days of hostilities, that the dictator is most vulnerable to criticism – by contrast with his later over-all achievement as war-time Leader, which eventually became formidable indeed. This important distinction is somewhat blurred by the fact that Stalin's deficiencies as a pre-war military leader were still coming to light long after war had broken out: in the glare, as it were, of German tank headlights and of burning Soviet cities. It is a measure of the Soviet leader's resilience that he contrived to digest the awful lessons of summer 1941 quickly and battle through to eventual victory.

Here, as in so many other spheres, we find a marked contrast between Stalin and Hitler. A talented but less professional dictator, Hitler had scored his most brilliant victories in 1939–41: the years when Stalin's mind does not appear to have been on his job as a war leader in potential. Then Hitler, his self-esteem inflated by a series of successful inspirations, begins to feel infallible, even as his instincts begin to betray him . . . while Stalin in his modest fashion is patiently acquiring the knack of managing a nation at war. Ten years older than Hitler, Stalin yet retained what his arch-enemy had lost: the capacity to learn from his mistakes. While Hitler was unlearning the art of warfare, Stalin was patiently learning it – at the expense of unnumbered casualties among his underlings.

Neither leader could, in the end, claim any superhuman degree of consistently applied strategic wisdom; still less does the reputation of either gain when one contemplates their many tactical interventions, through inept telephoned instructions, in the activities of commanders on the spot. It is for their victories over their own military establishments, which each skilfully converted into the instrument of an amateur desk-bound will, that Stalin and Hitler are best remembered by such of their generals as contrived to outlive them.

The Campaigns of 1941

In the first stage of the invasion of Russia, Hitler's forces enjoyed spectacular success. Even their previous year's victories in the west seemed eclipsed as vast German pincer movements enveloped the apparently helpless Soviet enemy in one great pocket after another. The most formidable and initially effective of the three main invasion hordes was von Bock's Army Group Centre, which followed a general thrust-line pointed at Moscow, reaching Smolensk on 16 July. Bock crushed Soviet resistance in Belorussia in less than a month, taking about six hundred thousand prisoners, covering five hundred miles in three weeks, and reaching a point about 250 miles from the Soviet capital.[1] Had he been permitted to continue his triumphant advance, Moscow might well have fallen to his forces by autumn. Fortunately for the Russians, however, it was at this point that Hitler made a particularly ill-judged intervention, halting Army Group Centre in the Smolensk area, while concentrating on operations by the two flanking formations. Of these, von Leeb's Army Group North surged triumphantly through the Baltic states towards Leningrad, while on the right wing, far to the south, von Rundstedt's Army Group South was biting deep into the Ukraine.

In many areas Soviet communities – disillusioned with Stalinism, as yet ignorant of Hitlerism – enthusiastically welcomed an invader who (it was supposed) might abolish the hated collective farms and tolerate ancestral religious practices. Elsewhere Soviet resistance was stubborn from the outset. Between these extremes the bulk of the population met the shock of German invasion and occupation with stunned apathy: the outcome of so many years of brutal regimentation.

That Stalin himself was at first stunned into inaction by the German invasion we have already noted. Within a few weeks, however, he was revealing his usual resilience, and was presiding over organizational changes designed to enable the Soviet Union to improvise a defence out of chaos. In this grave crisis this arch-bureaucrat's first instinct was – as might have been predicted – to create new committees. On 30 June 1941 he established a State Defence Committee vested with absolute authority over all Party, governmental, military and other organizations throughout the country.[2] The new body thus took precedence over both Politburo and Secretariat, and was chaired by Stalin himself. The other members were Molotov, Voroshilov, Malenkov and Beria. Among these Malenkov and Beria were relatively junior figures, now exalted over six full Politburo members. Thus Stalin streamlined the top leadership, ensuring that it contained his chief of political police, but no military specialist apart from Voroshilov. Among especially important organs subordinate to the State Defence Committee was Supreme Command Headquarters, also chaired by Stalin. Alongside these two bodies, newly formed during the war, two older military establishments continued to function: the Defence Commissariat and the General Staff, headed at the outbreak of hostilities by Timoshenko and Zhukov respectively. On 19 July 1941, however, Stalin himself assumed the post of Defence Commissar, and on 8 August he promoted himself Supreme Commander-in-Chief. Cautious as ever, he did not publicize his tenure of the second office until his forces began to win victories in the field,[3] after which he was also to assume the ranks of Marshal and Generalissimo.

As recently as April 1941, Stalin had held only one high office: that of Secretary, formerly Secretary-General, to the Party's Central Committee. Now he had added four more key posts affecting the direction of the war, having picked them up at the rate of one a month. He had – to recapitulate – been Prime Minister since May 1941; Chairman of the State Defence Committee since June; People's Commissar for Defence since July, and Supreme Commander-in-Chief since August. Thus equipped, the future

Generalissimo was ready to relearn the rudiments of the military art which he had originally studied during the Russian Civil War.

Stalin directed the general course of the war during the four hazardous years which eventually culminated in Allied victory. He determined Soviet strategic policy, controlling its diplomatic, political, economic, military and other ramifications. Having equipped himself with the interlocking committees, commissariats and headquarters listed above, he characteristically made little formal distinction between them in his working practice. As in time of peace, so too in wartime, he was apt to meet succeeding crises by improvising groups of advisers on an *ad hoc* basis – without greatly troubling about their precise status in his various hierarchies. Surrounded by an assortment of high-ranking officers and officials from the bodies named above, and also summoning generals as needed from sensitive areas at the front, Stalin sounded opinion and took his decisions. His interventions ranged from war theatre and army group down to army, corps and – such was his appetite for detail – far below that: on occasion down to company level.

Innumerable examples occur in the sources of the close watch maintained by the dictator over day-to-day operations on the fronts. An early instance involved the defence of Leningrad, as hastily put together when von Leeb's Army Group North was rolling towards the city in August 1941. Since no pre-war provision had been made to supply Leningrad with a defence system in the south, the beleaguered population was hurriedly mobilized (as was the usual practice in towns menaced by the German advance) to construct trenches and anti-tank ditches, civilians being enrolled in a volunteer militia. In order to control these operations in detail, Voroshilov and Zhdanov – Stalin's key satraps on the spot – decided to form a so-called 'Soviet for the Defence of Leningrad'. It was no more than a junior committee charged with organizing such things as the siting of tank traps, the issue of Molotov cocktails and the sandbagging of machine-gun posts, while leaving Voroshilov and Zhdanov free to concentrate on the broader aspects of the city's defences. But when Stalin learnt that such a Soviet had been set up, and without prior reference to himself, his deepest suspicions were aroused. Perhaps it was the bogy of popular participation which scared him, especially since Zhdanov and Voroshilov had not themselves chosen to serve on the newly-established organ, being fully occupied with more important matters. They soon learnt of their mistake when the Leader telephoned in a great rage. He insisted that these two proconsuls should themselves sit on their own suspicious-sounding Soviet; he would not or could not understand that they had only set up this body in the first place so that it could deal with problems of detail which they were too busy to handle.[4]

The incident belongs to the continuing saga of Stalin's hyper-sensitivity to developments in the second city of his realm.

Whether Stalin's interventions did or did not handicap Leningrad's defences as seriously as has been asserted,[5] it seems likely that his decisions contributed to the débâcle which occurred shortly afterwards on his southern flank. On 20 September, Kiev fell to yet another great enveloping movement from which the Germans claimed nearly seven hundred thousand prisoners.[6] Many of these might have escaped from the trap had it not been for a peremptory order from Stalin countermanding a decision by the local commander-in-chief, Budyonny, and his political adviser Khrushchev, to abandon the city when its fall appeared inevitable, and to withdraw their forces to the east. Incensed by their intention to retreat, the Supreme Chairman dismissed Budyonny as Theatre Commander, appointing Timoshenko in his stead – and with orders to hold on at all costs. Meanwhile the German pincers were closing more menacingly round the Kiev pocket with every passing hour until General Tupikov – Chief of Staff to Army Group South-West – appealed for permission to withdraw; he addressed the General Staff directly, over the head of his own superior, General Kirponos, who refused to authorize the message. A reply was received calling Tupikov a panic-monger and instructing the commanders of Army Group South West not to lose their heads, but to carry out Comrade Stalin's order. By 17 September, when the Supreme Command did finally authorize the retreat from Kiev, it was already too late to save the bulk of the beleaguered army group.[7] In this appalling rout the rash Tupikov and the prudent Kirponos both perished. Thus was the greatest single Soviet defeat of the war aggravated, if not actually caused, by Stalin's personal intervention, though it seems probable that his culpability has been exaggerated by the Khrushchevite sources on which we partly depend for our knowledge of this incident. It is also arguable that Hitler's victory at Kiev cost him dear by continuing to divert his forces from the most important strategic target of all: Moscow.

In early November Stalin attempted to make the best of a bad job by boasting that no country except the Soviet Union could have lost so much territory and survived.[8] After four weeks of warfare Hitler was master of an area twice the size of France.

Never relaxing his grip on the general conduct of the war, Stalin showed awareness of his own limitations by taking increased note of his leading generals' views. From the ordeal of the first few months certain commanders emerged with reputations enhanced, and the dictator took to sending such trusted figures to the crisis battlefront of the moment as his personal emissaries. His use of mobile trouble-shooters, particularly Vasilevsky and

Zhukov, made its contribution towards victory. Similarly Lenin had once dispatched Stalin to Tsaritsyn, Perm and Petrograd during the Civil War, just as Stalin himself had more recently employed mobile purgers from the Centre to give bite to the Great Terror on the periphery of his empire. While some of the most experienced German generals were dismissed during the first months of the Russo-German war, competence was less severely penalized on the Soviet side. Thus Stalin began, early in the war, to distinguish himself from Hitler by a superior ability to handle his top military leadership.

Among many outstanding Soviet commanders who emerged during the war none played a more crucial role than Georgy Zhukov: a tough fighting general who tempered deference to the dictator with occasional resistance to his demands on major issues. During the Civil War, Zhukov had served with First Cavalry Army, Stalin's favourite military formation. When, a few years later, the time came to motorize Zhukov's branch of the service he was picked by Stalin to command a newly formed tank regiment. In 1939 delayed but rapid promotion brought Zhukov command of the Soviet forces at Khalkhyn-Gol, where he defeated the Japanese Sixth Army. Not until May of the following year did he first meet Stalin personally.[9] In February 1941 Zhukov was appointed Chief of Staff, but resigned in July because he disagreed with Stalin over the feasibility of holding on to Kiev.[10] On 11 September 1941 Stalin rushed Zhukov to besieged Leningrad, where he took over from Voroshilov – now so desperately harassed that he was said to be at the front seeking death in battle. Within three days the new commander had stabilized the city's defences and the main danger had moved to Moscow.[11] It was, accordingly, to Moscow that Stalin switched Zhukov, on 6 October, to organize the capital's defences. Thus did Zhukov prove an exception to the rule that no one could survive after being proved right where Stalin was proved wrong – in this instance by the fall of Kiev after Stalin had decided, against Zhukov's advice, to hold on there at all costs.

Occupying several months during winter 1941–2, the Battle of Moscow was the first of the three decisive engagements which were to settle the outcome of the Soviet-German war, the other two being the Battles of Stalingrad and Kursk. Each of these operations involved an initial major German offensive converted into Soviet victory by a successful major counter-offensive. On each occasion Stalin took or sanctioned the main decisions, and on each occasion Zhukov was one of his chief executants.

The Battle of Moscow was joined on 30 September 1941 when the Germans launched Operation Typhoon: a massive assault designed to encircle the Soviet capital. It was Hitler's intention to isolate the city, and to allow its inhabitants to starve to death – treatment which he also intended to apply to besieged Leningrad. During the first few days a German victory seemed assured. Crashing forward against ineffective resistance, Hitler's armies encircled yet another great Soviet pocket at Vyazma, collecting yet another batch of several hundred thousand prisoners. By mid-October, however, their initial attack was becoming bogged down as the churned mud of autumnal Russia immobilized the *Wehrmacht*'s vehicles, thus depriving the German infantry of armoured support. Since these were predictable seasonal conditions, Hitler's folly in mounting this assault was an important factor in his eventual defeat before Moscow. And yet, despite the mud, it was far from obvious in October 1941 that the Battle of Moscow would be won by the Russians. As German troops pressed ever nearer to the Soviet capital there were signs of confusion and panic among the city's inhabitants, many of whom fled to the east without waiting for orders from above. In the middle of the month certain government departments, and all diplomatic missions, were evacuated to Kuybyshev on the middle Volga. On 19 October a state of emergency was declared in the capital by a proclamation which Stalin personally composed.[12]

While many others quitted Moscow, the dictator himself remained in the Kremlin all along: a symbol of Soviet determination to resist Hitler to the end. Aware of the political importance of the public gesture, Stalin went ahead with the customary 7 November parade commemorating the anniversary of the Revolution. Far from cancelling that annual ritual, he took the salute in person, even as German armies already ringed the western suburbs of the capital at a distance of some forty miles. On the previous evening he had addressed a large gathering in the Mayakovsky Station of the Moscow Metro. As these two speeches illustrate, the lower Russian military fortunes sank the less was the emphasis placed by Stalin on Marxist ideology, and the greater the attention which he paid to traditional Russian patriotism. In his Red Square speech of 7 November he again addressed his audience as his 'brothers and sisters', and went on to evoke the memory of six victorious Russian military leaders of pre-revolutionary days: St Alexander Nevsky, who had routed a Teutonic invader in 1242; Grand Prince Dmitry Donskoy, vanquisher of Tatars in 1380; Minin and Pozharsky, who had expelled the Polish occupying army from Muscovy in 1612; General Suvorov, subjugator of north Italy under Catherine the Great; Kutuzov, conqueror of Napoleon.[13] Then again, in Stalin's eve-of-parade speech, various non-ideological Russian cultural figures – Chekhov, Pushkin and Tchaikovsky – were invoked in the same breath as Lenin.[14]

In mid-November, Stalin forced Zhukov to attempt a counter-offensive on the Moscow front, overruling all objections – soon justified in the event – that this was premature and doomed to fail. Berating Zhukov for resistance to his plan, Stalin accused him of being too big for his boots: 'But we'll find a way of dealing with you.'[15] Of the extent to which Zhukov was indeed liable to give himself airs at this period, evidence is provided by one of his subordinates, General P. A. Belov, whom Zhukov took to the Kremlin at about this time for consultations on the defence of Moscow. Not having seen Stalin since 1933, Belov found him greatly changed; he looked tired and haggard, seeming to have aged twenty years rather than eight. Stalin's eyes were unsteady, his voice lacked confidence. Meanwhile the ebullient Zhukov was addressing his master in a sharp voice of command, as if he were the superior officer! Stalin, whose face periodically expressed a look of bafflement, seemed to accept a subordinate position.[16]

Whatever Stalin's posture may have been on this particular occasion, he continued to keep Zhukov firmly in his place, often treating him with a certain petulance. This was particularly evident at one point of the Battle of Moscow when Stalin showed an uncharacteristic lack of prudence. He had received the information – incorrect, as it later turned out – that a village called Dedovsk, situated only fifteen miles from the capital, had fallen into enemy hands. Thus informed, he at once telephoned Zhukov and ordered him to organize – in person – a counter-attack on this minor locality, despite the fact that Zhukov was overwhelmed with the problems of the front as a whole. On making enquiry, Zhukov discovered that it was not Dedovsk, but quite another – similarly named, but less tactically sensitive – village which had fallen: Dedovo. All attempts to explain the misunderstanding to Stalin were like butting one's head against a brick wall. In a towering rage the dictator repeated his order that Zhukov should recover the offending village, and do so in person. The result was that Zhukov and two other senior generals had to leave their headquarters to supervise the action, by a rifle company and two tanks, which restored Dedovo to Soviet possession at dawn on 1 December. This futile operation, ordained from on high, removed the main organizers of Moscow's defences from their operational duties at a time of acute crisis.[17]

Farcical though this particular intervention was, it was soon followed by a favourable change in the fortunes of war. Local Soviet counter-attacks, mounted on 5 December and initially conceived as defensive operations, revealed that the German troops facing Moscow were in poor shape.[18] Exhausted and depleted by a *Blitzkrieg* which had turned into a war of attrition, they had battled their way into the autumn slush, only to find that superseded by winter conditions harsh even by Russian standards. German vehicles – as ill designed for intense cold as for intense mud – were immobilized, while German troops lacked winter clothing such as the Red Army possessed in quantity. The Germans also lacked prepared positions in their rear, since the Fuehrer had expressly forbidden the construction of such defences; he believed exclusively in the virtues of attack, a faith which Stalin tended to share.

In keeping with this urge, Stalin now decided to exploit German embarrassments by again ordering a general Soviet counter-offensive along the entire front. And again Zhukov disagreed, preferring a massive but more concentrated counter-attack aimed at the destruction of Army Group Centre.[19] He may well have been right, for though the general Soviet counter-offensive of winter 1941–2 did indeed fling the Germans back between a hundred and two hundred miles on a broad front, it was far indeed from annihilating the invading forces, which coiled back and were to strike again with renewed venom in summer 1942. Stalin's winter offensive did, however, achieve two vital secondary aims: it relieved Moscow from immediate pressure, and it proved to the Red Army that the Germans – lice-ridden, freezing, starving and desperate – were no superhuman conquerors, but could be beaten at their own game.

Stalin the war-lord maintained a punishing work schedule and imposed the same on others. As already noted, his peacetime habit of toiling through the night had disrupted the timetable of administrative Moscow. Now, in wartime, he continued this practice, fixing exacting schedules to fit his own no less exacting routine. His contacts were by no means confined to his immediate subordinates, for – later in the war, at least – he made it his business to meet all his senior commanders personally.[20] He also made extensive use of the high-security telephone to demand reports and issue orders, often by-passing the regular chain of command. Such interventions could be disastrous – not least some of those ordering harassed troops to hold every inch of ground in contexts where this was tactically inappropriate. It was indeed fortunate for Stalin that he had in Hitler an opposite number possessed of a similar obsession with holding ground at all costs.

When discussing military matters, Stalin cultivated his usual terseness, combining this with a power of rapid, often inflexible decision, yet remaining sporadically open to advice. Wrong or right, his decisions were not taken – as, to a considerable extent, were Hitler's – by 'feel', but involved careful operational planning, even if subordinate planners did not necessarily have the last word. In dealing with his subordinates, Stalin could be remarkably courteous, while insisting that their reports should be brief, factual and relevant. He could also be rude and peremptory, to the extent of frequently losing his temper . . . yet never so uncontrollably as a Hitler. Laconic and taciturn by nature, the Soviet Supreme Commander would not always bother to reply on occasions when a subordinate questioned his telephoned orders, but would simply replace the receiver as a sign that the matter must be considered settled.

Possessing no specially constructed field headquarters, Stalin largely directed the war from his Kremlin office, which might be entered by passing through the office of his assistant Poskryobyshev, and then through a small chamber manned by the head of his personal bodyguard. Brightly lit, spacious, panelled in stained oak and with an arched ceiling, Stalin's room contained a long table covered with green cloth. There were icons of Marx and Engels; there was a plaster-of-Paris death mask of Lenin in a glass case; to these embellishments portraits of the rehabilitated Imperial Russian generals Suvorov and Kutuzov were added during the war. The chairs were hard, the room was uncluttered by superfluous objects. Stalin's desk was usually covered with documents, papers, maps, telephones and a stack of sharpened pencils. The dictator wrote his notes fast and legibly in blue pencil, and was well known for his habit of doodling when seated during conferences; but when receiving reports from his generals, who usually remained standing, he was apt to pace the room with rapid, silent strides.[21]

In this room – but also occasionally in the Kremlin air-raid shelter, or at his country villa at Kuntsevo – Stalin directed the war by day and by night, generally sleeping between about five a.m. and noon. He usually wore a simple military tunic, baggy trousers and brightly polished top boots, and he would puff away incessantly at a short pipe into which it was his practice to break the contents of two ravaged cigarettes; an *unlit* pipe in Stalin's hands was a storm signal which his subordinates quickly learnt to read. When interviewing generals, commissars, industrial managers, diplomats, designers and the like, the Commander-in-Chief usually preferred to do so in the presence of such close advisers as Molotov, Voroshilov, Malenkov and Beria. Should any conflict of opinion develop, one or other of these underlings would often draw some awkward customer to one side and warn him not to cross Stalin's will. For this reason it was much easier to deal with the dictator if one had the rare luck to catch him on his own.[22]

Polite and considerate though Stalin could be when the fancy took him, he never lost the habit of threatening his underlings; nor did he part with that underlying suspiciousness with which he had always regarded other human beings. Generals questioning his orders were apt to be accused of treachery and sabotage, however firmly their objections might be founded on a serious attempt to read the military situation and on a genuine concern for the success of Soviet arms. Those who queried Stalin's instructions were perhaps the bravest of all his subordinates, for what Soviet commander would not rather face any conceivable combination of armed Germans than the wrath of his Commander-in-Chief? And yet there remained this lack of ultimate consistency in the dictator which sometimes led him to respect and tolerate the very independence of mind which – at other times – he would crush with unrelenting ferocity. Admiral Kuznetsov reports several occasions on which Army Group Commanders disagreed with Stalin, and found their views accepted. 'I suspect [Kuznetsov adds] he even liked people who had their own point of view and were not afraid to stand up for it.'[23] Zhukov too insists – repeatedly – that it was possible to carry one's point in argument with Stalin, and himself claims to have done so frequently during the course of the war.[24] Moreover, there were times when Stalin called for greater initiative from his underlings.

There are many who love to hide behind my back [he complained to Yakovlev]. In every detail they refer to me and do not want to take responsibility on themselves. You are a young man. You are still unspoiled, and you know your business. Don't be afraid to act in your own name. Your authority will be greater and people will respect you.[25]

Thus did Stalin occasionally lament the lack of that very spontaneity which he continued to suppress even as he deplored its absence. Nor was personal initiative encouraged by the dictator's habit of severely restricting even his most senior colleagues' access to vital strategic intelligence. Extremely security-conscious, as befitted a veteran political conspirator, he repeatedly impressed on his generals the need for discretion, while also ensuring that they had as little as possible to be indiscreet about. He observed particularly stringent secrecy in respect of military reserves. Unbriefed on the availability of resources, army group and army commanders were ill placed to argue with the Supreme Commander-in-Chief, and were thus compelled to await reinforcements like manna from heaven. So jealously did Stalin guard his own prerogative that he would not discuss naval matters with his Defence Commissar and Chief of General Staff.[26] He also maintained, in wartime, through the NKVD and the army's Political Administration, two independent intelligence networks . . . independent both of each other and of army intelligence proper. By such means the dictator sought to keep the threads exclusively in his own hands, so that he alone was in a position to take far-reaching strategic decisions.

As Hitler had said, Stalin was indeed indispensable.

Pre-Stalingrad Foreign Entanglements

By no means exclusively concerned with Soviet military campaigning, Stalin also took part in many wartime negotiations with foreign statesmen.

Relations with Britain and the United States, as also with the Polish Government-in-Exile, were the Commander-in-Chief's main diplomatic preoccupations during the war.

On 18 July 1941, Stalin replied to the offer of British co-operation extended by Churchill on the day of Hitler's invasion of the USSR.[1] The dictator's letter remains unique in his correspondence with the Prime Minister in containing an apology for the Soviet-Nazi Pact on grounds of military expediency. Stalin's letter also contained the first of many demands that Britain should open a Second Front against the Germans in northern France: a theme which was to recur monotonously throughout the next three years. Attempting to build up by personal messages a friendly relationship such as he already enjoyed with the American President, Churchill often waited in vain for Stalin to answer his telegrams: he met with 'many rebuffs and only rarely a kind word' from the Soviet dictator. 'The Soviet government had the impression that they were conferring a great favour on us by fighting in their own country for their own lives. The more they fought the heavier our debt became.' Bearing Moscow's reproaches with patience, Churchill tried to make allowances for the pressures under which Stalin was labouring.[2]

Despite such difficulties, British and Soviet military missions were exchanged at an early stage, and the foundations of the later 'grand' alliance were slowly laid. Of this the USA, still nominally neutral, was not yet a member. However, President Roosevelt was quick to offer extensive aid to the Soviet Union. His representative, Harry Hopkins, reached Moscow on 30 July 1941 and had two long discussions with Stalin, who welcomed American help, displaying little of his usual suspiciousness. The talks covered many technical matters, revealing Stalin's continued grasp of detail and making it clear to his guest that he alone possessed a power of decision on military and other matters such as Roosevelt and even Churchill were accustomed to delegate. Hopkins also noted that: 'There is literally no one in the whole [Soviet] Government who is willing to give any important information other than Mr. Stalin himself.'[3] Besides stating his most urgent immediate needs – light anti-aircraft guns, heavy machine-guns, rifles and aluminium – Stalin also explained his policy of 'blooding' as many of his divisions as possible in battle; this was the only way to teach his troops that Germans could be defeated. Stalin also stated that he would welcome American troops under American command at any part of the Russian front. He was soon to propose to Churchill that twenty-five or thirty British divisions might be landed at Archangel 'without risk', or else sent through Iran to southern Russia:[4] a suggestion which bore no relation to the British military situation in late 1941. Stalin was of course too busy to study other nations' strategic problems, but it is significant that he was willing, at this desperate stage of the war, to contemplate an extensive allied military presence on Russian soil. At a later and more hopeful stage he was to object to the mere presence of allied observers on the Soviet fronts.[5]

At the time of the Stalin-Hopkins talks, global military pundits were everywhere predicting the swift collapse of Russia. Yet Stalin greatly impressed Hopkins with his confidence in the future; would any leader facing imminent defeat have shown himself so eager to acquire vast stocks of aluminium for aircraft production ? Stalin impressed Hopkins by talking as he knew his troops were shooting: straight and hard without any wasted word, gesture or mannerism. Though the dictator had a warm smile, he yet made the impression of a perfectly co-ordinated machine. 'Stalin knew what he wanted, knew what Russia wanted, and he assumed that you knew.' In his tight blouse, baggy trousers and glistening boots, Stalin impressed Hopkins as a formidable figure, 'built close to the ground like a football coach's dream of a tackle'. Somewhat dazzled by the aura of power emanating from the jackbooted Chairman, Hopkins yet did not fail to notice Stalin's penetrating sense of humour.[6]

Stalin's next important meeting with allied representatives took place on 28–30 September 1941, when he spent three evenings in the Kremlin with Lord Beaverbrook and Averell Harriman: emissaries of Churchill and Roosevelt respectively. Their discussions followed a characteristically Stalinist pattern which was to be repeated again and again in the future. Cordiality at the first meeting was followed by unexpected rudeness at the second encounter, while a third confrontation produced yet another *volte face*, culminating in a dinner with the usual vodka, smiles and macabre *bonhomie*. Such oscillation reveals something of Stalin's long-standing technique of secretly manipulating colleagues and rivals. On the present occasion agreement was reached in the end, and Stalin for once made little play with the idea of a Second Front – apart from suggesting that the British might send troops to the Ukraine; when Beaverbrook spoke of a contingent to reinforce the Caucasus, Stalin told him tartly that there was no fighting in the Caucasus.[7]

Calculated discourtesy alternating with broad smiles has rarely failed Soviet representatives in their task of establishing that weird ascendancy over foreigners which some foreigners seem over-anxious to grant them. On the present occasion Stalin succeeded, as he usually did, in making a memorable personal impression on alien potentates. Even the rugged Beaverbrook melted. 'We had got to like him,' Beaverbrook noted. Stalin was

a kindly man, with a habit, when agitated, of walking about the floor with his hands behind his back. He smoked a great deal and practically never shows any impatience at all.[8]

The British Foreign Secretary, Anthony Eden, conferred with Stalin between 16 and 21 December 1941. This visit pursued the usual oscillatory course, with Stalin alternatively purring and growling as the two statesmen attempted – inconclusively – to negotiate an Anglo-Soviet alliance. Dismayed at one stage by Stalin's unco-operative attitude, Eden adopted an unorthodox technique of putting pressure on his host. He staged a conversation with the British Ambassador in the apparent privacy of their rooms ... calculating that the talk would be 'bugged', and that its contents would be immediately relayed to the Kremlin. By such indirect means Eden told, or tried to tell, Stalin that he found it impossible to work with the Russians and regretted having made the journey to Moscow. But the choice of his car as a place in which to plot this conversation ('we could be pretty confident of not being overheard') shows that Eden was poorly initiated into the potentialities of 'bugging' as practised by the NKVD.[9]

Bugged or not bugged, the Foreign Secretary's tirade did not remove his main point of disagreement with Stalin. This revolved around Britain's refusal to recognize the Soviet Union's 1941 frontiers – so notably advanced on those of 1939 – as the basis for a peace settlement after victory over the Germans; having gone to war in defence of Polish independence, the British could hardly give away half of their ally's territory in the middle of hostilities. In the end the Russians were to concede this important point. When the Anglo-Soviet Treaty of Alliance was eventually signed, on 26 May 1942, it contained no recognition by the British of Stalin's numerous annexations from the period of the Soviet-Nazi Pact. That the dictator should eventually yield to resolute opposition was characteristic of his diplomatic style. So, too, was his tenacity in arguing over a post-war settlement which might well have seemed academic to a statesman less hard-headed, for German troops were encamped on Moscow's western approaches even as these disputes raged around areas now deep in the enemy hinterland.

Eden's visit culminated in the usual farewell Kremlin banquet, lasting until 5 a.m. on 21 December 1941: Stalin's sixty-second birthday. The diversions included an inebriated Timoshenko, and the teasing of Molotov, whom Stalin affected to hold solely responsible for 'his' pact with Hitler. Straight-laced by the standards of carousing Kremlinites, Eden found the sturgeon, sucking-pig and champagne embarassingly sumptuous in the context of beleaguered, half-starved Moscow.[10] As for Eden's personal impression, he clearly had the obvious contrast with Hitler at the back of his mind when describing Stalin as a quiet dictator, who neither shouted nor gesticulated, so that one could not guess his meaning or general tenor until the translation was given.[11]

332

Long and intricate discussions marked the first round of meetings between Stalin and Premier Churchill – a heartier trencherman than his Foreign Secretary. These talks began on 12 August 1942 and ended in the small hours of 15 August. Having once tried to strangle 'this sullen, sinister Bolshevik state' at birth, Churchill had approached Moscow from Teheran with the feeling of one 'carrying a large lump of ice to the North Pole'. His bleak and sombre interview with the 'great Revolutionary Chief and profound Russian statesman and warrior' did little to dispel this impression. Churchill now had to explain the impossibility of mounting, in 1942, a Second Front, which the Russians claimed – in defiance of documentary evidence – to have been promised. Stalin received the unwelcome news with ungraciousness understandable in the context of Russia's sufferings, accusing Churchill of being afraid of the Germans; but admitted in the end that he must accept the Prime Minister's decision while rejecting his arguments.[12] To soften the blow, Churchill initiated Stalin into Anglo-American plans to invade Vichy-held northern Africa. At once grasping the strategic significance of the north African operation, Stalin listed four advantages: it would hit Rommel in the back; overawe Spain; set Germans and Frenchmen fighting in France and expose Italy to the full force of the war. Churchill was much impressed by this remarkable statement:

It showed the Russian dictator's swift and complete mastery of a problem hitherto novel to him. Very few people alive could have comprehended in so few minutes the reasons which we had all so long been wrestling with for months.'[13]

On the following day Stalin showed himself less sympathetic, taunting the British with cowardice in refusing to face the enemy. The Prime Minister excused these remarks on account of the Red Army's courage, as he informed his host, while protesting vigorously at having come so far to establish working relations without evoking any ring of comradeship in his opposite number. Before these remarks could be translated Stalin commented that he liked the tone of what Churchill had said, even if he could not understand it.[14] On the following evening the two leaders adjourned for drinks in the intimacy of Stalin's domestic quarters, and discovered over their cups a common taste for chaffing the stuttering Molotov. Churchill made much of the fact that Molotov had come back later than expected from a recent visit to Washington, and whimsically attributed the delay to unilateral action on the part of the stone-bottomed one in sneaking off to sample the night life of New York. Many a subordinate of Stalin's had been shot for an offence less sinister, and the sally left Molotov looking 'rather serious' until Stalin counter-quipped that it was not to New York that his Foreign Commissar had sneaked off, but 'to Chicago, where the other gangsters live'.[15]

It was on this occasion that Stalin unbent sufficiently to describe to Churchill the dragooning of peasants and kulaks which had attended the collectivization of agriculture: a struggle more terrible, according to the Soviet dictator, than the war against Hitler. After explaining in effect how necessary it had been to starve several million peasants, Stalin demolished a considerable sucking-pig before stepping into an adjoining room to receive routine reports from the fronts.[16]

One of Churchill's reflections is especially valuable as a comment on the dictator's *modus operandi*: 'I suppose he [Stalin] is not used to being contradicted repeatedly, but he did not become at all angry or even animated.'[17] As this indicates, when Stalin was urging an immediate Second Front or pressing any other controversial issue, he was skilfully employing a practised technique; rarely, indeed, does he appear to have mixed emotion with politics – except, of course, on the many occasions when some emotion might profitably be simulated.

Claiming, in his ignorance, that there was no truth in the 'silly tales' about how Soviet dinners often turned into drinking bouts, the British Prime Minister revealed another more serious misconception when he pictured Stalin as subject to effective backstage pressures from *Sovnarkom*. Though the Leader did admittedly choose to consult senior colleagues on occasion, these certainly did not (in Churchill's phrase) 'have more power than we suppose', for they did not have any power at all except what Stalin might from time to time choose to lend them.[18] This pretended obligation to defer to shadowy forces behind the scenes provided the dictator with a staple operating ploy. Repeatedly invoking the need to consult Molotov, Soviet public opinion, the Commissar of Justice and other phantoms, he somehow contrived to persuade even the shrewdest observers that these were genuine repositories of a power which he was helpless to defy.

Among Stalin's wartime preoccupations the Polish problem loomed large. Since September 1939 nearly a million and a half Polish citizens had been deported to Russia: prisoners-of-war captured during the lightning Soviet campaign against Poland, and civilian victims of the ensuing NKVD-organized mass kidnappings carried out on Soviet-occupied Polish territory.[19] Then, suddenly, Hitler's attack on the Soviet Union had converted these survivors of Stalin-sponsored outrage into Stalin's allies; the Soviet Government entered into diplomatic relations with the London-based Polish Government-in-Exile, and steps were taken to free or grant an amnesty to the countless Poles imprisoned or exiled on Soviet soil. From these released captives it was proposed to form a Polish National Army under General Wladyslaw Anders, who received his appointment in quint-essentially Stalinist style. After twenty months in Soviet prisons, he was suddenly hailed from his crowded cell to take tea with the NKVD chief Beria and learn of his abrupt metamorphosis from dirty, beaten, down-trodden, inconsidered convict into Commander-in-Chief of an as yet non-existent army, with effect from 4 August 1941.[20]

Converging on their rallying points from well over a hundred places of detention, the released Poles were ragged, exhausted and starving. By no means all those covered by the amnesty were in fact released, for in many cases Soviet concentration camp commandants would not disgorge able-bodied Polish slaves. Then again, Soviet distances being as immense as Soviet wartime transport facilities were primitive, the released Poles found it difficult to move to their destinations. Their rations were pitifully in-adequate and had to be shared with the accompanying Polish women and children, for whom the Soviet authorities made no provision. Starvation was aggravated by typhus and malaria epidemics, until it seemed that the National Army would never become a fighting force under such appalling conditions. The only possible course – the Polish authorities felt – was to evacuate their forces to Iran, where they could be properly fed, equip-ped and trained with British and American aid.

Stalin personally negotiated these matters with Anders, revealing his usual suspiciousness. From the transcript of their discussions it seems likely that the atrocious sufferings of the Poles were due less to any deliber-ate policy of Stalin's than to his preoccupation with more pressing problems. Such at least was the impression which he himself sought to convey when savagely reprimanding the Soviet general who was responsible for victual-ling his new allies, and who turned red and white by turns as the dictator's accusations rained down on him. 'Do you think the Poles can eat your directives?' Stalin jeered. No less roughly did he handle the attendant Poles. Did they really want to fight? Or did they want to run away. Couldn't they see that the British were about to exploit them? That they might be sent to fight the Japanese instead of driving the Germans out of their homeland? It was in bringing the results of his own maladministration directly to his attention that the Poles' chief offence lay, in Stalin's eyes. They were, in effect, telling him – they were forced by their plight to tell him – something which no Soviet adviser would have dared to point out: that the Soviet Union of the early wartime period was a mess created by misman-agement, lack of foresight and faulty planning. No wonder that the main creator of the mess was annoyed to have his nose rubbed in it; no wonder that he hit back at the Poles. They evidently thought the Russians savages, he argued. But at other points of the conversation Stalin appealed to

Slavonic racial solidarity. He invited the Poles to agree that Slavs made the best fighting airmen, belonging as they did to a young, unspoilt race; the Jews, by contrast, were poor soldiers because they were so unreliable. Anders concluded that Stalin was as anti-Semitic as Plehve, that notorious pogrom-promoter under the last Tsar. True enough, perhaps. But on this occasion Stalin was probably less concerned to air prejudices of his own than to 'needle' the General into displaying the traditional anti-Semitism associated with the Polish officer caste.[21]

Anders describes Stalin as short, heavily built and broad-shouldered; his eyes were remarkably cold, his gestures soft and feline; he spoke Russian slowly, with a strong Caucasian accent, carefully weighing every word while his whole being radiated the consciousness of power. By contrast with the stuttering and malign Molotov, the dictator was always – or nearly always – amiable in manner. Surrounded by uniformed officers and civilians garbed in blue suits, the grey-tunicked Supremo, with his grey breeches tucked into jack-boots, made a modest impression. Yet his commissars, generals and admirals, though self-confident enough outside the Presence, cringed before him in obvious readiness to execute his every order with blind fanaticism.[22]

Less subservient by training, Anders deduced from his discussions with Stalin that the Poles on Soviet territory were faced with annihilation. He therefore sought, and eventually obtained, permission to evacuate a sizeable contingent, including civilians. Once the sole source of all decisions had signified assent, and once the NKVD – the only effective organization in the Soviet Union – had been put in charge, swift action resulted, and a large convoy of Poles proceeded to Iran. Thus did Anders bring a hundred thousand fellow-countrymen out of Muscovite thraldom; but he had to leave a far larger number behind.

As Soviet-Polish discussions proceeded, one sinister shadow began to loom ever larger: the fate of the fifteen thousand Soviet-captured Polish prisoners, chiefly officers, of whom the Poles had extensive records up to May 1940, at which point all traces abruptly vanished. It was not yet realized that these missing persons had been exterminated, about one third of them by mass execution in the woods at Katyn near Smolensk; as stated above, this very probably occurred at the initiative of Stalin or Beria, and at least with their prior knowledge.[23] Questioned on the whereabouts of these absentees by Polish representatives, Stalin claimed – improbably enough – that they must have escaped to Manchuria. Alternatively, said he, *a rumour was afoot* that they had turned up in Franz Josef Land![24] One is reminded of the Russian Tsar-Emperor Paul, during whose reign Siberian deportees frequently disappeared without trace: but only as individuals, never on so large a scale. Yet such was the vastness of Russia, such the slovenliness of her administrative methods – except when locally galvanized into savage simulated activity by the random impact of a sovereign will – that (it seemed for a time) the missing fifteen thousand might have become genuinely mislaid. As will be shown below, their posthumous saga was to complicate relations between Stalin and his allies in the later part of the war.

Stalingrad

In late March 1942, Stalin held a combined conference of the State Defence Committee and leading generals to determine future strategy – or, rather, to confirm a plan on which he himself was already resolved. This again envisaged multiple counter-attacks at widely separated points of the front: a procedure yet again opposed by Zhukov, who would have preferred to concentrate on a single devastating offensive in the centre, while remaining on the defensive elsewhere. This advice was rejected by the Commander-in-Chief: 'Are we supposed to sit . . . idling away our time and wait for the Germans to attack first?' Stalin asked, stressing the need to strike several spoiling blows over a wide front and probe the enemy's readiness.[1]

Unfortunately Stalin's broad-front strategy proved unsuccessful. The collapse of a local Soviet offensive in the Crimea was followed by the German capture of the whole peninsula. An attempt by Soviet Army Group North-West to seize the initiative near Demyansk also failed, and an ambitious bid to recapture Kharkov ended in downright disaster. It was on the Kharkov campaign of 1942 that Khrushchev, another re-writer of history, based a serious criticism of Stalin as a military leader. Himself then leading political officer in the area, Khrushchev claims to have urged Stalin to discontinue the drive against Kharkov once this had begun to threaten the attackers, rather than the attacked, with encirclement. Khrushchev says that he telephoned Vasilevsky, asking him to tell Stalin that the Kharkov operations must be cancelled; he also advised explaining the situation to the Commander-in-Chief on a map – as opposed to the globe on which Stalin always planned his operations. Informed that Stalin's mind was made up, Khrushchev next tried to telephone him personally at his villa – only to be fobbed off by Malenkov, who repeated the order to continue the offensive as planned. Stalin was standing close by, but could not even bother to pick up the receiver. The outcome was a defeat involving the loss of Soviet troops by the hundred thousand. Such, says Khrushchev, was the military genius of one who demanded incessant frontal attacks and the capture of village after village . . . of one whose generals did eventually succeed in imposing a more flexible approach, but only to be downgraded after victory by a Leader who insisted that every triumph at the front should be credited to himself. Khrushchev also accused Stalin of maligning Zhukov, chief among the generals degraded after the war, by attributing to him the habit of smelling a handful of earth as a means of deciding whether or not to order an attack.[2]

Zhukov's memoirs give an entirely different version of these events. It is Stalin whom Zhukov describes as worried about the Kharkov envelopment in May 1942 . . . and as reassured by Khrushchev.[3] Moreover, while it is true that Stalin did keep a terrestrial globe in his office, nothing could be more misleading than to suggest that he dispensed with situation maps. It is, however, also true that widely spaced spoiling offensives, as imposed by Stalin on his generals in spring 1942, were based on an over-optimistic reading of the situation. Stalin further erred in mid-1942 by misreading the *Wehrmacht*'s impending strategy. The Soviet leader believed that Moscow would remain the chief target, as during the previous winter. But Hitler – unwisely, one may feel – had decided to concentrate a dual thrust on the south, aiming both to capture the Caucasian oil fields and to cut the Volga, that vital Soviet artery, at Stalingrad. Had this two-pronged offensive succeeded, as for two months seemed likely, the fall of Moscow might indeed have been an indirect consequence.

Launching the German summer offensive, Hitler won a series of devastating victories until a conclusive German victory once again seemed likely. On 23 August, Hitlerite forces reached the Volga on a five-mile front north of Stalingrad. Severely bombing the city itself, they temporarily severed its communications with Moscow, whereupon the Soviet Commander-in-Chief jumped to the conclusion that Stalingrad had immediately fallen; when radio contact was at last re-established, he gave Vasilevsky a dressing-down memorable even by Stalinist standards.[4] But the city had not in fact fallen, and was not to do so entirely, although the Germans did manage to occupy the greater part of it after a few weeks' heavy fighting. Further south they had earlier captured Rostov and Novorossiysk, and were swiftly driving through the northern Caucasus. They planted a swastika flag on the summit of Mount Elbrus, almost in sight of Stalin's birthplace, and the road to Baku and the oilfields seemed to lie open to them.

Impressive though such gains were, making October 1942 the blackest month of the war for the Russians, Hitler was in fact committing himself beyond his resources. It was as an embattled nation of seventy-eight million, assisted by several half-hearted allies, that Germany had invaded the ill-prepared Soviet Union with its eve-of-war population of 190 million. Now this immense difference was at last beginning to tell. Depleted and ravaged by over a year's hard fighting in Russia, the *Wehrmacht* had over-extended its energies, its supplies and its communication links. Now the dissipation of effort was further aggravated by concentration on two separate targets: the oil of the Caucasus (so sorely needed by the strained German economy) and Stalingrad. On the capture of that city Hitler had staked his prestige, and it might indeed have been possible for the Germans to take either Stalingrad or the Caucasian oil-fields. The trouble was that they could not manage both. In any case, as it turned out, the Fuehrer's error was less that of selecting Stalingrad as a target in the first place than that of seeking to hold the city's devastated rubble long after strategic retreat had become imperative. After three months' intensive fighting, Stalingrad developed into the swivel on which initiative decisively passed from Hitler to Stalin, and – in the world at large – from Axis to Allies.

By now Stalin had begun to learn the folly of dictating too imperiously to his senior generals. On 26 August, shortly after the Germans had reached the Volga, he appointed Zhukov to the new and specially created post of Deputy Supreme Commander-in-Chief, and sent him to Stalingrad to co-ordinate the defences in conjunction with Vasilevsky. At the beginning of September a Soviet counter-plan began to take shape in the minds of General Headquarters, at the very time when Stalingrad's fortunes were at their lowest ebb. The over-all conception was Zhukov's and Vasilevsky's. No hasty improvisation, their grand design involved accumulating massive reserves over a forty-five-day period during which the enemy must be held off by 'active defence'. It was with the Battle of Stalingrad that Stalin at last began to show a true understanding of military strategy.[5] Such, at least, is the testimony of Zhukov, who naturally equates the acquisition of this skill with willingness to give greater heed to his own advice.

On 17 November a curious incident occurred, reflecting the aberrations to which Stalin's leadership remained liable. A mere forty-eight hours before the scheduled start of operations to relieve Stalingrad, the Commander-in-Chief suddenly summoned Vasilevsky from that front to the Kremlin. It turned out that a subordinate general on the Stalingrad front – Volsky, Commander of 4 Mechanized Corps – had written directly to Stalin over Vasilevsky's head in order to complain that the forthcoming offensive was doomed owing to inadequate preparation. In reply, Vasilevsky assured Stalin of his continued confidence in the agreed plan, and insisted that operations should proceed accordingly. Then Stalin telephoned Volsky: not to threaten the execution of that harassed general as a panic-monger, but to speak a few kindly, reassuring words. He also asked Vasilevsky to keep a keen eye on 4 Mechanized Corps and make a personal report on its progress to himself.[6] Thus two generals – one the other's subordinate – were encouraged to report on each other to Stalin while, as a matter of routine, the NKVD and the army's Political Administration were simultaneously reporting on both . . . and, incidentally, on each other too. Such was the nature of Stalinist controls, military and civilian alike.

Despite these preliminary alarms the Soviet counter-offensive duly opened on 19 November, when the Germans in Stalingrad found themselves seized by a vast enveloping movement. The more powerful pincer came curling round from two Soviet army groups in the north-west, and within four days this north-western claw had met the southern. German Sixth Army was now surrounded in Stalingrad, trapped as so many Soviet armies had been trapped during earlier campaigns. The doomed pocket was eventually cleaned out by 2 February 1943. Defeated at Stalingrad, the Germans began to extract their exposed forces from the Caucasus, and the Red Army could begin the slow process of driving the invader out of Soviet territory.

At the time of the Stalingrad campaign Stalin was much concerned to boost two institutions on which war-winning morale depended: the Red Army and the Orthodox Church.

Ornate epaulettes – previously reviled for their association with the Imperial Russian class system – were added to Soviet officers' uniform, large consignments of gold braid being ordered from Britain – much to the surprise of the suppliers.[7] More effective, perhaps, as a morale-booster was the decision – implemented at the height of the Stalingrad battle – to abandon the system of dual control whereby each Commanding Officer was flanked by a Political Commissar enjoying comparable status to himself. Military discipline was tightened, and commanders were instructed to shoot cowards and traitors on the spot. Then, in March 1943, Stalin identified his person more closely with the Red Army by promoting himself Marshal of the Soviet Union.

Always a pragmatist, Stalin recognized the importance of religion as a morale-building factor. Propaganda against the Russian Orthodox Church was suspended at the outbreak of war, and the Church responded by blessing the war efforts of the atheist state now converted into a champion of Christendom. Believers subscribed to supply the army with a tank column named after an early Russian military-ideological hero, Grand Prince Dmitry Donskoy, and a ceremony followed during which the Metropolitan Nikolay preached an informal sermon on the Christian's duty to hate his enemies. Further abandoning strict theological doctrine, the Metropolitan also alluded to Stalin as '*our common Father* [*sic*; capital in the original] Joseph Vissarionovich', thereby suggesting that the system of dual command – so recently abandoned by the Red Army on earth – had now been adopted in spheres more exalted. In the following year Stalin was to receive three Metropolitans, establishing in effect a concordat which permitted the Church to elect a Patriarch and governing body (the Holy Synod) and to publish a journal. Stalin also set up a Soviet for the Affairs of the Russian Orthodox Church . . . headed by a secret police official.[8] The clergy was encouraged to underwrite Stalinist propaganda by sponsoring international 'peace offensives', and by assuring foreigners that Soviet citizens enjoyed greater freedom to practise religion than was in fact the case. One by-product of the new policy towards the Church was a decrease in the antipathy with which the non-Soviet world regarded the avowedly atheist Soviet state. Official toleration of Russia's national religion lent colour to a view of Stalin which he himself had long fostered: that of a fervent nationalist who had abandoned Marxist dogma and the goal of world revolution.

By disbanding the Comintern in May 1943, Stalin further encouraged this misconception. He was careful, though, to keep the Comintern apparatus secretly in being, tightening rather than relaxing Moscow's iron control over foreign Communist parties.

All these measures played their part in strengthening Soviet resistance to German aggression. However, as the war developed, another factor was seen to play an overwhelmingly dominant role in boosting the Soviet will to win: Hitler's ruthless policy towards occupied Stalinist territory. Operating partly through the Gestapo and the SS, the German dictator proceeded to enslave and exterminate the occupied Soviet peoples in quantity, treating them as inferiors fit only to serve the German *Herrenvolk*. Thus did Hitler accomplish the truly spectacular feat of persecuting Stalin's subjects more cruelly than Stalin. In the end Hitler may have killed almost as many Soviet citizens – between twenty and thirty million – in a mere four-year period as Stalin contrived to destroy during a quarter of a century. Under these circumstances the Soviet population had no alternative but to rally to its own dictator as the lesser of two appalling evils.

Thus paradoxically did Hitler – perhaps the only man whom Stalin ever trusted – repay Stalin in the end by rendering his position yet more impregnable . . . for in 1945 Stalin was to add to the many other advantages which he already enjoyed as a wielder of totalitarian power the immense prestige of victory over another, yet more intensely detested, political psychopath.

Family Life

Stalin's family life, never a very prominent feature in his biography, dwindled during the war.

Of his elder son, Yakov Dzhugashvili – an army officer – the dictator saw no more after Yakov had been taken prisoner by the Germans on the Belo-russian front, early in the war. Stalin then conceived the idea, typical of his mentality, that his son had deliberately betrayed him. As we remember, all captured Soviet troops were presumed guilty of treason under Stalinism, and the dictator saw no reason why his first-born should be the sole excep-tion. Yakov's Jewish wife must also, surely, have had a hand in the plot? For good measure she was imprisoned by the NKVD, one among many of Stalin's relatives by marriage to suffer that fate. Meanwhile the German authorities were making much of having Yakov Dzhugashvili as their prisoner. They dropped leaflets on Moscow displaying the young officer's photograph, but they did not succeed in extorting anti-Stalinist statements from him. At one stage they contrived to propose exchanging this very special prisoner for some valued German captive in Soviet hands – an overture turned down by Stalin on the grounds that 'war is war'.[1]

So utterly did the dictator reject his first-born that he even claimed to have no son called Yakov. Broadcast by the German radio, these words reached Yakov Dzhugashvili in his prison camp, whereupon he reputedly committed suicide by throwing himself on electrified barbed wire; another version of his death (that credited by his father) has him shot by the Ger-mans.[2] Always a weakling in his father's view, Yakov showed himself extremely callous in his comments, made in German captivity, on the Poles massacred at Katyn in 1940. Not questioning Soviet responsibility for this affair, he considered the slaughtered officers to have been patently ripe for elimination as members of the intelligentsia: 'the most dangerous element to us'.[3] If correctly reported, this comment of Stalin's first-born helps to temper the regrets due from posterity over his untimely liquidation.

Yakov's half-brother Vasily, born to Stalin and his second wife Nadezhda in 1921, was less prone to exasperate his father than the inoffensive Yakov, for the dictator always did tend to feel at home with those rare individuals who appeared to operate on a lower moral plane than himself. To create such an impression Vasily worked hard, if at nothing else. Described by one witness as a 'beastly, pampered schoolboy',[4] the young man was thought to suffer from a surfeit of fast cars, girls and alcohol. He joined the air force and was fawned on by his fellow pilots, openly trading on his father's name. But Stalin did not indulge Vasily; indeed, he was continually finding fault with the youth. It was the dictator's toadies, from Beria downwards, who attempted to ingratiate themselves by fostering the second son's spec-tacular promotion. Beginning the war as a twenty-year-old captain, Vasily Stalin ended it as a prematurely dissipated lieutenant-general aged twenty-four.[5]

Of Stalin's three children, Svetlana had always been his favourite. After her mother's death in 1932, the dictator saw less and less of her too, but she did occasionally figure as hostess at his famous improvised supper parties; in fact, 'hostess' (*khozyayka*) was one of Stalin's nicknames for her. Winston Churchill recalls a social occasion in Moscow at which the dictator unexpectedly produced his handsome, red-haired, sixteen-year-old daughter with a twinkle in his eye and the air of one wishing to show that Bolsheviks too were capable of having a family life.[6]

Officiating occasionally at suppertime orgies less 'cultured' than those staged for the British Prime Minister, Svetlana usually felt constrained to leave the room at some point owing to the obscene language cultivated in that company. It was perhaps as well that ladies were generally excluded from these appalling stag parties. But when, exceptionally, feminine company did appear at the villa, the dictator would comport himself with studious gallantry: he was apt to proffer a magnificent spray of lilac to the wife of some marshal or aircraft designer. That Stalin's drinking habits were moderate his daughter also confirms, recalling only one occasion on which she ever saw her father the worse for drink: he was singing folk-song duets with a tipsy Minister of Health. Svetlana Alliluyeva also speaks of the crude practical jokes which were usual at these orgies. Without lowering his dignity by direct participation, her father would look on benignly as some prankster placed a ripe tomato on the chair of an unsuspecting guest, while another wit might be lacing someone's wine with salt or vodka. Mikoyan and Poskryobyshev were the licensed buffoons and butts of Kuntsevo, the latter often having to be carried home dead drunk after vomiting in the bathroom.[7]

Stalin's daughter also confirms that these macabre saturnalia became increasingly indecorous in course of time.

During the war a serious breach occurred between father and daughter when Stalin discovered that Svetlana had been meeting a man some twenty years older than herself, and that the two had fallen in love. The object of her affections, a certain Kapler, happened to be Jewish – which struck the jealous father as an added aggravation when the friendship was reported to him by his police. Why, he must repeatedly have wondered, must all his relatives be so compulsively philosemitic? Himself least of all liable to this particular foible, he had Kapler sent to an arctic concentration camp as a British spy, thus blighting his daughter's first love affair. Not surprisingly, Svetlana could never again think of her father with her old affection after this.[8]

12
Generalissimo

From Kursk to Berlin

IN mid-1943 Stalin's chief military anxieties were focussed on the Battle of Kursk, which took place over a huge area centred three hundred miles south of his capital. This was the third – after Moscow and Stalingrad – in the trio of great engagements which contributed most to driving the invaders out of the Soviet Union. The battle began – like its predecessors – with a German attack: on 4 July, Hitlerite forces began to assail the large Soviet salient around Kursk. But the Soviet command was ready for the Germans, having already appreciated that they would make their main effort here. Once again Stalin had accepted a plan jointly proposed by Zhukov, Vasilevsky and others: to let the enemy take the initiative and batter himself against well-prepared Soviet defences, after which powerful Red Army reserves would be launched in a devastating counter-offensive.[1]

Anxious and keyed up over what was to prove the greatest armoured engagement in military annals, Stalin occasionally showed himself eager to commit his forces prematurely – but remained open, says Zhukov, to the sound professional advice offered by Vasilevsky and Zhukov.[2] During the crucial two months following the German attack the plan proved its worth, the main enemy momentum subsiding after the first few days of massed tank clashes. By 5 August Soviet troops had taken Oryol and Belgorod, much-disputed Kharkov following on the 23rd of the same month. This counter-offensive was better prepared than those of Moscow and Stalingrad; larger forces were involved; it was the first occasion on which Soviet commanders effectively controlled massed tanks and mechanized units.

During this period Stalin came nearest to paying his one and only visit to the 'front': a curiously stage-managed episode. On 3 August he suddenly turned up at a place called Yukhnov, about 120 miles south-west of Moscow, and gave audience in a small hut to Marshal Voronov, who had been specially summoned to this rendezvous from the firing line. Yukhnov

344

itself was at least seventy miles away from the action. But – with or without Stalin's knowledge – the area had been rigged to simulate proximity to combat conditions: an inversion, as it were, of the 'Potemkin villages' once used to conjure up the image of non-existent peacetime prosperity and thus to feed the ego of an earlier autocrat, Catherine the Great. Stimulated by this synthetic exposure to combat conditions, the supreme ruler demanded a report on the current military situation before twice uttering an oracular statement about the need to capture Smolensk by spring 1944. Then conversation lapsed. As Voronov retraced his route to the front over rutted roads barely passable, he found himself wondering why on earth this arduous journey had been deemed necessary.[3]

Can this have been the episode which Khrushchev had in mind when he stated that Stalin 'never visited any section of the front or any liberated city except for one short ride on the Mozhaysk Highway during a lull in the fighting'?[4] Tough and intrepid in so many ways, the Supreme Commander-in-Chief clearly had no relish for the whiff of cordite. Meanwhile, since early in the war, Soviet propaganda had been fabricating a martial image more suitable for the warrior-leader of a nation in arms than that of a Kremlin-bound recluse. A painting, *Stalin at the Front near Moscow, 1941*, was widely reproduced on posters and postcards; it showed the fur-coated Commander-in-Chief standing at the edge of a wood and training his binoculars on Soviet troops engaged in assaulting German positions.[5] Stalin's failure ever to visit – in any real sense – the Soviet front line did not of course prevent him from invoking such an obligation as an occasional pretext for his inability to quit Moscow for conferences with allied statesmen. In August 1943 he excused himself from meeting Churchill and Roosevelt at Scapa Flow, or some other distant place, on the ground that he had to visit the fronts 'more often than usual'.[6] A year later the Soviet leader is found complaining to Churchill that he never felt well except in Moscow, and that 'even his visits to the front did him harm.'[7]

It was after returning from the Yukhnov Expedition that Stalin first commemorated a victory in the field by solemn radio announcement, artillery salvo and multicoloured pyrotechnics in Moscow. The first salute, in honour of the liberation of Oryol and Belgorod, was by twelve salvos from 124 guns. On 23 August the recapture of Kharkov earned twenty salvos from 224 guns. Stalin reserved to himself alone the right to sanction such salutes, of which some three hundred were to follow in the course of the war. He also took a keen interest in the text of the preceding radio announcements, as mellifluously intoned by the star announcer Levitan. On one occasion the dictator raged and swore because the name of Marshal Konev had been accidentally omitted from Levitan's text; the broadcast had to be stopped and re-started so that Konev could be included, the staff officer responsible for the faulty script being very lucky to escape dismissal. [8]

The war's victorious progress, as viewed from the Kremlin, is charted in speeches and Orders of the Day delivered by Stalin on dates of ritual significance: Red Army Day (23 February), Labour Day (1 May) and the anniversary (7 November) of the 'October' Revolution. His anniversary speech of November 1943 commemorated the first major Soviet summer counter-offensive:[9] that which followed the victory at Kursk.

Such was the success of Russian arms that, by the end of the year, Germany stood virtually alone; her various allies, Finland and Rumania in particular, were already seeking means of escaping from the Hitlerite camp. And 1944 saw Soviet victories yet more devastating. In Stalin's Order of the Day of 7 November ten such major blows are listed. Finland has been knocked out of the war. In Belorussia three German armies have been smashed, and more than half a million German prisoners taken. Further south the Red Army has encircled and destroyed two German armies, capturing over a quarter of a million prisoners. Routed in Rumania and flung out of Bulgaria, the *Wehrmacht* is beginning to suffer defeat in Hungary even as Stalin is speaking, while German forces in the Baltic have also been crushed. Through these and other Soviet triumphs the enemy has been entirely expelled from the pre-war territory of the USSR, and is now fighting on his home ground.[10] Within a few months his capital city, Berlin, will have fallen, and Germany will have surrendered unconditionally to Stalin and his allies.

Such had been the rigours of Stalinism in the late 1930s that many Soviet citizens had even experienced relief on becoming involved in one of the most savage wars of modern times. Among those welcoming Soviet-German hostilities were those Soviet concentration camp inmates who were permitted to volunteer for service in front-line punitive battalions. The hazards of warfare were bliss compared to the horrors of camp. Nor were these most abject of the dictator's victims alone in welcoming the war. 'Everyone without exception, at home, and at the front . . . all took a deep breath and flung themselves into the furnace of this deadly, liberating struggle with real joy, with rapture.'[11] Among the various advantages conferred by wartime conditions were: a reduction in the quota of nocturnal arrests carried out by NKVD raiding parties; freedom to practise religion without undue molestation; a reduction in the psychological burden imposed by Soviet propaganda now that its chief theme was no longer Marxist ideology but Russian nationalist sentiment.

Despite such relaxations, the Stalinist state did not change its essence. The Red Army remained subject to ferocious punitive discipline applied through the NKVD as well as through more regular military channels. Evolving the dreaded field security organ known as Smersh, the Soviet political police also maintained from the beginning of the war blocking battalions, which operated behind the fronts and were charged with shooting down Red Army troops retreating before the German onslaught. To be cut off by the enemy, to be encircled, to be taken prisoner . . . all these misfortunes were officially regarded as treason, rendering the culprit liable to imprisonment or shooting. In the early months of the war, ill-equipped and tactically mishandled Soviet troops again and again showed themselves capable of improvising a desperate defence against overwhelming odds. But on fighting their way out of encirclement these heroes were liable to be shot as traitors by other Soviet units freshly arrived from the rear; then, often enough, these very executioners would themselves fall into enemy encirclement and battle their way out in turn: only to fall victims to the same ferociously misapplied disciplinary syndrome.[12] As noted above, Soviet officers and commissars were empowered to shoot out of hand those subordinates whom they cared to identify as cowards and traitors. As for the several millions of Red Army personnel captured, starved and cruelly misused by the Germans, Moscow's official view was that all were traitors whose fate was of no importance. Later, on 'liberation' by the Red Army, such unfortunates often found themselves exchanging a German for a Soviet concentration camp. Even members of a soldier's family were responsible in law for his conduct in the field, relatives of prisoners of war being liable to long terms of imprisonment.[13] That Stalin himself had been rendered liable to prosecution under this head, owing to the capture by the Germans of his son Yakov, no one in the dictator's entourage was (one presumes) rash enough to point out.

The war period also witnessed the deportation of whole nations within the vast confines of the Soviet Union. Trucked to Siberia or Central Asia under atrocious conditions, the freight was, as ever, liable to perish in transit. The total of Soviet peoples deported in their entirety during the war is eight, so far as has yet been discovered, making a rough tally of some 1,650,000 souls.[14] First to go were the Germans of the Volga German Autonomous Republic, removed in accordance with a Supreme Soviet decree of 28 August 1941. A characteristic Stalinist trick was played on the victims at the outset, when an NKVD battalion parachuted into the area disguised as Hitlerite Germans; Volga denizens showing sympathy with these simulated Teutons were then massacred on the spot,[15] thus easing the pressure on available transport and assisting the complex logistics of the operation.

347

Between October 1943 and November 1944 seven more small nations or peoples were deported: the Chechens, the Ingushes, the Karachays and the Balkars of the northern Caucasus; the Kalmyks from the steppelands north-west of the Caspian; the Crimean Tatars; the Meskhetians. Not until the late 1960s did the deportation of this last-named people, who lived near the Soviet-Turkish border, become known to the world: an index of the strict security clamp imposed on these measures as a whole. Where else but in Russia could 200,000 persons vanish without trace . . . and so effectively that no clinching evidence of their disappearance was picked up for a quarter of a century? The Meskhetians were presumably deported for military reasons: the need to clear a frontier area of potentially disaffected peoples. By contrast, the other six uprooted nations of 1943-4 probably suffered for collaboration with the invading Germans, by whom all had been partly or wholly overrun. Most of these peoples also had a record of opposition to Russian rule stretching back into the pre-Soviet period, such indiscipline being particularly obnoxious to the Tsars' latest heir. That the decision to exile whole nations was primarily Stalin's may be inferred from the scale of these operations. An account does, however, exist of a joint meeting, on 11 February 1943 between the Politburo and the Soviet High Command, during which Stalin supported a postponement of the Chechen deportation . . . and this against the advice of Molotov and others who wished to see the Chechen-Ingush Republic liquidated immediately.[16]

Two additional, classically Stalinist features of this affair may be noted. The first is the stratagem whereby the Chechens were collectively kidnapped. They had been induced to forgather in celebration of Red Army Day on 23 February 1944 in association with locally billeted army units purportedly engaged on harmless manoeuvres in the mountains – but secretly charged with kidnapping duties. At a prearranged moment these police troops suddenly turned on the roistering natives, shooting down many and removing others in American Lease-Lend trucks.[17] Secondly, this particular deportation well illustrates the perverted symmetry of Stalin's mind. Back in 1913, Stalin had described this small nation – which he himself was to persecute so severely three decades later – as doomed to incredible suffering and extinction . . . by Tsarist oppression.[18]

So much for the peoples deported by Stalin in their entirety, to which it must be added that other extensive but selective deportations – of Greeks, of Jews, of Balts, of Ukrainians – also took place during or after the war. In all these operations Stalin showed himself a true heir, not merely of the Russian Emperors and Tsars, but also of the Muscovite Grand Princes who preceded the Tsars. Since the days of Ivan the Great, who ruled Muscovy from 1462 to 1504, it had been customary for Russian sovereigns to decree the large-scale forcible redistribution of their populations for political reasons.

To Stalin these deportations were no more than minor administrative adjustments, since his chief energies were naturally reserved for the victorious prosecution of the war. After Hitler's suicide and after the storming of Berlin and the defunct Fuehrer's bunker by Russian troops, Germany surrendered unconditionally on 7 May 1945. On 24 May, Stalin spoke at a Kremlin reception in honour of assembled Red Army officers. Never had the Georgian dictator shown himself a more fervent Russian patriot by adoption than now, as he singled out the Russians as outstanding for their wartime record among the many peoples of the USSR. He toasted the Russians as the guiding force within the USSR, and as remarkable for steadfastness of mind and character. Stalin also admitted that his government had made many mistakes during the war, referring to moments of despair which had been experienced during the great retreat of 1941–2. He said that any other people might have told their government that it had let them down, and must give way to an administration which would seek peace with Germany; but the Russian people had not shown such lack of faith, and its confidence in the Soviet Government had proved the decisive force in achieving victory over Fascism, the enemy of humanity.[19] Thus Stalin, now rendered immeasurably more powerful than before by his triumph over Hitler, apologized in his own characteristic manner for the gross errors through which he had involved his country in the early disasters of the war.

Stalin's toast to the Russian people was the prelude to a determined post-war campaign to denigrate the conquering Soviet marshals and other military heroes whose dangerously accumulating prestige threatened to rival his own. To counteract this the dictator had himself increasingly publicized as the supreme military genius who had won the war almost single-handed: a propaganda campaign which gathered way from the victory of Stalingrad onwards. On 24 June 1945 a victory parade was held in the Red Square, and was followed by a banquet during which Stalin remarked, according to one witness, that he was thinking of retiring in two or three years' time:[20] a thought which, as we remember, he was apt to express at not infrequent intervals. Shortly after this episode Stalin assumed the newly created supreme military rank of Generalissimo, also receiving the title of Hero of the Soviet Union to add to the Order of Suvorov and two Orders of Victory also conferred upon himself.

Under Western Eyes

The dictator's handling of relations with his allies continued to reflect his methods and personality throughout the war. In contacts with the West it was Stalin who made the running; Stalin who imposed the pattern of negotiation and fraternization; Stalin in the end who emerged the victor, almost, over his own allies as well as over Hitler. This success the Soviet dictator owed to his single-minded pursuit of long-term advantage, combined with the fact that he represented an unfamiliar and little understood phenomenon; one could devote a lifetime to politics in London or Washington without ever encountering a Dzhugashvili. Stalin was also ruthless in exploiting the natural sympathy, or even guilt, with which his Anglo-American allies contemplated the appalling sufferings inflicted on the Kremlin-ruled peoples by Germany: sufferings such as the British and American populations were mercifully spared. That Stalin had done his best during nearly two years of alliance with Hitler to deflect these agonies on to his new allies rather than to combine in averting them, British spokesmen tactfully failed to point out, though their country had stood alone against the might of Hitler and Stalin during much of that period.

Exploiting this situation, Stalin and his agents were inclined to treat their Western contacts with condescension, ungraciousness or downright rudeness. When, as so often happened, foreign representatives reacted by attempting to placate the surly dictator, he would only become more surly still. There were occasions, though, when someone chose to snap back, whereupon Stalin would give way gracefully, bringing into play the formidable social charm which he held in reserve.

These general features were to be observed at all levels of Soviet-Western wartime contact. Clamouring incessantly for a Second Front to be opened in western Europe, and having all his underlings briefed to do the same, Stalin seemed to think that an invasion of the Hitler-occupied coast could be launched on words alone, and without regard to concrete military possibilities. That his own troops were actually fighting what might be called a second front, having been engaged on the other side in the days of the first (Polish, French and other) fronts, Stalin's allies did not feel inclined to point out. When the new front, already demanded by Stalin in 1941, still failed to develop in 1942, Britain became the target for a virulent Soviet press campaign which included newspaper cartoons depicting the country as dominated by 'Colonel Blimps'. The British were charged with providing a refuge for gangsters: an accusation based on the flight to Scotland of Rudolf Hess, which still rankled with Ribbentrop's former host.[1]

As the tide of victory began to run against Hitler, Stalin's attitude to his alien associates – one can hardly call them allies – only became more grudging and ungenerous, until the impression was even created that the Soviet leaders were deliberately undermining all enterprises jointly undertaken with foreigners. Such an attitude appeared, for example, to dominate Soviet treatment of British naval personnel stationed at the Soviet arctic port of Murmansk. Engaged in servicing the convoys which brought much-needed supplies to Russia, these sailors were deliberately harassed by the Soviet authorities after Stalin had taken it into his head that they refused to treat the local population as their equals. This, to the dictator, only added insult to the injuries inflicted (he suspected) on the Soviet Union by the British, whose power and malignancy he had always been prone to exaggerate. In the end the irritations caused and received in Murmansk, together with associated disputes over British convoys to Russia, led to a serious quarrel between Moscow and London; one particularly rude letter from Stalin was handed back to his ambassador on Churchill's orders. Prepared in the last resort to stop the convoys to Murmansk rather than subject the Royal Navy to continued humiliation, Churchill eventually obtained the concessions which were usually forthcoming in the end whenever an allied statesman dared to defy Stalin.[2] As has been well noted, 'Soviet officials are much happier, more amenable and less suspicious when an adversary drives a hard bargain than when he succumbs easily to Soviet demands':[3] an attitude which, like most things in the Soviet Union, percolated down from the summit.

The United States Navy, by contrast – having no Churchill to defend it – signally failed to budge Stalin when thwarted in its turn at a later stage of the war. The Russians had now captured the important German experimental submarine station at Gdynia, but refused access to American naval experts. They thus prevented the Americans from investigating technical means whereby their convoys – still running the highly dangerous German submarine blockade, and with vital supplies to Russia – might be protected. Had the decision depended on General Deane, head of the US Military Mission to the USSR, these convoys would have been suspended until such time as the Russians should give way over Gdynia. But other counsels prevailed. Unfortunately, 'there were still some people in Washington who lived in dire fear of risking Soviet displeasure.'[4]

In keeping with his general suspiciousness, Stalin became obsessed with the notion that Western statesmen were seeking a separate peace with Hitler. Perhaps he projected into their minds the policy which he himself would have been following in their place; for the greater German resistance in the west during the last phase of the war, the brighter became the prospects for Soviet encroachments in the east such as ultimately menaced British and American interests. Stalin's suspicions inspired a *Pravda* article of January 1944 claiming that peace talks between Ribbentrop and two leading Britons were taking place in a Spanish or Portuguese coastal town.[5] Similarly, an acute crisis of nerves developed in the Kremlin when Stalin was informed of the surrender of German forces in Italy to the British; this affair led to a bitter exchange between Moscow and London, as recorded in Churchill's memoirs.[6] Flimsily based or not, such suspicions evidently caused the Soviet dictator genuine suffering. They were more than a histrionic device craftily designed to extract some advantage, though – Stalin being Stalin – they were always liable to be converted at any moment into just such a ploy.

There were, however, also occasions – rare enough – when the dictator was willing to make amends for his surliness. For example, in November 1942, he praised – albeit condescendingly – the Anglo-American invasion of North Africa.[7] Nor had he any objection to the associated Allied deal with the French Admiral Darlan, who was tainted by links with Vichy. 'Military discipline [Stalin told Churchill on 27 November] should know how to use ... not only the Darlans, but even the devil and his grandmother.'[8] The remark happens to echo a similar better-known comment made by Churchill – and with regard to his own co-operation with Stalin – to the effect that: 'If Hitler invaded hell I would make at least a favourable reference to the Devil in the House of Commons.'[9]

The Anglo-American invasion of German-held France, which began with the Normandy landings of 6 June 1944, at last created the Second Front for which Stalin had so long clamoured. His response, recorded in *Pravda* of 14 June, was suitably generous: 'Military history knows no other enterprise comparable in its breadth of conception, the grandeur of its dimensions and the mastery of its execution.'[10] Visiting Moscow a year later, the Allied Supreme Commander General Eisenhower was questioned in detail by Stalin and others on the logistics of operations in France and the Low Countries: the questioners' manner suggested that, of all the spectacular feats of the war – even including their own – allied success in organizing the supply services for the pursuit of the Germans across France would go down in history as the most astonishing.[11]

Veering between skilfully modulated cordiality and truculent assertiveness, Stalin's negotiating techniques enabled him to dominate even his two most powerful opposite numbers, Roosevelt and Churchill, with whom he held three conferences in the later part of the war: those of Teheran (November-December 1943), Yalta (February 1945) and Potsdam (July-August

1945). As the only member of the 'Big Three' who appears, in retrospect, to have known what he wanted all along, Stalin set himself – at these conclaves and in the associated diplomatic moves – to make the post-war world safe for Stalinism. His aim was not only to reincorporate into the Soviet Union all the various European lands annexed in 1939-41, but also to extend Soviet control further into central Europe and thus create an additional *cordon sanitaire* to protect the original protective belt snatched during the period of the Nazi-Soviet Pact. In the event only small portions of these newly incorporated areas were to be annexed outright, the remainder being converted into satellite states nominally independent, but ruled by puppet governments subservient to Moscow. In Stalin's appreciation the key to control of these future marionettes lay in the centre of his western frontiers – not on their northern and southern fringes. This meant that Poland – the largest and potentially most powerful of his earmarked dependencies – was to play the most crucial role of all. If Stalin could assert full control there, adding such other centrally placed eastern European states as Rumania, Bulgaria and Hungary, he was prepared to let the periphery go, permitting Finland in the extreme north and Greece in the extreme south to retain their independence.

We have no evidence enabling us to define exactly when Stalin decided to swallow large new tracts of eastern Europe. That the whole operation was scheduled long in advance in exact detail we may be permitted to doubt. More probably the pragmatical Stalin stumbled into the programme step by step, prompted by what – to repeat – was the guiding principle of his wartime diplomacy: that of making the post-war world safe for himself and his political system. As for the methods of achieving this goal, the dictator depended, as usual, on force and the threat of force, being well poised to do so in eastern Europe since it was he alone among the major Allies who had his troops on the ground in that part of the world. But force was only one element in the armament of a politician as complete as Stalin. He also set himself to 'sell' his conquest of eastern Europe to his main allies, among whom the British had gone to war specifically in order to safeguard Polish sovereignty. Even Stalin could not of course infuse Churchill and Roosevelt with active enthusiasm for his takeover of eastern Europe. But by using stubbornness, patience and various wiles he could, and eventually did, induce them to acquiesce in his carefully phased and camouflaged piecemeal annexations.

It was unfortunate for the Poles, as also for Stalin's other victims in eastern Europe, that the most powerful potential champion of their cause should have been a statesman as insensitive to the Soviet dictator's true nature – and as handicapped by ill health – as Franklin D. Roosevelt. The

American President was consistently outwitted by Stalin whenever their paths crossed. He seemed, indeed, eager to outwit himself without even putting Stalin to the trouble. With phenomenal complacency, Roosevelt had decided that the master of the Kremlin was what he called 'getatable'.[12] It was an error of the first magnitude, for if there is one consistent feature in the career of the elusive Stalin it is – if we may adapt the President's own colloquialism – that of *un*getatability. Stalin could and would make a deal if he could be shown that it was to his advantage; he would keep it, given the same condition. But he could not and would not be charmed or 'kidded along', though he was quite clever enough to gain advantages by persuading others that he was seducible in this way.

Stalin's invulnerability to American-style *bonhomie* emerged clearly at a Yalta luncheon when Roosevelt chose to reveal, in a jocular manner, the not very closely guarded secret that the Soviet dictator was known by the nickname 'Uncle Joe', also explaining that Stalin was always referred to by this title in secret telegrams between the British and American leaders. Stalin felt 'got at', not getatable. He was furious and made to leave, being mollified only when a member of Roosevelt's team pointed out that Uncle Joe was no worse than Uncle Sam. The Marshal 'understood the joke', Molotov later assured Churchill.[13] So much for attempts to woo the grim tyrant by jolly banter and to make him feel 'one of the boys'.

Another of Roosevelt's contrivances – a bid to win the dictator over by inducing him to join in teasing Churchill – was, in the Soviet context, a serious political blunder. Always formidable, the British Prime Minister would indeed have made a worthwhile butt. In view, however, of the need for Britain and the USA to present a united front against Stalin's encroachments, Roosevelt's stratagem was ill-conceived at best. It was rendered downright nauseating by the main topic around which the Churchill-baiting operation chanced to pivot: a proposal, made by Stalin, to round up fifty thousand German officers and technicians after the war and shoot them. To this lure Churchill majestically rose, remarking that he would prefer to be taken out into the garden there and then, and be shot himself, rather than 'sully my own and my country's honour by such infamy'. Undeterred, Roosevelt proposed a whimsical compromise: not fifty thousand, but only forty-nine thousand Germans should be shot! After Roosevelt's son Elliott had also chimed in, supporting the proposal on behalf of the United States Army, Churchill rose, left the table and stalked into the next room. He was pursued by a smiling and apologetical Stalin, who insisted that the remarks had been made entirely in jest, and used the full force of his 'very captivating manner' to clinch the point. But though Churchill consented to return, he was by no means fully convinced that

Stalin had not been speaking seriously.[14] As Churchill evidently realized, jokes about shooting prisoners of war come ill from a Stalin. As one also notes, Stalin's 'needling' of Churchill over this issue typically steered a calculated course between open malice and good-humoured banter. To resent the malice was to be a bad sport; to accept the banter was almost to find oneself Stalin's accomplice in condoning atrocities.

Churchill had behaved as a decent man, but unfortunately this unsavoury jape was not yet over. At Yalta the ailing Roosevelt revived it by suggesting that Stalin might propose a toast to the execution of fifty thousand German army officers. Roosevelt went on to offer some comments – possibly true in substance, but ill-advised in the political context – on the peculiarity of the British people in always wanting to have their cake and eat it. As has been well noted, such deliberate indiscretions – combined with Roosevelt's ostentatious avoidance of Churchill's company on certain occasions during the Big Three meetings – were unlikely to incline the Soviet leader to yield when presented with apparent British-American unity on an issue like Poland.[15]

Roosevelt's miscalculated indiscretions were by no means confined to the banqueting table, for he also informed Stalin in conference of his belief that American troops would not stay in Europe for more than two years after the war. Moreover, Roosevelt clearly implied a willingness to accept the Soviet annexation of Polish territory when he informed Stalin of the extent to which he himself was hampered, in a pre-election period, by the presence of a large number of Polish voters in the United States.[16] Nothing, perhaps, could have prevented Stalin from swallowing Poland in the end; but why should an American statesman go out of his way to make it easy for him? Behind such concessions to the Soviet point of view there lay, of course, a hope of lulling Stalin's ingrained suspicions: arguably an essential prerequisite for creating a safer world. It was all meant for the best, no doubt. But what gross insensitivity it shows towards the dictator's methods and character. No less insensitive was the ailing American President in clinging to his long-standing assumption that British imperialism was more dangerous than Soviet.

Churchill had his own technique of putting himself on terms with Stalin: a technique no less inept, politically, than the American President's. At a dinner given during one of the Big Three conclaves, Churchill decided that it was time for Stalin to abandon his namby-pamby practice of drinking toasts out of tiny glasses. Soviet-British goodwill might be better promoted by two claret glasses brimming with brandy. Twin bumpers having been provided, Prime Minister eyed Generalissimo significantly, the swill was quaffed and approving glances were exchanged. It would have been a better way than Roosevelt's to Stalin's heart – if he had one – but Stalin's follow-up shows how useless this sort of approach always remained. Far from lapsing into shared conviviality, he at once said to Churchill: 'If you find it impossible to give us a fortified position in the Marmora, could we not have a base at Dedeagatch ?'[17] As this remark shows, power politics were never very far from Stalin's mind. Did he ever wholly unbend ? Certainly not in a context where he might hope to pick up a base or two between the cheese and the nuts.

Among the least original of Stalin's bargaining techniques – though by no means the least effective – was the fuss which he would deliberately create around issues to which he was in fact secretly indifferent . . . his intention all along being to concede these non-essential points in the end: an interest in Tangier, say, or some former Italian colony. Having yielded these bargaining counters graciously, the dictator would of course expect to be accommodated with some substantial counter-concession in return. Similarly, he turned to excellent account Roosevelt's obsession with plans for an international post-war peace-keeping organization: the eventual United Nations. That a realist such as Stalin attached little importance to this project might be assumed on general grounds, were there not also documentary evidence on the point. At Yalta, it turned out, the usually well-briefed Soviet dictator had already been in possession of the American proposal on voting procedures in the United Nations Security Council for two months, but had not bothered to read it; and, as one observer correctly concluded, Stalin 'could not be greatly interested in the United Nations.'[18] That the Americans *were* interested in it Stalin could not fail to note, however, being quick to realize that concessions over voting methods in a notional organization might form a basis for extracting compensating concrete gains – the odd satellite or so – which might not otherwise have come his way so easily.

Throughout the Big Three negotiations Stalin continued to draw immense dividends from the continuing myth that he was ultimately answerable to various Soviet forces behind the scenes: public opinion, governmental institutions and the like. When Roosevelt once requested the postponement of recognition by the Soviet Union of its own puppet régime – the Lublin-based Polish Government – Stalin stated that he was powerless to sanction this because the Presidium of the Supreme Soviet had already decided to accord such recognition.[19] Then again, the Soviet people would not (said Stalin) support a declaration of war against Japan unless he could promise them such concessions as the Manchurian Railway, Port Arthur and Darien; these prospective gains would also make it 'much easier to explain the decision to the Supreme Soviet'.[20] Similarly, Stalin once told

Churchill that a failure by the Anglo-Americans to undertake the invasion of France, under the Overlord plan, would create 'bad feeling' in the Red Army.[21] So too, no doubt, had Stalin's massacre of its officer corps in 1937–8 – but without proving an effective obstacle to that operation.

The myth of implacable Soviet pressures in the background deceived the *rusé* Churchill no less than the complacent Roosevelt.[22] Stalin once told the Prime Minister that he himself and Molotov were alone among those with whom he worked in favouring gentle treatment of the London Poles. 'I was sure [Churchill comments] there were strong pressures in the background, both Party and military.'[23] This impression ran contrary to evidence which was already abundantly available at the time to those who had eyes to see: that Stalin was the sole, unchallenged source of authority. As we have noted, he listened to his colleagues' dissenting views often enough, and by no means always ignored their advice. It was the pretence of being irrevocably bound by such contrary opinions which formed the nub of this oft-repeated confidence trick. No doubt Stalin's frequent abrupt changes of front (between one meeting and another) helped to deceive Churchill over this matter. In selling the idea that he was fettered by mysterious unseen forces, Stalin secured an important tactical advantage over Churchill, particularly as the Prime Minister liked him personally, and was willing to join him in lamenting the intractability of background pressures which in fact barely existed.

To these devices Stalin also added juggling with democratic terminology and purportedly democratic institutions. To the Poles, for example, he readily conceded the right to hold free elections in which all anti-Nazi and democratic parties could take part. It soon became clear, though, that the Soviet authorities were to be sole arbiters of whether a given Polish party or politician might be deemed democratic, besides also retaining a monopoly over interpretations of the word 'free'. In Stalin's mind – as became clear far too gradually in the West – 'democratic' and 'free' were both rough synonyms for 'Kremlin-dominated'. The dictator would not have appreciated in the least Roosevelt's favourite, whimsical definition of democracy as 'the hole in the stuffed shirt through which the sawdust slowly trickles . . . the dent in the high hat'.[24] One would not wish to find oneself as the interpreter who had to make that ignobly phrased sentiment intelligible to any Soviet official, let alone to a Stalin.

Following the usual behavioural code of effective aggressors, Stalin repeatedly disclaimed designs against his future victims' sovereignty even as he was engaged in engineering their downfall. He repeatedly expressed, during the later stages of the war, his desire to see Poland free, strong and independent; and he was also particularly insistent that any Warsaw government should be *friendly towards the Soviet Union*. This seemed only reasonable – for had not Poland served, twice with living memory, as the corridor through which the Germans had struck at Russia? That *friendly towards* was Stalinist Hieratic for 'controlled by' only became clear in the fullness of time.

As a consideration of Stalin's negotiating career shows, there was nothing startlingly original about his technique of getting his own way, unless it was the stubborn persistence with which he exploited every available leverage, and the patience with which he could wait – for years if necessary – until an unfavourable context should change in his favour. The combination made him a bargainer formidable indeed. This was conceded by virtually all of those who clashed with him over the conference table, not least by the British Foreign Secretary Anthony Eden. Before the Yalta Conference, Eden recorded his fear that the meeting would lead to no worthwhile results, Stalin being the only one among the Big Three who 'has a clear view of what he wants and is a tough negotiator.'[25] Had Eden himself been required, after thirty years' experience of international negotiations, to pick a team to go into the conference room, his first choice would have been Stalin. The Soviet dictator was ruthless, says Eden, continuing in words which might seem to imply a criticism of Churchill: the Soviet leader never wasted a word; never stormed: was seldom even irritated. Calm, never raising his voice, he avoided the repeated negatives of Molotov, achieving his ends by methods more subtle. But superior though Stalin might be to Molotov, the two formed a well co-ordinated team; often teasing Molotov, Stalin was yet careful to uphold his Foreign Secretary's authority.[26]

General de Gaulle, who visited Moscow in late 1944, has described Stalin as a guileful dictator, a conqueror with an affable smile, a past-master at deception, also referring to the Soviet leader's ambitions, cryptic policy and underlying political passion: a passion so fierce that it often gleamed through his armour and lent him a certain sinister charm.[27] Having come to Moscow in order to negotiate a Soviet-French pact, de Gaulle found Stalin unwilling to concede this unless the French would grant recognition to the Kremlin-instructed Lublin Poles in return. Though French counsels could carry little effective weight at this time, de Gaulle flatly refused – for the time being – to side with Stalin over the Polish question; he regarded such a course as dishonourable, and believed that all things were possible: even that political integrity might, in the long run, prove a prudent investment.[28] Despite sustained Soviet pressure and prolonged ordeal by Muscovite hospitality, de Gaulle eventually carried his point after stalking out of a

Kremlin reception to mark his inflexible determination not to be manipulated. Stalin showed himself a good loser. He congratulated de Gaulle on playing his hand so well. 'I like dealing with someone who knows what he wants, even if he doesn't share my views.'[29]

De Gaulle's account adds to the rich literature on Stalin's table habits. During Franco-Soviet junketings the dictator ate heavily, serving himself from a bottle of Crimean wine, yet never relaxing the posture of a fighter engaged in a merciless struggle. Watchful and constrained, the surrounding Russians had their eyes always on their leader. And when the time came for toasts, Stalin stood up no less than thirty times to propose the health of the leading commissars and marshals around him. This ludicrous ritual was clearly designed to impress the French guests with Soviet strength. It also emphasized the degrading subservience imposed on Stalin's entourage, for each of these well-drilled satraps was obliged – on completion of the speech in his honour, and on the order 'come here' – to scuttle round the table and clink glasses with his master.

De Gaulle quotes some of the Generalissimo's toasts, such as that addressed to his chief artillery marshal: 'Voronov! To your health! You are in charge of deploying our large and small bore guns on the battlefields. . . . Go to it! Bravo for your artillery!'[30] In other instances threats were mingled with praise, as when Stalin spoke of the Quartermaster-General charged with supplying the fronts with men and material: 'He'd better do his best. Otherwise he'll be hanged . . . that's the custom in our country.' All in all, it was a great day for gallows humour. Stalin called for a machine-gun so that he could mow down the diplomats at his table, since they chattered to excess. In milder vein, he begged de Gaulle not to put the French Communist leader Thorez in prison: 'at least, not right away'. He was also heard threatening to send his own interpreter to Siberia because he 'knew too much'.[31]

On such occasions it indeed is the humble translator who sees most of the game, and we are therefore fortunate to have the comments of A. H. Birse, who interpreted regularly in British-Stalin confrontations during this period. Stalin was in general (Birse notes) a genial dictator, but opposition to his will could at any moment change the atmosphere to one of gloom and hostility. Stalin showed more friendliness to Birse than did other high-ranking Russians and enjoyed chatting with the interpreter informally in Russian as a relief from translated conversations. No admirer of Stalin the politician, and repelled by the adulation of Stalin the demigod, Birse was impressed and fascinated by the dictator's alertness and grasp of essentials. Stalin was always well briefed. He would pounce like a bird of prey on any weakness in his opponents' arguments. From an interpreter's point of view Stalin's slow and simple diction made the task of translating congenial and easy.[32]

Post-Stalingrad Foreign Entanglements

Among Stalin's victims to whom he was nominally allied, Poland remained the most important since it offered the key to the domination of post-war eastern Europe. Though we cannot trace in detail the imposition of Soviet control on Poland, three episodes call for examination as illustrating Stalin's style and methods: the inquest on the Katyn massacre; the exploitation of the Warsaw rising; the kidnapping of certain Polish politicians.

The world at large first heard the name Katyn on 13 April 1943, when Goebbels's propaganda apparatus broadcast the news that mass graves had been unearthed in that neighbourhood, which had now been under German occupation for nearly two years: they contained the bodies of thousands of Polish officers executed by the NKVD in May 1940. Goebbels's purpose in making the announcement was by no means humanitarian concern for the murdered Poles, but a wish to sow dissension between two of Germany's enemies: the Soviet Union and the Polish Government-in-Exile. In achieving this goal Nazi propaganda was entirely successful, since the Polish Government-in-Exile believed the accusation; it showed as much by immediately asking for an investigation by the International Red Cross ... and without requesting prior consultations with the Soviet Government. These developments played into Stalin's hands. With the humanitarian aspect of the Katyn affair he was as little concerned as Goebbels, especially as it may well have been he who ordered the executions in the first place. By now the Supreme Commander-in-Chief had become thoroughly weary of Poles. For two years they had been pestering him for information about missing officers and others, numbering fifteen thousand persons, who had disappeared after incarceration in three Soviet camps: they had made no less than two hundred enquiries, formal or informal, about this matter by the time when the corpses (accounting for 'approximately 4,443 bodies') were disinterred at Katyn.[1]

In the short term the Soviet authorities reacted to Goebbels's disclosures by indignantly denying Soviet reponsibility, and by claiming that it was not the Soviet authorities in 1940, but Germans in occupation of the area from summer 1941, who had shot the Polish officers. This assertion was later 'confirmed' by the findings of a Soviet Commission of enquiry, instituted – and personally briefed with its conclusions in advance – by Stalin after the German withdrawal from Katyn.[2] So much for immediate face-saving measures. As for longer-term prospects, Stalin was already determined to dominate post-war Poland. But he could not hope, in the context which was developing, for a post-war Polish government of Communist or fellow-travelling complexion – the less so as he had himself virtually destroyed the Polish Communist Party during the Great Terror. How welcome, therefore, was the opportunity now offered by Goebbels to accuse the Polish Government-in-Exile of collaborating with Hitler, and to sever diplomatic relations with that London-based administration, as was done on 26 April 1943. Needing Poles of his own as a counterweight to the London Poles, Stalin proceeded to set up the so-called Lublin Committee, which was eventually to form the basis of a Stalin-dominated Warsaw Government.

Meanwhile there were far too many Poles, whether located in Poland or elsewhere, who did not wish to see their country converted into a Soviet dependency. But then, suddenly, a lucky opportunity occurred to have such recalcitrants exterminated by someone else: the Warsaw rising of August-September 1944 in German-occupied Poland. At the time when this revolt broke out the Red Army had reached the eastern bank of the Vistula opposite the Polish capital, and the inhabitants had reason to believe that the German army was already preparing to evacuate the city. Anti-Nazi, but also anti-Soviet (in the sense of wishing to preserve Polish independence from totalitarian control of whatever complexion), the Polish underground Home Army attempted to assert national independence by attacking the German occupying forces on 1 August. In taking this fatal step the Poles had been encouraged, to an extent which remains controversial, by Soviet radio messages. Though we do not know whether Stalin had or had not cynically provoked the rising in the first place, we do know that he halted his troops on the Vistula and allowed events in Warsaw to take their sanguinary course. Nor would he even grant landing facilities on Soviet territory to Western-based allied planes which might have dropped supplies to the beleaguered Polish patriots. Actual instigator of the uprising or not, the dictator accordingly showed himself ready to exploit its political advantages to the full. His decision enabled the Germans to destroy the ill-equipped Home Army in a bitter two-month battle, partly fought in the sewers of the city. By a feat of masterly inactivity Stalin had allowed Hitler to perform the task of liquidating over 150,000 independent-minded Poles whom he might otherwise have had to liquidate himself.

According to a contrary view less damaging to Stalin's reputation, the Polish rebellion took place against the express wishes of the Soviet High Command, which had reached a natural obstacle on the Vistula and now needed time to consolidate. Not indeed until 17 January 1945 – more than three months after the Germans had suppressed the Warsaw rising – did the Red Army in fact take Warsaw, which can be interpreted to suggest that Stalin's chief motive for halting on the Vistula was military rather than political. It is also true that Stalin failed, similarly, to succour a rising – comparable, but on a smaller scale – which broke out during the same period in German-occupied Slovakia. Since the Slovakian rising (by contrast with the Polish) was firmly under local Communist direction, it has been plausibly argued that Stalin's refusal to aid the Slovaks cannot have been politically motivated.[3] However, this contention ignores the Communist dictator's long-standing record as the world's most ruthless suppressor of Communists – especially of those who (like the Slovaks now in revolt against Germany) were not firmly under his personal control. As the dictator well knew, the more successful Communist-dominated partisans might prove in German-occupied territory, the greater the degree of their potential emancipation from Soviet discipline. From his failure to aid the Communist Slovaks we are not, therefore, entitled to deduce that his simultaneous failure to aid the non-Communist Warsaw Poles was dictated by purely military rather than by political factors. Even Soviet anti-German partisans were treated with scant consideration by Stalin to the extent that, 'according to rumours which are hard to substantiate definitely, suspect or recalcitrant elements were screened out and sent to concentration camps.'[4]

March 1945 witnessed another episode in the saga of Poland's subjugation by Stalin when sixteen non-Communist Polish politicians were kidnapped on their native soil by the NKVD and taken to the Lubyanka. Here they were duly processed for the only Stalinist show trial to be staged in Moscow after the Bukharin affair of 1938. They were accused of diversionary activities against the Red Army during its advance across Poland, and were induced to confess by intensive, prolonged interrogation accompanied by carefully calculated deprivation of sleep, warmth and food. One of their number, Zbigniew Stypulkowski, became the only person to undergo public trial in Moscow without pleading guilty at any stage of the interrogation.[5] Released after receiving a short prison sentence, he published in the West a uniquely valuable account of Stalinist processing procedures. As such lenient treatment of a trial victim shows, Stalin still retained some degree of sensitivity to dwindling Western concern for the fate of Poles not subservient to the Kremlin.

Ruthless though Stalin was in handling non-Communist opponents, he was apt – as we have noted – to be yet more severe in dealing with political co-believers, as his wartime clashes with the Yugoslav partisans further illustrate. Head of the most substantial resistance movement in any German-occupied country, the Yugoslav Communist leader Tito naturally looked to Moscow for aid. But for years he waited in vain, receiving help from the

Top left: Stalin, 1920

Above: Stalin, 1927

Below: Stalin unbeautiful. Two photo-graphs–in effect 'candid camera' shots which escaped the vigilance of Stalin's censors–showing the dictator complete with pockmarks and looking exhausted

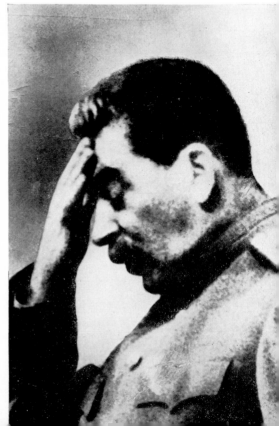

Left: Stalin's mother, Yekaterina Dzhugashvili (d. 1936)

Below: Stalin with Svetlana: Kuntsevo, 1935

Right: Stalin's elder son, Yakov Dzhugashvili, as a German prisoner during the Second World War

Below: Stalin's younger son, Vasily Stalin, as an air force commander during the Second World War

Opposite top: At a Supreme Soviet meeting, January 1938; left to right: Bulganin, Zhdanov, Stalin, Voroshilov, Khrushchev

Opposite bottom: Molotov signs the Frontier and Friendship Treaty between the USSR and Germany, 4 October 1939, watched by Ribbentrop (left) and Stalin

Right: Churchill and Stalin at the Kremlin, 1942.

Below: Roosevelt, Churchill, Stalin and Major Birse (right) celebrate Churchill's sixty-ninth birthday (30 November 1943) during the Teheran Conference, 28 November–1 December 1943

Opposite top: Churchill, Roosevelt and Stalin during the Yalta Conference, February 1945

Opposite bottom: Attlee, Truman and Stalin during the Potsdam Conference, July–August 1945

Above: Mao Tse-tung, Ulbricht, Stalin and Khrushchev on Stalin's seventieth birthday, 21 December 1949

Right: Stalin lies in state: Hall of Columns (House of Unions, near the Kremlin), 10 March 1953

Above: Soviet leaders (including Voroshilov, Malenkov, Molotov, Beria, Khrushchev) follow Stalin's glass coffin, on 12 March 1953, to the dictator's penultimate resting place: the Red Square Mausoleum

Left: The Red Square Mausoleum, during the period when it bore Stalin's name as well as Lenin's

Bottom: The monument was later destalinized by a decision of the Twenty-Second Party Congress, taken on 30 October 1961

British while Stalin was inclined to favour King Peter's Government-in-Exile rather than the Yugoslav Communist partisans. Stalin was also inclined to support the anti-Communist resistance group under Mihailovic, whom Tito denounced as a collaborator with the Germans. On one occasion Tito went so far as to cable Stalin: 'If you cannot send us assistance, then at least do not hamper us', a message which caused the Soviet leader to stamp with rage.[6] Nor did Tito's visit to Stalin of September 1944 lead to any harmony of views, for the Soviet leader was now urging the reinstatement of King Peter; after all, as Stalin sagely pointed out, that monarch could always be stabbed in the back at a later stage. On this and many other matters Tito found himself at cross purposes with Stalin, who – as the Yugoslav leader noted – showed himself intolerant of all contradiction.[7] Thus were sown the seeds of Tito's later defection from the Soviet camp: an event so damaging in its impact on world Communist unity as to demonstrate Stalin's farsightedness in seeking to curb the Yugoslav Communists at an earlier stage . . . but also his shortsightedness in dealing with them so autocratically.

Of Stalin's reluctance to see the Yugoslav partisan movement exclusively dominated by Communists, one of Tito's leading associates, Milovan Djilas, has provided further evidence. In spring 1944, during Djilas's first visit to Moscow, Stalin advised him to play down the revolutionary nature of the Yugoslav partisan movement, since the British might otherwise be frightened off. For example, the partisans should not wear red stars on their caps. 'By God, there's no need for stars,' Stalin angrily explained.[8]

During later meetings Djilas clashed with Stalin over assaults on Yugoslav citizens committed by soldiers of the Red Army who had recently entered Yugoslavia to fight alongside the partisans against the Germans. More than a hundred local women had been murdered by Soviet rapists, according to the Yugoslavs . . .[9] who tactlessly explained to Soviet representatives that English officers had a record less unchivalrous. Enraged by this gross 'insult' to the Red Army, Stalin did not trouble to deny the accusations of murder, rape and looting. All that seemed to him perfectly right and natural. Could Djilas not understand a soldier who 'has fun with a woman or takes some trifle', after fighting his way over hundreds of kilometres through blood, fire and death? Conveniently ignoring so many instances in which the fun had proved fatal to one of the playmates, and working himself up into a lather of tragic pathos, Stalin kissed Djilas's wife, exclaiming that he made this 'loving gesture at the risk of being charged with rape'.[10] In a more serious vein he expressed surprise that Djilas should be so shocked at the thought of a soldier amusing himself with a woman; Djilas had read

Dostoyevsky, after all, and must therefore possess some insight into the human soul! Stalin also said that he himself had once intervened to pardon a Red Army major sentenced to death for shooting a fellow-officer who was in the act of protecting a woman from violation. For good measure Stalin also told Djilas how much he approved the Red Army's alleged practice of wantonly massacring German civilian refugees, including women and children.[11]

There are few other recorded instances of Stalin speaking in so provocatively bloodthirsty a manner, for he remained essentially one who discreetly arranged massacres behind the scenes, not one who boasted about them openly. In the present instance he was clearly concerned to 'needle' the sensitive Djilas. He also called Djilas a 'German', basing this imputation on the Yugoslav guerrillero's liking for beer. Djilas was not amused. Nor did Tito, on the same occasion, appreciate Stalin's assertion that the Bulgarian army had fought better than the Yugoslav. On Stalin's characteristic teasing of his dinner guests, Djilas has commented that one never knew how large an element of rancour the dictator's jokes contained. With Stalin it was impossible to separate malice from humour, for play-acting came so naturally to him that he always seemed convinced of the truth of what he was saying.[12]

Djilas also provides valuable evidence on the suppers which Stalin was wont to improvise at his small country villa at Kuntsevo. These orgies, to which frequent reference has been made above, were casual affairs; the guests served themselves and sat wherever they liked. Servants appeared only when Stalin himself rang, and he himself never took the head of the table. But relaxed though the atmosphere might seem, it was at such gatherings that supreme policy was often decided. The guest-list varied, Molotov being the only regular; he was also, according to Djilas, the only member of the Politburo to be addressed by Stalin with the familiar second person singular form *ty*.[13] On the whole, though, Stalin cultivated a certain underlying formality in his contacts: he disliked (according to one military witness) being accosted in the normal Russian semi-familiar style by first name and patronymic;[14] it was as 'Comrade Stalin' rather than 'Joseph Vissarionovich' that he preferred to be addressed.

Formal or informal, Stalin's supper parties created the impression of 'a patriarchal family with a crotchety head whose foibles always made his kinsfolk somewhat apprehensive'.[15] As for the patriarch's table habits, Stalin ate enormous quantities, especially of meat, but drank in moderation, usually mixing red wine and vodka in little glasses; he never appeared inebriated in Djilas's presence – unlike Molotov and Beria, the latter being practically a drunkard.

The Potsdam Conference of 16 July–1 August 1945 was chiefly important in assisting Stalin's unavowed intention of dominating and – in effect –
annexing the eastern European states which came to be known as Soviet
satellites. By the end of this, the third and last of the wartime summit
conferences, the Soviet leader was the sole member of the Big Three to
survive, politically, from Teheran and Yalta. The succeeding United States
President, Truman, took the place of Roosevelt, who had died in office in
April, while the Churchill-Eden team was replaced by Attlee and Bevin as
the result of a British general election occurring in the middle of the Potsdam proceedings.

Stalin had no cause to welcome these changes. Truman made up for his
relative lack of experience by a greater sophistication of political approach.
No one seems to have told him about the famous 'getatability' of Uncle Joe,
and he therefore defended American interests more robustly than had his
predecessor. As for the British negotiators, Stalin had neither predicted nor
welcomed the appearance of a left-wing team. On the eve of the British
general election he had forecast a Conservative majority of about eighty;
he had also made it clear that he himself was counting on a Churchillian
victory. When the vote went the other way, Stalin was so disappointed that
he fell ill and was obliged to absent himself from the conference for a time;
such at any rate is the unlikely interpretation of his indisposition offered by
President Truman.[16] But it is certainly true that Stalin would have preferred
a Conservative to a Labour victory in Britain, if only because of his long-
standing tendency to discriminate against all left-wing governments other
than those dominated by the Kremlin. Molotov, too, was amazed at the
result of the British elections, and the new British Prime Minister had the
impossible task of explaining to him how 'we could not tell what would be
the result.'[17] The Soviet assumption was that Churchill, like any other
respectable statesman, would have had the sense to rig the election in
advance; his fall from office therefore cast grave doubts on his professional
competence.

Both new recruits to the Big Three found the sitting member impressive.
Truman was struck by Stalin's good humour, by his politeness and by the
fact that one could talk to him 'straight from the shoulder'.[18] To Attlee,
Stalin was 'a man you could do business with because he said yes and no
and he didn't have to refer back. He was obviously the man who could make
decisions, and he was going to be difficult. . . . He could make jokes and
take jokes. But I was under no illusion as to his readiness to co-operate or
as to his liking for us.'[19]

The change of negotiators at Potsdam could make little difference to the
fate of eastern Europe, now controlled by Stalin's armies. So long as the

dictator was determined to enforce Soviet control in Poland and bordering states, nothing short of direct military action could dislodge him. His main achievement at Potsdam was to remain on reasonably friendly terms with his allies while yet persuading them to swallow this bitter pill. By now Stalin already had a Polish government subservient to himself, and was prepared to tolerate no more than nominal temporary concessions to the principle of a coalition containing non-Kremlinized representatives. He also fought hard to secure recognition for the incorporation in newly Stalinized Poland of German territory up to the Oder and Western Neisse line. Next in priority came Bulgaria, Rumania and Hungary. Provided that these countries, together with Soviet-occupied Germany and Tito's Yugoslavia, were firmly inside the Stalinist camp, the dictator was prepared to make concessions in other areas. However, superb negotiator as he was, he had no intention of allowing his allies to realize this, permitting himself to be prised out of Austria and Iran, while reluctantly yielding claims to Soviet bases on the Bosphorus and in Tangier: claims which had no doubt been put forward in the first place as bargaining counters suitable for surrender in due course. Stalin also yielded ground on the quantity of Soviet reparations to be exacted from Germany, Italy and other defeated enemy states.

The ultimate effect of Stalin's policies, as promoted at Potsdam and during the immediate post-war period, was to reveal him as the main victor in the war so far as expansion of territory and influence in Europe was concerned.

Among the topics discussed at Potsdam was the continuing war against Japan. Though atomic bombing was soon to bring this conflict to a dramatically swift conclusion, such an outcome could not be predicted at the time of the Conference. Consequently the prospect of Stalin's military aid against the Japanese (with whom he was still at peace) remained attractive to his Western allies, and was another reason for conciliating him during the negotiations. The potential need for Soviet participation in the far eastern theatre had, however, already been somewhat eroded – and on the opening day of the Potsdam conclave – by the successful American explosion, in New Mexico, of the first experimental atomic bomb. Obviously Stalin must be informed of this vital development, and Truman decided to tell him in as casual a manner as possible. On the afternoon of 24 July he drew the Soviet dictator aside in the conference room to explain that the Allies had developed a new bomb far more destructive than anything yet known, and that they planned to use it very soon unless the Japanese should surrender. Stalin showed no great interest, merely remarking that he was glad to hear of the bomb; he hoped that it would indeed be used. He asked for no further information, and did not appear to grasp the importance of the new development.[20] In playing the inscrutable Oriental over this episode, Stalin was following his normal style, and we can only speculate about what may have been going on in his mind. Perhaps Truman's announcement was so casual that the Soviet leader genuinely failed to grasp its import? Perhaps he thought that the American President was lying or exaggerating for some diplomatic reason? Perhaps he already knew about the bomb through Soviet spies? Or perhaps he was just rather tired.

On 8 August – two days after the first atomic bomb had been dropped, on Hiroshima – the Soviet Union duly declared war on Japan. During the four weeks which followed, and which were interrupted by the Japanese surrender on 2 September, hostilities were prosecuted energetically by the Red Army, with considerable Soviet losses which might have seemed worth avoiding in a war already won. The episode abundantly illustrates Stalin's zest as empire-builder, as also does his rejection of a Japanese proposal – secretly extended at the time of the Potsdam Conference – that the Soviet Union should act as mediator in bringing about peace in the far east: Stalin turned down the suggestion before informing the Western leaders that it had been made.[21] In conformity with this jingoistic drive, Soviet propaganda insisted on claiming exclusive credit for victory over the Japanese: a foe already vanquished in all but name by Moscow's allies at the time when Moscow declared war. In an address commemorating the victory over Japan, Stalin revealed a vengeful mood. He exulted in the retribution exacted for Japanese aggression in the undeclared border war of 1938–9, as also for Japanese intervention in Siberia during the Civil War. He even delved back into Imperial Russian history by suggesting that he had taken revenge for the Japanese attack on Tsarist Russia in 1904.[22] Can he have forgotten that the Bolsheviks had been pro-Japanese at the time?

Though Stalin did retain certain small territorial gains through his belated attack on Japan, he was eventually compelled to disgorge many of his far eastern encroachments to Maoist China. Nor did he succeed, as he wished, in obtaining allied agreement for a Soviet zone of occupation in defeated Japan. This was one of those areas in which the Soviet dictator was prepared, when pressed, to make concessions. In any case he had Truman and General MacArthur to reckon with now, not Roosevelt.

13

Stalinism Reasserted and Defied

First Shocks of Peace

VICTORIOUS over Germany and her allies in the west through his subjects'
blood, toil, tears and sweat – victorious also in the far east through his
swift pounce on the defeated Japanese – Stalin embarks in autumn 1945
on the last, the most mysterious and in some ways the most fascinating
phase of his career: the seven-and-a-half years which culminate in his death
on 5 March 1953.

The evidence for this period is more elusive than that bearing on any
other phase of the Leader's post-revolutionary activities. No longer, in
these last years, was he habitually closeted with foreign statesmen, officials
and interpreters such as have given intimate glimpses of Stalin the warlord
in action. No longer did Trotsky survive to maintain archival record of the
tyrant's crimes. As for post-war Soviet witnesses, they had learnt to keep
their lips sealed, opening them only to intone officially scripted litanies in
the stiff Hieratic idiom. In the absence of better evidence we now depend
heavily on sources made available since Stalin's death: Soviet-published
posthumous 'revelations' about the dictator; the memoirs of Djilas,
Dedijer, Svetlana Alliluyeva and others. Aided by such testimony, by
documents of the period recently published in the Soviet Union, and by
painstaking Kremlinological analysis, we can crack the code of Stalin's last
years with fair confidence, at least supplying informed speculation at the
many points where hard fact is lacking.

The evidence shows the elderly leader still locked in combat with his
environment. Within the central Soviet power apparatus we find him
carefully manipulating his senior colleagues as he favours now one individual or group, now another ... only to switch his allegiance whenever
any particular combination waxes unduly potent. On a wider level we find
the Leader sponsoring a cultural witch-hunt directed by Andrey Zhdanov

– a protégé newly restored to favour – against Soviet intellectuals as a whole. On a level wider still the Soviet peasant masses suffer the cancellation of concessions permitted in wartime. As for non-Russians within and without the dictator's orbit, these remain the object of his deepest suspicions. Non-Russian Soviet citizens – Ukrainians, Jews, Tatars and many others – fall foul of renewed xenophobic drives. On the western borderlands – annexed in 1939-40, lost to Hitler in 1941, reconquered from Hitler at the end of the war – Stalinist persecution falls with especial severity. These repressions are also extended to the eight nations of eastern Europe which he annexes – in certain cases partially or temporarily – as colonial dependencies termed (according to point of view) People's Democracies or Soviet satellites. For a time revolutionary China, too, assumes the aspect of a Stalinist satellite. As for the world outside the Communist orbit, that becomes the object for virulent Stalin-sponsored propaganda barrages and for attacks on its territorial integrity mounted through the blockade of West Berlin and the invasion of South Korea. In all these areas of activity the theme is now more than ever that of Stalin against the whole world, whether personified by Soviet police chiefs, by his sisters-in-law . . . or by such distant bogymen as American imperialists engaged in polluting the peace-loving masses of North Korea with germ-infected spiders scattered from the skies.

Though Stalin maintains totalitarian rule of extreme severity throughout this post-war period, we can yet register five phases of greater or lesser repressiveness, as chiefly reflected in the dictator's internal policies, but also in his attitude to satellite and foreign affairs. Until the summer of 1946 controls remain loose by Stalinist standards, the comparatively easy-going atmosphere of wartime being very largely preserved. A two-year period of severe repression follows: that associated with the name of Zhdanov. But Zhdanov's death, in 1948, by no means terminates persecutions generally considered Zhdanovite, for 1949 becomes the harshest of all the post-war years. In 1950-2, however, certain slight relaxations may be observed . . . until, in late 1952, tension mounts again as Stalin seemingly prepares a new Great Terror on the basis of a so-called Doctors' Plot: a nightmare from which his death in 1953 provides a merciful release.

What were Stalin's strengths, what were his weaknesses when the war ended in 1945?

Among his advantages was a greater degree of internal mastery over his subjects than had been exercised by any previous despot. His unique system of controls, built up in the 1930s and based on a powerful terror apparatus, was still functioning effectively. But by now Stalin was reaping an additional advantage which had been denied to him in pre-war years.

He had become an accepted national leader: a status conferred by victory in what he himself has called the cruellest and hardest of all Russia's many wars, a conflict unparalleled in the annals of mankind.[1] His prestige thus enhanced, his position secure from challenge, post-war Stalin found himself wielding yet greater political power than ever before. In his seventh and eighth decades, accordingly, he still retained his special flair for rendering what already seemed absolute rule yet more absolute.

Supremely in control of his empire, Stalin enjoyed an advantage denied to foreign rivals such as Truman and Attlee, whose decisions must allow for public opinion in their own countries. There was a point, for example, beyond which they could not afford to delay or reverse the demobilization of their armed forces; nor was the American President free – even had he wished – to unleash on the Soviet Union a preventive nuclear war, despite the phobias which must have plagued the Soviet dictator on this score. Stalin, by contrast, commanded a regimented community responsive to his lightest whim. He also enjoyed the advantage – and despite considerable demobilization – of having on the ground in eastern Europe the vast land armies which placed the political future of Poland, and of the other eastern European candidates for satellitization, outside the area which the West could effectively influence.

As for Stalin's post-war weaknesses, the most obvious of these was his lack of nuclear weapons: a deficiency which his spies and researchers were busily repairing. A further handicap lay in the extreme devastation wrought on Soviet soil by enemy action. Both in absolute and in relative terms the USSR had suffered more grievously than any of her major allies in World War Two. An unknown total – between twenty and thirty million – of her soldiers and civilians had perished. A comparable number of survivors had been rendered homeless as they faced the ordeal of their first peacetime winter amid ruined cities, factories and transport facilities ... not to mention the ravaged countryside, which had been ill equipped to feed the nation as a whole even before Hitler's tanks had rolled over its ploughlands and pastures.

It is probable, however, that neither the appalling devastation of his realm, nor his embarrassing lack of nuclear weapons, caused Stalin as much anxiety as a third feature of the early post-war Soviet scene: the widespread contamination of so many millions of his subjects through wartime contact with various categories of foreigner. Always suspicious – as recorded above – of interactions between races, nations and cultures, the Leader had sought to quarantine his subjects within the frontiers of the USSR during the 1930s. But then war had burst his *cordon sanitaire* asunder, bringing the newly Stalinized masses into confrontation with a rabble of ideological plague-carriers from a score of 'bourgeois' countries, enemy and allied. Over sixty million Soviet citizens had suffered under some form of occupation by Germans or German allies during the war; entire Soviet armies had been taken prisoner, and vast numbers of Soviet civilians had been freighted to the *Reich* as forced labourers; hundreds of thousands of Soviet partisans had fought against Germans, Rumanians, Italians, Finns, Spaniards and others. Though casualties among all these groups had been heavy, some five million or more Soviet citizens had contrived to survive hostilities in the area west of the pre-war Soviet frontiers. About half of these survivors suffered liberation by the advancing Red Army; a little under half underwent repatriation to the Soviet Union by Britain, America and other Western countries, often against their will;[2] and some five hundred thousand were able to avoid returning, choosing to make their homes in 'bourgeois' countries.

Stalin's security forces had orders to harass such non-returning Soviet citizens on foreign soil, but it was the far larger mass of the repatriated which received most careful attention. All these many millions were suspect. So too were those millions of Red Army soldiers and officers who – far from having been forcibly removed to the West by the Germans – had fought their way into eastern Europe and Germany with Stalin's conquering armies in 1944-5. They too had been able to observe that citizens of so-called capitalist countries enjoyed higher living standards, and more extensive civil liberties, than were available within Stalin's jurisdiction. Even Hitlerite Germany seemed like a haven of freedom to Soviet invading forces ... especially in view of the veil drawn by Stalin's censorship over Hitlerite persecution of the Jews. As for American, British and other 'bourgeois' troops unregimented even by the crude and limited political disciplines of Fascism ... such contacts had naturally been more polluting still.

Unaware of the extent to which they had (by Stalin's standards) become corrupted or liable to corruption, the victorious soldiers and officers of the Red Army were in a frame of mind similar to that of the Emperor Alexander I's Russian armies triumphant over Napoleon in 1812-15. As conquering heroes they felt entitled to privileges comparable at least to those enjoyed by the conquered. Also feeling that they had fully proved their loyalty to Stalin, they hoped and expected that political relaxations – such as had been introduced in the Soviet Union to a limited extent during the war – would be further extended and developed in time of peace.

There could be no question, unfortunately, of a Stalin permitting such licence, or of his allowing returning heretics-presumptive – whether war heroes or war victims – to be welcomed home with open arms. Absolute though the dictator's control of Soviet public opinion remained, he knew that the price of despotism is eternal vigilance, and that early post-war conditions made such vigilance more necessary than ever. All returning prisoners of war and forced labourers were accordingly greeted with institutionalized Stalinist suspicions, as also was the vast Soviet population – including active anti-German partisans – restored to Stalinist normalcy by the recovery of enemy-occupied Soviet territory. Intensively screened and interrogated by political police, returnees were liable to be freighted in bulk, as also were suspect residents from former occupied areas, to concentration camps constantly depleted through high mortality. Thus did many a newly 'liberated' Soviet prisoner of war immediately exchange Hitlerite for Stalinist captivity. What proportion was executed, consigned to camps, or reindoctrinated by techniques less drastic, we have no means of determining. That the total of persons arrested in the immediate post-war period was enormous we know; that it would have been even greater if Stalin could have had his way, we also know. But even the beloved Leader was compelled to adjust his appetite for repression to the technical possibilities of his age. Otherwise he would have deported the Ukrainians – all forty million of them – *en masse*;[3] how fortunate, then, that insufficient rolling stock was available for the purpose.

The western borderland territories, originally annexed by Stalin before the war, were among those to suffer most grievously from the early post-war Stalinist repressions. In return many of these areas maintained sporadic partisan activity against the Soviet authorities long after the war; in some places such resistance even outlasted the dictator himself. Yet another reservoir of victims for Soviet concentration camps was to be provided in the early post-war years by the satellite states of eastern Europe incorporated in Stalin's dominions. By such means the post-war Stalinist slave colonies – of northern European Russia, the Siberian far east, Central Asia and elsewhere – were maintained as a flourishing concern with booming mortality statistics.

Bureaucrat, Host and Puppet-Master

During the years 1945–53 Stalin's real power continued to rest, as it had during the war, on his specially devised system of interlocking terroristic and terrorized bureaucracies: those of police, Party, army, police-within-Party, Party-within-police, police and Party-within-government/army, and so on. Meanwhile the Leader's nominal authority still derived from his continuing tenure of three major offices: those of Politburo member; of

Prime Minister; of chief among several Secretaries of the Party's Central Committee.

In fact, though not in form, Stalin was still ruling – as he had before and during the war – by despotic fiat. This practice by no means precluded frequent consultations with leading colleagues temporarily in favour, besides which the dictator was still delegating important matters to chosen subordinates who could always be disavowed and removed at some convenient moment. As for the elaborate democratic pretences which had always formed an integral part of Bolshevik tradition, these were still preserved to the extent that decrees were issued in the name of the Party's Central Committee or of the Council of Ministers (as *Sovnarkom* was renamed in 1946). Nor did Stalin openly assert the kind of divine right and status which he permitted his sycophants to claim for him. His public posture – in so far as he had one, for he became more and more of a recluse in his declining years – was still that of the modest servant of the community, the humble elect of people and Party.

Rarely during his declining years did Stalin even go through the motions of consulting the party which he nominally served as its elected representative. After the Eighteenth Congress of March 1939 over thirteen years elapsed until the convocation of the Nineteenth Congress in October 1952 . . . and this in defiance of a provision whereby new congresses were to convene at three-yearly intervals. Such was Stalin's treatment of the institution which remained, in theory, the sovereign Party's governing organ. The Central Committee was similarly flouted. Until a new congress should 'elect' a new committee, nominal responsibility for policy continued to rest with the survivors of those 'elected' in 1939. But this made little difference, since Stalin permitted only one Central Committee plenum between 1945 and 1952.[1]

As for the Politburo – itself nominally responsible to the now dormant Central Committee – Stalin continued to offer lip-service to this former repository of power: that is, he paid it the respect of manipulating it in a particularly outrageous manner. At the end of the war the Politburo consisted of nine full members (Andreyev, Kaganovich, Kalinin, Khrushchev, Mikoyan, Molotov, Stalin, Voroshilov, Zhdanov) and of four candidates (Beria, Malenkov, Shvernik, Voznesensky). Whether this body ever convened in full conclave we do not know; Khrushchev has said that Politburo sessions occurred only occasionally.[2]

Already consisting of persons selected by and subservient to the dictator, the Politburo was further emasculated by the practice of appointing subcommittees nominated by Stalin (varying in size from five to nine members) to deal with important areas of policy. Thus, as the Leader's gusts of alternating suspicion and benevolence played over a dozen colleagues, he was able to bypass the temporarily disgraced and give prominence to his favourites of the hour. On 3 October 1946, for example, Stalin 'proposed' (i.e. ordered) that the special Politburo Commission, appointed to supervise foreign affairs and known as 'the Six', should henceforward also be empowered to deal with internal reconstruction and domestic policy.[3] Its terms of reference were thus expanded to include more or less the entire length and breadth of Soviet administration. The result was to suspend, in effect, those Politburo members who were not honoured with membership of the chosen sextet. A further shift saw the Six expanded to a septemvirate through co-option of the top planner Voznesensky.

Since Stalin's will could always be made to prevail, both inside the Seven and outside it, the other leaders remained equally powerless whether included in or excluded from such vacillating combinations. And though it was naturally less alarming to find oneself in the swim than out in the cold, such indications meant very little in practice. Voznesensky, for example, had not long been elevated to membership of the Seven before Stalin had him dismissed and shot during the Leningrad Affair, to be described below. As this isolated example reminds us, post-war Stalin did not find it necessary to persecute his closest political colleagues with the extreme severity practised in the 1930s. In those palmy days he had killed off about half among the score of individuals who had at any time held either full or candidate Politburo membership – it is impossible to be more precise owing to the mystery which still cloaks the dictator's responsibility for the death of Kirov and certain others. By contrast, Voznesensky remains the only Politburo member or candidate (among four from the 1945 vintage who predeceased the dictator) of whom we can be certain that he was killed on Stalin's orders.

Though the composition of the Politburo was relatively stable in 1945–52, the same cannot be said of the Central Committee's Secretariat. In size this body was roughly constant, varying between four and six members. But the only secretary to serve uninterruptedly throughout these years was Stalin himself. Two among the various other secretaries of the period (Popov and Kuznetsov) were to be removed during the Leningrad Affair. As for the other senior Party bodies, the Orgburo continued to function, at least nominally, and the claim has been made that it became more important than the Politburo.[4] That would not be saying much, however, for it must be repeated that under the Stalin dictatorship – especially during its post-war years – no institution or person enjoyed decision-making power except to the degree which Stalin might from time to time choose to permit. That these senior bodies themselves controlled vast subordinate bureaucratic empires made no difference to the fact that all were, in the last analysis, impotent.

While maintaining so complex an array of interdependent committees, Stalin yet continued – as in earlier days – to take and communicate many of his decisions informally at the Kuntsevo supper parties to which he was still inviting senior colleagues. These social events were apt to be interrupted by administrative orders which happened to float into the Leader's mind. Chancing to glance at a map on one occasion, and noticing the numerous German names (dating from the time of Peter the Great) of places near Leningrad, Stalin gave instructions for them to be russified . . . and there was Zhdanov ready with his notebook to record his master's wishes.[5] It also occurred to the dictator to build a canal uniting the Volga with the Don; on that occasion it was the doomed chief planner Voznesensky who meekly produced a pencil and jotted down the off-hand ukase.[6] With similar casualness Stalin would pick up various territorial and racial problems of the day. Germany must be divided between the USSR and the West, he told the Yugoslav Communist leader Djilas in early 1948: the first occasion on which he is known to have mooted such a possibility. Boasting that there were no Jews in the Soviet Party's Central Committee, he called for Djilas's applause for this anti-Semitic statement; but Djilas recognized a deliberate attempt to provoke him into indiscretion, and wisely made no comment.[7]

It is principally through such Yugoslav evidence that we are able to monitor Stalin's *modus operandi* during the early post-war years. Soviet-Yugoslav negotiations of the period – especially those of 1948 leading to the rift between the two states – must be discussed below at the proper place. For the moment they are important as showing us the techniques employed by Stalin in *tête-à-tête* negotiation: a topic on which native Soviet witnesses are lacking, except for the highly suspect *Khrushchev Remembers*.

This evidence reveals the elderly dictator employing tried methods of the past rather than pioneering new devices. For example, he was still exploiting every opportunity of promoting ill feeling among his associates. In May 1946 he attempted to sow dissension between two visiting satellite representatives, Tito and Dimitrov: leaders, respectively, of the Yugoslav and Bulgarian Communist parties. On this occasion Stalin went out of his way to disparage the defunct Comintern, of which Dimitrov had been Secretary-General until its dissolution in 1943, and tried to provoke a quarrel between Dimitrov and Tito by suggesting that it should be Tito who sponsored the foundation of the projected new Communist international body: the Cominform. Stalin further tried to set his Bulgarian

and Yugoslav guests squabbling over the wine which he offered them at
his table; though labelled as Bulgarian, it was really Yugoslav, said the
host – claiming that it came from an area stolen by Bulgaria from Yugoslavia during the war. *Bonhomie*, simulated or not, and horseplay also had
a role to play on these occasions, the same orgy witnessing the ceremonious
drinking of *Bruederschaft*, at Stalin's command, between himself and Tito.
With intimate terms thus established between Soviet Generalissimo and
Yugoslav Marshal, Stalin proceeded to give proof of his physical strength
by three times lifting this signally honoured guest off the ground to the
strains of Russian folk music from his gramophone. But such cordiality
could turn into sudden fits of rage. When a minor hitch – affecting transport arrangements – occurred during the same evening, the dictator lost
his temper with some attendant Soviet colonel. Quivering with fury,
shouting and gesticulating brusquely, Stalin abused this pale, trembling
uniformed flunkey who stood there 'as if struck by heart failure'.[8]

Two years later Stalin was in less sprightly mood. He looked very much
changed, and was complaining that old age had crept up on him. Gone
were his former liveliness, his quick wit, his pointed sense of humour. The
powerful intellect appeared to be in decline; there were conspicuous signs
of senility. Always a hearty trencherman, the dictator had now become
downright gluttonous, though he was drinking less than before. His
character remained unchanged: stubborn, angular and suspicious. Everyone fawned on him; everyone waited for him to express his opinion first . . .
and then hurried to agree with him.[9] The description is that of Djilas, who
had once more been invited to supper at Stalin's out-of-town *dacha*,
where he now found himself obliged, as were all the other guests, to guess
the temperature as recorded on an outside thermometer; they were then
'sconced' one glass of vodka for each degree of error. Later in the proceedings Beria pressed a glass of pepper gin on Djilas and explained with
a sniggering leer that it had a 'bad effect' on the sex glands. Not to be
outdone, Stalin called for a solemn toast to the memory of Lenin, 'our
Leader, our Teacher, our All'; he then demonstrated his musical taste or
his sense of humour, or both, by playing a gramophone record which combined the warbling of a coloratura soprano with a hideous yelping descant
furnished by the barking of a pack of dogs.[10] Between such interruptions
talk roved idly from one topic to another. For a time literature attracted
Stalin's attention. He dismissed Dostoyevsky as a great writer whose
works must be kept out of the clutches of the young because he was also
a great reactionary. The Generalissimo also discoursed of Gorky and
Sholokhov, while some attendant toady quoted to him his own former

bon mot on the love poems of Simonov – that no more than two copies of these should be published: 'One for Him and one for Her'.[11]

Such was the atmosphere in which the Yugoslav visitors were immersed only temporarily, but in which Soviet leaders (who have left no reliable evidence) had to operate on a long-term basis as they jockeyed for position during the years 1945-53. They were not so much rivals for direct power as for influence over a dictator whose position could not conceivably be challenged so long as he retained control of his faculties. While competing for the boss's ear, his underlings were also discreetly seeking to improve their chances in the struggle for the succession which was bound to break out when he died.

In our survey of the post-war ebb and flow of Soviet top persons, we may first note Stalin's characteristic prudence in removing from the highest military office his most distinguished soldier, Zhukov, who might conceivably have become the focus for some Bonapartist *coup*. Dismissed as Commander-in-Chief over the Soviet land forces in 1946, the great Marshal was relegated to a series of obscure provincial appointments. Wild rumours surrounded Zhukov's disappearance from the Centre: he was said to have plotted against Stalin and to have been imprisoned in an isolator in the far north.[12] Though nothing so dramatic had occurred, Zhukov's wartime role was henceforward underplayed in Soviet histories, novels and other propaganda handouts issued during Stalin's lifetime: a penalty for the Marshal's widespread popularity as a major architect of victory over Hitler.

As for inner-Politburo manoeuvres, Stalin's capacity for reducing an individual's political influence, without necessarily resorting to drastic methods, was also shown in his treatment of Malenkov and Beria. During 1945-8 he relegated both these powerful figures, who were to some extent political allies, to the background. To the student of Stalin's methods, Beria's evolution is particularly instructive. As will be remembered, Beria had been appointed NKVD boss in 1938: the most sensitive office in the power structure, and to Stalin the most dangerous of all in potential. There was no position from which a *coup* could more easily be mounted against the dictator than from the political police establishment which supplied his bodyguards, his doctors, his chauffeurs and his household servants . . . and which also controlled vast armies consisting of various kinds of police troops all completely independent of the military chain of command. As will also be recalled, Beria's two immediate predecessors at the head of the NKVD had both been liquidated by Stalin after a brief tenure of office. By surviving his appointment for fifteen years, contriving eventually to outlive his master, Beria was to demonstrate durability of the highest order.

377

Beria did indeed physically survive his appointment to the NKVD. But to what extent did he survive as the active wielder of police powers? There are indications that Stalin was already seeking to detach him from that private empire even before the outbreak of war. In February 1941, Beria's Commissariat of the Interior (NKVD) lost direct control of the political police proper when this was removed from him and elevated to the status of a separate commissariat: the NKGB. Retaining the NKVD at this stage, Beria lost the NKGB . . . but to a personal protégé. Six months later, however, in the grave crisis caused by the outbreak of war, this split was countermanded, the NKGB reverting to its subordinate position as part of the NKVD: a sign that, at this disastrous stage, Stalin attached more importance to over-all political security than to the clipping of Berias' wings. But then, in 1943, with the tide of war at last turning in the Soviet Union's favour, Stalin reconstituted the NKGB as a commissariat nominally independent of Beria.[13] In January 1946, Beria's domestic powers were again reduced: now the NKVD too was taken away from him and given to a General Kruglov, who was not a Beria man and who retained this office until Stalin's death. Thus was Beria detached, at least formally, from his earlier satrapy. In March 1946 the NKVD and NKGB became the MVD and MGB respectively: the result of a decision to call all the 'people's commissariats' ministries; (it was through the same provision that the *Sovnarkom*, of which Stalin remained Chairman, became the Council of Ministers).

Despite the formal removal of internal affairs from Beria's direct grasp, several authorities have claimed that he still continued to exercise general control over political security.[14] But it seems hard to reconcile this claim with Krushchev's assertion that Stalin entrusted the over-all supervision of the post-war security organs – including Kruglov's MVD – to a complete outsider: the newly rising Party Secretary A. A. Kuznetsov.[15] Appointed to the Secretariat in 1945, Kuznetsov was a protégé of Beria's resurgent rival Zhdanov. It therefore seems safer to assume that Beria was removed from effective control over the security forces during the period of Zhdanov's ascendancy in 1946-8. Beria was far from downgraded, however, being entrusted with responsibility in the especially vital area of nuclear development. He also received promotion – in March 1946 – to full Politburo membership, perhaps as a consolation prize. Nor had Beria been so drastically detached from his former security fief as to prevent him from reasserting control over the political police complex in 1949-50, and again after Stalin's death in 1953 – as will be related in due course.

Malenkov's fortunes also form an instructive commentary on Stalin's last years. By the end of the war Malenkov seemed to have become the dictator's chosen heir. He was, after Stalin himself, the most important Secretary of the Central Committee, and he was given economic responsibilities which included chairmanship (from 1943) of the influential Committee on the Rehabilitation of Liberated Areas. He had thus taken over the mantle of crown prince which, in the late 1930s, had been that of Zhdanov: a precarious status, as Zhdanov had himself discovered when removed from the Centre and made responsible for beleaguered and starving Leningrad. But in the immediate post-war period it was Malenkov's turn to be taught the same lesson when Zhdanov returned to Moscow and the Secretariat, assuming a degree of ascendancy such as Stalin at no other time conceded to any other subordinate. There was a corresponding decline in Malenkov's influence. His policy of dismantling German industry and removing the pieces to Russia was discredited, and between 1946 and 1948 he even ceased to be listed as a Central Committee Secretary.[16]

Neither Malenkov nor Beria was openly disgraced in 1946. But both had been reminded, in a manner gentle by Stalin's standards, that one man was still in full control.

The Zhdanov Period at Home

Though the Stalinized Soviet Union at no time ceased to suffer regimentation intolerably harsh by 'bourgeois' standards, Stalin's subjects could (as we have noted) mark variations in severity from one period to another. In cultural life the comparatively easy-going atmosphere of the war was maintained for nearly twelve months after the Japanese surrender. So lax had censorship conditions become that many books and articles, published with official blessing during this phase, were destined to be denounced as heretical during the following years.

It has been suggested that the Leader served advance notice of an impending cultural crackdown in his speech to the electors of the Stalin District of Moscow on 9 February 1946.[1] In this, Stalin's last personally delivered policy-making oration of any importance, certain truculent remarks about the capitalist West helped to mark the passing of the anti-Hitlerite alliance and the consequent division of the world into two coldly warring camps, capitalist and communist. Nor did the Stalin of 9 February miss the opportunity to boast of his political achievements at home, as tested by the greatest war in history. The Soviet system had passed that examination with flying colours, he claimed, and had proved itself a going concern. But though Stalin's February speech was indeed boastful and menacing by turns it no more than dimly foreshadowed the ideological war which Zhdanov was to launch on the unprepared Soviet public six months later.

In claiming that Zhdanov 'launched' this campaign, and in accepting the label 'Zhdanovite' for the period 1946-8 – more strictly, for the period from summer 1946 onwards – we are following normal practice and using a convenient term. But it is important to stress that Zhdanov no more bore ultimate responsibility for the *Zhdanovshchina* (Soviet domestic policies from 1946 onwards) than the unfortunate Yezhov had borne responsibility for the *Yezhovshchina* of 1937-8. Not least among Stalin's skills was that of associating his own most unpopular measures with the names of their chief executants rather than with his own. On the briefing which Zhdanov may have received from his master we can only speculate. The most plausible assumption is that Zhdanov was chosen for this particular assignment because it accorded with his known propensities, and that Stalin let Zhdanov 'have his head' – closely monitoring implementation of the new policies, but without issuing detailed directives. Having other protégés available, the dictator could always replace his chief implement: a step which appears to have been contemplated at the very point when Zhdanov was to make it unnecessary by conveniently dying.

However closely he may or may not have been supervised by Stalin, Zhdanov did not infuse Stalinism with new ideas. He merely took elements long established as part of the system and injected them with increased virulence. The essence of his campaign was to insist – more stridently than had been insisted before – that all those active in the Soviet cultural and intellectual world, from authors and film-producers to philosophers and economists, were in effect advertising copywriters or executives employed on the greatest 'account' in the history of their profession: that of the Stalinized USSR as a whole. Their task was to 'sell' Stalin and his system with the same parade of devotional fervour with which others have launched detergents, canned beers and breakfast cereals. That the vehicle for this promotional offensive might be an eight-hundred-page novel, a three-hour film, or every page of every daily newspaper and other periodical – this consideration merely emphasizes the unlimited resources supporting a campaign such as Madison Avenue would have reduced to catchwords and television 'spots'. Stalinist publicity executives could afford to be more stately, long-winded and Victorian in their methods than their Western counterparts. But the simulated ecstasy of these acolytes, their claim to have solved the riddle of existence, their promise to open the gates of paradise on earth, their repetitive insistence on points already repeated *ad nauseam,* the helpless boredom generated in any sensitive recipient ... these features were identical. So too was the concentration on accumulating material objects (whether individually owned motor cars and washing machines or collectively owned combine harvesters and hydro-electric stations) which these two theoretically opposed philosophies each offered as the key to everlasting bliss.

Zhdanov's task as Stalin's senior ad-man was to remind Soviet intellectuals as brusquely as possible that they had been conscripted in the service of this great promotional drive. As was typical of Stalinist methods, an offensive ultimately directed against the entire Soviet cultural world began with the strafing of two individual scapegoats: the writers Zoshchenko and Akhmatova. They were the main targets for the Central Committee decree of 14 August 1946 ('On the Journals *Zvezda* and *Leningrad*') which opened the cultural assault, and which was followed one week later by a fighting speech from Zhdanov in person. Zoshchenko and Akhmatova were rebuked for standing aloof from politics; for propagating pessimism; for poisoning the minds of the young; for pursuing art for art's sake; for subservience to the West; for ignoring ideology. Akhmatova was denounced as a mixture of nun and whore who composed personal poetry accessible only to the few; Zoschchenko's sketch *Adventures of a Monkey* was condemned for implying that the ape house of a zoo might be a better place to live than the Soviet Union at large.[2]

Zhdanov next moved against the Soviet theatre and film world. Theatre managements were criticized for showing plays by Somerset Maugham and Arthur Pinero instead of works by Soviet playwrights on contemporary themes. Among films selected for condemnation was Part Two of Sergey Eisenstein's *Ivan the Terrible*. Eisenstein was accused of belittling the great sixteenth-century tyrant, and of slandering his murderous private army known as the Oprichnina: this, the MVD/MGB of sixteenth-century Muscovy, was now declared a 'progressive' phenomenon. We note how keenly sensitive Stalinism had become to attacks on the Leader such as were inevitably implied in any serious attempt to portray a historical tyrant.

The basic elements in Zhdanov's campaign were the glorification of everything Russian and the vilification of everything foreign. Targets for abuse embraced the entire decadent West, and especially the United States, while Soviet offenders included all those who allegedly 'kow-towed' to foreigners, even if this offence went no further than recognizing foreign influences on Russian writers. To have engaged in the comparative study of literature was now, it seemed, to have conspired against the State – except of course that literary influences described as emanating *from* Russia remained untreasonable all along. Philosophers and economists also fell under the lash. G. F. Aleksandrov – a protégé of Zhdanov's rival

Malenkov and author of a *History of West European Philosophy* – was rebuked for overrating alien thought systems; the economist Varga was assailed by Voznesensky (an ally of Zhdanov) for proclaiming the unduly soft line that world capitalism was not necessarily doomed to perish in the near future as the result of its inner contradictions.

Many academic and literary works were now rewritten to conform with Zhdanovite requirements, one high-placed victim being Aleksandr Fadeyev. In 1946 his war novel *The Young Guard* had received a Stalin Prize, first class, only to be denounced in the following year for failure to give adequate credit to the Party as an organizing force in the early period of the Hitlerite invasion. Fadeyev was compelled to rewrite the novel, and this despite his exalted status as premier author-hatchetman: he had been appointed Secretary-General of the Union of Writers in the wake of the Zoshchenko-Akhmatova scandal. Himself disgraced over *The Young Guard,* Fadeyev yet retained his new post, continuing to discipline fellow-writers while submitting to the discipline which he himself was administering. As for humbler culprits, they were compelled to make public recantations as abject as anything in the previous history of Stalinism. But though many intellectuals lost their posts, and some were arrested, the campaign impinged far less drastically on individuals than had the Terror of the late 1930s.

Tito's Breakaway

Far from confining his trouble-shooting activities to the Soviet Union, Zhdanov was also employed to regiment the Soviet satellites of eastern Europe. By early 1948, Stalin controlled eight of these dependencies, containing about a hundred million people: Albania, Bulgaria, Czechoslovakia, eastern Germany, Hungary, Poland, Rumania and Yugoslavia. Neither in the tempo nor in the technique of Stalinization did these communities follow an identical pattern of development, and the last Soviet takeover of all – that of Czechoslovakia in February 1948 – was followed within months by the dramatic breakaway of Titoist Yugoslavia from the Stalinist system.

On the satellites as a whole colonialist rule of a newly evolved type was imposed gradually and in three distinct phases: firstly, that of genuine coalition government including Communists; secondly, that of spurious coalition government dominated by Communists; and, thirdly, that of outright Stalinist totalitarianism.[1] The third stage, monolithic Stalinism, was achieved by Yugoslavia and Albania as early as 1945, but in other areas Stalinization took longer to establish. By the end of 1948 it had been everywhere imposed, but with the important reservation that Yugoslavia's defection had now reduced the total of satellites from eight to seven. When fully established, the typical Stalinist satellite consisted of a nominally independent country known as a People's Democracy. It was ruled by native-born puppet 'leaders' who were chosen for their subservience to Moscow, and who were manipulated from behind the scenes by a variety of threats and levers: occupation or threat of occupation by the Soviet Army; the subordination of local political security forces to the Kremlin; Communist party links; ruthless economic exploitation; imposed show trials.

Yet another instrument for controlling the satellites was forged in September 1947 with the creation of the Cominform: an operation for which Zhdanov – under Stalin – was chiefly responsible. Unlike the Comintern (disbanded in 1943), this new international Stalinist association was limited in membership to nine parties, all European. Nor did the Cominform's advertised aims include the fomenting of global revolution, since its ostensible purpose was the exchange of officially sponsored information – for which facilities more than adequate already existed. The real function of the new body was, presumably, to enable Stalin to issue orders in the name of an international authority whenever he might find it inconvenient to instruct his satellites through his numerous other channels of command. It was Stalin who fixed Belgrade as the Cominform's official home, wishing either to flatter Tito or to enmesh him more closely in the Stalinist system. Stalin also personally invented a long-winded title for the Cominform's official newspaper: *For a Lasting Peace – For a People's Democracy*. The intention was to compel the 'bourgeois' press to repeat the whole rigmarole every time reference was made to the periodical, and thus to provide free advertisement for the Stalinist system.[2] In fact, however, the paper was so tedious, even by the standards of Stalin-sponsored publications, that there was rarely occasion to allude to it at all.

Soon after the foundation of the Cominform, Soviet-Yugoslav relations began to move towards a crisis. January and February 1948 saw the third and last of Djilas's expeditions to Moscow, where he had two discussions with Stalin: the first suspiciously affable, the second chillingly hostile. Not yet ready, in January, to quarrel with the Yugoslavs outright, Stalin quickly disposed of one problem which had been causing tension between Moscow and Belgrade: that of Albania, which seemed to hover between the status of satellite to Stalin and satellite to Tito. 'We agree to Yugoslavia swallowing Albania,' Stalin now obligingly told the Yugoslavs. He then gathered the fingers of his right hand together, brought them to his mouth, licked them and pretended to swallow them.[3] It was a gesture of shattering vulgarity, not least shocking because of the casual way in which the dictator seemed to be arbitrating the destiny of a nation on the spur of the moment. Singled out on the same occasion for an ostentatious display of benevolence by the Soviet leader, Djilas quickly realised that this was an attempt to turn him against his senior political comrades in Yugo-slavia,[4] and to recruit him as Stalin's chief man in Belgrade. Divide-and-rule had ever been the dictator's motto, but in this instance his splitting tactics were unsuccessful. They were to remain so throughout the Soviet-Yugoslav dispute, during the whole of which Tito and his colleagues maintained unbroken solidarity.

Having resisted Stalin's blandishments in January 1948, Djilas found a distinct chill in the air when the Moscow discussions of Stalin's relations with his satellites were resumed, after an interval, on 10 February.[5] By now the Soviet leader's attitude towards the Titoists had hardened, and it is from this February meeting that we must date the beginning of a serious Moscow-Belgrade split. Once again Stalin is found 'needling' a favourite butt – the red-faced Dimitrov, who was derided for a recent indiscretion: approving at a press conference the idea of an eastern European federation excluding the Soviet Union. Stalin also jointly rebuked the Bulgarian Dimitrov and the Yugoslav Foreign Minister Kardelj for signing a friendship pact between their two countries without previously clearing this with the Soviet Union. As was now abundantly evident, Stalin no longer intended to tolerate any inter-satellite relations whatever except those supervised in detail by himself; and he forced Kardelj to sign an agreement to this effect. Constantly interrupting and brow-beating the satellite representatives, Stalin denied – in one famous exchange of discourtesies – that Holland formed part of the Benelux community. Kardelj tried to correct this solecism, but was angrily informed: 'When I say no it means no!'[6] As the episode shows, the truth was still, to Stalin, whatever he might at any moment declare it to be.

Meanwhile the world at large had no inkling that Russia was about to lose what seemed the brightest jewel in her satellite crown. Yugoslavia had all along appeared to conform with every bend and twist in the Kremlinite line. She had already staged her own trials of political dissidents, and she had shot down certain intruding American aircraft. Behind the scenes, however, her quarrel with the Soviet Union was simmering dangerously. The Yugoslavs had annoyed Stalin by objecting to the extensive recruiting of Yugoslav citizens by the Soviet intelligence services.[7] Tito also resented Soviet economic exploitation, while his penchant for taking political initiatives in the area of inter-satellite relations was a further offence. Not only had the Yugoslav leader been treating Albania as his personal satellite

– and that before receiving Stalin's contemptuous permission to do so – but he had also toyed with federative plans envisaging Belgrade as the centre of a Balkan empire excluding the Soviet Union. Tito's post-war attempts to annex Trieste had also irritated the Soviet leader by complicating his relations with his western former allies over a trivial issue.[8] Then again, on a personal level, although the Yugoslav leaders had always deferred to Stalin, the trouble was that the respect of these battle-hardened partisans had stopped short of abject servility. As disciplined Stalinists they were fully prepared for Yugoslavia to remain a political and economic dependency of Moscow; but they did object to the extreme degree of colonial subjugation which Stalin wished to impose.

Clinging to a fragment of independence in his relations with Moscow, Marshal Tito enjoyed certain advantages denied to his opposite numbers in the other satellites. The Yugoslavs had made their own revolution; their partisans had fought and defeated the Germans on a scale unmatched in any other occupied country; Tito's heroic wartime feats had earned him kudos in the other satellite countries as well as in Yugoslavia – popularity which was enough of an offence in Stalin's eyes to warrant the humbling of the Yugoslav marshal.

Proceeding from words to deeds, Stalin took the first concrete step towards precipitating a Moscow-Belgrade showdown on 18–19 March 1948 by suddenly removing all Soviet military advisers from Yugoslavia: a gesture intended to symbolize the withdrawal of his favour. This development provoked an acrimonious correspondence (since published) between the Central Committees of the two Communist Parties concerned. Signed by Molotov and Stalin,[9] the Soviet letters to the Yugoslavs show the same crudely bullying tone which the Generalissimo was also apt to take in *tête-à-tête* discussions with underlings. In content, too, the Soviet letters have Stalin's stamp. Tito and his associates are accused of Trotskyism, Bukharinism and Menshevism: a combination of errors such as might have seemed a logical impossibility to any mind less flexible than the Leader's. On a more mundane level, Stalin's old complaint against Djilas – for irresponsibly harping on the Red Army's formidable record of rape in Yugoslavia – is dredged out.[10] Among innumerable other accusations made against the Yugoslav Party none is more typical or traditional than the charge of adopting *undemocratic methods*. Accused of maintaining a disgraceful terrorist régime, the Titoists were further denounced for appointing their officials from above instead of permitting them to be elected by the rank-and-file; they were also accused of stifling self-criticism. These charges have a long familiar ring, for Stalin had often resorted to the same tactics when dealing with recalcitrant underlings – one recalls, for example, his strictures of 1928 against the Soviet trade-union chief Tomsky and against the Moscow Party leader Uglanov.

Elsewhere in his correspondence with the Yugoslavs, Stalin even goes so far as to threaten Tito with assassination: 'We think that the political career of Trotsky is quite instructive.'[11] It is not surprising, then, that Tito refused to put his head in the lion's mouth after his last meeting with the Soviet dictator in 1946. He would not visit Moscow in person in early 1948, despite Soviet pressure on him to do so; later in the same year he declined Muscovite invitations to discuss Soviet-Yugoslav differences on Stalin-held territory. The final excommunication of the Yugoslavs by the Cominform, in Bucharest on 28 June 1948, accordingly took place without Titoist participation as Stalin's assembled vassals from the eight remaining Cominform parties appealed to healthy elements in the Yugoslav party, loyal to Marxism-Leninism, to convert their leaders to internationalism (that is, Stalinism) or to replace them.[12] Thus Stalin called for a Stalinist *coup* in Belgrade, being slow to appreciate the temper of Yugoslav resistance to his imperious demands. He boasted that he had only to shake his little finger and there would be no more Tito.[13] But however much the Generalissimo might huff and puff, and however often Stalinist propaganda might assail the Titoist clique with vituperation of the choice brand reserved for political dissidents within the Communist camp, Tito's house yet remained standing. Neither verbal threats, nor menacing troop movements, nor staged border incidents could break the Yugoslav will to resist. From the military invasion which he could easily have mounted in the period immediately following the break, the cautious Generalissimo held back until (by 1950) a Yugoslavia associated with the West no longer stood alone against the might of Stalin.

According to Khrushchev, the Soviet-Yugoslav quarrel was grossly and wilfully bungled by Stalin, who played a 'shameful role'; the affair could easily have been settled by discussion.[14] No doubt it could, for Belgrade was only too willing to compromise. But could the matter have been settled along lines satisfactory to Stalin, whose temperament brooked no element of disobedience in his political associates? Anxious to preserve world Communism as a monolith dominated by himself alone, the Generalissimo preferred to rule over a truncated empire rather than abate one jot of his dictatorial power. Stalinism must be preserved in pristine purity untainted by any hostile element. Hence the Leader's pre-war and wartime opposition to Communist revolutionary movements in so many countries of the world – in Spain, China and Greece, as well as in Yugoslavia. Hence, too, Stalin's failure to encourage the large post-war French and Italian Communist parties to seize power at junctures when such a course appeared to offer some prospect of success. Stalin had no interest in seeing new Communist régimes established if these were to be no more than quasi-Stalinist and quasi-subservient to the Kremlin. They must be completely under his control or they were worse than useless to him: a policy of which the wisdom has been confirmed by developments since the dictator's death. Pluralism has long replaced monolithism within the world Communist movement, as first Yugoslavia, later Albania and China, and also Poland, Hungary, Rumania and Czechoslovakia have – with varying degrees of success and for varying periods of time – asserted a degree of independence from Kremlinite control . . . not to mention the considerable licence taken since Stalin's death by Communist parties within countries not ruled by Communist governments. The process now seems irreversible.

Though Stalin never went so far as to yield independent power to Zhdanov, he yet permitted that senior trouble-shooter to promote policies – foreign as well as domestic – which by no means echoed every nuance of his master's voice. Reviewing the period 1946–8 in the context of what preceded and followed it, we see in the admittedly russo-centric Zhdanov a mentality more international-minded and more concerned with ideology than that of the pragmatical Stalin, whose addiction to Russian chauvinism was even greater than that of his latest protégé. This is evident from the tone of Zhdanov's cultural witch-hunt at home, and also from the policies simultaneously promoted by him as Stalin's temporary handler-in-chief of eastern European satellites. In both areas we can trace what appear to be Zhdanovite emphases differing from essentially Stalinist emphases.

That both Zhdanov and Stalin favoured Soviet expansionism is clear, but there seems to have been a disagreement about the kind of militancy which the situation required. Pioneering the Cominform – he made the key speech at its founding conference in September 1947 – Zhdanov appears to have placed more trust than his master in the potentialities of Communist parties outside the Soviet Union. It seems likely, for instance, that Zhdanov wanted to give all-out support to the Communist partisans in Greece: a line also promoted by the Yugoslavs. But though Stalin may have been willing to let Zhdanov have his head over such matters for a while, his instinct was to put his main trust in Soviet political and military power, rather than in the doings of satellite or foreign Communist parties in faraway countries of which he knew next to nothing. Cautious by instinct, pugnacious only in contexts of his own careful choosing, Stalin once admitted himself reluctant to support the Greek Communists, saying that he did not want to antagonize Great Britain and the USA. ('the most powerful state in the world') in an area vital to Western interests.[15] That Zhdanov clashed with Stalin over this issue seems likely. If so we can dimly discern the phantom of a Zhdanov-Tito axis directed against Stalin: a suggestion which is confirmed to some extent by the suspicious interest which visiting Yugoslavs showed in Leningrad when received there by Zhdanov's faction in early 1948.[16] Promoting militancy in areas inadequately controlled by the Kremlin, and seeking to advance Communism locally by reliance on imperfectly controlled native forces such as the Greek and Yugoslav parties, Zhdanov antagonized his master. Then came Tito's defection from the Soviet camp: an event which could only confirm Stalin in his growing mistrust of Zhdanovism. It was now that Stalin began to restore Zhdanov's rival Malenkov to his former prominence. He also brought a new Soviet spokesman, Suslov, into the East European orbit: perhaps as a replacement for Zhdanov. When, therefore, Zhdanov presided over the excommunication of Tito at the Cominform Bucharest conference of June 1948, he was probably being compelled, by a typical Stalinist manoeuvre, to demolish his own discredited policies.[17]

That Zhdanov would have fallen from power in any case, even if his death had not intervened two months later, seems a likely assumption from signs of disfavour which had been accumulating. There is also the point that Zhdanov had, by now, been given quite enough latitude for any one man. He had run through the two or three years of grace which – the careers of Yagoda and Yezhov suggest – were the most that any Stalinist favourite could count on without expecting to be pushed into the background, if not disgraced and executed. Always mindful of the need to keep his entourage unbalanced, Stalin might well have been ready to drop Zhdanov in mid-1948, even if Zhdanov's satellite policies had not been discredited by then.

Zhdanov's death, on 31 August 1948, came as no surprise. He was known to be in bad health, and he had told Djilas in the previous January that he might die at any moment.[18] Still, the fact remains that this was yet another in the catalogue of highly convenient fatalities with which Stalin's career is studded – convenient in this case because the dictator was able to modify Zhdanovite policies without dealing the blow to corporate high-level Soviet morale which the public disavowal of a living Zhdanov might have inflicted. The defunct Zhdanov was always to remain in good odour – like the defunct Kirov before him – with the Stalinist publicity machine ... and this despite the savage secret persecution of Zhdanovites, known as the Leningrad Affair, which was to follow shortly.

Though the suspicion still persists that Zhdanov may have been liquidated on Stalin's orders, a mere suspicion it remains. It rests solely on the sinister circumstances surrounding the spurious 'Doctors' Plot' as fabricated by or for the declining Stalin in 1952-3. At that time certain eminent Kremlin physicians were to be accused of having murdered Zhdanov by medical means: on the instructions of British and American intelligence operating through international Jewry. As in earlier cases – those of Gorky and Kirov – one has the uneasy feeling that Stalin may have been impelled by a certain orderliness of mind to saddle others with a crime committed by himself. It would have appealed to him as a neat way of rounding off such political murders, if murders they indeed were, and it would certainly have tickled his famous sense of humour.

14
Peacemonger

Stalin in his Seventies

As we trace Stalin's progress from the onset of his eighth decade, we shall begin by considering his public image as it was now being presented to the Soviet Union and the world at large. We shall then turn from the official to the domestic plane to review his private life during these declining years.

Zhdanov's death signals no reduction in the campaign to 'sell' Stalin's image. On the contrary, Stalin worship – first fully launched on the dictator's fiftieth birthday – reaches its peak exactly twenty years later, on 21 December 1949, with extravagant celebrations in honour of the newly septuagenarian genius. From every corner of the Soviet Union, from the satellites, from the Stalinist faithful all over the globe, countless gifts – tapestries, ornamental weapons, carpets, embroideries – flow towards Moscow, there to be housed in a special museum. On the sacred date artillery salutes assail the ears of stunned Muscovites, even as their eyes are beguiled by acres of scarlet bunting and by Red Square processions. Do they look up into the heavens? Lo! He is there also, resplendent in inflated rubber ... for the occasion is also marked by a special release of balloon effigies of the bewhiskered deity; tethered near the Red Square and floodlit by night, they brood benignly over the worshippers below. Journalistic celebrations culminate in a *Pravda* nativity edition full of Hieratic felicitations:

Beloved Leader and Teacher ... progressive people of the entire world ... tocsin calling for vigilance ... gratitude ... network of meat combines ... mankind ... banner ... mighty voice of the Great Stalin ... powerful columns of fighters for peace ...

The authors of these stylized tributes are surviving Politburo members whose piecemeal extermination the deified Generalissimo will shortly be plotting in detail.

Converted into full-time propagandists by the Cult, Soviet authors of what purport to be *belles lettres* have long been glorifying Stalin until it has now become almost impossible to publish a novel, a story or a poem on a contemporary theme without making lengthy obeisances to the Leader. Drama contributes its share to the Cult, as also to the continued rewriting of history. Ivan Popov's play *The Family* (1950) has the Lenin of 1897 asking about the revolutionary situation in Transcaucasia. Eliciting a reply pregnant in its limpid simplicity ('Stalin is there'), the Leader's great forerunner can only gasp 'Magnificent!'[1] It need hardly be said that Stalin had been a seventeen-year-old schoolboy in 1897; that it is doubtful whether he had even heard of Lenin at the time; and that Lenin had quite certainly never heard of him.

Another work of the period, Pyotr Pavlenko's novel *Happiness,* employs techniques borrowed from the medieval Russian Lives of the Saints to depict Stalin at Yalta in 1945. The novel's hero, Voropayev, is a war veteran accustomed to facing German tanks undaunted; yet even this battle-hardened hero's knees give beneath him as he sees the godhead approach. Stalin's arms are outstretched, his smile is beatifically devastating. He has not aged .... And yet, and yet ....

His face, still the same face as it always had been, still that dear counterance so familiar down to its tiniest adored wrinkle, has taken on new traits of majesty and solemn seriousness . . . a change inevitable since the People is accustomed to gaze into that beloved visage as into a mirror.

Overwhelmed by Stalin's warm, friendly nature, keen interest in humanity and amazing grasp of actuality, Voropayev timidly removes from his coat pocket the tiny handkerchief in which are wrapped a few humble snowdrops ... freshly picked 'for Stalin' by a dear little girl whom Voropayev has chanced to meet on his way to the Leader's residence. After sending the infant donor some biscuits in return, the Great Friend of Children Everywhere looks Voropayev straight in the eye, man to man, while his face lights up as if touched by a ray of sunshine. The meeting makes Voropayev feel a thousand years younger.[2]

In such a context it comes as no surprise to find the leading novelist Leonid Leonov – an original creative writer and a Christian believer – proposing in *Pravda* the introduction of a new calendar based on Stalin's nativity instead of Jesus Christ's![3]

Occasionally Stalin can be seen contributing to the Cult in person – as when he intervenes to edit the *Short Biography* of himself, composed in 1948. Not content merely to approve the existing scriptural text – with its references to 'the greatest leader' and 'the sublime strategist of all times and nations' – he also makes insertions in his own hand, rendering the devotional message yet more devotional. The sentence 'Stalin is the Lenin of today' is expanded to read: 'Stalin is the worthy continuer of Lenin's work, or, as it is said in our party, Stalin is the Lenin of today.' Stalin also inserts passages lauding Stalin's genius as military strategist and theoretician. And it was as part of this same essay in editorship that Stalin produced the richest and most ironical jest of his career: 'Stalin never allowed his work to be marred by the slightest hint of vanity, conceit or self-adulation.'[4]

What of the dictator's private life, such as it was, during his old age? What of his hobbies, relaxations and domestic entourage; his attitudes to friends and relatives? The general picture is of an old man in whom only the political passion still persists; his family affections – never strong – now barely survive, while even his few leisure pursuits are heavily tinged with politics.

Stalin liked watching pre-war films, especially those featuring Charlie Chaplin ... but with the eloquent exception of Chaplin's *Great Dictator*, which was never shown in the Soviet Union.[5] Nor did the Leader scorn the Soviet cinema, even after his cultural persecutions had virtually brought film production to a halt within his empire. Apt to take his private movie shows more seriously than they deserved, Stalin formed a wildly optimistic assessment of Soviet rural prosperity on the basis of idyllic celluloid bumpkins who were shown feasting at tables laden with turkeys and geese.[6] Still, even this must have made a change from the table talk of Beria, Zhdanov, Malenkov and the like. It was with these and other Politburo members that the dictator still liked to spend his evenings at those interminable informal buffet suppers which were so tastelessly spiced with horseplay, practical jokes, compulsory potations and the needling of some chosen butt or licensed buffoon. Even during his rare holidays from Moscow, Stalin continued to command the presence of these boon companions at extended semi-working supper parties which continued whenever he visited his residences in the Sochi area or other parts of the southern USSR. He had once regularly taken his summer holidays in that region, but had been unable to do so during the troubled years 1938–45. Travelling south by car in 1946 after so long an interval, the dictator obtained for the first time glimpses of the appalling devastation wrought in southern Russia by the war.[7]

In summer 1951, Stalin took the last vacation trip of his life: to Borzhomi, in Georgia. Retaining the bulk of a capacious palace for his personal use, he forced his enormous staff to huddle in cramped servants' quarters. Sometimes he would stride briskly through the park, his generals panting after him; but the spry old man was liable to make a sudden swerve at any moment and bump into these senior flunkeys, cursing them for their clumsiness. No less exasperating was his reception by the local inhabitants, who flocked to welcome the return of Georgia's most famous native product. For once Stalin was greeted with unfeigned enthusiasm: here, after all, was the boy from Gori who had mastered the long detested Russians. But Stalin loathed public adulation at close quarters. His face twitched when he sighted the huge welcoming crowd assembled in his honour – fawning, shouting and throwing bouquets – at Kutaisi railway station. Attempting, later, to take a trip from Borzhomi, he found himself kidnapped by hospitable villagers; carpets were laid on the road, and he was compelled to join them in a banquet. This display of emotion disgusted Stalin, and he returned to his palace in high dudgeon. Imprisoned there by his own fame, the august holidaymaker was unable to visit Tiflis or his home town of Gori, where his birthplace – the one-time shack of cobbler Vissarion Dzhugashvili – now stood encapsulated in the pretentious colonnaded shrine erected by Beria.[8]

As his life drew towards its close, Stalin became ever more lonely, ever more solitary.

For twenty-seven years [his daughter has stated] I was witness to the spiritua. deterioration of my own father, watching day after day how everything human in him left him and how gradually he turned into a grim monument to his own self.[9]

His closest intimate during his last years was one Nikolay Vlasik. Stalin's butler – in effect – at Kuntsevo, Vlasik was also responsible for security arrangements in that household, being a general of political police. Somehow this major-domo – 'incredibly stupid, illiterate and uncouth', according to Stalin's daughter – had become a power behind the throne, being used by the dictator to pass on his views about films, operas, architectural projects and the like. But Vlasik, too, was eventually arrested on Stalin's orders.[10] Meanwhile the dictator had become a prey to paranoid fantasies. Lest attempts be made to poison him, all his food was chemically analysed at a special laboratory. A specially appointed doctor would periodically sample the air of the dictator's dwelling ... perhaps to prevent the shade of Yagoda from spraying the curtains with the deadly mercury vapour to which allusion had been made at his trial in 1938.

Owing to the large staffs maintained at so many unused residences, Stalin's living expenses were inordinately high, but were footed by the State. He continued all along to receive monthly wage packets; from the Central Committee; from the Defence Ministry; from the Council of

Ministers; and from the numerous other bodies which had J. V. Stalin on their pay roll. Unopened in sealed envelopes, these funds accumulated in the drawers of his villa. After the dictator's death the whole hoard was to disappear without trace.[11]

Having driven his second wife, and possibly his eldest son, to suicide (as described above) and having also liquidated several relatives-by-marriage during the *Yezhovshchina*, Stalin continued during the post-war period to persecute surviving members of his family. For sixteen years he brooded on his second wife's self-inflicted death before taking revenge, in 1948, by ordering the imprisonment of the three women who – as he himself was apt to complain – bore the guilt of *knowing too much* about that scandal.[12] Two of these victims were sisters-in-law of Stalin's: Nadezhda's elder sister Anna Redens, *née* Alliluyeva, and Yevgeniya, widow of Nadezhda's brother Pavel Alliluyev. Also arrested for guilt by association with the suicide was Polina, Molotov's Jewish wife – a close friend of Nadezhda's and her confidante on the fateful night of her last quarrel with Stalin. Only after the dictator's death were these unfortunate women to be released.

Among this trio of Stalin's victims his widowed sister-in-law Yevgeniya had incurred Stalin's additional displeasure by choosing (after the death of her first husband, Pavel Alliluyev) a second spouse who was of Jewish extraction. After the war both Yevgeniya and her new husband were arrested – she on suspicion of poisoning her former husband Pavel. As for Anna Alliluyeva, she was not only guilty of being Stalin's sister-in-law, but had also offended by publishing a book of memoirs about him in 1946. This work had been converted into Hieratic prose by someone else, but the text does not consist of Legend material unalloyed. It was, perhaps, the over-intimate picture of the dictator which gave offence . . . the pages, for instance, on which he is described as a jocular occasional lodger in the Alliluyevs' Petrograd apartment during the pre-revolutionary period. The author makes much of Stalin's penchant for mimicry, and even records his habit of mocking the tub-thumping revolutionary orators of that age. She also describes in detail his main physical disability: the weakness in one arm which led the Imperial Russian authorities to reject him for military service. By inference, too, Anna Alliluyeva accuses Stalin of neglecting his ageing mother. All these were blemishes unsuitable for the image of a deified tyrant.

The pogrom against Stalin's 'in-laws' was provoked or intensified by Beria, who craftily worked up the dictator's suspicions; on this point Svetlana's testimony accords with Khrushchev's accusations.[13] Svetlana's aunts told her that they blamed Beria for the arrest of the Svanidzes (relatives of Stalin's first wife) in the late 1930s, and also for their own.

Her aunt by marriage, Yevgeniya, had drawn Beria's anger upon herself by indiscreetly mocking his crude sexual advances.[14]

Liquidating, temporarily or permanently, these and many other relatives by marriage, Stalin at least left the elder Alliluyevs (his father-in-law and mother-in-law) in peace, though they too found themselves banned from his presence, lest they intercede on behalf of kinsfolk less favoured. Had they had the chance to plead for their daughter Anna, they would no doubt have reminded Stalin of her kindness to him during his days as a hunted revolutionary, when she had helped him with food, clothing and shelter. Such an appeal might very well have succeeded, for Stalin found it hard to resist the few suppliants who managed to penetrate his defences; hence the care which he took to protect himself from confrontations so embarrassing. On this his daughter Svetlana's memoirs provide evidence – describing, for example the occasion on which a diplomat, M. M. Slavutsky (father of one of Svetlana's schoolfriends) was arrested, whereupon the victim's wife immediately composed a letter to Stalin appealing for clemency. The missive was given to Slavutsky's daughter for transmission to Stalin via Svetlana – who indeed fulfilled this errand of mercy. All turned out well: the victim was duly released, returning home a few days later. But Stalin severely rebuked his daughter for acting as a go-between; he strictly forbade her to do anything of the kind again.[15]

To the dictator in decline his daughter was proving a grievous disappointment. As recounted above, he had already consigned to a concentration camp the first man for whom Svetlana had formed a serious attachment: the Jewish cinematic script-writer Kapler. Then, several years later, Svetlana announced her intention of marrying a certain Grigory Morozov, and it turned out that Morozov too was Jewish. Whence, Stalin must yet again have wondered, the fatal fascination exercised over his relatives by a race for which he himself felt such antipathy? Giving his grudging consent to the match, he refused to meet his new son-in-law.[16] Svetlana has well described the terror which she felt as she first introduced her little son Joseph, aged three, to his terrible forbear and namesake . . . who, luckily, took a fancy to the child and played with him for half an hour. Since Stalin agreed to meet only three of his eight grandchildren, the infant had been exceptionally favoured.[17] But the dictator – increasingly isolated and crotchety in his declining years – became more and more estranged from his daughter, who eventually lost all feeling for him.

Stalin's surviving son Vasily was turning out yet more unsatisfactory. After ending the war as a precociously dissipated twenty-four-year-old lieutenant-general, he was appointed Air Commander of Moscow Military District. But in 1952 he caused grave scandal by failing to call off a May

Day fly-past during stormy weather, with the result that several planes crashed, their pilots being killed. For this offence Stalin dismissed the young general, whose behaviour had long been outrageously indecorous.[18] By now Vasily was already an advanced alcoholic; he stood in urgent need of treatment, not of the humiliating reprimands which his angry father would administer to him in public. After an ignominious further career, which included dismissal from the air force and prolonged spells in prison and hospital, Stalin's second son was to die of alcoholism in 1962.

Fighting for Peace

On 24 June 1948, a few days before having Yugoslavia expelled from the Cominform, Stalin struck out in a different direction by imposing a blockade on the sectors of Berlin occupied by his former Western allies: an enclave surrounded by Soviet-controlled East Germany. Following so closely on the recent Soviet takeover of Czechoslovakia, this challenge almost seemed an act of war, especially as it was accompanied by other alarming activities: by threats to Turkey and Iran; by Communist partisan activity in countries as diverse as Greece, Malaya, Indonesia, Burma, the Philippines and China; by the apparent intention to invade Yugoslavia. The Western allies countered the Berlin blockade by organizing a massive airlift. They also pressed on more urgently with measures to unite non-Stalinist Germany. Thus did the Generalissimo's 'brinkmanship' over Berlin help to stiffen Western resistance, also hastening the formation of an anti-Stalinist military bloc, NATO. As an exercise in aggression the Berlin blockade therefore proved a failure, but it at least served Stalin well as a probing operation. For some three years he had pursued the policy of extending Stalinism in widespread areas of eastern and central Europe by all means short of war; now, in Berlin, he at last met determined opposition. Always accustomed to withdraw when resolutely resisted, he served notice of his willingness to back down over Berlin in *Pravda* of 27 January 1949, encoding this concession in four face-saving answers to questions put to him by an American journalist.[1] A few months later, in May, the Soviet blockade was duly lifted.

With the raising of the Berlin blockade, Stalin's period of extreme post-war pugnacity in eastern and central Europe came to an end. Meanwhile, in the far east, Communist expansion still continued apace; but without the Soviet Generalissimo's blessing. Autumn 1949 saw the swift conquest of mainland China completed by Communist armies under Mao Tse-tung, and on 1 October China was officially proclaimed a People's Republic.

Mao's outright victory was unwelcome to the Soviet dictator. Never an automatic sponsor of upheaval for upheaval's sake, Stalin was interested in seeing foreign governments overthrown only if they were to be replaced by régimes which he could hope to dominate totally and permanently. At the moment the Chinese Communists might be comparatively weak, and thus dependent on Stalin's good will; but the huge country which they ruled was nearly three times as populous as the Soviet Union, and even Stalin could hardly conceive of keeping so gigantic a puppet perpetually dancing at his touch. Neither desiring a Communist takeover in China, nor yet striving vigorously to thwart it, Stalin had taken a middle position, treating hostilities between Nationalist and Communist Chinese as one of those running sores which – like the earlier Spanish Civil War and the later Korean campaign – were best kept open as long as possible. So long as Mao had a fair edge over Chiang, but without actually winning, there had always been hope that the USA might sacrifice vast resources to the Nationalist cause while the Soviet Union stood, benignly uncommitted, on the side lines. A few years earlier – perhaps with some such calculation in mind – Stalin had even advised the Chinese Reds to call off their insurrection; to disband their armies; and to make a deal with Chiang.[2] But by now the Chinese Communists had had the advantage of studying Stalin's methods for twenty years. Knowing their man only too well, they had blandly agreed to follow his advice by reducing their military activities; but they had then gone ahead regardless with their all-out anti-Chiang campaign. In July 1948, Stalin was still found trying to restrain the too-successful Chinese Reds through an emissary who reached their armies in southern Hopei. They should not embark on any large scale offensive against the Nationalists, he told them, but should confine themselves to continuing guerrilla warfare.[3] Once again, though, the Chinese comrades courteously ignored Big Brother's counsel.

In keeping with Stalin's policy of non-involvement in China, the Soviet press of 1949 had little to say about Mao's successes, concentrating rather on the villainy of Tito; even the Greek Communist partisans (whom Stalin also deplored) received more prominence from the Soviet propaganda machine than did the victorious Chinese comrades. Maintaining 'correct' diplomatic relations with the Chiangists long after their defeat seemed certain, the Soviet government correspondingly delayed official recognition of Mao's republic until the last moment. Then, a few months later, Chinese delegates headed by the victorious Mao were indeed invited to Moscow, but found themselves treated as representatives of a second-class power. And it was an unenthusiastic Stalin, not the usual smiling host, who allowed himself to be photographed for *Pravda* with the Chinese.

The extraordinary length of Mao's stay in Moscow (from 16 December 1949 until 17 February 1950) provoked rumours of Stalin detaining the Chinese leader against his will. In any case much hard bargaining must have taken place. It led to a treaty relaxing the Soviet hold on Port Arthur, Dairen and the Manchurian Railway, previously conceded by Chiang in the Soviet-Chinese treaty of 1945. The Chinese also received financial credits from Russia, but on an insultingly inadequate scale.[4]

While Western countries were increasingly alarmed by Soviet Russia's huge (though considerably demobilized) land armies in Europe, and by her sophisticated techniques of territorial aggrandizement, Stalin had fears of his own to contend with. The economic strength of the Soviet Union was immeasurably less than that of the USA, which also possessed long-range aircraft and a powerful navy such as Stalin lacked. Above all, America held a monopoly of nuclear weapons. So long as this situation persisted, Stalin could hope to win a war against the West only if his enemies should practise atomic self-denial. Meanwhile, behind the scenes, he was trying to promote Soviet nuclear development by all possible means.

As will be recalled, Stalin had reacted with apparent lack of interest to President Truman's announcement, made to him at Potsdam in July 1945, that the USA had developed an atomic bomb. Having no nuclear weapons of his own for the time being, the Soviet leader did his best in the early post-war years to pretend that no such things existed. Soviet military journals passed over the topic in total silence,[5] and Stalin himself rarely picked it up. Among his few allusions is a statement made on 17 September 1946. Stalin then claimed that he personally did not consider the atomic bomb as serious a factor as certain other statesmen believed it. Atom bombs were well equipped to terrify the weak-nerved; but they did not exist in sufficient numbers to determine the outcome of a war. The American monopoly of atomic weapons did create a threat, of course, but that monopoly would not continue long; and in any case use of the bomb would be banned.[6] Such was the low profile which Stalin preferred to maintain in public on this delicate theme. In private conversation, however, the Soviet leader was known to express a very different attitude; he spoke of the atom bomb with enthusiasm, allowing it to be understood that he would never rest until he had one of his own.[7]

On 23 September 1949 the world learnt that the Soviet Union had at last exploded her first nuclear device, but the Stalinist publicity machine made no attempt to exploit this achievement; there was no cause for alarm, Moscow radio told its listeners.[8] And in any case the fact was that the gap between the first experimental explosion and the stock-piling of deliverable bombs had yet to be filled. Neither now nor later in his life did Stalin threaten other countries with Soviet nuclear attack: a distasteful habit which Khrushchev was to cultivate after his master's death. By then Soviet hydrogen bombs and effective delivery systems had been added to the modest beginnings achieved under the Generalissimo.

It is no coincidence, perhaps, that the explosion – so underplayed in propaganda – of the Soviet Union's first nuclear device, in late 1949, coincided with the adoption of a slightly less aggressive foreign policy. Now the dictator at last unavowedly jettisoned the militant expansionism of his early post-war years and adopted a posture still admittedly militant, but comparatively defensive in essence. While maintaining the traditionally truculent Soviet tone, he abandoned from 1950 onwards the further extension of his European empire. Though this change of attitude was chiefly brought about by an increased Western will to resist, the growing strength of the Soviet Union also played its part by removing the need for bluster designed to distract attention from nuclear vulnerability. From now onwards Stalin was to aim less at stretching the bounds of his satellite Empire in the West than at subverting the capitalists from within through propaganda. His main instrument was the great Stalinist Peace Campaign, which invited the gullible and unwary in countries outside his orbit to identify a love of peace with support for his foreign policy objectives. Agitation against colonialism was increasingly used to weaken the Western hold on global military bases, while attempts were also made to disrupt the Western alliance by sowing discord between the USA and her partners. Thus did short-term Stalinist aggression give way to long-term Stalinist subversion.

In one area of the world, however – the far east – Stalinist aggression continued unabated until halted by the dictator's death. On 25 June 1950, Communist North Korea launched a sudden attack across the Thirty-Eighth Parallel against non-Communist South Korea: a massive onslaught preceded by a considerable military build-up. That Stalin had advance knowledge of the North Korean attack may be assumed; that he could have vetoed it, had he wished, is certain. What we do not know is the extent to which he was responsible for unleashing the Korean War in the first place. One leading authority has him as the prime mover;[9] another inclines to see China as the pacemaker, inferring that Mao may have insisted on the Korean adventure during the long Soviet-Chinese negotiations of 1949–50 in Moscow.[10] In the absence of evidence both views tend to be expressed cautiously, but it is at least common ground that the North Koreans did not launch the war on their own unprompted initiative.

Whatever the degree of Stalin's sponsorship, the Korean adventure offered him an evident advantage in the quick gains which seemed to be going for nothing. Had not American statesmen openly proclaimed Korea inessential to the USA's vital interests?[11] In any case, what likelihood could there be of armed intervention in Korea by an America which had so recently failed to lend Chiang Kai-shek massive support in the Chinese conflict: a conflict far more fraught with foreign policy implications? How tempting for Stalin, then, to sanction – or, at least, not to countermand – the swift annexation of South Korea by the North; such a *coup* might quickly neutralize American influence on Japan, now threatening to become Asia's main anti-Communist bulwark. But though the Generalissimo evidently miscalculated American intentions in Korea, he was all along hedging his bets with typical caution. He had no intention of committing Soviet troops. When the briefly victorious invaders were flung back far to the north, seeming to face utter rout, it was the Chinese – not the Soviet – army which intervened to avert a Communist defeat. Thus was the Korean War turned into an infection weakening bodies politic other than Stalin's. American and other Western resources were wastefully committed under United Nations authority, and the beauty of it was that their blows were directed against a target so satisfactory to the Soviet dictator: the Stalinized – but imperfectly Stalinized – Communists of Korea and China! Meanwhile the dictator and his propaganda machine could sanctimoniously condemn American aggression from the side lines. Stalin did so personally, with his usual lofty dignity, in a *Pravda* interview of 17 February 1951 – also confirming his intention of continuing the attempted disruption of Western public opinion through the Soviet 'peace' campaign. There was only one way of avoiding war, claimed the active instigator or passive sponsor of the Korean conflict: the People (Hieratic for 'pro-Stalinists') must everywhere make the Cause of Peace (Hieratic for 'Soviet foreign policy objectives') their own cause and defend it to the end.[12]

Despite offering opportunities for such flagrant peace-mongering, the Korean War did not pay off for Stalin. Against the massive wastage of American resources in the far east must be set the West's vastly increased will to resist Soviet encroachments, reflected in a much boosted armaments drive. As in Berlin, so too in Korea, Stalin's probings had struck resolute resistance – and had thus served a useful function as a reconnaisance operation. Both exercises told the Soviet dictator that it was time to back down. He was able to do so without loss of face, and without even having to pay with the lives which he was always ready to squander so generously if necessary. If Berlin and Korea must be numbered among Stalin's failures, they were the failures of a still skilful and still – despite the occasional reckless gamble – ultra-cautious operator.

Party Discipline, Satellite and Soviet

In the months immediately following Zhdanov's death Stalinist oppressions grew still harsher as the dictator resumed his old habit of executing top Communists. This practice, neglected since the beginning of the war, was not only revived at home, but was also extended to the satellite countries.

The persecution of satellite Communist leaders was Stalin's response to Yugoslavia's defection, being designed to prevent the Titoist rot from spreading to the seven remaining eastern European dependencies. As his main disciplinary procedure the Leader chose to revive the show trial. So far all such trials of any importance had taken place in Moscow, but now Stalin felt that the time had come to export the institution to the satellite capitals. For each trial an arch-villain was indicted, together with a select entourage of accomplices. Death sentences pronounced in a rigged court were swiftly followed by executions, the procedure being accompanied from start to finish by carefully scripted spontaneous meetings of 'indignant' workers, and by the howling of the world's Communist publicity media. Thus, by judicial murder – such as they might themselves have inflicted on their colleagues had Stalin so instructed them – were liquidated Albania's Koci Xoxe, Hungary's Laszlo Rajk and Bulgaria's Traicho Kostov: in May, September and December 1949 respectively. Other persecutions, for the moment less spectacular, had also taken place in Rumania and Poland.[1]

The early satellite show trial victims tended to be nationalist deviants only in the sense of having sought certain minimal relaxations in the harsh colonial régime imposed by Moscow. They also tended to be selected from among Communists with non-Soviet international affiliations: those who had fought in the Spanish Civil War, or who had later resisted occupying Germans. As ever, contact between persons of different nationalities still aroused Stalin's suspicions – not least when undertaken in the Soviet interest; one is reminded of the repressions reputedly suffered by Soviet partisans who had campaigned against the German invader in the western USSR. The satellite survivors and show trial riggers, by contrast, tended to be persons such as the Hungarian Rakosi, who had spent extensive periods in the Soviet Union, and who were accordingly nicknamed 'Muscovites'. But it was not, of course, on the charge of fighting in Spain – or on that of resisting German occupation – that Stalin's satellite victims of 1949 were arraigned. They were indicted, rather, for collusion with

Tito, and for acting as imperialist agents. As with the Moscow trials, interrogators worked hard behind the scenes to extort abject public confessions; but at least one senior traitor – the Bulgarian Kostov – held out against pre-trial conditioning, and refused to incriminate himself.

As for the surviving satellite leaders, no more effective way could have been devised of harnessing them to Stalinism than by thus completing the process of their corruption. Aware that failure to play their role in these farces would implicate themselves as spies, mad dogs and imperialists, they had been compelled to sanctify in Hieratic pronouncements the execution of comrades on charges known to be false. They had thus entered the category least mistrusted by the Soviet dictator: that of persons driven to the ultimate limit of publicly demonstrated self-degradation. On the lower echelons, too, the show trial ritual was outstandingly successful, compelling the masses as it did to assemble at collective hate sessions where political deviants could be conveniently singled out by police and informers on the basis of face-crime: failure to dispose one's features in the prescribed mask of rage on mention of a Xoxe, a Kostov or a Rajk.

In implementing judicial terror, Czechoslovakia – the last European country to be swallowed by Moscow – had shown herself deplorably backward. So laggard were the Czechoslovak Communist leaders that they had to be prodded by the ultra-Stalinist Hungarian party boss Rakosi into seeking suitable victims. Not until October 1949 did Soviet 'advisers' reach Prague. And only after complaints by these newly-arrived Kremlinite emissaries – who expressed amazement that no 'enemies' had yet been discovered in the Czechoslovak Party – did the search for a 'Czechoslovak Rajk' begin in earnest.[2] Soon the Foreign Minister, Vlado Clementis, had been cast for that villain's role – qualifying, as one with a modest record of opposition to Stalinist policies, for grooming as a self-confessed Titoist. Not until February 1951, however, was Clementis's arrest announced. By that time Stalin's rancour had spread beyond nationalist deviants – his first satellite targets – to Moscow-trained satellite leaders: the very 'Muscovites' who had previously been employed to frame nationalist colleagues of the Clementis-Rajk variety. Thus it came about that Rudolf Slansky, one of Czechoslovakia's principal Moscow-trained Communists, was arrested in November 1951. By that time – if he had been discharging his duties efficiently – Clementis would long ago have been tried and hanged, and on charges which would have included plotting the assassination of Slansky! Now, owing to inexcusable Czechoslovak lack of vigilance, it had become necessary to telescope both categories of victim: the earlier nationalist and the later 'Muscovite'.[3] In November 1952, Slansky and Clementis together with their associates were tried in Prague and duly imprisoned or hanged.

The most striking feature of the new satellite persecutions was their deliberately emphasized Jewish accent. The Jewishness of Slansky, and of the majority among his co-defendants, was constantly stressed at the Prague trial and in the attendant publicity campaign. Here we clearly discern the personal intervention of Moscow's senior anti-Semite, who – as will be noted in due course – was simultaneously sponsoring the persecution of Jews in the Soviet Union.

In 1949 Stalin also sanctioned the liquidation of leading Communists at home through an extensive purge of the defunct Zhdanov's followers. This was the notorious Leningrad Affair, which – by contrast with the eastern European show trials – was to remain a closely guarded secret for several years. Khrushchev states that this campaign of arrests and liquidations was personally supervised by Stalin after Beria and his protégé Abakumov had primed the dictator with fabricated evidence.[4] The other organizer of the Leningrad Affair was Malenkov. Only after Stalin's death was the complicity of the Malenkov-Beria-Abakumov triad gradually leaked.

No city in Stalin's realm more easily aroused his lurking suspicions than Leningrad. Once the seat of Zinovyev, then of Kirov, then of Zhdanov, the former metropolis still retained some shreds of a pro-Western bias deriving from its days as St Petersburg. It was in order to equip himself with a 'window on Europe' that Peter the Great had first founded this city on the bogs of the Neva estuary. But Stalin disapproved of windows: and especially of any which might open on Europe. He had cold-shouldered Leningrad during its appalling wartime ordeals. More recently, in early 1948, the Leningrad Party – a nest of Zhdanovites – had offended by welcoming certain Yugoslav visitors too warmly ... and this at the very time when Stalin was already quarrelling with Tito. There were also rumours that the Leningraders plotted to restore their city to its original role as the Russian capital; and however unfounded these reports might be, it was precisely on such phantoms that the declining dictator's paranoid fantasies battened.

Though details of the Leningrad Affair still remain obscure, it is likely that the tally of those shot or arrested ran well into four figures.[5] They included all the main figures in the Leningrad Province and City Party secretariats, town councils and trade union organizations.[6] The two senior victims were both Zhdanovites who had graduated from Leningrad to the Centre: the top planner N. A. Voznesensky, who had become a full Politburo member in 1947; and A. A. Kuznetsov, the Central Committee Secretary to whom Stalin had temporarily transferred some of Beria's political security responsibilities. Kuznetsov and Voznesensky were shot, as were many other senior figures, while lesser victims 'disappeared' by their thousands – executed or freighted to the camps. Malenkov and Beria could feel that they had staged a comeback. Beria strengthened his position still further in 1950, when certain key security forces – the independent police armies – were transferred from the MVD (commanded by a non-Beriaite) to the MGB, where they came under Beria's crony Abakumov. Not long afterwards, however – probably in November 1951 – Stalin dismissed Abakumov as MGB boss, replacing him with the party *apparatchik* Ignatyev, who was no Beria man. Thus did the wary dictator neatly remove the striking arm of the political police from Beria's recently reasserted control.[7]

That the tide was now running against Beria – that Beria had already become, in Stalin's mind, the premier martyr-designate of a projected new terror – is suggested by the unleashing, in 1951, of a local persecution confined to the victim's supporters within Georgia. This, yet another of the late Stalinist 'Affairs', was directed against the Mingrelians: an ethnical variant of the Georgian stock to which Beria – but not Stalin – happened to belong. Helpless to intervene, as the Mingrelian Affair developed, Beria saw his fellow-tribesmen and allies disappearing from influential positions in Tiflis. This persecution was undertaken at the initiative of J. V. Stalin unhampered by consultations with the Politburo, and claimed thousands of 'innocent' victims.[8] They were accused of conspiring to detach the Georgian Republic from the USSR and join it to Turkey.

This charge against the Mingrelians carries the same paranoid whiff as that simultaneously levelled by Stalin against the Jews executed (as will be described below) for plotting to turn the Crimea into a world Zionist centre. That persecution, too, may have been aimed against Beria, who – despite his avowedly Georgian origins – was commonly thought to be Jewish, and who had long ago contaminated himself in Stalin's eyes by sponsoring the Soviet wartime Anti-Fascist Jewish Committee, since liquidated as a nest of Zionist-Imperialist spies. Was the Slansky trial conceived by Stalin as a pilot scheme for another, greater trial which never took place because it was frustrated by his own death: that of Beria? Was Stalin now preparing for Beria the doom of his predecessors Yagoda and Yezhov?

Turning back to late 1949, we find Stalin restoring Nikita Khrushchev – now a Politburo member of ten years' standing – to Moscow from the Ukraine, where he had been operating as proconsul-in-chief since 1938. Reinstalled in the capital, Khrushchev became a Secretary of the Central

Committee and First Secretary of the Moscow Party's provincial organization. Stalin was thus filling the vacuum left by Zhdanov with a formidable power-contender who could be balanced against the resurgent Malenkov and a Beria not yet openly menaced. Khrushchev returned to Moscow primed with managerial experience in the Ukraine: a grain-producing area of capital importance. Holding strong views on farm organization, he helped to overthrow the policies of Andreyev – hitherto the Politburo's main agricultural specialist, an advocate of decentralization and of incentives for individual peasants. Khrushchev would have none of this, but sponsored the rapid amalgamation of collective farms, to such effect that their total was drastically reduced – from 250,000 to under 100,000 – within three years.[9] In January 1951, however, this arch-centralizer became so afflicted by dizziness from success that he launched an ambitious scheme to settle Soviet peasants in 'agro-towns' while converting them into farming proletarians or rural mechanics. This project was soon tactfully disavowed in *Pravda*; for a time Khrushchev's agricultural policies also came under attack from Beria's henchmen in the Caucasus; they were to be disavowed yet again by Malenkov at the Nineteenth Party Congress of October 1952. But though discredited as a would-be super-regimenter of muzhiks, Khrushchev yet suffered no serious loss of status. No doubt he remained necessary as a reserve favourite whom Stalin, after undermining Beria, could pit against the still-favoured Malenkov.

Malenkov's prestige as heir-presumptive was enhanced by the decline of his former ally Beria. For that very reason it might soon become necessary to phase out Malenkov by favour shown to the rival power-contender Khrushchev – who was, however, occasionally reminded, by twitches on the thread such as those noted above, that he must not aspire to any status other than that of Stalin's marionette.

The Cultural Front

Increasingly militant in his satellite and foreign policies after Zhdanov's death, Stalin also intensified the continuing cultural witch-hunt at home. He permitted this to build up maximum tension in 1949, after which a very slight degree of relaxation was to be conceded. As in foreign and satellite affairs, so too on the domestic front we can detect a slight change of emphasis – such as enables us to distinguish, however tentatively, Zhdanovite Stalinism from Stalinism of a purer strain. Designed principally to boost the Communist Party and world revolution, the earlier drive had been ideological in essence ... with a strong seasoning of Russian nationalism. Now, after Zhdanov's death, the proportions of the mix are varied, the continuing cultural holy war being waged chiefly in the interests of xenophobic Russian chauvinism ... with a strong seasoning of Marxist ideology. Now, as never before, the pre-eminence of everything Russian over everything foreign is asserted. Russians turn out to have invented printing before Gutenberg: they have anticipated Stephenson's Rocket with some Puffing Billy of their own; the flying Wright brothers were forestalled by Russian birdmen; Russians have invented the bicycle, the telegraph, the telephone, the tank, the tractor and radio. Taken as a whole, these claims were wildly ludicrous, though not all the individual assertions were equally far-fetched.

So much for the master race. Lesser breeds, whether inside or outside the Soviet Union, were put firmly in their place. The decadent West, and especially its Anglo-American imperialist component, was attacked with sustained abuse more venomous by far than had ever been directed against Hitlerite Germany. Non-Russian minorities within the Soviet Union also came under more severe attack, for bourgeois nationalism: that is, for praising their own native heroes, traditions and history. They were censured, too, for failure to give due appreciation to the 'progressive' role played (according to the latest Stalinist dogma) by Imperial Russia when she had annexed their territories in the first place.

From this anti-minority drive Ukrainians, Tatars and Caucasians suffered greatly. The prime victims, however, were Soviet Jews. Many of these spoke no other language but Russian, yet continued to be regarded in law as belonging to a separate Jewish nationality: one which lacked any self-contained territory such as the other main Soviet minorities possessed. Though Stalin never developed into a persecutor of Jews on the Hitlerite scale, Jews certainly appear to have been his least favoured people all along. His daughter repeatedly attests his ingrained anti-Semitism – an element which increased towards the end of his life, when he became irritated by his relatives' habit of marrying into his least chosen race.[1] Suspicious, as ever, of all contacts between different peoples and cultures, the dictator particularly resented the people whose centuries-old diaspora ensured that they, of all races, had the widest possible range of global contacts, Soviet and non-Soviet, with all manner of other communities.

In Stalin's Jewish policies we again detect a shift of emphasis coinciding with Zhdanov's departure. In May 1948, at the time of Zhdanov's continuing ascendancy, the Soviet Union had been quick to recognize the newly-founded state of Israel. A few months later, though – in autumn of the same year – scenes alarming to Stalin took place in the streets of Moscow as thousands of Soviet Jews staged a demonstration in honour of Golda Meir when she visited the Soviet capital as Israeli Foreign Secretary.

His suspicions deeply stirred by such unheard-of initiative from below, especially since it was in favour of a foreign power, Stalin was seized with a profound distrust of the world Zionist movement, switching from his initial benevolence towards Israel to an anti-Israeli and pro-Arab policy.

With Zhdanov's departure an anti-Jewish element became a more noticeable feature of the continuing cultural witch-hunt. The Soviet press went out of its way to print the recognizably Jewish surnames of various cultural figures, notably drama critics, who were accustomed to write under Russian-sounding pseudonyms; another device was the publication of cartoons depicting Wall Street financiers as ostentatiously hook-nosed. In a country with so heavily-controlled a press these features appeared to give official sanction to the expression of anti-Jewish feelings which had long been present in areas of the Russian Empire. Thus Stalin spiced cultural warfare with anti-Semitism, but without going so far as to make the baiting of Jews the main ingredient; as noted above, Jews were by no means the only cultural victims, while the hounding of victim-Jews as 'rootless cosmopolitans' (the main abusive anti-Semitic label) was often carried out by other, eagerly Stalinizing Jews.

On those Jews who represented a specifically Yiddish culture (as opposed to the many Jews who were culturally Russian) Stalin's rancour fell with particular severity. Yiddish publications were banned, and Yiddish-orientated cultural figures were liquidated. One of these, the actor Mikhoels, appears to have been murdered by Stalin's political police, the crime being disguised – on the dictator's express telephoned instructions, overheard by his daughter – as a car accident.[2] Mikhoels had been a member of the Soviet wartime Jewish Anti-Fascist Committee – now suspected of espionage because of its record of collecting American donations to the Soviet war effort. Other members of that committee too were arrested, including the poet Fefer, who probably perished in a concentration camp.[3] The campaign also involved the widespread arrest of Jewish intellectuals and extensive deportations of Jews to outlying regions. Eventually, on 12 August 1952, Stalin's pogrom culminated in the shooting of various leading Jews, including Solomon Lozovsky: once a prominent member of the Party Central Committee. They were charged with planning to detach the Crimea from the USSR, and to turn it into a Jewish national home.[4] Not until Stalin was in his grave did the facts about these executions become known, for the dictator's anti-Semitic feelings were never publicly acknowledged during his lifetime. Now we learn, from Khrushchev's alleged memoirs – for what they may be worth – that Stalin was accustomed to tell funny stories about Jews in private, skilfully mimicking and caricaturing their characteristic manner of speaking Russian; he is also reported as encouraging Soviet factory workers to amuse themselves in the evenings by beating up Jews.[5]

In summer 1948, Stalin brought into increased prominence the noted pseudo-scientist Trofim Lysenko, who had enjoyed varying degrees of vogue since the 1930s. This fast-talking charlatan, an exploiter of bogus genetical and agrobiological theories, was thereafter able to maintain an extensive reign of terror within the Soviet scientific world at large. Lysenko bewitched Stalin with various miracle-working schemes, all purporting to effect dramatic short-term rises in food productivity on the basis of minimal outlay. He offered to boost wheat production through 'vernalization'; to crop tomatoes in the tundras; to foster sugar-beet in the torrid deserts of Central Asia; to create great climate-transforming oak forests in the steppes by planting acorns in clusters of thirty, rather than singly. Extensively promoted in the field, these plans all failed signally, wasting many a billion roubles. But to say so aloud was to risk one's neck or one's job. And in any case, no one was interested: by the time when Lysenko's vernalized wheat, or other latest project, turned out to be collapsing about its ears, this senior Soviet medicine-man would be busily selling his master some new and even more exciting scientific wonder. Though Lysenko was never able to demonstrate the viability of his miracles by repeatable experiments, it was perhaps for this very reason that his claims appealed to Stalin, purporting as they did to transcend the laws of cause and effect. There was also the flattering assertion that all these marvels proceeded ultimately from the Leader himself. Had Stalin not made the philosophical claim that 'gradual, concealed, unnoticeable quantitative changes lead to rapid, radical qualitative changes'? From that it was but a small step to Lysenko's assertion that one species could be transformed into another: wheat into rye, pines into firs and so on. Following this line of reasoning, one minor sycophant even gave Stalin priority over Lysenko for the inspired discovery that acquired characteristics are inheritable.[6] It is not surprising that the dictator should have found the concept alluring – offering, as it seemingly did, scope for transforming and revolutionizing human, animal and plant nature to an extent hitherto considered impossible.

Lysenko's scientific reign of terror was ushered in by his presidential address, delivered on 31 July 1948, to a witch-hunting assembly of the Lenin All-Union Academy of Agricultural Science. This grand oration, 'On the Situation in Biology', had been carefully edited in advance (and discussed in detail with Lysenko) by the Leader himself; Lysenko kept in his office a draft which included corrections in Stalin's hand – he would show it to visitors as a special mark of favour.[7] The burden of this harangue was a vicious attack on orthodox genetics as a reactionary, bourgeois pseudo-science opposed to the new, true, Stalinist-Lysenkoite school of genetics, which asserted the inheritability of acquired characteristics. After Lysenko's oration the Soviet scientific world was flooded with heresy denunciations. Non-Lysenkoists were assailed for idealism, sabotage, metaphysics, racism, cosmopolitanism, formalism, anti-Marxism, anti-Darwinism, anti-Michurinism, Mendelism, Morganism, Weismannism, complicity with the imperialist bourgeoisie, kow-towing to the West and a host of other crimes. Investigated by Lysenkoite commissioners, numerous geneticists, physiologists, soil scientists, agrobiologists, biochemists and others had their laboratories closed down; lost their posts; were forced to make humiliating public recantations.

Around the arch-quack orbited dozens of minor prophets, including another agricultural witch-doctor, V. R. Williams, and a medico-scientific charlatan, O. B. Lepeshinskaya. It was the latter's good fortune, at a time when she was hard pressed by vicious Weismannist-Morganists, to receive an unexpected telephone call from Stalin himself. She has described the experience in Hieratic prose:

> I lifted the receiver and heard such a familiar, such a dear voice, that of Joseph Vissarionovich. . . . Encouraging me with friendly, fatherly words, Stalin gave me advice. And in His wise counsel there was such crystal clarity, such power of scientific prevision that my heart stood still with pride . . . pride that there is on this large planet a Man intimate and dear, for whom all complex questions and problems are an open book, for whom, in all detail, the path of development of Soviet progressive science is clear.[8]

Lepeshinskaya's most notable scientific discovery was that old age might be postponed indefinitely through bicarbonate of soda enemas.

By mid-1950 Stalin seemed established as a remote despot. Never visiting factories or farms, he appeared in public seldom, and then only on official occasions. He rarely sought, nowadays, to commit his thoughts to paper, his recorded utterances of 1946–50 being sparse in the extreme. They consist largely of official messages, or of magisterial 'answers' to 'questions' addressed to him by foreign journalists and public figures, most of whom he did not bother to meet. As for the cultural witch-hunt, the Leader still remained loftily aloof from its frenzied development, characteristically leaving the management of it to his underlings. But then, suddenly, Stalin is seized by a mysterious urge to communicate! *Pravda* of 20 June 1950 carries a ten-thousand-word article by him on 'Marxism and Linguistic Problems'; this is later followed by four shorter contributions from the same pen on the same theme.

Stalin is not himself a philologist, as he humbly explains, but has been asked by certain young people to clear up the relationship between linguistics and Marxism, the latter being a subject in which he can claim a modest competence. He begins by discussing whether language belongs, in Marxist terms, to the basis or to the superstructure of society. To neither, he argues. His thesis becomes more impassioned when he leaves Marxist theory to assault the Soviet linguistics establishment, which was committed to the ideas of the defunct Georgian philologist, N. Ya. Marr. Marr was by no means a mere linguistic Lysenko, and there was more to his achievement than his oft-quoted reduction of all human speech to the four basic elements SAL, BER, YON and ROSH.[9] One pronounced feature of his teaching, which had hitherto made it seem a Marxist brand of philology, was the argument that the chief element differentiating one language from another was the stage of social development attained by its speakers. Around this assertion a clique of epigones had established a linguistic empire comparable to that of the Lysenkoites in the scientific world; persecuting non-Marrite philologists who continued to follow linguistic techniques as practised in the West, they had converted Marrism-Leninism into an important branch of Marxism-Leninism.

Now unexpectedly humbling these former favourites, Stalin claims that Marr's followers have set up an 'Arakcheyev régime' in linguistics: a régime, in other words, like that of General Count Arakcheyev, the notorious instrument of tyranny under the Tsar-Emperor Alexander I during the first quarter of the nineteenth century. More remarkable still, coming from so wholehearted a regimenter of opinion as Stalin, is the following claim: 'No science can develop and prosper without the clash of opinions, without freedom of criticism. But this generally recognized rule has been ignored and violated in the crudest manner. A closed group of infallible leaders has been created, which, while insuring itself against any possible criticism, has begun to act in a wilful, high-handed manner.'[10] The statement was true, of course, and not only of the linguistics world. But it was very much in Stalin's style that he, the very creator of all these Arakcheyev régimes, should suddenly begin devouring his own progeny. In denouncing the cult of infallible leaders, the most infallible leader of all was only conforming with a pattern familiar from his earlier career. We are reminded of his high-minded strictures on the cult of his own personality, as recorded above. We are also reminded of the occasions on which he had blandly condemned various excesses inspired by himself, ascribing them to the exuberance of over-enthusiastic followers; such an episode had been the denunciation of ultra-zealous collectivizers in his article of March 1930, 'Dizziness from Success'. Nor must it be forgotten that the Leader disliked *all* entrenched positions: not least those occupied by Stalinists more Stalinist than Stalin.

Despite these links with a long familiar operating technique, Stalin's pronouncements on linguistics do signal yet another slight but definite variation of policy. Having first sanctioned Zhdanov's cultural repressions, and having then proceeded to intensify those repressions after Zhdanov's death, the dictator was now, perhaps, beginning to feel that things had gone too far. He was nowhere near ready to demolish his entire network of Arakcheyev régimes, but he was trying – tentatively – to cut back their most extreme manifestations. As can be traced in retrospect, post-war cultural stringencies did begin to fall off slightly after reaching their peak in 1949, and the propaganda campaign against the bourgeois imperialist West was also somewhat moderated after that year. Now it was, too, that certain ultra-fanatical, Stalin-quoting Soviet denouncers of heresy found themselves pilloried in *Pravda* – and for their very fanaticism – by spokesmen enjoying official favour.[11] An official attempt was also made to revive literature by calling (in vain) for works satirizing Soviet shortcomings in the manner of those nineteenth-century scourges of bureaucracy Gogol and Shchedrin. Attacks were also made on ultra-tame Soviet playwrights who had believed themselves to be following the official line by depicting contemporary Soviet society as so perfect that no conflict could conceivably arise within it. Yet another sign of the times was a decline in Lysenko's status: first came a decrease in his quota of praise in the press; then, in 1952, it even became possible to print attacks on his theories.[12]

Though such signs seemed to bode ill for entrenched Stalinists, the new concessions to moderation yet remained tentative, and at no time was an all-out cultural thaw created. That liberal sentiments buried among his linguistic pronouncements should not become the signal for general relaxation, Stalin himself carefully ensured by repeating in those same scriptures certain chilling arguments already advanced by him in the late 1930s. Now, as then, he sternly warned anyone who might be waiting for the State to 'wither away' under established Communism (in accordance with Marxist doctrine). He repeated that such withering-away must remain a dream so long as the USSR was surrounded by capitalist enemies.[13] He also gave a new twist to Marxist revolutionary theory by indicating that from now onwards no sweeping change could be expected to occur in the Soviet Union except through 'revolution from above': that is, in effect, on orders issued by himself! He also repeated a claim – previously advanced in the notorious *History of the All-Union Communist Party (of Bolsheviks): A Short Course* of 1938 – to the effect that the collectivization of agriculture had been just such a 'revolution from above'.[14] While dethroning N. Ya. Marr in certain sections of his linguistic articles, the author was thus serving notice in other parts of the same writings that J. V. Stalin had no intention of abdicating.

411

15
His Last Plot

Final Months

In October 1952, Stalin steps up what appear to be preparations for launching a new Great Terror. So far the dictator's post-war repressions have embraced Jews, intellectuals, satellite Titoists and many others; totalitarian controls have been continuously enforced with impressive rigour, while the concentration camps still show no signs of disgorging their millions or tens of millions. And yet, even as the country groans under these impositions, there are many who still remember the years 1937–8, when fear had more openly stalked the land. Now, in the last months of his life, Stalin seems bent on reviving such wholesale atrocities. Post-war persecutions hitherto isolated, tentative or imperfectly co-ordinated, are – it seems – about to be united in a renewed holocaust *à la* Yezhov.

To inject premonitions of impending disaster the dictator exploited the Nineteenth Party Congress of 5–14 October. As over a thousand congress delegates – representing over six million Party members – assembled in the Kremlin, one idea must have been present in the secret thoughts of all: even Stalin could not go on for ever. That the tyrant was fast ageing, if not ailing, seemed evident enough. But which of his senior subordinates was likely to succeed him? Malenkov still remained heir presumptive, as was clear from the decision to entrust him with delivery of the Central Committee's report to the Congress: a function regularly performed by Stalin himself during the preceding quarter of a century. Second in the ranking list established at the Congress was Khrushchev, who spoke to introduce changes in the Party statutes. An unusually prominent role was also assigned to Poskryobyshev: head of the dictator's personal secretariat, and commonly regarded as his main *aide* in administering the most savage persecutions of the past. Such was the apprehension evoked by this widely feared boon companion of Stalin's that his emergence from the shadows greatly enhanced the general panic which must now be intensified if arrests and shootings were to avalanche. Meanwhile two declining power-contenders – Beria and Molotov – found themselves allotted comparatively modest roles in keeping with their position as martyrs-designate. Beria's declining status was further emphasized by the failure of the Congress to re-elect certain of his identified associates to the Central Committee.

While prominence was conferred on or withheld from lesser figures, the dictator himself dominated an assemblage which – apart from a brief concluding speech – he scorned to address in person. However, as almost every word pronounced by other orators seemed to emphasize, even a silent Stalin still enjoyed supreme authority. From the body of the house the usual ritual grovellings before the Great Leader were received with the usual ritual ovations: Stalin-worship echoed, as usual, in diapason by publicity media throughout the Soviet Union. It was the Leader's most recent thinking, too, which dominated the speeches. That this should be so he had ensured by publishing a policy statement on the eve of the gathering: 'Economic Problems of Socialism in the USSR'.

In one respect this work shows Stalin adopting a moderate line. Having long ago embraced the theory that political enthusiasm could transcend the laws of cause and effect, and having also sponsored the associated claim that there were no fortresses which Bolsheviks could not conquer, the dictator was at last beginning to turn his back on such supernatural solutions. There *were* such things as economic laws, he now insisted, and it was no use Party members pretending that they could be ignored or rewritten to suit their convenience. To say this was to apply, in a new sphere, the tactic of theoretical retreat, as already sounded in Stalin's denunciation of Marr and in the latitude recently extended to critics of Lysenko. But encouraging though this retreat to common sense might seem, it made little practical difference, for Stalin's economic article gave no indication that the Soviet citizen was to have an easier time. Far from that, the dictator showed himself bent on yet tougher regimentation of the peasantry; as for industry, he indicated that the priority given to production of the means of production was to be further stressed . . . not relaxed in favour of the consumer. That Stalin still, in his eighth decade, saw himself beset by ever more menacing enemies both inside and outside the Soviet Union the text of the article also shows.[1]

Stalin's minions, from Malenkov downwards, echoed these abrasive sentiments in their speeches to the Congress. Calls for vigilance – long familiar as a tension-creating signal – resounded in the orations of all leading speakers, including those presumably earmarked as purge-victims. Among those who still basked in the dictator's fickle favour, Malenkov spoke ominously of the leadership's wisdom in recognizing danger in embryo, and in preventing it from assuming threatening dimensions.[2] The newly voluble Poskryobyshev focused attention on embezzlers of state property, whom he pilloried as enemies of the people no better than traitors and spies hired at tremendous expense by brazen US imperialists.[3] Through these and many other speeches the Congress fulfilled its function of whipping up ever increasing anxiety within the Party and outside.

One especially noteworthy achievement of the late 1930s – Stalin's slaughter of the Leninist Old Guard – was celebrated at the Congress through the removal of the once honoured word Bolshevik from the Party's official title. What had, since 1925, been called the 'All-Union Communist Party (of Bolsheviks)' now became the 'Communist Party of the Soviet Union'. The Congress also sanctioned more ominous changes affecting organization: the abolition of the Orgburo and the Politburo. These were now replaced by a new body – or at least by a body bearing a new name: the Presidium of the Central Committee. This emerging, vastly expanded organ had twenty-five full and eleven candidate members. It represented a continuation of the superseded Politburo to the extent that ten of the abolished Politburo's eleven members (all except Andreyev) went straight on to the Presidium – which was small comfort to them, though, since they were now outnumbered by so many upstarts. That the new recruits had been brought in with the ultimate intention of ousting the old was obvious. Thus trebling his pool of potential top favourites – or victims – Stalin had vastly increased his scope for liquidating or promoting individuals close to the summit in accordance with the day-to-day requirements of any developing high-level purge. This flexibility was further extended by a simultaneous increase in the size of the Central Committee's Secretariat – from four to ten persons – as also by a corresponding expansion of the Central Committee itself. Increasing the membership of all these bodies, and consequently impairing such vestigial powers as they might still possess, Stalin was following a technique dating back to the early 1920s.

Did the newly elected giant Presidium ever meet in full conclave? There is no evidence that it did. Typically enough, Stalin preferred to deal with a smaller, shadowy, also newly established body, the so-called 'Bureau' of the Presidium.[4] This probably had a variable membership: an advantage to the dictator, who could change its composition in accordance with his whim of the moment – maintaining his normal practice of conferring with favoured protégés on an *ad hoc* basis, while dignifying such consultations with the disyllable which so aptly begins the word bureaucracy.

That Stalin conceived the sudden expansion of the renamed Politburo, and of the Party Secretariat, as a prelude to a drastic purge of top

Communists was confirmed over three years later in Khrushchev's Secret Speech. Khrushchev pointed to Molotov and Mikoyan as prospective victims, claiming that both were denounced by Stalin to the new Central Committee of October 1952 on certain 'baseless charges'. Another victim-designate had been Voroshilov. Suspecting that veteran marshal of spying for the British, Stalin had arranged for his home to be 'bugged' with a listening device; for several years, too, Voroshilov had been forbidden to attend the Politburo, and had been denied access to official documents.[5] In indicating Molotov, Mikoyan, Voroshilov and possibly Andreyev as the main targets for Stalin's plans to 'finish off' the old members of the Politburo, Khrushchev omitted to list Beria among senior figures earmarked for liquidation. By no means, however, does it follow from this omission that Beria had forfeited the role assigned to him by Stalin: that of chief victim-designate. The fact is that Khrushchev, speaking in 1956, could not possibly disclose the imminence (in 1952) of Beria's disgrace without conferring on him the credit which (according to Soviet logic) automatically accrued, in the context of a denunciation of Stalin, to all those named as targets for the expiring tyrant's malice. Far from conceding Beria the honour of having been singled out as prime victim, Khrushchev goes out of his way to associate Beria with Stalin's worst crimes. Khrushchev claims that the secret police chief had egged Stalin on to ever greater atrocities:[6] an accusation which one has no difficulty in believing.

After laying the groundwork for a new and possibly greater terror at the Nineteenth Party Congress, Stalin immediately proceeded to the second, more acute, stage: the rigging of the so-called Doctors' Plot. It was probably between 4 and 9 November 1952 that certain Kremlin physicians, mostly Jewish, were quietly taken into custody:[7] an event of which the public was to remain ignorant for over two months. The arrests had been prompted by a certain Dr Lidiya Timashuk, radiologist and grandmother, who had written to Stalin denouncing the doctors' use of improper medical treatment to exterminate certain high Soviet officials and officers. Timashuk was a police informer, according to Khrushchev, who says that the initiative for her denunciation of the doctors came from elsewhere. Perhaps her letter to Stalin was commissioned by Stalin himself? In any case it was Stalin who ordered the doctors' arrest, and it was Stalin who controlled their processing in custody with the aim of extracting confessions designed to implicate others and thus form the basis for a new purge. It was Stalin who ordained that one of the doctors should be put in chains. Stalin also defined the technique to be applied by the investigating authorities as: 'beat, beat, and beat yet again'. He told his latest security chief, Ignatyev, that if he could not extract the required admissions: 'We will shorten you by a head.' These methods produced the usual suitable confessions. Circulating copies to members of the defunct Politburo, Stalin told them: 'You are blind like young kittens. What will happen without me? The country will perish because you do not know how to recognize enemies.'[8]

As these details suggest, the only plotting connected with the Doctors' Plot was that of Stalin himself, and of those who assisted or encouraged him. Yet, even as the dictator launched this devious scheme, he was also planning – or pretended to be planning – to withdraw from the scene entirely. Twice in late 1952 he asked the newly elected Central Committee to sanction his retirement. And twice the Committee unanimously turned down this request.[9] Thus was repeated a pantomime which had been enacted several times earlier in Stalin's career, when his offers of resignation – sincere or not – had always been rejected by his colleagues. These were the only occasions on which it was prudent to disagree with the Leader in public.

Unaware, as yet, of the special role assigned by Stalin to Jewish doctors, the Soviet public could not fail to sense the general increase of officially fostered tension as the year 1952 moved towards its close. There were calls for a tightening of Party discipline, and – as always on the eve of intensified repression – there were yet more strident demands for vigilance. Industrial managers came under the lash, as did economists too. So also did those Soviet officials who were said to have allowed personal relationships to mar their professional efficiency. Even the closest family ties must not be permitted to impede watchfulness, *Pravda* dinned into its readers, adding that everyone must learn to prevent his nearest and dearest from falling into political errors and crimes. A similar claim – that loyalty to Stalin must transcend love of wife, husband, children and parents – had been made repeatedly in the late 1930s.

While this campaign was gathering way, Svetlana Alliluyeva paid a birthday visit to her father: on 21 December 1952. It was his seventy-third and last birthday, being also the last occasion on which his daughter was to see him in possession of his faculties. Stalin looked terrible. He, who could have summoned the best medical treatment in the Socialist Sixth of the World, was now dosing himself on pills or drops of iodine taken from the cupboard in his bed-sitting room at Kuntsevo. He would not allow any doctor near him. How could he ever trust a doctor again, now that such a leading light of the medical profession as Academician V. N. Vinogradov (his own personal physician for more than twenty years) had turned out to be a British spy? Vinogradov it was who now lay chained in some dungeon on the express order of his most august patient.

Besides dosing himself with quack nostrums, the failing Stalin also attempted to give up tobacco after so many years as a much publicized smoker of pipes and cigarettes, and even of cigarettes crumbled into pipes. But he made no attempt to throw off another form of self-indulgence which he had acquired during Siberian exile in the old days: the traditional Russian steam bath. By exposing himself to this ordeal until the very end he may well have shortened his life, according to his daughter.[10]

Was Stalin mad? Or did he become so? The more one contemplates his growing eccentricities the more the question seems to arise. That he suffered to some extent from paranoid delusions, which increased as he grew older, seems clear. However ill-grounded his fears of the medical profession may have been, they must – like all paranoid fears – have been genuinely felt: would he otherwise have banished doctors from his presence when he stood most in need of their aid? Nor can one dismiss as merely delusional the apprehension from which Stalin constantly suffered – or pretended to suffer – of omnipresent danger from multifarious enemies. If the tyrant's associates were not actually plotting his assassination, working through doctors, maids, gardeners, guards, or anyone else who could have access to him, then they should have been. Such was the logic of their situation as it must have appeared to Stalin. Knowing what he was capable of doing to his colleagues, he had every reason to cultivate apprehension about what they might do to him. To some extent, therefore, his 'delusions' of persecution were not delusions at all. Sensing the dangers around him – which were genuine enough, if only in potential – Stalin had successfully protected himself against them throughout a long career. If, therefore, a continuing ability to cope with one's environment is to be taken as a criterion of sanity, then the despot surely remained sane until the end of his days.

The impression – true or false – that the post-war USSR had fallen into the clutches of a lunatic was much increased when (on 13 January 1953) *Pravda* at last proclaimed the discovery of a sinister medical conspiracy. Some time previously, it was stated, the Soviet security authorities had uncovered certain terrorist-doctors who had sought to exterminate Soviet public figures through medical sabotage. Nine guilty physicians were listed, six of whom bore what appeared to be Jewish surnames. They had allegedly caused the death of Comrade A. A. Zhdanov, and also of Comrade A. S. Shcherbakov, a Secretary of the Central Committee. They had also tried, but failed, to put out of action three marshals of the Soviet Union, one general and one admiral. Five of the accused doctors had been working for American intelligence through the international bourgeois Jewish organization known as *Joint*; three had been British agents.[11]

As was usual with Stalin's major aggressive moves, the charges were designed to serve a variety of purposes. By including spy scares, the dictator reintroduced a theme which had often proved its worth as a terror-building force in the past. Then there was the new spiking of overt anti-Semitism, which might soon come to excuse the arrest of anyone who had ever been seen talking to a Jew. Ground was also laid in the indictment for accusations against the former police establishment, since the deaths of Shcherbakov (1945) and Zhdanov (1948) had occurred during the period when Beria, and then Beria's crony Abakumov, had headed political security. This point was underlined by press attacks on the political police launched at the time of the doctors' arrest; never before had the Soviet security forces been publicly censured in this way, and the campaign thus reinforced the growing impression that Stalin had selected Beria as senior candidate for martyrdom.

Not that Beria's Presidium colleagues could take much comfort. Since no living civilian leader had been named in the list of the doctors' alleged victims-designate, all members of Stalin's top political entourage must have felt themselves ultimately menaced ... and no doubt that was the intention. Only the army and navy might draw a little comfort – from the naming of five high-ranking living officers among the doctors' supposed targets. By implying that the armed forces were not immediately endangered in the coming holocaust, Stalin was perhaps attempting to insure himself against the danger of a military *coup*.

Having served public notice, in his own peculiar code, of intention to mount a new Terror, Stalin allowed the press campaign to gather momentum during the five-and-a-half weeks following *Pravda's* denunciation of the doctor-conspirators. The dictator was not yet ready for the mass arrests which he presumably intended to introduce with a new show trial based on concocted medical material. Still bent only on increasing tension, he was carefully reviving and sensitizing memories of the terrible 1930s.

Since the methods of the Great Terror had never been wholly abandoned, the campaign of early 1953 largely involved the increased use of techniques which already lay to hand. No newspaper – it almost seemed – now dared print a single paragraph without invoking the hoary concept of vigilance, that classic stimulant of the *Yezhovshchina*. Now, as in those heroic days, radio and press thundered against spies, poisoners, murderers, enemies of the people, mad dogs and beasts in human shape. Only by shouting louder than everyone else could an individual hope to prove that he did not belong to any of these suspect categories. Meanwhile more and more scapegoats were being singled out and pilloried by name as a warning to their social group, the whole operation being presumably designed in part to distract attention from the parlous economic and political condition in which the Soviet Union found itself after seven years of peacetime Stalinism. Among those variously accused of non-vigilance, negligence, cosmopolitanism, kow-towing to the West, foisting alien ideologies on the Soviet people, subjectivism, objectivism, and of other fashionable crimes, were officials of Party, Government and *Komsomol*; those tainted by contact with foreigners; dignitaries of the Soviet minority republics; former Mensheviks and Trotskyites; Jews; the Soviet intelligentsia as a whole from doctors, journalists, librarians and museum-keepers to academicians, jurists and economists. For five-and-a-half weeks these, and all other subjects of Stalin's empire, cringed under the verbal lash and awaited their fate. The more enterprising, as usual, sought to avert disaster by zeal in denouncing their fellows: public-spiritedness which received official encouragement when, in late January, Dr Lidiya Timashuk received an Order of Lenin. A yet more celebrated informer, the boy-hero of the 1930s Pavlik Morozov – martyred by kulaks after denouncing his father as an enemy of the people – was commemorated in a play newly staged in Moscow and furiously applauded by any theatre-goer who did not wish to compromise his reputation for vigilance.

In one feature, though, the latest campaign showed a marked divergence from its predecessors: Stalin's top colleagues had quietly dropped out. None of them was now signing articles calling for greater vigilance:[12] a silence deafening in the context.

Final Weeks

The last independent witness – that is, the last person from outside the Kremlin-instructed world – known to have set eyes on the living Stalin was the Indian Ambassador to Moscow, K. P. S. Menon, whom the dictator received on the evening of 17 February 1953. Greeting his guest, Stalin added that it was his duty as Prime Minister to meet foreign ambassadors; but (as Menon has noted) it was a duty which he had chiefly honoured in the breach, having received only three foreign diplomats during the preceding five years. The dictator seemed alert and fully in possession of his faculties as he discoursed of world affairs, including India's national and linguistic problems. He criticized Americans for seeing politics exclusively in terms of business and profits. It was no use preaching morals to such people, the dictator sanctimoniously claimed, adding a homely yet ominous comparison typical of his personal idiom: that the Russian peasant was

a very simple man but a very wise man. When the wolf attacks him he does not attempt to teach it morals, but tries to kill it. And the wolf knows this and behaves accordingly.[1]

419

As was his custom during such conversations, Stalin had been doodling with a pencil, producing on the present occasion sketches – which the Indian Ambassador was able to observe – of wolves in various postures. Who or what precisely these dangerous quadrupeds may have symbolized in Stalin's mind is not clear. The Americans? Soviet doctors? World Jewry? His innumerable 'enemies' in their sinister and fanged totality? Whatever may have been at the back of his mind, the doodled wolves seemed to bode mischief.

The doodling of the wolves was to be Stalin's last recorded conscious act. Within three weeks his embalmed corpse was lying in state in the Hall of Columns in Moscow, as a prelude to display alongside Lenin's remains in the Red Square sepulchre.

What had happened in the meantime? What was the precise course of events between the Menon interview of 17 February and the announcement, made on 6 March 1953, that Stalin had breathed his last? We may discard such rumours as that which has the dictator perishing in a fit of rage while quarrelling in his office with members of the defunct Politburo.[2] A variant which portrays Molotov, of all people, handing his master a glass of poisoned brandy must also be rejected for lack of evidence – not because such a thing is beyond the bounds of possibility. Never, one may suspect, have so many individuals from Molotov outwards and downwards had motives so urgent to desire the death of the one man whose existence menaced all his subjects, not excluding a single member of his immediate entourage. As the individual most threatened, Beria had the strongest motive of all, and also happened to possess the ripest experience as a dispenser of sudden death. It is certainly conceivable that he found the means to hasten, artificially, the tyrant's end.

Though such suspicions cannot be entirely discounted, any serious reconstruction of Stalin's death must take note of his daughter's evidence, since she is the only witness of these events who has published an account outside the orbit of Kremlinite censorship. On 2 March she was called out of a French class at the academy where she was studying, and taken to Stalin's *dacha* at Kuntsevo. She found him there lying on a sofa. She was told that he had had a stroke during the night, and had been found at 3 a.m. lying on a rug. Stalin had lost the power of speech, but his daughter saw him open his eyes several times. Could he recognize anyone? She could not tell. His death, occurring three days later, was 'difficult and terrible'. The choking tyrant's lips went black, the final agony was appalling. At the last moment Stalin suddenly opened his eyes, lifted his left hand as if to pronounce a curse . . . and died.[3]

This account confirms what might otherwise have remained for ever in doubt – that Stalin's death did indeed occur at roughly the time officially attributed to it: 9.30 in the evening of 5 March. Had it not been for Svetlana's testimony, we might have deduced an earlier death from certain indications bearing on the period following the Menon interview of 17 February. Most significant of these was the abandonment by all Soviet publicity media of the vigilance campaign. It was suspended – abruptly – on 22 February, and in full career, while the printer's ink was barely dry on such rabid purge-stimulating material as yet another laudatory article on the police nark Timashuk. This had appeared on 20 February, and the conclusion seems inescapable that Stalin somehow lost control of his machine immediately afterwards. An event which occurred on 21 February may – or may not – confirm this: the announcement that General Shtemenko had been replaced by Marshal Sokolovsky as Chief of Staff to the Soviet armed forces. Since Shtemenko had been one of the five senior officers named (and thereby politically honoured) in the communiqué of 13 January as an alleged victim-designate of the alleged doctor-murderers, he was presumably – whether he knew it or not – one of those on whom Stalin relied to support the projected new terror; and Shtemenko had in any case long been one of the senior generals most closely associated with Stalin.[4] Another military move behind the scenes – the announcement by the military command of the Kremlin (on 17 February) of the death of a Major-General Kosynkin – may or may not also have a bearing on these events. Was some hidden hand removing Stalin's protectors?

Whatever may be thought of such speculations, the abandonment in full career of the doctor-centred witch-hunt suggests that Stalin suffered on or about 21 February some form of incapacitation which removed him from the control of events. Perhaps the stroke officially reported as occurring on the night of 1–2 March had in fact occurred a week earlier. Or perhaps there had been a previous, less severe stroke.

It remains possible that Beria or some other menaced individual found means to poison the dictator. No faith need be placed in the three official medical bulletins of 4–5 March. Signed by a battery of senior doctors or medical officials from the Minister of Health downwards, these ascribed Stalin's fatal illness to a sudden cerebral haemorrhage. But what conceivable credence need be placed in the statement of Kremlin-instructed physicians acting in this nightmarish context? As for Svetlana Alliluyeva's testimony, though this certainly appears to confirm the official version of Stalin's death, and though her integrity is above suspicion, she was not medically qualified to assess the allegation that the father whom she saw die – of what were described to her as natural causes – might possibly have perished from some slow-acting poison. However, the very fact that Stalin died a lingering death makes it improbable that he was so assassinated. Here, if ever, was a case for over-kill: one does not half-liquidate a liquidator who, even in his last agonies, may yet find some means of striking back at his slayer.

Given these circumstances, it is not surprising that the announcements and medical bulletins recording Stalin's fatal illness should leave much to be desired. The dictator's original stroke on the night of 1–2 March (if indeed that is when it took place) was hushed up for more than two days, being first proclaimed over the radio in the early morning of 4 March. Though the 'best medical brains' were reported as attending the ailing dictator, it was far from clear why they described Stalin as having been robbed of consciousness before losing the power of speech;[5] one does not need a medical degree to judge such a claim suspicious. And why, if Stalin indeed suffered the attack in his Moscow apartment (as reported in the first radio communiqué) was he removed to his Kuntsevo villa – from an area bristling with excellent hospital facilities – which is where Svetlana Alliluyeva found her father dying? A marked contrast was also evident between the lavish technical details supplied in the first medical bulletin (of 4 March) – details of pulse rate, blood pressure, temperature, circulation – and a failure even to indicate the hour at which the 'sudden cerebral haemorrhage affecting vital areas of the brain' had taken place. Succeeding bulletins were yet more technical in content, being apparently addressed to a specialist audience ... yet containing obvious absurdities. Why, for instance, was the normal ratio of albumen and red corpuscles stated to be present in the urine?[6] These substances are not normally present in the urine at all! Surely communications so replete with mumbo-jumbo must have been designed less to inform the Soviet and world public than to lull it into a 'soporific, deeply unconscious state' comparable to that of the dying dictator?

It would be idle to expect the highest professional standards from members of a terrorized profession – some of whose colleagues lay beaten, and even chained, in Stalin's dungeons – as they attempted to do what was expected of them, whatever that might seem to be, around a deathbed which was already the focus for political manoeuvrings among Stalin's potential successors. Doctors or laymen, all those involved had been accustomed for a quarter of a century to leave ultimate decision-taking in the hands of one man. Now each of them had become, suddenly, a potential wielder of initiative in his own right: a discovery terrifying indeed.

Finally, at about 4 a.m. on Friday, 6 March, after a solemn drum roll and the playing of the Soviet National anthem, an official triply sponsored communiqué – of the Central Committee, Council of Ministers and

Presidium of the Supreme Soviet – was proclaimed on the Soviet radio. Stalin was dead. The time of death was registered as 21.50 hours in the previous evening and the passing was suitably proclaimed in impeccable Hieratic prose such as the dead man himself might have composed:

The heart of Joseph Vissarionovich Stalin – Lenin's Comrade-in-Arms and the Genius-endowed Continuer of his Work, Wise Leader and Teacher of the Communist Party and of the Soviet People – has ceased to beat.[7]

Surprising though it may seem, it must be recorded that the tyrant's death was ostentatiously mourned by those who witnessed it: cooks, gardeners, chauffeurs, maids and guards mingled their tears – if only of relief – with those of Malenkov, Khrushchev, Voroshilov, Kaganovich and Bulganin.[8] As for Stalin's two surviving children, the tipsy Lieutenant-General Vasily Stalin lurched around the bungalow, accusing his expiring father's entourage of murdering him by poison or other means. His sister Svetlana could not bring herself to kiss her dead father's forehead, as (she implies) was expected of her.[9]

As for the nation which Stalin had ruled so ruthlessly and so long, though his death did indeed make a profound impression, the general reaction was by no means unmixed jubilation. Not that signs of mourning were especially evident. Bonfires and balalaikas appeared here and there in the streets. Places of entertainment remained open, and the death of Boris Godunov (portrayed – probably unfairly – as a murderous tyrant in Moussorgsky's opera of the same name) was greeted that night with prolonged applause. Far away in the north, we are told, warders and inmates of the Vorkuta concentration camps combined to get gloriously drunk on liquor which became mysteriously available in quantity.[10]

To their master's death the long-dragooned Soviet masses responded not so much with extremes of joy or sorrow as with sensations of dazed shock, tension, anxiety and wary expectation. Huge crowds converged on the centre of Moscow to pay their last respects or disrespects.[11] The situation was potentially explosive, for might not the dead man's empire burst asunder after so sudden a relaxation of the mighty pressures which had constricted it? Alarmed by such fears – and also, no doubt, by the obligation to show initiative such as had been stunted for many a long year – the surviving leaders moved swiftly to contain the 'disarray and panic' which they feared, and which they openly invoked as a possible danger in an official communiqué of 7 March.[12]

Until the first shock wave should subside, these potential legatees of power were bound to huddle together in unity simulated or genuine. Whether through general agreement amongst colleagues, or by a secret *coup,* Beria at once grasped control of his old political security fief. He brought massive formations of MVD troops into Moscow within hours of his master's death, sealing off the Red Square and important buildings. But though wholesale disarray and panic were kept within manageable bounds, central Moscow yet witnessed appalling scenes involving widespread loss of life. Using MVD lorries as crush-barriers, Beria's security forces rendered confusion worse confounded as millions of mourners or celebrators jostled and pressed ever tighter against each other and against these obstacles. Among the mob was the young poet Yevtushenko, who found himself in Trubnaya Square on his way to see Stalin lying in state. Protected by his height and physique, the poet heard the bones of a young girl crack – and noticed her 'insanely bulging, childish blue eyes' – as she was slammed into the standard of a traffic light. Soon afterwards he found himself stepping on something soft: a human body. These were only two among many hundreds – perhaps thousands – of victims claimed by Stalin even in death as they were choked and crushed between the walls of houses and the police trucks – of which the sides were dripping with blood, but which the MVD drivers refused to move because they had 'no instructions'. Yevtushenko joined other robust young men who formed a chain and passed women and children inside the trucks, where they were comparatively safe. When things quietened down the distraught poet went home without bothering to inspect the corpse displayed in the Hall of Columns. But Yevtushenko had indeed 'seen Stalin', as he told his mother on his return.[13]

Stalin's obsequies were hustled through with unseemly haste. For three days only – by contrast with the full week allotted to the ceremonies following Lenin's death – did the embalmed despot, wearing his medal ribbons and Generalissimo's uniform, his facial pock-marks decently concealed by cosmetic treatment, remain on view in the Hall of Columns in Moscow's House of the Unions: once a club for the pre-revolutionary gentry, and afterwards the setting for Stalinist show trials. Then, on the morning of 9 March, the body was solemnly conveyed to the Red Square, being lifted on to a gun-carriage by nine pall-bearers, of whom one was the dead man's son Vasily, while the others were the top Politburo veterans. Perfunctory speeches – from Malenkov, from Beria and from a sobbing Molotov – followed. Then the body was slotted into the granite Red Square sepulchre on which the inscription had already been altered to include the great Georgian's name. Thus Stalin's remains took their place beside Lenin's. Thirty salvos of gunfire, and an orgy of uproar from riverboat and factory sirens lent additional dignity to the proceedings.

Far from receiving impressive obituary notices, Stalin was commemorated in the press only by satellite spokesmen or junior officials.[14] Among the funerary articles was one in a medical journal by Dr Lidiya Timashuk, whose role as Public Watchdog Number One now had little time to run. By comparison with all the celebrations which Stalin had dominated in 1924 after Lenin's death, the obsequies of Stalin himself (staged by Khrushchev in 1953) were rushed through with scant ceremony.

Thus the great dictator died: not with a bang, but to a chorus of whimpers.

Life after Death

Leaderless

EMERGENCY responses to Stalin's death included extensive and hasty organizational measures taken by the surviving leaders. The recently established giant Presidium of the Central Committee was reduced from twenty-five full members to a mere ten, eight of whom (Malenkov, Beria, Molotov, Khrushchev, Voroshilov, Kaganovich, Bulganin and Mikoyan) were veterans from the old Politburo days. It was among these seasoned Stalinists that many of the key ministries were also distributed. As a minor but significant detail, Marshal Zhukov was quickly restored from the obscurity to which Stalin had relegated him, and became Deputy Minister of Defence; his great prestige was presumably valued as bolstering the vulnerable new leadership with vital army support.

From the top leaders Malenkov at once seemed to emerge as full heir to the Stalin dictatorship. Not only did the chief secretaryship of the Central Committee automatically fall to him on Stalin's death, but he also took over Stalin's old position of Prime Minister. Thus equipped, Malenkov seemed well poised to establish himself as a second Stalin. In the press, too, the new potentate received prime billing, being given especial prominence in *Pravda*-published photographs. Among these was the notorious fake showing the newly fledged dictator Malenkov in triune communion with Stalin and Mao; other Soviet leaders (present in the original, dating from 1950) had been carefully expunged. Great prominence was also given to Malenkov in published photographs of Stalin's obsequies.

That Malenkov's programme was Stalinist business as usual – the only difference being that a new idol would preside from the Kremlin – was suggested by revived press agitation about vigilance . . . though there was also conciliatory talk of cultivating international harmony and improving the Soviet standard of living. It was not long, however, before the apparent successor showed himself incapable of grasping supreme power. By 11 March, Malenkov was evidently losing the campaign to make himself an absolute totalitarian despot, as became clear from a noticeably reduced press cult. Then, on 14 March, at the first post-Stalin plenum of the Central Committee, Malenkov was relieved of his Central Committee secretaryship 'at his own request'. It was a big step-down, but he still retained the premiership, and he was still the front-runner . . . though now only the first in a field of potential equals. The second most powerful individual remained Beria, whose control over the security machine gave him especially effective leverage. Meanwhile Molotov (the senior surviving Bolshevik) either would not or could not make his prestige tell, while Khrushchev – elevated to the senior Party secretaryship by Malenkov's demotion – appeared, for the moment, to be comfortably placed in fourth position.

Proclaiming themselves a collective leadership, Stalin's heirs first combined to unscramble the Doctors' Plot, which was repudiated in early April – the informer Timashuk being incidentally forced to disgorge her Order of Lenin. Then the leaders began to quarrel among themselves. The first victim was Beria, who fell to a combination of colleagues – all potentially menaced by his grip on the secret police. With Beria removed – and executed as a British spy in December 1953 – the decreasingly collective leadership was riven by a variety of intrigues which eventually, by 1957, gave Khrushchev controlling power . . . but never mastery supreme and unalloyed such as Stalin had enjoyed.

Destalinization and Restalinization

Stalin is dead. But Stalinism, in various forms, lives on. We shall now consider the use made of the defunct dictator's reputation in the Soviet Union by his successors, after which we shall review interpretations of his achievement which have been put forward in the West, and attempt a summing up.

During the two decades following the Leader's death the Soviet political scene has been overshadowed by traumatic memories of his rule and has continued to be haunted by his ever-present ghost.

The most sensational event in Stalin's posthumous biography has been the so-called 'secret' speech delivered by Nikita Khrushchev – his successor as leading Party Secretary – to the Twentieth Party Congress on 24–25 February 1956. Never officially acknowledged – nor yet officially repudiated – by Soviet authority, the text has been published in English by the American State Department . . . unauthenticated![1] But it has been accepted as genuine by non-Soviet specialists all over the world, and has frequently been used as a source for the present study.

In the Secret Speech, Khrushchev attacks Stalin for abusing his great powers; for injuring the Party; for dealing in violence and terror, thus abandoning Lenin's allegedly more civilized methods; for riding roughshod over the Soviet legal system; for deliberately refraining, over long periods, from allowing Party congresses and Central Committee plenums to meet; for violating the Leninist principle of collective leadership; for framing and killing 'honest' Communists after meaninglessly and arbitrarily labelling them enemies of the people; for shooting 98 out of 139 members of the Central Committee elected at the Seventeenth Party Congress of 1934; for arresting 1,108 out of 1,966 delegates to that same Congress; for his pathologically suspicious nature ... but also for a culpable lack of suspiciousness towards Hitler; for his failure to heed warnings of impending German attack in 1941, and for the inadequate state of Soviet defences at that time; for indecision and hysteria in the early days of the war; for planning his military campaigns on a globe; for pretending to be infallible; for his isolation from the people; for the growing deterioration, during the post-war years, of a character already markedly capricious and brutal; for provoking an unnecessarily severe conflict with Titoist Yugoslavia. Khrushchev also accuses Stalin of rigging the notorious Doctors' Plot affair and of doing so as a pretext for ushering in a new great terror campaign in 1953 ... a project which was called off after the dictator's death in March of that year.

Khrushchev further censures Stalin for glorifying his own person; for having Politburo members tortured and killed; for preventing Voroshilov and Andreyev from attending Politburo meetings; for plotting the downfall of Mikoyan and Molotov.

As this summary of charges indicates, Khrushchev fell short of a full indictment of Stalin in two major respects. Firstly, he said nothing of the dictator's slaughterous record as a collectivizer of agriculture from 1929 onwards, but confined his strictures to the period from the assassination of Kirov (1934) onwards. Secondly, the concern expressed by Khrushchev was discriminatory, being bestowed almost exclusively on the leading Communist Party members liquidated or otherwise inconvenienced by the tyrant. About the appalling sufferings inflicted on the Soviet population at large Khrushchev said virtually nothing, also ignoring the repression of the Party rank and file. To the pioneering destalinizer Khrushchev, it would appear, Stalin's concentration camps – in which, besides Party members, untold millions of non-party citizens also perished – were less of a blemish on the defunct dictator's record than the crime of having Voroshilov's home 'bugged' with a listening device.

As these reservations suggest, the sensational impact – both within the

Soviet Union and in the world at large – of Khrushchev's Secret Speech derived hardly at all from such information about Stalin as it purveyed, since most of this was already known or suspected. The impact was due, rather, to what the speech implied about the lengths to which the Soviet authorities were now prepared to go in telling the truth about their own past . . . and hence about the degree of liberalization which they might now be contemplating. The spectacular aspect of the secret speech did not, therefore, lie in Khrushchev's disclosures as such, but in the fact that the chief representative of a system so rigid was prepared to make any disclosures at all . . . rather as if a person deemed to be in *rigor mortis* should suddenly be seen to twitch a toe. Another factor limiting the scope of 'destalinization' and associated relaxations, as implemented from 1956 onwards, was the motive driving the main sponsor. Khrushchev was not – to put it mildly – himself galvanized by powerful liberalizing urges. He was, rather, attempting to bolster his own power by simulating liberal postures. While denouncing Stalin – but within carefully defined limits – Khrushchev was aiming to entrench his own position . . . and perhaps, even, seeking Stalinist powers for himself.

That Khrushchev's was indeed a delicate balancing act became clear later in 1956 through two outbreaks of indiscipline in Soviet-dominated eastern Europe: outbreaks stimulated in part by Soviet destalinization. These events were the Hungarian rising and the widespread expression of anti-Soviet dissent in Poland. Khrushchev reacted by reversing destalinization. Now – as was to happen regularly whenever uncontrollable libertarian forces seemed to loom on the horizon – a few favourable, restalinizing references to the dead dictator proved a quick and effective means of encoding the announcement of a crackdown otherwise enforced in Budapest by Soviet tanks. Thus did Stalin's name become the powerful symbol which it still remains in the Soviet Union and eastern Europe.

Another significant episode in the revaluation of Stalin by his heirs was the Twenty-Second Party Congress of 1961. In a further, shorter destalinizing oration – non-secret in that it was officially published on the Soviet side – Khrushchev returned to the attack.[2] The most scandalous element in his new pronouncement was the suggestion – previously insinuated in the Secret Speech, but now more broadly hinted – that Kirov's assassination (the event which had sparked off the mass repressions of the late 1930s) had been carried out at Stalin's behest. Then, by a decision taken at the same Congress, the disgraced Georgian's corpse was summarily removed from the Red Square sepulchre, where it had lain alongside Lenin's since 1953, and interred in modest obscurity by the Kremlin wall.

This second destalinization campaign pulsated on until the end of Khrushchev's ascendancy in October 1964 – and beyond that in the sense that the years 1965–6 remained rich in newly-published, relatively frank historical and memoir material relating to Stalin. However, even in the most extreme phases of so-called destalinization nothing remotely approaching a full and free public discussion of his record ever took place in the Soviet Union. The widespread horrors instigated by the great dictator still continued to be described in soothing officialese as 'phenomena associated with the cult of J. V. Stalin'. Attempts to break this taboo – for example in Solzhenitsyn's novels – led either to the banning, or to the severe censoring, of the works in question.

After Khrushchev's removal from high office a policy of discreet restalinization was adopted under the succeeding duumvirate of Brezhnev and Kosygin. This has, on the whole, been a 'low profile' operation with the accent on ignoring the great dictator – not on overt attempts to rehabilitate his memory in full. The mild bromide has thus replaced the mild aperient. But however eager Soviet authority may be to ignore Stalin, it has proved impossible to relegate a historical figure of such proportions to the status of 'unperson'. For example, the article (1971) on Stalin in the *Soviet Historical Encyclopaedia* still quotes Lenin's famous comments of 1922–3 on the rough-hewn Georgian's defects of character and on the need to remove him from the office of Secretary-General. 'The mistakes and distortions associated with the cult of Stalin's personality' did – the article concedes, repeating a long familiar formula – inflict a certain harm on the cause of Communist construction. 'But [it is added] they did not, and could not, change the nature of Socialist society.'[3] In this sentiment even foreign observers least sympathetic to Soviet governmental techniques can readily concur, for it is arguable that Stalin was indeed a true heir of Lenin. The catastrophic 'phenomena associated with the cult of J. V. Stalin' were, according to this view, a natural development of – rather than a deviation from – the course of by no means dissimilar phenomena associated with the cult of V. I. Lenin.

Twenty years after Stalin's death, the handling of his image by Soviet communications media is still a useful key to fluctuations in the political climate. This remains evident from the most cursory examination of the many documents involved – such as encyclopaedia articles and memoirs – in which the dread symbol occurs. Praise of Stalin, abuse of Stalin, *failure to mention Stalin in a context where his name might have been expected to occur* . . . all these symptoms help to locate the current position of the barometric needle on the scale between political relaxation (to be equated with destalinization) and repression (to be equated with restalinization).

Perhaps, in a way, Stalin left no more deadening legacy than an atmosphere in which such trivialities could acquire major significance.

Stalin through 'Bourgeois' Eyes

So much for the treatment of Stalinism and of Stalin in the Soviet Union by his Soviet successors. What of the reaction of the non-Stalinist world to J. V. Stalin and the phenomena associated with his cult?

In fixing the dictator's international reputation a particularly prominent role has been played by his great rival Trotsky. Between 1917 and 1940 (as we have observed) the careers, ambitions and intrigues of these two arch-foes were intimately intertwined . . . until Trotsky, who had argued from emigration against the need to assassinate Stalin,[1] was himself assassinated by an emissary of his reigning competitor.

Though Trotsky once refused to describe Stalin as a nonentity, he many times assessed him as a mediocrity.[2] Stalin was (Trotsky wrote) neither a thinker, nor a writer, nor an orator. Stalin did not owe his rise to supreme power to personal qualities, but to the functioning of an impersonal bureaucratic machine . . . of a machine which had 'created him'.[3] Love of power, ambition, envy, a desire to impose his will . . . these were Stalin's outstanding characteristics, Trotsky claimed. Caught unawares by his own rise to pre-eminence which no one could have predicted, Stalin was (Trotsky said) unworthy to stand comparison even with a Hitler or a Mussolini, let alone with the great Lenin to whom his minions would often compare him.[4] Stalin had created a privileged caste of creatures blindly loyal to himself, possessing as he did an almost faultless instinct for exploiting antagonisms between others.[5] It was wrong, though (said Trotsky), to describe Stalin as 'just a small town politician': Kamenev's phrase for him.[6] Stalin's strong, yet treacherous character – even his very incapacity for logical thinking and lack of creative imagination – had given him a modestly formidable stature. As for Stalin's policies, Trotsky found himself in a dilemma, approving as he did in principle of mass industrialization and collectivization . . . considering, too, that the main force of Stalin's sweeping economic measures was progressive.[7]

These views of Stalin have been widely accepted, partly because of the polemical force with which they are expressed. A contributory cause, helping to establish the Trotskyite view, has been a very natural reaction against the exaggerated claims made for genius-Stalin by the Stalin Legend. The two most influential 'bourgeois' interpreters of Stalin – E. H. Carr and Isaac Deutscher – have both, broadly, accepted the Trotskyite thesis about the great dictator, though each has developed it creatively and imparted his own particular twist.

No moulder of events (according to Carr), Stalin 'moulded himself to them. . . . More than almost any other great man in history, Stalin illustrates the thesis that circumstances make the man, not the man the circumstances.'[8] Stressing Stalin's practical bent, his Russia-centredness, his contempt for intellectuals, and his 'dislike of democratic procedures',[9] Carr maintains that Stalin's aims were dictated by the dynamic force inherent in the revolution itself. Stalin – claims Carr – carried the revolution forward to its 'appointed conclusion' by rapid industrialization:[10] a thesis characteristic of its author's extreme devotion to the principle of historical determinism. If Stalin was a great man, he was great (according to Carr, quoting Trotsky) only in the sense of Helvetius's dictum: 'Every period has its great men, and if it has none it invents them.' But Carr does dissociate himself from the extreme position taken up by Trotsky: whereas Trotsky portrays Stalin as exclusively the creation of an impersonal machine, Carr admits that: 'It required something more than a machine to "create" Stalin and put him in power.'[11]

To Isaac Deutscher, similarly, Stalin was 'a man of very ordinary stature and of middling thoughts. Only his fists and feet contrasted with his real stature – they were the fists and the feet of a giant.'[12] Like Trotsky, Deutscher attributes Stalin's success to his domination of a 'machine'.[13] Like Trotsky, too, Deutscher underestimates Stalin's skill and originality in creating the machine in the first place. The unspoken – and unconvincing – implication of the Trotskyite school is that practically anyone could have risen to supreme power in the fledgling Soviet Union, had he but been willing – as only an earth-bound and limited creature like Stalin could be – to stoop to such low and unfair devices as the exploitation of a political machine . . . devices too contemptible to be taken up by such free-ranging, noble and generous spirits as a Kamenev, a Zinovyev, a Trotsky or a Bukharin.

As Robert McNeal has pointed out – and as we have also argued above – Trotsky greatly underestimated Stalin, bemused as he was by his successful rival's inability or unwillingness to adopt the behaviour patterns of the typical Russian radical intellectual. Trotsky, in McNeal's portrayal, failed to detect the swiftness, acuteness and sureness of Stalin's power-accumulating intelligence . . . failed, too, to credit Stalin with holding sincere ideological beliefs.[14] As indicated above, the degree of sincerity with which Stalin was, in his heart, a devotee of Marxist ideology remains one of the great unsolved mysteries about this 'most puzzling and elusive personality of his age'.[15] There is no need either to accept or to reject wholeheartedly the thesis implied by McNeal: that Stalin's chief motive force may have been a sincerely held political faith rather than mere cynical power-seeking. That both elements were present – were indissolubly fused – in his mentality it seems safe to assert; of the degree to which one preponderated over the other we cannot be certain. And in any case, whatever Stalin's deepest feelings about ideology may have been, we must surely agree with Carr that he 'never allowed doctrine to stand in the way of the demands of common sense.'[16] Yet to leave it at that would be to underestimate the stature of one who by no means always allowed common sense to hamper unpredictable political fantasy-structures. What common sense was there about the Moscow trials of 1936–8? Or about the anti-cosmopolitan campaign, the Lysenkoite persecutions and the Doctors' Plot? These were more like the nightmares of a psychopathic witch-doctor than manoeuvres in which rationality and sobriety were the predominant elements.

Many of the more exotic aspects of Stalin's character are brought out in Robert Conquest's study *The Great Terror*. Conquest rejects the Trotsky-Carr-Deutscher picture of Stalin as a ruler of limited intelligence and ability, who yet conferred enormous benefits on Soviet society . . . even if he also, admittedly, caused untold loss and suffering. Where Trotsky and his followers had been prepared to allow Stalin credit for his crash indus-trialization programme – as also for the collectivization of agriculture and for the mass liquidation of illiteracy – Conquest emphatically rejects the view that comparable goals could only have been achieved by Stalinist methods. Far from representing Stalin's reign as a necessarily stern pre-condition for the country's economic development, Conquest portrays it as a cataclysmic disaster – pointing out that 'economically speaking . . . milder measures could have produced equally good results, as they had in Meiji Japan, for example.'[17] It is also worth repeating that Stalin's indus-trial achievements brought few tangible benefits indeed to the rank-and-file Soviet consumer and citizen. The Stalinized Soviet man-in-the-street might derive satisfaction from the thought of belonging to a powerfully armed industrial complex possessing a high capacity for production of the means of production and for the destruction of the human race. But from his own living conditions he could derive only meagre satisfaction – so little of the country's growing economic wealth did the loving Leader-Genius make available to the average citizen. Since the Leader's death Soviet citizens have, it is generally conceded, enjoyed a modest rise in their standard of living and a relaxation of extreme totalitarian controls. But in neither sphere have developments during the two decades following

Stalin's demise conferred benefits sufficiently marked to justify, post-humously, the inferno of the great dictator's reign.

Conquest and other interpreters – among whom Leonard Schapiro is outstanding – have also undermined the Trotskyite thesis whereby Stalin is portrayed, essentially, as a deviant from the path originally pioneered by Lenin. Viewed from this non-Trotskyite angle, Stalin no longer appears as an aberrant Leninist. It is Lenin, rather, who emerges as a somewhat ineffectual Stalin-in-embryo! Despite the earlier leader's extreme personal modesty, and despite his preference for genuine consultations with senior colleagues, he also employed violence and deceit on a scale which reveals these qualities, in retrospect, as outstanding proto-Stalinist features of his rise to power and exercise of rule.

With his enthusiastic exploitation of deceit and violence Stalin did indeed show himself Lenin's faithful disciple. Yet one of the paradoxes of the 'unimaginative' Georgian's achievement was his extension of these Leninist techniques beyond what the most daring fantasy might have believed possible. Both Lenin and Stalin were accustomed to talk of 'destroying hostile elements', and both arranged for droves of victims arbitrarily designated antagonistic to be corralled and shot in the back of the head. Stalin, however, did so on a scale exceeding that of Lenin by many a hundredfold. As has been said by Andrey Sinyavsky – himself a victim of post-Stalinist Soviet persecution – Stalin translated into action Lenin's often extravagant figures of speech: 'When Lenin spoke about the enemies of our ideology, he used metaphors. Stalin put these metaphors into effect, and we had the horrors of the year 1937.'[18] While recording this comment we must, however, add that Lenin's bloodier metaphors by no means always remained in the realm of metaphor (as Sinyavsky claims) – even though Stalin did far outstrip Lenin as a sponsor of massacres.

By such methods Stalin made Leninism work on a permanent basis: something which Lenin himself had showed few signs of achieving during his five years as active political Leader. After 1917, it has been pointed out, Lenin 'failed to make the transition from revolutionary to statesman, from the battlefield to the peace conference table. A great revolutionary, he had not managed to develop the qualities required of a statesman.'[19] Still less had the same great revolutionary succeeded in creating an effective institutional foundation on which to stabilize the peacetime government of a vast, complex and heterogeneous country. Stalin it was who realized that the solution lay in maximized bureaucratic terrorism: an element already prominent during Lenin's brief reign, but imperfectly and ineffectively geared to the machinery of power. Also sensing that bureaucratic terrorism could be intensified, under twentieth-century conditions, beyond any level attainable in an earlier age, Stalin pioneered – may indeed be said to have invented – the political control technique known as totalitarianism. Only terroristic, bureaucratic, totalitarian methods, we may surmise, could have made russified Marxism viable as a permanent basis for a governmental and social organization. Without Stalin – with only the Trotskys, Zinovyevs, Kamenevs, Bukharins and Molotovs to steer the fortunes of Bolshevism – Lenin's system, so imperfectly realized and consolidated during his lifetime, might well have collapsed. Thanks to Stalin, however, the system was given an institutional and administrative grounding so solid that it has held firm during the decades following his death. Since then Leninism-Stalinism – little modified in essence by the various much publicized post-Stalinist concessions and relaxations – has remained the basis of the Soviet system of government. An individual's over-all assessment of Stalin's achievement must therefore depend in no small measure on his assessment of the Soviet way of life, as lived during and after Stalin's dictatorship. Good, bad or indifferent, the Soviet Union of today is the Georgian dictator's creation. An attainment gigantic in terms of the skill, ingenuity and determination required to bring it about, it represents, perhaps, the most difficult feat achieved by one man in the whole of recorded history. From the fact that the achievement was difficult, however, it by no means follows that it was necessarily worthwhile.

Not least among Stalin's attainments was that of mounting an assault on the very basis of truth, an aspect well brought out in Roman Redlikh's *Stalinism as a Spiritual Phenomenon*: perhaps the most illuminating philosophical discussion of the topic. Redlikh lists various officially imposed fictions or myths concocted and advertised by the dictator: that Bolshevik theory is scientifically based; that Socialism had been achieved by the late 1930s; that the Soviet people was morally and politically united; that the 'most democratic constitution in the world' (the Soviet Constitution of 1936) had some practical function in conferring civil rights; that life in the Stalinist Soviet Union had become happy and prosperous; that the Soviet Union was the most progressive country in the world; that political power was in the hands of Soviet workers; that Soviet labour was invariably performed with feelings of profound enthusiasm . . . and so on.[20] To this array of fabrications were appended such further fictional concepts as 'capitalist encirclement', 'enemies of the people' and 'the people's wrath' . . . this last being supposedly directed against all those designated by Stalinist formulae of disapproval. The main point behind Redlikh's analysis is that Stalin's subjects *were by no means expected to believe* in these preposterous claims and fraudulent concepts, but *were merely required to affirm their acceptance* of such myths and fictions in public as a form of ritual obeisance. 'By restricting the public utterances of Soviet citizens almost solely to reciting parts of the theory and glorifying its creator, Stalin demonstrated the extent to which they were in his power.'[21] The recital of prescribed fictions was, in other words, a form of verbal goose-step which Stalin imposed on his subjects as a disciplinary technique.

From such analyses as those of Conquest, Schapiro and Redlikh – which are closer to that adopted in the present study than those of the other leading authorities mentioned above – Stalin emerges as a potent but ultimately sterile political manipulator ... one whose originality as a pioneer of behavioural control contrasts vividly with the posture of pedestrian mediocrity so assiduously simulated by himself and so misleadingly publicized by Trotsky and his school. In his own highly specialized and essentially destructive field, Stalin was indeed a genius – no less so, perhaps, than a Mozart or an Einstein. Never, surely, has one man shown such skill and tactical flexibility in manoeuvring sections of a large, potentially harmonious community into an orgy of mutual annihilation by methods ranging from semantic jugglery, card indexing, bribery, intimidation, blackmail and corruption to jackbooted kicks, torture, starvation, exposure, exhaustion, bullets, bayonets and other 'phenomena associated with the cult of J. V. Stalin'. Above all, Stalin had the wit to discern that humanity's collective political brain can often be most effectively bamboozled by the crudest of tricks and the simplest of verbal devices. He was intelligent enough not to squander his efforts on ingenious forms of chicanery when coarser methods could be made to achieve more power for less effort. Stalin was, in short, almost always clever enough to avoid being clever for the sake of being clever.

Was J. V. Stalin – were the 'phenomena' associated with his Cult – really necessary? Yes, if Leninism was to survive. But was it desirable that Leninism – that Leninism-Stalinism – should survive? Would the world now be a worse place if that remarkable and original technique of government had somehow fallen by the wayside in the early days? It depends on what criterion of good government is adopted. If, we repeat, the prosperity and freedom of the governed – that is of Soviet or satellite individuals, rather than ideological and notional abstractions – are to be accepted as the determinant, then Stalinism was an utter disaster. In non-Stalinized countries, however, (and in non-Stalinized countries alone) the erosion of privilege, and consequent improvement in the workers' status, owes much to the great Georgian. The bogy of Stalin – and of his legacy, Stalinized Russia – has played no small part in persuading capitalism in 'bourgeois' states to yield up entrenched positions to the workers. This, in the end, may come to be recognized as the chief advantage to flow from one of the most remarkable and harmful political careers on record. If, then, this self-appointed champion of the global proletariat achieved anything worth while for the working masses it was those of the capitalist, not the Communist, world to whom he brought tangible benefits.

To his own subjects the Marvellous Georgian brought – on a scale greater than that caused by any other ruler in history – suffering, degradation and death.

Reference Notes

For full titles of works to which reference is made, see Bibliography. The following abbreviations are used:

CPSU: *The Communist Party of the Soviet Union*
ed.:   edited (by)
PTsK: *Protokoly Tsentralnogo komiteta RSDRP(b),*
            avgust 1917–fevral 1918
SIE: *Sovetskaya istoricheskaya entsiklopediya*
Svet. (1967): ALLILUYEVA, Svetlana, *Twenty Letters to a Friend*
Svet. (1969): ALLILUYEVA, Svetlana, *Only One Year*
tr.:   translated (by)
W.:   STALIN, *Sochineniya*

Preface (pp. xi–xiii)

1, De Gaulle, 65. **2,** Blackstock, *The Secret Road to World War Two,* 284.

Introduction (pp. xvii–xxii)

1, Rigby, 71. **2,** Kennan, 'Certain Questions from the Early History of the Bolshevik Faction,' 9.

Chapter One

1. *Childhood* (pp. 1–9)

1, Iremaschwili, 9–10. **2,** Svet. (1967), 211–12. **3,** Information from a recent (1972) visitor to Gori. **4,** Private Soviet source. **5,** Iremaschwili, 11–12. **6,** W., 1: 314–15. **7,** Svet. (1967), 164. **8,** Knickerbocker; *Pravda,* 27 October 1935. **9,** Svet. (1967), 164. **10,** Svet. (1969), 340. **11,** Svet. (1967), 164. **12,** Okhrana files, cited in Smith, E., 28–9. **13,** Uratadze, 209. **14,** Knickerbocker; Svet. (1969), 345. **15,** Svet. (1967), 165. **16,** Souvarine, 44. **17,** Kaminsky, 37. **18,** *Alliluyev*

438

Memoirs, 189. **19,** Trotsky, *Stalin*, 1:26. **20,** Iremaschwili, 5. **21,** Souvarine, 3. **22,** Iremaschwili, 5–6. **23,** Trotsky, *op cit.*, 1:24–5. **24,** Iremaschwili, 6. **25,** Smith, E., 19; Svet. (1967), 38. **26,** Kaminsky (see Bibliography). **27,** Ibid., 35–6. **28,** Yaroslavsky, 8. **29,** Smith, E., 20. **30,** Yaroslavsky, 8. **31,** W., 13:113. **32,** Yaroslavsky, 9. **33,** Abramov, 4. **34,** *Pravda*, 27 October 1935. **35,** Knickerbocker. **36,** Iremaschwili, 8. **37,** Ibid., 8, 16.

2. *Seminarist* (pp. 9–18)

1, Svet. (1969), 340. **2,** Yaroslavsky, 16–17. **3,** *Iz vospominany russkago uchitelya.* **4,** W., 13:113. **5,** W., 13:114. **6,** Souvarine, 112. **7,** Kaminsky, 84–5. **8,** Smith, E., 38–42; Payne, 46–51. **9,** Ibid., 47. **10,** Iremaschwili, 22. **11,** Abramov, 6. **12,** Vakar. **13,** P. Kapanadze in *Rasskazy starykh rabochikh Zakavkazya o velikom Staline*, 26. **14,** Iremaschwili, 19. **15,** W., 8:174. **16,** Beria, 23. **17,** Vakar. **18,** Iremaschwili, 20. **19,** Yaroslavsky, 17. **20,** Ibid., 17–18. **21,** Iremaschwili, 20. **22,** Knickerbocker. **23,** W., 1:416. **24,** Iremaschwili, 24. **25,** Deutscher, *Stalin*, 26.

Chapter Two
1. *Urban Guerrillero* (pp. 19–32)

1, Alexandrov, 9; Spiridovich, 239. **2,** Kaminsky, 88–9. **3,** Iremaschwili, 24. **4,** Barbusse, 8. **5,** *Alliluyev Memoirs*, 27–30. **6,** W., 1:417. **7,** Smith, E., 78. **8,** *Alliluyev Memoirs*, 49–50. **9,** Beria, 27. **10,** Iremaschwili, 27. **11,** Ibid., 28. **12,** Beria, 27–8; Yaroslavsky, 27. **13,** Smith, E., 88. **14,** Souvarine, 43; Uratadze, 66–7; Vakar. **15,** W., 1:418. **16,** Payne, 76; Smith, E., 90; Trotsky, *Stalin*, 1:58. **17,** Beria, 30. **18,** W., 1:419. **19,** W., 1:418. **20,** W., 1:28. **21,** Payne, 75. **22,** W., 1:25. **23,** W., 1:419. **24,** Barbusse, 20. **25,** Vakar. **26,** Ibid. **27,** Beria, 36. **28,** Smith, E., 108. **29,** Iremaschwili, 28; Smith, E., 104–06; Trotsky, *op. cit.*, 1:63. **30,** Smith, E., 106. **31,** Beria, 36. **32,** Uratadze, 66. **33,** *Batumskaya demonstratsiya 1902 goda*, 195–6. **34,** W., 1:420. **35,** Ivanov. **36,** W., 1:420; Smith, E., 116. **37,** Smith, E., 121–4. **38,** Ibid., 67, 120. **39,** W., 6:53–4. **40,** Iremaschwili, 30. **41,** Ibid., 39–40.

2. *Police Spy?* (pp. 33–39)

1, Smith, E., 61. **2,** Arsenidze, 221–2. **3,** Smith, E., 67. **4,** Arsenidze, 224. **5,** Kennan, 'Certain Questions from the Early History of the Bolshevik Faction', 9. **6,** Smith, E., 306–08. **7,** Arsenidze, 219–20. **8,** Smith, E., 70. **9,** Arsenidze, 221–2. **10,** Ibid., 224. **11,** Vakar. **12,** Arsenidze, 222 and *passim.*

3. *Journalist and Agitator* (pp. 39–43)

1, McNeal, *Stalin's Works*, 9–10. **2,** Ibid., 10. **3,** Arsenidze, 227. **4,** Ibid., 225.

5, McNeal, *op. cit.*, 9. **6,** Alexandrov, 13. **7,** Beria, 42. **8,** Smith, E., 92–4. **9,** W., 1:424. **10,** Lyadov and Pozner. **11,** Glenny, 'Leonid Krasin', 194–7. **12,** Bas, 109–11. **13,** Kennan, 'Certain Questions from the Early History of the Bolshevik Faction', 4. **14,** *Avlabarskaya nelegalnaya tipografiya*. **15,** Smith, E., 143–4. **16,** Trotsky, *Stalin*, 1:362. **17,** Arsenidze, 222. **18,** Ibid., 228–31. **19,** Pokrovsky; Makharadze. **20,** Maglakelidze; Smith, E., 137. **21,** W., 1:422–5.

4. First Meetings with Lenin (pp. 44–51)

1, Alexandrov, 32; Yaroslavsky, 52. **2,** Krupskaya, 128–9. **3,** W., 6:54. **4,** *Chetvyorty (obyedinitelny) syezd RSDRP*, 81. **5,** Ibid., 82. **6,** Ibid., 374. **7,** W., 1:206–35. **8,** Reshetar, 66. **9,** W., 6:56. **10,** *Chetvyorty (obyedinitelny) syezd RSDRP*, 547. **11,** Futrell, 47. **12,** Shaumyan, 50. **13,** Glenny, 'Leonid Krasin', 204. **14,** Smith, E., 186. **15,** Lyadov, 213. **16,** W., 2:50–1. **17,** Arsenidze, 221. **18,** *Pyaty (londonsky) syezd RSDRP*, 241. **19,** Trotsky, *Stalin*, 1:144. **20,** Glenny, *op. cit.*, 205. **21,** Wolfe, *Three who Made a Revolution*, 387. **22,** W., 6:57.

5. Expropriator (pp. 51–55)

1, Shaumyan, 9–10. **2,** Bibineishvili, 130. **3,** Smith, E., 399. **4,** Arsenidze, 232. **5,** Souvarine, 100. **6,** Vakar. **7,** Arsenidze, 232. **8,** Wolfe, *Three who Made a Revolution*, 470–1. **9,** Shub, 'Kamo', 247. **10,** Ludwig, *Staline*, 41–2. **11,** Smith, E., 204. **12,** Souvarine, 100. **13,** Iremaschwili, 37. **14,** Wolfe, *op. cit.*, 471. **15,** Vakar.

6. Prisoner and Exile (pp. 55–61)

1, Barbusse, 44. **2,** W., 2:408–11. **3,** Trotsky, *Stalin*, 1:176. **4,** Dubinsky-Mukhadze, *Shaumyan*, 124–57. **5,** Souvarine, 110. **6,** Vereshchak. **7,** Trotsky, *Stalin*, 1:180–1. **8,** Vereshchak, cited in Trotsky, *op. cit.*, 1:182. **9,** Yaroslavsky, 72. **10,** Trotsky, *op. cit.*, 1:182. **11,** Vereshchak, cited in Souvarine, 114. **12,** Vereshchak, cited in Smith, E., 221. **13,** Smith, E., 222. **14,** Alliluyeva, A. S., 110–12. **15,** W., 2:412–14. **16,** Trotsky, *op. cit.*, 1:188. **17,** Beria, 185–6. **18,** W., 2:209–12. **19,** Smith, E., 232. **20,** W., 2:209–10. **21,** Trotsky, *Stalinskaya shkola falsifikatsy*, 183. **22,** Dubinsky-Mukhadze, *Ordzhonikidze*, 91–6. **23,** Smith, E., 241.

Chapter Three

1. Central Committeeman (pp. 62–65)

1, W., 2:416. **2,** Smith, E., 251. **3,** Reshetar, 98–9; Schapiro, CPSU, 127; Ulam, *Lenin and the Bolsheviks*, 283. **4,** Smith, E., 250. **5,** Alexandrov, 42; Trotsky,

Stalin, 1:206. **6,** SIE, 12:353. **7,** Alexandrov, 42; Smith, E., 251. **8,** W., 2:417–18. **9,** Arsenidze, 232. **10,** Smith, E., 255–7. **11,** SIE, 5:643–4; Trotsky, *op. cit.,* 1:208. **12,** Ibid., 208–09. **13,** Ibid. **14,** Alliluyeva, A. S., 113. **15,** Lenin, fifth edition, 48:53. **16,** Smith, E., 259–61.

2. *Lenin's Man in St Petersburg?* (pp. 66–70)

1, Badayev, *Bolsheviki v Gosudarstvennoy dume,* 21, 36. **2,** Alexandrov, 43–4; Trotsky, *Stalin,* 1:214; W., 2:419. **3,** Trotsky, *op. cit.,* 1:215–33. **4,** Krupskaya, 202. **5,** W., 2:248–9. **6,** Lenin, fifth edition, 48:62–79. **7,** Smith, E., 267–8. **8,** Elwood, 369; *Iz epokhi 'Zvezdy' i 'Pravdy',* 3:201–02. **9,** Lenin, *op. cit.,* 48:127. **10,** Ibid., 114–72; *Iz epokhi 'Zvezdy' i 'Pravdy',* 3:194–221.

3. *The Austrian Episode* (pp. 70–74)

1, Krupskaya, 204–05. **2,** Alliluyeva, A. S., 116. **3,** Anders, 140. **4,** Ibid., 139. **5,** W., 2:310–11. **6,** W., 2:356. **7,** *KPSS v rezolyutsiyakh,* 1:388–9. **8,** Smith, E., 294. **9,** Lenin, fifth edition, 48:135. **10,** Byalik, 110. **11,** Trotsky, *Stalin,* 1:233–5. **12,** Pipes, 40–1; W., 2:300. **13,** W., 2:329. **14,** Deutscher, *The Prophet Armed,* 209. **15,** W., 2:279.

4. *Final Exile* (pp. 74–78)

1, W., 2:421. **2,** *Iz epokhi 'Zvezdy' i 'Pravdy',* 3:217. **3,** Ibid., 219. **4,** Shotman, 175 ff. **5,** *Alliluyev Memoirs,* 190. **6,** Svet. (1969), 351, 359. **7,** Shveytser, 18–20. **8,** Alliluyeva, A. S., 117–18. **9,** Shveytser, 31; Sverdlov, 1:266. **10,** Smith, E., 314–16. **11,** Shveytser, 22–3. **12,** *Proletarskaya revolyutsiya* (Moscow), 1936, 7:168. **13,** *Leninsky sbornik* (Moscow), 1931, second edition, 11:193. **14,** Samoylov, 351. **15,** Sverdlova, 266. **16,** Alliluyeva, A. S., 167; Yaroslavsky, 88. **17,** Baikaloff, 27–30. **18,** Smith, E., 324–5.

Chapter Four

1. *March and April* (pp. 79–86)

1, Alliluyeva, A. S., 166. **2,** Schapiro, CPSU, 172–3; SIE, 7:664–6. **3,** Alexandrov, 55. **4,** *Voprosy istorii KPSS* (Moscow), 1962, 3:143. **5,** Burdzhalov, 44. **6,** *Voprosy istorii KPSS,* 1962, 3:150. **7,** W., 3:2, 7. **8,** Trotsky, *Stalin,* 1:275–6. **9,** Smith, E., 413; Snegov, 22–5. **10,** W., 6:333. **11,** *Voprosy istorii KPSS,* 1962, 5:112. **12,** Snegov, 29. **13,** Raskolnikov, 63. **14,** Trotsky, *op. cit.,* 1:285. **15,** Alexandrov, 50. **16,** Trotsky, *op. cit.,* 1:291. **17,** Burdzhalov, 51. **18,** Rabinowitch, 40. **19,** Snegov, 30; Trotsky, *op. cit.,* 1:294–5. **20,** Burdzhalov, 56. **21,** Trotsky, *op. cit.,* 1:284. **22,** Sukhanov, 230.

2. *June and July* (pp. 86–90)

1, W., 3:88. **2**, Sovokin, 46. **3**, Rabinowitch, 60, 72. **4**, Sovokin, 52. **5**, Rabinowitch, 105–06; W., 3:96–9, 159. **6**, W., 3:109. **7**, Tsereteli, 2:266–7. **8**, W., 3:109. **9**, Rabinowitch, 150. **10**, Tsereteli, 2:305. **11**, Ibid., 2:344. **12**, W., 3:111–12.

3. *Lodger and Orator* (pp. 90–94)

1, Alliluyeva, A. S., 177–8. **2**, Ibid., 184. **3**, Berger, 56–7. **4**, Tsereteli, 2:334. **5**, Alliluyeva, A. S., 185, 190. **6**, Ibid., 191. **7**, Trotsky, *Stalin*, 1:315. **8**, McNeal, *Stalin's Works*, 51. **9**, W., 3:174, 186–7. **10**, Trotsky, *op. cit.*, 1:322. **11**, Sverdlova, 329. **12**, PTsK, 6. **13**, Trotsky, *op. cit.*, 1:323. **14**, PTsK, 20, 24–5.

4. *October* (pp. 94–101)

1, PTsK, 55. **2**, Deutscher, *Stalin*, 159. **3**, SIE, 11:552–6. **4**, Daniels, *Red October*, 55; PTsK, 65, 261–2. **5**, Ibid., 85–6. **6**, Ibid., 86. **7**, Ibid., 104. **8**, Trotsky, *Stalin*, 1:342. **9**, PTsK, 100. **10**, Ibid., 114. **11**, Ibid., 107, 115. **12**, Ibid., 107. **13**, Daniels, *Red October*, 108–10. **14**, W., 3:390. **15**, PTsK, 119. **16**, Trotsky, *op. cit.*, 1:341. **17**, Alliluyeva, A. S., 194–6. **18**, McNeal, *Stalin's Works*, 80. **19**, W., 4:154.

Chapter Five

1. *First Taste of Power* (pp. 102–115)

1, W., 13:108–09. **2**, Pestkovsky, cited in Shub, *Lenin*, 306–07. **3**, Trotsky, *Stalin*, 2:13–14. **4**, Deutscher, *The Prophet Armed*, 333–4; PTsK, 133–4. **5**, Lenin, third edition, 22:69–71. **6**, Trotsky, *op. cit.*, 2:19. **7**, Ibid., 18. **8**, PTsK, 157. **9**, Trotsky, *op. cit.*, 2:19. **10**, W., 4:22–4. **11**, W., 4:8–9. **12**, McNeal, *Stalin's Works*, 60; W., 4:31–2. **13**, PTsK, 160, 279; Schapiro, *The Origin of the Communist Autocracy*, 84–5. **14**, *Leninsky sbornik* (Moscow-Leningrad, 1931), second edition, 11:38. **15**, PTsK, 171–2. **16**, Ibid., 200, 202. **17**, Pipes, 113. **18**, Pestkovsky, cited in Trotsky, *op. cit.*, 2:30–1. **19**, Pestkovsky, cited in Pipes, 113.

2. *Military Trouble-Shooter* (pp. 115–127)

1, Trotsky, *Stalin*, 2:49. **2**, W., 4:419. **3**, *Dokumenty o geroicheskoy oborone Tsaritsyna v 1918 g*. **4**, W., 4:118. **5**, W., 4:116. **6**, *Dokumenty (op. cit.)*, 94. **7**, W., 4:118, italics added. **8**, W., 4:121. **9**, W., 4:127. **10**, *Dokumenty (op. cit.)*, 84. **11**, Trotsky, *op. cit.*, 2:61. **12**, W., 4:118. **13**, W., 4:121. **14**, Trotsky, *My Life*, 377. **15**, Ibid. **16**, Pipes, 198. **17**, Ibid., 203. **18**, *Pravda*, 20 September 1963, cited in R. Medvedev, *Let History Judge*, 15. **19**, W., 4:420. **20**, *Dokumenty* *(op. cit)*, 80–1. **21,** Trotsky, *Trotsky's Diary in Exile*, 81. **22,** W., 4:128. **23,** Trotsky, *My Life*, 378. **24,** Trotsky, *Stalin*, 2:54, 79, 81. **25,** W., 4:186, 208. **26,** Erickson, 58. **27,** W., 4:211. **28,** Lenin, third edition, 25:112. **29,** SIE, 12:594–6. **30,** Lermolo, 220. **31,** W., 4:263. **32,** Luckett, 303. **33,** W., 4:268. **34,** Lenin, fifth edition, 50:325. **35,** W., 4:261. **36,** W., 4:262. **37,** Deutscher, *The Prophet Armed*, 436. **38,** W., 4:464–5. **39,** Trotsky, *op. cit.*, 2:119. **40,** Deutscher, *op. cit.*, 442–3; Luckett, 319. **41,** Lenin, fifth edition, 51:409. **42,** Ibid., 140.

3. *Poland and the Caucasus* (pp. 127–132)

1, Lenin, fifth edition, 51:247. **2,** Ibid., 51:249. **3,** Trotsky, *Stalin*, 2:128. **4,** W., 4:475. **5,** Davies, N., 67–9. **6,** Pipes, 229–30. **7,** Bessedovsky, cited in Pipes, first edition, 236. **8,** Pipes, 235.

Chapter Six
1. *Peace Breaks Out* (pp. 133–140)

1, W., 5:7. **2,** *Desyaty syezd RKP(b)*, 98. **3,** Carr, *The Bolshevik Revolution*, 1:200; Lenin, third edition, 26:267. **4,** *KPSS v rezolyutsiyakh*, 2:220–1. **5,** Schapoir, *The Origin of the Communist Autocracy*, 320. **6,** Ibid., 264. **7,** *KPSS v rezolyutsiyakh*, 2:346. **8,** Schapiro, *op. cit.*, 322. **9,** Carr, *op. cit.*, 1:207; *Odinmadtsaty syezd RKP(b)*, 722–5. **10,** Schapiro, *op. cit.*, 336. **11,** *Odinnadtsaty syezd RKP(b)*, 89. **12,** Ibid., 150–1. **13,** Emmott, 26. **14,** Lenin, third edition, 27:289. **15,** Ibid., 27:542–3. **16,** Pipes, 250.

2. *Lenin Thwarted* (pp. 140–147)

1, Fotiyeva, *Iz vospominany o Lenine*, 28–9. **2,** Lenin, fifth edition, 45:339. **3,** Ibid., 54:327–8. **4,** Ibid., 45:608. **5,** Ibid., 54:674–5. **6,** Ibid., 54:329–30. **7,** Ibid., 45:344–6. **8,** Ibid., 45:356–62. **9,** Pipes, 269. **10,** Lewin, *Lenin's Last Struggle*, 56. **11,** Lenin, *op. cit.*, 45:356–62. **12,** Ibid., 45:346. **13,** Trotsky, *My Life*, 409. **14,** Carr, *The Interregnum*, 264. **15,** Lenin, *op. cit.*, 45:389–406. **16,** Carr, *op. cit.*, 265. **17,** Lenin, *op. cit.*, 54:329–30. **18,** Ibid., 54:329, 674. **19,** Ibid., 54:330. **20,** Trotsky, *Stalin*, 2:187–99.

3. *Around Lenin's Death-Bed* (pp. 147–156)

1, Deutscher, *The Prophet Unarmed*, 87, 91. **2,** Carr, *The Interregnum*, 272. **3,** W., 5:206–08. **4,** W., 5:183. **5,** W., 5:262. **6,** Carr, *op. cit.*, 274–5. **7,** W., 5:235. **8,** Bajanov, 152. **9,** *Chetyrnadtsaty syezd VKP(b)*, 455. **10,** Carr, *op. cit.*, 292–4. **11,** Schapiro, CPSU, 353; Trotsky, *Stalin*, 2:249. **12,** W., 5:305. **13,** Carr, *op. cit.*, 289; Pipes, 262–3. **14,** Bajanov, 74–7. **15,** Ibid., 91. **16,** Deutscher, *op. cit.*,

118. **17,** *Sotsialistichesky vestnik* (Berlin), 24 May 1924, 9–10. **18,** Ibid., 28 May 1924, 11. **19,** Carr, *op. cit.*, 310; Deutscher, *op. cit.*, 121–3. **20,** W., 5:384–5. **21,** Carr, *op. cit.*, 317. **22,** *Pravda*, 28, 29, 30 December 1923; 1, 4 January 1924. **23,** W., 6:14–21. **24,** W., 6:24. **25,** *Pravda*, 24 January 1924. **26,** Trotsky, *My Life*, 433. **27,** W., 6:46–51. **28,** Carr, *op. cit.*, 348.

Chapter Seven

1. *Trotsky Extruded* (pp. 157–164)

1, Wolfe, *Khrushchev and Stalin's Ghost*, 258–9. **2,** Bajanov, 46; Carr, *The Interregnum*, 359–61; Trotsky, *The Suppressed Testament of Lenin*, 13. **3,** Bajanov, 46. **4,** Carr, *op. cit.*, 361–2; *Trinadtsaty syezd RKP(b)*, 629–33. **5,** Eastman, *Since Lenin Died*, 128. **6,** W., 10:175–6. **7,** Bajanov, 19–31. **8,** Ibid., 34–6, 49, 145. **9,** Ibid., 156–8. **10,** Carr, *Socialism in One Country*, 2:8–10. **11,** W., 6:328. **12,** W., 6:358–401. **13,** *Pravda*, 20 January 1925. **14,** W., 7:9–10. **15,** W., 7:380. **16,** Carr, *op. cit.*, 2:35. **17,** Payne, jacket. **18,** Bajanov, 26–7. **19,** Chamberlin, 2:119; Erickson, 39. **20,** Avrich, 176–8, 211. **21,** Deutscher, *The Prophet Armed*, 425–6.

2. *Kamenev and Zinovyev Quelled* (pp. 164–168)

1, Carr, *Socialism in One Country*, 2:64. **2,** Lang, 243–4; W., 6:308–09. **3,** W., 7:382. **4,** Trotsky, *Stalin*, 2:250–1. **5,** Ibid. **6,** Carr, *op. cit.*, 2:108; ibid., 1:302. **7,** W., 349–50. **8,** *Chetyrnadtsaty syezd VKP(b)*, 274–5. **9,** W., 7:391. **10,** *Chetyrnadtsaty syezd VKP(b)*, 186.

4. *Socialism in One Country* (pp. 173–177)

1, Deutscher, *Stalin*, second edition, 290. **2,** Carr, 6:51.

5. *The United Opposition Vanquished* (pp. 177–185)

1, Trotsky, *My Life*, 445. **2,** Deutscher, *The Prophet Unarmed*, 274. **3,** *Pyatnadtsaty syezd VKP(b)*, 2:1659. **4,** Serge, *Vie et Mort de Trotsky*, 180–1. **5,** W., 8:214–356. **6,** *Khrushchev Remembers*, 46; Orlov, 266. **7,** *Pyatnadtsataya konferentsiya VKP(b)*, 486. **8,** Ibid., 601. **9,** Carr, *Foundations of a Planned Economy*, 2:21–2. **10,** Trotsky, *Stalinskaya shkola falsifikatsy*, 137, 143, 149. **11,** Ibid., 179. **12,** W., 10:175–7. **13,** *Pravda*, 1 November 1927. **14,** W., 10:190. **15,** W., 10:191. **16,** W., 10:209–11; 234–5. **17,** W., 10:217–18. **18,** W., 10:349. **19,** Popov, 2:327. **20,** W., 10:336. **21,** W., 10:327. **22,** W., 10:328.

6. *Bukharin Overwhelmed* (pp. 185–198)

1, Deutscher, *Stalin*, 312. **2,** Trotsky Archives, cited in Erlich, 94. **3,** W., 11:3–4. **4,** Rigby, 76. **5,** Orlov, 28. **6,** Avtorkhanov, 28–9. **7,** Lyons, *Assignment in Utopia*, 117, 123. **8,** Ibid., 127. **9,** W., 12:14. **10,** Daniels, *The Conscience of the Revolution*, 329. **11,** W., 11:159. **12,** Carr, *Foundations of a Planned Economy*, 1:80–2; 2:64. **13,** Ibid., 2:65–6; Deutscher, *The Prophet Unarmed*, 441–2. **14,** Schapiro, CPSU, 371. **15,** Carr, *op. cit.*, 2:77; *Pravda*, 20 October 1928. **16,** W., 11:288. **17,** W., 11:236. **18,** Daniels, *op. cit.*, 342. **19,** W., 11:279. **20,** W., 11:286. **21,** Daniels, *op. cit.*, 344–8. **22,** Trotsky Archives, cited in Deutscher, *op. cit.*, 396. **23,** Deutscher, *op. cit.*, 456. **24,** Ibid., 468. **25,** Deutscher, *The Prophet Outcast*, 89. **26,** W., 11:318–21. **27,** Carr, *op. cit.*, 2:89–90. **28,** W., 12:1–107.

7. *Quinquagenarian* (pp. 199–201)

1, Schapiro, CPSU, 368. **2,** Souvarine, 577.

Chapter Eight

1. *Peasant and Worker Regimented* (pp. 202–213)

1, Deutscher, *Stalin*, 406. **2,** W., 6:282. **3,** W., 16:141–2. **4,** Conquest, *The Great Terror*, 22. **5,** W., 12:170. **6,** Lewin, *Russian Peasants and Soviet Power*, 514. **7,** W., 12:192–3. **8,** Lewin, *op. cit.*, 514–15. **9,** Prokopovich, 1:204; Schapiro, CPSU, 389; SIE, 7:495. **10,** Conquest, *op. cit.*, 21. **11,** Swianiewicz, 123; Lewin, *op. cit.*, 508. **12,** Conquest, *op. cit.*, 23. **13,** Churchill, 8:78. **14,** Fainsod, *Smolensk under Soviet Rule*, 240. **15,** *Kollektivizatsiya selskogo khozyaystva*, 107. **16,** W., 12:265. **17,** W., 13:161–215. **18,** Deutscher, *Stalin*, 341. **19,** Schapiro, CPSU, 387. **20,** Conquest, *op. cit.*, 496. **21,** W., 13:38–9.

2. *Patterns of Oppression* (pp. 213–219)

1, Lewytzkyj, 76. **2,** Williams-Ellis, *passim*. **3,** Lyons, *Assignment in Utopia*, 370 **4,** Ibid., 372. **5,** *Wrecking Activities at Power Stations in the Soviet Union*, 427. **6,** W., 13:84–102. **7,** Serge, *Memoirs of a Revolutionary*, 250. **8,** Lyons, *op. cit.*, 447–64; Tchernavin, 199–204. **9,** *Pravda*, 2 December 1930. **10,** Nicolaevsky, 28–9. **11,** Ibid. **12,** Ibid., 29–30. **13,** Conquest, *The Great Terror*, 30. **14,** Rigby, 39–40.

3. *Patron of Literature and Interviewee* (pp. 219–226)

1, Muchnic, 94–5. **2,** W., 12:173–7. **3,** Nicolaevsky, 46. **4,** Mandelstam, N., 339. **5,** Khrushchev, cited in Johnson, 161–2. **6,** Lyons, *Assignment in Utopia*, 383. **7,** Ibid., 381–90. **8,** Forbes, 75. **9,** Blackstock, *The Secret Road to World War*

Two, 284. **10**, W., 13:104–23. **11**, *Oxford Classical Dictionary*, 103. **12**, W., 13:116–17. **13**, Ludwig, *Leaders of Europe*, 372. **14**, Lyons, *op. cit.*, 428–9. **15**, Ibid., 431–3. **16**, Ervine, 518; Pearson, 329–31. **17**, Shaw, 4. **18**, Wells, 799–807. **19**, Foreign Office Records, cited in Hyde, 315–18.

4. *Family Man* (pp. 226–232)

1, Svet. (1967), 113. **2**, Orlov, 317–18. **3**, Barmine, 264. **4**, Ibid., 256, 264; Svet. (1967), 119. **5**, Lermolo, 229. **6**, Svet. (1967), 122–3, 204; Svet. (1969), 141–2. **7**, Ibid., 142. **8**, Ibid., 351. **9**, Iremaschwili, 40. **10**, Serge, *Portrait de Staline*, 94–5. **11**, Hyde, 260. **12**, Lermolo, 226–7. **13**, Barmine, 264. **14**, Svet. (1969), 360. **15**, Forbes, 63–4. **16**, Ibid., 70–2. **17**, Svet. (1969), 143. **18**, Lermolo, 225. **19**, Hyde, 251. **20**, Svet. (1967), 105. **21**, Ibid., 154. **22**, Ibid., 165; Svet. (1969), 362. **23**, Ibid., 344. **24**, Barmine, 262–3. **25**, Svet. (1967), 111, 170–1.

5. *The Seventeenth Congress* (pp. 232–235)

1, Rigby, 38. **2**, W., 13:347. **3**, W., 13:305. **4**, W., 13:302. **5**, W., 13:355. **6**, Schapiro, CPSU, 402; but see Rush, 95. **7**, Rigby, 37. **8**, Leonhard, 95. **9**, Nicolaevsky, 93–4. **10**, Fainsod, *How Russia is Ruled*, 364. **11**, Prokopovich, 1:254; Schapiro, CPSU, 404. **12**, Shirer, 279. **13**, Kennan, *Russia and the West under Lenin and Stalin*, 285. **14**, Ulam, *Expansion and Coexistence*, 194.

Chapter Nine

1. *Kirov Assassinated* (pp. 236–244)

1, Ouralov, 17–18. **2**, Orlov, 31–2; Rigby, 39, 97. **3**, Bukharin Trial, 376. **4**, Ibid., 572. **5**, See Conquest, *The Great Terror*, 44; Schapiro, CPSU, 405. **6**, Rigby, 39, italics added. **7**, Ibid., 97–8, italics added; Conquest, *op. cit.*, 47–9; Orlov, 37. **8**, Armstrong, *The Politics of Totalitarianism*, 22. **9**, Conquest, *op. cit.*, 42. **10**, Nicolaevsky, 91. **11**, Rigby, 39. **12**, Conquest, *op. cit.*, 47. **13**, Rigby, 39. **14**, *Pravda*, 6 December 1934. **15**, Ciliga, 71. **16**, Conquest, *op. cit.*, 57–8; *Pravda*, 16, 18 January 1935. **17**, Schapiro, CPSU, 406. **18**, See Conquest, *op. cit.*, 83, 538–9. **19**, Nicolaevsky, 46. **20**, W., 14:128. **21**, W., 14:131. **22**, W., 14:49. **23**, W., 14:67–9. **24**, W., 14:60, italics added. **25**, W., 14:99, italics added. **26**, W., 14:89.

2. *Zinovyev Framed* (pp. 244–249)

1, Orlov, 108. **2**, Ibid., 73. **3**, Ibid., 120–1. **4**, Ibid., 129. **5**, Ibid., 129–30. **6**, Ibid., 139–40. **7**, Conquest, *The Great Terror*, 111. **8**, Ibid., 102. **9**, Orlov, 179. **10**, Rigby, 39–40. **11**, Krivitsky, 166; Orlov, 220. **12**, Ibid., 350. **13**, Ibid. **14**, Nicolaevsky, 63.

3. *Pyatakov, Plenum and Police Disciplined* (pp. 250–257)

1, Kravchenko, 239. **2,** Ibid. **3,** Nicolaevsky, 64. **4,** Conquest, *The Great Terror,* 112; *Not Guilty,* 76–96. **5,** Conquest, *op. cit.,* 169–70. **6,** Orlov, 82. **7,** Ibid., 81. **8,** Ibid., 189–91. **9,** Avtorkhanov, 229. **10,** Conquest, *op. cit.,* 187; Kravchenko, 240. **11,** Conquest, *op. cit.,* 189; Dubinsky-Mukhadze, *Ordzhonikidze,* 6–7; Rigby, 70. **12,** Krivitsky, 228–9. **13,** Conquest, *op. cit.,* 194; Rigby, 42. **14,** Krivitsky, 228. **15,** Coates, 262. **16,** Ibid., 257. **17,** Ibid., 271. **18,** *Pravda,* 27 January 1937. **19,** Orlov, 222. **20,** Ibid., 221–2. **21,** Krivitsky, 166–7. **22,** Orlov, 225. **23,** See Conquest, *op. cit.,* 199.

4. *The Generals Shot* (pp. 257–265)

1, Garthoff, 221. **2,** Ibid. **3,** Medvedev, R., *Let History Judge,* 213–14. **4,** Erickson, 367. **5,** Ibid., 374. **6,** Barmine, 88–90. **7,** Krivitsky, 239. **8,** Petrov, Yu., 299. **9,** Conquest, *The Great Terror,* 205. **10,** Krivitsky, 251. **11,** Conquest, *op. cit.,* 224. **12,** Erickson, 473. **13,** Barmine, 6. **14,** Ibid., 8. **15,** SIE, 5:473; *Malaya sovetskaya entsiklopediya,* 3:791. **16,** *Pravda,* 17 February 1964. **17,** Conquest, *op. cit.,* 462. **18,** Wolin, 194. **19,** Ekart, 244. **20,** Davies, J., 192, 202. **21,** Ibid., 132. **22,** Ibid., 194. **23,** Ibid., 192. **24,** Blackstock, *The Secret Road to World War Two,* 309. **25,** Deutscher, *Stalin,* first edition, 379. **26,** Deutscher, *Stalin,* second edition, 379. **27,** See Conquest, *op. cit.,* 207. **28,** Bukharin Trial, 188. **29,** See further Bailey, Blackstock *(op. cit.),* Erickson, Nekritch.

5. *The Party Smashed* (pp. 265–268)

1, Fainsod, *Smolensk under Soviet Rule.* **2,** Conquest, *The Great Terror,* 256; Dedijer, *Tito Speaks,* 102. **3,** Conquest, *op. cit.,* 241. **4,** Orlov, 249. **5,** Conquest, *op. cit.,* 242, 247. **6,** Mandelstam, N., 356. **7,** Rigby, 46. **8,** Ibid., 45. **9,** Schapiro, CPSU, 440. **10,** Conquest, *op. cit.,* 525–35.

6. *Stalinism Exported* (pp. 268–272)

1, See Bailey, Blackstock *(The Secret Road to World War Two),* Dewar, *passim.* **2,** Poretsky, 235. **3,** Dewar, 94. **4,** Ibid., 49–59. **5,** Ibid., 64. **6,** Orlov, 237–8. **7,** Thomas, 284. **8,** Bolloten, 99. **9,** Thomas, 419. **10,** Krivitsky, 126. **11,** Thomas, 460–1. **12,** *Pravda,* 17 December 1936. **13,** Thomas, 637. **14,** Conquest, *The Great Terror,* 230.

7. *Bukharin Agonistes* (pp. 272–275)

1, Nicolaevsky, 3–65; Dan. **2,** Ibid., 181–2. **3,** Pasternak, 453. **4,** Weissberg, 425. **5,** Bukharin Trial, 576. **6,** Ibid., 49. **7,** Katkov, *The Trial of Bukharin,* 125. **8,** Feuchtwanger, 144. **9,** Maclean, 119–20.

8. *Man of Letters, Home Lover and Commuter* (pp. 275–282)

1, Solzhenitsyn, 179. **2,** Ivanov-Razumnik, 220, 308. **3,** Conquest, *The Great Terror,* 323. **4,** Brown, 124. **5,** Conquest, *op. cit.,* 323. **6,** *Malaya sovetskaya entsiklopediya,* 1:714. **7,** Mandelstam, N., 146. **8,** Ibid., 147. **9,** Mandelstam, O., 1:lxix. **10,** Conquest, *op. cit.,* 278. **11,** *Literaturnaya gazeta* (Moscow), 17 November 1932. **12,** Conquest, *Courage of Genius,* 20. **13,** Glenny, 'Mikhail Bulgakov', 18. **14,** Private Information. **15,** Ehrenburg, *Novy Mir* (Moscow), 1965, 4:60. **16,** Ibid., 1962, 5:154. **17,** Ibid., 1965, 4:60. **18,** Ibid., 1962, 4:58. **19,** Ibid., 1965, 4:60. **20,** W., 14:274. **21,** See Rigby, 73. **22,** Svet. (1969), 347. **23,** Svet. (1967), 139; Svet. (1969), 370. **24,** Svet. (1967), 28. **25,** Ibid., 134. **26,** Kravchenko, 399. **27,** *Khrushchev Remembers,* 298–9. **28,** Svet. (1967), 28. **29,** Kravchenko, 398.

9. *Post-Mortem* (pp. 282–288)

1, Conquest, *The Great Terror,* 465. **2,** Bialer, 168. **3,** Svet. (1967), 16, 27. **4,** Conquest, *op. cit.,* 525–35. **5,** Nicolaevsky, 89.

10. *The Eighteenth Congress* (pp. 288–290)

1, Conquest, *The Great Terror,* 471; Rigby, 38. **2,** Ibid., 37. **3,** W., 14:374. **4,** W., 14:385. **5,** W., 14:338–9. **6,** W., 14:341.

Chapter Ten

1. *Prelude to a Pact* (pp. 291–295)

1, Hitler, *Mein Kampf,* cited in Shirer, 952. **2,** 'Moscow and the Nazis', 129 ff. **3,** Petrov, V., 'The Nazi-Soviet Pact', 43. **4,** Krivitsky, 249. **5,** W., 14:345. **6,** Rossi, 20–1. **7,** Ibid., 27. **8,** Shirer, 600. **9,** Hilger and Meyer, 290–1. **10,** Ibid., 300. **11,** Ibid., 301. **12,** Ibid., 304. **13,** *Nationalsozialistische Deutschland und die Sowjetunion, Das,* 83. **14,** Ibid., 84.

2. *Honeymoon and Disillusion* (pp. 295–303)

1, Schulenburg dispatch, cited in Shirer, 757. **2,** Hilger and Meyer, 302–03. **3,** Ibid., 314. **4,** Ibid., 313. **5,** Tarulis, 154–5. **6,** Tanner, 41. **7,** Cited in Werth, 89. **8,** *Velikaya otechestvennaya voyna Sovetskogo soyuza,* 46–7. **9,** *Documents on German Foreign Policy,* cited in Shirer, 802. **10,** Ulam, *Expansion and Coexistence,* 292. **11,** Hilger and Meyer, 317. **12,** Rossi, 88. **13,** Ibid., 90. **14,** Ibid. **15,** *Hitler's Table Talk,* 8, 587, 666. **16,** Ibid., 624, 657, 661, 684. **17,** Sherwood, 782; Avon, 413. **18,** Shirer, 951; Rossi, 136–7. **19,** Shirer, 954. **20,** Schmidt, 214. **21,** Cited in Shirer, 969.

3. *Infringements of Socialist Legality* (pp. 303–307)

1, Hingley, 185. **2,** Herling, 59. **3,** Buber-Neumann, 179. **4,** Zawodny, 127. **5,** Ibid., 162. **6,** Ulam, *Expansion and Coexistence,* 344. **7,** Deutscher, *The Prophet Outcast,* 337–8. **8,** Levine, *The Mind of an Assassin,* 30. **9,** Ibid., 80. **10,** Ibid., 108–09. **11,** Ibid., 86. **12,** Ibid., 131–2. **13,** Trotsky, *Stalin,* 1:7, 16. **14,** Cited in Conquest, *The Great Terror,* 449. **15,** See McNeal, 'Trotsky's Interpretation of Stalin', *passim.* **16,** Levine, *op. cit.,* 62.

4. *Have we Really Deserved This?* (pp. 307–312)

1, Shirer, 986. **2,** *Documents on German Foreign Policy, 1918–1945,* Series D, 12:537; Hilger and Meyer, 327. **3,** Ulam, *Expansion and Coexistence,* 310. **4,** Shirer, 1002. **5,** *Novy mir* (Moscow), 1962, 6:150. **6,** Hilger and Meyer, 330; Werth, 132–3. **7,** 'Sovetskiye organy bezopasnosti v gody Velikoy otechestvennoy voyny', 27. **8,** Bialer, 180. **9,** Ibid., 227. **10,** Rigby, 55. **11,** *Pravda,* 14 June 1941. **12,** Boldin, 64–7. **13,** Erickson, 587. **14,** Bialer, 196. **15,** Nekritch, 209. **16,** Kennan, *Russia and the West under Lenin and Stalin,* 324.

Chapter Eleven

1. *The Lessons of 22 June* (pp. 313–320)

1, Bialer, 205. **2,** Rigby, 57. **3,** *Novy mir* (Moscow), 1964, 12:162–3. **4,** Zhukov, 268. **5,** W., 15:1–10. **6,** W., 15:3. **7,** Maysky in *Novy mir* (Moscow), 1964, 12:165. **8,** Ulam, *Expansion and Coexistence,* 316. **9,** Grigorenko, 91, 95. **10,** W., 15:19. **11,** Erickson, 584. **12,** Grigorenko, 71–2; Seaton, 92–3. **13,** Bialer, 101–02. **14,** Ibid., 155–7. **15,** Ibid., 157–8. **16,** Ibid., 158, 577. **17,** Ibid., 173–4. **18,** Grigorenko, 67–9, 163. **19,** Bialer, 63; Conquest, *The Great Terror,* 490. **20,** Bialer, 238. **21,** Conquest, *op. cit.,* 489–90. **22,** Artemyev, 108–09; Lewytzkyj, 191–2. **23,** Meretskov, 168–9.

2. *The Campaigns of 1941* (pp. 320–329)

1, Seaton, 131. **2,** *Pravda,* 1 July 1941. **3,** Bialer, 348. **4,** Salisbury, 217–18. **5,** Ibid., 219. **6,** Werth, 203. **7,** Bialer, 393; Werth, 199–202. **8,** W., 15:16. **9,** Ruslanov, 127; Zhukov, 168. **10,** Ibid., 288–9. **11,** Werth, 289. **12,** Bialer, 305. **13,** W., 15:35. **14,** W., 15:24. **15,** Bialer, 290. **16,** Ibid., 296. **17,** Zhukov, 341–2. **18,** Seaton, 224. **19,** Zhukov, 352–3. **20,** Bialer, 41. **21,** Zhukov, 280–1. **22,** Bialer, 135. **23,** Ibid., 349. **24,** Zhukov, 281. **25,** Bialer, 104. **26,** Zhukov, 205.

3. *Pre-Stalingrad Foreign Entanglements* (pp. 329–337)

1, Churchill, 6:6–7. **2,** Ibid., 6:10–11. **3,** Sherwood, 342. **4,** Churchill, 6:77.

5, Ulam, *Expansion and Coexistence*, 319. 6, Sherwood, 343–4. 7, Ibid., 387–8. 8, Ibid., 391. 9, Avon, 297. 10, Ibid., 302. 11, Ibid., 289. 12, Churchill, 8:60–3. 13, Ibid., 8:65. 14, Ibid., 8:69. 15, Ibid., 8:78. 16, Ibid., 8:78–9. 17, Ibid., 8:69. 18, Ibid., 8:71. 19, Zawodny, 5. 20, Anders, 76–7. 21, Ibid., 112, 129–34. 22, Ibid., 141. 23, Zawodny, 127, 155. 24, Anders, 120, 159.

4. Stalingrad (pp. 337–341)

1, Zhukov, 366. 2, Rigby, 57–60. 3, Zhukov, 368. 4, Seaton, 293. 5, Zhukov, 285, 376–84. 6, Seaton, 309–10. 7, Werth, 382. 8, Kolarz, 50–3; Wolin, 23.

5. Family Life (pp. 341–343)

1, Svet. (1967), 172–3. 2, Ibid., 173; Svet. (1969), 349. 3, Zawodny, 157. 4, Conquest, *The Great Terror*, 68. 5, Svet. (1967), 223. 6, Churchill, 8:77. 7, Svet. (1969), 361–3. 8, Ibid., 145; Svet. (1967), 185–93.

Chapter Twelve

1. From Kursk to Berlin (pp. 344–349)

1, Zhukov, 445. 2, Ibid., 464. 3, Voronov, 384–5. 4, Rigby, 57. 5, Bialer, 608. 6, Churchill, 9:247–8. 7, Ibid., 11:190. 8, Bialer, 362–7; Werth, 619. 9, W., 15:109. 10, W., 15:173. 11, Pasternak, 453. 12, Grigorenko, 111–12. 13, Seaton, 90. 14, Conquest, *The Nation Killers*, 65. 15, Anders, 114. 16, Conquest, *op. cit.*, 99–100. 17, Ibid., 102. 18, Stalin, cited in Conquest, *op. cit.*, 31. 19, W., 15:203–04. 20, Bialer, 563.

2. Under Western Eyes (pp. 350–360)

1, *Pravda*, 19 October 1942; Werth, 445–6. 2, Churchill, 9:228–44. 3, Deane, 297. 4, Ibid., 298. 5, Werth, 690. 6, Churchill, 12:100–13. 7, W., 15:83. 8, Cited in Werth, 450. 9, Churchill, 5:336. 10, W., 15:150. 11, Eisenhower, 339–40. 12, Sherwood, 799. 13, Churchill, 12:57–8. 14, Ibid., 10:42–3. 15, Ulam, *Expansion and Coexistence*, 369. 16, Sherwood, 796. 17, Churchill, 12:300. 18, Byrnes, 37. 19, Ulam, *op. cit.*, 366–7. 20, Ibid., 371. 21, Churchill, 10:48. 22, Ibid., 9:241. 23, Ibid., 11:210. 24, Sherwood, 735. 25, Avon, 504. 26, Ibid., 514–15. 27, de Gaulle, 65. 28, Ibid., 76. 29, Ibid., 81. 30, Ibid., 77. 31, Ibid., 67, 82. 32, Birse, 212.

3. Post-Stalingrad Foreign Entanglements (pp. 360–367)

1, Zawodny, 24, 35. 2, Ibid., 158, 167. 3, Kolko, 120. 4, Armstrong, *Soviet*

Partisans in World War II, 65. **5,** Stypulkowski, 5. **6,** Dedijer, *Tito Speaks,* 233.
7, Ibid., 234. **8,** Djilas, 70. **9,** Ibid., 82. **10,** Ibid., 88. **11,** Ibid., 102. **12,** Ibid.,
89–90. **13,** Djilas, 60, 72–3. **14,** Bialer, 113. **15,** Djilas, 74. **16,** Truman, 331.
17, Attlee, 149. **18,** Truman, 267. **19,** Williams, 71. **20,** Byrnes, 263. **21,**
Treadgold, *Twentieth Century Russia,* 400. **22,** W., 15:213–14.

Chapter Thirteen

1. *First Shocks of Peace* (pp. 368–372)

1, W., 16:4–5. **2,** Armstrong, *The Politics of Totalitarianism,* 174. **3,** Rigby, 62.

2. *Bureaucrat, Host and Puppet-Master* (pp. 372–379)

1, SIE, 7:693. **2,** Rigby, 80; Schapiro, CPSU, 510. **3,** Rigby, 80. **4,** Armstrong,
The Politics of Totalitarianism, 202. **5,** Djilas, 134. **6,** Ibid., 141. **7,** Ibid., 139–41.
8, Dedijer, *Tito Speaks,* 281–5, 301. **9,** Djilas, 137–8, 146. **10,** Ibid., 136, 143,
145–6. **11,** Ibid., 143. **12,** Meissner, *Sowjetrussland zwischen Revolution und
Restauration,* 148. **13,** Hingley, 188. **14,** Conquest, *The Soviet Police System,* 21;
Lewytzkyj, 217. **15,** Rigby, 63. **16,** Schapiro, CPSU, 512–13.

3. *The Zhdanov Period at Home* (pp. 379–382)

1, Swayze, 32. **2,** Struve, 423–6.

4. *Tito's Breakaway* (pp. 382–389)

1, Seton-Watson, 169–71. **2,** Djilas, 117. **3,** Ibid., 129. **4,** Ibid., 123. **5,** Ibid., 156
6, Dedijer, *Tito Speaks,* 330. **7,** Djilas, 118. **8,** Ulam, *Expansion and Coexistence,*
384. **9,** Dedijer, *op. cit.,* 343. **10,** Bass, 29–30. **11,** Ibid., 10. **12,** Ibid., 46.
13, Rigby, 65. **14,** Ibid. **15,** Djilas, 164. **16,** Armstrong, *The Politics of Totalitarianism,* 201. **17,** Conquest, *Power and Policy in the USSR,* 93. **18,** Djilas, 140.

Chapter Fourteen

1. *Stalin in his Seventies* (pp. 390–396)

1, Struve, 456. **2,** Ibid., 454–5; Slonim, 289. **3,** Payne, 658. **4,** Rigby, 71. **5,** Svet.
(1967), 201; Svet. (1969), 366. **6,** Rigby, 76. **7,** Svet. (1967), 199–200. **8,** Ibid.,
210–13. **9,** Svet. (1969), 138. **10,** Ibid., 370; Svet. (1967), 138. **11,** Svet. (1969),
365. **12,** Ibid., 150. **13,** Rigby, 101. **14,** Svet. (1969), 352. **15,** Svet. (1967), 159;
Svet. (1969), 146. **16,** Svet. (1967), 197–8. **17,** Ibid., 76. **18,** Ibid., 224–5.

2. *Fighting for Peace* (pp. 396–401)

1, W., 16:108–09. **2**, Dedijer, *Tito Speaks*, 331. **3**, Shulman, 107. **4**, Ulam, *Expansion and Coexistence*, 489–95. **5**, Shulman, 21. **6**, W., 16:56. **7**, Djilas, 138. **8**, *New York Times*, 25 September 1949. **9**, Ulam, *op. cit.*, 518. **10**, Shulman, 141. **11**, Whiting, 39. **12**, W., 16:180.

3. *Party Discipline, Satellite and Soviet* (pp. 401–405)

1, Seton-Watson, 314–15. **2**, Kaplan, 101. **3**, Conquest, *Power and Policy in the USSR*, 173. **4**, Rigby, 63. **5**, Conquest, *op. cit.*, 100. **6**, Ibid., 96. **7**, Hingley, 211–12. **8**, Rigby, 65. **9**, Conquest, *op. cit.*, 125.

4. *The Cultural Front* (pp. 405–411)

1, Svet. (1967), 171, 193, 197, 206. **2**, Svet. (1969), 149. **3**, Struve, 441. **4**, Conquest, *Power and Policy in the USSR*, 438–9. **5**, *Khrushchev Remembers*, 263. **6**, Medvedev, Zh., *The Rise and Fall of T. D. Lysenko*, 134–5. **7**, Ibid., 116–17. **8**, Ibid., 135. **9**, Payne, 664. **10**, W., 16:144. **11**, Struve, 478–9. **12**, Joravsky, *The Lysenko Affair*, 156–7. **13**, W., 16:165. **14**, W., 16:141–2; Schapiro, CPSU, 537.

Chapter Fifteen

1. *Final Months* (pp. 412–419)

1, W., 16:188 ff. **2**, Leonhard, 68. **3**, *Pravda*, 13 October 1952. **4**, Schapiro, CPSU, 525. **5**, Rigby, 81. **6**, Ibid., 67. **7**, Conquest, *Power and Policy in the USSR*, 165–6. **8**, Rigby, 66–7. **9**, Svet. (1969), 370. **10**, Svet. (1967), 217. **11**, *Pravda*, 13 January 1953. **12**, Leonhard, 79.

2. *Final Weeks* (pp. 419–425)

1, Menon, 27–9. **2**, Hyde, 592. **3**, Svet. (1967), 13–18. **4**, Bialer, 636–7. **5**, Payne, 690. **6**, Ibid., 695. **7**, Leonhard, 57. **8**, Svet. (1967), 19. **9**, Svet. (1969), 151. **10**, Leonhard, 83. **11**, Medvedev, R., *Let History Judge*, 559. **12**, *Pravda*, 7 March 1953. **13**, Medvedev, R., *op. cit.*, 559; Yevtushenko, 89–90. **14**, Leonhard, 95.

Chapter Sixteen

2. *Destalinization and Restalinization* (pp. 427–431)

1, *The Anti-Stalin Campaign and International Communism*, 2. **2**, Rigby, 94–106. **3**, SIE, 13:784.

3. *Stalin through Bourgeois Eyes* (pp. 431–437)

1, McNeal, 'Trotsky's Interpretation of Stalin', 148. **2,** Trotsky, *Stalin*, 2:215. **3,** Ibid., 1:16. **4,** Ibid., 2:138–9. **5,** Ibid., 2:205–07. **6,** Ibid., 2:215. **7,** McNeal, *op. cit.*, 149. **8,** Carr, *Socialism in One Country*, 1:176–7. **9,** Ibid., 1:182. **10,** Ibid., 1:185. **11,** Ibid., 1:177. **12,** Deutscher, *Stalin*, 295. **13,** Ibid., 235. **14,** McNeal, *op. cit.*, 144–5. **15,** Deutscher, *op. cit.*, 360. **16,** Carr, *op. cit.*, 1:181. **17,** Conquest, *The Great Terror*, 496. **18,** Labedz, 208. **19,** Schapiro and Reddaway, 18. **20,** Redlikh, 67–101. **21,** Ibid.

Select Bibliography

Wherever more than one edition is cited – e.g. '(London, 1951; New York, 1951)' – page references in the Reference Notes, above, are always to the edition which is mentioned first.

ABRAMOV, A. *Nachalo revolutysionnoy deyatelnosti I. V. Stalina, 1894–1902* (Leningrad, 1939)

ABRAMOVITCH, RAPHAEL, R. *The Soviet Revolution, 1917–1939* (London, 1962; New York, 1962)

ALEXANDROV, G. F. *et al.*, compilers *Joseph Stalin: a Short Biography* (Moscow, 1949)

ALLILUYEV, S. YA. *Proydyonny put* (Moscow, 1956)

Alliluyev Memoirs, The: Recollections of Svetlana Stalin's Maternal Aunt Anna Alliluyeva and her Grand-Father Sergei Alliluyev, tr. from the Russian and ed. by David Tutaev (London, 1968; New York, 1968)

ALLILUYEVA, A. S. *Vospominaniya* (Moscow, 1946)

ALLILUYEVA, SVETLANA *Twenty Letters to a Friend*, tr. from the Russian by Priscilla Johnson (London, 1967; New York, 1967)

Only One year, tr. from the Russian by Paul Chavchavadze (London, 1969; New York, 1969)

ANDERS, WLADYSLAW *Mémoires, 1939–1946*, tr. from the Polish into French by J. Rzewuska (Paris, 1948)

Anti-Stalin Campaign and International Communism, The: a Selection of Documents, ed. by the Russian Institute, Columbia University (New York, 1956)

ARMSTRONG, JOHN A. *The Politics of Totalitarianism: the Communist Party of the Soviet Union from 1934 to the Present* (New York, 1961)

ed., *Soviet Partisans in World War II* (Madison, 1964)

ARSENIDZE, R. 'Iz vospominany o Staline', *Novy zhurnal* (New York), 1963, No 72

ARTEMYEV, VYACHESLAV P. *Rezhim i okhrana ispravitelno-trudovykh lagerey MVD* (Munich, 1956)

ATTLEE, C. R. *As it Happened* (London, 1954; New York, 1954)

Avlabarskaya nelegalnaya tipografiya Kavkazskogo soyuznogo Komiteta RSDRP, 1903–1906 gg: sbornik materialov i dokumentov (Tbilisi, 1954)

AVON, THE EARL OF *The Eden Memoirs. The Reckoning* (London, 1965; New York, 1965)

AVRICH, PAUL *Kronstadt 1921* (Princeton, 1970)

AVTORKHANOV, ABDURAKHMAN *Stalin and the Soviet Communist Party: a Study in the Technology of Power* (London, 1959; New York, 1959)

BADAYEV, A. *Bolsheviki v Gosudarstvennoy dume: bolshevistskaya fraktsiya v IV Gosudarstvennoy dume i revolyutsionnoye dvizheniye v Peterburge: vospominaniya* (Moscow, 1937)
The Bolsheviks in the Tsarist Duma (London, n.d.; New York, n.d.)

BAIKALOFF, ANATOLE V. *I Knew Stalin* (London, 1940)

BAILEY, GEOFFREY *The Conspirators* (London, 1961; New York, 1960)

BAILEY, SYDNEY D. 'Stalin's Falsification of History: the Case of the Brest-Litovsk Treaty', *The Russian Review* (Hanover, N. H.), January 1955, Vol 14, No 1

BAJANOV, BORIS *Avec Staline dans le Kremlin* (Paris, 1930)

BARBUSSE, HENRI *Stalin: a New World Seen through One Man*, tr. from the French by Vyvyan Holland (London, 1935; New York, 1935)

BARMINE, ALEXANDER *One who Survived: the Life Story of a Russian Under the Soviets* (New York, 1945)

BARTON, PAUL *L'Institution concentrationnaire en Russie, 1930–1957* (Paris, 1959)

BAS, I. 'Muzey bolshevistskogo pechatnogo slova', *Istorichesky zhurnal* (Moscow,) 1937, No 11

BASS, ROBERT and ELIZABETH MARBURY, ed. *The Soviet-Yugoslav Controversy, 1948–58: a Documentary Record* (New York, 1959)

BASSECHES, NIKOLAUS *Stalin*, tr. from the German by E. W. Dickes (London, 1952; New York, 1952)

Batumskaya demonstratsiya 1902 goda (Moscow, 1937)

BAUER, OTTO *Die Nationalitaetenfrage und die Sozialdemokratie* (Vienna, 1907)

BECK, F. and W. GODIN *Russian Purge and the Extraction of Confession*, tr. from the German by Eric Mosbacher and David Porter (London, 1951; New York, 1951)

BERGER, JOSEPH *Shipwreck of a Generation: the Memoirs of Joseph Berger* (London, 1971)

BERIA, L. *K voprosu ob istorii bolshevistskikh organizatsy v Zakavkazye: doklad na sobranii partaktiva 21–22 iyulya 1935 g.*, 9th edition (Moscow, 1952)

BIALER, SEWERYN, ed. *Stalin and his Generals: Soviet Military Memoirs of World War II* (Indianapolis, 1969)

BIBINEISHVILI, B. *Kamo* (Moscow, 1934)

BIRSE, A. H. *Memoirs of an Interpreter* (London, 1967; New York, 1967)

BLACK, C. E. ed. *Rewriting Russian History: Soviet Interpretations of Russia's Past* (New York, 1956)

BLACKSTOCK, PAUL W. ' "Books for Idiots": False Soviet "Memoirs" ', *The Russian Review* (Hanover, N.H.), July 1966
The Secret Road to World War Two: Soviet versus Western Intelligence 1921–1939 (Chicago, 1969)

BOLDIN, I. V. 'Sorok pyat dney v tylu vraga', *Voyenno-istorichesky zhurnal* (Moscow,) 1961, No 4

BOLLOTEN, BURNETT *The Grand Camouflage: the Communist Conspiracy in the Spanish Civil War* (London, 1961; New York, 1968)

BOR-KOMOROWSKI, T. *The Secret Army* (London, 1950; New York, 1951)

BRANDT, CONRAD *Stalin's Failure in China, 1924–1927* (New York, 1966)

BROWN, EDWARD J. *Russian Literature Since the Revolution* (New York, 1963)

BRZEZINSKI, ZBIGNIEW K. *The Permanent Purge: Politics in Soviet Totalitarianism* (Cambridge, Mass., 1956)

BUBER-NEUMANN, MARGARETE *Als Gefangene bei Stalin und Hitler: eine Welt im Dunkel* (Stuttgart, 1958)

BUDUROWĬCZ, BOHDAN B. *Polish-Soviet Relations, 1932–1939* (New York, 1963)

BUDYONNY, S. M. *Proydyonny put*, 2 vols (Moscow, 1959, 1965)

'Bukharin Trial': *Report of Court Proceedings in the Case of the Anti-Soviet 'Bloc of Rights and Trotskyites'* (Moscow, 1938)

BUNYAN, J., ed. *Intervention, Civil War and Communism in Russia, April–December 1918: Documents and Materials* (Baltimore, 1936)

BUNYAN, J. and H. H. FISHER, ed. *The Bolshevik Revolution, 1917–1918: Documents and Materials* (Stanford, 1934)

BURDZHALOV, E. N. 'O taktike bolshevikov v marte-aprele 1917 goda', *Voprosy istorii* (Moscow), 1956, No 4

BYALIK, B. A., *et al.*, ed. *V. I. Lenin i A. M. Gorky*, 3rd, enlarged edition (Moscow, 1969)

BYRNES, JAMES F. *Speaking Frankly* (London, 1947; New York, 1947)

CADOGAN, ALEXANDER *The Diaries of Alexander Cadogan, 1938–1945* (London, 1971; New York, 1972)

CARR, E. H. *A History of Soviet Russia*, as follows:
The Bolshevik Revolution, 1917–1923, 3 vols (London, 1952-54; New York, 1951–53)
The Interregnum, 1923–1924 (London, 1954; New York, 1954)
Socialism in One Country, 1924–1926, 3 vols (London, 1958–64; New York, 1958–60)
Foundations of a Planned Economy, 1926–1929, 2 vols, vol 1 in collaboration, with R. W. DAVIES (London, 1969–71; New York, 1970)

CHAMBERLIN, WILLIAM HENRY *The Russian Revolution, 1917–1921*, 2 vols (New York, 1935)

Chetvyorty (obyedinitelny) syezd RSDRP, 23 aprelya – 8 maya (10–25 aprelya) 1906 g. (Moscow, 1934)

Chetyrnadtsaty syezd VKP(b), 18–31-dekabrya 1925 g. (Moscow-Leningrad, 1926)

CHTÉMENKO, SERGUÉI *L'Etat-Major Général Soviétique en Guerre, 1941–1945* (Moscow, 1971), tr. from the Russian into French by Jean Champenois

CHUIKOV, VASILI I. *The End of the Third Reich*, tr. from the Russian by Ruth Kisch (London, 1967; New York 1968 as *The Fall of Berlin*)

CHURCHILL, WINSTON S. *The Second World War*, 12 vols (London, 1964; New York, 1948–53)

CIANO, G. *Ciano's Diary, 1939–1943*, ed. Malcolm Muggeridge (London, 1947)

CIECHANOWSKI, JAN *Defeat in Victory* (London, 1948; New York, 1947)

CILIGA, ANTON *The Russian Enigma*, tr. from the French by Fernand G. Renier and Anne Cliff (London, 1940)

COATES, W. P. and ZELDA K., compilers *The Moscow Trial (January, 1937) and Two Speeches by J. Stalin* (London, 1937)

COLLARD, DUDLEY *Soviet Justice and the Trial of Radek and Others* (London, 1937)

CONQUEST, ROBERT *Courage of Genius: the Pasternak Affair* (London, 1961; New York, 1962)
  Power and Policy in the USSR: the Study of Soviet Dynastics (London, 1961; New York, 1962)
  The Great Terror: Stalin's Purge of the Thirties (London, 1968; New York, 1968)
  The Nation Killers: the Soviet Deportation of Nationalities (London, 1970; New York, 1971)
  ed., *The Soviet Police System* (London, 1968; New York, 1968)

Correspondence between the Chairman of the Council of Ministers of the USSR and the Presidents of the USA and the Prime Ministers of Great Britain (Moscow, 1957)

CRANKSHAW, EDWARD *Khrushchev: a Biography* (London, 1966; New York, 1966)

DALLIN, DAVID J. *Soviet Russia and the Far East* (London, 1949; New Haven, 1948)
  The New Soviet Empire (London, 1951; New Haven, 1951)
  Soviet Espionage (New Haven, 1955)

DALLIN, DAVID J., and BORIS I. NICOLAEVSKY *Forced Labour in Soviet Russia* (London, 1948, New Haven, 1947)

DAN, L. 'Bukharin o Staline', *Novy zhurnal* (New York), March 1964, No 75

DANIELS, ROBERT VINCENT *The Conscience of the Revolution: Communist Opposition in Soviet Russia* (Cambridge, Mass., 1960)
  Red October: the Bolshevik Revolution of 1917 (London, 1968; New York, 1969)

DAVIES, JOSEPH E. *Mission to Moscow* (New York, 1941)

DAVIES, NORMAN *White Eagle, Red Star, the Polish-Soviet War, 1919–20* (New York, 1972)

DE GAULLE, GENERAL *War Memoirs. Salvation, 1944–1946*, tr. from the French by Richard Howard (London, 1960; New York, 1960)

DEANE, JOHN R. *The Strange Alliance: the Story of American Efforts at War-time Co-operation with Russia* (London, 1947; New York, 1947)

DEDIJER, VLADIMIR *Tito Speaks: his Self Portrait and Struggle with Stalin* (London, 1953; New York, 1953)
  The Battle Stalin Lost: Memoirs of Yugoslavia, 1948–1953 (New York, 1971)

DELBARS, YVES *The Real Stalin*, tr. from the French by Bernard Miall (London, 1953)

Desyaty syezd RKP(b), mart 1921 goda: stenograficheskiy otchot (Moscow, 1963)

DEUTSCHER, I. *Stalin: a Political Biography*, 1st edition (London, 1949); 2nd edition (London, 1967; New York, 1967)
  The Prophet Armed: Trotsky, 1879–1921 (London 1954; New York, 1954)
  The Prophet Unarmed: Trotsky, 1921–1929 (London, 1959; New York, 1951)
  The Prophet Outcast: Trotsky, 1929–1940 (London, 1963; New York, 1963)
  Ironies of History: Essays on Contemporary Communism (London, 1966; New York, 1966)

DEWAR, HUGO *Assassins at Large: a Fully Documented and Hitherto Unpublished Account of the Executions outside Russia Ordered by the GPU* (London, 1951; Boston, 1952)

DJILAS, MILOVAN *Conversations with Stalin*, tr. from the Serbo-Croat by Michael B. Petrovich (London, 1962; New York, 1962)

Documents on British Foreign Policy, 1919–39, ed. E. L. Woodward and Rohan Butler, 2nd series, vol 7; 3rd series, vols 4–7 (London, 1951–58)

Documents on German Foreign Policy, 1918–1945, series D, vols 8–12 (Washington and London, 1954–62)

Dokumenty o geroicheskoy oborone Tsaritsyna v 1918 g. (Moscow, 1942)

DUBINSKY-MUKHADZE, I. M. *Ordzhonikidze* (Moscow, 1936)
Shaumyan (Moscow, 1965)

DURANTY, WALTER *Stalin & Co: the Politburo – the Men Who Run Russia* (London, 1949; New York, 1949)

Dvadtsat pyat let bakinskoy organizatsii bolshevikov (Baku, 1924)

EASTMAN, MAX *Since Lenin Died* (London, 1925, New York, 1925)
Leon Trotsky: the Portrait of a Youth (London, 1926; New York, 1925)

EHRENBURG, ILYA *Men, Years – Life*, 6 vols, tr. from the Russian by Anya Bostock and others (London, 1961–66; Cleveland, 1965)

EISENHOWER, DWIGHT D. *Crusade in Europe* (London, 1948; Garden City, NY, 1948)

EKART, ANTONI *Vanished without Trace* (London, 1954)

ELLIS, C. H. *The Transcaspian Episode 1918–1919* (London, 1963; New York, 1963)

ELWOOD, RALPH CARTER 'Lenin and *Pravda*, 1912–1914', *Slavic Review* (New York), 1972, Vol 31, No 2

'Emmott': *Report (Political and Economic) of the Committee to Collect Information on Russia*, Lord Emmott, Chairman (London, 1921)

ERICKSON, JOHN *The Soviet High Command: a Military–Political History, 1918–1941* (London, 1962; New York, 1962)

ERLICH, ALEXANDER *The Soviet Industrialization Debate* (Cambridge, Mass., 1960)

ERVINE, ST JOHN *Bernard Shaw* (London, 1956; New York, 1956)

ESSAD-BEY *Stalin: the Career of a Fanatic*, tr. from the German by Huntley Paterson (London, 1932; New York, 1932)

FAINSOD, MERLE *How Russia is Ruled* (Cambridge, Mass., 1956)
Smolensk under Soviet Rule (London, 1959; Cambridge, Mass., 1958)

FEIS, HERBERT *Churchill, Roosevelt, Stalin: the War they Waged and the Peace they Sought* (Princeton, 1957)
Between War and Peace: the Potsdam Conference (Princeton, 1960)

FEUCHTWANGER, LION *Moscow, 1937: My visit Described for my Friends*, tr. from the German by Irene Josephy (London, 1937; New York, 1937)

FISCHER, GEORGE *Soviet Opposition to Stalin: a Case Study in World War II* (Cambridge, Mass., 1952)

FISCHER, LOUIS *The Life and Death of Stalin* (New York, 1952)
The Life of Lenin (London, 1965; New York, 1964)

FISCHER, RUTH *Stalin and German Communism: a Study in the Origins of the State Party* (Cambridge, Mass., 1948)

FORBES, ROSITA *These Men I knew* (London, 1940; New York, 1940)

FOTIYEVA, L. A. *Iz vospominany o Lenine* (Moscow, 1964)
Iz zhizni V. I. Lenina (Moscow, 1967)

FUTRELL, MICHAEL *Northern Underground: Episodes of Russian Revolutionary Transport and Communications through Scandinavia and Finland, 1863–1917* (London, 1963; New York, 1963)

GAFENCU, GRIGORE *Prelude to the Russian Campaign: from the Moscow Pact . . . to the Opening of Hostilities in Russia*, tr. by Fletcher-Allen (London, 1945)

GALLAGHER, MATTHEW P. *The Soviet History of World War II: Myths, Memories amd Realities* (New York, 1963)

GARIBDZHANYAN, G. B. *V. I. Lenin i bolshevistskiye organizatsii Zakavkazya, 1893–1924* (Yerevan, 1967)

GARTHOFF, RAYMOND L. *How Russia Makes War: Soviet Military Doctrine* (London, 1954; Glencoe, Ill., 1953)

GATHORNE-HARDY, G. M. *A Short History of International Affairs, 1920–1934* (London, 1934)

GERASSIMOFF, ALEXANDER *Der Kampf gegen die erste russische Revolution* (Frauenfeld, 1934)

GETZLER, ISRAEL *Martov: a Political Biography of a Russian Social Democrat* (London, 1967; New York, 1967)

GINZBURG, EVGENIA SEMYONOVNA *Into the Whirlwind*, tr. from the Russian by Paul Stevenson and Manya Harari

GLENNY, MICHAEL 'Mikhail Bulgakov: Return from Obscurity', *Communist Affairs* (Los Angeles), 1968, vol 6, No 2
'Leonid Krasin: the Years before 1917: an Outline', *Soviet Studies* (Glasgow) 1970, vol 22, No 2
'About Mikhail Bulgakov, his Novel, the Moscow Art Theatre and Stanislavsky', Preface to *Black Snow: a Theatrical Novel by Mikhail Bulgakov* (Harmondsworth, 1971)

GOLDMAN, EMMA *My Disillusionment in Russia* (London, 1925; Garden City, NY, 1923)

GRAHAM, STEPHEN *Stalin: an Impartial Study of the Life and Work of Joseph Stalin* (London, 1931)

GREY, IAN *The First Fifty Years: Soviet Russia, 1917–1967* (London, 1967; New York, 1967)

GRIGORENKO, PJOTR *Der sowjetische Zusammenbruch, 1941* (Frankfurt am Main, 1969)

HART, B. H. LIDDELL, ed. *The Soviet Army* (London, 1956; New York, 1956)

HERLING, GUSTAV *A World Apart*, tr. from the Polish by Joseph Marek (London, 1951; New York, 1951)

HILGER, GUSTAV *Stalin: Aufstieg der UdSSR zur Weltmacht* (Berlin, 1959)

HILGER, GUSTAV and ALFRED G. MEYER *The Incompatible Allies: a Memoir-History of German–Soviet Relations, 1918–1941* (New York, 1953)

HINGLEY, RONALD *The Russian Secret Police: Muscovite, Imperial Russian and Soviet Political Security Operations, 1565–1970* (London, 1970; New York, 1971)

History of the Communist Party of the Soviet Union (Bolsheviks): Short Course, ed. by a Commission of the Central Committee (Moscow, 1943)

Hitler's Table Talk, 1941–1944, tr. from the German by Norman Cameron and R. H. Stevens (London, 1953)

HULL, CORDELL *The Memoirs of Cordell Hull*, 2 vols (New York, 1948)

HYDE, H. MONTGOMERY *Stalin: the History of a Dictator* (London, 1971; New York, 1971)

IKONNIKOV, S. N. *Organizatsiya i deyatelnost RKI v 1920–1925 gg.* (Moscow, 1960)

IREMASCHWILI, JOSEPH *Stalin und die Trageodie Georgiens: Erinnerungen* (Berlin, 1932)

IVANOV, B. 'V Novoy ude', *Pravda*, 25 December 1939

IVANOV-RAZUMNIK *The Memoirs of Ivanov-Razumnik*, tr. from the Russian by P. S. Squire (London, 1965; New York, 1965)

Iz epokhi 'Zvezdy' i 'Pravdy', 1911–1914 gg., 3 vols (Moscow, 1921–23)

Iz vospominany russkago uchitelya Pravoslavnoy gruzinskoy dukhovnov seminarii (Moscow, 1907)

JASNY, NAUM *Soviet Industrialization, 1928–1952* (Chicago, 1961)

JOHNSON, PRISCILLA *Khrushchev and the Arts: the Politics of Soviet Culture, 1962–1964* (Cambridge, Mass., 1965)

JORAVSKY, DAVID *Soviet Marxism and Natural Science, 1917–1932* (London, 1961; New York, 1961)

The Lysenko Affair (Cambridge, Mass., 1970)

Joseph Stalin: a Short Biography (Moscow, 1941)

KAMINSKY, V. and I. VERESHCHAGIN 'Detstvo i yunost vozhdya: dokumenty, zapisi, rasskazy', *Molodaya gvardiya* (Moscow), 1939, No 12

KAPLAN, KAREL 'Anatomy of a Show Trial', *Studies in Comparative Communism* (Los Angeles), April, 1969, pp. 97–117

KATKOV, GEORGE *Russia 1917: the February Revolution* (London, 1967; New York, 1967)

The Trial of Bukharin (London, 1969; New York, 1969)

KENNAN, GEORGE F. *Russia and the West under Lenin and Stalin* (New York, 1960) 'Certain Questions from the Early History of the Bolshevik Faction, 1906–1912', Seminar Notes, 15 March 1966, Russian Research Center, Harvard University, Cambridge, Mass.

'Excerpts from a Draft Letter Written at Some Time During the First Months of 1945', *Slavic Review* (New York), September 1968

KERENSKY, A. F. *The Kerensky Memoirs: Russia and History's Turning Point* (London, 1965; New York, 1965)

KHARMANDARYAN, S. V. *Lenin i stanovleniye Zakavkazskoy federatsii, 1921–1923* (Yerevan, 1969)

Khrushchev Remembers, tr. from the Russian and ed. by Strobe Talbott (London, 1971; New York, 1971)

KNICKERBOCKER, N. R. 'Stalin, Mystery Man Even to his Mother, Post Interviewer Finds', *New York Post*, 1 December 1930

KOCHAN, LIONEL, ed. *The Jews in Soviet Russia Since 1917* (London, 1970; New York, 1970)

KOLARZ, WALTER *Religion in the Soviet Union* (London, 1961; New York, 1961)

KOLKO, GABRIEL *The Politics of War: Allied Diplomacy and the World Crisis of 1943–1945* (London, 1969; New York, 1968)

Kollektivizatsiya selskogo khozyaystva (Moscow, 1957)

KONDRATYEV, NIKOLAY *Marshal Bluykher* (Moscow, 1965)

KORYAKOV, M. 'Termometr Rossii', *Novy zhurnal* (New York, December 1958, No 55

KPSS v rezolyutsiyakh i resheniyakh syezdov konferentsy i plenumov TsK, vols 1–7 (Moscow, 1970–71)

KRAVCHENKO, VICTOR *I Chose Freedom: the Personal and Political Life of a Soviet Official* (London, 1947; New York, 1946)

KRIVITSKY, W. G. *I was Stalin's Agent* (London, 1940; New York, 1939, as *In Stalin's Secret Service*)

KRUPSKAYA, NADEZHDA *Memoirs of Lenin* (London, 1970)

KUZNETSOV, N. G. 'Na Potsdamskoy konferentisii', *Voprosy istorii* (Moscow), 1965, vol 8

LABEDZ, LEOPOLD and MAX HAYWARD, ed. *On Trial: the Case of Sinyavsky (Tertz) and Daniel (Arzhak)* (London, 1967; New York, 1966)

LABIN, SUZANNE *Stalin's Russia*, tr. by Edward Fitzgerald (London, 1949)

LANG, DAVID MARSHALL *A Modern History of Georgia* (London, 1962; New York, 1962)

LAQUEUR, WALTER *Russia and Germany: a Century of Conflict* (London, 1965; Boston, 1965)

LAURAT, LUCIEN *Staline, la linguistique et l'impérialisme russe* (Paris, 1951)

LEAHY, WILLIAM D. *I was There: the Personal Story of the Chief of Staff to Presidents Roosevelt and Truman Based on his Notes and Diaries Made at the Time* (London, 1950; New York, 1950)

LENIN, V. I. *Sochineniya*, 3rd edition, 30 vols (Moscow, 1935–37)

Polnoye sobraniye sochineny, 5th edition, 55 vols (Moscow, 1958–65)

Leninsky sbornik, 37 vols (Moscow-Leningrad, 1924–59)

LEONHARD, WOLFGANG *Kreml ohne Stalin* (Cologne, 1959)

LERMOLO, ELIZABETH *Face of a Victim*, tr. from the Russian by I. D. W. Talmadge (London, 1955; New York, 1955)

LEVINE, ISAAC DON *Stalin* (New York, 1931)

Stalin's Great Secret (New York, 1956)

The Mind of an Assassin (London, 1959; New York, 1959)

LEWIN, MOSHE *Russian Peasants and Soviet Power*, tr. from the French by Irene Nove (London, 1968; Evanston, Ill., 1968)

Lenin's Last Struggle, tr. from the French by A. M. Sheridan Smith (London, 1969; New York, 1970)

LEWYTZKYJ, BORYS *Die rote Inquisition: die Geschichte der sowjetischen Sicherheitsdienste* (Frankfurt am Main, 1967)

LUCKETT, RICHARD *The White Generals: an Account of the White Movement and the Russian Civil War* (London, 1971; New York, 1971)

LUDWIG, EMIL *Leaders of Europe* (London, 1934)
Staline: Essai biographique (New York, 1942)

LYADOV, M. *Iz zhizni partii v 1903–1907 godakh: vospominaniya* (Moscow, 1956)

LYADOV, M. N. and S. M. POZNER *Leonid Borisovich Krasin ('Nikitich'), gody podpolya: sbornik vospominany, statey i dokumentov* (Moscow-Leningrad, 1928)

LYONS, EUGENE *Assignment in Utopia* (London, 1937; New York, 1937)
Stalin: Czar of All the Russias (London, 1941; New York, 1940)

MACLEAN, FITZROY *Eastern Approaches* (London, 1966)

MCNEAL, ROBERT H. *Lenin, Stalin, Khrushchev: Voices of Bolshevism* (New Jersey, 1957)
'Trotsky's Interpretation of Stalin', in *Stalin*, ed. T. H. Rigby (Englewood Cliffs, 1966)
Stalin's Works: an Annotated Bibliography (Stanford, 1967)
Bride of the Revolution: Krupskaya and Lenin (London, 1973; Ann Arbor, 1972)

MAGLAKELIDZE, S. and A. IOVIDZE *Revolyutsiya 1905–1907 gg. v Gruzii: sbornik dokumentov* (Tbilisi, 1956)

MAISKY, IVAN *Memoirs of a Soviet Ambassador: the War, 1939–43* (London, 1967)

MAKHARADZE, F. YE. *Ocherki revolyutsionnogo dvizheniya v Zakavkazye* (Tiflis, 1927)

MAKHARADZE, F. YE. and G. V. KHACHAPURIDZE *Ocherki po istorii rabochego i krestyanskogo dvizheniya v Gruzii* (Moscow, 1932)

Malaya sovetskaya entsiklopediya, 3rd edition, 10 vols (Moscow, 1958–1960)

MANDELSTAM, NADEZHDA *Hope against Hope: a Memoir*, tr. from the Russian by Max Hayward (New York, 1970)

MANDELSTAM, OSIP *Sobraniye sochineny*, 2 vols (Washington, D.C., 1964)

MAREK, FRANZ *Was Stalin wirklich sagte* (Vienna, 1970)

MARIE, JEAN-JACQUES *Staline* (Paris, 1967)

MEDVEDEV, ROY *Faut-il réhabiliter Staline?* tr. from the Russian into French by François Olivier (Paris, 1969)
Let History Judge: The Origins and Consequences of Stalinism (London, 1972; New York, 1972)

MEDVEDEV, ZHORES A. *The Rise and Fall of T. D. Lysenko*, tr. from the Russian by I. Michael Lerner (New York, 1969)

MEISSNER, BORIS *Sowjetrussland zwischen Revolution und Restauration* (Cologne, 1956)
Die Sowjetunion, die baltischen Staaten und das Voelkerrecht (Cologne, 1956)

MENON, K. P. S. *The Flying Troika: Extracts from a Diary* (London, 1963; New York, 1963)

MERETSKOV, K. A. *Na sluzhbe narodu: stranitsy vospominany* (Moscow, 1970)

MONTGOMERY, BERNARD LAW *Memoirs* (London, 1958; Cleveland, 1958)

MOORE, BARRINGTON *Terror and Progress USSR: Some Sources of Change and Stability in the Soviet Dictatorship* (Cambridge, Mass., 1954)

MORAN, LORD *Winston Churchill: the Struggle for Survival, 1940–1965* (London, 1966; Boston, 1966)

'Moscow and the Nazis', *Survey* (London), October 1963, No 49

MOSKALYOV, M. *Russkoye byuro TsK bolshevistskoy partii, 1912—mart 1917* (Moscow, 1947)
Byuro Tsentralnogo Komitta RSDRP v Rossii (Moscow, 1964)
MUCHNIC, HELEN *From Gorky to Pasternak: Six Writers in Soviet Russia* (New York, 1961)
MURPHY, J. T. *Stalin, 1879–1944* (London, 1945; Englewood, NJ, 1946)
Nationalsozialistische Deutschland und die Sowjetunion, Das, 1939–41: Akten aus dem Archiv des Deutschen Auswaertigen Amts (Berlin, 1948)
NEKRITCH, ALEXANDRE *L'Armée Rouge assassinée: 22 juin 1941*, tr. from the Russian into French by Marie Bennigsen (Paris, 1968)
NICOLAEVSKY, BORIS I. *Power and the Soviet Elite: 'The Letter of an Old Bolshevik' and Other Essays* (London, 1966; New York, 1965)
Not Guilty: Report of the Commission of Inquiry into the Charges Made against Leon Trotsky in the Moscow Trials (New York, 1938)
NOVE, ALEC *Was Stalin Really Necessary?: Some Problems of Soviet Political Economy* (London, 1964)
An Economic History of the USSR (Harmondsworth, 1972; Baltimore, 1972)
Odinnadtsaty syezd RKP(b), mart-aprel 1922 g. (Moscow, 1936)
ORLOV, ALEXANDER *The Secret History of Stalin's Crimes* (London, 1954; New York, 1953)
OURALOV, ALEXANDRE *Staline au Pouvoir*, tr. from the Russian into French by Jacques Fondeur (Paris, 1951)
PANKOV, D. V. *Komkor Eydeman* (Moscow, 1965)
PASTERNAK, BORIS *Doctor Zhivago*, tr. from the Russian by Max Hayward and Manya Harari (London, 1958; New York, 1958)
PAYNE, ROBERT *The Rise and Fall of Stalin* (London, 1968; New York, 1965)
PEARSON, HESKETH *G.B.S.: a Full Length Portrait* (New York, 1942)
PETROV, VLADIMIR 'The Nazi-Soviet Pact', *Problems of Communism* (Washington, D.C.), January–February 1968
PETROV, VLADIMIR and EVDOKIA *Empire of Fear* (London, 1956; New York, 1956)
PETROV, YURY P. *Partiynoye stroitelstvo v Sovetskoy armii i flote* (Moscow, 1964)
PIPES, RICHARD *The Formation of the Soviet Union: Communism and Nationalism, 1917–1923* (Cambridge, Mass.), 1st edition, 1954; 2nd, revised edition, 1964
POKROVSKY, M. N., ed. *1905: materialy i dokumenty* (Moscow, 1925)
POLIKARPOV, V. D., ed. *Etapy bolshogo puti: vospominaniya o grazhdanskoy voyne* (Moscow, 1963)
POPOV, N. *Outline History of the C.P.S.U.(b)*, tr. from the 16th Russian edition (London, n.d.; New York, 1934)
PORETSKY, ELISABETH K. *Our Own People: a Memoir of 'Ignace Reiss' and his Friends* (London, 1969; Ann Arbor, 1970)
POSSONY, STEFAN T. *Lenin: the Compulsive Revolutionary* (Chicago, 1964)
PROKOPOVICH, S. N. *Narodnoye khozyaystvo SSSR*, 2 vols (New York, 1952)
Protokoly Tsentralnogo komiteta RSDRP(b), avgust 1917—fevral 1918 (Moscow, 1958)

Pyatnadtsataya konferentsiya VKP(b) (Moscow-Leningrad, 1927)

Pyatnadtsaty syezd VKP(b), 2 vols (Moscow, 1962)

Pyaty (londonsky) syezd RSDRP, aprel–may 1907 goda: protokoly (*Moscow*, 1963)

RABINOWITCH, ALEXANDER *Prelude to Revolution: the Petrograd Bolsheviks and the July 1917 Uprising* (Bloomington, 1968)

RANDALL, FRANCIS B. *Stalin's Russia: an Historical Reconsideration* (New York, 1965)

RASKOLNIKOV, F. F. *Na boyevykh postakh* (Moscow, 1964)

Rasskazy starykh rabochikh Zakavkazya o velikom Staline (Moscow, 1937)

RAUCH, GEORG VON *A History of Soviet Russia*, 5th, revised edition, tr. from the German by Peter and Annette Jacobsohn (New York, 1957)

REDLIKH, ROMAN *Stalinshchina kak dukhovny fenomen* (Frankfurt am Main, 1971)

REED, JOHN *Ten Days that Shook the World* (Harmondsworth, 1966; New York, 1967)

RESHETAR, JOHN S. *A Concise History of the Communist Party of the Soviet Union*, revised edition (New York, 1964)

RIGBY, T. H., ed. *The Stalin Dictatorship: Khrushchev's 'Secret Speech' and Other Documents* (Sydney, 1968)

ROEDER, BERNHARD *Der Katorgan: Traktat ueber die moderne Sklaverei* (Cologne, 1956)

ROSSI, A. *Deux ans d'alliance germano-soviétique, août 1939—juin 1941* (Paris, 1949)

RUFFMANN, KARL-HEINZ *Sowjetrussland: Struktur und Entfaltung einer Weltmacht* (Munich, 1967)

RUPERT, RAPHAEL *A Hidden World* (London, 1963; Cleveland, 1963)

RUSH, MYRON *The Rise of Khrushchev* (Washington, D.C., 1958)

RUSLANOV, P. 'Marshal Zhukov', *The Russian Review* (Hanover, N.H.), April and July 1956, vol 15, Nos 2–3

SALISBURY, HARRISON E. *The Siege of Leningrad* (London, 1969; New York, 1969)

SAMOYLOV, F. N. *Po sledam minuvshego* (Moscow, 1954)

SCHAPIRO, LEONARD *The Origin of the Communist Autocracy: Political Opposition in the Soviet State, First Phase, 1917–1922* (London, 1955; Cambridge, Mass., 1955)

The Communist Party of the Soviet Union, 2nd, revised and enlarged edition (London, 1970; New York, 1971)

SCHAPIRO, LEONARD and PETER REDDAWAY, ed. *Lenin: the Man, the Theorist, the Leader: a Reappraisal* (London, 1967; New York, 1967)

SCHELLENBERG, WALTER *The Schellenberg Memoirs*, tr. from the German by Louis Hagen (London, 1956; New York, 1956 as *The Labyrinth: Memoirs*)

SCHMIDT, PAUL *Hitler's Interpreter*, tr. from the German (London, 1951; New York, 1951)

SCHWARTZ, HARRY *Russia's Soviet Economy* (London, 1951)

OMON M. *The Russian Revolution of 1905: the Workers' Movement and the Formation of Bolshevism and Menshevism* (Chicago, 1967)

SEATON, ALBERT *The Russo-German War, 1941–1945* (London, 1971; New York, 1971)

SERGE, VICTOR *Destin d'une Révolution: U.R.S.S., 1917–1936* (Paris, 1937)
Portrait de Staline (Paris, 1940)
Vie et Mort de Trotsky (Paris, 1951)
Memoirs of a Revolutionary, 1901–1941, tr. from the French by Peter Sedgwick (New York, 1963)

SETON-WATSON, HUGH *The Eastern European Revolution*, 3rd edition (London, 1956; New York, 1956)

SHAUMYAN, L. *Kamo: zhizn i deyatelnost professionalnogo revolyutsionera S. A. Ter-Petrosyana* (Moscow, 1959)

SHAW, GEORGE BERNARD *Shaw on Stalin: a Russia Today Pamphlet* (London, 1941)

SHERWOOD, ROBERT E. *Roosevelt and Hopkins: an Intimate History* (New York, 1948)

SHIRER, WILLIAM L. *The Rise and Fall of the Third Reich: a History of Nazi Germany* (London, 1964; New York, 1960)

SHOTMAN, A. *Kak iz iskry cozgorelos plamya* (Leningrad, 1935)

SHUB, DAVID 'Kamo: the Legendary Bolshevik of the Caucasus', *The Russian Review* (Hanover, N.H.), July 1960
Lenin: a Biography (Harmondsworth, 1966; Baltimore, 1967)

SHUKMAN, HAROLD *Lenin and the Russian Revolution* (London, 1966; New York, 1967)

SHULMAN, MARSHALL D. *Stalin's Foreign Policy Reappraised* (New York, 1966)

SHVEYTSER, V. *Stalin v turukhanskoy ssylke* (Moscow, 1943)

SLONIM, MARC *Soviet Russian Literature Writers and Problems* (New York, 1964)

SMITH, EDWARD ELLIS *The Young Stalin: the Early Years of an Elusive Revolutionary* (London, 1968; New York, 1967)

SMITH, WALTER BEDELL *Moscow Mission, 1946–1949* (London, 1950; New York, 1950)

SNEGOV, A. V. 'Neskolko stranits iz istorii partii, mart—nachalo aprelya 1917 g.' *Voprosy istorii KPSS* (Moscow), 1963, No 2

SOLZHENITSYN, ALEXANDER 'An Open Letter to the Fourth Congress of Soviet Writers from Alexander Solzhenitsyn', *Survey* (London), July 1967, No 64

SOUVARINE, BORIS *Stalin: a Critical Survey of Bolshevism*, tr. by C. L. R. James (London, 1939; New York, 1939)

Sovetskaya istoricheskaya entsiklopediya, ed. Ye. M. Zhukov and others, vols 1–13 (Moscow, 1961–71)

'Souvetskiye organy gosudarstvennoy bezopasnosti v gody Velikoy otechestvennoy voyny', *Voprosy istorii* (Moscow), May 1965

SOVOKIN, A. M. 'K istorii iyunskoy demonstratsii 1917 g.', *Voprosy istorii KPSS* (Moscow, 1966, No 5

SPIRIDOVICH, A. L. *Istoriya bolshevizma v Rossii ot vozniknoveniya do zakhvata vlasti, 1883–1903–1917* (Paris, 1922)

STALIN, I. *Voprosy Leninizma*, 11th edition (Moscow, 1945)
Sochineniya, vols 1–13 (Moscow, 1946–51), also; in effect a continuation of this edition.
Sochineniya, vols 14–16 (1–3) ed. Robert H. McNeal (Stanford, 1967)

STETTINIUS, EDWARD R. *Roosevelt and the Russians: the Yalta Conference* (London, 1950; New York, 1949)

STRIK-STRIKFELDT, WILFRIED *Against Stalin and Hitler: Memoir of the Russian Liberation Movement, 1941–1945*, tr. from the German by David Footman (London, 1970; New York, 1971)

STRONG, ANNA LOUISE *I Change Worlds* (London, 1935; New York, 1935)

STRUVE, GLEB *Geschichte der Sowjetliteratur* (Munich, 1957)

STYPULKOWSKI, Z. *Invitation to Moscow* (London, 1951; New York, 1962)

SUKHANOV, N. N. *The Russian Revolution 1917: a Personal Record*, ed., abridged and tr. from the Russian by Joel Carmichael (London, 1955; New York, 1962)

SVERDLOV, YA. M. *Izbrannyye proizvedeniya*, 4 vols (Moscow, 1957)

SVERDLOVA, K. T. *Yakov Mikhaylovich Sverdlov* (Moscow, 1957)

SWAYZE, HAROLD *Political Control of Literature in the USSR, 1946–1959* (Cambridge, Mass., 1962)

SWIANIEWICZ, S. *Forced Labour and Economic Development: an Enquiry into the Experience of Soviet Industrialization* (London, 1965; New York, 1965)

SZAMUELY, T. 'The Elimination of Opposition between the Sixteenth and Seventeenth Congresses of the CPSU', *Soviet Studies* (Glasgow), 1966, vol 17, No 3

TANNER, VAINO *The Winter War: Finland against Russia, 1939–1940* (Stanford, 1957)

TARULIS, ALBERT N. *Soviet Policy towards the Baltic States, 1918–1940* (Notre Dame, 1959)

THOMAS, HUGH *The Spanish Civil War* (Harmondsworth, 1968; New York, 1961)

TOKAEV, G. A. *Betrayal of an Ideal* (London, 1954)
Comrade X (London, 1956)

TREADGOLD, DONALD W. *Lenin and his Rivals: the Struggle for Russia's Future, 1898–1906* (London, 1955; New York, 1955)
Twentieth Century Russia (Chicago, 1964)
Trinadtsaty syezd RKP(b) (Moscow, 1924)

TROTSKY, LEON *My Life: the Rise and Fall of a Dictator* (London, 1930; New York, 1930)
Stalinskaya shkola falsifikatsy: popravki i dopolneniya k literature epigonov (Berlin, 1932)
The History of the Russian Revolution, tr. from the Russian by Max Eastman, 3 vols (London, 1932–33; New York, 1932)
The Suppressed Testament of Lenin (New York, 1935)
The Revolution Betrayed: What is the Soviet Union and Where is it Going? tr. from the Russian by Max Eastman (London, 1937; New York, 1937)
Trotsky's Diary in Exile (Cambridge, Mass., 1953)
Stalin: an Appraisal of the Man and his Influence, tr. from the Russian by Charles Malamuth, 2 vols (London, 1969)

Select Bibliography

TRUMAN, HARRY S. *Year of Decisions, 1945* (London, 1955; New York, 1955)

TSERETELI, I. G. *Vospominaniya o fevralskoy revolyutsii*, 2 vols. (Paris, 1963)

TSYAVLOVSKY, M. A. ed. *Bolsheviki: dokumenty po istorii bolshevizma s 1903 po 1916 gody byvsh. Moskovskogo Okhrannogo otdeleniya* (Moscow, 1918)

TUCKER, ROBERT C. *The Soviet Political Mind: Studies in Stalinism and Post-Stalin Change* (London, 1963; New York, 1963)

TUCKER, ROBERT C. and STEPHEN F. COHEN, ed. *The Great Purge Trial* (New York, 1965)

ULAM, ADAM B. *Titoism and the Cominform* (Cambridge, Mass., 1952)
Lenin and the Bolsheviks: the Intellectual and Political History of the Triumph of Communism in Russia (London, 1966; New York, 1965)
Expansion and Coexistence: the History of Soviet Foreign Policy, 1917–1967 (London, 1968; New York, 1968)

UMIASTKOWSKI, R. *Poland, Russia and Great Britain, 1941–1945: a Study of Evidence* (London, 1946)

URATADZE, GRIGORY *Vospominaniya gruzinskogo sotsial-demokrata* (Stanford, 1968)

UTECHIN, S. V. *Everyman's Concise Encyclopaedia of Russia* (London, 1961; New York, 1961)
Russian Political Thought: a Concise History (New York, 1964)

VAKAR, N. 'Stalin: po vospominaniyam N. N. Zhordania', *Posledniya novosti* (Paris), 16 December 1936

Velikaya otechestvennaya voyna Sovetskogo soyuza, 1941–1945: kratkaya istoriya (Moscow, 1967)

VERESHCHAK, S. 'Stalin v tyurme: vospominaniya politicheskogo zaklyuchonnogo', *Dni* (Paris), 22, 24 January 1928

VICKERY, WALTER N. *The Cult of Optimism: Political and Ideological Problems of Recent Soviet Literature* (Bloomington, 1963)

VORONOV, N. N. *Na sluzhbe voyennoy* (Moscow, 1963)

WARTH, ROBERT D. *Joseph Stalin* (New York, 1969)

WEINBERG, GERHARD L. *Germany and the Soviet Union, 1939–1941* (Leiden, 1954)

WEINGARTNER, THOMAS *Stalin und der Aufstieg Hitlers: die Deutschlandpolitik der Sowjetunion und der Kommunistischen Internationale, 1929–1934* (Berlin, 1970)

WEISSBERG, ALEX *Conspiracy of Silence*, tr. by Edward Fitzgerald (London, 1952; New York, 1951 as *Accused*)

WELLS, H. G. *Experiment in Autobiography: Discoveries and Conclusions of a Very Ordinary Brain*, 2 vols (London, 1934; New York, 1934)

WERTH, ALEXANDER *Russia at War, 1941–1945* (London, 1965; New York, 1964)

WETTER, GUSTAV, A. *Sowjetideologie heute, I: Dialektischer und historischer Materialismus* (Frankfurt am Main, 1962)

WHITING, ALLEN S. *China Crosses the Yalu: the Decision to Enter the Korean War* (New York, 1960)

WILLIAMS, FRANCIS *A Prime Minister Remembers: the War and Post-War Memoirs of the Rt. Hon. Earl Attlee* (London, 1961; New York, 1962)

WILLIAMS-ELLIS, ANNABEL, ed. *The White Sea Canal: Being an Account of the Construction of the New Canal between the White Sea and the Baltic Sea* (London, 1935)

WOLFE, BERTRAM D. *Three Who Made a Revolution: a Biographical History* (London, 1956; New York, 1948)
Khrushchev and Stalin's Ghost: Text, Background and Meaning of Khrushchev's Secret Report to the Twentieth Congress on the Night of February 24–25, 1956 (London, 1957; New York, 1957)
The Bridge and the Abyss: the Troubled Friendship of Maxim Gorky and V. I. Lenin (London, 1967; New York, 1967)

WOLIN, SIMON and ROBERT M. SLUSSER *The Soviet Secret Police* (New York, 1957)

Wrecking Activities at Power Stations in the Soviet Union: the Case of N. P. Vitvitsky etc. (London, 1933)

YAKIR, PYOTR *A Childhood in Prison* (London, 1972; New York, 1973)

YAKIR, P. I. and YU. A. GELLER compilers *Komandarm Yakir: vospominaniya druzey i soratnikov* (Moscow, 1963)

YAKOVLEV, A. S. *Tsel zhizni* (Moscow, 1966)

YAROSLAVSKY, E. *Landmarks in the Life of Stalin* (London, 1942)

YEMELYANOV, V. S. 'O vremeni, o tovarishchakh, o sebe', *Novy mir* (Moscow), 1967, No 2

YEVTUSHENKO, YEVGENY *A Precocious Autobiography*, tr. from the Russian by Andrew R. MacAndrew (London, 1963; New York, 1963)

ZAMYATIN, YEVGENY *A Soviet Heretic: Essays*, tr. from the Russian by Mirra Ginsburg (Chicago, 1970)

ZAWODNY, J. K. *Death in the Forest: the Story of the Katyn Forest Massacre* (London, 1971; Notre Dame, Ind., 1972)

ZHORDANIA, NOAH *My Life*, tr. into Russian from the Georgian by Ina Zhordania (Stanford, 1968)

ZHUKOV, G. *The Memoirs of Marshal Zhukov*, tr. from the Russian (London, 1971; New York, 1971)

ZUBOV, N. *F. E. Dzerzhinsky: biografiya* (Moscow, 1963)

Index

Index

Index

Compiled by Patricia Utechin

Index

Emigration, émigrés, xx, 24, 37, 60, 78, 85, 175, 179, 216, 220, 264, 269, 272, 305

Emmott Committee, 138

Engels, F., 41, 177-8, 222, 328

Expropriations (financial), 33, 37, 47-8, 51-4, 63

Eykhe, R. I., 255, 267

Fadeyev, A. A., 382

Famine:
  1921-2, 133, 144, 204
  1932-3, 204, 206, 209, 212, 215, 224, 227, 229, 232

February Revolution, 56, 78-84, 92

Fefer, I., 407

Feuchtwanger, L., 275

Finland:
  Stalin, 43, 110, 353; 1st Party Conference, 44-5; Lenin, 52, 92, 95; Brest-Litovsk Treaty, 105, 113; Nazi-Soviet Pact, 294, 302-03; Soviet-Finnish War, 296-8, 301, 315; World War Two, 346

Five Year Plans, 196, 199, 210-11, 214, 218, 220, 230

Forbes, R., 222, 229-30

France:
  Civil War intervention, 115; Stalin, 183, 233, 289; Trotsky, 196; Spanish Civil War, 270; Nazi-Soviet Pact, 293; World War Two, 298-9, 301, 311, 313, 333, 357-9; Communist Party of, 386

Frumkin, M., 194

Frunze, M. V., 165-6, 276

Gamarnik, Ya. B., 179, 260, 263, 274

Gaulle, C. de, xii, 358-9

Georgia, Georgians:
  Stalin, 1, 4-5, 10, 13, 28, 41, 43, 64, 72, 120, 392-3; russification, 8-9, 12; Marxism, 14; Bolsheviks, 51; Civil War, 132; USSR, 139; Communist Party, 143-6, 148-9; Trotsky, 153; peasants, 165; Beria, 283; Mingrelians, 404

Germany, Germans, 52, 79, 82, 270, 292-7, 299, 302, 307-09; peace negotiations, 1917, 112-13; Civil War, 119; internal events, 152, 164, 203, 235, 289; Stalin, 183, 233; Pyatakov trial, 251; Tukhachevsky, 261, 264; Bukharin, 273; World War Two, 310-12, Chs. 11 and 12 passim, 371; post-war, 375, 379; East Germany, 382, 396; see also Brest-Litovsk, Treaty of; Hitler, Nazi-Soviet Pact, World War Two

Germogen, 12

Glurdzhidze, G., 7

Gnedin, Ye., 292

Godunov, Boris, Tsar, 423

Goebbels, J., 360-1

Gogol, N. V., 411

Gorbatov, A. V., 317

Gori, 1-12, 17-18, 25, 29, 53

Gorky, A. M., 73, 166, 215, 220-2, 241-2, 265, 273, 376, 389

GPU, 269, 283

Great Terror, 172, 202, 243, 269, 272, 275, 282, 284-8, 418, 433; survivors, 69, 119, 221, 279; Stalin's responsibility, 143, 162, 219, 236, 251, 298, 324, 361, 434; intelligentsia, 214-15, 220, 279-80, 382; Party, 232, 240, 254, 265-8, 290, 374; Yezhov, 234, 256; military, 257-8, 262-3, 357; Beria, 283-4

Greece, 307, 311, 353, 386-7, 396

Grigorenko, P., 319

Gryaznov, General, 54

Harriman, A., 331

Henderson, L., 264

Hess, R., 308, 350

Hitler, A.:
  Germany, xii, 109, 203, 235, 285, 289; invasion of Russia, 127, 258, 307, 309-12; Shaw, 225; Spanish Civil War, 270-1; Nazi-Soviet Pact, 287-8, 291-304, 311; World War Two, 311, Chs. 11 and 12 passim; Khrushchev's revelations, 428; Trotsky, 431

Hoover Institution (California), 39

Hopkins, H., 330-1

Hungary, 346, 353, 366, 382, 387, 401, 429

474